UTILIZING SWITCH INTERFACES

WITH CHILDREN WHO ARE

SEVERELY PHYSICALLY

CHALLENGED

# UTILIZING SWITCH INTERFACES

## WITH CHILDREN WHO ARE SEVERELY PHYSICALLY CHALLENGED

an emphasis on communication strategies

**Carol Goossens'**
**Sharon Sapp Crain**

pro·ed
8700 Shoal Creek Boulevard
Austin, Texas 78757

Cover artwork and illustrations by Carol Goossens'



Printed in the United States of America

**Library of Congress Cataloging-in-Publication Data**

Goossens', Carol.
Utilizing switch interfaces with children who are severely physically challenged / Carol Goossens' and Sharon Sapp Crain.
p. cm.
Includes bibliographical references and index.
ISBN 0-89079-516-9
1. Handicapped children—Rehabilitation. 2. Computerized self-help devices for the handicapped. 3. Electric switchgear. I. Crain, Sharon Sapp, 1959- . II. Title.
RJ138.G66 1992
617.1'03—dc20 91-35836
CIP

pro·ed
8700 Shoal Creek Boulevard
Austin, Texas 78757

3 4 5 6 7 8 9 10 98 97 96 95

*To our friendship*

# Contents

# Acknowledgments

NOW THAT THIS project is finally completed, we would like to thank a number of people who helped to lighten the load. We wish to thank Anita Ingram, Johnnie Martin, and Kim Storey for their assistance in manuscript preparation. Appreciation goes to PRO-ED for their editorial assistance.

Because this project spanned four states (Alabama, Pennsylvania, Texas, and New York), we wish to thank the telephone company, the airlines, and express mail, without which this long-distance project would not have survived. Appreciation also goes to the breakfast establishments in each of these states for giving us the incentive for "getting up and at 'em."

Thank you to Jennifer Angelo for her valuable input regarding several of the motor aspects of this text. The section on commercially available adaptive fixtures (Chapter 4) is very much a tribute to the expertise of Larry Weiss. Larry is, in large part, responsible for our early interest in fabricating switch mounts. Thank you Larry for being such a wonderful teacher. Caroline Musselwhite . . . where do we begin? We thank her for her insightful content review, her moral support, her wit, and above all her friendship.

Much appreciation is extended to Andrea Schirmer Jensen and Joan Bergman for their contribution of Chapter 2, which is pivotal to the text. We thank them not only for their contribution to the text but also for all that we've learned from our working relationship. Their creativity and willingness to share their knowledge have made them a joy to work with.

A special thank-you is extended to family and friends who continued to show their support long after they had surely given up hope of ever seeing a finished copy. In particular, we would like to acknowledge Pam Elder, Roger LeMoine, Carolyn Edwards, and Gene Sapp. Bob Crain is worthy of special mention. Out of necessity Bob had the opportunity to put the high-gloss polish on his already glowing parenting skills. His sense of humor never let us take it all too seriously.

And last but not least, a special thank-you goes to the person who coined the phrase, "and this too shall pass."

chapter 1

# INTRODUCTION

THERE'S A BATTLE *ahead, many battles are lost*
*But you'll never see the end of the road*
*While you're travelling with me.*

(from "Don't Dream It's Over,"
N. Finn, Crowded House, 1986)

In our role as facilitators we will never see the end of the road "traveling" with nonspeaking children who are severely physically challenged. Our learning will be a never-ending process.

The task of serving children who are functionally nonspeaking is often difficult and overwhelming due to the demands it places on our skills and time. To ensure that these children achieve their full potential, augmentative communication programming requires (a) considerable foresight and long-range systematic planning, (b) a significant investment of time for preplanning and system design, (c) a considerable amount of teamwork involving a variety of facilitators, and (d) above all, creativity. Nowhere are these needs more apparent than with children for whom switch technology is vital to meeting their communication, academic, mobility, recreational, and daily living needs. By way of example, consider the following hypothetical case study in which switch technology was systematically implemented very early, and with considerable foresight and creativity.

Keisha is a 10-year-old who is severely physically challenged due to cerebral palsy. Between the ages of 4 months and 3 years, Keisha and her family received interdisciplinary services through a combined center- and home-based early intervention program. Within this program Keisha's parents assumed an active role as members of an extended interdisciplinary team that included a physical therapist, an occupational therapist, a speech/language pathologist, a developmental psychologist, a nutritionist, a nurse, and a social worker. In general, emphasis was placed on empowering Keisha's family to address multiple needs.

Prior to 8 months of age, considerable attention was directed toward assisting Keisha's family with various handling and positioning techniques; that is, how to hold and carry Keisha in a therapeutic manner. Feeding and oral motor stimulation were also emphasized (Figure 1.1a). At 8 months of age attention was directed toward encouraging Keisha to bring her hands toward midline and eventually to bring her hands toward her mouth (Figure 1.1b). As Keisha was unable to grasp objects, lightweight objects were positioned in her hands via Velcro straps.

Emphasis was eventually placed on encouraging Keisha to reach for objects. Initially, toys were selected that could be easily activated by light touch (e.g., adapted glow baby, electronic keyboard, vibrating switch). Adapted battery-operated toys played a vital role in Keisha's therapeutic scenario. Whenever Keisha touched the battery-operated toy placed within easy reach, the facilitator activated the toy via an interconnecting switch (Figure 1.1c). Later, in keeping with a progression outlined by Van Tatenhove (1985), a switch was introduced in a hand-activated format (Figure 1.1d). Initially, the switch was placed on, or in close proximity with, the adapted battery-powered toy. Later, the toy was

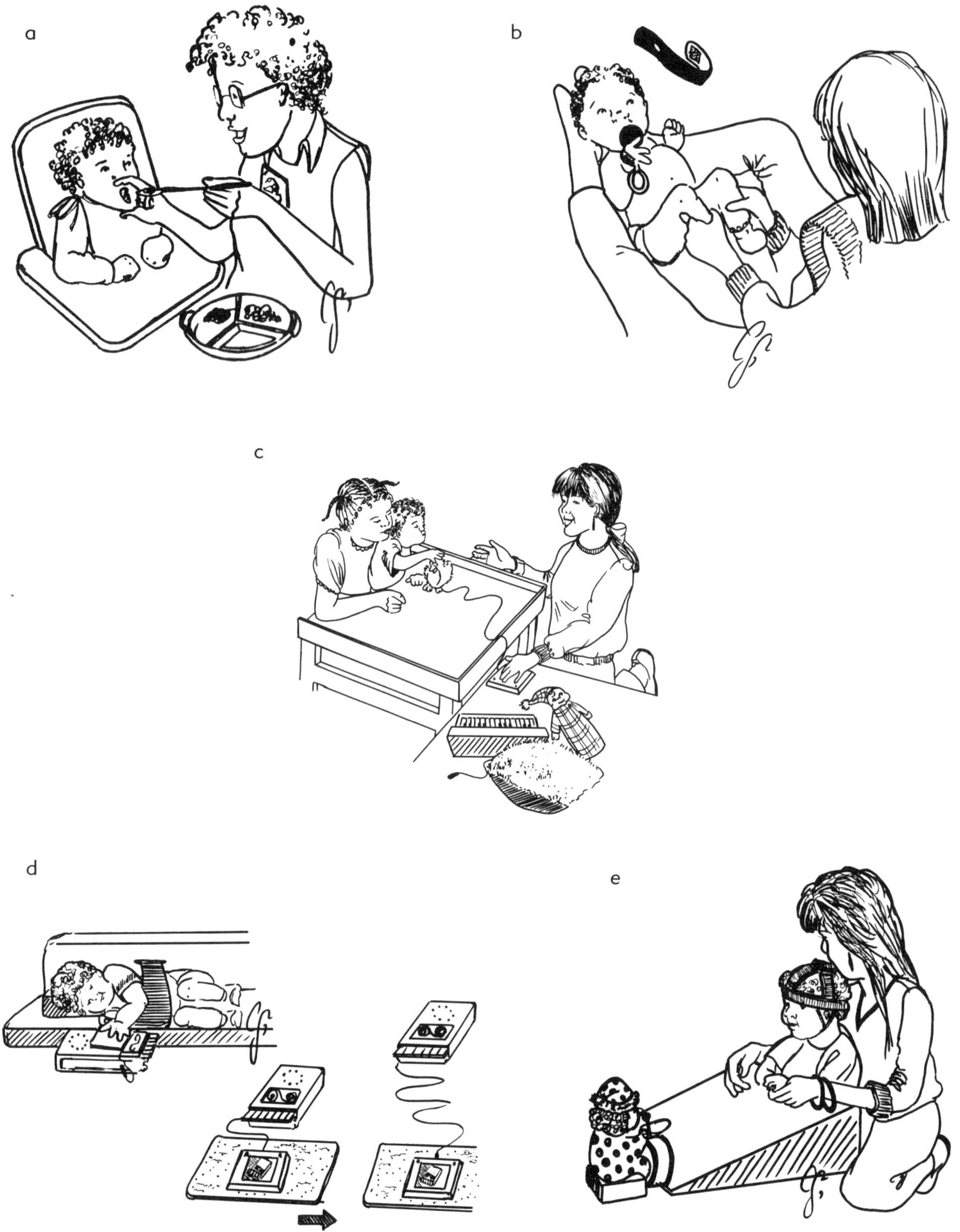


**FIGURE 1.1.** Programming prior to 8 months.

placed at increasingly greater distances from the end reward. When Keisha had successfully acquired the concept of cause and effect relative to early switch use, this newly acquired knowledge was applied to the training of various motor skills such as head lifting (Figure 1.1e). By 8 months of age communication programming focused on training Keisha to indicate a desire for more of a pleasurable activity by vocalizing and making eye contact with her facilitator. Vocal turn taking continued to be a focus throughout the first year of life.

Two parallel strands of intervention became evident between 8 and 12 months of age (Figure 1.2). One strand of intervention focused on training Keisha to communicate through eye pointing. The second parallel strand focused on preparing Keisha for using the technology that would, long range, play a vital role in her future. As visually depicted in Figure 1.2, intervention within the eye-pointing, direct-selection strand focused attention on training Keisha to follow an index finger point to the left and right (Figure 1.2a). Adapted battery-powered toys played an important role in this therapeutic scenario. Whenever Keisha successfully followed the adult's cross-body point to the left or right, she was rewarded with an interesting spectacle (i.e., a battery-operated toy, switch-activated by the facilitator). Later, Keisha was taught to eye-point toward or reach for real objects in her environment to signal a desire to interact with that object (Figure 1.2b). When Keisha appeared to have understanding of eye pointing or reaching to request, choice making with real objects was introduced into her therapeutic plan (Figure 1.2c). In keeping with the team's holistic, environmental approach to intervention, all facilitators (regardless of their professional affiliation) provided Keisha with opportunities to make meaningful choices throughout daily home routines as well as a range of therapeutic play activities (Figure 1.2d). Toward the latter part of the 8- to 12-month developmental period, photographs were paired with the real objects in these previously established choice-making paradigms (Figure 1.2e and f). To facilitate the process of making picture choices readily accessible for choice making throughout the day, storage displays were incorporated throughout the home environment. Examples are illustrated in Figure 1.3.

Shifting to the parallel, switching/scanning strand of intervention, emphasis during the 8- to 12-month range continued to focus on using switch-accessed rewards to address various motor and cognitive goals (Figure 1.4a and b). A variety of non-electronic adaptive play materials were also used to facilitate the development of cognitive, play, and motor skills (Figure 1.5).

During the 12- to 18-month age period, expressive communication continued to focus on choice making using photographs as the visual representations (Figure 1.6). It was during the latter part of this intervention period that aided language-stimulation displays were superimposed on all daily routines such as mealtime, dressing, bath time, playtime (Figure 1.7). These displays allowed the family to point out key picture symbols on the display as they interacted with Keisha. During a diaper changing activity, for example, the following scenario might unfold.

> "Oh Dirty. You got a DIRTY DIAPER . . . TAKE OFF . . . gotta TAKE OFF that DIAPER . . . CLEAN . . . we NEED a CLEAN DIAPER . . . look what daddy found . . . a CLEAN DIAPER . . . OK here we go . . . PUT ON . . . let's PUT ON this CLEAN DIAPER . . . whoops we're NOT FINISHED . . . MORE . . . we gotta do MORE . . . PANTS . . . gotta PUT ON your PANTS."

At this point aided language stimulation was provided primarily for the purposes of conducting symbol comprehension training in context. Despite the fact that at this early point Keisha was unable to relate to line drawing symbols, she was being exposed to their use much like the normal child is exposed to speech during the first year of life despite the child's initial lack of understanding. Throughout this period many of the basic principles of good verbal language stimulation remained operative while aided language stimulation was being provided. Recognizing the importance of therapeutic positioning to Keisha's overall functioning, the positioning specialist on the team recommended a wheelchair, an upright-stander, a side-lyer, and a bath chair to be used in the home environment.

Parallel to Keisha's advancements in learning to eye-point to request preferred objects or activities, she continued to undergo systematic programming relative to switch access. It was at this point in intervention that it became apparent to the team that

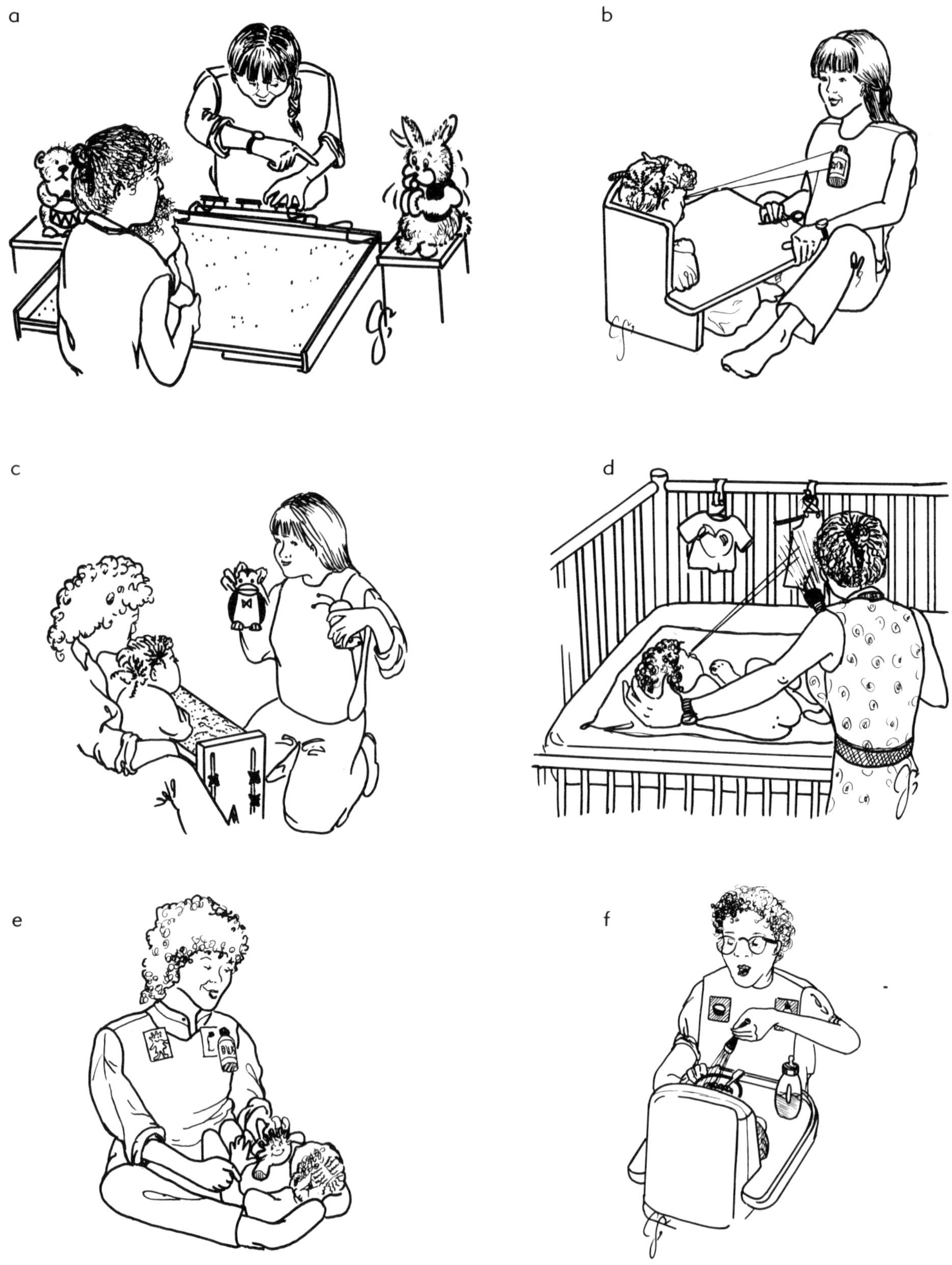


**FIGURE 1.2.** Programming 8 to 12 months—Eye pointing.

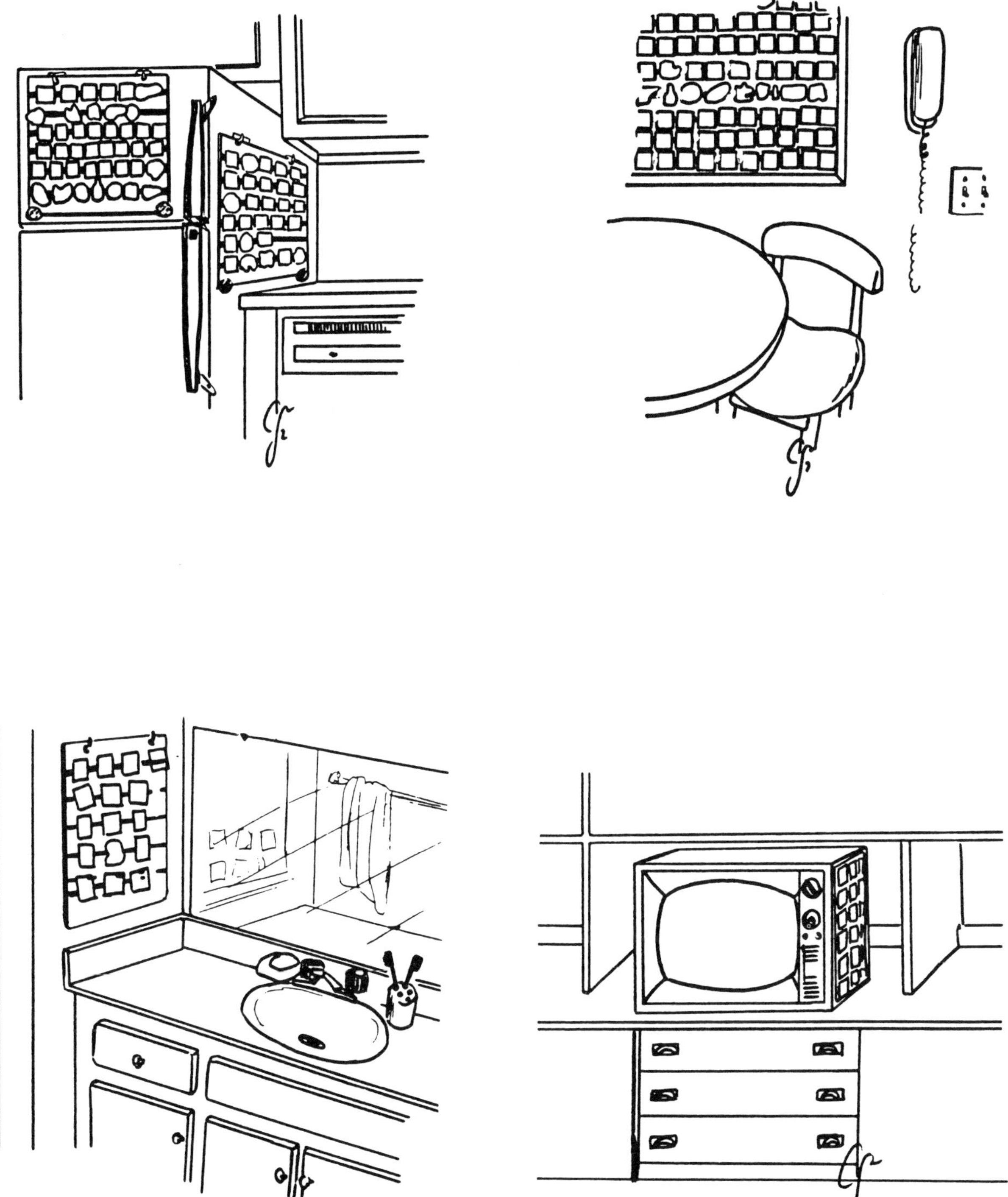

**FIGURE 1.3.** Making visual representations accessible within the home environment.

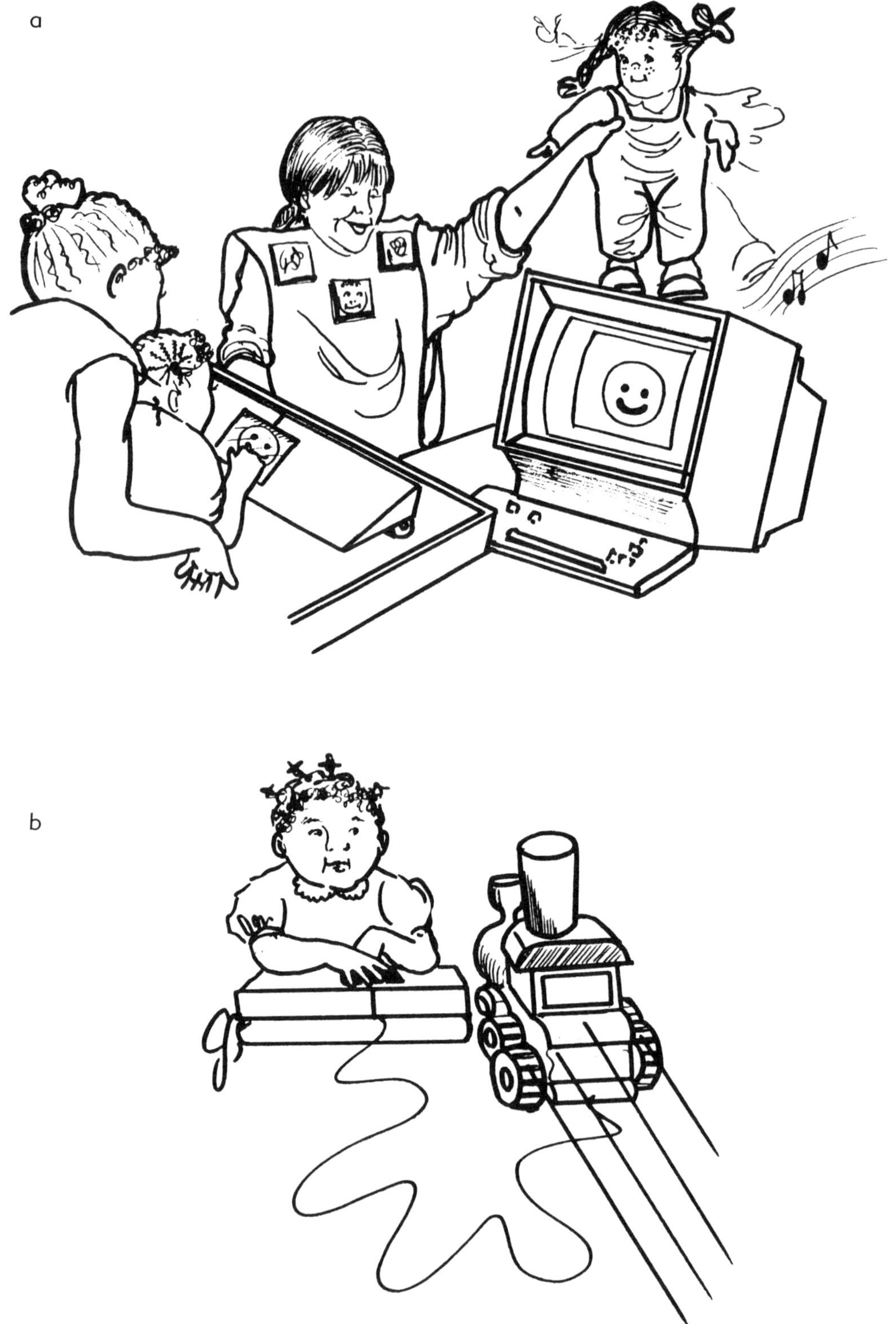

**FIGURE 1.4.** Programming 8 to 12 months—Switching.

**FIGURE 1.5.** Programming 8 to 12 months—Adapted play materials.

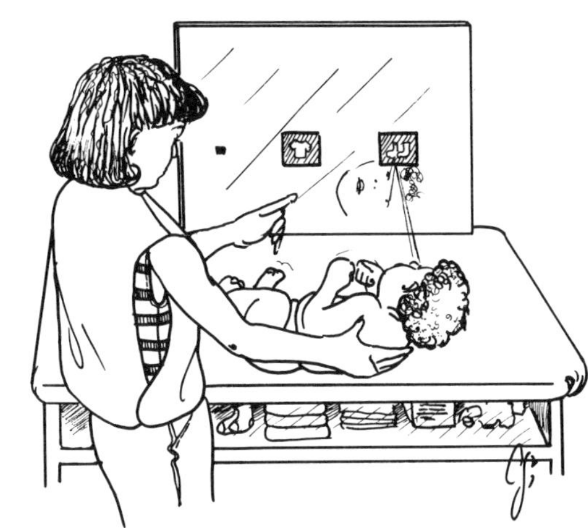

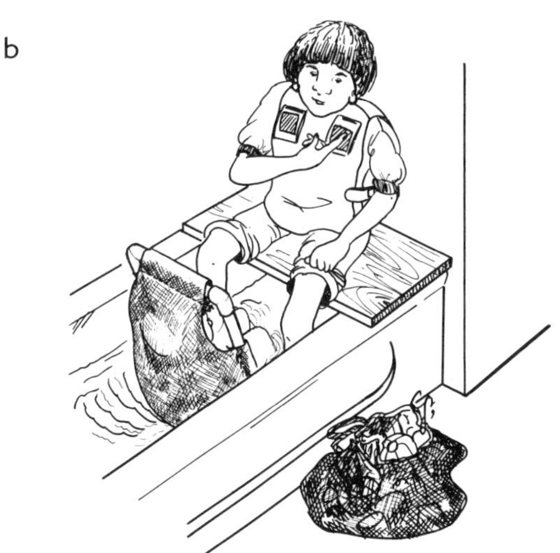

**FIGURE 1.6.** Programming 12 to 18 months—Eye pointing (choice making).

Keisha's head control was superior to her arm and hand control. Although able to initiate and maintain contact with the switch within a hand-activated format, Keisha continued to experience difficulty with the release aspect of switch access. CPVC pipes and fittings were used to position a switch to the left of Keisha's head allowing her to use a lateral head-turn to access her switch. Therapeutic attention was then directed toward training a volitional release, first within untimed formats and later with a timing component overlaid. As illustrated in Figure 1.8, this was addressed in a variety of tasks such as "freeze-frame dancing" (Figure 1.8a), adapted slide projector (Figure 1.8b), and timing device (Figure 1.8c) used with battery-operated toys that required Keisha to release contact with the switch in order to reinitiate the reward.

It was also during this 12- to 18-month period that various computer software programs designed for single-switch use were introduced using the family's home computer and an interface box that

a

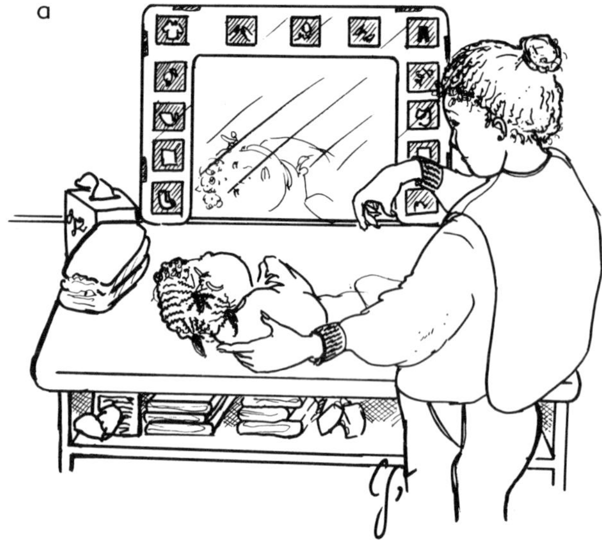

b

**FIGURE 1.7.** Programming 12 to 18 months—Eye pointing (aided language stimulation—symbol comprehension training in context).

allowed the computer to accept switch input (Figure 1.8d). This software thus served not only a motor training role but a recreational role as well.

As depicted in Figure 1.9, a hand-activated format was not completely abandoned. Keisha's hand-activated format continued to be used in communication tasks in which the release aspect of switch access was not a critical feature of the task.

Between 18 and 24 months of age (Figure 1.10), choice making was achieved using line drawings (commercially available symbols) paired with the previously employed photos. It was also during this period that a small flashlight was used to light-cue expressive communication on the aided language stimulation displays.

Parallel to this program using eye pointing as the primary means of communication, Keisha began to receive her first exposure using switch access in single-cell targeting tasks in the absence of a scan pattern (Figure 1.11). This practice was achieved within the context of computer software. It was also during this period that Keisha was first exposed to partner-assisted scanning involving an array size greater than two. By 24 months of age, step scanning was being employed as the scanning selection technique for computer access. In addition to using various public domain and commercially available software programs to serve a recreational and motor training role, choice making relative to play began to be conducted within an electronic format using the home computer and a language-empty software program (Figure 1.12).

Between 2 and 3 years of age (Figure 1.13), emphasis was placed on expanding Keisha's activity-based vocabulary. When face-to-face communication was possible, combined display formats (vest + frame) were used to give Keisha access to a larger vocabulary array (Figure 1.13a). During this time span Keisha began training in self-feeding using an adapted spoon. As side-by-side assistance was required, a mirror eye-gaze format was required during mealtime (Figure 1.13b).

Parallel programming during the 2- to 3-year age period focused on using a joystick to achieve powered mobility (Figure 1.14). Initially, training was conducted outdoors minimizing potential obstacles; later training was conducted indoors with the assistance of a facilitator-manipulated override switch. It was during this period that a portable voice output communication device was purchased through third-party payment. Although able to use a joystick for beginning powered mobility, Keisha did not possess the refined timing skills necessary for accessing her voice-output device using directed scanning. She was, however, able to perform element scanning using a step-scan mode. That is, each switch activation advanced the cursor one cell until the target cell was reached. In keeping with Keisha's chronological age at the time, the device was programmed with multiple sets of messages (sentences and phrases),

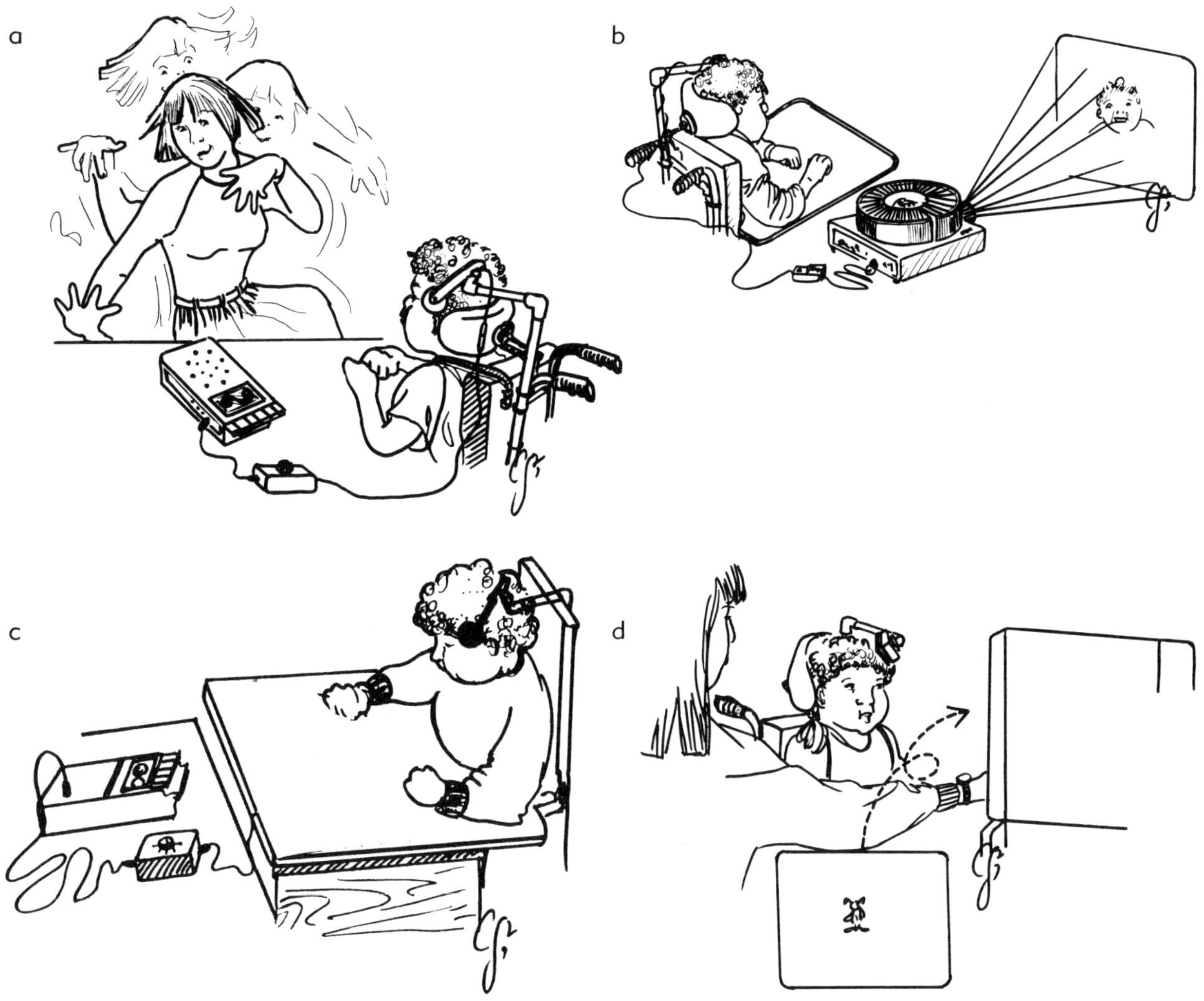


**FIGURE 1.8.** Programming 12 to 18 months—Switching/scanning (head-activated).

each set being assigned to its own unique level on the device and each set having its own unique overlay that served as a mnemonic for calling forth the underlying messages.

Between 3 and 5 years of age, Keisha was enrolled in an integrated preschool, served by an interdisciplinary team. As depicted in Figure 1.15, communication was achieved through a combination of techniques (scanning electronic device + eye pointing). Depending on the activity, eye pointing was frequently mediated through voice output made possible through the use of a partner-assisted Talking Eye-Point Board (InvoTek; an external peripheral interfaced with the family's Apple computer). Whenever Keisha eye-pointed to a symbol on the Talking Eye-Point Board frame, her selection was confirmed by the facilitator shining a penlight on its adjacent light-sensitive cell. The computer then spoke the underlying message.

Concurrent to this training, Keisha underwent intervention in learning to access both the family's home computer and her portable voice-output device using an automatic scan mode. Initially, this targeting was conducted solely in the context of play. Later, a choice-making paradigm was reintroduced to provide Keisha with practice accessing her device using an automatic as opposed to a step-scan mode. By the time Keisha entered elementary school at the age of 5, she was using an automatic scanning selection technique to access her device (configured within a level-based, 8-location format).

The fact that Keisha possessed numerous reliable response modes (eye pointing, scanning) allowed her to be mainstreamed within her new educational set-

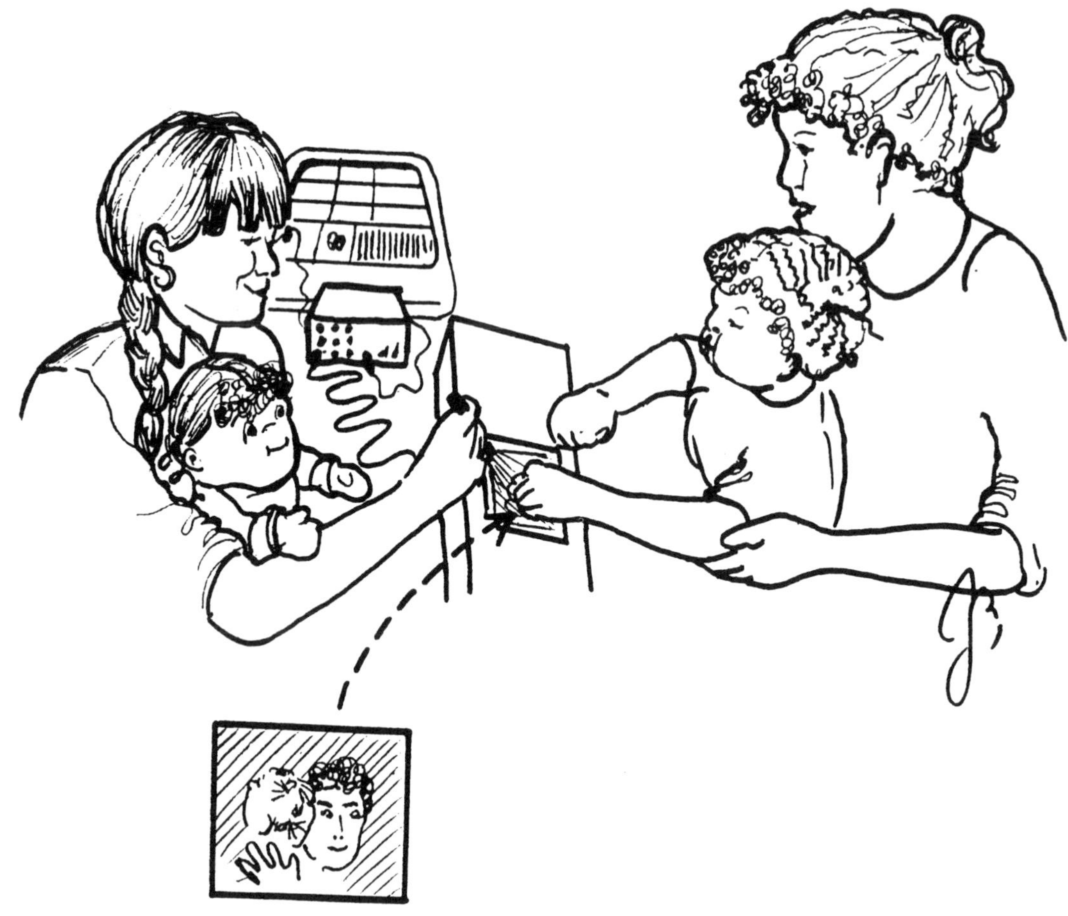

**FIGURE 1.9.** Programming 12 to 18 months—Switching/scanning (hand-activated).

ting. At this point in time attention was directed toward programming her voice-output device to allow her to mediate communication during all classroom routines plus interaction during recess. It should, however, be noted that eye pointing continued to play an important role in Keisha's therapeutic plan. Using a software authoring program called Brainz (Bainum Dunbar, Inc.), many of the work sheets used by the other children in the class were retooled into a scanning format accessible using Keisha's head-activated switch setup.

Parallel to her basic communication and literacy training program utilizing eye pointing and automatic scanning within an 8-location format, Keisha began motor training in accessing her device using a faster, more complex scanning selection technique called row-column scanning. Supplementing this motor training involving Keisha's dedicated voice-output device, software programs for the Apple computer were selected that allowed Keisha to practice her row-column scanning while playing games such as tic-tac-toe and Scancentration (Interaction Games Software; Don Johnston Developmental Equipment) (Figure 1.16). At the age of 6 years, Keisha was demonstrating mastery of row-column scanning using several 32-location, activity-based communication displays, each programmed into a level on her dedicated voice-output scanning communication device. Concurrent with Keisha's communicative use of a 32-location format accessed through row-column scanning, she began parallel motor training accessing her device more directly using an optical head-pointer (Figure 1.17). Training was initiated first within an 8-location format and

**FIGURE 1.10.** Programming 18 to 24 months—Eye pointing (choice making and beyond choice making).

later within a 32-location format. When Keisha demonstrated proficiency accessing her device using an optical head-pointer with the device configured in a 32-location format, row-column scanning was replaced by the optical head-pointer, a faster selection technique. Later, parallel programming was conducted to achieve motor skill in accessing the device configured in a 128-location format. At this point Keisha began using her device as an alternate keyboard to access the class and home personal computer. Keisha's written homework was now accomplished using either the device's on-board printer or the computer printer available in both the school setting and the home.

At the age of 9 years, Keisha's facilitators began transitioning her to the use of a code-based as opposed to a level-based format on her dedicated communication device. Using a code-based format, Keisha was afforded the generative power of word-by-word message compilation at speeds not possible using letter-by-letter message compilation.

Currently, Keisha is 10 years old and "holding her own" in a regular fifth-grade classroom. Keisha is an example of what can occur but is not occurring on a routine basis. Given an interdisciplinary team approach, systematic programming, long-range parallel programming, and above all creativity, Keisha was able to realize a potential above and beyond what typically occurs. Keisha epitomizes what we as facilitators hope for all the children we are attempting to serve—the chance to achieve their fullest potential regardless of their degree of handicap. Typical of many children who are severely physically challenged, the ability to use a switch interface is a vital key to opening many doors to future success. It is important to note, however, that switch technology was not solely responsible for Keisha's favorable outcome. As illustrated, Keisha's communication needs were successfully realized using a variety of selection techniques (facial expressions, eye pointing, scanning, using both nonelectronic and electronic direct selection and scanning techniques). In the final analysis, it was the skillful manipulation of these various options depending on Keisha's needs and abilities at the time that provided Keisha with a viable communication system.

The task of providing a child like Keisha with switch access for communication requires a broad knowledge base, typically drawing on the expertise of many individuals in an interdisciplinary team (par-

**FIGURE 1.11.** Programming 18 to 24 months—Switching/scanning.

ent, teacher, speech/language pathologist, physical therapist, occupational therapist, rehabilitation specialist). If such children are to achieve viable switch access, they must be therapeutically positioned in a manner that maximizes their motor strengths while compensating for their motor weaknesses (such as lack of trunk stability, poor head control, interfering abnormal reflexes, or heightened postural tone). The intent of Chapter 2 is to familiarize the reader with the basic principles of seating, irrespective of the type of seating system employed. Although switch access can and does occur in many alternate therapeutic positions such as upright standing, supine, side-lying, prone over a wedge, the focus of Chapter 2 is the seated position, the position most frequently employed when engaged in switch access.

In delineating a viable switch setup, attention must be directed toward delineating what movement pattern and what switch interface will promote reliable access with minimal effort. Chapter 3 focuses on the task of delineating a viable switch setup.

The child's ability to reliably access a switch interface is highly dependent on the facilitator's skill in securely positioning the switch interface in the path of the child's most reliable movement pattern. Chapter 4 is designed to summarize information regarding how to achieve stable switch mounts using (a) commercially available adaptive fixtures, (b) CPVC pipe and fittings, (c) Ethafoam for hand-activated switch setups, and (d) various switch mounts positioned directly on the child's body.

A broad range of scanning selection techniques is available. Chapter 5 provides the reader with an overview of these techniques and discusses the component skills required for each.

When learning the motor aspects of a scanning selection technique, training frequently occurs in motivating gamelike formats, purposely minimizing the communicative and cognitive load. Chapter 6 presents a systematic format designed to assist children in acquiring motor access skills in a time-effective manner.

The task of setting up an augmentative communication system to address the child's communicative needs is challenging for even the most experienced facilitator. Chapters 7 and 8 are, therefore, devoted to designing and training the use of systems that promote frequent, self-initiated use. In Chapter 7, emphasis is primarily directed toward extending the skills established in Chapter 6 to early choice making using an environmentally based approach. In Chapter 8, emphasis is placed on designing a system to serve as a conversational tool. Although scanning communication devices can be used to address literacy, language, and academic goals, the focus of Chapters 7 and 8 is solely on "conversational" concerns. A glossary of terms has been provided in Appendix E for the reader unfamiliar with out-of-field terminology used throughout the text. A listing of distributors and trademarks is also available (Appendix F) to facilitate the process of tracking down equipment and materials.

**FIGURE 1.12.** Programming 18 to 24 months—Switching/scanning (choice making).

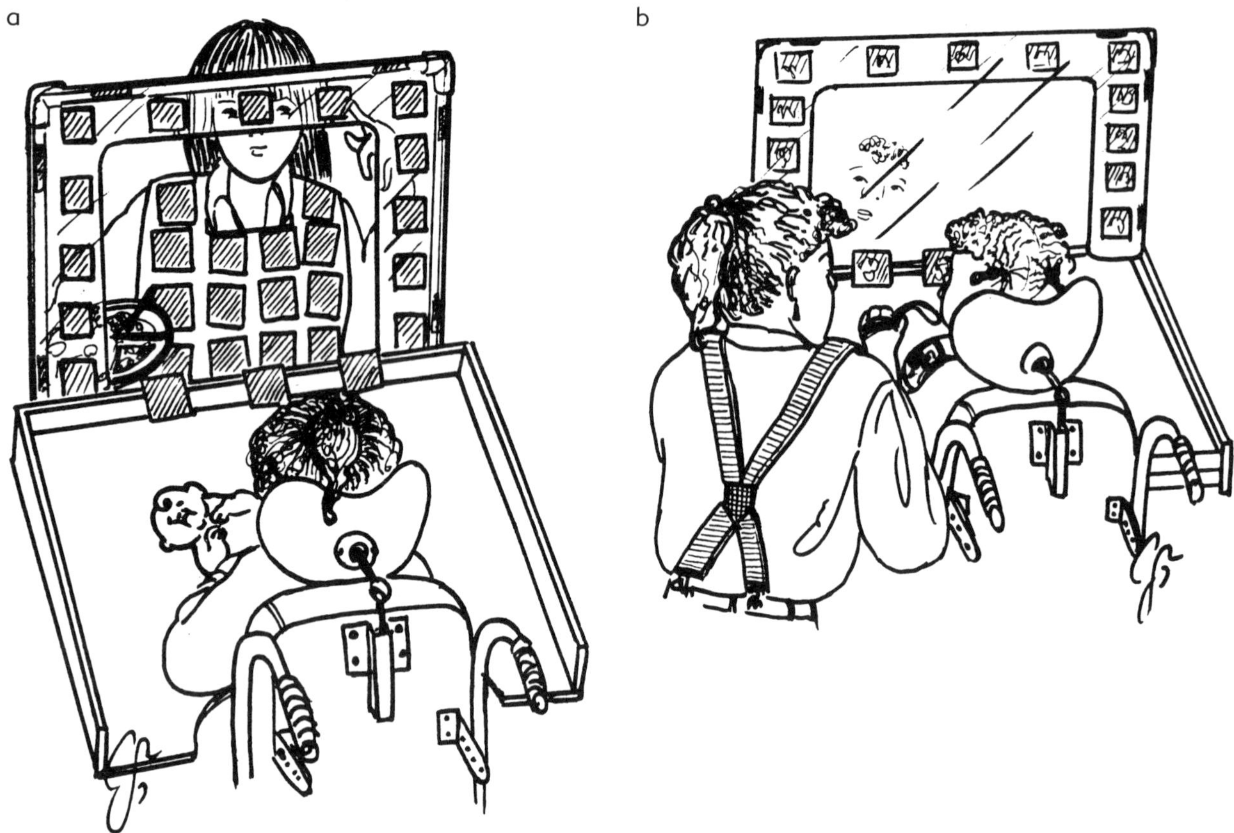


**FIGURE 1.13.** Programming 2 to 3 years of age—Eye pointing.

**FIGURE 1.14.** Programming 2 to 3 years of age—Switching/scanning (powered mobility).

**FIGURE 1.15.** Programming 3 to 5 years of age—Communication training (combined techniques).

**FIGURE 1.16.** Programming 3 to 5 years of age—Motor training (row-column scanning).

**FIGURE 1.17.** Programming 6+ years of age—Motor training (direct selection using an optical head-pointer).

chapter 2

# Positioning the Child for Viable Switch Access

*Andrea Schirmer Jensen*
*and Joan S. Bergman*

A NUMBER OF SKILLS are required to successfully use a switch interface. Motorically, the child must initiate, release, and/or maintain contact with the switch interface to input or control a target system such as an adapted toy, environmental control unit, microcomputer, dedicated communication device, or powered wheelchair. When a switch interface is used to input a visually based scanning communication device, additional visual skills must be coordinated with the motor skills of switch access. In general, the child is required to visually monitor the movement of an indicator scanning through an array and must either initiate or release switch contact within a certain time frame when the indicator has highlighted the desired item.

The child's ability to successfully coordinate the motor and visual skills required for functional switch use is in large part dependent on the manner in which the child is therapeutically positioned. More specifically, therapeutic positioning can better enable a child who has severe physical disabilities to

1. Perform the movement pattern needed to reliably access a switch interface
2. Achieve the head control needed to visually monitor the target system
3. Disassociate head and eye movements to visually monitor the path of the scanning indicator
4. Disassociate head and upper extremity movements, allowing visual monitoring to continue irrespective of the use of the upper extremities for switch access
5. Better coordinate the motor and visual skills required to select a target item when it is highlighted by the scanning indicator
6. Perform all of the above as reliably and as effortlessly as possible, thereby promoting frequent use of the target system

In the case of a scanning communication device, frequent use is required to produce the multiple conversational turns that characterize typical communicative exchange. By way of example, consider the following cases.

In her previous seating system (Figure 2.1a), Amanda was unable to perform a reliable movement pattern to access a switch interface. She also lacked the head control necessary to visually monitor the scanning indicator on her communication device. When provided with adequate postural support (Figure 2.1b), Amanda was able to motorically select the desired item while visually tracking the scanning indicator.

Similar to Amanda, Danielle experienced difficulty accessing a head-activated switch interface as she lacked appropriate stabilization (Figure 2.2a). As her body was in constant motion, a great deal of energy was expended in attempting to initiate contact with her switch interface. When provided with adequate stabilization (Figure 2.2b), Danielle was able to use a relatively effortless movement pattern to activate her head switch. As shown by these brief examples, appropriate therapeutic positioning is vital to promoting success in using a switch interface. Attention must therefore be directed toward

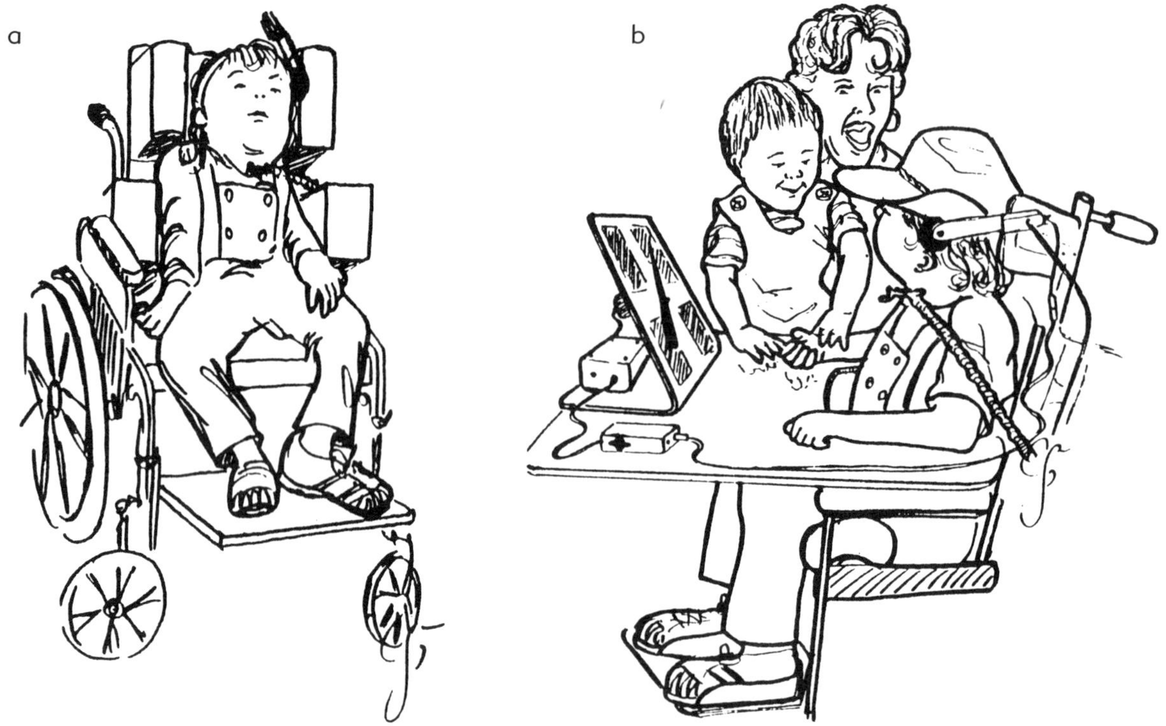

**FIGURE 2.1.** Amanda (a) in previous seating system and (b) operating a scanning device after being therapeutically positioned.

**FIGURE 2.2.** Danielle (a) experiencing difficulty with stabilization and (b) provided with adequate stabilization.

therapeutically positioning the child prior to assessing or training the ability to use a switch interface.

As depicted in Figure 2.3, children who are severely physically challenged often require a variety of therapeutic positions. Although switch access can and does occur in many alternate therapeutic positions, this chapter will focus on the seated position, the position most frequently employed when engaged in switch access. For additional information on therapeutic positioning, the reader is referred to Bergen and Colangelo (1985); Bergen, Presperin, and Tallman (1990); Bergman (1990); Bergman, Drews, and Jensen (1990); Henderson (1989); Trefler (1984); and Ward (1984).

## Normal and Abnormal Motor Development

To understand the importance of therapeutic positioning and its role in promoting function, a basic understanding of normal motor development is required. As depicted in Figure 2.4, motor control normally develops in a predictable developmental sequence. In general, children develop control of *proximal* body parts before *distal* body parts (Figure 2.4a). That is, the child learns to control his or her trunk before his or her hands. Control also develops in a *cephalo* (head) to *caudal* (tail) sequence (Figure 2.4b). That is, the child is typically able to control the head before he or she is able to control the trunk, and is able to control the trunk before the legs (Illingworth, 1975; Smart & Smart, 1977).

The children described in this chapter have physical disabilities because of an insult to the neuromotor system. This damage interferes with their ability to develop normal motor control. Although such children generally develop motor skills along the same developmental sequence as able-bodied children, they tend to do so at a much slower rate. For example, it is not unusual for a child with cerebral palsy to develop adequate head control but continue to demonstrate poor trunk control. Development of motor control may also be arrested at a certain point in the developmental sequence. For example, a child may be 12 years old but continue to demonstrate poor head control.

Several factors interfering with normal motor function must be taken into account when designing a therapeutic seating system. Such factors include lack of proximal stability, abnormal muscle tone, abnormal reflexes, and skeletal deformities (Bergman, 1990; Bergman et al., 1990).

### Lack of Proximal Stability

Movement can be divided into two components, stability and mobility. Simply stated, a body part is either in motion (mobility) or it is not in motion (stability). Heavy work activities such as walking and running are accomplished when stability is superimposed on mobility. In contrast, fine-motor movements such as writing or talking are accomplished when mobility is superimposed on stability. To perform a fine-motor movement, the child must be able to stabilize proximal body parts to achieve controlled mobility of distal body parts (Stockmeyer, 1967).

For children with severe physical disabilities, the act of operating a switch interface can be considered a fine-motor movement. That is, the child must be able to stabilize proximal body parts to reliably move distal body parts such as the head, the hand, or the foot to access a switch interface. If the child is unable to satisfactorily stabilize proximal body parts on his or her own, assistance should be provided with therapeutic positioning.

As shown in Figure 2.5a, Joey is unable to sit independently and therefore experiences difficulty accessing a switch. In the absence of proximal stability Joey adopted an *abnormal posture* to stabilize his body to improve his ability to access a switch. As illustrated, Joey extends, adducts, and internally rotates his arms (Figure 2.5b) or elevates his shoulders to stabilize his neck (Figure 2.5c) to achieve better head control. Periodically, Joey may be observed to adduct, internally rotate, and extend his hips in an attempt to stabilize his lower body to better control his trunk and head. Therapeutic positioning is needed to provide Joey with the proximal stability required for him to initiate movement distally, without resorting to abnormal posturing to create stability. Abnormal posturing is not only inefficient, but it leads to secondary disabilities such as joint abnormalities and pain.

### Abnormal Muscle Tone

Children with central nervous system dysfunction often demonstrate abnormalities of muscle tone. A

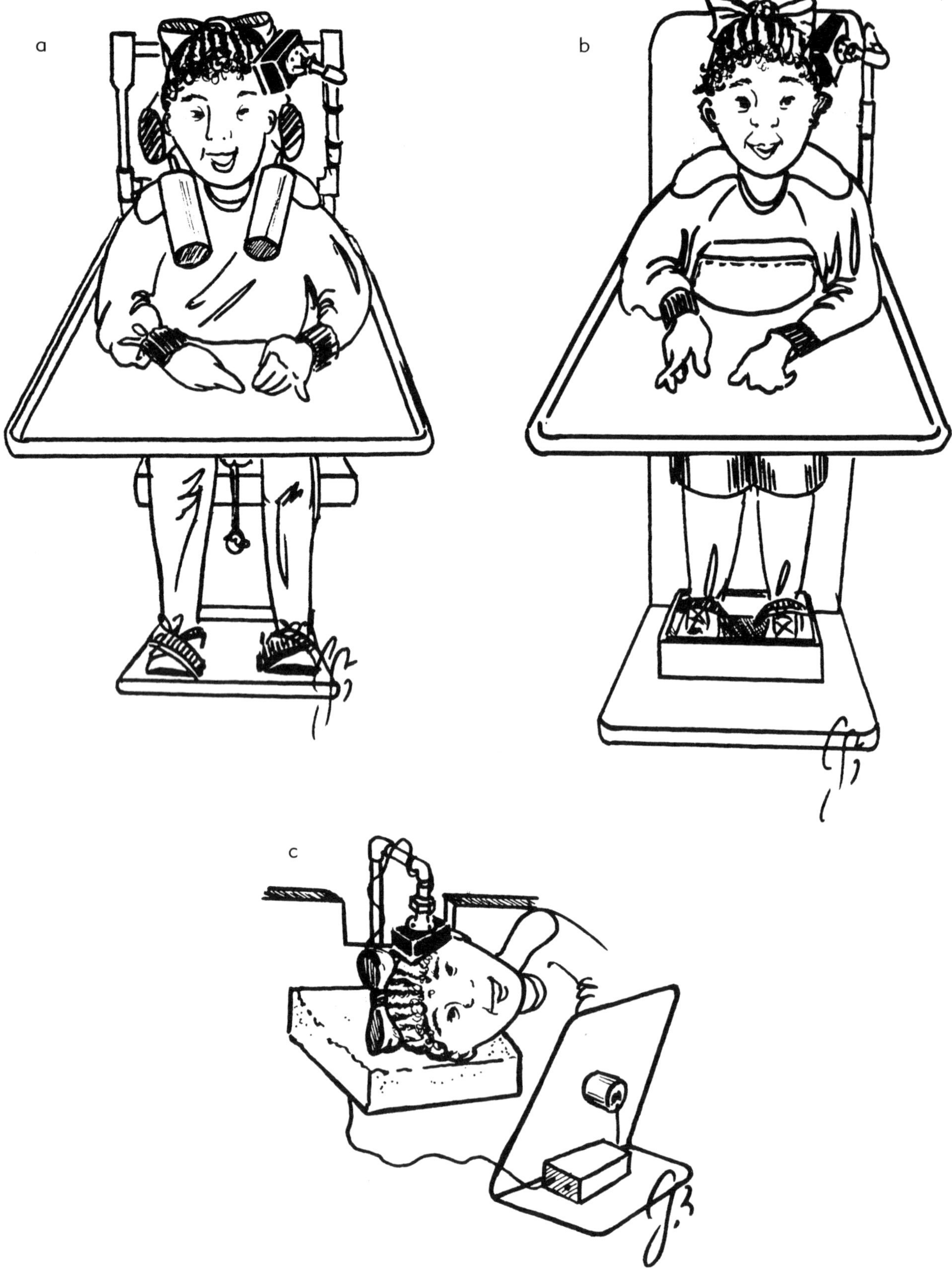


**FIGURE 2.3.** Various therapeutic positions: (a) seated, (b) standing, and (c) side-lying.

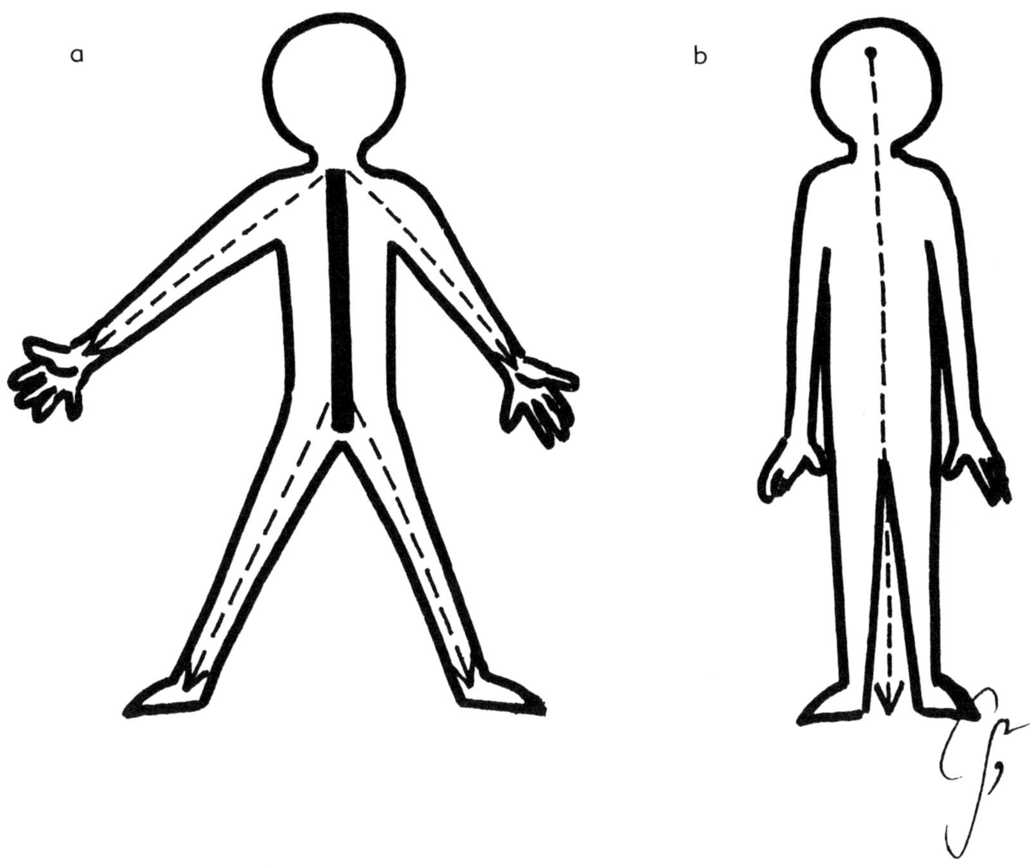


**FIGURE 2.4.** Development of normal motor control: (a) proximal to distal sequence and (b) cephalo to caudal sequence.

child who feels "stiff" or "tight" has too much tone (*hypertonia*). Such children typically experience difficulty with precise movements. Another child may have low tone (*hypotonia*). The child with hypotonicity often lacks sufficient muscle tone to initiate movement. Such children are typically dominated by gravity and experience difficulty moving against it. Muscle tone can also be fluctuating (*athetosis*). A child with athetosis may appear to have a body that is in constant motion. Children with athetosis often experience difficulty eliminating extraneous movements of distal body parts. In addition, children may demonstrate associated movements. That is, the child may seem to be in good control of his or her body until a voluntary movement, at which time many body parts engage in uncontrolled nonstereotypic movements. For example, Julie experiences difficulty in isolating the movement required to activate a hand switch from other body movement. Upon initiation of the desired movement pattern using her hand, her other arm and both legs also engage in movement.

Various degrees of muscle tone may be evidenced in different body parts. For example, a child may be hypertonic in his or her extremities but hypotonic in his or her trunk. This child may rely on his or her arms to hold the trunk up in order to sit independently. Another child may have athetoid muscle movement that is masked by increased extensor tone (tone that causes extension of the extremities). This child's athetosis may not be readily observed, because the increased tone causes the child to have difficulty with movement. Once the child is therapeutically positioned, however, and the extensor tone reduced, the child may demonstrate athetoid movements. Muscle tone may also vary across all four extremities. A child may have more tone in his or her legs than his or her arms, or have greater tone on one side of the body than on the other side of the body.

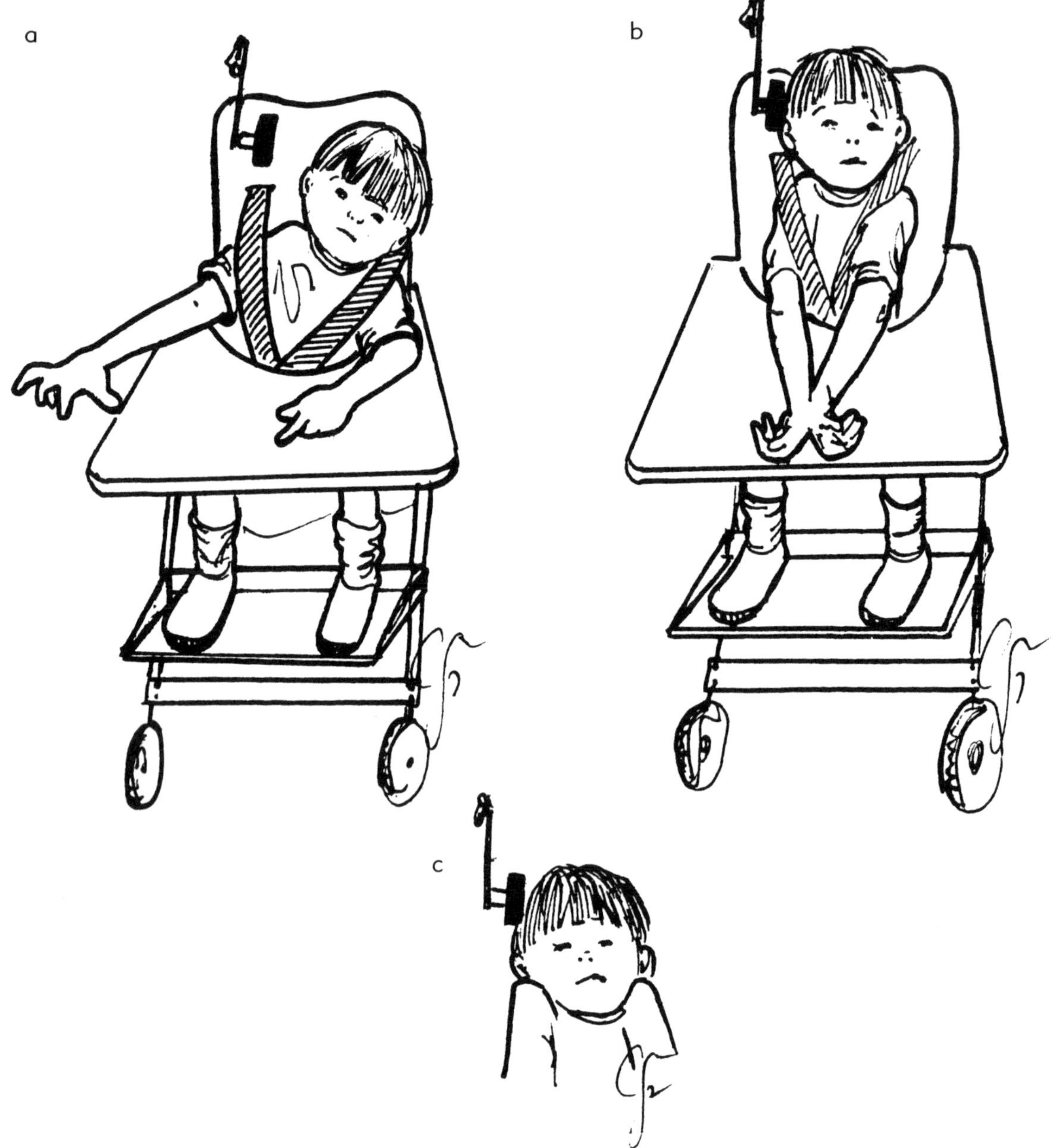


**FIGURE 2.5.** Joey shown using abnormal posturing to promote better head control: (a) Joey has difficulty accessing a switch; (b) he extends and rotates his arms to achieve stability; (c) he elevates his shoulders to stabilize his head.

In general, therapeutic positioning attempts to normalize muscle tone by decreasing tone that is too high and facilitating tone that is too low. It can also help to limit extraneous movement. Positions that promote flexion are often used to relax extensor tone. The latter is especially important for a child like Will, who tends to extend or push up in his chair as illustrated in Figure 2.6. In contrast, positions that promote extension are often used to facilitate tone that is too low.

## Abnormal Reflexes

Reflexes are normal at some point in a child's life and play an important role in normal motor devel-

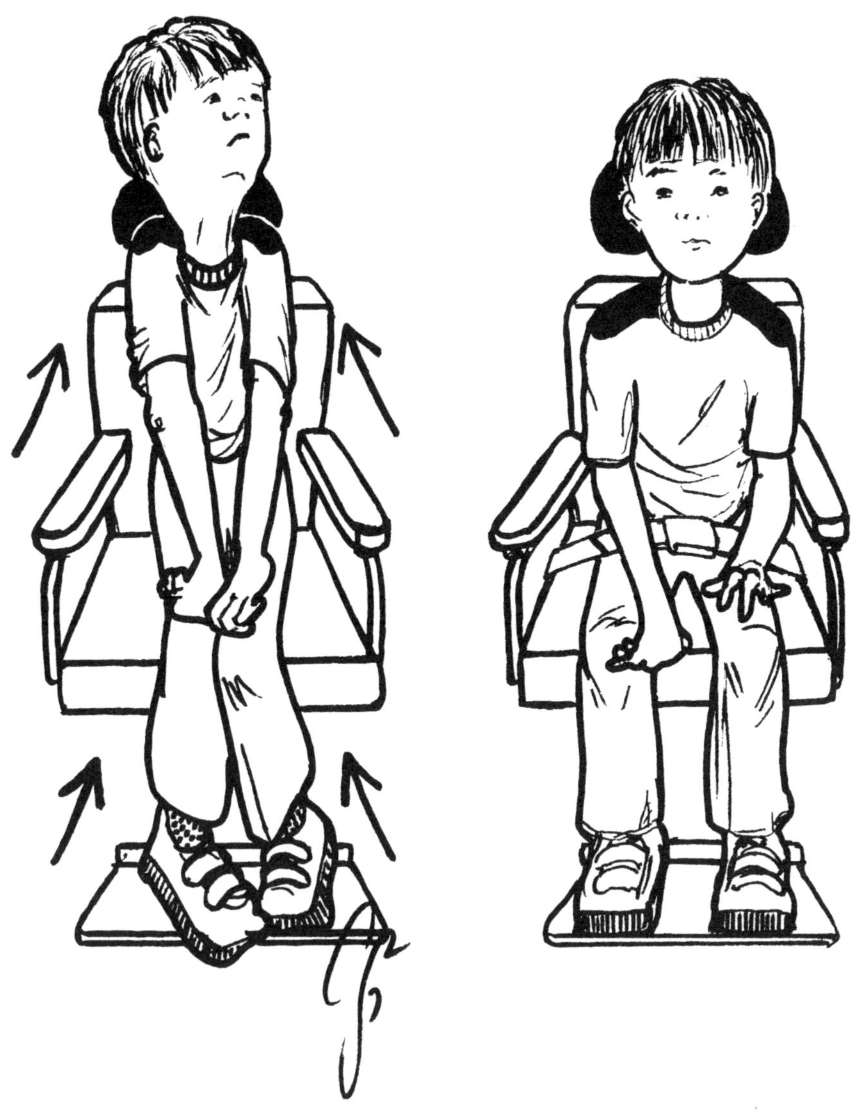

**FIGURE 2.6.** Will demonstrates extensor thrust.

opment. When retained beyond the time they are normally integrated, however, such reflexes can interfere with motor function and motor development (Fiorentino, 1976). Careful observation is required to determine what reflexes are operative and to what degree. This will vary from child to child. For some children a reflex may be obligatory (consistently triggered), and for others a reflex may be triggered inconsistently. Having determined what reflexes are still operative, the positioning system can then be designed to minimize the interfering effects of the operative reflexes. Five reflexes worthy of more in-depth discussion are:

- ❑ Asymmetrical tonic neck reflex
- ❑ Symmetrical tonic neck reflex
- ❑ Positive supporting reaction
- ❑ Tonic labyrinthine supine reflex
- ❑ Tonic labyrinthine prone reflex

**ASYMMETRICAL TONIC NECK REFLEX (ATNR).** ATNR (see Figure 2.7) may be elicited when the child's head is turned to the side (sometimes when a hand is brought to the mouth). *Extensor* tone increases in the extremities on the face side, and *flexor* tone increases in the extremities on the skull side.

**FIGURE 2.7.** Asymmetrical tonic neck reflex (ATNR).

**SYMMETRICAL TONIC NECK REFLEX (STNR).** Extension of the child's neck causes extension in the upper extremities and possible flexion in the lower extremities (Figure 2.8a). Flexion of the child's neck causes flexion in the upper extremities and possible extension of the lower extremities (Figure 2.8b). Flexion or extension of the upper extremities may also elicit this reflex.

**POSITIVE SUPPORTING REACTION.** This reflex is elicited when pressure is applied to the ball of the foot. When this occurs the child's tone will involuntarily increase throughout the body causing extension in the spine and extremities.

**TONIC LABYRINTHINE REFLEXES.** When the child is lying supine, body tone increases as the child assumes a posture of full extension. Voluntary flexing by the child will be difficult if not impossible when the reflex is operative. Lying prone has the opposite effect on the child. In prone, the child experiences increased flexor tone and active extension is limited (Fiorentino, 1976).

### Skeletal Deformity

When abnormal muscle tone and abnormal reflexes continue to have their effect on the child's body, they can produce changes that lead to skeletal deformities. These skeletal deformities in turn can limit range of motion and muscle function. In some instances deformities of the rib cage and spine can compromise body function by compressing internal organs such as the lungs and heart (Bergman, 1990; Bergman et al., 1990). If a child has a severe deformity such as a *scoliosis* (lateral curvature with rotation of the spine) or *kyphosis* (posterior curvature of the thoracic spine when viewed from the side), the seating system must be designed to accommodate the deformity, help prevent further progression, and, over time, possibly reduce the deformity.

## General Principles of Seating

A therapeutic positioning system should enhance proximal stability, normalize muscle tone, eliminate or minimize the effects of abnormal reflexes, minimize the emergence of skeletal deformities, and, in general, promote optimal function. Given today's resources, it is possible for every child who has severe physical disabilities to be positioned comfortably and therapeutically. Since no one line or type of equipment is suitable for every child, it is imperative that the positioning specialist (usually a physical or occupational therapist) be knowledgeable about what is available so as to choose objectively and intelligently among the numerous seating alternatives. Ideally, the selection process should be conducted with input from the child, the child's family, therapists, as well as equipment specialists and other care providers. Adequate time should always be allotted to try various positioning options with sufficient time allowed to observe their effects on the child's posture and functional abilities.

Although some individuals will require considerable additional equipment, others may require only minimal support. It is important to provide all the support a child needs without ''overpositioning'' the child. As a general rule, children should be encouraged to use the motor control that they possess. When, however, such control requires a child to expend an enormous amount of energy thereby precluding the child's ability to engage in functional activities, support should be provided.

In general, positioning can be considered an exercise in fine-tuning where change in the support of one body part may be reflected in changes throughout the body. These changes can either positively or negatively affect the child's ability to reliably access a switch interface.

General guidelines for positioning can be discussed with respect to the following six categories:

- ❑ Pelvic stability
- ❑ Lower extremity support

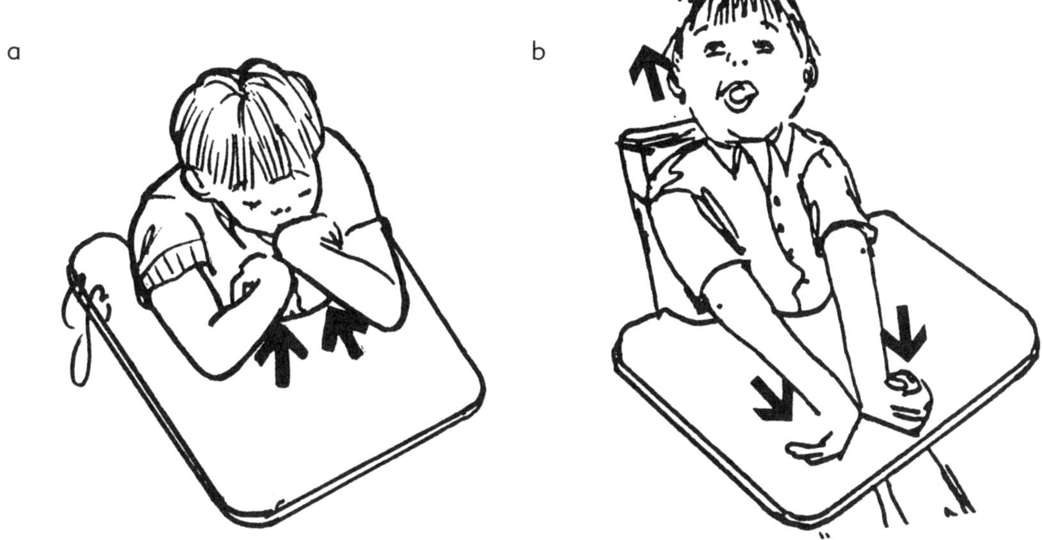


**FIGURE 2.8.** Symmetrical tonic neck reflex (STNR).

- ❑ Trunk stability
- ❑ Head support
- ❑ Upper extremity support
- ❑ Manipulation of orientation in space

### Pelvic Stability

In the seated posture, the hip joints are near the mid-range of motion, which allows for maximum pelvic mobility. The pelvis is free to move when the upper sacrum is not supported by the backrest (Zacharkow, 1988). Branton (1966) concluded that, while seated, the body will adopt postures in order to achieve stability. The need for stability, even if it requires muscular activity, predominates over the need for relaxation. Therefore, it is important to provide adequate support to stabilize the pelvis in the seated position.

The chair seat and back should be constructed of a firm material to provide support and promote stability. As illustrated in Figure 2.9, a sling seat and back provide a hammocking effect that tends to inhibit function and promote deformity. Special seat cushions of air or a gel substance can be used in conjunction with a firm seat for children who may not have adequate sensation or have a history of skin breakdown or pressure sores.

As depicted in Figure 2.10, the child's buttocks should be positioned well back in the seat/back angle of the chair. For the child with hypertonicity, attaining this position can be facilitated by greatly flexing the child at the hips. While keeping the child flexed, the buttocks should be placed in the back of the chair flush with the seat back and the pelvis should be secured with a seat belt. The seat belt should always be snug and should be anchored to the chair in a manner that allows the belt to bisect

**FIGURE 2.9.** Sling seat and back.

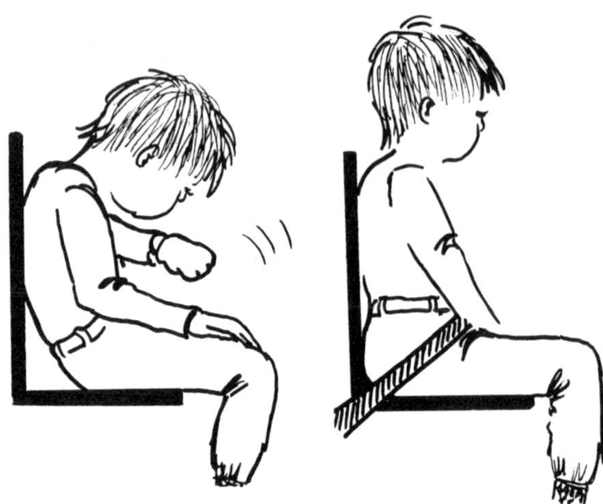

**FIGURE 2.10.** Buttocks positioned back in the seat and pelvis secured.

**FIGURE 2.11.** Extensor thrust.

the seat/back angle with a posterior/inferior force as illustrated in Figure 2.10. Some children will demonstrate an extensor thrust whereby they extend and raise their buttocks off the seat (Figures 2.11 and 2.6). An extensor thrust is especially detrimental to head-activated switch setups. For such children, if a standard seat belt is not sufficient to stabilize the pelvis, a *rigid pelvic restraint* (subasis bar) (Margolis, Jones, & Brown, 1985) may be helpful (Figure 2.12). This should be used in conjunction with other seating components (to be discussed later in the chapter) that are designed to help reduce the child's tone. Hip guides are useful in preventing lateral shifting of the pelvis.

Another component used to stabilize the pelvis is a *proximal pelvic positioner* (Figure 2.13). Proximal pelvic positioners can assume a variety of forms and are successful only if the individual has anterior/posterior mobility of the pelvis. As illustrated, a roll can be placed at the top of the pelvis causing a slight anterior tilt of the pelvis which causes a normal *lordosis* (anterior curve of the spine when viewed from the side) of the lumbar spine. When a seating system has a multipiece back, the lower pad can often be tilted to serve as the proximal pelvic positioner. It is important to note that the lower pad should be small enough that it does not extend past the top of the child's pelvis. As the tilted lower pad can be positioned to maximize contact with the sacrum, this option is highly successful in tilting the

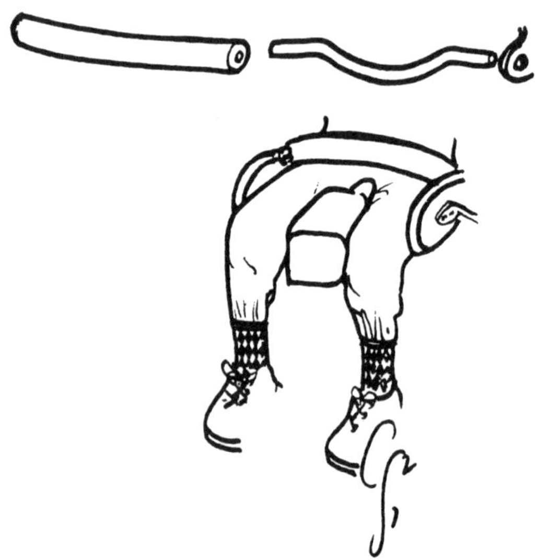

**FIGURE 2.12.** A rigid pelvic restraint.

pelvis slightly anteriorly. The pelvis can also be stabilized using a Bi-Angular Back (a two-part back system) (Wengert & Margolis, 1987). For the child with increased extensor tone, anterior tilting of the pelvis causes the pelvis to be flexed on the thighs. As flexion tends to be tone-reducing, this procedure frequently helps to reduce the extensor thrust. For the child with a hypotonic trunk, this same component also facilitates extension of the spine, thereby

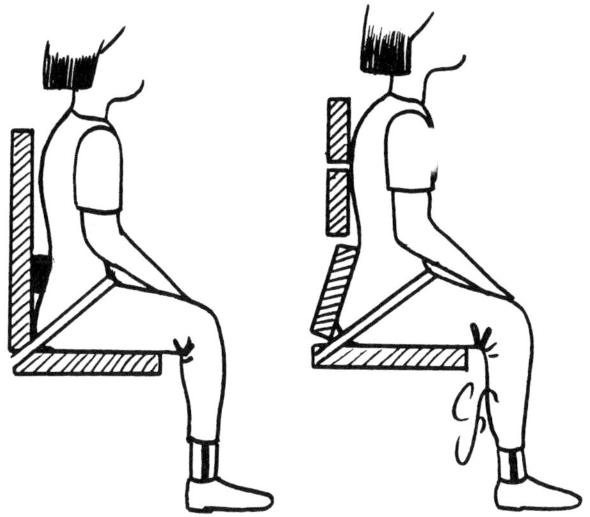

**FIGURE 2.13.** Proximal pelvic positioners.

assisting the child in holding the trunk upright against gravity.

Another option for pelvic positioning that has been used successfully is a *sacral pad* (Monahan, Taylor, & Shaw, 1989). This pad is placed at the base of the pelvis and is used to stabilize the lumbosacral joint. As illustrated in Figure 2.14, the pad is curved and widens laterally to maintain the pelvis in midline. This pad is used in conjunction with a lap belt.

### Lower Extremity Support

Chair depth is considered optimal when the space between the back of the knees and the front of the seat approximates the width of one to two fingers. By maximizing the surface area in contact with the child's thighs, pressure can be more equally distributed. When the child's legs are of unequal length and/or the hips have fixed deformities of unequal amounts, custom seats can be prescribed to accommodate this discrepancy (Figure 2.15). Pelvic stability can also be enhanced through the use of a *distal pelvic positioner.* As illustrated in Figure 2.16, the chair seat can be wedge-shaped or constructed with a rolled edge, causing the knees to be positioned higher than the hips. As distal pelvic positioners decrease the hip/back angle, they promote flexion at the hips which in turn reduces the child's extensor tone. A child may benefit from using both proximal and distal pelvic positioners to promote flexion at the hips, thereby reducing extensor tone.

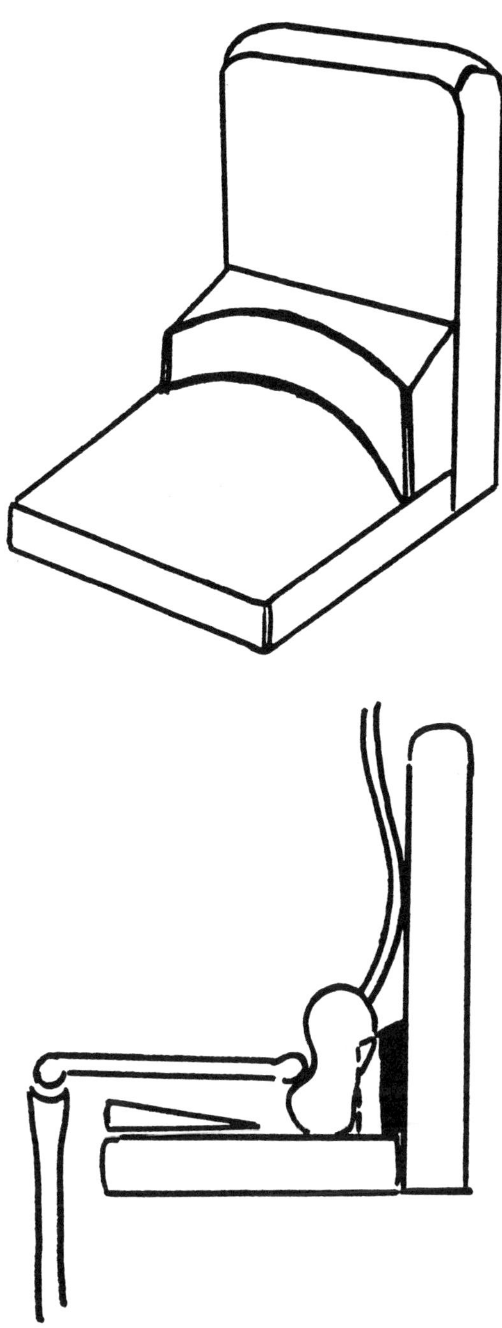

**FIGURE 2.14.** Sacral pad.

As illustrated in Figure 2.17, knee blocks can also be used to stabilize the pelvis (Monahan et al., 1989). The blocks apply pressure on the patellar tendon of the knee, which forces the pelvis to be maintained in a neutral position. This option has been used with individuals who have limited pelvic mobility.

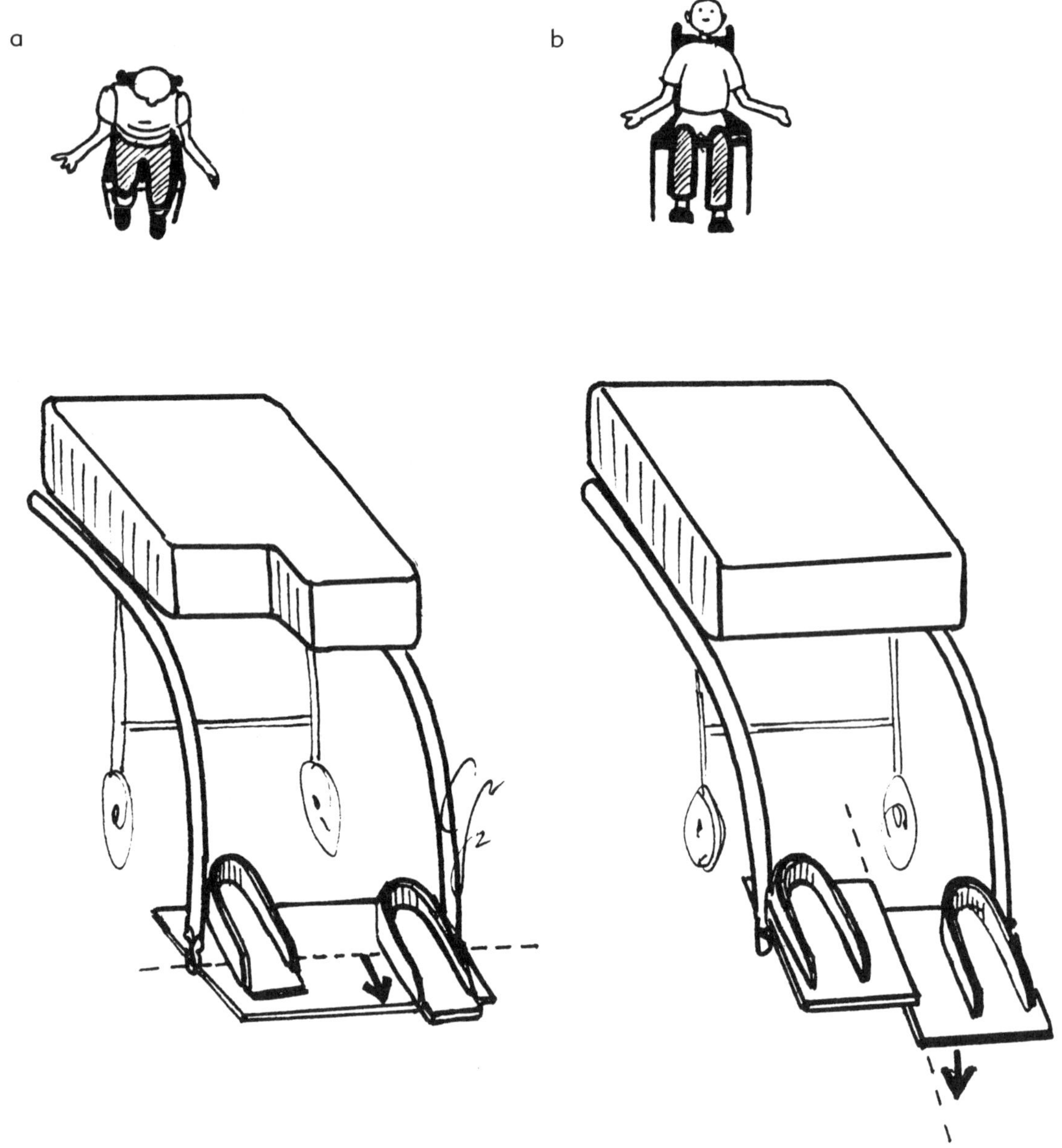


**FIGURE 2.15.** Accommodating unequal thigh (a) and calf (b) lengths.

When the child assumes a seated position, the thighs should be maintained in a neutral position of slight abduction. As illustrated in Figure 2.18, an abductor pommel may be positioned between the child's knees to prevent the legs from coming together or crossing. A child who is hypertonic will often adduct the thighs while extending. In some instances, this extension can be prevented by widening the abductor pommel as illustrated in Figure 2.19. Adductor pads can be placed on the outside of the child's knees to prevent the child's thighs from assuming a position of excessive abduction. This is especially evident with children demonstrating low tone. An abductor pommel and adductor pads are often used together to stabilize the thighs as illustrated in Figures 2.18 and 2.19. Knee blocks, previously discussed, also maintain the thighs in neutral alignment.

In some instances, further lower extremity and pelvic support can be achieved through the use of a *custom molded seat cushion.* This cushion is molded to the specific client and is often useful to accommodate fixed pelvic or hip deformities. As the support is within the seat cushion, additional pads are

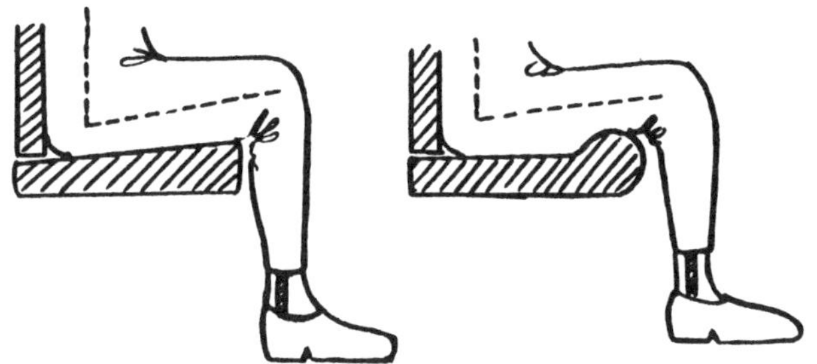

**FIGURE 2.16.** Distal pelvic positioners.

not usually necessary. Other types of seat cushions allow for some custom tailoring by using component pieces such as hip guides and abductor and adductor pads. These pieces are adhered to the base of the seat and concealed under a unifying cover.

When seated, the child's feet should be supported. In addition to support, many children require stabilization to minimize extraneous movements of the lower extremities. As such movements tend to negatively alter the position of the pelvis thereby destroying the child's stable sitting base, failure to stabilize the feet can have an adverse effect on the child's ability to reliably access a switch. As previously depicted in Figure 2.15b, unequal leg length may necessitate the use of individual foot plates. Some foot plates also allow for adjustability in the angle of the ankle. This is especially important for children possessing fixed deformities of the ankle. As the angle of the foot plate can be adjusted, contact with the bottom of the child's foot can be maximized, thereby promoting greater distribution of pressure. Angle adjustability is also important for some children with increased extensor tone. With such children the angle of the foot plate can be adjusted to position the foot in slight dorsiflexion, which in turn may help to reduce the child's tendency to extend (Figure 2.20). If the child has a strong positive supporting reaction, the positioning specialist may wish to shorten the depth of the foot plate thereby eliminating contact with the ball of the child's foot (Figure 2.21). With a shortened foot plate, the child should wear firm-soled shoes to avoid drop-foot deformity.

## Trunk Stability

Lateral supports or scoliosis pads are often used to prevent the child's trunk from falling to either side. These pads can be planar (flat) or curved. Since

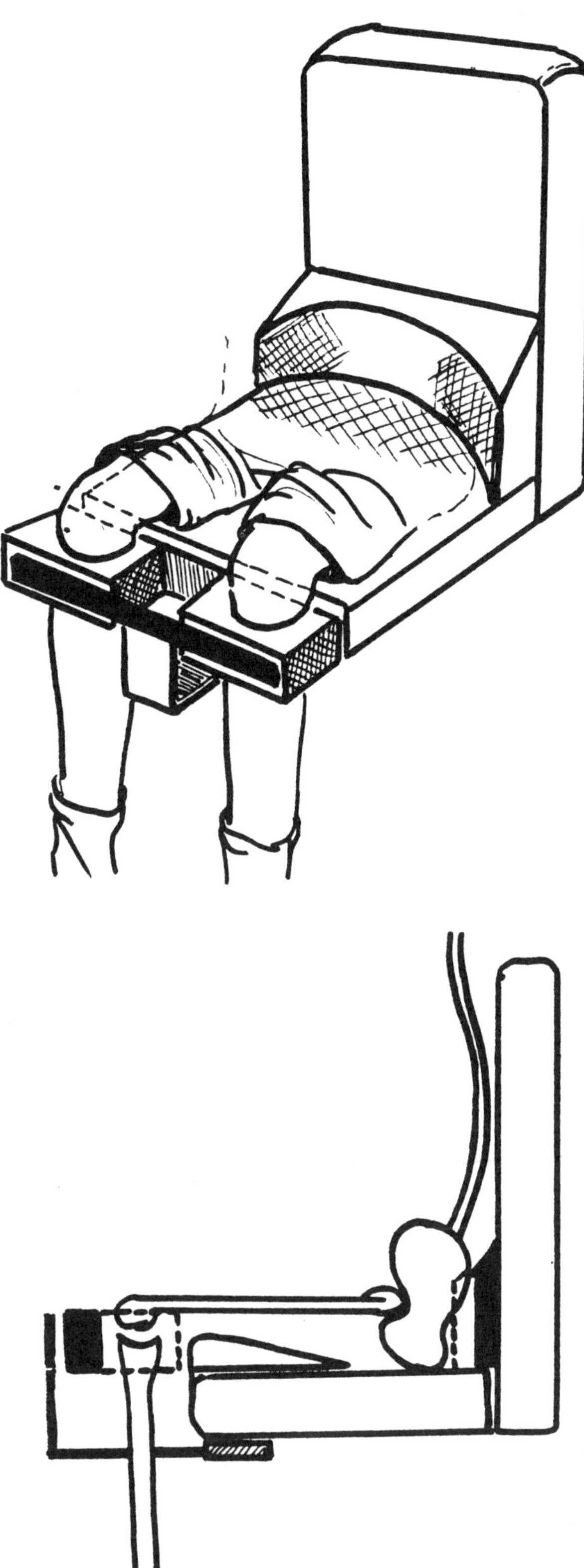

**FIGURE 2.17.** Knee blocks.

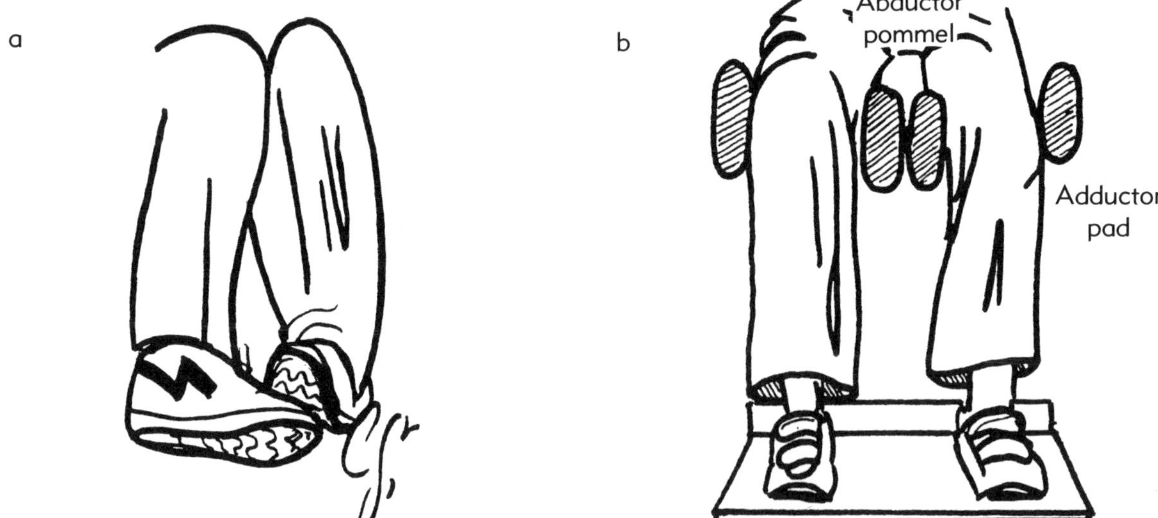


FIGURE 2.18. Abductor pommel and adductor pads maintain the thighs in neutral alignment.

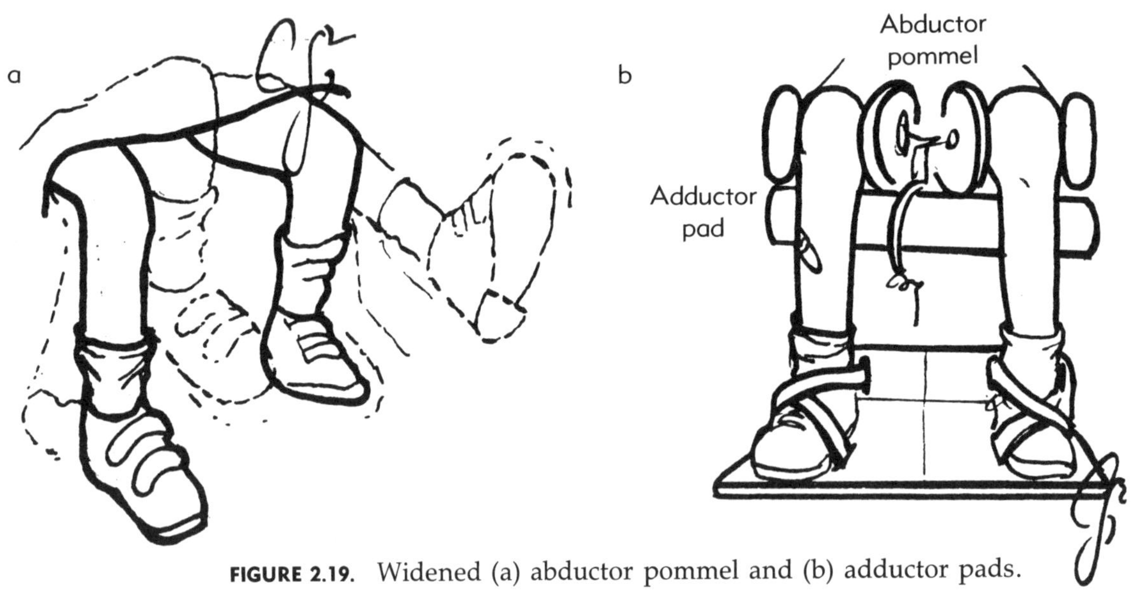


FIGURE 2.19. Widened (a) abductor pommel and (b) adductor pads.

curved thoracic pads follow the contour of the child's thorax, they must be constructed in a manner that allows them to be easily removed or swung away when transferring the child in or out of the chair. When contoured back cushions are used, the lateral pads may be built into the seat back. When a scoliosis is present, a multiple point system of control is required. As illustrated in Figure 2.22, one lateral pad is placed just below the apex of the curve on the convex side. On the concave side, the other lateral pad is placed above the apex of the curve,

FIGURE 2.20. Angle adjustable foot plate.

**FIGURE 2.21.** Shortened foot plate.

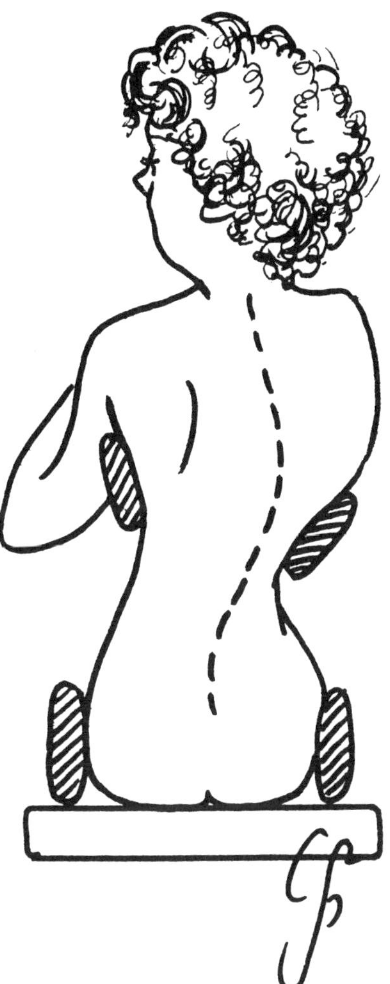

**FIGURE 2.22.** Four-point system to support a scoliosis.

while a hip guide is placed below the apex (Trefler & Taylor, 1984). Additionally, a second hip guide may be placed on the other side of the pelvis to prohibit any lateral movement of the pelvis that could produce curvature of the lower spine. If the scoliosis is severe, individual pads may not be sufficient. In such cases a custom-molded system that maximizes contact with the body may be necessary to provide support to the bony deformity.

As illustrated in Figure 2.23, trunk stability can also be enhanced through the use of chest supports, available in a variety of styles. In addition to providing lateral trunk support, curved thoracic pads (Figure 2.23a) assist with anterior support by cupping around the front of the trunk.

In general, a "V" harness (Figure 2.23b) does not offer adequate support and the upper straps often cause areas of irritation on the side of the neck. In direct contrast to the "V" harness, a butterfly harness (Figure 2.23c) applies pressure on the sternum. This anterior pressure on the sternum assists in keeping the trunk erect. When adjusting the top straps of the chest support, care should be taken to ensure that the straps do not cause irritation on the side of the neck (Figure 2.23d). This is especially true for the "H" harness, as the straps run vertically. With most types of butterfly harnesses, the top straps are angled slightly to cross over the shoulder away from the neck. The top strap should also come over the child's shoulder and anchor to the seat back equal to or below the level of the shoulder (Figure 2.23e). This helps to distribute pressure over the shoulder and prevent irritation to the neck.

As illustrated in Figure 2.23f, it is important to note that the lower strap of the chest support should be separate from the pelvic belt. If the support is anchored to the pelvic belt, the pelvic belt will not adequately stabilize the pelvis. Instead, the pelvic belt tends to shift upward exerting unwanted pressure on the abdomen.

The center pad of a butterfly harness is typically fabricated from material that is more rigid than the straps. Another type of support, the Danmar harness (Figure 2.23g), is constructed from a firm but bendable substance that is on the sternum and continues over the top of the shoulder.

For some children, the chest support may be insufficient as these children may continue to roll their shoulders forward. For these children, shoulder retractors (Figure 2.23h) may be necessary to

a. Curved thoracic pads

f. H-harness: Separate lower chest harness strap and pelvic belt

b. "V" harness

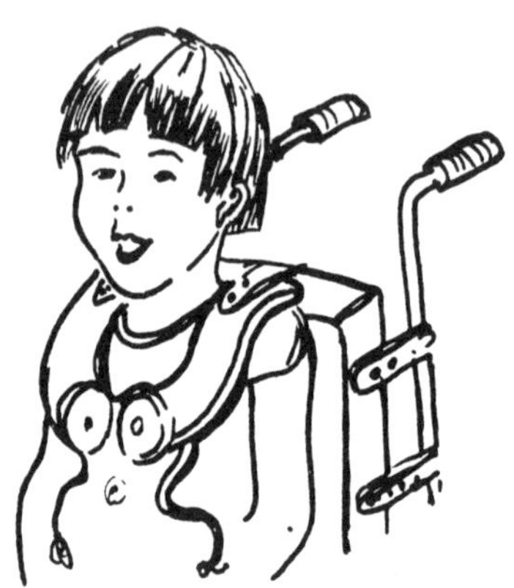

g. Danmar harness

c. Butterfly harness

d. Straps should not be positioned to cause irritation to neck.

e. Shoulder harness should be anchored lower than the shoulder level.

h. Shoulder retractors

**FIGURE 2.23.** Trunk stability.

hold the shoulders back thereby assisting the child in keeping the trunk erect. Trunk stability can also be enhanced when a lap tray is employed. This is especially true when the lap tray cutout follows the contour of the child's thorax. As will be discussed in greater detail in Chapter 3, the height of the tray should be adjusted to allow the child's forearms to rest comfortably, as children often use their forearms as a weight-bearing surface to assist with keeping their trunk erect. As head control is dependent on adequate trunk stability, the importance of trunk stability to children's ability to control their head for switch access cannot be overstated.

## Head Support

Head support is critical for the child who lacks good head control. Adequate head control is necessary for a child to access a head-activated switch and visually monitor a target system. Many types of headrests are available. As is the case with other equipment components, a single type is not appropriate for every child. Several head support options are depicted in Figure 2.24. As illustrated, the use of an extended seat back as a headrest is rarely appropriate for children with severe physical disabilities, because an extended back tends to push the head forward (Figure 2.24a). Similarly, large pads placed on each side of the head should be avoided because they compromise the child's peripheral vision and do not provide adequate stability for the head and neck (Figure 2.24b).

A slightly curved headrest (Figure 2.24c) is typically used with the child who does not require a lot of support but simply requires an area to rest the head. The neck ring illustrated in Figure 2.24d provides support under the occiput. A collar headrest (Figure 2.24e) is most appropriate for children who demonstrate strong tonic neck reflexes and tend to habitually hold their heads down. If steps are not taken to promote a more upright head posture, overstretching of neck extensors may occur and structural deformities may be forthcoming. The collar provides neck and occipital support, while simultaneously reducing movement and thereby maintaining an upright and midline orientation of the head. A neck collar can also be used on an as-needed basis throughout the course of the child's day.

Illustrated in Figure 2.25 is an Otto Bock headrest that provides support under the occiput and curves around the sides of the head. This type of headrest generally works well for a child using a head switch. The headrest should come in contact with the bottom of the skull and back of the head. If the headrest is too far back or too far forward, head control will not be optimal. The hardware of the headrest enables the headrest to be adjusted in all directions, allowing appropriate placement behind the child's head. For the child who has some head control, a headrest can also serve as a "home base." For the child capable of using a lateral head turn for switch access, contoured headrests often serve as a guide, facilitating movement on and off the switch interface.

The lap tray frequently plays an important role in promoting head control. As illustrated in Figure 2.26a and b, Julie is not able to keep her head in the headrest without a lap tray. When, however, a lap tray is employed, Julie is able to prop on her elbows and forearms, thereby increasing stability throughout her trunk, shoulders, and neck and enabling her to have better head control (Figure 2.26c).

## Upper Extremity Support

A lap board or tray is also vital to optimizing upper extremity control. As will be discussed in greater depth in Chapter 3, care should be taken to ensure that the tray is not too high (causing the child to elevate his or her shoulders, thereby restricting head movement) or too low (compromising the child's ability to weight bear on the forearms). Weight bearing on the forearms is sometimes desirable, because it provides receptive stimulation to the shoulder girdle, producing greater head, upper extremity, and trunk control. In some cases the positioning specialist may select an angled or easel lap tray (Figure 2.27). For some children, the easel lap tray serves to inhibit an active symmetrical tonic neck reflex by positioning the forearms in elbow flexion thus preventing the arms from assuming a posture of extension. The head is free to operate more independently from the arms while accessing a head-activated switch or visually monitoring the target system. An easel tray may also prove beneficial for displaying materials for children with visual problems. It also assists children with muscle weakness

a. Extended seat back

b. Large lateral head pads

c. Curved headrest

d. Neck ring

e. Hensinger head collar

**FIGURE 2.24.** Head supports.

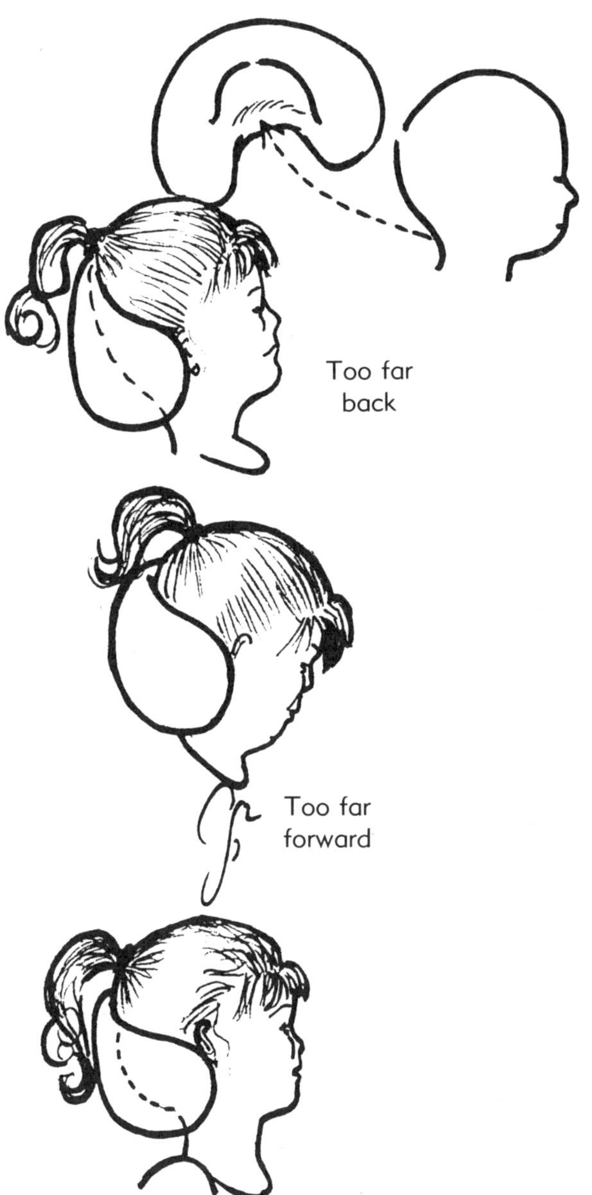


**FIGURE 2.25.** Curved two-step headrest.

of the trunk or neck who experience difficulty returning to an upright trunk position.

As illustrated in Figure 2.28, a bumper can be placed behind the child's elbow and along the forearm to promote a more functional forward arm posture. Such pads can also be used to limit horizontal abduction: a tendency to habitually extend the arms out to the side. In some cases, bumpers may be positioned behind the upper arm or shoulder to prevent excessive shoulder retraction promoting a more forward arm posture. Some children may require stabilization of their forearms when they are attempting the motor task of switch access. Options for stabilizing the upper extremities are discussed in greater detail in Chapter 3.

### Manipulation of Orientation in Space

Children who have severe physical disabilities frequently benefit from a seating system that allows for specificity of orientation in space. As illustrated in Figure 2.28, this is achieved by holding the seat-to-back angle constant, while tilting the entire seating system. Nwoabi (1987) found that upper extremity function is influenced by the body's orientation in space and that the clients in that study performed better in a neutral orientation than they did at 30° and 15° of posterior inclination or 15° of anterior inclination. However, many children may benefit from small degrees of inclination to facilitate upper extremity function (Bergman et al., 1990).

When the tonic labyrinthine supine reflex is still active, the child tends to assume a position of full extension when seated with a backward tilt. The effect of this reflex can be eliminated by bringing the child into a more upright position. When tilted too far forward, the child will assume a posture of flexion if the tonic labyrinthine prone reflex is active. Tilting the seating system slightly back may eliminate the effect of this reflex.

When provided with appropriate postural stability, many children begin to demonstrate appropriate righting reactions. Righting reactions maintain the normal position of the head in space and maintain the body in line with the head and neck. When tilted too far back, a child may be observed to actively flex his or her neck and upper body in an attempt to right himself or herself. In many instances, bringing the child more upright or slightly forward may actually increase postural extension as the child attempts to bring the body into upright alignment.

A third factor that is important when manipulating a child's orientation in space is the effect of gravity. Gravity can be a strong force, especially for children who have little volitional movement. When tilted too far back, a child may not be able to flex his or her body to move against gravity. When tilted too far forward, the child may be pulled further forward by gravity, and he or she may not have suffi-

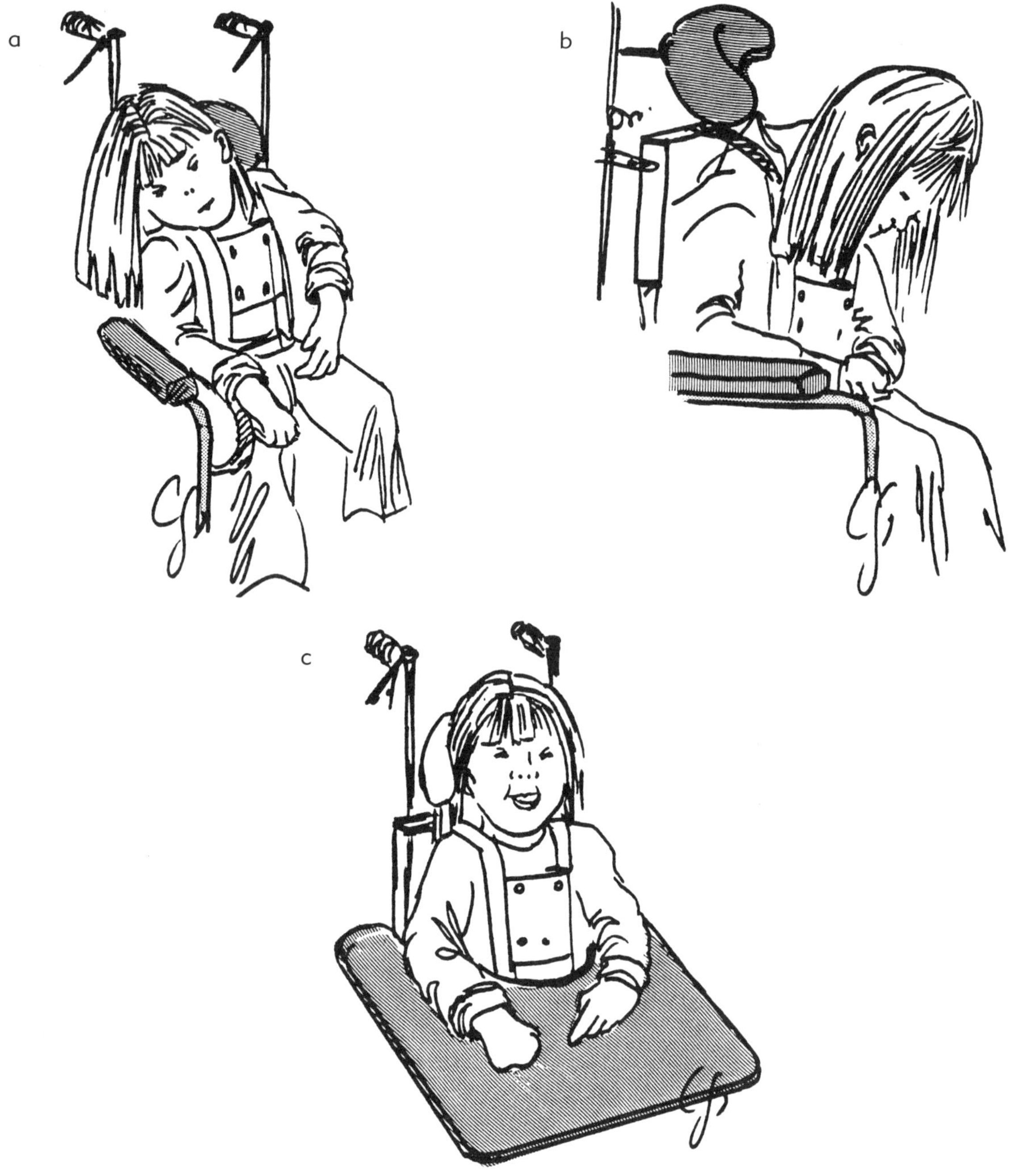


**FIGURE 2.26.** Julie uses a lap tray to promote better head control.

cient muscle strength to lift the head up into the headrest.

All three factors—the labyrinthine reflexes, development of righting reflexes, and gravity—are important considerations when determining a child's optimal orientation in space. A child should be observed for changes in postural tone or volitional activity as he or she is moved through several angles. The optimal orientation for a child is the angle in which the child is not having to work too hard to counteract gravity or to right himself or herself. It is also the point at which muscle tone becomes as close to normal as possible. It is important to note that some children may require a vari-

**FIGURE 2.27.** Angled easel lap tray.

ety of orientations in space. The optimal position may vary during the day as the activities change, tone changes, or as the child fatigues.

### Summary

Appropriate therapeutic positioning is considered crucial to delineating a viable switch setup. A therapeutic positioning system comprises many components that have been determined to enhance overall function. In general, stability is provided where needed; the effects of abnormal muscle tone and reflexes are eliminated or minimized; and skeletal deformities are accommodated. It is important to note that removal or alteration of any one of the components can change the individual's function drastically. Caregivers and therapists should therefore monitor the completeness of the system for missing or broken parts, and care should be taken to keep the system clean, operating smoothly, and readily accessible. Children must be seen for reevaluation as they grow, as they develop motorically, and as their needs change.

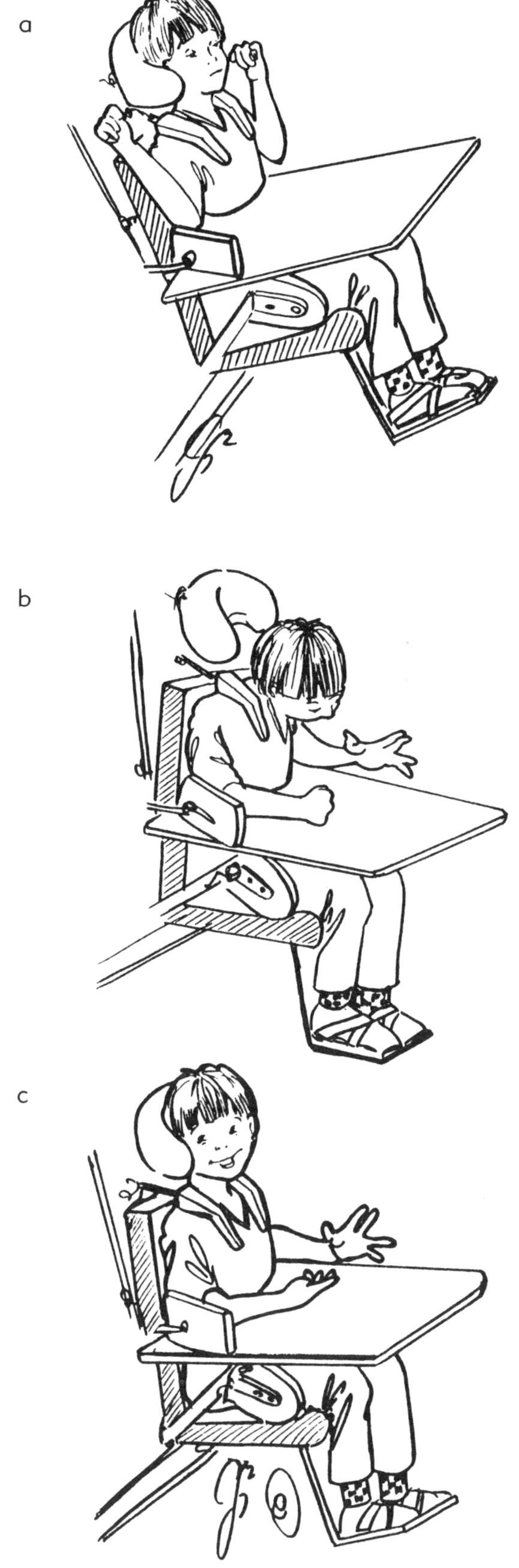


**FIGURE 2.28.** Manipulating orientation in space.

chapter 3

# Determining a Viable Switch Setup

A VIABLE SWITCH SETUP is defined as one that the child can control reliably with minimal fatigue. In determining a viable switch setup, several factors must be taken into consideration. First and perhaps foremost, the facilitator must delineate what movement pattern can be used for reliable switch access. Having delineated a potentially viable movement pattern, attention is then directed toward determining what switch interface will be placed in the path of the previously designated movement pattern. These general issues are the primary focus of Chapter 3.

Many children who are severely physically challenged use their hand as the control site for switch access. Considerable attention is therefore devoted to formats using the hand as the control site. The more motor-involved the child is, however, the greater the likelihood that a control site other than the hand will be required for switch access. In keeping with this need, Chapter 3 also devotes considerable space to a discussion of formats involving alternate control sites.

## Movement Pattern Selection

The process of movement pattern selection is typically a combination of two components:

- ❑ Informal observation/background information
- ❑ Screening for potentially viable movement patterns

### Informal Observation/Background Information

Information regarding the child's typical motor performance when engaged in various functional everyday activities can provide the facilitator with valuable insight into which movement patterns hold promise for viable switch access. As suggested by Lee and Thomas (1990), this informal observation is best achieved by observing the child perform familiar tasks in a familiar environment with a familiar person. With the ready availability of camcorders in many homes and schools, it is now feasible to supplement information derived from the traditional intake questionnaire with videotape segments of the child engaged in functional activities such as dressing, feeding, grooming, and playing with toys. When observing the child involved in these tasks, either live or on videotape, the facilitator is able to glean information regarding the presence and nature of three broad types of movement patterns:

- ❑ Involuntary abnormal movement patterns
- ❑ Voluntary abnormal movement patterns
- ❑ Voluntary normal movement patterns

**INVOLUNTARY ABNORMAL MOVEMENT PATTERNS.** The movement of severely physically challenged children is frequently dominated by involuntary abnormal reflexes—that is, reflexes that, due to cerebral damage, have persisted beyond that time when they are typically integrated in able-bodied babies. Two reflexes worthy of more in-depth discussion are the asymmetrical tonic neck reflex (ATNR) and the symmetrical tonic neck reflex (STNR) (Figure 3.1). As illustrated in Figure 3.1, the ATNR and STNR result in differential patterns of tone that are elicited in response to specific stimuli.

When the child is dominated by an ATNR, turning the head and/or eyes to one side triggers extension of the child's arm on the "faceside" of the head and flexion of the opposite arm. When an STNR is operative, extension of the child's neck causes extension in the arms and possible flexion in the child's legs; flexion of the child's neck results in flexion of the arms and possible extension in the legs. When these reflexes are operative, the child is locked into these positions and must either wait for their influence to weaken or must receive assistance from an adult to release from the reflex.

The consistency with which a given reflex is triggered in response to its eliciting stimuli may vary greatly from child to child. For some children, a given reflex may be obligatory, that is, it is consistently triggered in response to its eliciting stimuli. For many children, however, these reflexes are manifested inconsistently.

When attempting to delineate a viable movement pattern for switch access, it is extremely important to know what involuntary reflex patterns are operative and to what degree. In general, the presence of a reflex may:

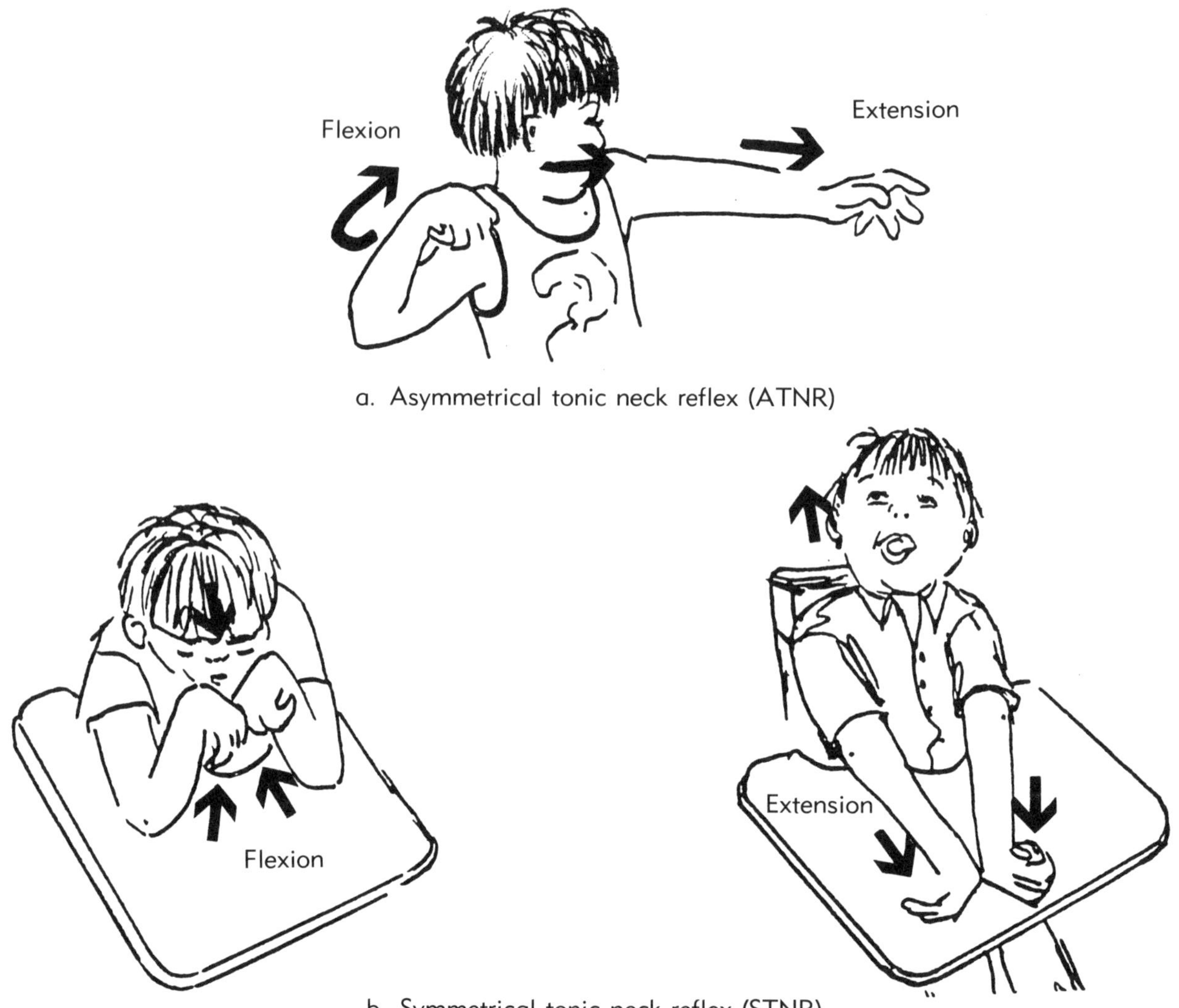


**FIGURE 3.1.** Involuntary movement patterns.

- ❑ Contraindicate the use of certain movement patterns for head-activated switch setups
- ❑ Mandate modification of switch presentation for hand-activated switch setups
- ❑ Mandate special placement of the facilitator and the switch-controlled target system relative to the child

**Contraindicate the Use of Certain Movement Patterns for Head-Activated Switch Setups.** The presence of an obligatory ATNR or STNR may contraindicate the use of certain movement patterns. As illustrated in Figure 3.2, the presence of an obligatory ATNR may preclude the use of a lateral head turn for switch access. Whenever Joey turns his head laterally to activate the switch, an ATNR is triggered (Figure 3.2a). Similarly, the presence of an obligatory STNR may preclude the use of head flexion for Joana (Figure 3.2b). When Joana drops her chin to activate the switch, an STNR is triggered. Although these reflexes may assist these children in maintaining contact with the switch interface, the release aspect of switch access (crucial to utilizing a scanning selection technique) is no longer under voluntary control when the reflex is operative. In cases in which an ATNR or STNR is not obligatory, use of a lateral head turn or head flexion for switch access is feasible. It should, however, be noted that responding may be less reliable than desired, due to the intermittent interference of the reflex.

In many instances, the facilitator may decide to select movement patterns less likely to trigger abnormal reflex patterns. As illustrated in Figure 3.2c, if an ATNR is operative for a child, a lateral head tilt may be selected over a lateral head turn, as the former is less likely to trigger an ATNR. It should, however, be noted that not all children are able to perform a lateral head tilt. Similarly, knowing that an STNR is operative, the facilitator trying to capitalize on a chin-activated switch setup might position the switch in an angled format, thus requiring the child to use a more forward gliding movement pattern, less likely to trigger an STNR (Figure 3.2d).

**Mandate Modification of Switch Presentation for Hand-Activated Switch Setups.** As illustrated in Figure 3.3, the presence of an ATNR or STNR may also affect the manner in which the facilitator presents a switch in a hand-activated switch setup. During the early stages of intervention, the process of activating a hand-activated switch setup is visually mediated, that is, children derive benefit from being able to visually monitor the movement of their hand relative to the switch interface. When an ATNR is operative (Figure 3.3a), lateral placement of the switch may exacerbate the appearance of the reflex. Whenever Brian turns his head laterally to monitor the activity of his hand, an ATNR is triggered. Knowing that an ATNR is still operative for Brian, the facilitator may strive to minimize the likelihood of triggering an ATNR by positioning the switch more midline, thus minimizing the need for Brian to turn his head laterally to visually monitor the activity of his hand.

The presence of a strong STNR can also confound the use of a hand-activated format (Figure 3.3b). Whenever Greta looks down to monitor the activity of her hand, an STNR is triggered pulling her arms back into flexion. Knowing that an STNR is operative, the professional might attempt to minimize the likelihood of triggering the reflex by presenting the switch in a vertically angled format. When the switch is presented vertically angled as opposed to flat, considerably less head flexion is required for Greta to visually monitor the activity of the hand relative to the switch.

**Mandate Special Placement of the Facilitator and/or the Switch-Controlled Target System Relative to the Child.** The presence of an abnormal reflex can also have therapeutic implications for how the target system (battery-operated toy, communication device, personal computer) and/or the facilitator are positioned relative to the child (Figure 3.4). When working with a child dominated by a strong ATNR (Figure 3.4a), it is recommended that the facilitator avoid positioning herself or himself on the side(s) prone to eliciting the reflex. Whenever possible, the facilitator should strive to work face-to-face with the child at the child's midline (Frazer, Hensinger, & Phelps, 1987). When conditions necessitate working behind the child, the facilitator might consider using a mirror to allow the child to view the interacting facilitator, without promoting the head turn likely to trigger an ATNR. This can be achieved by positioning a mirror (ideally lightweight mirrored Plexiglas) in front of both the child and the facilitator.

When working with a child prone to the interference of an STNR (Figure 3.4b), the facilitator should always be cognizant of the need to work at eye level. If the facilitator fails to lower herself or him-

**FIGURE 3.2.** Contraindicated use of certain movement patterns for head-activated setups.

self to eye level when interacting with the child, the act of looking up at the adult will inadvertently trigger an STNR. Similarly, if placement of the target system necessitates neck flexion or extension, switch access may be less than optimal, as the act of visually monitoring the target system elicits an STNR, which in turn confounds the child's ability to reliably control the switch interface. If such is the case, the facilitator might consider circumventing this dilemma by presenting the target system at eye level for the child.

As can be seen from these examples, it is important to know what involuntary abnormal reflex patterns are operative and to what degree. Presence of such reflexes may:

- ❑ Contraindicate the use of certain movement patterns for switch access
  - — If an ATNR is operative, the use of a lateral head turn may be contraindicated.
  - — If an STNR is operative, the use of head flexion may be contraindicated.

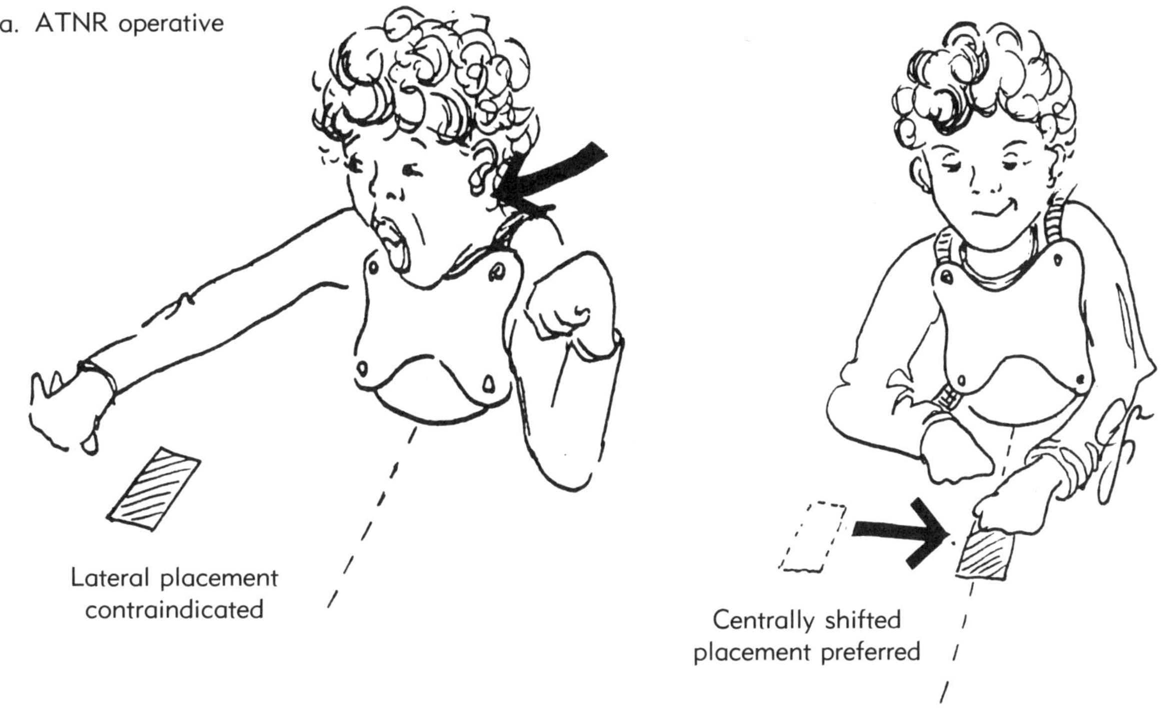


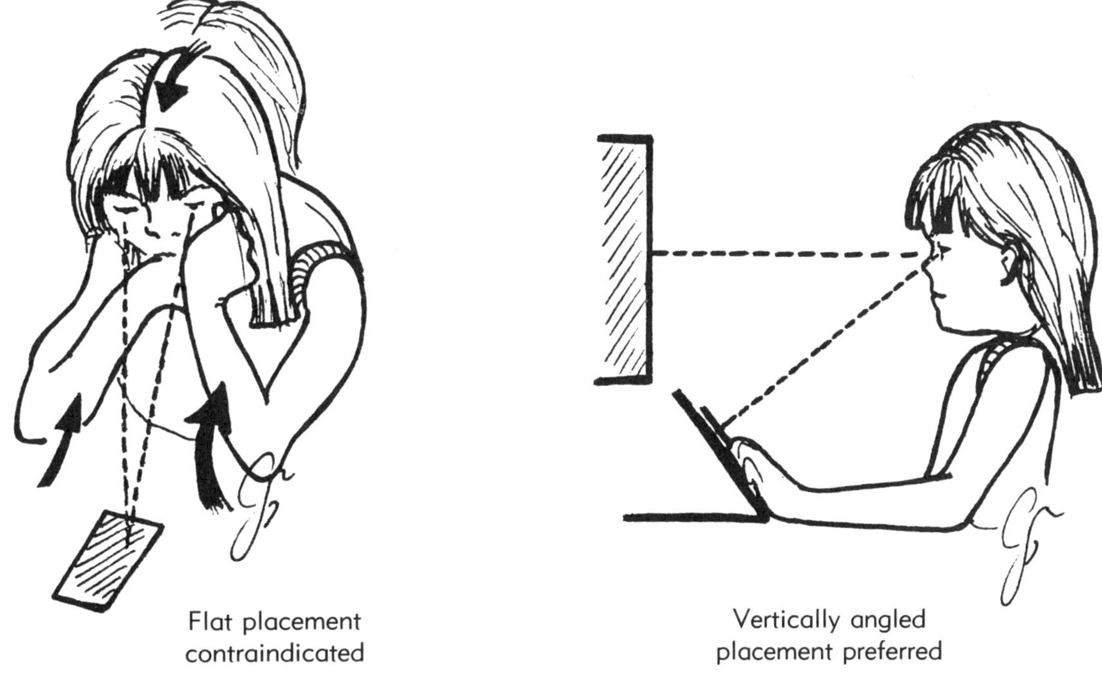


**FIGURE 3.3.** Mandated modifications of switch presentation for hand-activated switch setups.

a. ATNR operative

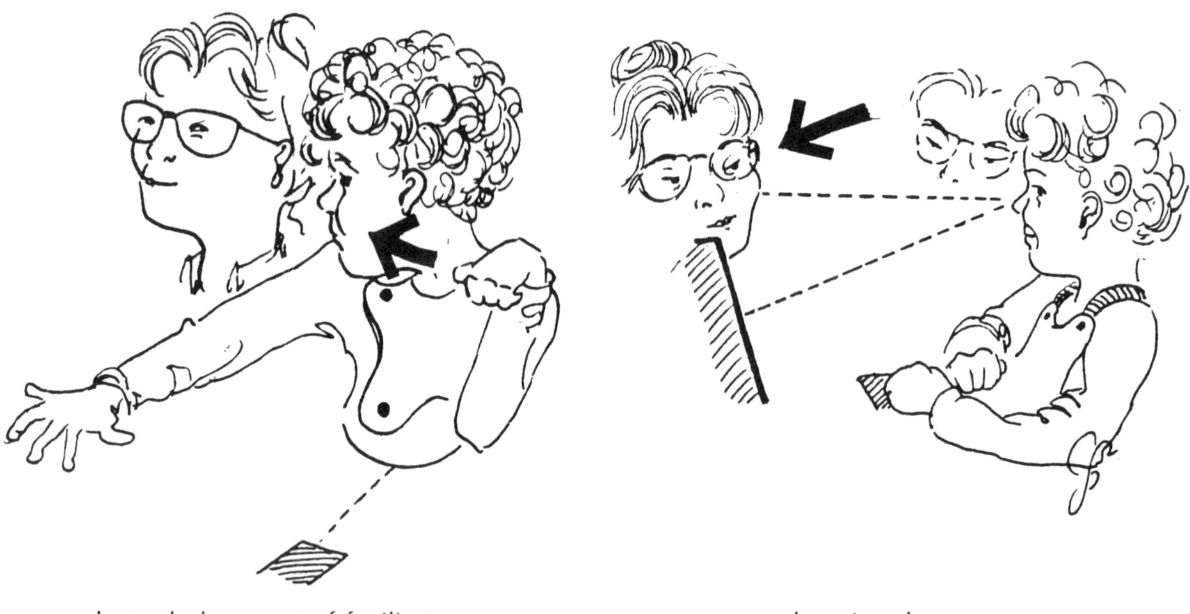

Lateral placement of facilitator and/or target system contraindicated

Anterior placement preferred

b. STNR operative

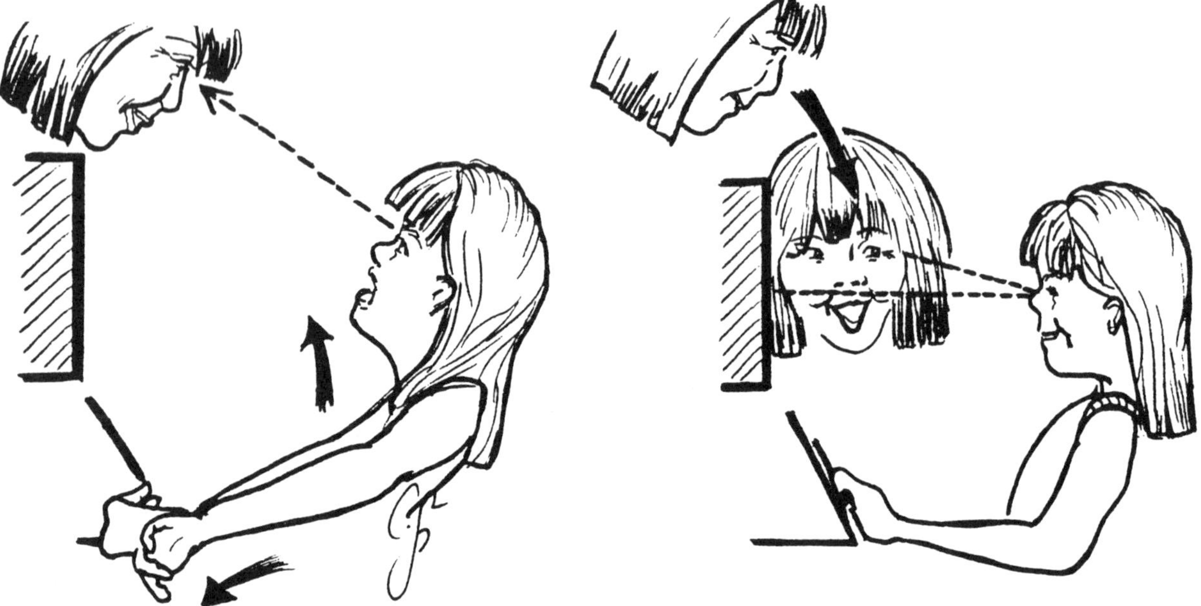

Place facilitator and/or target system at eye level

**FIGURE 3.4.** Mandated special placement of the target system or facilitator.

- ❑ Mandate the use of movement patterns less likely to trigger the reflex
  - — If an ATNR is operative, a lateral head tilt may be preferred over a lateral head turn.
  - — If an STNR is operative, a forward glide may be preferred over neck flexion.
- ❑ Dictate changes in the manner of presenting switches to be accessed in a hand-activated format
  - — If an ATNR is operative, more central placement may be preferred over lateral placement of a hand-activated switch.
  - — If an STNR is operative, an angled placement may be preferred over a flat presentation of a hand-activated switch.
- ❑ Dictate placement of the target system and/or the facilitator relative to the child
  - — If an ATNR is operative, the target system and interacting facilitator should be placed more midline.
  - — If an STNR is operative, the facilitator should strive to work at eye level and should position the target system in a location that does not require marked neck flexion or extension.

**VOLUNTARY ABNORMAL MOVEMENT PATTERNS.** Many of the movement patterns performed by children who are motorically involved are best described as voluntary but abnormal movement patterns. Basically, voluntary abnormal movement patterns can be discussed as those

- ❑ Using involuntary abnormal movement patterns as part of a voluntary movement pattern
- ❑ Using compensatory, posturing strategies to build in the stability
- ❑ Using synergy patterns instead of more integrated patterns

**Using Involuntary Abnormal Movement Patterns as Part of a Voluntary Movement Pattern.** Children with cerebral palsy will sometimes attempt to use their involuntary abnormal movement patterns (STNR, ATNR) to assist them in performing functional movement. As illustrated in Figure 3.5, Brian is unable to extend his arm to access a desired object presented at midline. He is then observed to turn his head to the right to trigger an ATNR, which in turn promotes extension of his arm. Once the reflex has weakened, Brian proceeds to move his extended arm toward midline to access the desired toy.

In Figure 3.6, Trevor is unable to move his arms toward midline to make contact with a desirable object. He is then observed to drop his head to trigger an STNR, which in turn moves his arms forward into a flexed posture. When the reflex has weakened, Trevor is observed to extend his head to force the arms into extension. Once the reflex has weakened, Trevor proceeds to access the desired target object.

**Using Compensatory Strategies to Enhance Stability.** Children with cerebral palsy typically demonstrate abnormalities of postural tone. Due to insult to the motor area of the brain, their muscles may have (a) too much tone (hypertonicity), resulting in "tight muscles"; (b) too little tone (hypotonicity), resulting in "floppy muscles"; or (c) fluctuating tone (Campbell, c. 1985), resulting in too much tone for a period of time then changing to too little tone. Because of this abnormal tone, the movements of such children are often performed in an abnormal fashion. Generally, children with cerebral palsy do not use a variety of controlled and graded movements. Instead, they have learned to use a small number of abnormal compensatory movement patterns (Burkhart, 1987).

The mobility required for switch access must be built on a stable base. The importance of therapeutic positioning that can help to normalize tone and thereby foster more functional normal movement patterns cannot be overstated. Often, children with cerebral palsy can be observed to invent compensatory strategies to promote increased stability. In so doing, however, mobility is often compromised. Illustrated in Figure 3.7 are two children who have adapted different strategies for holding their heads up. In Figure 3.7a, Deana is using extension of her arms on the lap tray surface to assist her in stabilizing her trunk and head in an upright position. In the process of using her arms for support, however, Deana has unwittingly compromised their use for object manipulation or switch access.

Ehren (Figure 3.7b) is also faced with the dilemma of poor head control. Attempting to compensate for this predicament, Ehren adopted a compensatory strategy of elevating his shoulders and tipping his head back. Although he can now hold his head erect, the fact that his head is tipped back compromises Ehren's field of vision. Furthermore, the fact that his shoulders are elevated severely limits

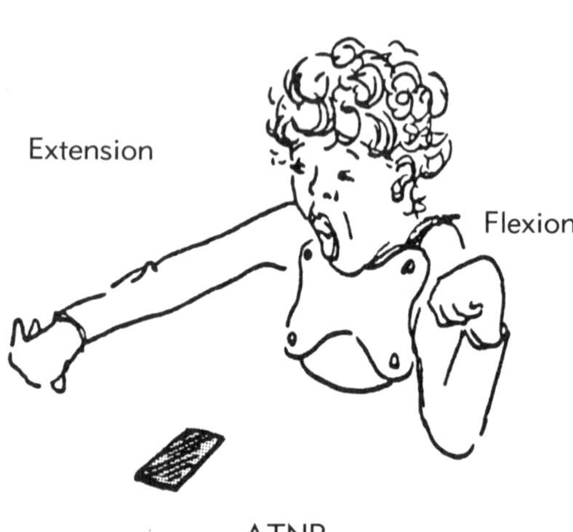

**FIGURE 3.5.** Voluntary abnormal movement patterns—Using an ATNR.

rotation of his head to the left or right and limits the use of his upper extremities.

These abnormal ways that severely physically challenged children move and hold their bodies against gravity can ultimately result in structural changes in the muscles and ligaments. These limitations, or contractures as they are called, inevitably impose further restrictions on the quality and range of movement possible. What initially was adopted as a "helping" strategy, in the long run only served to further exacerbate the initial problem.

**Using Synergy Patterns.** Children with cerebral palsy often experience difficulty isolating movement (Burkhart, 1987). As symbolically reflected in Figure 3.8, such children tend to perform movements as whole patterns as opposed to component parts that can be "mixed and matched" to create a wide range of movement patterns. These whole movement patterns are often referred to as synergy patterns. That is, when physically challenged children perform a voluntary movement they tend to do so in a preset, abnormal way (frequently with overflow of movement to other parts of the body). Because these abnormal synergy patterns reflect larger "prepackaged" units, they do not lend themselves to being flexibly combined and recombined to form a broad, varied array of movement patterns. It is therefore not surprising that the movement patterns of motor-involved children are much more limited in their generative scope than those of physically normal children. As illustrated in Figure 3.9a, an abnormal synergy pattern involving internal rotation of the shoulder, pronation of the forearm, and ulnar deviation of the hand is sometimes noted when attempting to establish a hand-activated switch setup. As this movement pattern is typically performed using abnormal tone, its use for switch access is considered to be less than desirable. As illustrated in Figure 3.9b and as is discussed later in the book, the manner in which a switch is presented can sometimes help break down these synergy patterns, allowing switch access to occur using motor patterns performed with more normalized tone.

**VOLUNTARY NORMAL MOVEMENT PATTERNS.** According to Campbell (c. 1985), those movement patterns most frequently performed by children with cerebral palsy are those that are abnormally coordinated. Move-

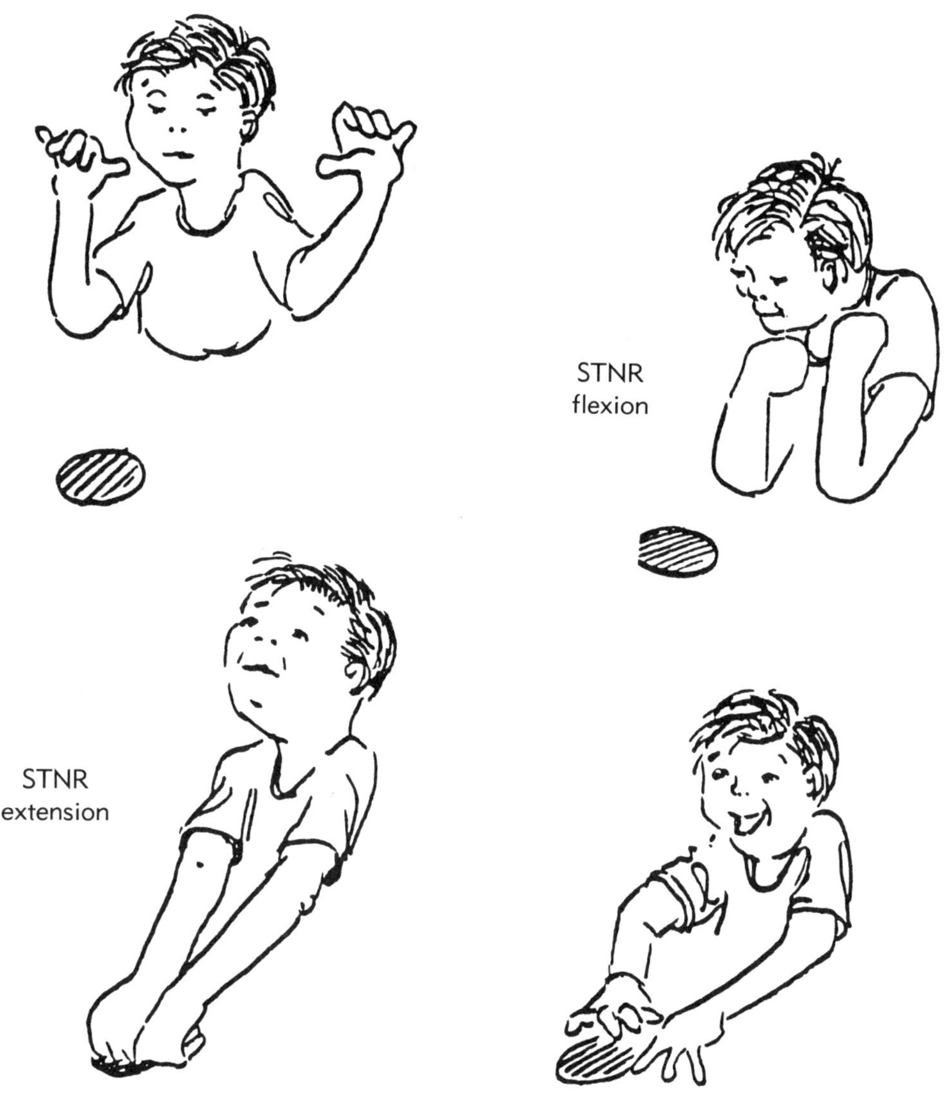


**FIGURE 3.6.** Voluntary abnormal movement patterns—Using an STNR.

ment patterns that are coordinated in a normal fashion tend to be infrequently performed.

Voluntary normal movement patterns are best described as those that look normal in their execution and appear to be performed effortlessly in the absence of abnormal increased tone. It is important to note that the more severely impaired the child, the fewer the voluntary normal movement patterns that are available for switch access. The manner in which the child is therapeutically positioned and the way in which a switch interface is presented are two factors that play a crucial role in promoting voluntary normal movement patterns.

When delineating a viable switch setup, the facilitator is ideally looking to achieve switch access using a voluntary normal movement pattern. Much of the challenge of delineating viable switch access, however, lies with the facilitator's ability to orchestrate those factors conducive to the appearance of voluntary normal movement patterns. In the event that a voluntary normal pattern of access is not forthcoming, the facilitator may be forced to settle for the use of a voluntary abnormal movement pattern. Although voluntary abnormal movement patterns can be considered as a second alternative to voluntary normal movement patterns, involuntary abnormal movement patterns (those that are reflexive in nature) are considered to be less than desirable for switch access (Burkhart, 1987; York, Nietupski, & Hamre-Nietupski, 1985). Although these patterns may assist the child in initiating and maintaining switch contact, they are not conducive to releasing

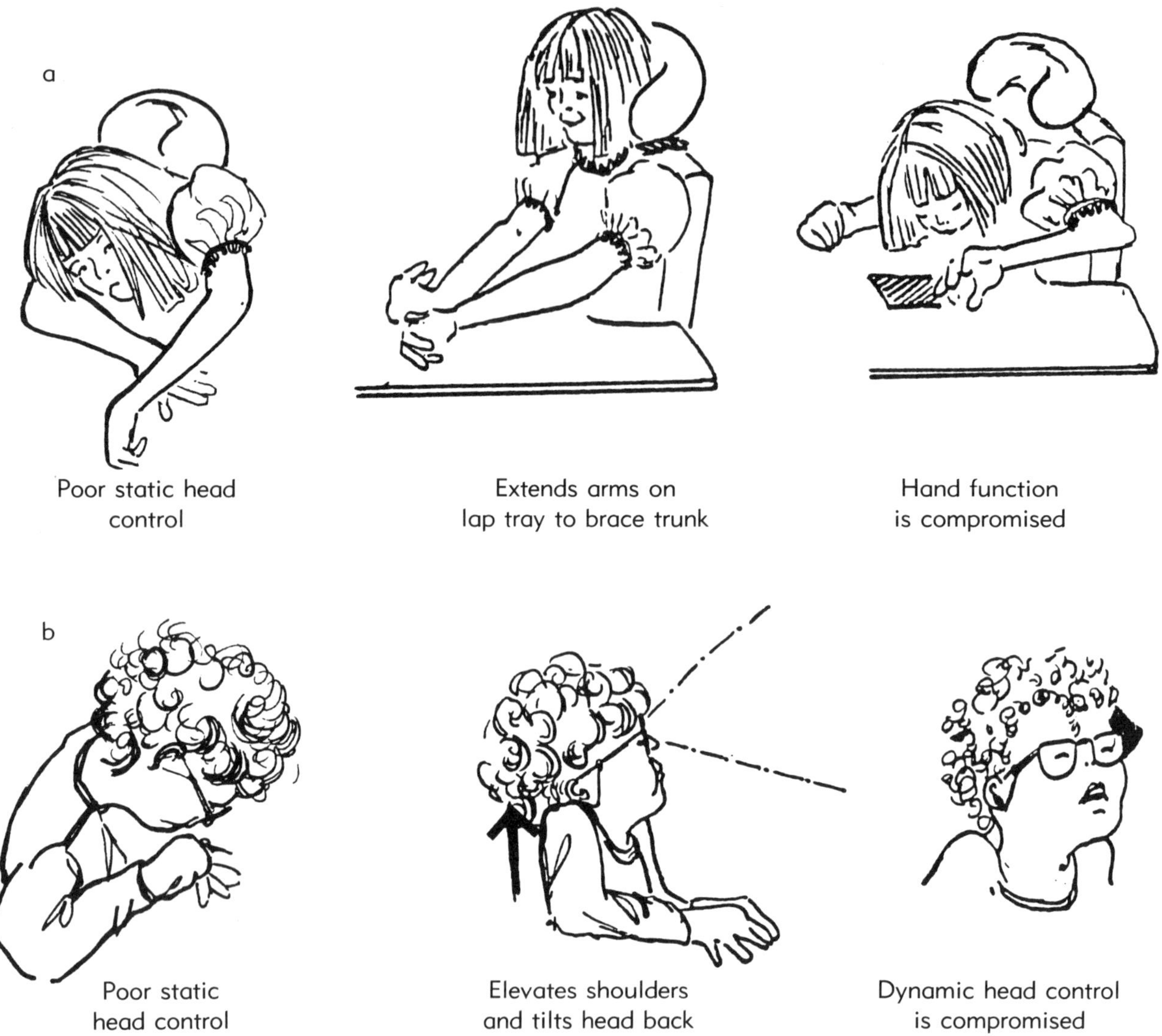


**FIGURE 3.7.** Compensatory strategies for promoting better head control.

switch contact in a timely fashion. Furthermore, they promote practice of a movement pattern that the motor specialist has worked hard to eliminate from the child's movement repertoire. As such, their use should generally be avoided.

When delineating a potentially viable movement pattern for switch access, background information regarding medical status is also vital to the selection process. Children with hypotonia, for example, are frequently susceptible to shoulder subluxation or dislocation. Similarly, many children with athetosis and severe spasticity are prone to hip subluxation or dislocation (Frazer et al., 1987). When the child's medical history confirms this to be the case, care should be taken to select movement patterns that decrease the likelihood of dislocation (e.g., knee abduction).

## Screening for Potentially Viable Movement Patterns

The informal observation and background information previously discussed are then supplemented by information derived from a cursory screening of the various movement patterns typically used for switch access. When conducting this screening, the facilitator should consider using a switch interfaced with a highly motivating end reward. As illustrated in Figure 3.10, a switch is required that can be easily

a. Normal development

Isolated movement components

Mixed and matched to form a variety of movement patterns

b. Abnormal development

Prepackaged movement components (synergy patterns)

Limited array of movements

**FIGURE 3.8.** Abnormal synergy patterns.

positioned relative to the various control sites (i.e., the body parts that will actually make contact with the switch). This can be achieved by using (a) a low-profile touch switch (as opposed to a force-sensitive switch) with a substantial nonactivating surface that permits easy handling by the facilitator (e.g., TASH plate switch) or (b) the more typical pedal or tread switch to which a handle is attached with Velcro to permit easy manipulation by the facilitator (Wright & Nomura, 1985). In an attempt to heighten the child's motivation to perform the task, the facilitator should consider interfacing the switch with a timer and a tape recorder containing a loop-tape (telephone answering machine tape cassette) of hysterical laughter. When conducting this task, the child is required to tickle "Mr. Tickle" (the switch) with various body parts. With each contact, the child is rewarded by Mr. Tickle's hysterical laughter. Mr. Tickle then proceeds to another control site. "Mr. Tickle! You come back here right now . . . Where is he going? . . . Oh look, he's hiding under your chin . . . (whispered) Tickle him with your chin . . . Yes! You got him . . . (whispered) Get him again. Oh no, he's running away. Mr. Tickle! Where are you going?"

As it has been speculated by various authors (Van Tatenhove, 1985; Wright & Nomura, 1985) that invisible movement patterns (i.e., movements that children are unable to see themselves perform) are cognitively more difficult than movement patterns that can be visually monitored, the facilitator may wish to perform this task with and without the benefit of a mirror. Although this screening can be conducted by a sole facilitator, it is ideally performed with two: one facilitator manipulating the switch and

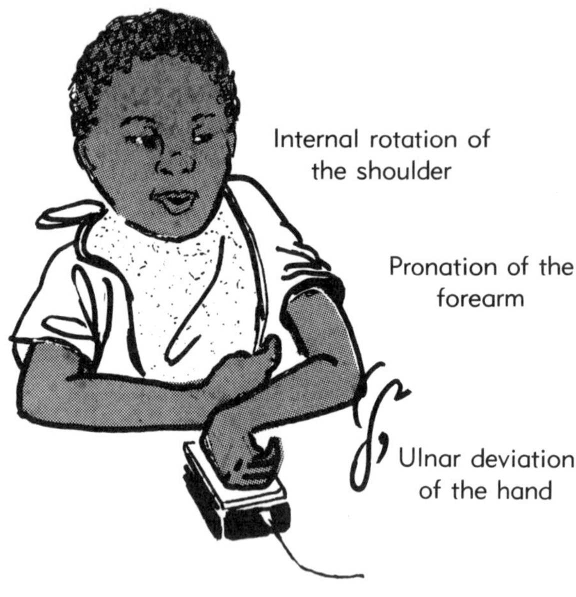

**FIGURE 3.9.** An abnormal synergy pattern involving the upper extremities.

a second facilitator noting (a) the child's ability to reliably perform the requested movement pattern, (b) the speed with which the child is able to initiate the movement pattern, and (c) the quality of that movement pattern. With respect to the latter, the facilitator is interested in the degree to which the targeted movement pattern is performed with abnormal movement patterns, an overall increase in body tone, and/or the overflow of movement to other parts of the body.

In general, the facilitator is looking for the movement pattern that holds potential for reliable access (Burkhart, 1987; York et al., 1985). Although switch contingencies can be used to train new motor responses, the movement pattern required for access to a communication system is usually one that is at least partially reliable. Within the context of this screening task, emphasis is placed solely on the child's ability to at least target or initiate contact with the switch when the switch is placed in close proximity to the control site. The movement patterns delineated in this screening process must later be subjected to more in-depth evaluation regarding the child's ability to maintain and release contact with the switch (skills crucial to communication device access).

This screening task thus serves to narrow the range of options to those that show high potential for viable access. In general, there appears to be consensus for the need to delineate more than one option for further evaluation. Lee and Thomas (1990) suggested identifying three options. Campbell (c. 1985), in her work with early contingency awareness training, suggested delineating two or more potentially viable options.

## Control Interface Selection

When the facilitator has successfully delineated several movement patterns with potential for viable switch access, attention is directed toward selecting which control interface will be placed in the path of the movement patterns previously designated for more in-depth evaluation.

As documented in Brandenburg and Vanderheiden (1987b), a broad array of switch interfaces are available commercially. Numerous resources also exist for constructing homemade switches (Burkhart, 1980, 1982). Given budgetary constraints, many programs opt for making homemade switches. Although homemade versions are considerably cheaper, they are more prone to failure than commercially available switches (Frazer et al., 1987; Wright & Nomura, 1985). This fact, however, by no means negates their use. Typically, if a person knows how to make a

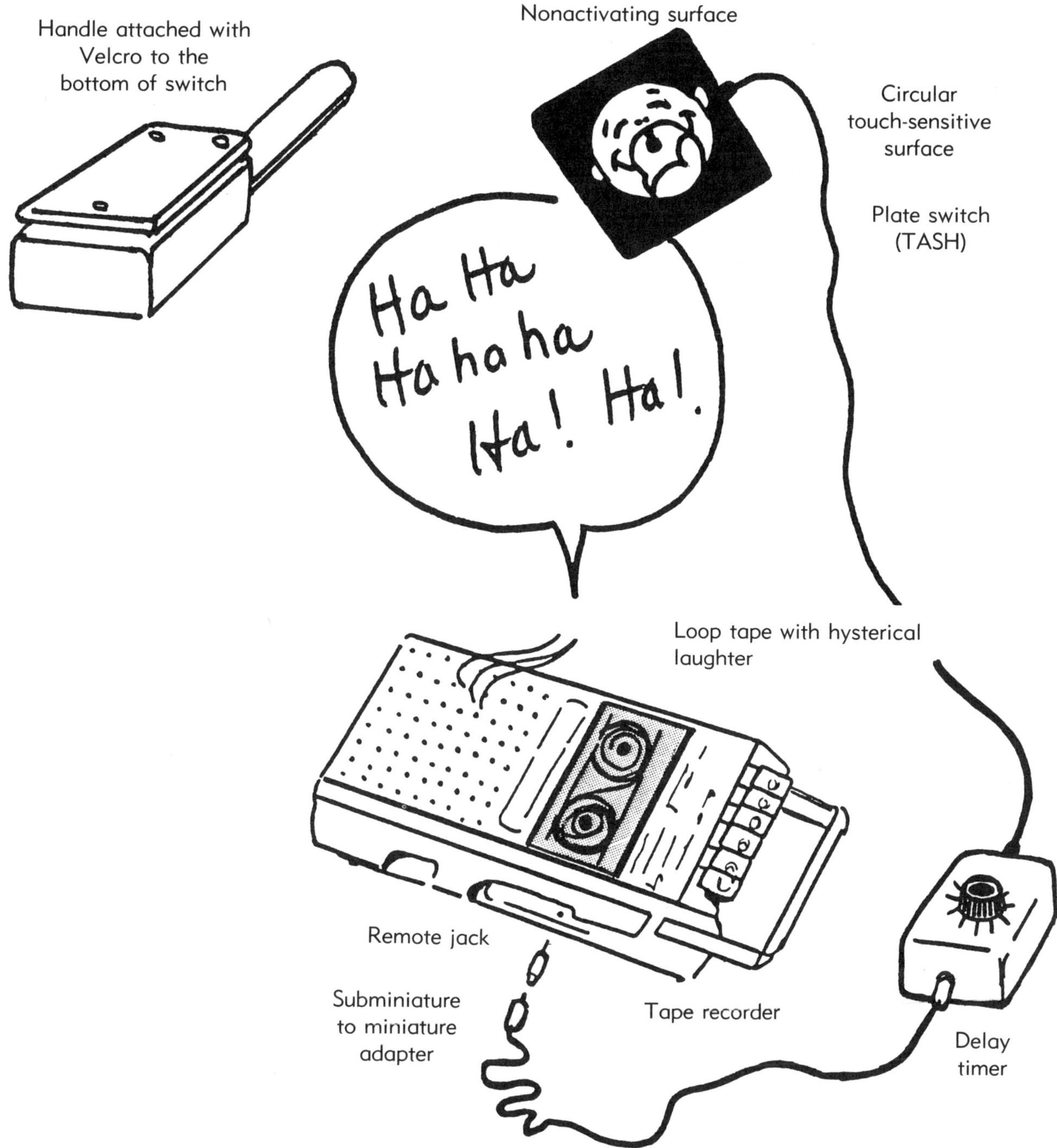


**FIGURE 3.10.** Screening for potentially viable movement patterns.

switch he or she also knows how to fix it. When making a decision to utilize homemade versus commercially available switch interfaces, the person-hours required to build and maintain homemade switches are definitely worthy of administrative consideration.

Switch interfaces vary greatly in their method of activation. Switch closure can be achieved through touch, detection of sound waves (i.e., voice-activated), changes in air pressure, disruption of an invisible infrared beam, muscle contraction, changes in the proximity of one body area relative to another, changes in moisture, and changes in switch orientation.

When selecting a switch interface, the facilitator should select the simplest switch interface capable of meeting the child's needs and abilities. As switches accessed through touch constitute the simplest type of control interface, it should not be surprising that switches accessed through touch (e.g., push, pedal switches) constitute the major type prescribed for use with severely physically challenged children (Wright & Nomura, 1985). Given the high frequency with which touch switches are employed with the target population of this book, minimal attention will be directed toward the use of specialty switches.

Touch switches vary with respect to several features. When delineating an optimal switch setup, attention is typically directed toward selecting the touch switch that possesses those features most likely to promote reliable, voluntary control of the target movement pattern. The following features reflect those dimensions most likely to be considered during the selection process:

- ❑ Force
- ❑ Feedback
- ❑ Amount of travel
- ❑ Amount of play
- ❑ Size
- ❑ Weight
- ❑ Moisture resistance
- ❑ Multiple switches
- ❑ Safety

## Force

Touch switches vary in the amount of force required to achieve switch closure. At the extreme end of the continuum are switches that can be activated by contact, in the absence of force. Moving away from this extreme are switches that reflect a continuum of force (measured in ounces or grams) to achieve switch closure. Most switches are not designed to be variable in force. Switches are typically classified as requiring light, medium, or heavy force for activation. A notable exception is the Zygo Lever Switch, which can be varied in force along a continuum.

Although most switches are not designed as adjustable switches, the force required to achieve switch closure can be altered. As illustrated in Figure 3.11, this can be achieved by removing the internal springs and inserting foam of various thicknesses or substituting or altering the internal springs. To reduce the force required, the professional would substitute a weaker or shorter internal spring; to increase the force required, a stiffer or longer internal spring would be used (Figure 3.11a). To decrease force the activation surface can also be lengthened relative to its point of pivot (Figure 3.11b). It is, however, important to note that many switches are designed with a particular force that takes into account the facilitative effect of gravity on the activation surface. Without this precaution the forces of gravity would promote switch closure when such closure is not desired.

The Don Johnston mounting switch requires 5 ounces of force to activate when its spring is intact. When the spring is removed, only 1 ounce of force is required for switch activation. To achieve a variable degree of force between 1 ounce and 5 ounces, the professional adjusts spring length by cutting the spring. (Small springs can be purchased at hardware and electronics stores.)

As illustrated in Figure 3.11c, joystick sensitivity can be modified by altering the length of the joystick shaft (Lee & Thomas, 1990; TASH catalogue, c. 1987). Shortening the shaft *increases* the amount of force required; lengthening the shaft *decreases* the amount of force required.

Force is an extremely important determinant in the switch selection process. As illustrated in Figure 3.12, switch force must be selected in keeping with the child's motoric strengths and weaknesses. If a child is hypotonic (Figure 3.12a), a sensitive switch requiring minimal force tends to be preferred over a switch requiring greater force. When working with children with degenerative conditions such as muscular dystrophy, attempts are made to minimize the movement and force required to achieve switch activation (Lee & Thomas, 1990). Touch-sensitive switches requiring minimal force are therefore frequently prescribed. When the switch is presented in a hand-activated format, a light-force switch allows gravity and the weight of the hand to maintain switch closure.

Children who demonstrate writhing hand movements on the switch interface (Figure 3.12b) frequently experience difficulty maintaining switch closure. When a switch requiring minimal force is employed, however, the weight of the hand becomes sufficient to maintain more constant switch closure.

In many instances, the use of a light-force switch may be contraindicated. When an individual demonstrates involuntary movements (Figure 3.12c), an

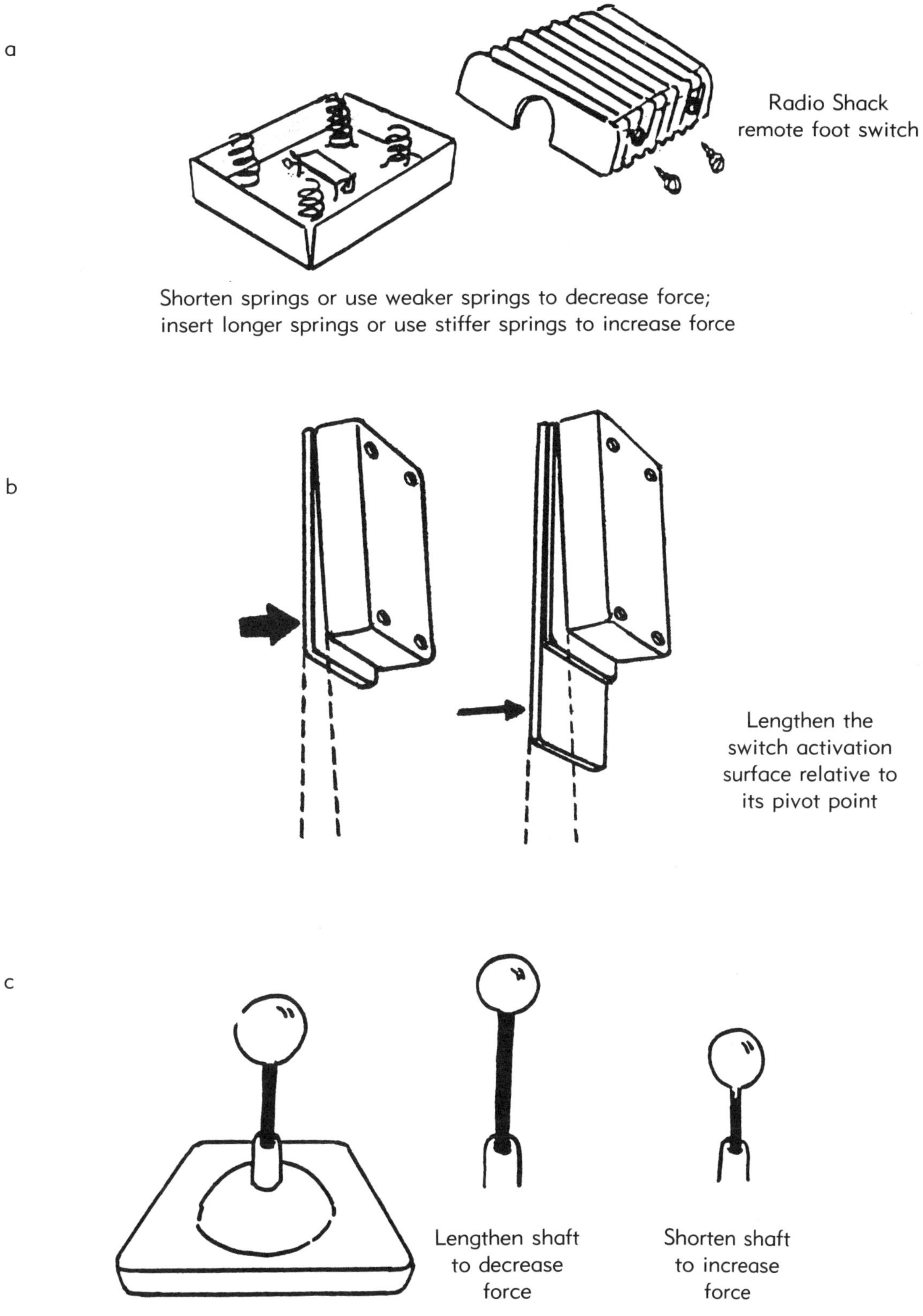
a
Radio Shack
remote foot switch
Shorten springs or use weaker springs to decrease force;
insert longer springs or use stiffer springs to increase force
b
Lengthen the
switch activation
surface relative to
its pivot point
c
Lengthen shaft
to decrease
force
Shorten shaft
to increase
force

**FIGURE 3.11.** Altering the sensitivity of switches.

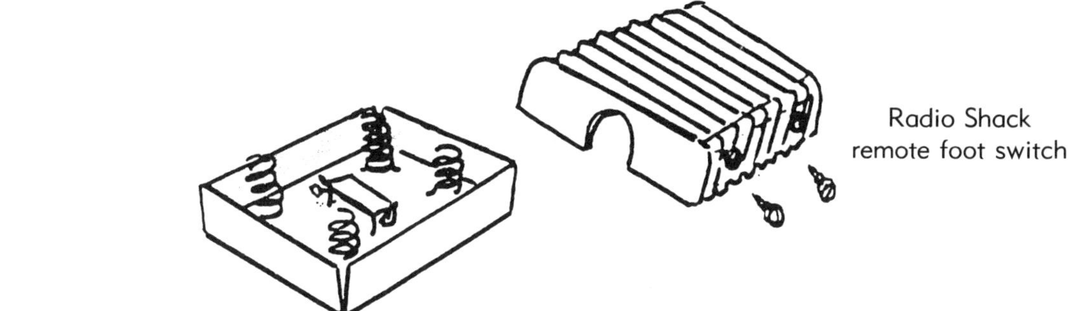

a. Hypotonia

Weight of hand is not sufficient to maintain activation of non-light-touch switch

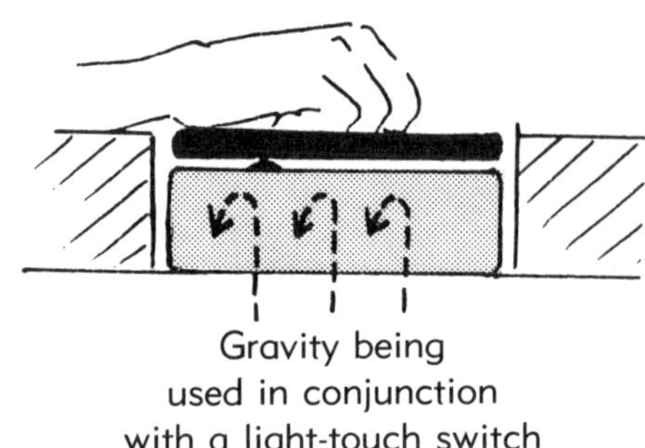

Gravity being used in conjunction with a light-touch switch

b. Athetosis

Weight of hand is not sufficient to maintain activation of non-light-touch switch

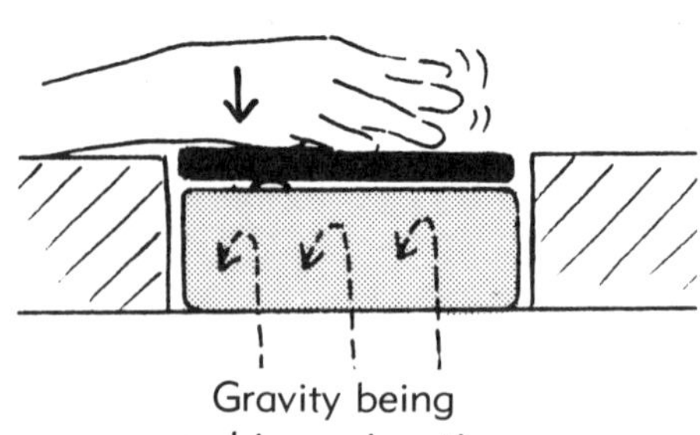

Gravity being used in conjunction with a light-touch switch

c

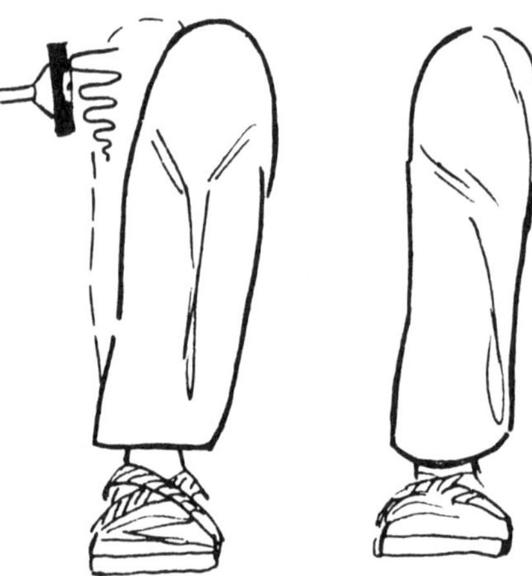

Involuntary extraneous movements and/or multiple activations may necessitate use of a switch requiring greater force

**FIGURE 3.12.** Using switch sensitivity to the child's advantage.

extremely sensitive switch mounted to utilize the head or knee as the control site can result in the frustration of frequent accidental activation. In such instances, a switch requiring greater force may be preferred, because involuntary movements will not reach the threshold required for achieving switch closure.

Some children with cerebral palsy demonstrate multiple activations; that is, attempts to perform a single switch activation may result in an initial activation followed by several rapidly produced, unwanted activations. To alleviate this problem, the professional might consider utilizing a switch that requires more force. While initial contact with the switch is sufficient to activate the switch, subsequent unwanted contacts (typically of decreasing force) are of insufficient force to achieve switch closure.

## Feedback

Feedback is a term used to describe information that a switch provides the user regarding a change in its on/off status. Feedback can assume many forms:

- auditory—When switch closure is achieved, it is accompanied by an audible click or beep.
- visual—When switch closure is achieved, a small light on the switch is activated or the entire switch activation surface becomes illuminated. When achieving switch closure, the switch activation surface can be observed to move to achieve the full excursion required for switch closure.
- tactile—When achieving switch closure, a portion of the child's body is making contact with the switch activation surface.
- kinesthetic—When achieving switch closure, the child's muscles receive feedback as they exert pressure on the switch.
- proprioceptive—When achieving switch closure, the child's muscles and tendons receive information regarding their relative change of position in space.
- vibrotactile—When switch closure is achieved, the switch activation surface begins to vibrate.

In general, there appears to be consensus among professionals that the use of a switch that is rich in feedback can facilitate motor performance (Lee & Thomas, 1990). Speed of access is frequently enhanced when feedback is provided. The younger the child, the greater the need for such feedback, especially auditory feedback. Not all switches, however, provide the user with auditory feedback. Switches activated by touch without force, for example, frequently provide no somatosensory (touch, kinesthetic, proprioceptive), visual, or auditory feedback (other than the auditory performance of the target system). If a switch interface lacks auditory feedback, it can be simulated via (a) some keyboard emulators (e.g., adaptive firmware card) (Lee & Thomas, 1990), (b) some software programs that provide the option of adding auditory feedback (e.g., TARGET software), or (c) a homemade device (inserted between the silent switch and the target system) that is capable of providing an audible click.

With visually impaired individuals, it may be advantageous to make the switch activation surface more salient by adding a textured surface (Lee & Thomas, 1990). Sometimes a layer of adhesive female Velcro or lamb's wool may be added to the surface to protect the head from forceful activation. For some children, however, such soft surfaces may elicit a protective tactile reaction. It is also important to note that some research suggests that children with cerebral palsy tend to prefer hard as opposed to soft objects when asked to indicate a preference for paired objects of different texture (Curry & Exner, 1988). It was speculated that the harder objects may have provided the children with more proprioceptive information than they receive from the softer, lighter weight, less resistive materials.

Although feedback is frequently advantageous, some children (especially children who are low functioning and multihandicapped) may fixate on the feedback characteristics of the switch, disregarding the end reward. For example, a child who is deaf-blind may repeatedly hit the switch, totally disregarding the music of its end reward. The clicking of the switch is more motivating than the end reward. In such instances, the facilitator should consider selecting a switch interface devoid of the specific problematic feedback characteristic.

## Amount of Travel

Travel is defined as the distance the activation surface of the switch must move from its resting position to the point of achieving switch closure. Touch switches vary in the amount of travel required for switch activation. The continuum ranges from touch switches that require no force and therefore no travel, to switches that require substantial travel to achieve switch closure. Lever switches in particular have definite trade-offs between the force required and the distance traveled. For example, Zygo Industries Inc. produces both a long-leaf and a short-leaf switch. Although the long-leaf version requires greater travel to activate, it requires considerably less force to activate than the short-leaf version.

Switches with short travel are often useful with individuals who are hypotonic or have a degenerative condition such as muscular dystrophy. If the selected switch, however, is a lever switch, it is important to remember that the reduced travel required might be counteracted by increased force. With such individuals switch access must often be achieved utilizing movements that are extremely limited in range (e.g., independent finger movement).

As a general rule, cognitively young children appear to benefit from the proprioceptive feedback derived from switch interfaces with noticeable travel. Substantial travel can also be beneficial in instances in which a child demonstrates frequent involuntary movements that inadvertently result in accidental switch activation. In such instances, the greater the travel required, the less the likelihood that extraneous involuntary movements will be of sufficient amplitude to cause accidental activation.

As depicted in Figure 3.13, touch switches may also vary in the direction of travel needed to achieve switch closure. Most switches are classified as being unidirectional—that is, the travel required for switch activation is achieved in only one plane. Some switches, however, are bi-directional (e.g., Rocker Switch, Prentke Romich Company) or multidirectional in nature (i.e., switch closure is achieved whenever the switch activation surface is deflected a predetermined distance in any direction from its neutral position) (e.g., Wobble Switch, Prentke Romich Company; Leaf Switch, Zygo Industries). According to the developers, multidirectional switches are believed to be useful with children demonstrating gross control of a control site.

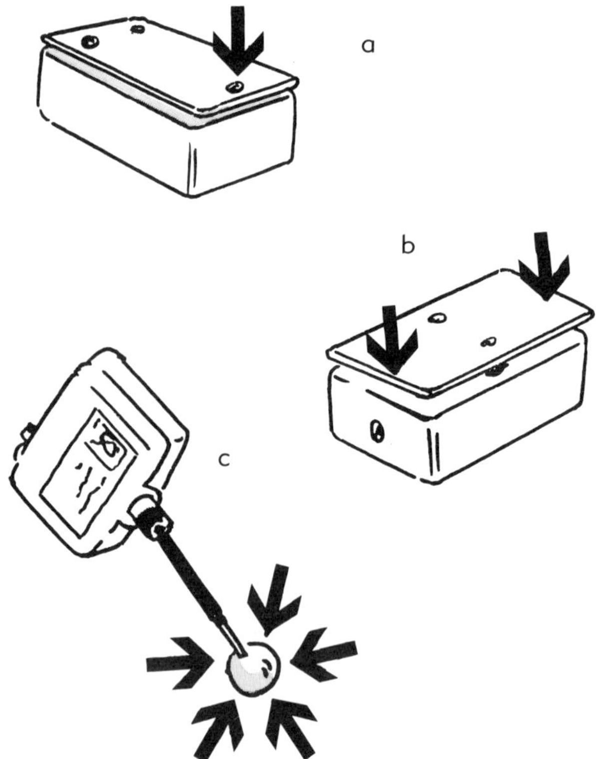


**FIGURE 3.13.** Switches employing (a) unidirectional, (b) bi-directional, and (c) multi-directional travel.

## Amount of Play

Switches vary in the amount of play or give that is inherent in the switch design. Some switches are rigid—that is, they do not give to the impact of switch activation. Others, due to the nature of the materials used (e.g., Kydex plastic) or the design employed, give on impact. The readily available Radio Shack Remote Foot Switch, for example, has considerable play or ''jiggle,'' especially when its springs are removed to diminish the amount of force required for activation. The TASH soft switch and flex switch and the Zygo Leaf Switch also possess considerable play and are reportedly designed in this manner to absorb unnecessary force (TASH, c. 1987). In the authors' experience, however, many children (especially children with athetoid movements) perform better when there is minimal play in the switch setup. When working with young children, attempts should be made to make the motor response for switch access as consistent as possible from one trial to the next. When the switch inherently allows for considerable play, the motor response required of the child tends to vary from one trial to the next. Children with athetoid movements tend to be especially prone to the negative effects of too much play in the switch interface. Because many of the child's movements are already highly variable in nature, the variability inherent in the switch only serves to further heighten the child's tone.

## Size

Two aspects of switch size appear to be relevant to the switch selection process: (a) the size of the switch activation surface and (b) the height of the switch interface. When working with children functioning below a 12-month level or when working with children who are both visually and physically impaired, a switch with a large switch activation surface is highly desirable. As therapeutic emphasis is usually focused on early cause and effect (contingency awareness training), attention is primarily directed toward teaching the child to initiate and maintain contact with the switch interface. Because gross-motor movements are frequently employed, a large activation surface is often advantageous. When, however, therapeutic attention later shifts to training the child to use a scanning selection technique, the ability to release switch contact becomes of equal importance to the ability to initiate and maintain switch contact. Whereas a large activation surface was previously advantageous, it may now be problematic, confounding the child's ability to quickly slide off or release contact with the switch activation surface.

When the child is involved in learning to use a scanning selection technique, a smaller activation surface is often desirable. Much of the difficulty that children experience in targeting a smaller switch interface, however, can often be attributed to the height of the switch interface. In recent years, several "low-profile" switches have appeared on the market. As illustrated in Figure 3.14a, low-profile switches are less than ¾ inch in height. They therefore require minimal shoulder elevation to target when presented in a hand-activated format. Although low-profile switches are highly desirable from a motor perspective, the reader should be aware of the fact that the thinner the switch, the greater the likelihood that the switch will provide minimal feedback (auditory, visual, kinesthetic, proprioceptive) to the user. For this reason, the professional may wish to present a high-profile switch (rich in feedback) within a simulated low-profile format. As illustrated in Figure 3.14b, this can be achieved by (a) cutting a hole in the lap tray or table surface to lower the switch activation surface relative to the surrounding, supporting surface or (b) building up the surface area around the switch activation surface, thereby allowing the switch to be presented in a low-profile format relative to the surrounding supporting surface. Options for simulating low-profile switches are discussed later in greater detail.

The child's therapeutic positioning equipment may also be a factor limiting the size and/or depth of the switch interface needed to capitalize on a specific motor pattern. When using a lateral head tilt, for example, the amount of space available between the child's head and the headrest may impose limitations on the size of the switch interface that can be employed. Similarly, when using the knee as the control site for switch activation, the presence of an abductor pommel (used to keep the legs separated) or the presence of leg adductor pads may mandate the use of a thinner or smaller switch interface.

### Weight

Typically, the weight of the switch interface is not an issue if the switch is to be supported by a lap tray or table surface. When, however, the switch is to be mounted on the child's body or suspended in free space relative to the control site, weight must be taken into consideration. As illustrated in Figure 3.15, an inordinate amount of weight on a chin bracket or collar can negatively affect the child's posture. Similarly, when a switch mount must cross a substantial distance through free space to position the switch in the path of the target movement pattern, the weight of the switch interface can have a negative effect on the stability of the supporting mount.

### Moisture Resistance

If a switch is to be used in the vicinity of the mouth, care should be taken to ensure that the selected switch is not negatively affected by saliva. As illustrated in Figure 3.16, the design of the switch, in large part, determines the extent to which its performance will be compromised by the presence of saliva. In general, switches that necessitate that one surface be moved relative to a second surface in which the exposed switch mechanism is embedded (Figure 3.16a) are especially susceptible to malfunction resulting from the two surfaces sticking together in the presence of moisture. In direct contrast, the switch design illustrated in Figure 3.16b is not subject to the interfering effects of saliva. As the switch mechanism is safely protected within the body of the switch, saliva cannot interfere with the operation of the switch. In addition to interfering with the general function of the switch, the presence of moisture can cause the internal mechanism to rust over time. Although some facilitators have attempted to coun-

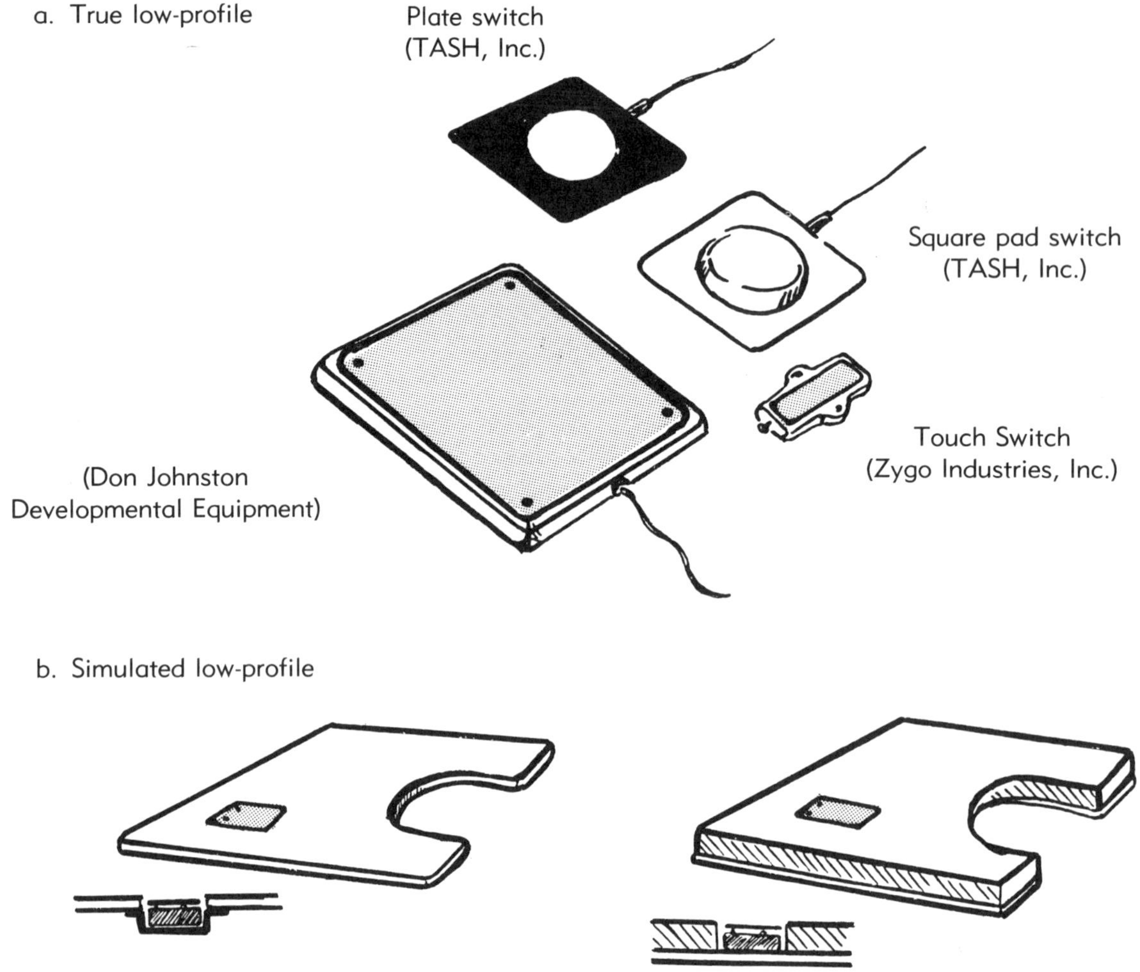


**FIGURE 3.14.** True and simulated low-profile formats.

teract this dilemma by covering the switch in a plastic Ziplock bag, this option is less than optimal as the bag tends to stick to the control site and can over time result in tissue breakdown. In other instances, the facilitator may reduce the likelihood of moisture reaching the internal mechanism by enlarging the activation surface of the switch thus providing some protection (Figure 3.16c). In general, switches that are hermetically sealed or moisture-resistant are relatively few in number. Notable exceptions are the TASH Round Pad Switch and the Zygo Touch Switch.

When a switch is located in the vicinity of the head, a tendency for the child to mouth on the switch may be noted. In such instances, all other factors being equal, the facilitator is faced with two options. The facilitator can either (a) maintain the control site prone to mouthing (e.g., cheek), selecting a moisture-resistant switch to counteract the potentially negative effects of this tendency, or (b) mount the switch higher on the child's head (e.g., side of the forehead area) to eliminate the child's ability to mouth on the switch, thereby eliminating the need for a moisture-resistant or hermetically sealed switch.

## Multiple Switches

The switch interfaces described thus far have been reflective of single-switch interfaces. As illustrated in Figure 3.17, multiple-switch interfaces are also available and are primarily used with directed scanning.

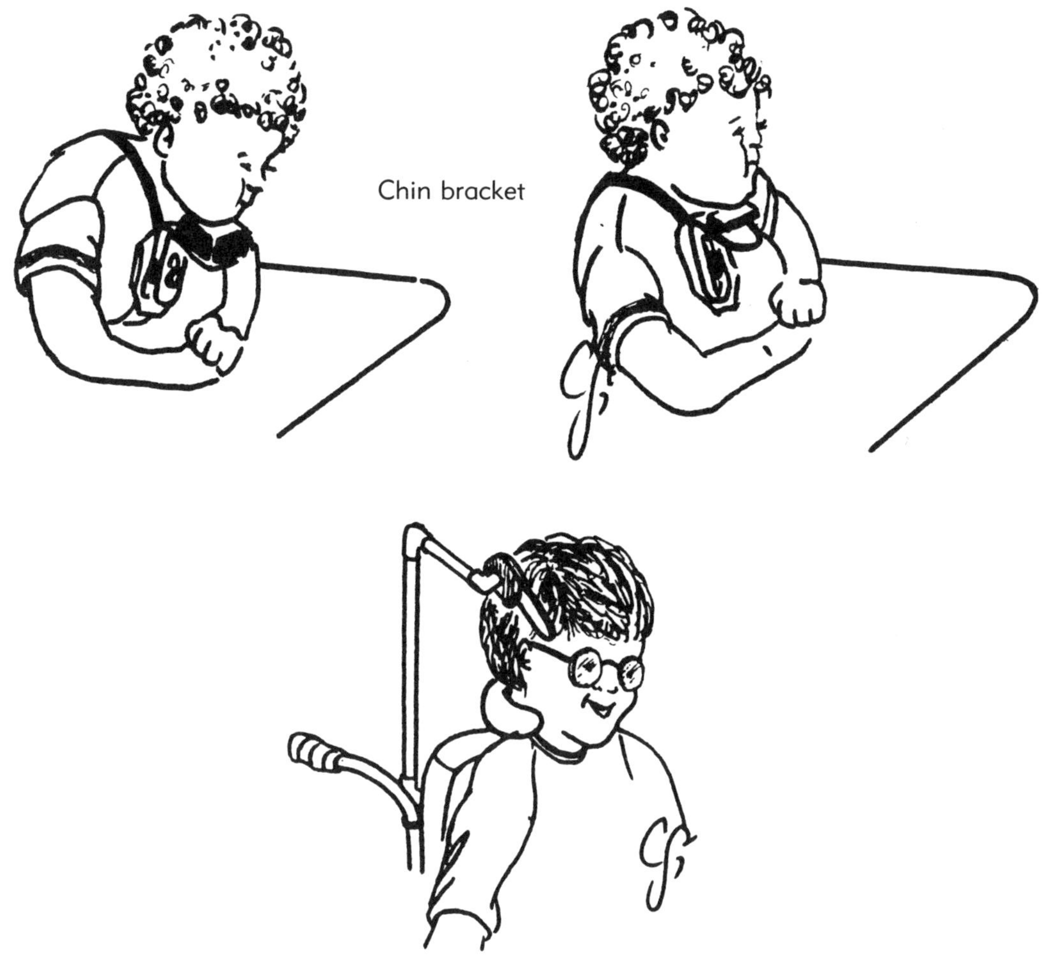


**FIGURE 3.15.** Switch setups necessitating minimal weight.

Directed scanning is a selection technique in which the child has some degree of control over the movement of the scanning indicator. Most professionals are familiar with the joystick interface commonly used in many arcade video games. Joysticks (Figure 3.17a) are available in either a gated or ungated format. With a gated joystick, the shaft of the joystick moves through definite slots. With an ungated joystick, the joystick shaft can be moved in any direction relative to its central resting position. Although some joysticks allow for movement in four directions, others include the diagonal directions as well. In the event the child is unable to coordinate motor planning in four directions, the facilitator might consider using multiswitch arrays (Figure 3.17b) or dual switches (Figure 3.17c). More specific information regarding the use of these switches relative to directed scanning is presented in Chapter 5.

### Safety

Some switches are specifically designed to buffer the blow of activation. As illustrated in Figure 3.18, such switches are often cushioned to buffer contact with the body part.

When selecting a switch interface, care should be taken to ensure that the selected switch interface does not have edges that will be potentially damaging within the context in which it will be used. Although a given switch may be relatively safe when used within a hand-activated format, this may not be the case when it is used in the vicinity of the head. If, for example, the child periodically loses head control and must reestablish his or her head in the headrest, the latter act may result in periodic contact with the corner or edge of the switch. If these corners are sharp, bodily harm becomes a possibility.

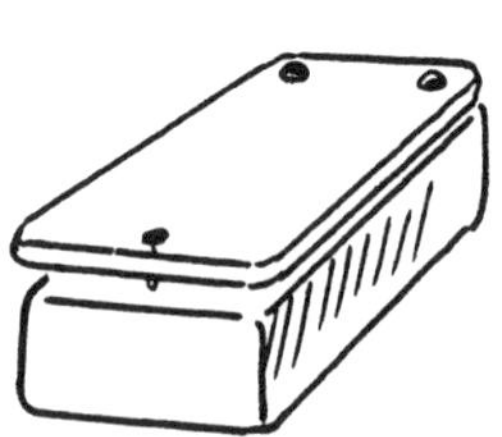

a. Negatively affected by saliva

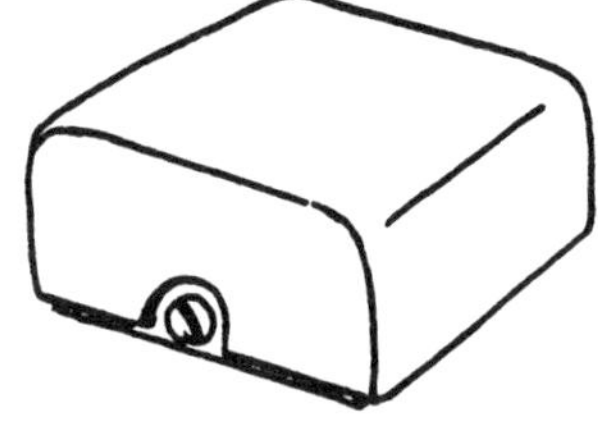

b. Not negatively affected by saliva

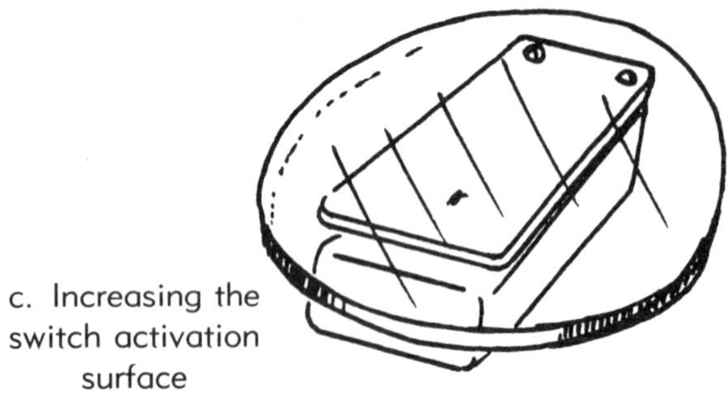

c. Increasing the switch activation surface

**FIGURE 3.16.** Accommodating the interference of moisture.

## Formats Using the Hand as the Control Site

Switch activation involving reach and touch using the upper extremities is generally considered to be cognitively easier than switch access involving alternate control sites such as the head, knee, and foot (Campbell, c. 1985). It is therefore not surprising that the hand is frequently selected as the control site for switch access.

When establishing a viable hand-activated switch setup, the facilitator strives to delineate the setup that enables the child to reliably initiate, maintain, and/or release contact with the switch interface with minimal fatigue. To achieve this goal, focus must be on

- ❑ Providing a supporting surface of optimal height and angle
- ❑ Promoting a more functional arm posture
- ❑ Stabilizing switch presentation on the supporting surface
- ❑ Determining the location of the switch on the supporting surface
- ❑ Simplifying and facilitating the motor response for switch access
- ❑ Delineating clear boundaries for the target motor pattern
- ❑ Focusing control
- ❑ Facilitating an open-hand posture

### Providing a Supporting Surface of Optimal Height and Angle

When utilizing the hand as the control site, a lap tray or table frequently serves as the supporting surface for the switch interface. As previously discussed in Chapter 2 and as illustrated in Figure 3.19, the height and angle of the supporting surface can greatly affect upper extremity use.

If the supporting surface is too high (Figure 3.19a), the child's shoulders are elevated, compromising optimal functioning of the upper extremities and restricting the child's ability to turn his or her head laterally. If the supporting surface is too low (Figure 3.19b), the forearms may not be receiving the support necessary for stabilizing the trunk, which in turn promotes better head control. In the absence of this additional support, head control may present as yet another motor act to be juggled, when ideally the child should be focusing his or her full attention on gaining proficiency using the hand for switch access.

Given the constraints of some wheelchair designs, lap tray height may be less than optimal. Lap tray height is typically dictated by the height of the wheelchair armrests. Although some brands of wheelchairs possess some built-in adjustability, the available range of adjustment for armrest height may be quite limited or totally absent. As illustrated in Figures 3.19c and 3.19d, wheelchair modifications may be necessary to approximate a more optimal lap tray height. If the supporting surface is too high, the lap tray can be lowered 1 to 2 inches by removing the armrest surface, allowing the lap tray to rest directly on the wheelchair structures supporting the armrests (Figure 3.19c). If the lap tray surface is too low, the height of the supporting surface can be raised by attaching wooden spacers and modifying the hardware for lap tray attachment to the wheelchair (Figure 3.19d).

Occasionally, the existing seating inserts such as thoracic pads and abductor pommels for the hips may interfere with the facilitator's ability to achieve an optimal lap tray height. The latter serves to highlight the need for the lap tray to be prescribed as a

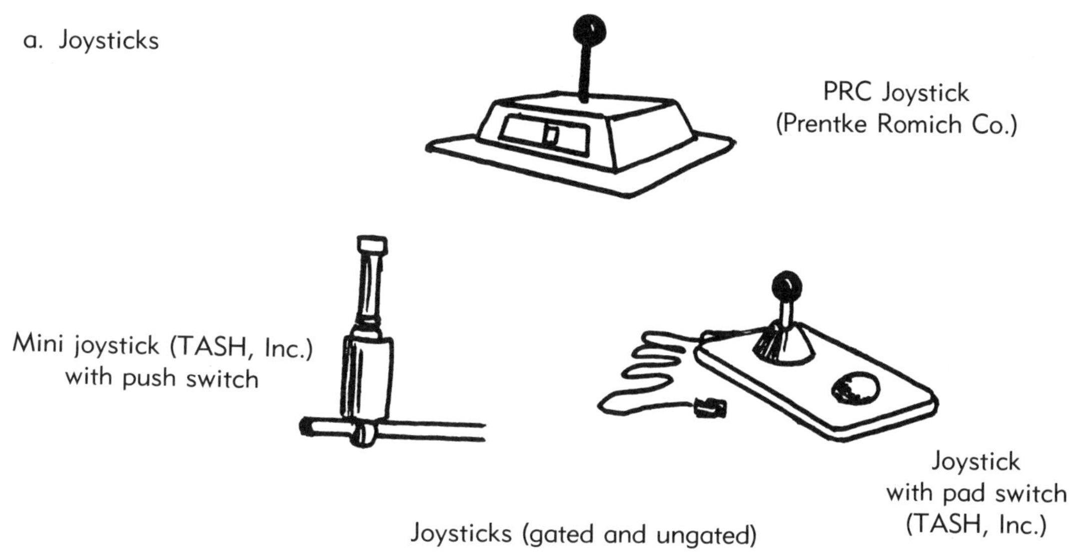


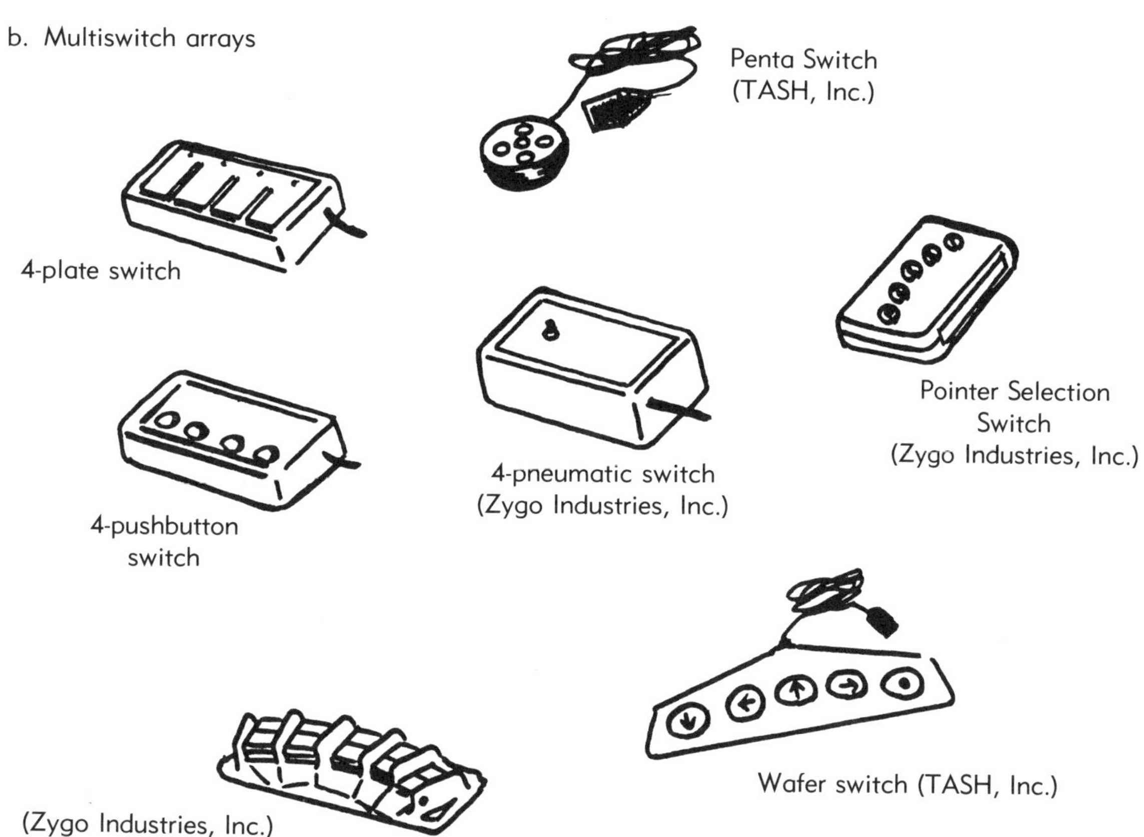


**FIGURE 3.17.** Multiple switches.

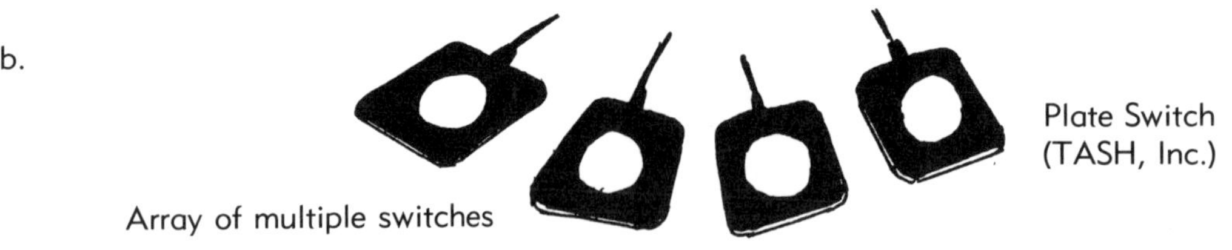


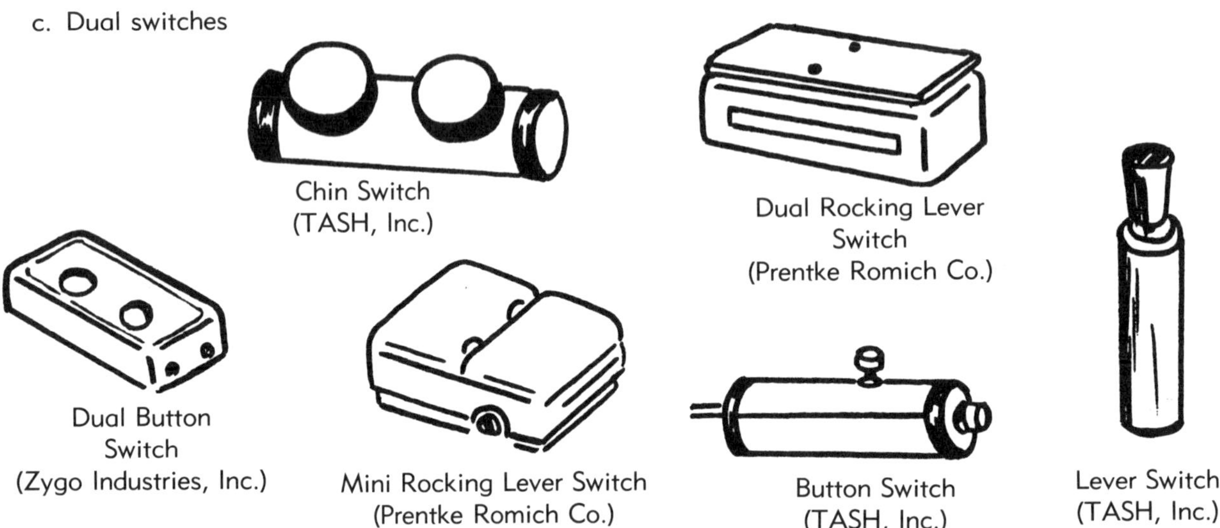


**FIGURE 3.17. (Continued)**

**FIGURE 3.18.** Cushioned or buffered switch interface.

vital part of the child's overall therapeutic seating evaluation. When considered as an integral part of the overall seating evaluation, seating inserts may be selected that allow the positioning expert to simultaneously address the need for therapeutic support and optimal lap tray height. When an abductor pommel interferes with the attainment of optimal lap tray height, an angled format may be necessary to allow the lap tray to clear the pommel, while simultaneously permitting lap tray height to remain optimal, proximal to the child. As illustrated in Figure 3.19e, an angled format can be achieved by attaching wedged wooden inserts to the underside of the lap tray.

In addition to facilitating the attainment of optimal lap tray height proximal to the child, an angled lap tray can positively affect upper extremity functioning for some children. A synergy pattern of increased extensor tone in the arms may be evidenced less frequently when an angled lap tray format is adopted (Figure 3.19e). In general, an angled format appears to allow gravity to pull the

a. Too high

b. Too low

c. Decreasing height

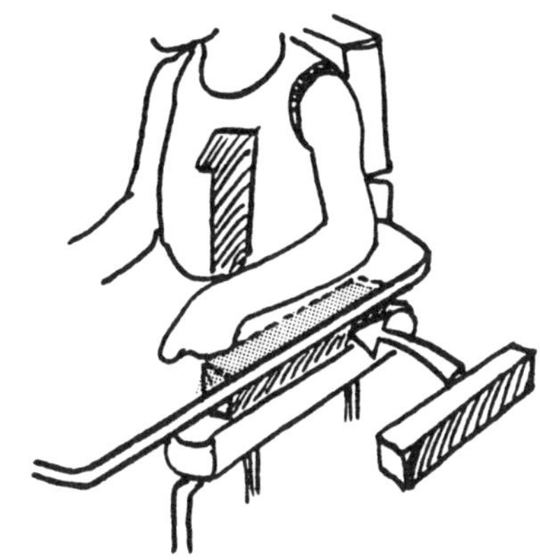
d. Increasing height

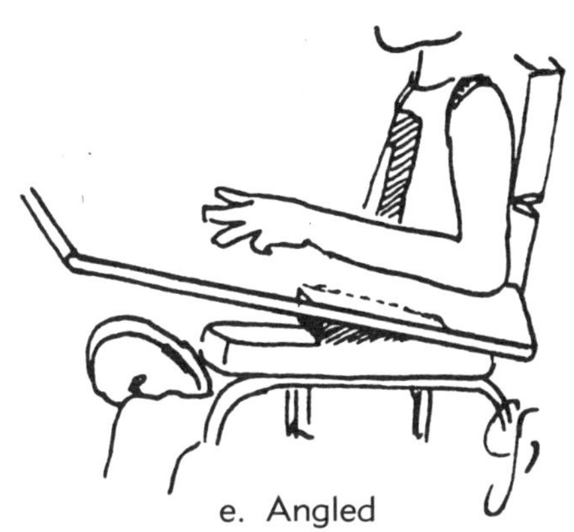
e. Angled

f. Abnormal synergy pattern of increased extensor tone

**FIGURE 3.19.** Achieving optimal height and angle of supporting surface.

arms back into a pattern of flexion, which may help to reduce tone in the upper extremities.

When working with children who are severely physically challenged, tables that are adjustable in height and angle are highly desirable, if not crucial, to the diagnostic process. Wheelchairs vary greatly in the height of the seat off the ground. When a non-adjustable table is employed, it may be necessary to alter the height relationship between the table and the wheelchair. The latter can be achieved using wooden platforms or a sheet of dense Ethafoam to alter the relative height of the wheelchair or the table (by placing the entire wheelchair on a platform or placing the table on a platform) as required to achieve an optimal height for the supporting surface. Because this process requires considerable extra steps, adjustable tables are definitely a more time-effective option.

When conducting an evaluation for a hand-activated switch setup, the process is greatly facilitated by using an adjustable table. In addition to allowing the facilitator to explore the potential benefits of an angled format, the use of a highly adjustable table eliminates the tendency for the facilitator to work within the constraints of a less than optimal lap tray arrangement. Having delineated a viable, hand-activated switch setup under conditions that are optimal, the facilitator can then take steps to modify the wheelchair–lap tray relationship to approximate this improved arrangement. A facilitator who witnesses the child's superior performance under optimal conditions using an adjustable table is less likely to settle for less than optimal.

## Promoting a More Functional Arm Posture

As diagrammed in Figure 3.20, many children with cerebral palsy experience difficulty achieving a functional forward arm posture. In some instances, extreme spasticity may be causing the arms to retract secondary to external rotation of the shoulders. In other situations, the child with athetosis may be experiencing difficulty controlling distal movement of the upper extremities. In many instances, the lack of a functional forward arm posture is a function of a less than optimal seating system. Assuming that the observed lack of a functional forward arm posture is not a function of poor therapeutic positioning, additional strategies may be implemented to achieve this goal. A more functional forward arm posture can be achieved by (a) attaching scapular wings to the wheelchair frame or (b) attaching angled bumpers to the lap tray or table surface.

In addition to the aforementioned suggestions, several options exist that serve a stabilizing or restrictive role, limiting extraneous movement of the child's upper extremities (Figure 3.21). As illustrated, the shoulder protractor belt (Erhardt, 1982, 1986) and arm restrainer (Reymann, 1985a; Riley, 1970) are potentially useful with children who demonstrate mild-to-moderate motor involvement. Although these options work well for some children, they are considered to be less than desirable in instances in which children "work against" the stabilizing bands, thus increasing their overall body tone. To circumvent this problem, Erhardt (1986) presented a third option in which wide bands of dressmaker elastic are slipped over the upper arms and are interconnected by a length of bootlace running through a central ring on the chest band. This option reportedly allows greater flexibility of movement while still restricting the overall range of movement.

Overhead slings and arm troughs (Figure 3.22) can also be used to promote functional use of the upper extremities for switch access. A mobile arm support or overhead sling (Figure 3.22a) is believed to be especially useful with individuals demonstrating low tone (Williams, Csongradi, & LeBlanc, 1982; Wright & Nomura, 1985), as it effectively minimizes the interfering effects of gravity, allowing the child to use extended fingers to access the switch.

An arm trough (Figure 3.22b) can also be used to position the arm for functional switch access. When utilizing this option, the switch is ideally mounted off the trough to ensure optimal positioning of the switch relative to the hand.

## Stabilizing Switch Presentation on the Supporting Surface

Stable presentation of the switch is crucial to evaluating its effectiveness for switch control. To facilitate the process of presenting the switch interface within a flexible yet stable format, it is recommended that the lap tray or adjustable table surface be covered with indoor/outdoor carpet. As visually depicted in Figure 3.23, carpet can be adhered to the supporting surface using carpet tape, duct tape (rolled in loops), or (more permanently) adhesive Velcro.

a. Retracted arm posture

b. Athetoid distal arm movements

Nonfunctional arm postures

c. Scapular wings attached to wheelchair frame

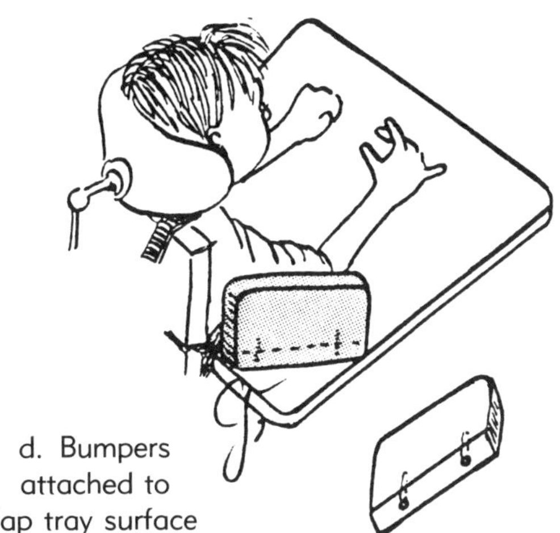

d. Bumpers attached to lap tray surface

**FIGURE 3.20.** Facilitative options for promoting a more forward arm posture.

When the bottom of a switch is lined with adhesive male Velcro (hook, mushroom), the switch can be temporarily, but securely, placed anywhere on the covered supporting surface. Furthermore, when the indoor-outdoor carpet is gridded with permanent felt-tip markers, the task of evaluating switch performance in one location relative to the next is greatly facilitated. Masking tape (Campbell, c. 1985) or chalk (Goossens' & Crain, 1986a) can be used to trace the outline of the switch at various locations on the carpet, thus providing a visual record of the locations investigated during the evaluation process.

When working in a diagnostic setting, the facilitator should consider keeping rolls of carpet remnants available (pregridded with permanent markers) to expedite the task of covering a lap tray with indoor/outdoor carpet. To construct an insert, the facilitator places the lap tray face down on the carpet and traces its outline. When placing the lap tray on the carpet, care should be taken to ensure symmetrical placement on the gridded carpet. That is, the center of the lap tray should be aligned with a grid line. An electric kitchen knife can then be used to cut the carpet.

### Determining the Location of the Switch Interface on the Supporting Surface

The location of the switch interface on the supporting surface is perhaps the most important single factor in delineating a viable hand-activated switch

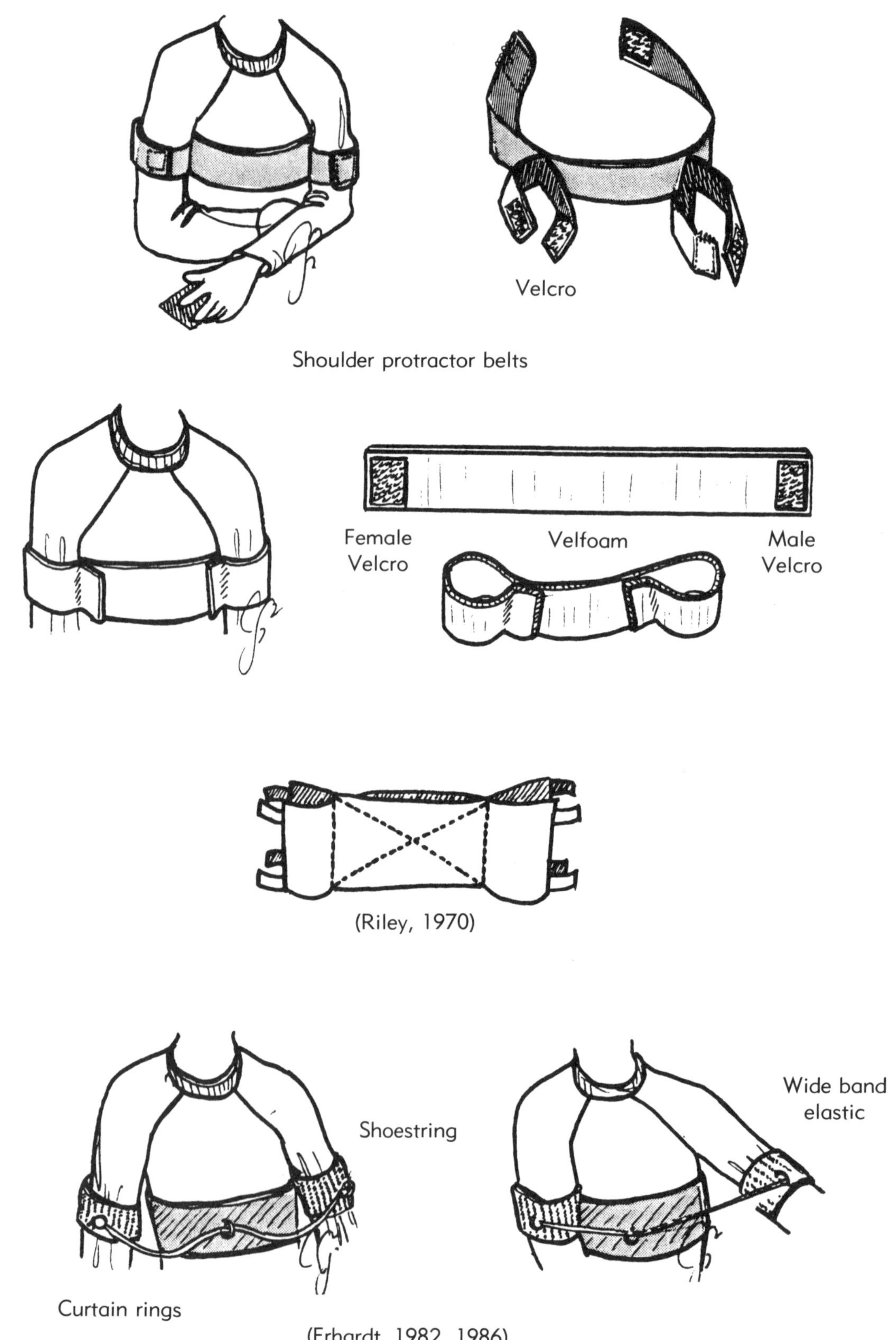


**FIGURE 3.21.** Restrictive options for promoting a more forward arm posture.

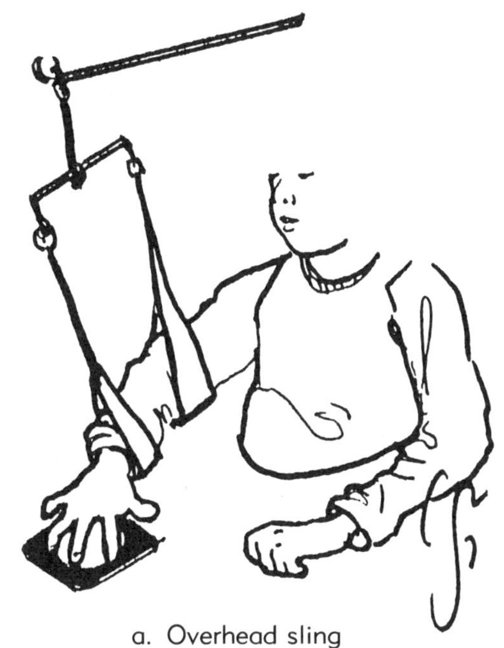


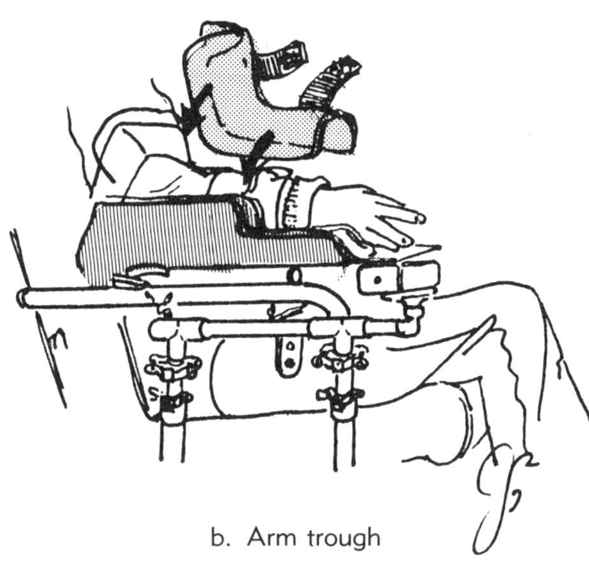


**FIGURE 3.22.** Mobile arm supports and stationary arm troughs.

setup. When determining a viable location, the facilitator should consider:

- ❑ Hand preference
- ❑ Typical resting location of the arms and hands
- ❑ Most frequent range of voluntary and involuntary movement of the arms and hands
- ❑ Formats that promote arm flexion

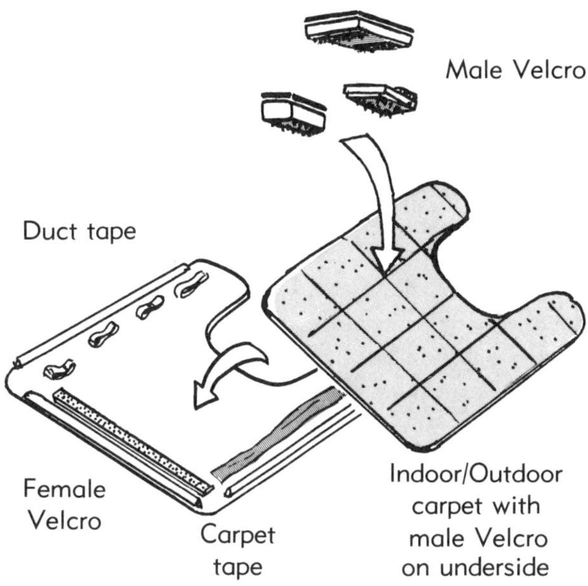


**FIGURE 3.23.** Stabilizing switch presentation through the use of indoor/outdoor carpet and Velcro.

- ❑ Formats that promote mirror images of abnormal synergy patterns
- ❑ Visual constraints

**HAND PREFERENCE.** Many children who are severely physically challenged experience difficulty crossing midline. If the child demonstrates a preference for using his or her right hand, the switch interface is typically positioned to the right of midline. If the child is left-handed, placement is usually to the left of midline.

**TYPICAL RESTING LOCATION OF THE ARMS AND HANDS.** Knowledge of the typical resting location of the arms/hands on the supporting surface can assist in delineating viable switch placement. Children with hypotonia typically demonstrate a restricted range of functional movement. Switch placement in close proximity to the typical resting position of the hands can greatly minimize the effort required for switch access.

**MOST FREQUENT RANGE OF VOLUNTARY AND INVOLUNTARY MOVEMENT OF THE ARMS AND HANDS.** When working with cognitively young children, the most frequent range of movement of the arms/hands on the supporting surface can assist in placement. When undergoing early contingency awareness training with switches, primary attention is directed toward placing the switch interface within the range of movement most likely to promote first accidental, and later purposeful, switch activation. With the cognitively older child for whom successful scanning is a concern, attention shifts to delineating a switch setup conducive to the release, as well as the initiating and maintaining aspects of switch access. In such instances, attention may be directed toward positioning the switch interface well within the maximum range of motion but just outside the range of most frequent extraneous movement.

**FORMATS THAT PROMOTE ARM FLEXION.** Hypertonicity in the upper extremities can greatly impede the child's ability to reliably and effortlessly access a switch interface. If the child is extensor tone dominant, flexion in the arms tends to be tone-reducing. Knowing this, the facilitator may wish to place the switch interface in locations that mandate or encourage arm flexion, thereby promoting a switch access movement pattern that is more normalized in tone.

**FORMATS THAT PROMOTE A MIRROR IMAGE OF AN ABNORMAL SYNERGY PATTERN.** In some instances a viable switch setup can be achieved by purposely placing the switch in locations that promote normal movement patterns that are the mirror image of abnormal synergy patterns. If, for example, the child frequently demonstrates increased extensor tone of the arms at midline (diagrammed in Figure 3.24), the professional might consider (a) utilizing an angled lap tray to allow gravity to assist in pulling the elbows back into flexion and/or (b) placing the switch more lateral and proximal to the typical position that the hands assume during the abnormal synergy pattern.

**VISUAL CONSTRAINTS.** Visual concerns (e.g., visual field deficits, ocular mobility restrictions) are also worthy of consideration when delineating a hand-activated switch setup (Wright & Nomura, 1985). If, for example, the child demonstrates a left visual field deficit, the switch would be positioned on the right side to accommodate this deficit. Placement of the switch in keeping with the child's visual strengths is especially crucial during the earliest stages of switch access. If the child is cognitively young, the switch should be placed where access can be visually monitored. Children are often better able to learn the required response if they are able to visually monitor the process.

### Simplifying and Facilitating the Motor Response for Switch Access

Ideally, the motor response should be as simple as possible. In general, most children are able to access a switch more reliably when (a) the range of vertical head control required for monitoring the activity of the hand and monitoring the target system is reduced; (b) the need for the arm or hand to move through free space is minimized; (c) the need for shoulder elevation has been eliminated; and (d) there is a guiding and/or stabilizing surface to assist the child in moving on and off the switch interface. Toward addressing these goals, the facilitator should consider presenting the switch in an angled and/or low-profile format.

**LOW-PROFILE FORMATS.** High-profile switches are often problematic because they require unsupported movement through space and some degree of shoulder elevation to "get on" the switch interface. Furthermore, such formats fail to provide the child with a guiding surface to assist the process of moving effortlessly on and off the switch. Currently, several low-profile switches are commercially available that are capable of addressing the aforementioned needs.

When selecting a low-profile switch, the importance of switch feedback characteristics should not be overlooked. Typically, the thinner the low-profile switch, the greater the likelihood that the feedback characteristics (e.g., auditory, visual, somatosensory) crucial to the learning process will be compromised. As an alternative to using a low-profile switch interface lacking in feedback, the facilitator might consider presenting a high-profile switch rich in feedback, within a simulated low-profile format. This can be achieved by (a) recessing the switch activation surface relative to the supporting surface (cutting a hole in the lap tray or table surface to allow the body of the switch to be recessed relative to the supporting surface) or (b) building up the supporting surface around the switch activation surface (positioning a wooden or Ethafoam platform around the switch interface). These options were previously depicted in Figure 3.14.

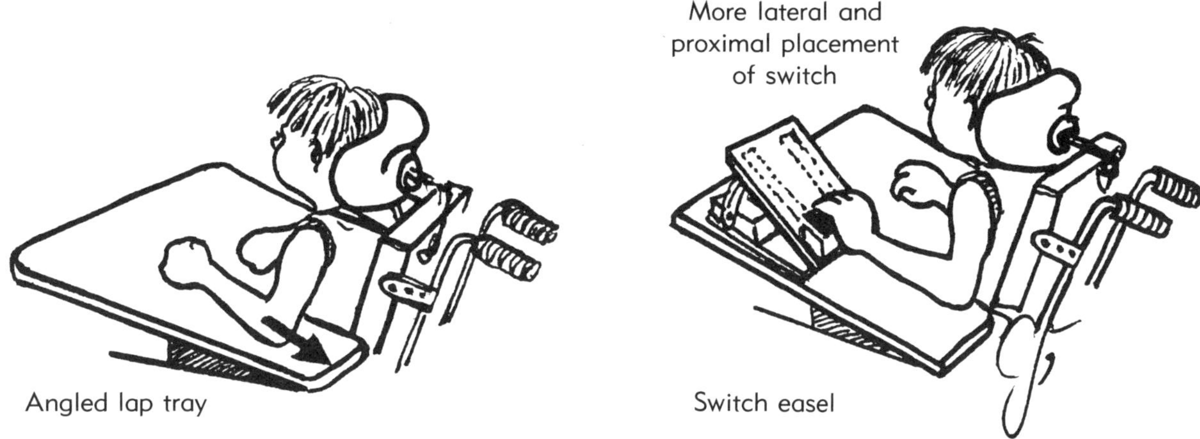


**FIGURE 3.24.** Using the mirror image of an abnormal synergy pattern.

When using the first option, difficulty is sometimes experienced in finding usable space beneath the lap tray to accommodate the body of the recessed switch. In addition, the changes thus derived are permanent, with no margin for error or changes over time. As a result, the "build-up" option is frequently preferred. When using the build-up option, attention should be directed toward ensuring that the surrounding built-up surface does not alter the optimal relationship between the child's shoulders and his or her supported elbows or forearms.

**ANGLED FORMATS.** Angled formats are facilitative for some children. As illustrated in Figure 3.25, they (a) reduce the range of vertical head movement required for alternately monitoring the switch and the target system and (b) may necessitate that the hand assume a mirror image version of the frequently observed abnormal synergy pattern of ulnar deviation of the hand. Angled formats can be achieved using a switch easel (Figure 3.25a), an Ethafoam mount (Figure 3.25b), or a Plexiglas easel lap tray (Figure 3.25c). Chapter 4 presents instructions for constructing a switch easel.

**COMBINED LOW-PROFILE AND ANGLED FORMATS.** In recent years, the authors have experienced considerable success using Ethafoam mounts that allow the switch to be presented in both a low-profile and an angled format. As depicted in Figure 3.26a, an angled-recessed format can greatly simplify and facilitate the motor response necessary for switch access by (a) reducing the need for unsupported movement of the arm/hand through free space; (b) reducing the need for shoulder elevation when accessing the switch; (c) providing a guiding or stabilizing surface to assist in moving the hand on and off the switch interface; and (d) promoting a "head-up" posture,

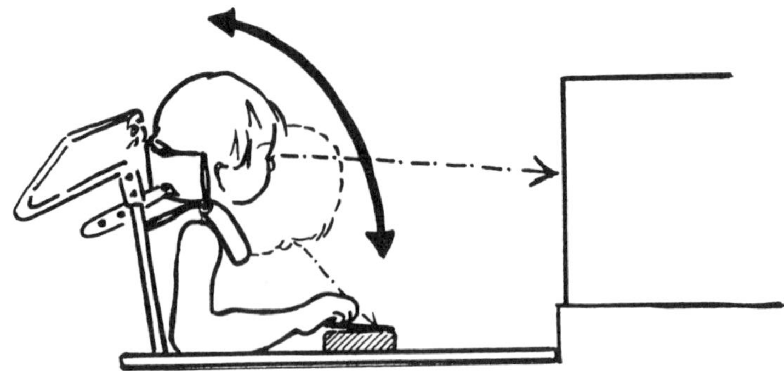

Full range of vertical head movement required

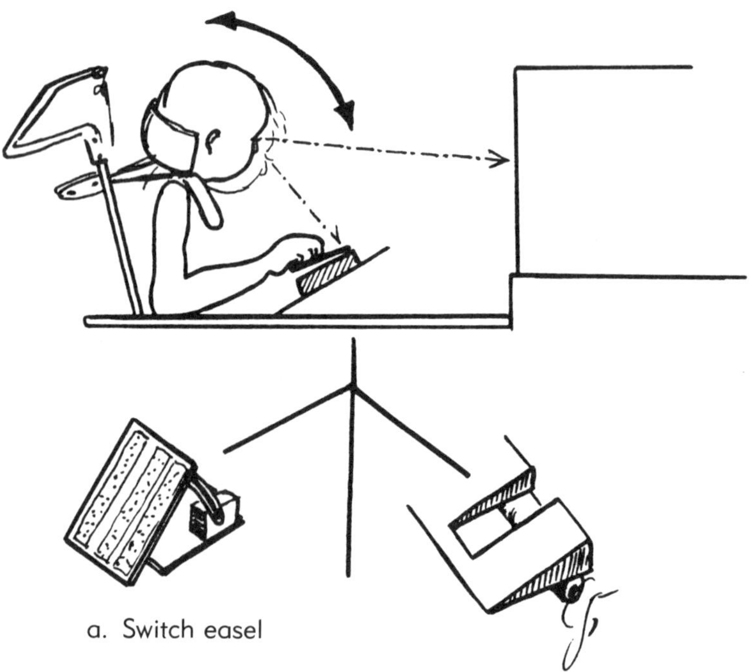

Reduced range of vertical head movement required

**FIGURE 3.25.** The facilitative effects of angled formats.

**FIGURE 3.26.** Ethafoam mounts.

thereby partialing out the confounding effects of poor graded vertical head control. Furthermore, the proposed formats do not inadvertently alter the lap tray height or necessitate that the lap tray be irreversibly altered. The efficacy of a recessed-angled format is typically evaluated using the three-part, angled Ethafoam mount illustrated in Figure 3.27a. Using these basic components, the professional is able to systematically alter the following variables.

1. The location of the switch cutout along a horizontal, left to right plane (Figure 3.27b). Many children with cerebral palsy experience difficulty crossing midline. If the individual is right-handed, the cutout is usually located midline or to the right of midline; if the child is left-handed, the switch cutout is typically located midline or to the left of midline. As the collective width of the three Ethafoam components is less than the width of most lap trays, the cutout can be simulated at any point along a horizontal continuum by manipulating the relative placement of the three component parts.

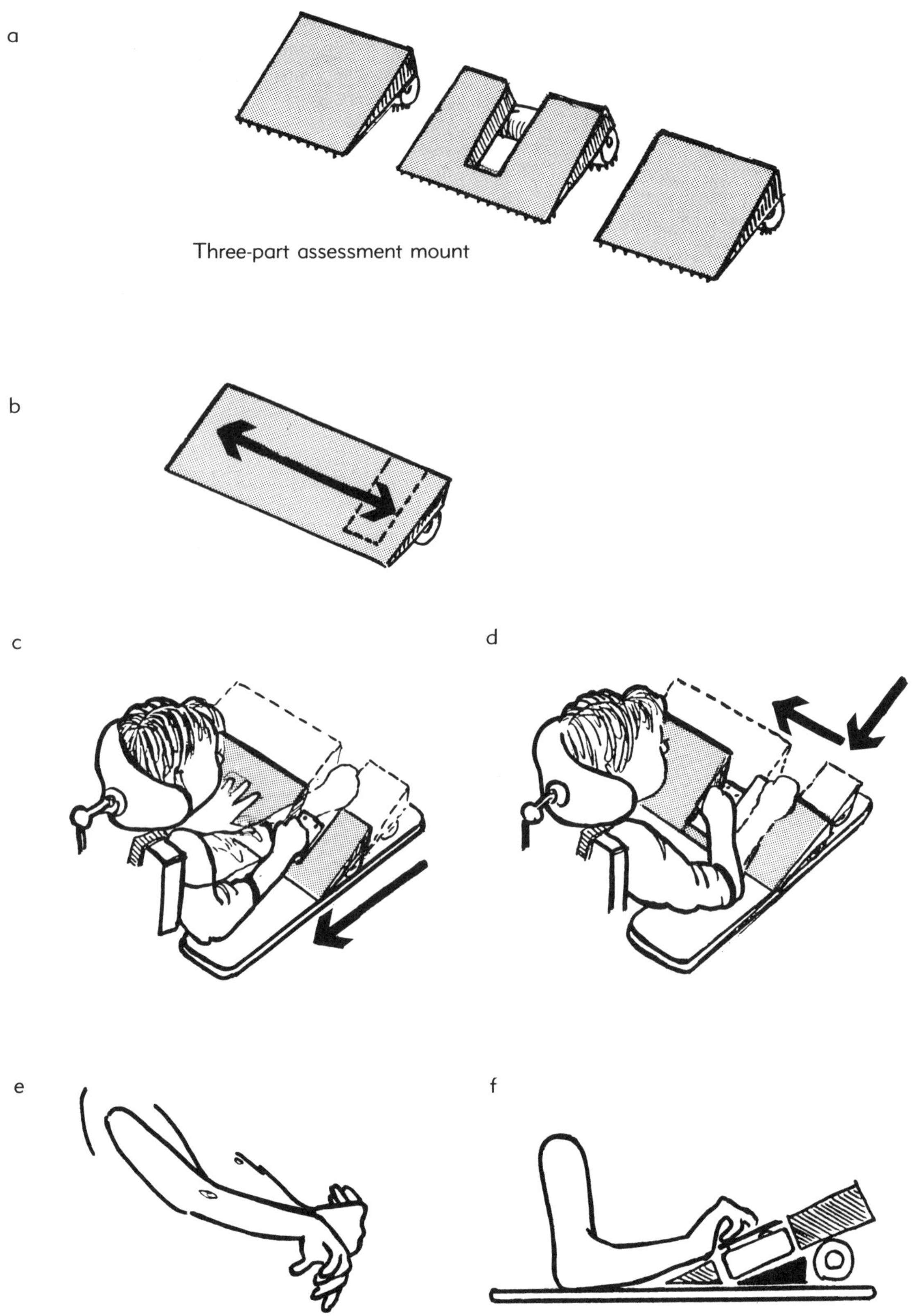


**FIGURE 3.27.** Assessing the efficacy of an Ethafoam mount.

2. The distance between the lower front edge of the Ethafoam mount and the child's body. Typically, the closer the mount is positioned toward the child's body, the greater the need for the child to (a) extend the shoulder pulling the elbow back into flexion (Figure 3.27c) or (b) demonstrate elbow flexion necessitating more midline placement of the switch in the angled Ethafoam mount (Figure 3.27d).
3. The height and angle of the Ethafoam mount. If the child demonstrates an abnormal synergy pattern that includes pronation of the forearm and ulnar deviation of the hand (Figure 3.27e), a more angled format may foster a more normalized hand posture, one that is opposite to the abnormal synergy pattern (Figure 3.27f).
4. The height or depth of the switch activation surface relative to the surrounding surface of the mount. Several options are included in Figure 3.28.

*Flush:* When utilizing a flush format, the switch activation surface is presented level with the surface of the surrounding Ethafoam mount. This format can facilitate the use of a sliding motion to move on and off the switch interface. Typically, the movement used to slide off the switch is the reverse of that used to slide on. Although gravity may be used to assist the child in achieving release, sequenced movement in a single plane appears to be motorically easier than sequenced movement in more than one plane. To further enhance effortless movement on and off the switch, the facilitator should consider adhering a wide strip of smooth plastic tape to the mount in the path of the sliding action.

*Recessed:* A recessed format presents the switch activation surface lower than the surrounding surface of the Ethafoam mount. This format works well with children who are

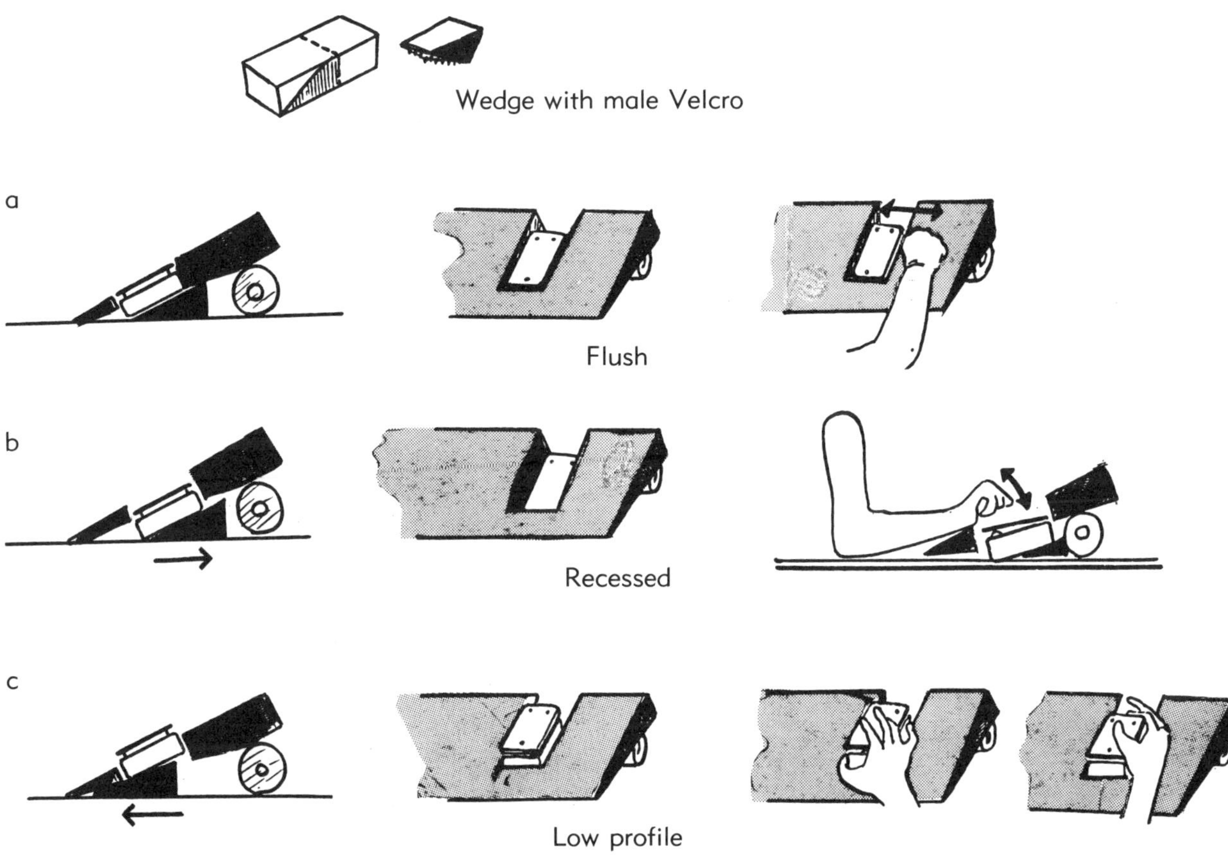


**FIGURE 3.28.** Simulating flush, recessed, and low-profile formats in Ethafoam mounts.

able to stabilize the proximal portions of their hand such as the wrist or base of thumb on the mount surface, while simultaneously mobilizing the distal portions of their hand (extended fingers, fingers flexed into a fist) to activate the switch activation surface. To assist in maximizing stability, the facilitator may consider (a) adding a textured surface such as adhesive female Velcro or a thin layer of Dycem to the point of hand contact on the mount or (b) sculpting a slight indentation for the hand at the point of its contact on the Ethafoam surface.

*Low Profile:* A low-profile format presents the switch activation surface slightly elevated relative to the surrounding Ethafoam surface. This format is especially useful with children capable of (a) stabilizing their thumb on the edge of the switch, freeing the fingers for switch access, or (b) stabilizing the ulnar side of the hand on the edge of the switch, freeing the thumb for switch access.

As illustrated, all options are achieved by manipulating the relative position of an Ethafoam wedge insert. For further information regarding the construction of Ethafoam mounts, the reader is referred to Chapter 4.

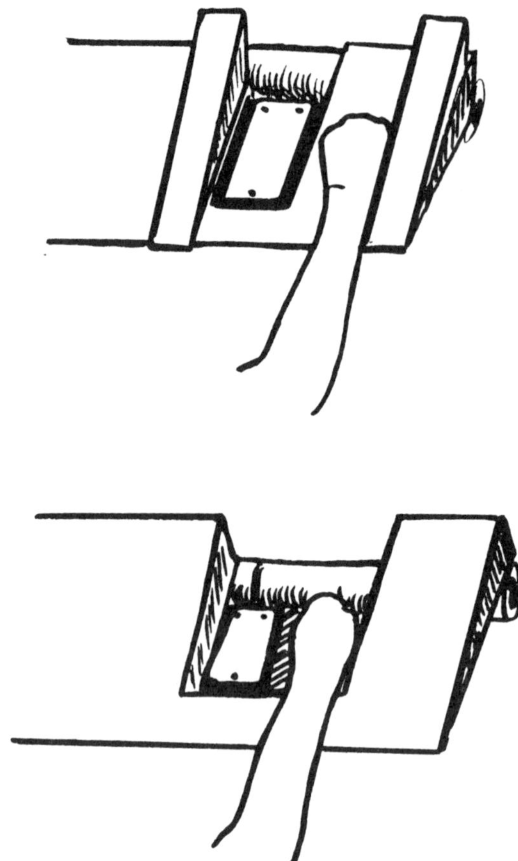

**FIGURE 3.29.** Incorporating boundary bumpers into hand-activated switch setups.

## Delineating Clear Boundaries for the Target Motor Response

When training a child to use a switch interface, performance can be greatly enhanced when clear boundaries are established for the required motor response. As illustrated in Figure 3.29, consistency of responding across trials can be achieved through the use of *boundary bumpers.* When a sliding action is used to move on and off the switch, children may experience difficulty grading the distance their hand must move to get on the switch. When a bumper is placed adjacent to the switch, ''oversliding'' is eliminated. Furthermore, this bumper can now serve as a rebound surface to assist the child in initiating movement off the switch. The release aspect of switch access is thus facilitated.

In some instances the facilitator may wish to incorporate a second bumper to help the child limit the maximum excursion of the hand away from the switch. Similar to the first bumper, this second bumper may serve as a rebound bumper assisting the child in initiating movement onto the switch. In many instances, the second boundary bumper serves to facilitate the release aspect of switch access. Many children who are severely physically challenged experience difficulty with the release aspects of switch access. When a second boundary bumper is incorporated into the switch setup, the task is cognitively altered from that of ''have to get off this switch'' to ''have to get over there.'' Thus, the task of release, often difficult for motor-involved children, has been cognitively transformed into an initiation task, a task that is typically easier for such children.

## Focusing Control for Switch Access

Children with cerebral palsy often perform motor acts as a whole body response. In addition, individuals with athetosis are often plagued with the dilemma of "too many moving parts." Thus, the act of switch access becomes a complex juggling act. Such children are often able to utilize a switch interface more reliably when extraneous movements of nonaccessing extremities are minimized (Frazer et al., 1987). Given this increased stability, children are better able to focus attention on using their hand to activate the switch. For this reason, hand function is frequently enhanced when (a) the child's feet are stabilized and (b) the nonaccessing hand is secured using "stabilizers" (Lee & Thomas, 1990).

Several options exist for stabilizing the nonaccessing hand. Generally, these options can be classified as those requiring the active participation of the child and those that are passively achieved (necessitating restraint of the child).

**ACTIVE OPTIONS.** When delineating a stabilizer for a particular child, priority is generally given to those options that are actively achieved by the child. As shown in Figure 3.30, active options include horizontal bars, vertical dowels, or even gripping the edge of the lap tray or switch mount. When pursuing active options, care should be taken to ensure that these options are not being achieved with heightened tone or abnormal hand or arm postures. Often the decision to use a horizontal versus a vertical dowel is the result of a trial-and-error process. When a child demonstrates ulnar deviation of the hand, a vertical format is frequently preferred, because it promotes the use of a hand posture that is a mirror image of ulnar deviation of the hand. Having delineated the relative efficacy of a vertical versus a horizontal format, considerable fine-tuning can be achieved by altering the thickness of the dowel or bar in keeping with the child's grasp. Thickness can be altered by adding foam or Aquaplast or by modifying bicycle handle bar grips to function as vertical dowels. For individuals demonstrating athetoid movements of the hand, a dowel or bar covered with a spongy foam may prove beneficial, as its elastic nature promotes a sense of maintaining contact with the dowel or bar to be gripped (S. Lane, personal communication, c. 1987). There is, however, some evidence in the literature to suggest that children with cerebral palsy prefer hard objects over soft objects (Curry & Exner, 1988) and children with spasticity are more likely to have sensory disturbances than those with athetosis (Trachdjian & Minear, 1958).

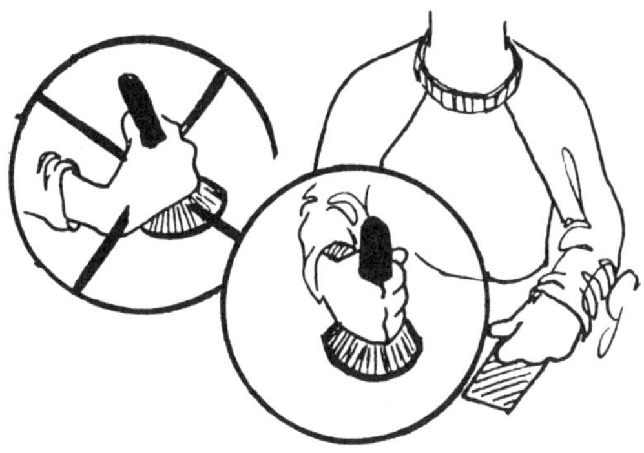

Stabilizing dowel

Stabilizing bar

**FIGURE 3.30.** Stabilizing the nonaccessing hand—Active options.

**PASSIVE OPTIONS.** When an active option is not viable, passive options are subjected to systematic evaluation. As a general rule, the facilitator should use only as much restraint as is necessary to enhance switch access. The more restraining the option and the more steps required to set the stabilizer in place, the less desirable the option. As depicted in Figure 3.31, passive options include weighted cuffs, beanbag weights, stabilizing cylinders, Velcro straps, placement under the lap tray, and arm trough restraints. As previously the case with active stabilizers, passive stabilizers should be positioned in a manner that promotes normal hand postures. Although a beanbag weight may effectively stabilize the nonaccessing arm, it would be unfortunate if this were being achieved with the underlying hand in an abnormal wrist posture.

When positioning stabilizers (whether active or passive) on the supporting surface, attention should

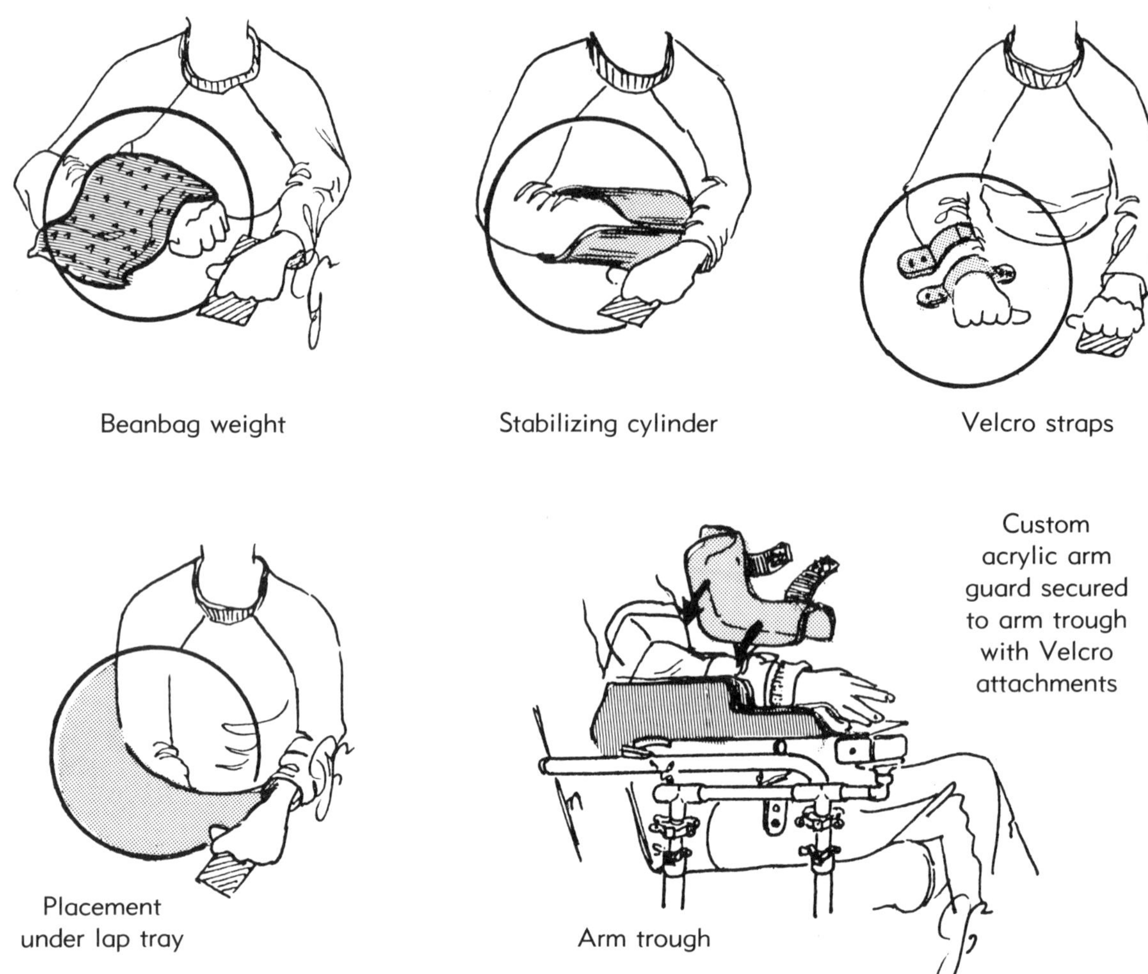


**FIGURE 3.31.** Stabilizing the nonaccessing hand—Passive options.

be directed toward noting the extent to which a setup promoting arm flexion has a tone-reducing effect on both the stabilizing and the accessing arms. In the authors' experience, setups that (a) promote arm flexion, (b) promote symmetrical placement of the "stabilized arm" and the "accessing arm" (thus promoting trunk symmetry), or (c) promote horizontal placement of the stabilized arm in close proximity to the trunk tend to be most successful with children with cerebral palsy.

## Facilitating an Open-Hand Posture

Most children are able to generate more force for switch access when using a fisted, as opposed to an open, hand. For some children, however, it may be advantageous to foster an open-hand posture. As indicated by several sources (Bobath, 1978; Farber, 1982; Frazer et al., 1987), facilitation of an open-hand posture can have a tone-reducing effect on the entire arm. Furthermore, when the hand is open and the fingers are released, they are free to access a switch presented in a recessed format. As illustrated in Figure 3.32, an open-hand posture can be facilitated using (a) a hand cone, (b) a sof-splint (Reymann, 1985b), (c) a thumb loop (Utley, in Boehme, 1988), (d) a spasticity reduction splint, or (e) a wrist cock-up splint with a thumb abductor.

According to Farber (1982), hand cones can be used to facilitate an open-hand posture. When positioning the cone, the wider end is positioned on the little-finger side of the hand (Frazer, Hensinger, & Phelps, 1983), while the Velcro straps used to attach the cone to the hand should be positioned snugly just below the metacarpophalangeal joint on the back of the hand.

Several sources note that thumb abduction can serve to decrease overall flexion or spasticity in the

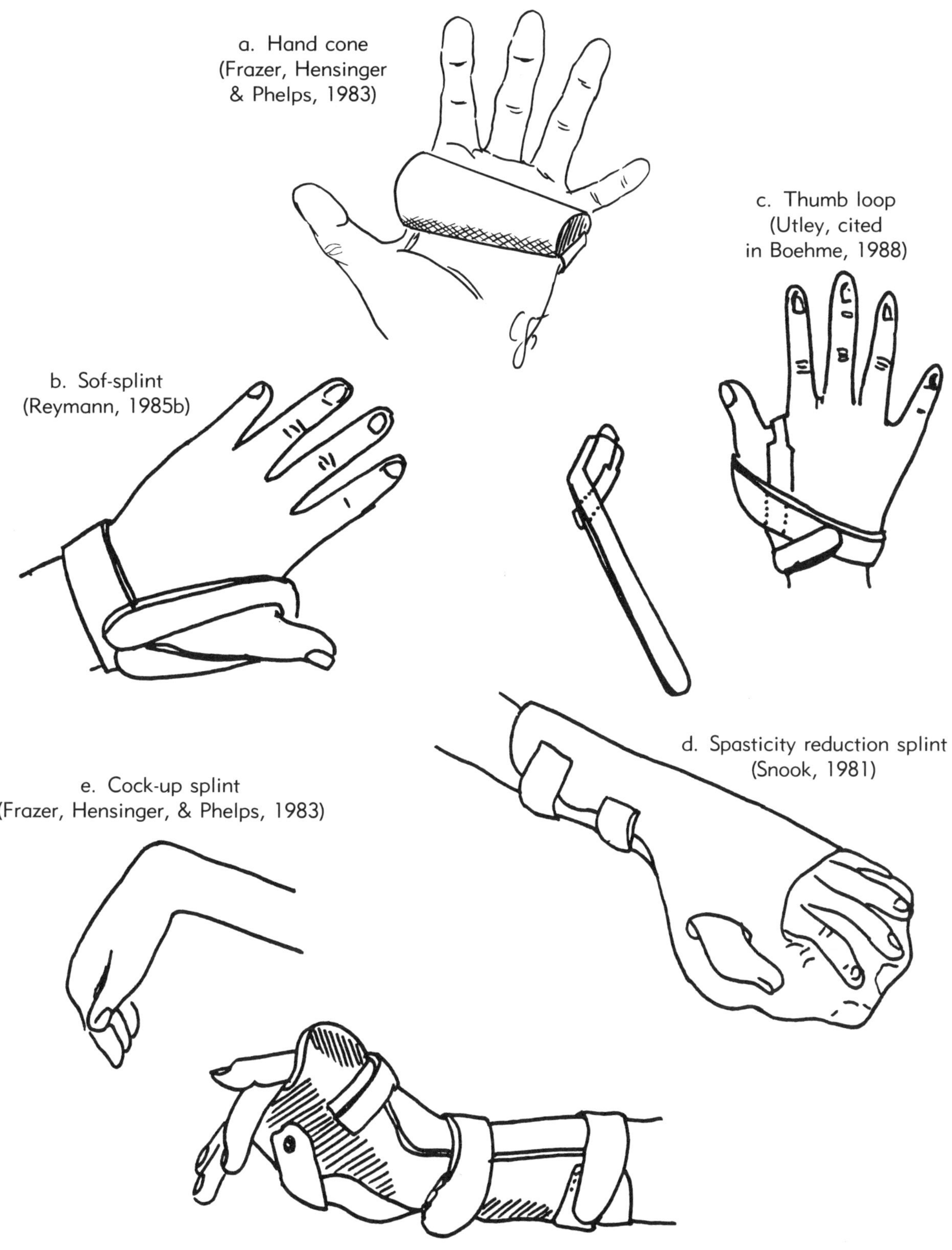


**FIGURE 3.32.** Facilitating an open-hand posture.

arm (Bobath, 1978; Frazer et al., 1987; Snook, 1981). Reymann (1985b) and Boehme (1988) have noted the use of a sof splint to achieve thumb abduction. Frazer et al. (1983, 1987) noted that a wrist cock-up splint with a thumb abductor can effectively reduce the tone in the wrist and thereby enhance overall hand function. Similarly, Snook (1981) noted that spasticity of the hand and arm can be effectively reduced through the use of a spasticity reduction splint, that is, a splint specifically designed to hold the wrist in extension with the thumb and fingers abducted and extended.

The use of hand splints appears to be controversial in the field of occupational therapy. Despite the controversy, there appears to be consensus that splinting is justified when used to prevent evolving deformities and enhance daily functioning. The recommendation to use a hand cone or a splint to optimize switch access should be considered only with input from an occupational therapist.

## Formats Using Alternate Control Sites

Many facilitators demonstrate a strong bias toward using the hand as the control site for switch access. Ease of presentation, the child's ability to visually monitor the motor act, and the child's need to gain proficiency in using his or her arms and hands are cited as reasons for preferring a hand-activated format over formats involving alternate control sites such as the head, knee, foot, or elbow. When selecting a control site, priority should always be given to the control site that promotes reliable and relatively effortless switch access. Although the hand is a viable control site for many children who are physically challenged, there are many children for whom the hand is not the preferred option. The use of a hand-activated switch setup involves considerably more than arm and hand control. Poor *static head control,* for example, can greatly confound the child's ability to effortlessly and reliably access a hand-activated switch setup. As illustrated in Figure 3.33a, many severely physically challenged children use their arms (supported by a lap tray or table surface) to help stabilize their upper trunk, which in turn provides the stable base for achieving better head control. When such children are required to use their upper extremities for switch access, the role their hands and arms typically play in promoting better head control is unwittingly compromised (Figure 3.33a). Head control, previously not a problem, now becomes a confounding factor. Given the interfering effects of poor head control, performance using a hand-activated switch setup is less than optimal.

The need for relatively good *dynamic head control* is also worthy of discussion. During the early stages of learning to access a hand-activated switch setup, the motor act is visually directed. Children are observed to split their attention between visually monitoring what their hand is doing with the switch and visually monitoring the activity of the target system (battery-operated toy, computer screen, or communication device). If a child is unable to dissociate eye movement from head movement, this need to "toggle" the gaze between the hand and the target system is accompanied by frequent movement of the head up and down and against the forces of gravity. If the child does not possess good graded vertical head control (Figure 3.33b), movement of the head down may eventually be achieved by merely letting the head drop rapidly; movement up may be achieved only with considerable effort and fatigue. In short, the need to alternately monitor the activity of the hand and the activity of the target system may necessitate movement of the head up and down, which in turn requires a certain degree of dynamic vertical head control. In the absence of refined vertical head control, hand-activated switch access may be greatly confounded by fatigue. If such is the case, access may be considerably better when the child uses an alternate control site. When using a head-activated format, for example, the head-up posture required for switch access is congruous with the head-up posture required for visually monitoring the target system. As the upper extremities are not required for switch access, they can continue to promote the trunk stability necessary for supporting the head movement patterns required for a viable head-activated switch setup.

In the final analysis, the performance of a hand-activated switch setup, relative to formats involving alternate control sites, should be the determining factor when selecting a viable control site for switch access. Unfortunately, the decision to use the hand as the control site is often made a priori in the absence of systematic data contrasting the relative efficacy of a hand-activated format with those involving alternate control sites. The head, knee,

a

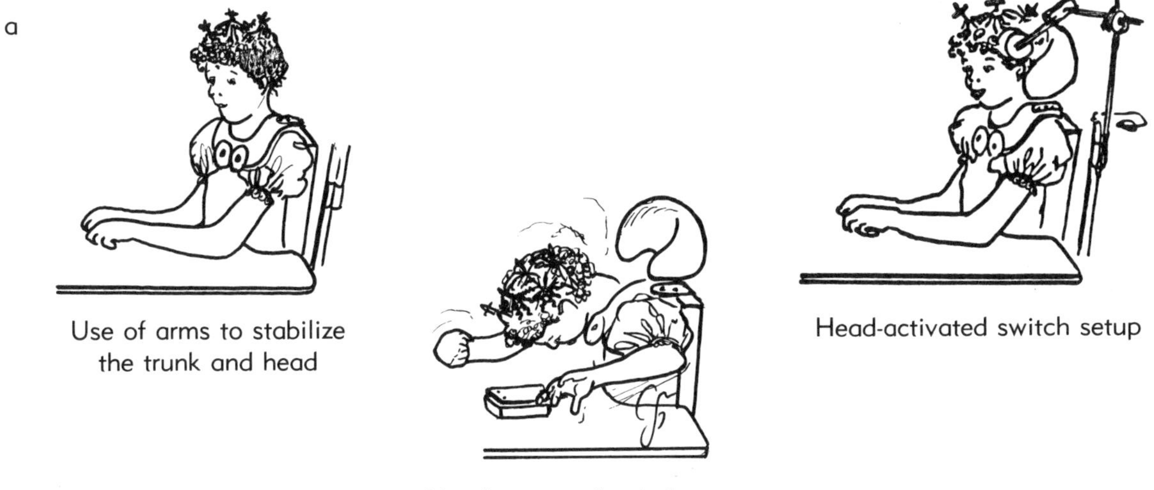


b

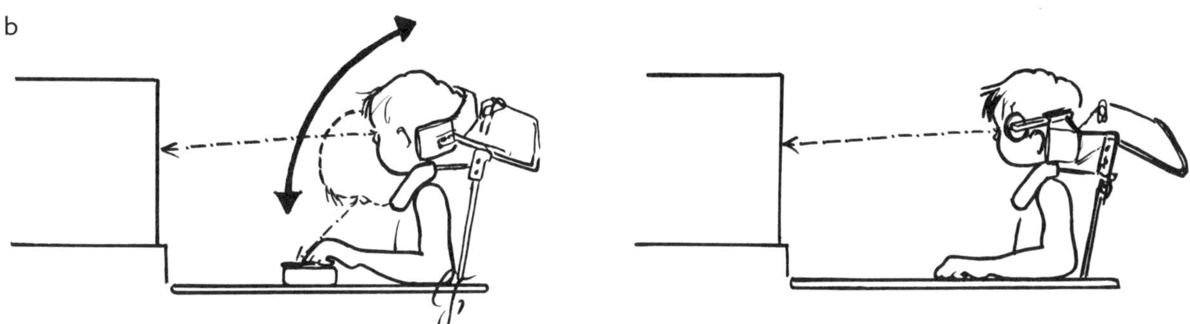

**FIGURE 3.33.** The confounding effects of poor head control on a hand-activated format.

and foot are alternate control sites worthy of more in-depth discussion.

## Head as a Control Site

Depicted in Figure 3.34 are four head movement patterns frequently used with severely physically challenged children:

- ❑ Lateral head turn
- ❑ Lateral head tilt
- ❑ Head flexion
- ❑ Head extension

**LATERAL HEAD TURN.** When a lateral head turn serves as the movement pattern for switch access, the head is rotated to the left or right in a horizontal plane while maintaining the head in vertical alignment (Figure 3.34a). Because a lateral head turn is an early developing and frequently used movement pattern for visual tracking and sound localization, it is considered to be motorically easier and less fatiguing than a lateral head tilt. Use of a lateral head turn, however, is frequently precluded when an ATNR is operative. In such instances, turning the head may trigger a reflexive movement pattern that greatly confounds the release aspect of switch access.

**LATERAL HEAD TILT.** When a lateral head tilt is employed for switch access, the head is tilted to the left or right in a vertical plane while the head is maintained in horizontal alignment (Figure 3.34b). In most instances, a lateral head tilt is preferred over a lateral head turn for the following reasons: (a) It is not subject to the interference of a nonverbal headshake "no"; (b) it is less prone to accidental activation (as it is a less frequent movement pattern and the switch

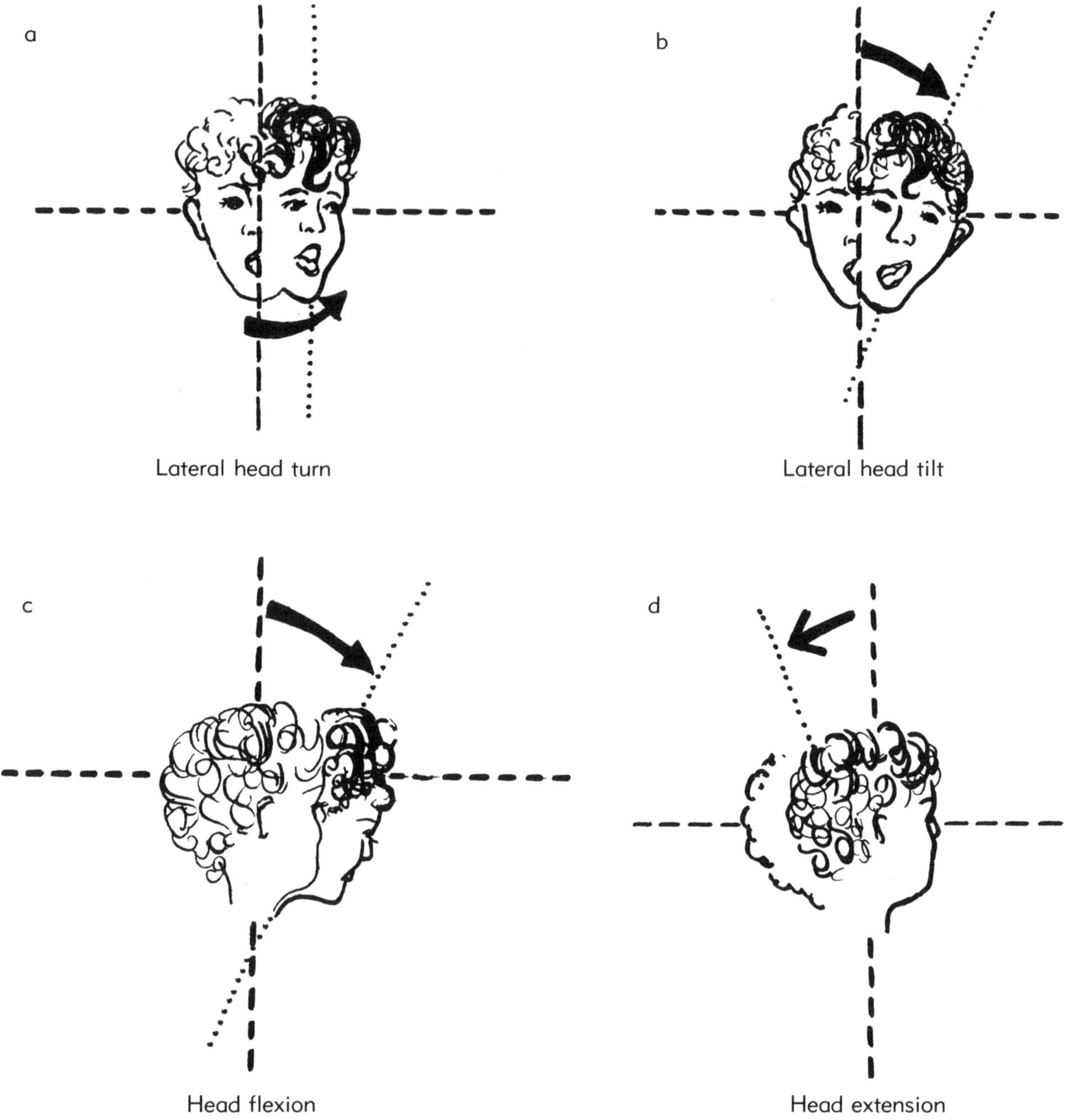


**FIGURE 3.34.** Head movement patterns.

interface is typically positioned farther from the head); (c) it allows the child unable to dissociate eye movements from head movements to more easily maintain visual contact with the target system; and (d) it is less prone to the interfering effects of an ATNR. As the lateral head tilt is less commonly performed in daily interaction with the environment, however, it is considered by some professionals to be more physically fatiguing.

**HEAD FLEXION.** When utilizing head flexion as the movement pattern for switch access, the head is rotated in a vertical plane while maintaining the head's horizontal alignment (Figure 3.34c). Because head flexion is a movement pattern performed at midline, it tends to promote (a) good body alignment and (b) a straight-ahead gaze ideally suited to visually monitoring the target system. Despite its many advantages, however, this movement pattern may be problematic for some children. First and foremost, the forward and down head posture often exacerbates drooling with many children. Furthermore, to capitalize on this movement pattern, the switch is typically placed in close proximity to the mouth. This close proximity may promote a tendency for the cognitively young child to mouth on the switch. For others, the presence of the switch in the vicinity of the face is best described as physically intrusive.

**HEAD EXTENSION.** When head extension serves as the movement pattern for switch access, the head is moved backwards in a vertical plane, leaving the head's horizontal alignment relatively unchanged (Figure 3.34d). Head extension is typically considered to be less desirable than other options, because it promotes a movement pattern that many therapists attempt to counteract (i.e., the tendency to tilt the head backwards to compensate for poor static head control). For many children, pressure on the back of the head can trigger extensor thrust (Frazer et al., 1987; Hehner & McNaughton, 1975). Although switch access is possible under such conditions, the resultant switch access would be achieved with heightened overall body tone, negatively affecting the child's ability to voluntarily release contact with the switch.

### Knee as a Control Site

Motor development typically evolves in a cephalocaudal direction. That is, the child usually achieves head control before upper extremity control, which in turn is typically achieved before lower extremity control. It is, therefore, not surprising that for most children with cerebral palsy, the head and upper extremities serve as control sites more frequently than the lower extremities. There are, however, instances in which a child with cerebral palsy may not be as involved in the lower extremities as the upper extremities. In such instances, movement of the knee may prove to be viable for reliable switch access. As illustrated in Figure 3.35, there are three movement patterns worthy of more in-depth consideration:

- ❑ Knee adduction
- ❑ Knee abduction
- ❑ Hip flexion

**KNEE ADDUCTION.** When knee adduction (Figure 3.35a) serves as the movement pattern for switch access, the knee is moved laterally toward midline. As represented, this lateral movement can be achieved by moving the entire leg laterally or by tilting the leg laterally when the foot is stabilized. With respect to the latter, the facilitator should be cognizant that children with motor involvement frequently experience difficulty dissociating the movement of one body part relative to another. For this reason, it may be necessary to loosely strap the foot of the leg being used for switch access. Of the two options presented, the lateral tilt is frequently easier, because the anchored foot serves as a stable base from which movement of the knee can be effectively achieved.

**KNEE ABDUCTION.** When knee abduction (Figure 3.35b) is being used as the movement pattern for switch access, the knee is moved laterally away from midline. As is the case with knee adduction, this can be achieved by moving the entire leg away from midline or by tilting the leg (stabilized at the level of the foot). All other factors being equal, knee abduction is preferred over knee adduction, because the latter can place the child at greater risk for hip subluxation. As abduction moves the femur into the hip, it typically poses less of a physical risk for individuals prone to hip subluxation or dislocation.

**HIP FLEXION.** When hip flexion (Figure 3.35c) serves as the movement pattern for switch access, the knee is moved vertically against gravity. To capitalize on this movement pattern, the switch interface is usually positioned above the knee. Because this movement pattern requires the child to raise the knee against gravity, it is generally considered to be more physically taxing than other movement patterns involving the knee. If hip flexion is to be used for switch access, complete stabilization of the foot is not recommended. Usually, the toe is stabilized, freeing the heel to assist in achieving hip flexion.

### Foot as a Control Site

Illustrated in Figure 3.36 are four movement patterns involving the foot as the control site for switch access:

- ❑ Foot abduction
- ❑ Foot adduction

a. Adduction

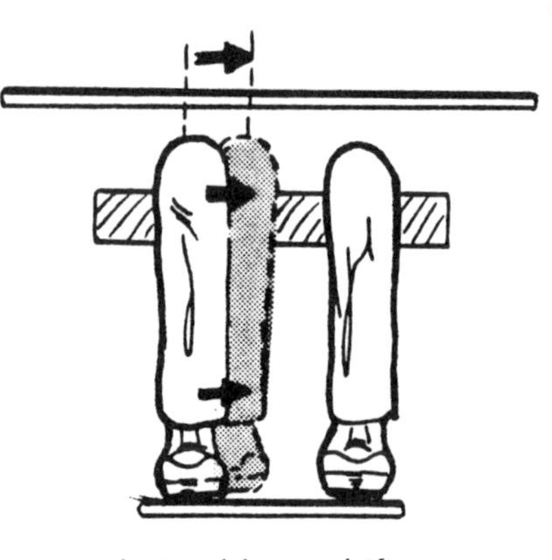

Lateral knee shift

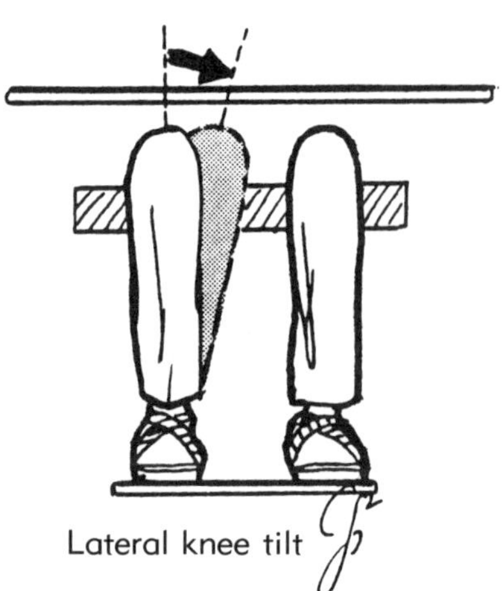

Lateral knee tilt

b. Abduction

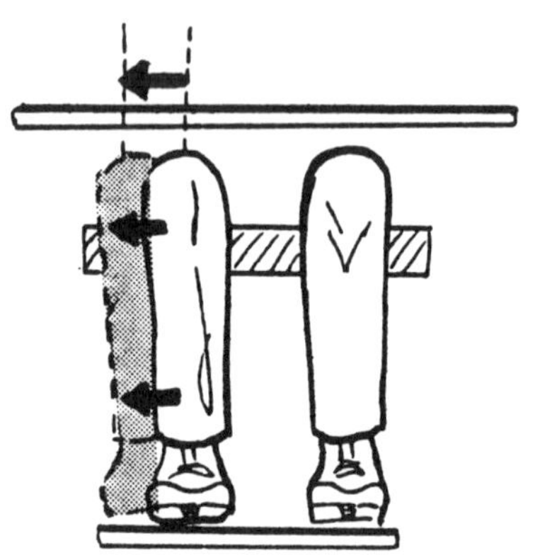

Lateral knee shift

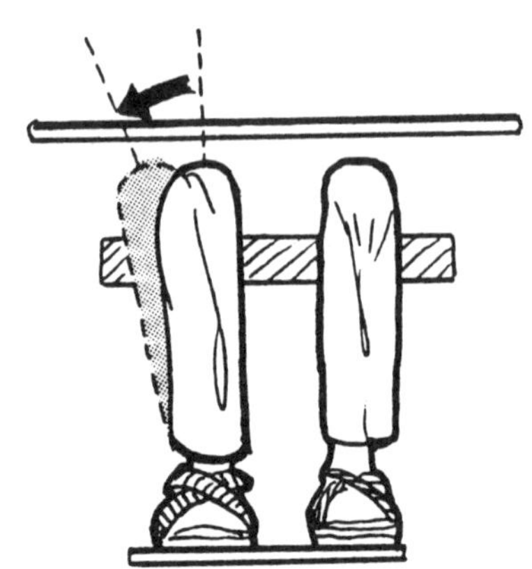

Lateral knee tilt

c. Hip flexion

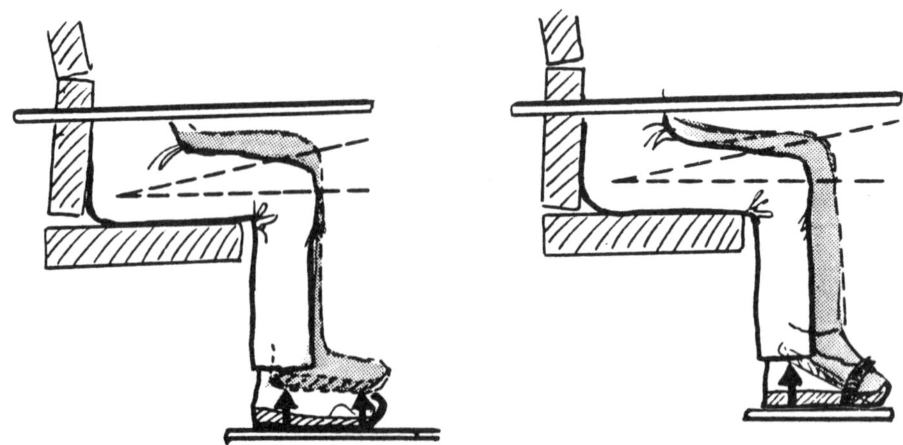

**FIGURE 3.35.** Knee movement patterns.

a. Abduction

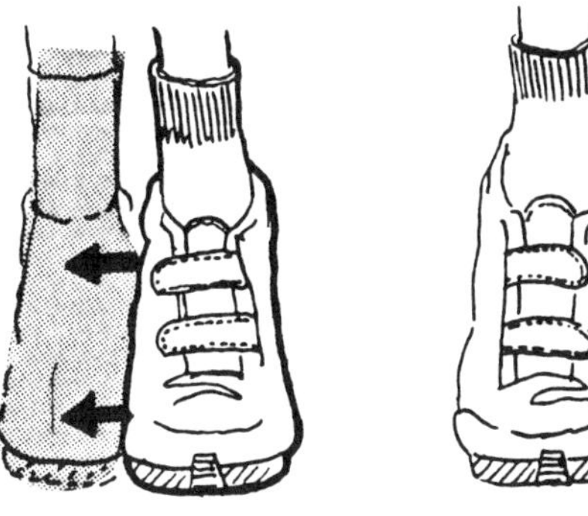
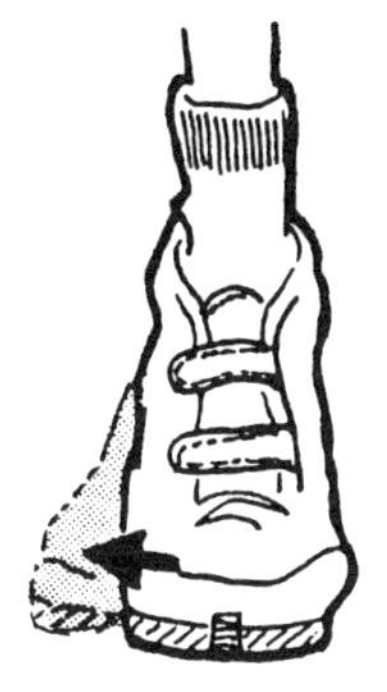

Lateral foot shift

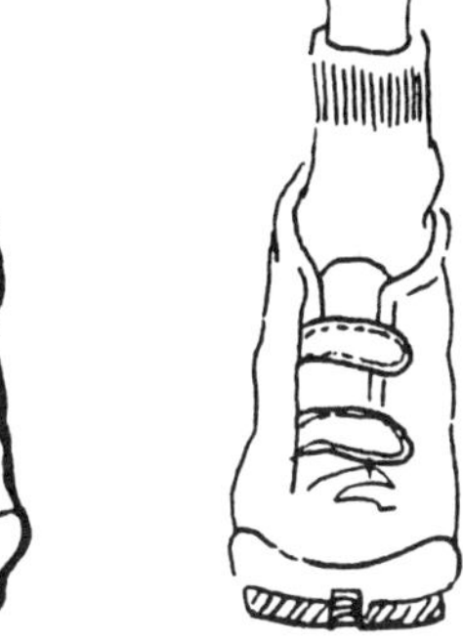

Lateral foot pivot

b. Adduction

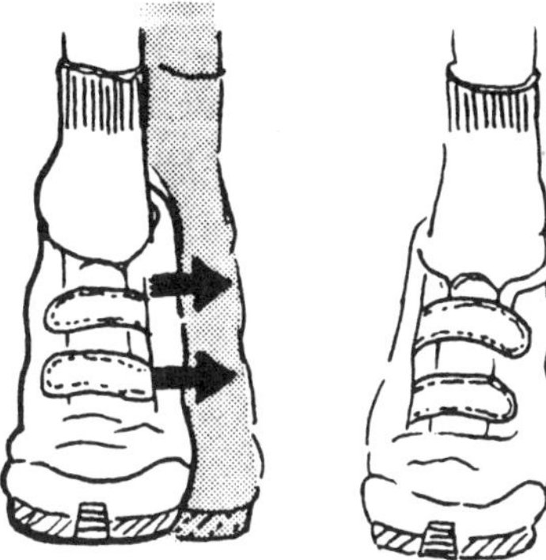
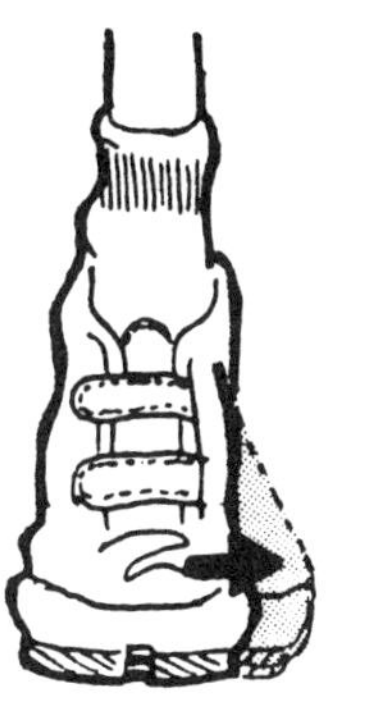

Lateral foot shift

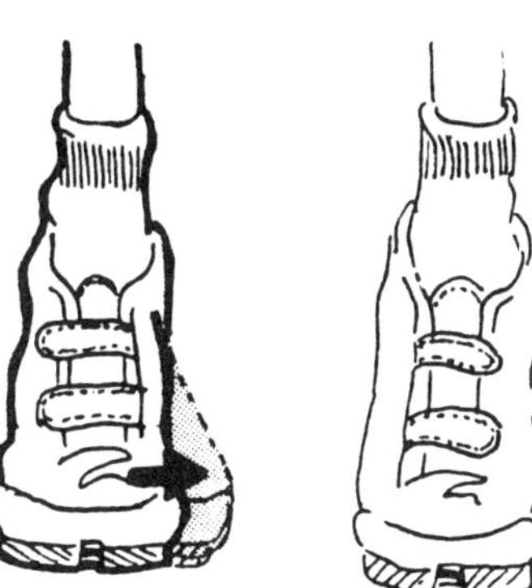

Lateral foot pivot

c. Dorsiflexion

d. Plantarflexion

**FIGURE 3.36.** Foot movement patterns.

- ❑ Dorsiflexion
- ❑ Plantarflexion

**FOOT ABDUCTION.** When foot abduction (Figure 3.36a) serves as the movement pattern for switch access, either the entire foot is shifted away from midline or the distal portion of the foot is pivoted relative to a stabilized heel.

**FOOT ADDUCTION.** When utilizing foot adduction (Figure 3.36b) to achieve switch access, the foot is moved toward midline. As is the case with foot abduction, this can be achieved by moving the entire foot medially or by pivoting the foot medially relative to a stabilized heel. All factors being equal, however, foot abduction is generally preferred over foot adduction, because it is less likely to promote hip dislocation.

**DORSIFLEXION.** When dorsiflexion of the foot (Figure 3.36c) is used for switch access, the switch is typically positioned in an inverted format. Because this movement pattern requires children to move their foot upward against the forces of gravity, switch action is typically latching in nature (i.e., the first activation of the switch activates the target system, which remains activated until a second activation of the switch turns it off). In contrast to previously discussed movement patterns, the dorsiflexion movement pattern tends to be more fatiguing.

**PLANTARFLEXION.** Plantarflexion (Figure 3.36d) requires the child to move the foot downward in a vertical plane. When utilizing this movement pattern, the switch interface is positioned beneath the foot. Typically, the switch employed is either a heavy-duty switch or is slightly recessed relative to its surrounding slightly spongy surface. When the foot rests on the switch, the switch is not activated; force must be exerted to activate the switch. In many instances, the facilitator may wish to strap the child's foot to the switch to build in greater stability for access (Beukelman, Yorkston, & Dowden, 1985). This movement pattern would, however, be contraindicated in instances in which a child demonstrates a positive supporting reaction. With such children, stimulation of the balls of their feet results in extension and the increase in overall body tone that typically accompanies this reflex.

## General Guidelines

Four general guidelines should be considered when establishing a switch setup involving an alternate control site.

1. Place the switch close enough to the control site to allow *effortless contact,* yet far enough away to *minimize accidental activation* due to extraneous, nonpurposeful movements or purposeful, nonverbal gestures such as a headshake or head nod.
2. Position the switch in a manner that *maximizes contact* between the switch activation surface and the control site when switch closure is being achieved. As illustrated in Figure 3.37, this can be accomplished by (a) reorienting the switch mount or (b) inserting a wedge between the switch and its attachment plate to promote more parallel alignment with the control site. As depicted in Figure 3.38, wedges are typically constructed of lightweight Ethafoam and are attached to the mounting plate with glue or adhesive Velcro. Adherence to this guideline (a) decreases the likelihood that slight changes in positioning will negatively affect viable switch access and (b) enhances the tactile feedback that is believed to be an important factor when working with cognitively young children. Although many options exist for achieving contact between the switch and the control site, the options that exist for maximizing contact are more restricted. Furthermore, it is only when care is taken to align the switch activation surface parallel with the surface of the body part/control site that maximum contact between switch and control site can be assured.
3. Consider incorporating a boundary bumper to clearly delineate for the child the maximum excursion of the control site away from the switch activation surface. The boundary bumpers for several control sites are presented in Figure 3.39. As depicted, the boundary bumpers for alternate control sites are often positioned in a manner that promotes the neutral resting position of the control site. When using a head-activated switch setup, the boundary bumper can be constructed of

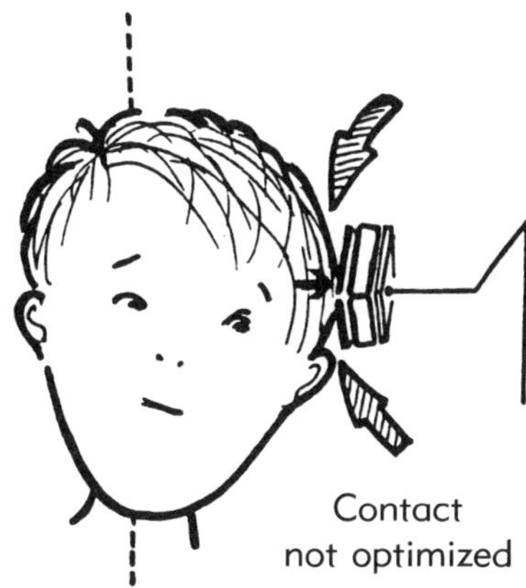

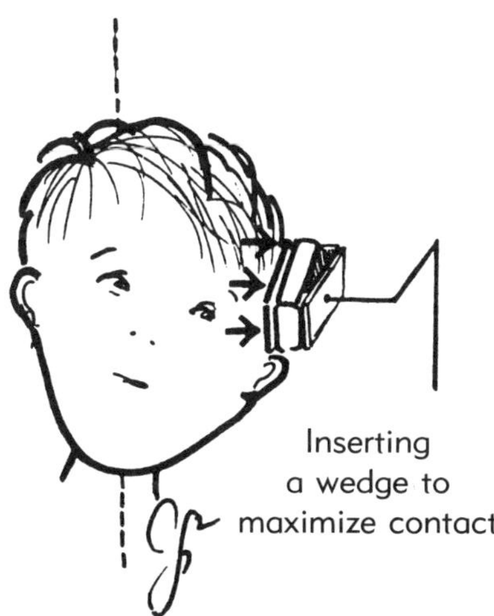


**FIGURE 3.37.** Maximizing contact between the switch interface and the control site.

Ethafoam or polyethelene foam (trade name Rubetex or Armaflex foam) attached to the mounting plate via adhesive Velcro. As depicted in Figure 3.40, a plush covering can be used to soften contact with the control site when Ethafoam is used. It is also possible to adhere a layer of ½-inch-thick foam derived from a camping mat to a mounting plate constructed of Plexiglas, Kydex plastic, or Masonite. As boundary bumpers promote *consistency of responding* from one trial to the next, they can greatly facilitate learning. Specifically, they may (a) assist the child in *initiating contact* with the switch by serving as a rebound surface; (b) assist the child in *releasing contact* with the switch by cognitively altering the task from "have to get off the switch" to "have to get over to the boundary bumper"; and (c) reduce or eliminate accidental activation by serving as a "home base" to position the control site when the child is not involved in the actual act of activating the switch. Boundary bumpers are much like trainer wheels on a bicycle. They help the child learn the required response and are later eliminated.

4. Consider focusing control by minimizing the extraneous movements of other body parts. Extraneous movements of the hands and arms can be stabilized using the suggestions previously presented in Figures 3.30 and 3.31. The professional may also consider stabilizing the trunk/arms by (a) positioning the arms below the lap tray (Trefler, 1982) or (b) using an angled Plexiglas easel lap tray (e.g., Safety Travel Chair lap tray, Figure 3.41b). Stabilization of the feet is typically achieved through the use of foot straps and/or heel cups.
5. Avoid accepting a movement pattern performed (a) with greatly increased body tone, (b) as part of an abnormal reflex or synergy pattern, or (c) forcefully. Appendix A presents additional information relative to the movement patterns most frequently employed in switch setups involving alternate control sites. Figure 3.42 visually summarizes steps taken to optimize head-activated switch setups.

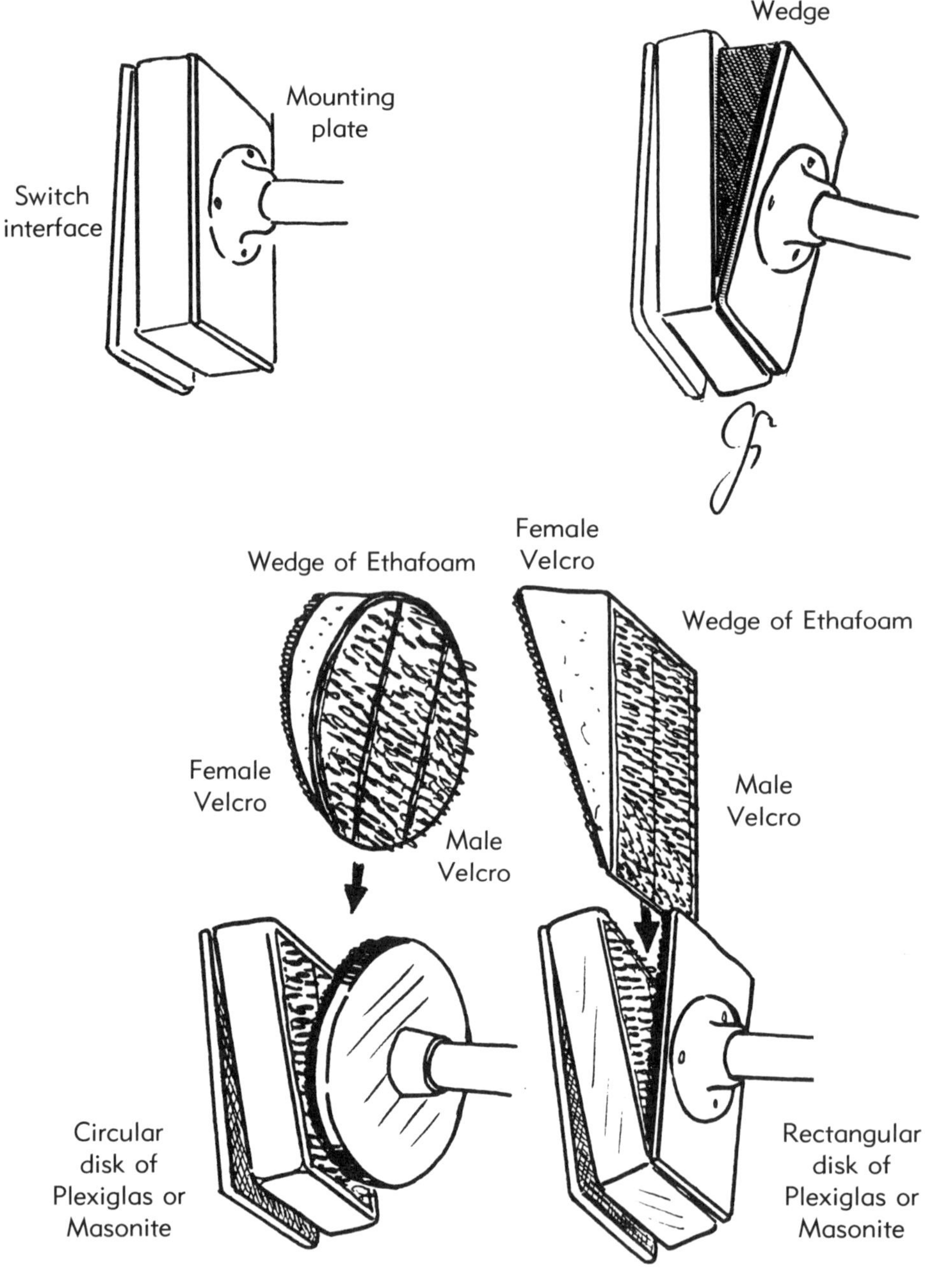


**FIGURE 3.38.** Constructing a wedge for a mounting plate.

## Summary

A number of factors must be considered when determining a viable switch setup. The two major factors addressed in this chapter are:

- ❑ What movement pattern can be used by the child for reliable switch access, and
- ❑ What switch interface will be placed in the path of the designated movement pattern.

The process of determining what movement pattern can be used for reliable switch access involves (a) informal observation of the child's typical motor performance during routine daily activities (e.g., dressing, mealtime, play) and (b) subsequent screening for potentially viable movement patterns. Through informal observation, the facilitator gathers information relative to three broad types of movement patterns:

Lateral head tilt

Head flexion

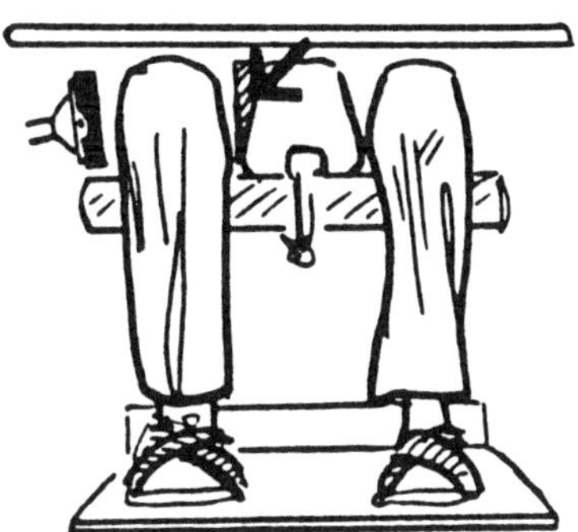
Lateral knee tilt (abduction)

**FIGURE 3.39.** Boundary bumpers for various movement patterns.

- ❑ Involuntary abnormal movement patterns
- ❑ Voluntary abnormal movement patterns
- ❑ Voluntary normal movement patterns.

When delineating a viable switch setup, the facilitator is ideally looking to achieve switch access using a voluntary normal movement pattern. In the event a voluntary normal movement pattern is not an option, the facilitator may be forced to settle for use of a voluntary abnormal movement pattern. Although sometimes used, abnormal movement patterns are considered less desirable for switch access.

Informal observation is supplemented by screening the various movement patterns typically used for switch access. Screening is conducted using a switch interface with highly motivating end rewards. Throughout the screening, the facilitator assesses:

- ❑ The child's ability to reliably perform the requested movement pattern
- ❑ The speed with which the child is able to initiate the movement pattern
- ❑ The degree to which the movement is performed with abnormal versus normal movement patterns, an undesirable increase in overall body tone, and/or overflow movement to other parts of the body

In general, the facilitator screens for movement patterns that can be performed as reliably and as effortlessly as possible, and without triggering abnormal reflex patterns. Having delineated movement patterns with potential for viable switch access, the facilitator focuses on selecting the switch interface to be placed in the path of the movement pattern(s).

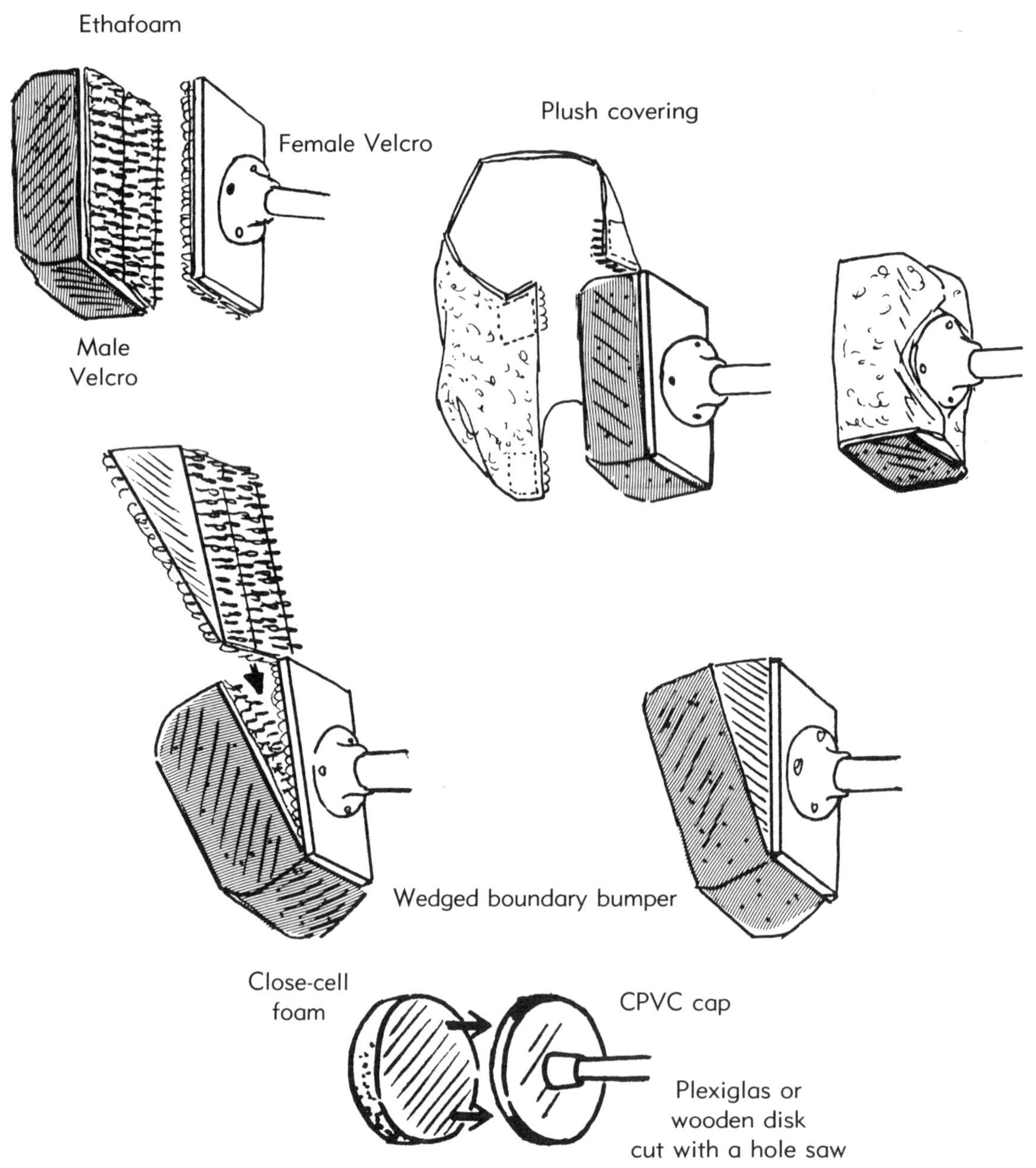


**FIGURE 3.40.** Constructing a boundary bumper on a mounting plate.

Switch interfaces vary according to a number of different features, each of which must be considered during the switch selection process. Switch features include force, feedback, amount of travel, amount of play, size, weight, moisture resistance, and safety.

For many children, the hand may be the control site of choice. For others, an alternate control site may be the preferred option. Considerations relative to using the hand and alternate control sites (head, knee, foot) for switch access were discussed in the latter part of this chapter.

Having (a) delineated a viable movement pattern for switch access and (b) selected an appropriate switch interface to be used with a particular movement pattern, the facilitator must now direct attention toward creating a supporting structure to position the switch in the desired location relative to the control site. Constructing the supporting structure or switch mount is the focus of Chapter 4.

a. Positioning arms below lap tray (Trefler, 1982)

b. Angled Plexiglas easel lap tray (Safety Travel Chair) lap tray

**FIGURE 3.41.** Using the lap tray to stabilize the upper trunk and extremities.

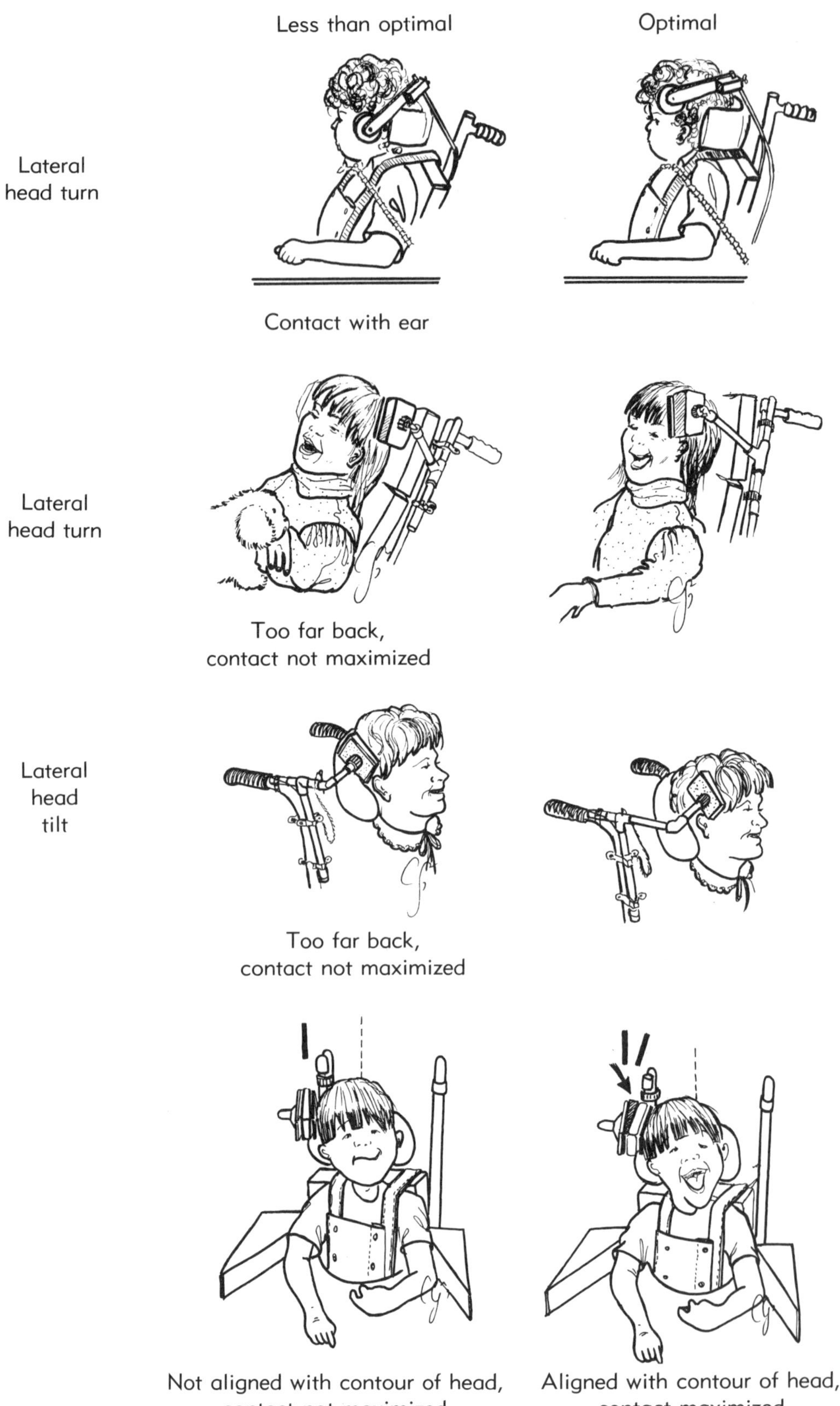


**FIGURE 3.42.** Optimizing switch setups involving head movement patterns.

chapter 4

# Constructing the Switch Mount

A SWITCH MOUNT CAN BE generally defined as a structure that positions a switch interface in a desired location relative to the control site. In the previous chapter, minimal attention was directed toward the mounting aspects of achieving a viable switch setup. Although the process of "delineating a viable switch setup" (Chapter 3) was addressed as if it occurred separately from that of "constructing the switch mount" (Chapter 4), the latter is an important subcomponent of the former. Because the switch mount serves as the supporting structure for switch placement, the importance of the mount to the viability of the switch setup cannot be overemphasized.

## Guiding Principles

The guiding principles for mount construction remain consistent regardless of the type of mount employed. In general, the switch mount should be:

- ❑ Stable
- ❑ Noninterfering
- ❑ Safe
- ❑ Flexible
- ❑ Cosmetically pleasing

### Stability

A switch mount should securely and consistently present the switch in an optimal position relative to the control site. When constructing a mount, care should be taken to ensure that the mount accommodates the target location for the switch interface, not the reverse. Too often, optimal switch placement is compromised as a result of limitations in mount design. When working with children who are severely physically challenged, small compromises in switch placement can result in large compromises in motor performance. In general, the more consistent the required response can be made for the young child, the greater the speed with which the skill is acquired. Hundreds, perhaps thousands, of trials may be necessary before a target motor response for switch access becomes effortless and automatic for the child who is severely physically challenged. An analogy for the able-bodied individual is learning to drive a car using a stick shift. Initially, every move is a conscious effort. With time and thousands of trials, the process becomes automatic, requiring minimal processing by higher level brain centers. Because the switch mount serves as the supporting structure for switch placement, a stable switch mount is considered crucial to the motor acquisition process.

### Noninterference

The switch mount should not interfere with the conduct of daily routines such as toileting and feeding (Wright & Nomura, 1985). In keeping with this guideline, the switch mount should never limit the child's visual field or compromise the range of upper extremity movement (Lee & Thomas, 1990; TASH,

c. 1987). When designing a wheelchair mount, care should be taken to ensure that the mount does not inadvertently increase the functional width of the wheelchair, thereby encumbering the process of moving effortlessly through doorways (Williams et al., 1982). Furthermore, the mount should not interfere with the client's ability to transfer or be transferred in and out of the wheelchair. Mount designs that allow the switch to be quickly and temporarily removed or moved out of the way to facilitate transfer are highly desirable.

### Safety

Switch mounts should be constructed in a manner that ensures that the switch interface can be used safely. In keeping with this goal, the mount should have no sharp edges or protruding hardware that might result in bodily harm to the child or damage to the vehicle required for wheelchair transport.

It is not unusual for some children to demonstrate forceful switch activation, raising concern for the child's safety when using the switch. In response to this dilemma, several facilitators advocate incorporating some "play" or "give" into the mount design to minimize the likelihood of injury. In the authors' experience, however, we have found such children to perform best when (a) steps are taken to ensure that the mount is extremely stable, with minimal play, and (b) boundary bumpers are employed to assist the child in clearly delineating the required motor response. During the early stages of intervention, children with motor involvement typically experience difficulty grading their motor movements. Forceful activation of the switch often reflects the child's attempt to enhance targeting accuracy by increasing speed of access. When steps are taken to enhance targeting accuracy (through the use of a highly stable switch mount and boundary bumpers), the need for increased speed of access is thus eliminated.

The cable connecting the switch interface with the target system is also subject to damage if care is not taken to prevent this cable from being caught in the wheels of the wheelchair or in the mechanism for adjusting the angle of the bed (switch brochure, Prentke Romich Company). Although the cable can be anchored securely with Velcro or pinch clamps, the facilitator may also consider drilling a hole in the switch mount and running the cable inside the mainframe of the mount.

### Flexibility

Children with cerebral palsy frequently require a variety of therapeutic positions throughout the course of the day. When constructing switch mounts for various therapeutic positions, attention should be directed toward delineating mounting fixtures amenable to use of a given switch interface in a variety of positions. Although this is not always feasible, attention to this need can greatly facilitate the ease of setting up a switch in a variety of positions.

Ideally, the mainframe of the mount should be permanently attached to the frame of the various therapeutic positioning options. This practice can greatly facilitate the process of quickly positioning the switch in its optimal location or removing the switch to facilitate transfer of the child in and out of the equipment.

### Appearance

When constructing a switch mount, care should be taken to make the mount as aesthetically pleasing and as unobtrusive as possible. A switch mount, like other pieces of equipment, can add or detract from the overall appearance of the individual.

## Types of Switch Mounts

Switch mounts can assume a variety of forms. Within this chapter five major types of switch mounts are discussed:

- ❑ Switch mounts made with commercially available adaptive fixtures
- ❑ Switch mounts made with CPVC pipes and fittings
- ❑ Headrest switch mounts
- ❑ Hand-activated switch mounts constructed of Ethafoam
- ❑ Switch mounts positioned on the body

## Switch Mounts Made with Commercially Available Adaptive Fixtures

Considerable creativity has gone into delineating hardware that will allow a switch to be securely positioned in the path of a child's most reliable motor response. Although some of the components employed have been designed specifically for building switch mounts, numerous components have been borrowed from industries producing camera mounting supplies, as well as studio and recording equipment.

Several companies have assembled switch mounting or adaptive fixtures kits. Most smaller kits are designed to achieve a specific purpose such as mounting a specific type of switch to a standard wheelchair frame. As illustrated in Figure 4.1, more comprehensive kits are also available. In general, the larger kits provide a collection of component parts useful for mounting a broad array of switches to a wide range of therapeutic positioning equipment.

The more comprehensive kits tend to be used in two ways. In small clinical programs, the kit is primarily used to delineate a viable switch setup. Having achieved this goal, duplicate parts are ordered, to be assembled for the client at a later date. In larger clinical programs providing diagnostic services to numerous clients, an inventory of adaptive fixtures is kept on hand. This inventory allows the child's mount to be constructed using kit components. The kit is later replenished using parts from the program's inventory. This procedure eliminates waiting for ordered parts and making a repeat visit to assemble the ordered parts. A switch setup can thus be provided in a more timely and cost-effective manner.

Switch mounts constructed with commercially available mounting hardware can be discussed with respect to these major components:

- ❑ Constructing the mainframe of the mount
- ❑ Adapting the switch to accommodate the mainframe
- ❑ Attaching the mainframe to therapeutic positioning equipment.
- ❑ Designing a stable mount
- ❑ Fine-tuning the mount
- ❑ Making the mount permanent
- ❑ Incorporating a removal joint

**CONSTRUCTING THE MAINFRAME OF THE MOUNT.** Switch type is the primary determinant of the mounting materials to be used in the mainframe of the mount. In general, the mainframe of the mount can be constructed using either rigid or flexible mounting materials.

**Rigid Mainframes.** Tubing and aluminum rods constitute the two main types of rigid materials employed in the mainframe of a switch mount.

*Tubing.* Five-eighths-inch (outer diameter) tubing is constructed of stainless steel and is available in a variety of pipe lengths and pipe angles (typically 45° or 90°). The ends of the tubes are threaded to allow them to be joined and to be coupled with components possessing a compatible thread. As illustrated in Figure 4.2, tube ends are typically classified as being either male (external threads) or female

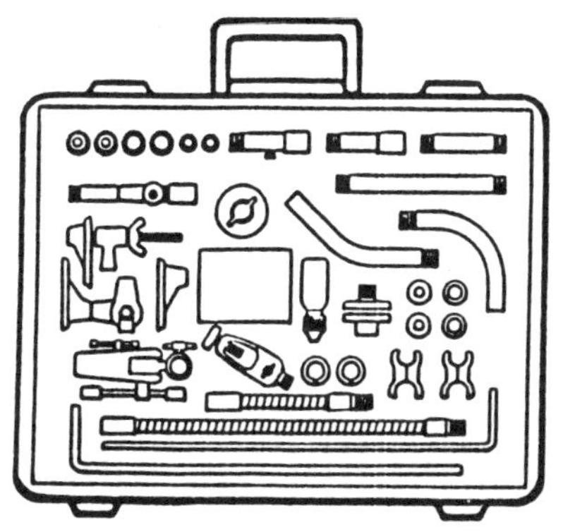

Zygo Industries, Inc.

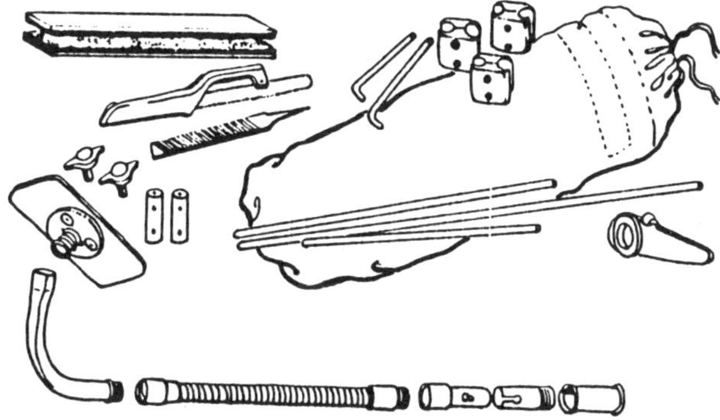

Don Johnston Developmental Equipment

**FIGURE 4.1.** Commercially available adaptive fixtures kits.

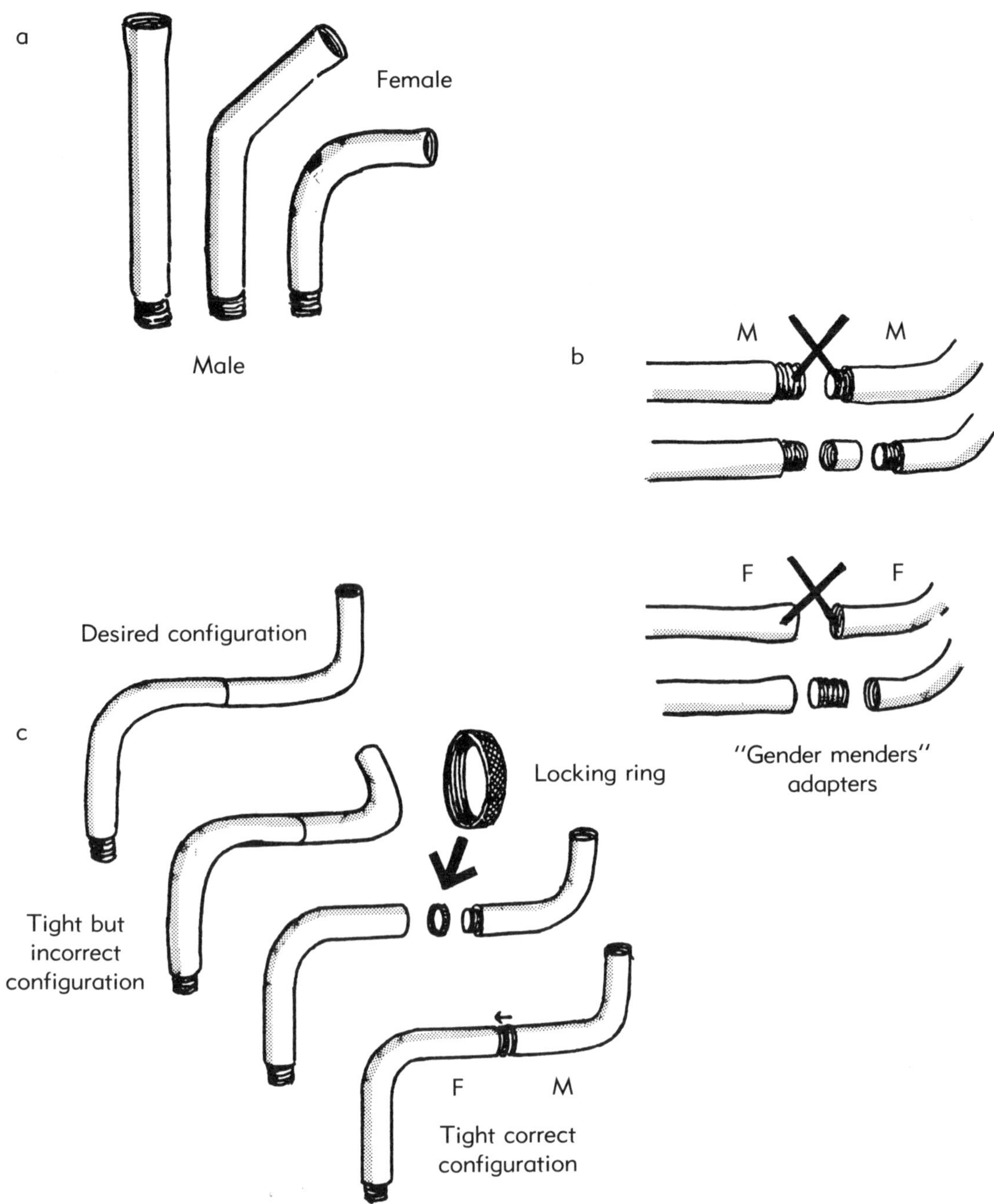


**FIGURE 4.2.** Rigid mainframes—Tubing.

(internal threads). By design, a male end can be directly coupled only with a female end. In instances in which two same-sex ends must be coupled, such as male to male or female to female, adapters or ''gender menders'' (Figure 4.2b) are required to convert one of the ends to the opposite sex.

When constructing a tube-based mount, two- and three- dimensional configurations are achieved by incorporating 90° and 45° angle tubes into the switch mount design. When tubes are tightly interfaced (required for stability), the resulting configuration is not always the desired configuration. As illustrated in Figure 4.2c, locking rings can be used to circumvent this problem. Prior to coupling two components, a lock ring is threaded on the male end of the tube to be coupled. The joint is then tightened to the point of achieving the desired (but slightly loose) configuration; that is, to a point just prior to achieving a tight, but incorrect, configuration. At this precise point, the locking ring is tightened in the direction of the female end of the coupled parts. Thus, a configuration can be achieved that is both tight and correct.

Tubing is capable of producing extremely stable mounts. The fact that tubing is available in fixed lengths and angles, however, necessitates considerable ingenuity in achieving a switch mount that does not compromise optimal placement of the switch relative to the control site. Although pipe can theoretically be cut to any length and rethreaded, this option is achieved with considerable additional expense and time.

*Rods.* Aluminum rods, available in ¼-inch and ⅜-inch (outer diameter) sizes, are available in straight lengths or lengths with a short (3-inch or 4-inch) 90° bend (Figure 4.3a). Thicker, ½-inch rods are also available from TASH, Inc. As the ¼-inch and ⅜-inch diameter rods are constructed of aluminum, their length can be easily altered by securing the pipe in a vise and cutting the rod with a hacksaw or jeweler's saw. A file can then be used to remove burrs from the cut end.

When using rods for the mainframe of the mount, three options exist for achieving two- and three-dimensional configurations:

- ❑ Bending the rods
- ❑ Using a single-plane swivel
- ❑ Using a universal swivel

*Bending the rods.* As illustrated in Figure 4.3, rods can be bent to any desired angle by (a) using the edge of a hard surface (Figure 4.3c), (b) securing the rod in a vise prior to bending (Figure 4.3d), or (c) using a pipe bender (available in most hardware stores).

*Using a single-plane swivel.* Several companies provide a coupling option called a ball swivel. As depicted in Figure 4.4a, this option consists of a sphere with two perpendicular shafts, each large enough to accommodate a ⅜-inch or ¼-inch rod. Each rod is secured in its shaft with setscrews and tightened with an allen wrench. Setscrews are inserted perpendicular to the rod and therefore exert lateral pressure on the rod within the shaft, preventing the rod from moving laterally or vertically within the shaft. By design, this mounting option allows one rod to be positioned perpendicular to a base rod and to be varied a full 360° in a single plane relative to this base rod. When two single-plane swivels are incorporated into a mount design, adjustability is possible in all planes.

*Using a universal swivel.* The universal swivel (Zygo Industries, Inc.) and universal swivel clamp (TASH, Inc.) allow two rods to be joined and positioned in any 360° configuration relative to each other in a 360° sphere. The Zygo universal swivel is constructed of two circular halves separated by a metal disk and joined by a central thumbscrew. Each half contains a variety of shafts (some semicircular, some square) that course through the entire width of the circular half. To utilize this mounting option, the central thumbscrew is loosened to allow one rod to be inserted through one half of the fixture and a second rod to be inserted through the second half. The previously discussed shafts of various sizes and shapes (semicircular, square) located on both halves allow the fixture to accommodate rods of different widths. With ¼-inch rods, the smaller semicircular openings are used; with ⅜-inch rods, the larger semicircular openings are used. Once inserted, rods can be configured into any arrangement relative to each other in a 360° sphere. The desired arrangement of rods is maintained by tightening the thumbscrew on the side of the adaptive fixture.

Similar to the Zygo universal swivel, the TASH universal swivel contains two halves capable of accommodating ½-inch diameter rods. When its central thumbscrew is loose, the two rods can be configured into any arrangement relative to each other in a 360° sphere.

**Flexible Mainframes.** As illustrated in Figure 4.5, flexible mainframes include:

- ❑ Goosenecks
- ❑ Flexbars
- ❑ Adjustable arms

*Goosenecks.* Goosenecks (Figure 4.5a) are a highly flexible option for achieving switch positioning. They are readily available in a variety of lengths (ranging from 6 inches to 24 inches). Due to their flexible nature, goosenecks can be used to quickly position a switch in the path of the targeted movement pattern. Unfortunately, the ease with which a gooseneck can be used to position a switch within the

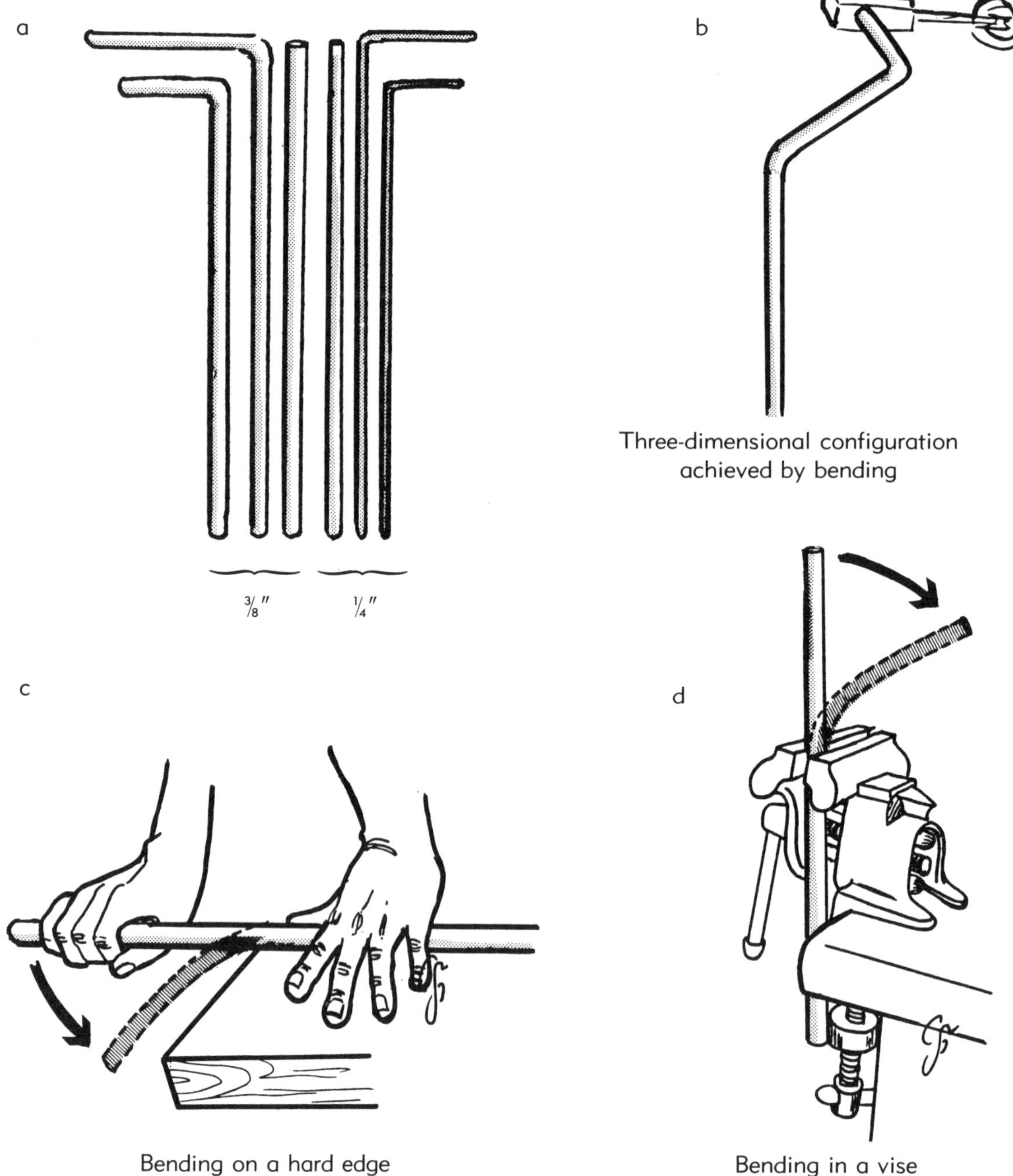


**FIGURE 4.3.** Rigid mainframes—Rods.

range of optimal access is equal to the ease with which force of switch activation can move a gooseneck-mounted switch out of the optimal range of access. Furthermore, with repeated use, goosenecks tend to lose their stiffness. Thus, the likelihood that a switch will be moved out of its optimal range will occur with increasing frequency over time.

As previously discussed, the process of learning to access a switch is greatly enhanced if switch placement remains highly consistent from one trial to the next. Because goosenecks cannot assure consistency of placement, they are generally not considered to be an optimal long-term mounting option for the majority of children requiring switch mounts. The long-term use of gooseneck switch mounts is often limited to use with children whose overall low tone exerts minimal pressure on a switch mount during switch activation. In view of these shortcomings, the

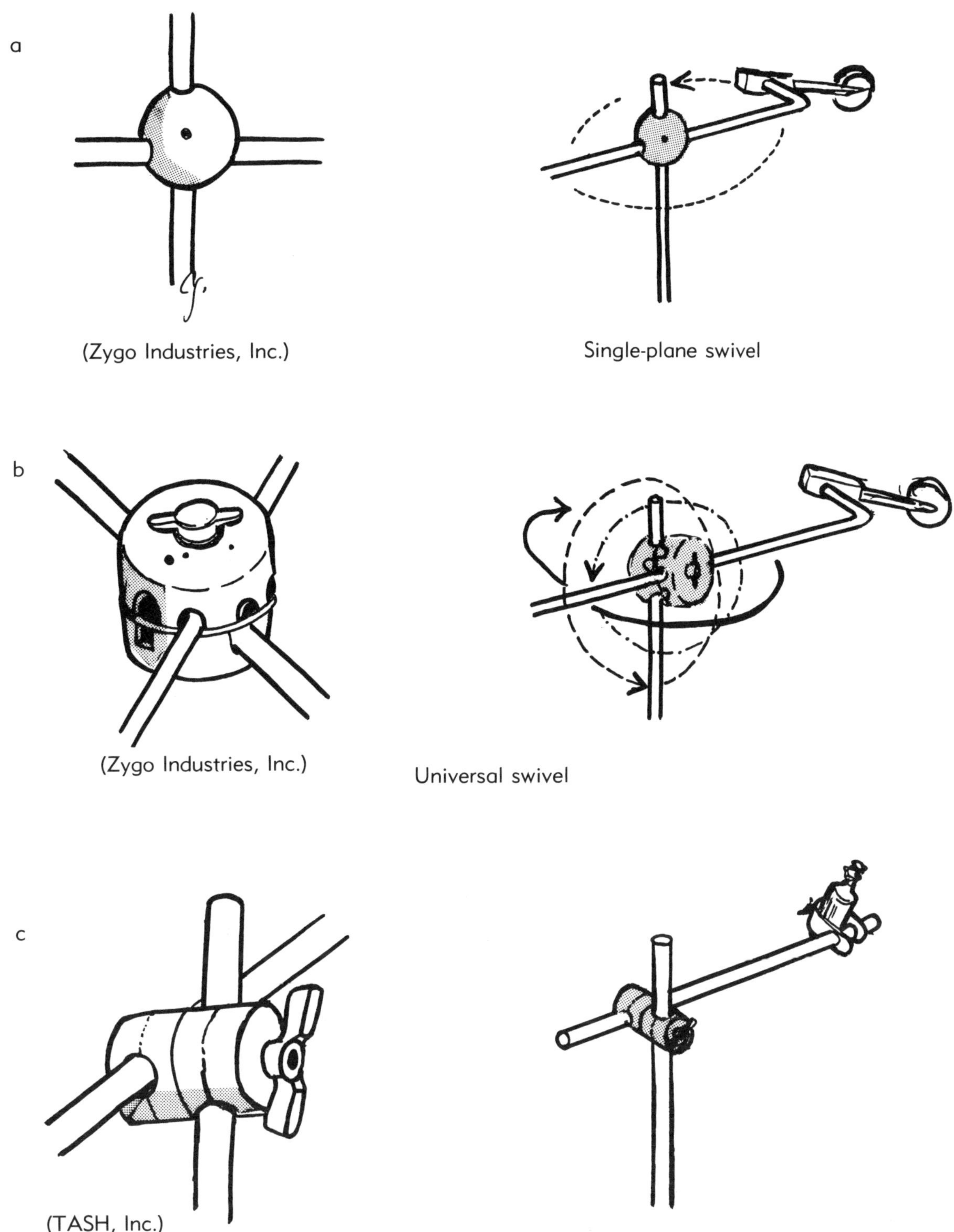


**FIGURE 4.4.** Single-plane and universal swivels.

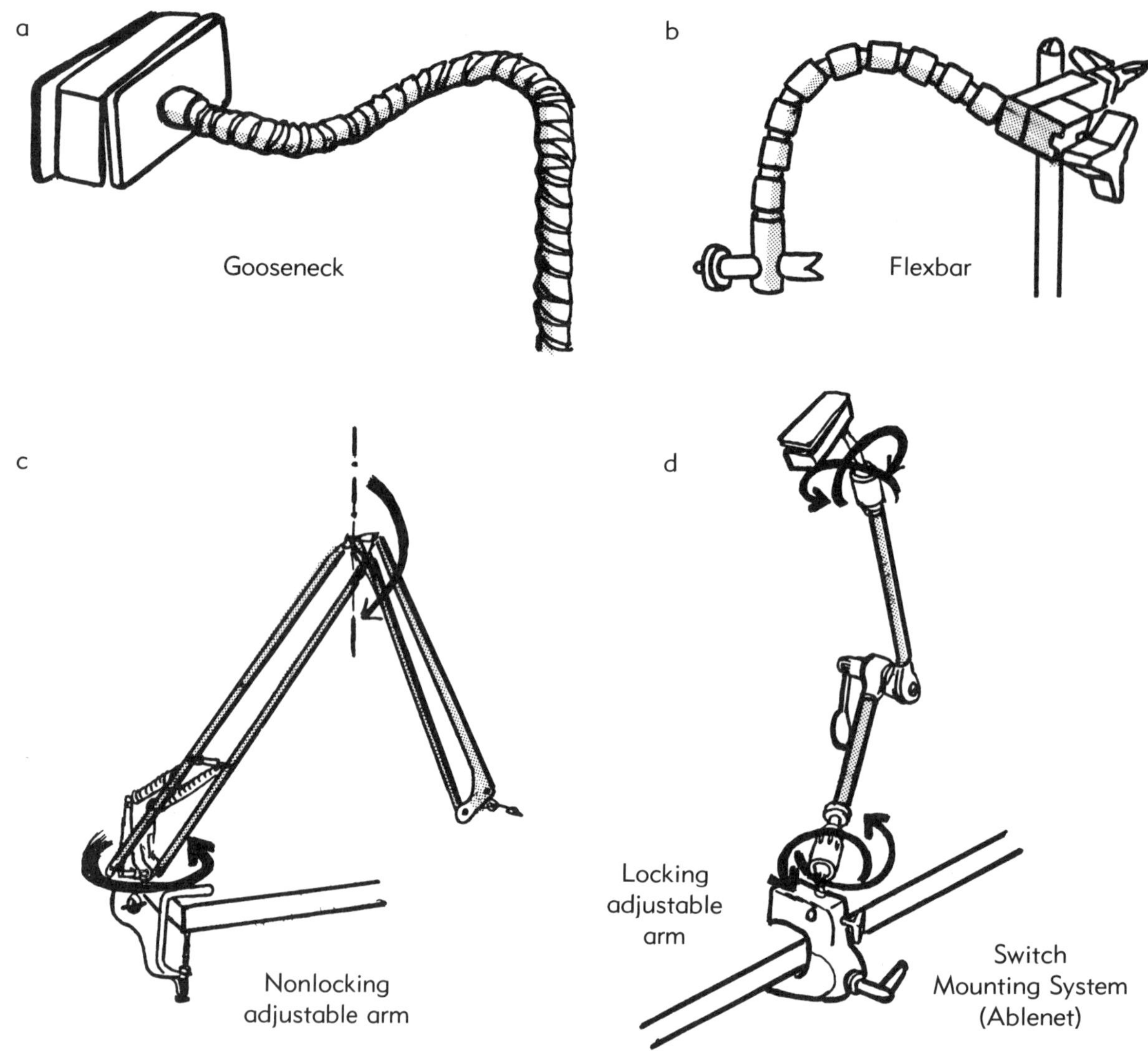


**FIGURE 4.5.** Flexible mainframes.

use of gooseneck mounts is often limited to that of assisting the process of screening for a viable control site. Having delineated a potentially viable control site using the gooseneck, steps can be taken to establish a more stable mount using mounting materials such as tubes or rods.

*Flexbars.* Flexbars (Brown & Sharpe Mfg. Co.) (Figure 4.5b) attempt to emulate the advantages of the gooseneck while rectifying its disadvantages. Similar to the gooseneck, a flextube is constructed of linked components that permit flexibility of placement. Unlike the gooseneck, however, the flextube can be "locked" into a stable position. When the lever is "unlocked," the flextube can be positioned in any curved configuration. When the desired configuration has been achieved, the lever is tightened to lock the flextube into a stable configuration. To achieve minor adjustments in the mainframe configuration, the lever of the flextube is released, modifications are made, and the new configuration is then locked into place via the lever.

*Adjustable arms.* As illustrated in Figure 4.5c, several distributors offer adjustable mounting arms, similar in concept to the adjustable arms of desk lamps. Most mounting arms contain two joints: One joint (usually the lower joint) permits 360° adjustments in a single horizontal plane; the other joint (midway in the arm) permits 180° to 360° adjustment in a vertical plane. When the joints of the arm are constructed with ball and socket joints, as is the case with the Universal Switch Mounting System (Ablenet) (Figure 4.5d), greater flexibility of positioning is possible. Similar to the flexbar, a lever can be loosened to free the joints, allowing the arm to be positioned in the desired configuration. Once the desired position is achieved, the lever is flipped back to secure the configuration. As one might expect, the increased flexibility afforded by the design greatly increases the cost of the arm.

Adjustable arms are typically available with either a clamp or a weighted base, allowing them to be mounted on a lap tray or table top. Although less common, some arms contain special clamps allowing attachment to a ⅞-inch-diameter wheelchair frame or a 1-inch-diameter bed rail.

Generally, nonlocking adjustable arms are beneficial only when the force of switch activation is not sufficient to move the switch out of the optimal range relative to the control site. Although they are more expensive, locking adjustable arms are preferred over their less expensive nonlocking counterparts.

**ADAPTING THE SWITCH TO ACCOMMODATE THE MAINFRAME.** Switches generally fall into two categories: (a) those that can accommodate a mainframe of ⅝-inch-diameter tubing (or a gooseneck) and (b) those that are designed to transition to ¼-inch- or ⅜-inch-diameter rods.

**Accommodating a Tube Mainframe.** As illustrated in Figure 4.6, the frequently used push or pedal switches are often interfaced with either ⅝-inch-diameter tubes or goosenecks. Options can be generally classified as semipermanent or detachable. As depicted in Figure 4.6a, semipermanent mounting can be achieved using several options, all requiring the use of a central screw. Although some pedal switches are factory-constructed with a threaded hole, the three mounting options depicted necessitate drilling a hole in the bottom of the switch. As one might suspect, this is feasible only when placement of the hole does not interfere with the internal switch mechanism.

When working with young children, the need for switch access in a variety of therapeutic positions and the need to conduct parallel programming (e.g., conducting head-accessed switch training parallel to hand-accessed switch training) necessitate the use of readily detachable mounting options. As illustrated in Figure 4.6b, such options include a mounting plate with hardware that allows the plate to be coupled with ⅝-inch-diameter tubing. Although mounting plates are commercially available from a variety of sources, relatively inexpensive homemade versions can be constructed using the fixtures and a rectangular or circular "plate" (depicted in Figure 4.6a) constructed of ¼- or ⅛-inch-thick wood, Plexiglas, or Kydex plastic, cut with a jigsaw or a hole saw (S. Matthews, personal communication, 1991). Adhesive Velcro (male Velcro on the switch bottom; female Velcro on the mounting plate) or Dual Lock ("industrial strength Velcro") is typically used to securely but temporarily attach the switch to the mounting plate. Similar to adhesive Velcro, Dual Lock is an adhesive-backed substance that consists of two visually distinct components: One component is a dense arrangement of mushroom-shaped stems (Type 400); the other is a looser arrangement of mushroom-shaped stems (Type 170). When a stable but easily detachable mount is required, the loose pattern is coupled with the dense pattern. When an "almost permanent" mount is required, the dense pattern can be coupled with itself. Dual Lock is stronger but considerably more expensive than adhesive Velcro (hook and loop fasteners). In our experience, adhesive Velcro more than adequately addresses the need for a stable but readily detachable mounting option. To maximize adhesion, it is recommended that (a) a hair dryer be used to heat the receiving surface before applying the Velcro (thus making it more receptive to a full seal) and (b) the Velcro, once applied, be kneaded into the receiving surface; and (c) the surfaces to be coupled (i.e., switch bottom and mounting plate) be covered completely, thus creating a larger coupling surface.

**Accommodating Rod Mainframes.** As depicted in Figure 4.7, many switches are designed to accommodate a mount constructed with either ¼-inch- or ⅜-inch-diameter aluminum rods. Most switches amenable to being coupled with rods (Figure 4.7a) are preconstructed with a shaft into which a rod can be inserted. A setscrew or thumbscrew, inserted perpendicular to the rod, is tightened on the rod to prevent it from shifting vertically or laterally in the shaft. In other instances, special adaptive fixtures employing a shaft setscrew design can be used to achieve a transition to the rod mainframe (Figure 4.7b). As

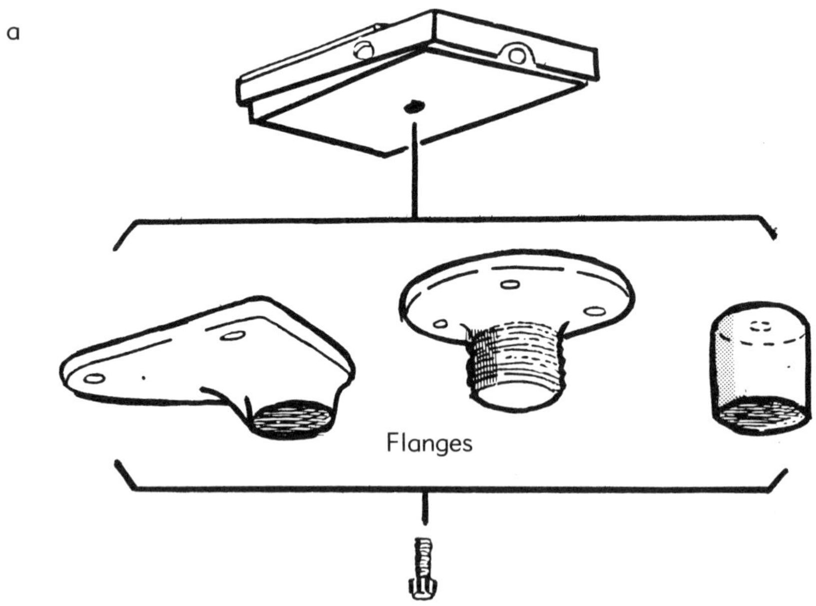


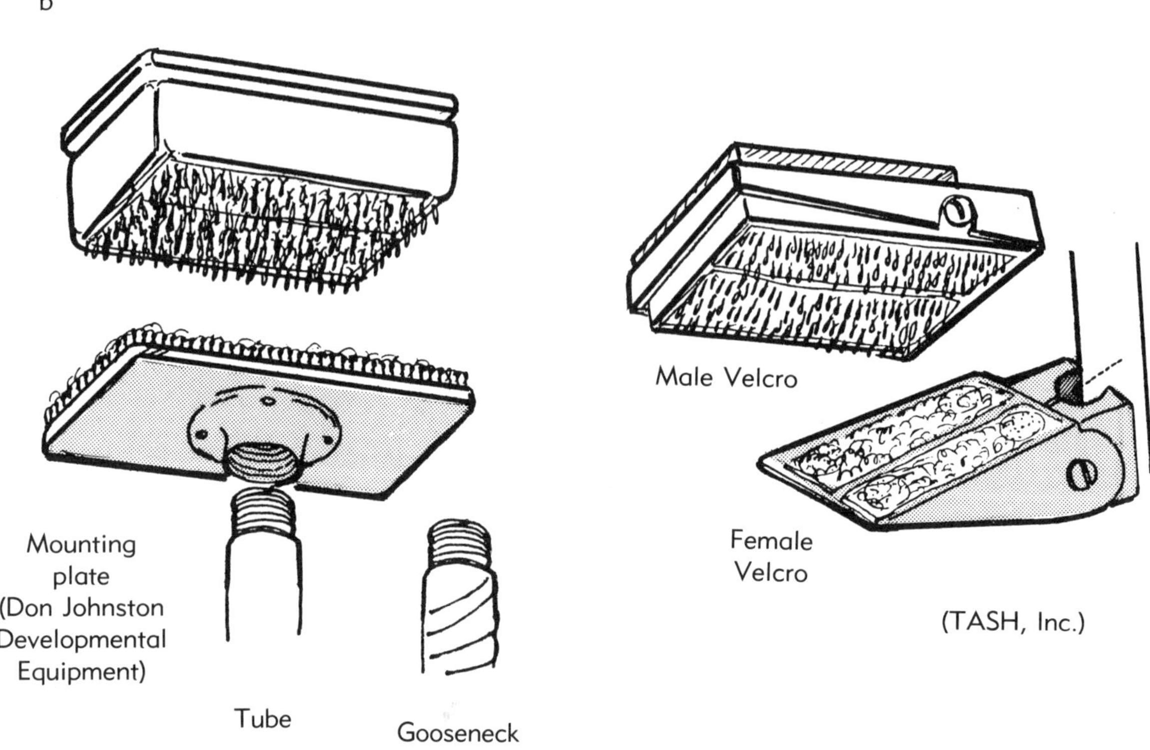


**FIGURE 4.6.** Interfacing a switch with a tube or gooseneck.

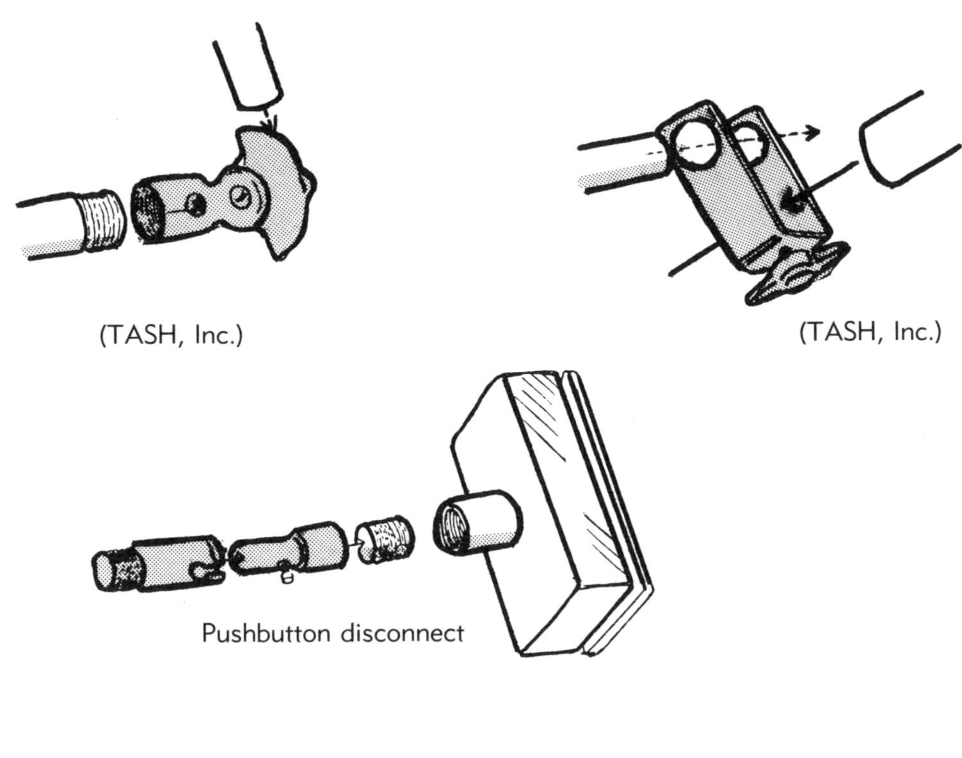


(TASH, Inc.) (TASH, Inc.)

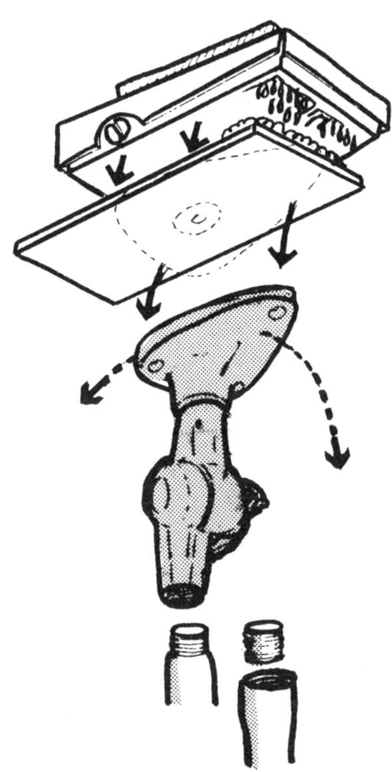

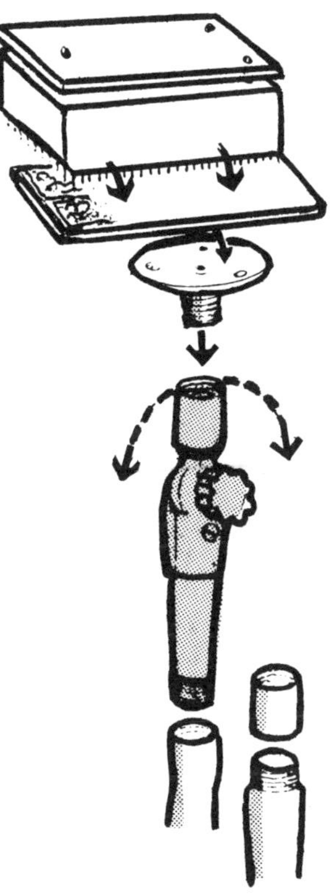

(Zygo Industries, Inc.) (Zygo Industries, Inc.)

**FIGURE 4.6. (Continued)**

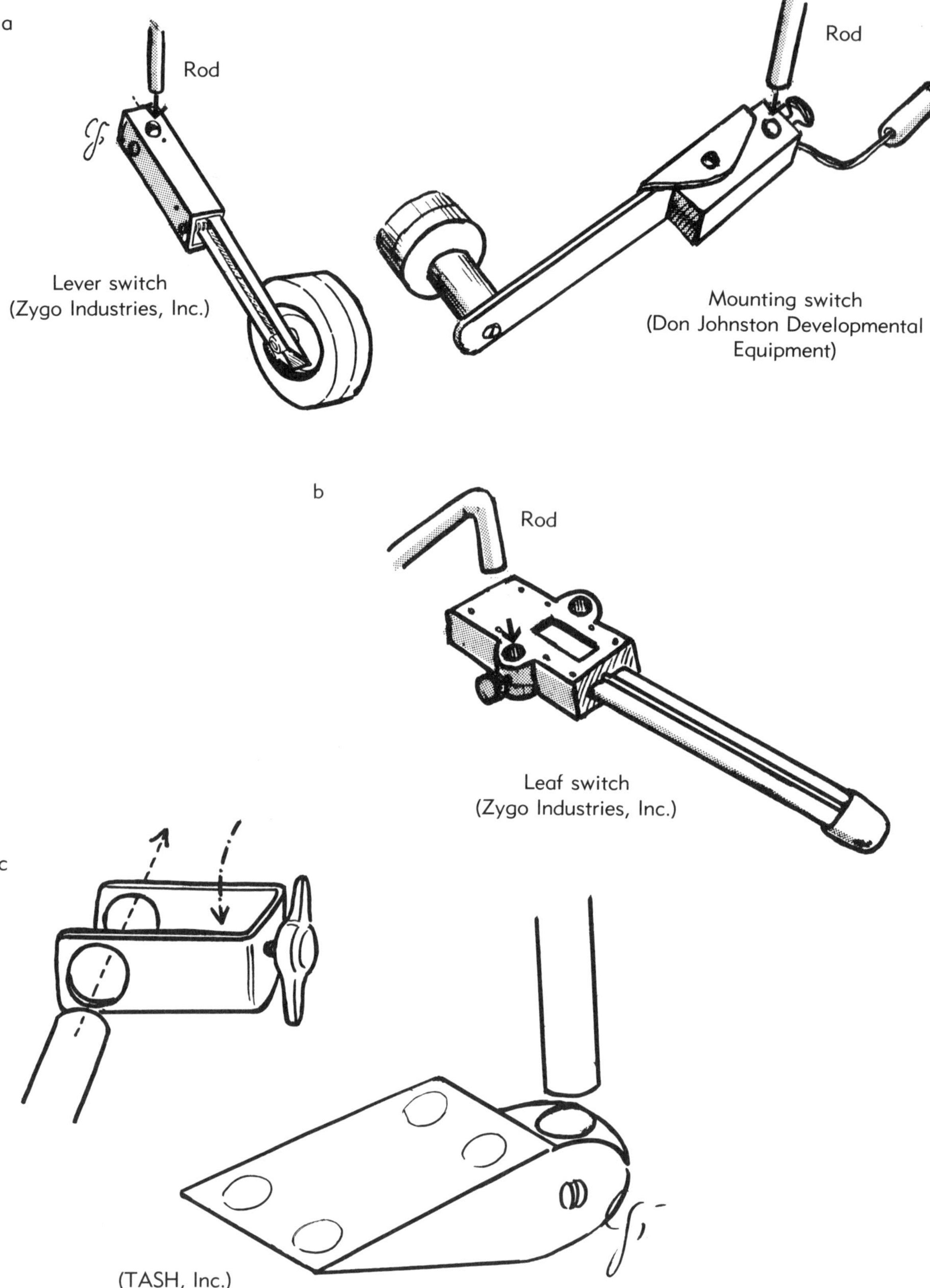


**FIGURE 4.7.** Interfacing a switch with a rod.

illustrated in Figure 4.7c, many such fixtures include a swivel component. Although swivel components tend to be costly, they allow for greater flexibility in fine-tuning switch placement. This capability for fine-tuning is especially helpful in instances in which slight variations in wheelchair positioning alter the optimal relationship between the switch and the control site. Although therapeutic positioning should ideally remain consistent from one moment to the next, changes in the child's overall body tone dictate otherwise. Although swivels provide flexibility of switch placement, they also introduce a weaker link into the switch mount. With children who strike their switch forcefully, swivels periodically lose their lock. Repositioning and relocking are thus necessary.

**ATTACHING THE MAINFRAME TO SUPPORTING THERAPEUTIC POSITIONING EQUIPMENT.** Several options exist for attaching the mainframe of the switch mount to therapeutic positioning equipment (e.g., wheelchair, lap tray, table, bed rail, prone stander, side-lyer). Options can be discussed in terms of those options accommodating a tube or gooseneck mainframe and those compatible with a rod mainframe.

**Accommodating Tube Mainframes.** Tubes and goosenecks can be attached to the supporting structures of therapeutic positioning equipment in three major ways:

- ❑ Wheelchair clamps
- ❑ Ground clamps and worm-drive clamps
- ❑ Table clamps and flanges

*Wheelchair clamps.* Wheelchair clamps are commercially available from a variety of sources. As shown in Figure 4.8a, the wheelchair clamp is constructed of two identical halves, joined by two machine screws held in place by nuts. A nut-retaining ridge allows the screws to be completely removed without dislodging the nuts. Each half of the clamp forms two circular openings: The larger opening is designed to accommodate a ⅞-inch-diameter wheelchair frame; the smaller opening accommodates the ⅝-inch-diameter tube or gooseneck mainframe. Prior to insertion of the tube into this opening, it is typically inserted into a sleeve adapter. This sleeve adapter (plus contained tube) is then positioned in the shaft with its slit facing the opening of the shaft (Figure 4.8b). When the screws of the wheelchair clamp are tightened using an allen wrench, the tube mainframe is securely attached to the wheelchair frame. Although wheelchair clamps are most commonly used to attach a ⅝-inch-diameter tube to a ⅞-inch-diameter wheelchair frame, one half of the clamp can be reversed to create two openings of equal size. This reconfiguration allows a ⅝-inch-diameter tube mainframe to be coupled with a ⅝-inch-diameter (nonstandard) frame.

*Ground clamps and worm-drive clamps.* These inexpensive mounting options can be readily found in the electrical and plumbing sections of your local hardware store. Ground clamps are available constructed of either copper or aluminum. Although aluminum ground clamps tend to be cheaper, they are not rustproof. Copper options are therefore preferred despite their higher cost. As depicted in Figure 4.8c, both ground clamps and worm-drive or hose clamps completely encircle the tube and the frame of the supporting equipment and are secured in place by tightening either one screw (in the case of the worm-drive clamp) or two screws (in the case of the ground clamp). In some instances, the diameter of the supporting structure may necessitate the substitution of longer screws. Although ground clamps and worm-drive clamps are inexpensive substitutes for the more expensive wheelchair clamp, their use is precluded in instances in which upholstery attaches directly to the wheelchair frame.

When utilizing ground clamps, care should be taken to ensure that the ends of the screws do not pose a safety hazard to the child. Similarly, care should be taken to select a worm-drive clamp of a size that is not so large that it results in a protruding length. The loose ends of the worm-drive clamps should always be anchored to prevent bodily harm or damage to the upholstery of vehicles in which the wheelchair is transported.

*Table clamps and flanges.* As represented in Figure 4.8d, a variety of table clamps and flanges are available to attach a tube mainframe to a flat supporting surface such as a lap tray or table. As can be discerned from the illustration, options vary in their degree of permanence and their ability to be swiveled to achieve various angles of presentation. When permanently bolting flangelike fixtures to polycarbonate plastic or Plexiglas, care should be taken to avoid shattering the acrylic. This can be avoided by (a) not forcing the drill bit, (b) gradually increasing the drill bit size to reduce the stress imposed on the plastic,

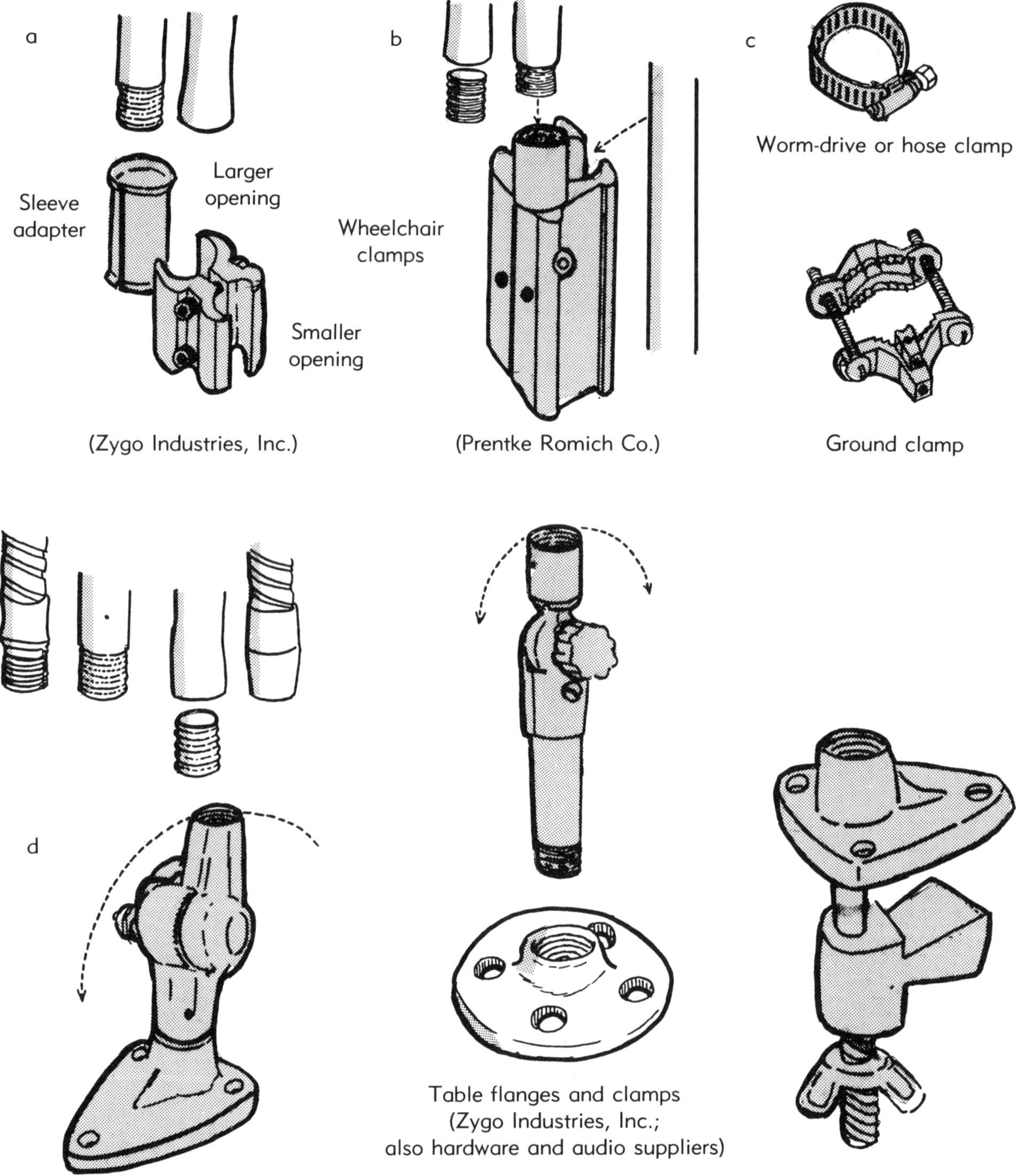


**FIGURE 4.8.** Attaching a tube or gooseneck mainframe to supporting therapeutic positioning equipment.

and (c) making sure the plastic surface is well supported when drilling. As previously discussed, adapters (male to female; female to male) may be necessary to allow same-sex ends to be coupled with table clamps and flanges.

**Accommodating Rod Mainframes.** Rod mainframes are mounted to supporting structures in three ways:

- ❑ Wheelchair clamps
- ❑ Ground clamps

- ❑ Pinch clamps
- ❑ Other clamps

*Wheelchair clamps.* As illustrated in Figure 4.9a, adapters (¼-inch adapter, ⅜-inch adapter) are required to couple a rod mainframe with the previously discussed wheelchair clamp. Each adapter consists of two or three setscrews (allowing screws to be inserted perpendicular to the inserted rod). When the setscrews are loosened using an allen wrench, a rod can be inserted into the adapter. The setscrews are then tightened to prevent the rod from shifting. The assembled adapter plus rod is then placed into the smaller opening of the wheelchair clamp. When positioning the adapter in the clamp, care should be taken to ensure that the setscrews are directed toward the opening. This allows the professional to more easily adjust rod height during the evaluation process (by loosening the setscrews), without having to loosen the wheelchair clamp (a much more involved process).

*Ground clamps.* A less expensive option for mounting ¼-inch rods can be achieved using a ground clamp. As illustrated in Figure 4.9b, some ground clamps include a shaft capable of accommodating a ¼-inch-diameter rod. The rod is secured using a screw that functions as a setscrew. The remaining ground clamp structure is then tightened around the frame of the supporting therapeutic equipment. As previously discussed, upholstery attached directly to the frame may not permit use of this inexpensive mounting option.

*Pinch clamps.* This fixture can be used to permanently attach rods to the frames of various pieces of therapeutic positioning equipment. As depicted in Figure 4.9c, the rod is inserted into the fixture and is pinched tightly in place via a screw inserted into both the fixture and the frame of the therapeutic equipment to which the mount is being attached. To prevent slippage care must be taken to ensure that the screw is very tight. An electric screwdriver can greatly facilitate the task of achieving a tight connection.

*Other clamps.* Illustrated in Figure 4.9d and 4.9e are other options capable of attaching a rod mainframe. Both options depicted use a setscrew concept to secure the rod in the adaptive fixture.

**DESIGNING A STABLE MOUNT.** Having determined the target location for the switch, the facilitator must next visualize the most direct path that the mount must assume to attach to supporting therapeutic positioning equipment (e.g., wheelchair frame, lap tray, table). The more direct the path (in terms of distance and number of turns), the more stable the mount.

As a general rule, mounts achieved with ⅝-inch-diameter tubing tend to be more stable than mounts achieved with aluminum rods or flexible goosenecks. Similarly, mounts achieved with ⅜-inch-diameter rods tend to have less play in the mounting system than mounts achieved with thinner, ¼-inch rods.

Above and beyond the intrinsic relative stability of the materials constituting mainframes, the manner in which the mount is designed can greatly affect its stability (Figure 4.10). As depicted in Figure 4.10a, mount stability can be greatly enhanced when (a) the distance between the switch and the attachment clamp is minimized (Don Johnston Developmental Equipment) and (b) double clamps are used to attach the mount to the supporting frame of the therapeutic positioning equipment. When rods are used as the mainframe, stability can be greatly enhanced by building a bilateral rather than a unilateral mount (Figure 4.10b). In addition to enhancing mount stability, such a format allows greater flexibility of switch placement. As depicted, flexibility of horizontal placement can be achieved by sliding the switch along the horizontal rod of the mount. Flexibility of vertical placement of the switch relative to the control site can be achieved by pivoting the orientation of the switch on the horizontal rod. Although the stability of the mount is greatly enhanced by such a design, it should be noted that the additional mounting hardware required not only increases the expense of the mount but is also more conspicuous. Furthermore, the position of the child's headrest may preclude the use of such a mounting option.

If goosenecks are to be incorporated into the mount design, the facilitator should be aware of the inverse relationship between gooseneck length and gooseneck stiffness. That is, the shorter the length of gooseneck, the stiffer the gooseneck. To increase mount stability while simultaneously maintaining flexibility of placement, the facilitator should consider a mount design that incorporates a shorter length of gooseneck in conjunction with the more stable ⅝-inch-diameter tubing (Figure 4.10c). As previously discussed, goosenecks tend to lose their stiffness with use. Stiffness can be restored by inserting a straightened metal coat hanger into the small cen-

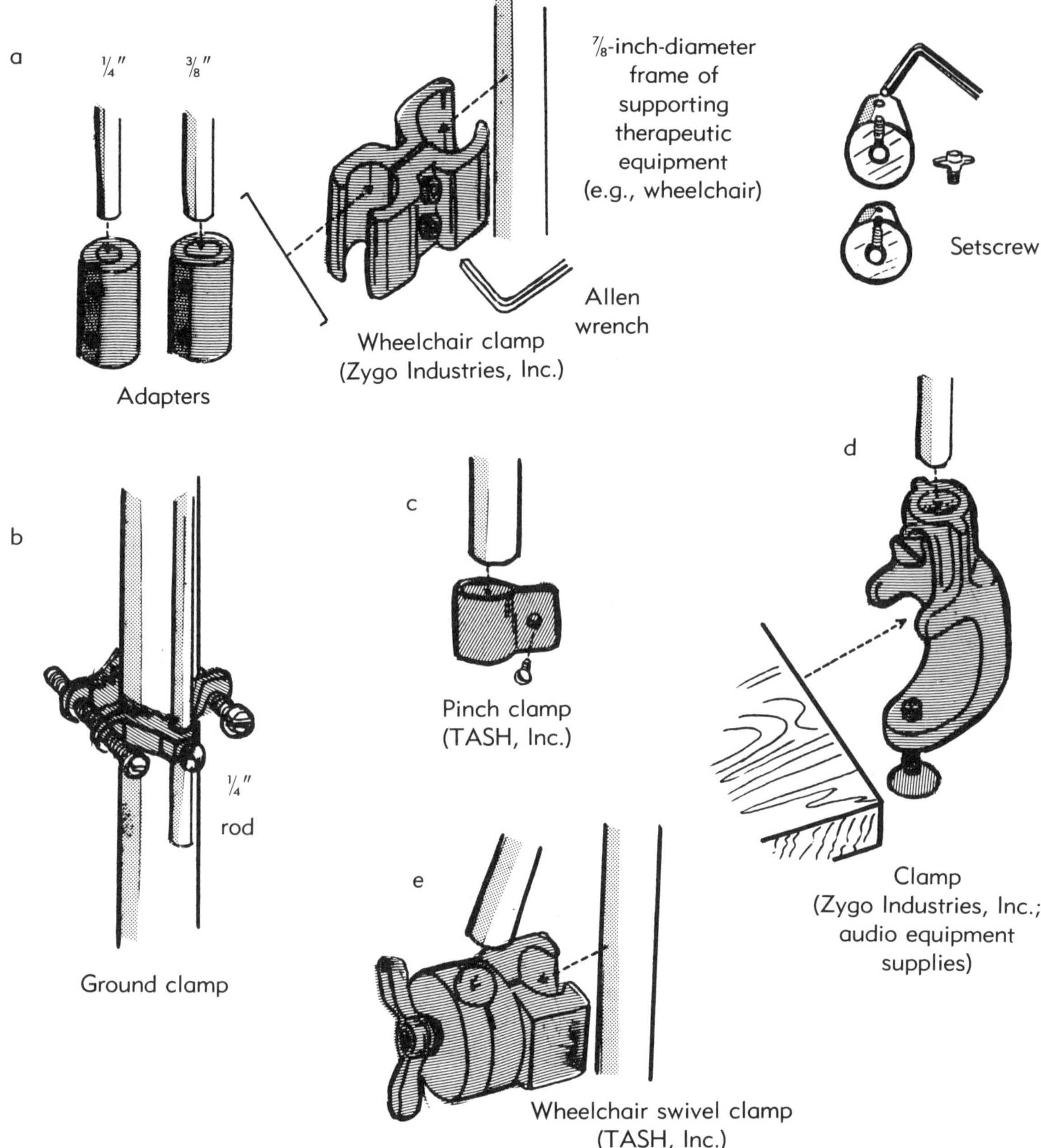


**FIGURE 4.9.** Attaching a rod mainframe to supporting therapeutic positioning equipment.

tral hole of the gooseneck (Prentke Romich Company) (Figure 4.10d.) It should be noted, however, not all goosenecks possess a central shaft.

When working with commercially available tubing, the facilitator is frequently working with fixed lengths. Although approximately 1 inch can be gained or lost in a configuration by placement of the tube/gooseneck/rod mainframe, relative to the frame of the supporting therapeutic structure (i.e., in front vs. to the outside vs. to the inside vs. behind the wheelchair frame), the fact that the facilitator is working with fixed lengths adds considerably to the challenge of achieving a mount configuration that places the switch within the optimal range of switch access. Although swivel components tend to weaken the mount somewhat, their inclusion in the mount

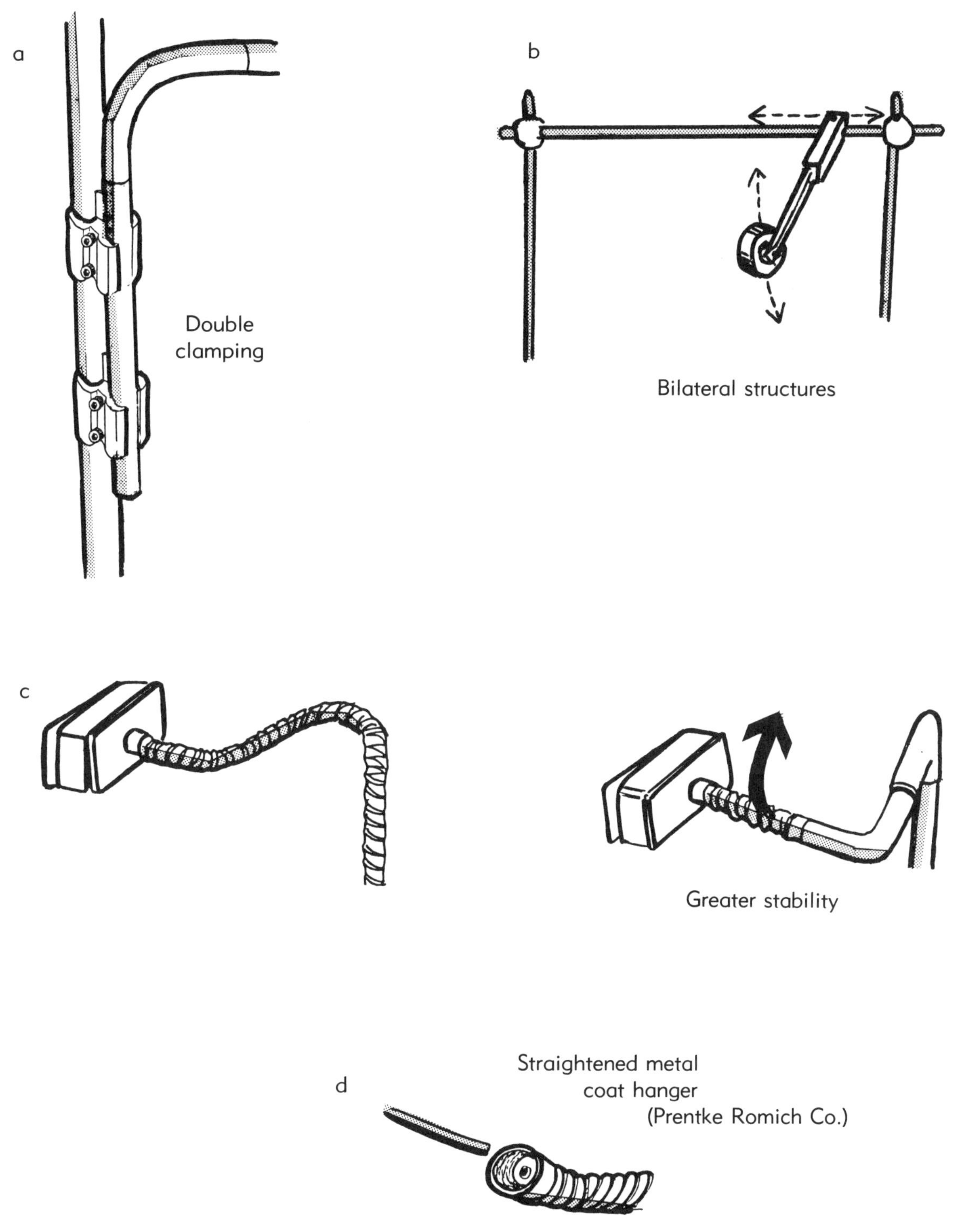


**FIGURE 4.10.** Designing a stable mount.

design can greatly enhance flexibility of switch placement, especially when the switch employed is one that can be activated from any angle (e.g., Wobble Switch, available from Prentke Romich Company). Swivel components have the additional advantage of allowing the switch to be swung out of the way to facilitate transfer of the child in and out of the wheelchair.

**FINE-TUNING THE MOUNT.** Once a temporary switch mount has been constructed, the resulting setup must undergo systematic evaluation to determine if it is functionally viable (see Chapter 6 for details). When fine-tuning a switch setup, a delicate balance exists between placement that is close enough to be effortless and placement that is too close and therefore prone to accidental activation. As represented in Figure 4.11, adjustments can be made at three levels of the mount:

- ❑ Switch
  - — Shift the switch on its Velcro base.
  - — Unlock or unscrew the lock on the swivel component to adjust the orientation of the switch relative to the control site.
- ❑ Mainframe
  - — Loosen the thumbscrew on the universal swivel and adjust the rod closer or farther away from the control site.
  - — Unlock the adjustable arm, reposition the mount, then relock when it approximates an optimal placement.
  - — Bend the gooseneck to the desired new location.
- ❑ Attachment to supporting therapeutic equipment
  - — Adjust the swivel component if the mount design includes such a component.
  - — Loosen the setscrews on the wheelchair clamp adapters, pivot the rod to the desired location, then retighten the setscrews.

When several switch setups are being contrasted, the facilitator should consider using photographs (ideally Polaroid) or a camcorder to document the various setups under consideration (Lee & Thomas, 1990). This practice can greatly facilitate the process of replicating the setup determined to be most viable for reliable access.

**MAKING THE MOUNT PERMANENT.** Once the mount has been subjected to a trial period validating its appropriateness for the child, steps must be taken to make the mount more permanent.

**Making Tube Mounts Permanent.** When ⅝-inch tubing serves as the mount mainframe, joints can be secured in four ways:

- ❑ Loctite
- ❑ Thread binder
- ❑ Sheet metal screws
- ❑ Pop rivets

*Loctite.* Loctite is a substance that can be applied to the threads of the tube prior to coupling the tube with another tube or interfacing component (e.g., flange, table clamp) (Figure 4.12a). As the joint is tightened, the air is removed, causing the Loctite to expand and harden into a tight seal. This tight seal can be undone only by applying heat directly to the joint using a lighter or a hair dryer.

*Thread binder.* Thread binder is a thin, celluloid tapelike substance that can be wrapped around the male threads prior to coupling the male end of one component with the female end of another component. When assembled this substance resists unthreading of the component parts (Figure 4.12b).

*Sheet metal screws.* When a more permanent option is desired, ⅜-inch holes can be drilled into the joint of two coupled tubes, allowing insertion of a ⅜-inch sheet metal screw with a hex head (Figure 4.12c). To assist the tubing in accepting the drill bit, it is recommended that a center punch be used to tap a small indentation in the tube.

*Pop rivets.* Pop rivets can be used to make joints more permanent. Pop rivets are available in a variety of sizes and are installed by first drilling a hole, then installing the pop rivet with a pop rivet gun.

**Making Rod Mounts Permanent.** Rod mounts can be made more permanent by using the following:

- ❑ Setscrew contact
- ❑ Universal swivel

*Setscrew contact.* As previously discussed, setscrews are the primary means for securing a rod in the shaft of a coupling component. As depicted in Figure 4.13a, the rod presents a curved surface to the flat end of the setscrew. As the setscrew is unable to bear fully and securely on the rod, the likelihood of slippage is great. To enhance stability, it is recommended that the setscrew be inserted tightly, then unscrewed to note the point of setscrew contact. The surface of the rod is then filed flat at this point to allow more stable contact between the setscrew and the rod (mounting switch literature; Don Johnston Developmental Equipment).

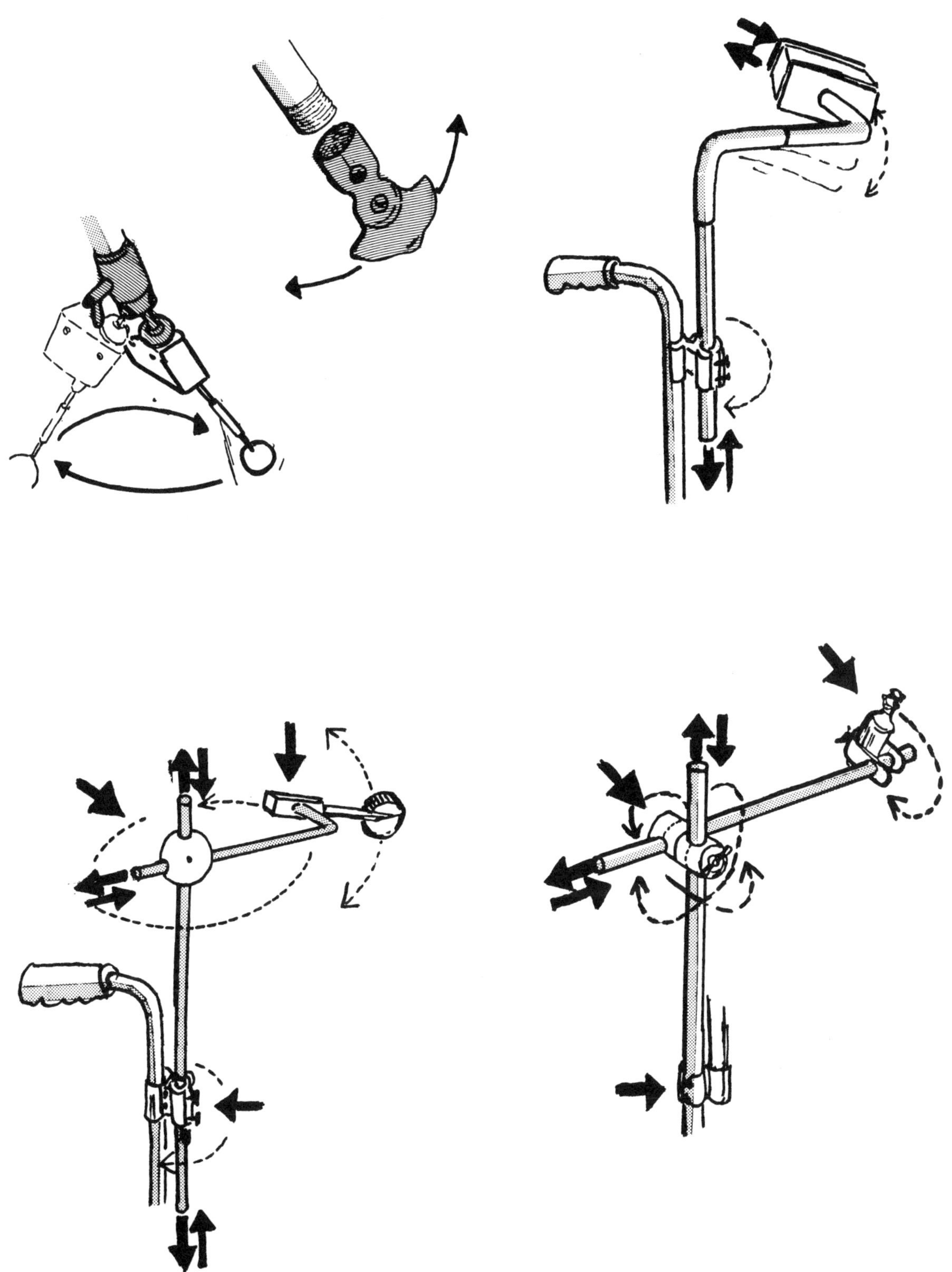

**FIGURE 4.11.** Fine-tuning the mount—Points of adjustment.

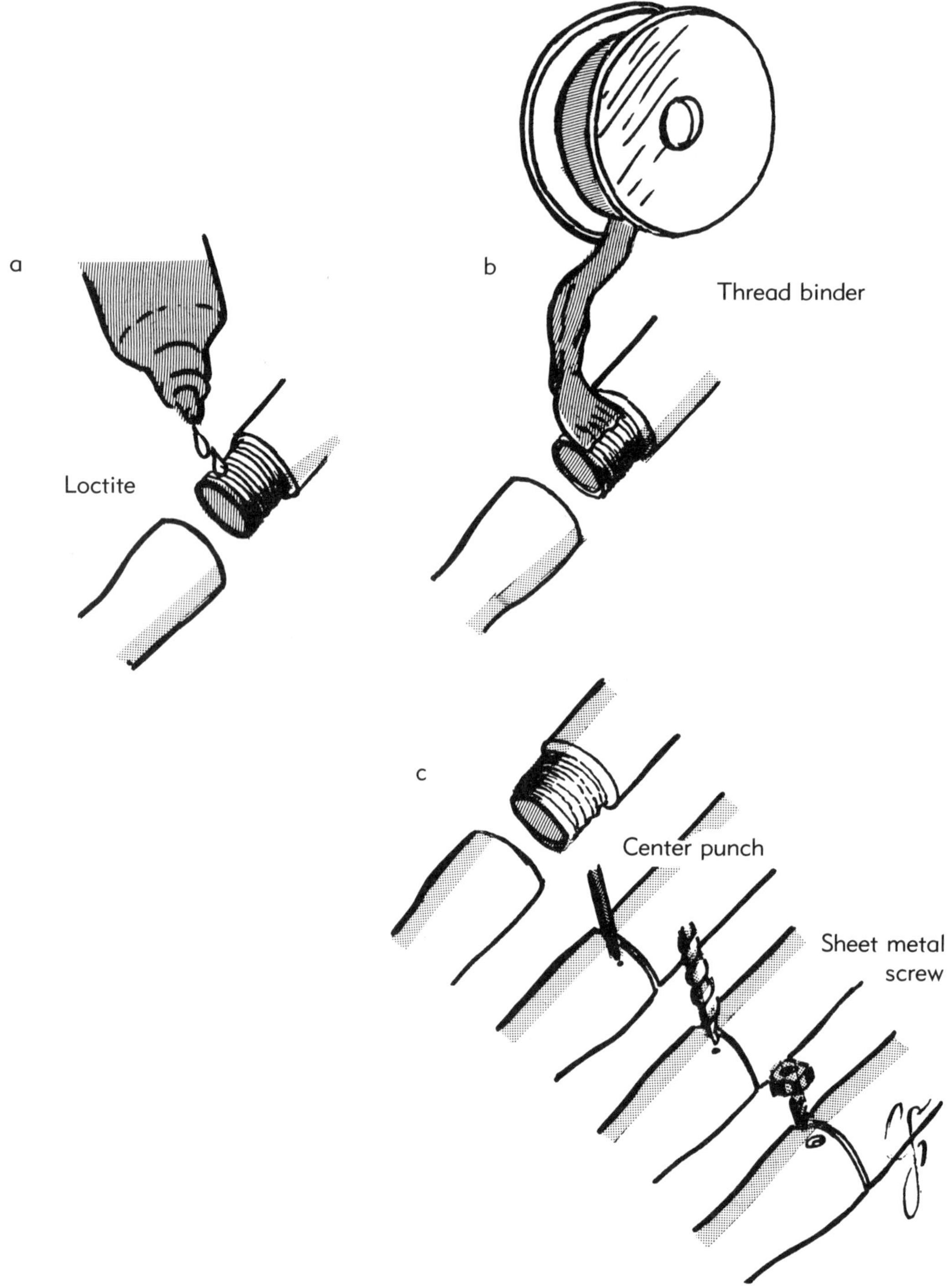


**FIGURE 4.12.** Making tube mounts permanent.

*Universal swivel.* When incorporating a universal swivel into the mount design, Loctite can be used to "lock" the thumbscrew to ensure that the relative orientation of the rods is maintained. If a more permanent option is desired, a hole can be drilled through both halves of the universal swivel to allow a sheet metal screw to be inserted to maintain the desired rod orientation. Frequently, however, the universal swivel serves as the point for pivoting the switch temporarily out of the way. This being the case, permanent stabilization of this joint would not be an option. Figure 4.13b visually summarizes strat-

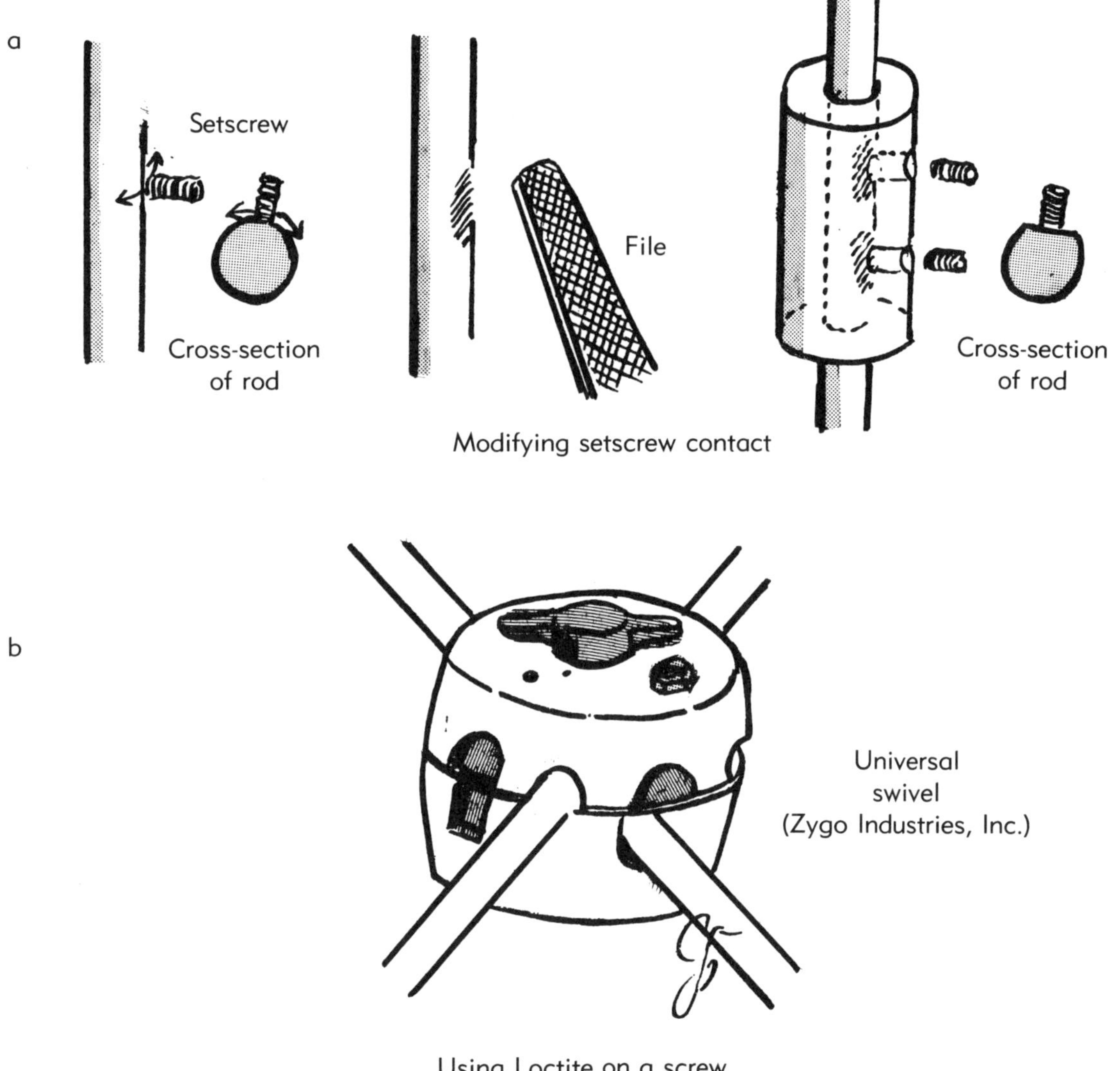


**FIGURE 4.13.** Making rod mounts permanent.

egies for making the universal swivel more permanent.

**INCORPORATING A REMOVAL JOINT.** Ideally, the mount design should allow the switch to be temporarily removed or swung out of the way to (a) facilitate transfer of the client in and out of the chair and/or (b) allow the switch to be transferred to an alternate therapeutic position. As previously discussed, consistency of switch placement is crucial to learning to use a switch interface reliably. Although many mounting alternatives (e.g., adjustable arms, universal swivel, swivel components) allow the mount to be readily swung out of the way, they generally offer no guarantee that consistency of switch placement can be maintained from one time to the next. As illustrated in Figure 4.14a, consistency of switch placement can be enhanced by using a permanent marker to mark off the relative position of the adjustable parts. These marks then serve as a visual guide to ensure consistency of switch placement.

When a wheelchair clamp is used in conjunction with adapters, thumbscrews can be substituted for the setscrews, allowing the mount to be quickly loosened and pivoted out of the way to facilitate transfer (Figure 4.14b). When using this method, however, care should be taken to mark the relative position of the moving parts to ensure consistency

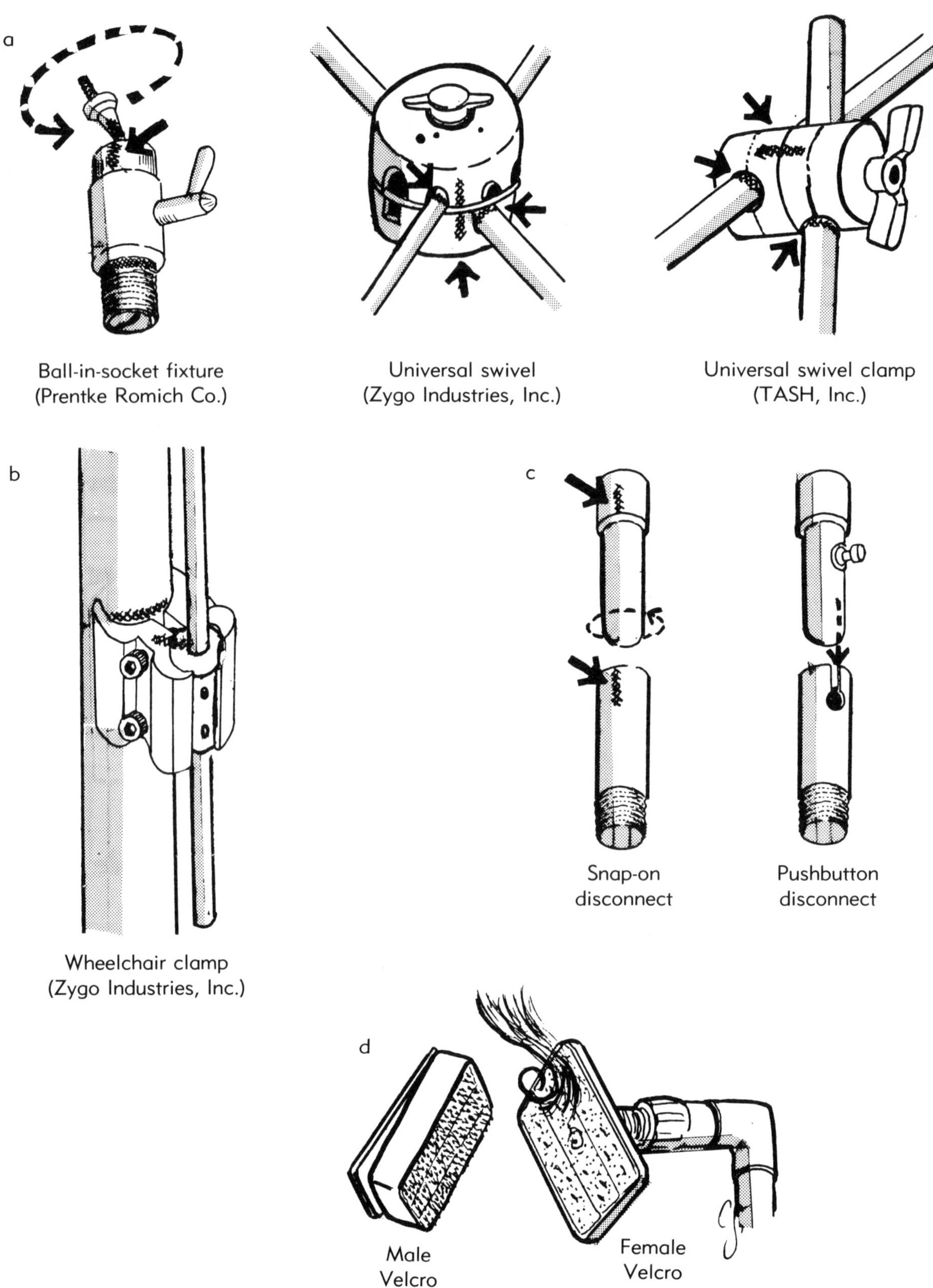


**FIGURE 4.14.** Incorporating a removal joint and ensuring consistency of placement.

of placement. As a general rule, however, the closer the removal joint is to the switch, the better.

When utilizing a tube mount, a snap-on disconnect or a pushbutton disconnect (Figure 4.14c) can be incorporated to promote flexibility of removal and reassembly. Of these two options, the pushbutton disconnect is the preferred choice, because it permits only one orientation (rather than 360° in a single plane, as is the case with the snap-on disconnect). This restricted orientation ensures consistent placement of the switch relative to its control site. When incorporating a removal joint into mount design, care should be taken to select a point that does not necessitate moving the switch into the control site to remove the switch. This also reduces the likelihood of having a protruding pipe with potential for causing bodily harm to the child.

When Velcro is used in conjunction with a mounting plate, the switch can be easily removed to facilitate transfer. Because removal of the switch leaves an exposed plate, the nonabrasive female component of Velcro is always used as the coupling material on the plate. In addition, the child's hair is not likely to be caught in the female Velcro.

### Switch Mounts Made with CPVC Pipe and Fittings

Commercially available mounting kits can be costly and frequently require considerable ingenuity when interfacing the various component parts to achieve that sometimes elusive stable, viable switch mount. As illustrated in Figure 4.15a, an inexpensive and easily constructed alternative to commercially available hardware can be found in the plumbing section of your local hardware store. CPVC (chlorinated polyvinyl chloride) pipe[1] is a cream-colored, rigid, heat-resistant tubing, typically used as hot and cold water supply pipes in residential homes. CPVC pipe is available in a range of diameters that are sized nominally according to the inside (not outside) diameter of the pipe. The ½-inch CPVC pipe is the diameter most amenable to building switch mounts. When ½-inch CPVC pipe is permanently assembled with solvent cement, it is able to withstand considerable force. Prior to permanent "gluing" of the component parts, the assembled mount is sufficiently stable to allow the switch setup to be subjected to systematic evaluation. Thus, the switch setup can be thoroughly tested prior to making the mount permanent.

CPVC pipe is typically purchased in 10-foot lengths that can be cut to any size using a hacksaw or a CPVC pipe cutter (Figure 4.15b). This ease of achieving variable pipe lengths is the feature that makes CPVC mounts easier to work with than most commercially available mounting hardware.

A variety of ½-inch CPVC fittings are included in the CPVC product line. As illustrated in Figure 4.15c, this line includes elbows (which allow the pipe to turn corners), straight couplers (which allow two lengths of pipe to be joined), and tees (which allow three pipe lengths to be joined at a shared focal point). CPVC male and female adapters and threaded caps are also available and are used extensively in adapting switch interfaces to accommodate a CPVC mount.

In addition to being a strong and easily assembled medium, CPVC materials are relatively inexpensive. Most switch mounts can be constructed at costs under $5.00. This feature is especially desirable when working with children. Growth spurts frequently necessitate changes in the child's seating and positioning. These changes, in turn, require repeated alterations in switch mount configurations. When CPVC materials are being used as the mounting medium, changes can be easily accommodated without inordinate long-range expense or time.

In this section, the reader will find information regarding:

- ❑ Assembling a basic CPVC mounting kit
- ❑ Constructing the mainframe of the mount
- ❑ Adapting the switch to accommodate the CPVC mainframe
- ❑ Attaching the CPVC mainframe to the supporting therapeutic positioning equipment.
- ❑ Designing a stable mount
- ❑ Fine-tuning the mount
- ❑ Making the mount permanent
- ❑ Incorporating a removal joint
- ❑ Making the mount aesthetic

**ASSEMBLING A BASIC CPVC SWITCH MOUNTING KIT.** An organized CPVC mounting kit can greatly enhance the process of quickly assembling switch mounts.

---

[1]The original concept of using CPVC pipe for switch mounts was obtained from J. Buchanan, the father of a client, Jessica Buchanan.

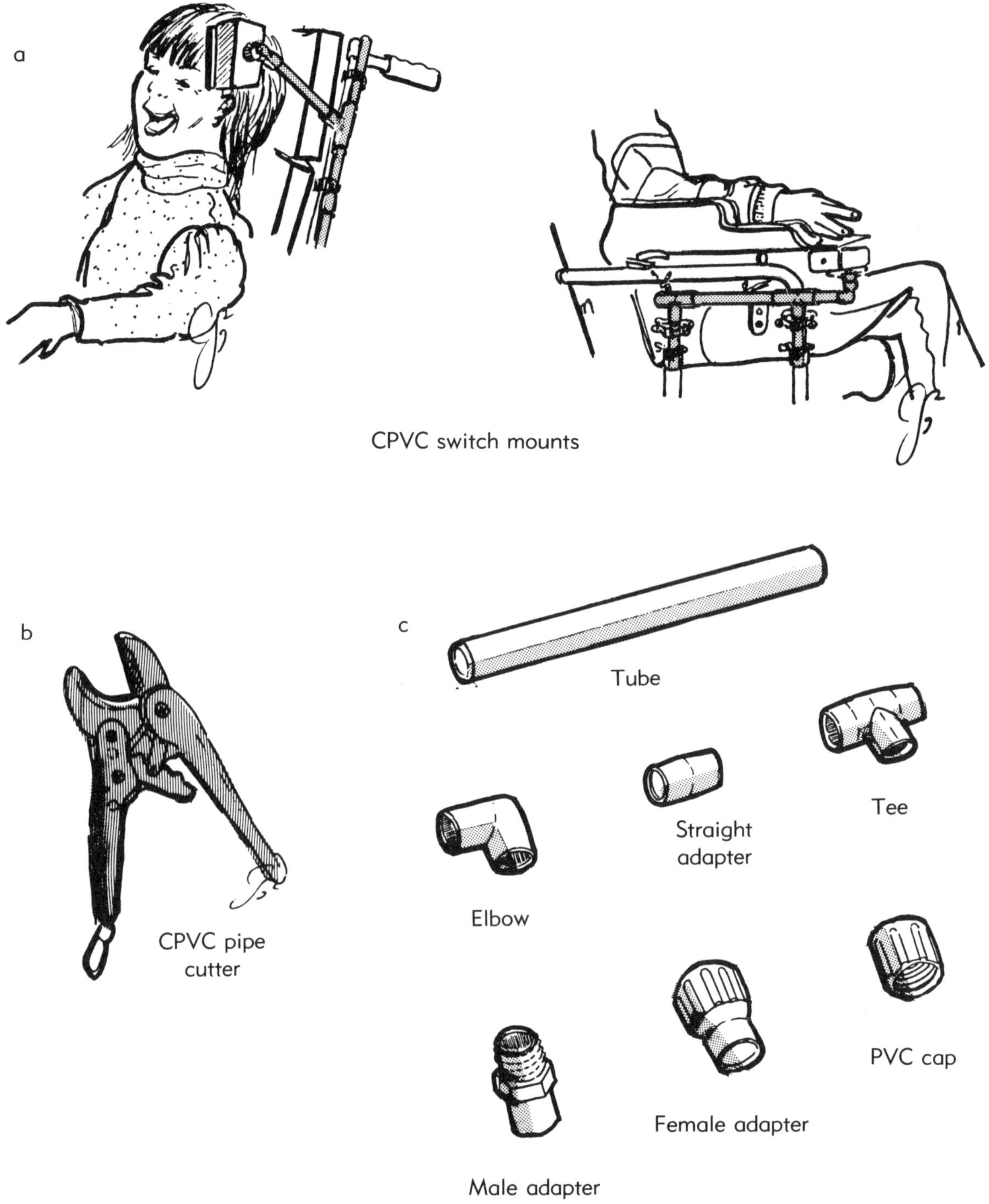


**FIGURE 4.15.** Using CPVC pipes to make switch mounts.

Presented in Appendix B are the component parts that make up a basic CPVC mounting kit. Ideally, the kit should include a range of the most frequently used switch interface types, preadapted to accommodate a CPVC mount. When preadapted switch interfaces are being used, a viable CPVC mount can be made in a matter of minutes with precut lengths of CPVC pipe. To facilitate this trial and error process, it is recommended that the basic kit include two sets of precut pipe lengths ranging in size from 1.0 inches to 12.0 inches (in .5-inch increments). To aid the facilitator in quickly locating a larger or smaller pipe as needed during the assembly process, each pipe length is numerically coded (e.g., .5, 1.0, 1.5) midway on the pipe. A multilevel fishing tackle or tool box (large enough to house a power drill and an electric screwdriver) can be used to keep components organized and readily accessible for assembly. When working in a busy diagnostic setting, the facilitator may wish to store component parts in larger quantities in organizer or storage bins. Figure 4.16 depicts the storage options for CPVC mounting materials.

**CONSTRUCTING THE MAINFRAME OF THE CPVC MOUNT.** When constructing the CPVC mount mainframe, it is advisable to handhold the switch interface in the desired location, relative to the control site (body part that will make contact with the switch interface). As discussed in Chapter 3, a position is required that (a) allows the child to reliably initiate, maintain, or release contact with the switch interface; (b) is close enough to the control site to allow activation without overexertion; (c) is far enough away to minimize accidental activation; and (d) does not reinforce abnormal movement patterns or promote excessive overflow movements.

While holding the switch interface in the desired location, the facilitator visualizes the most direct

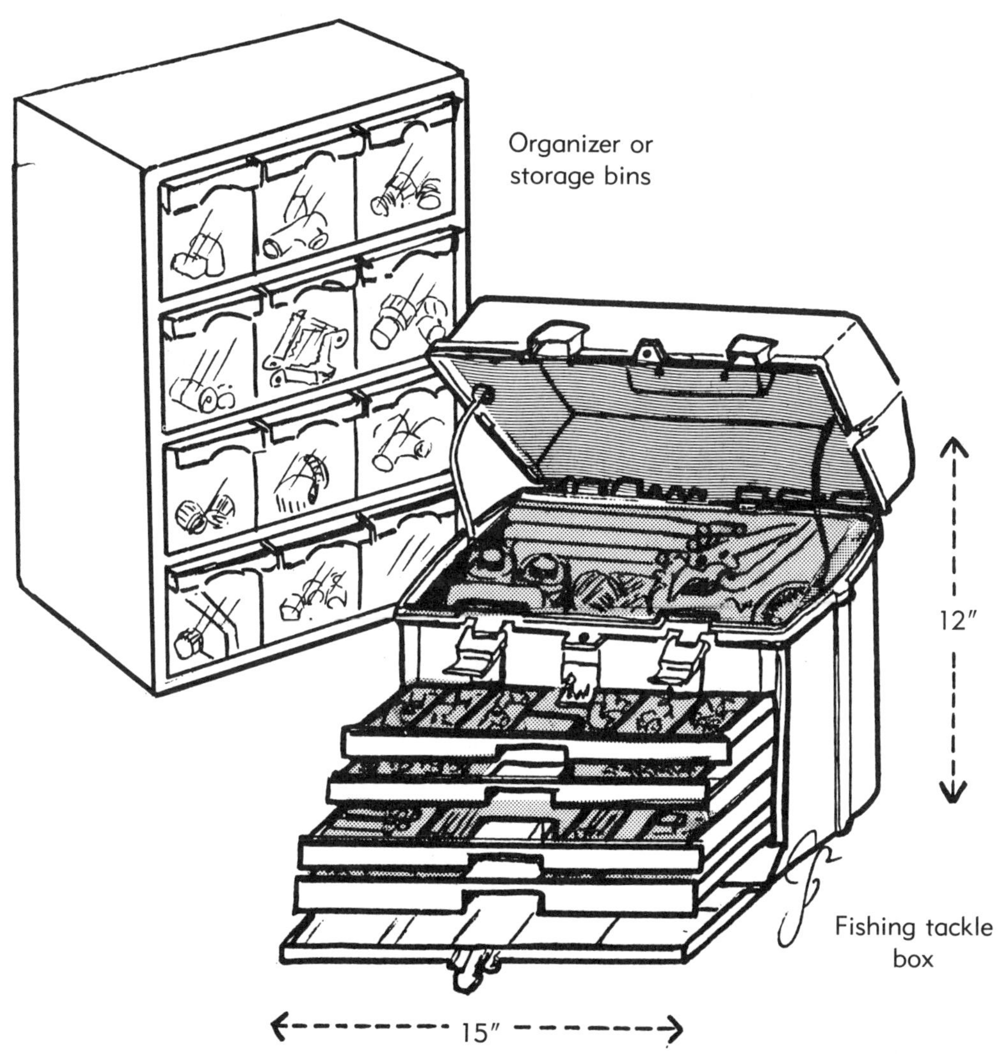


**FIGURE 4.16.** CPVC mounting kits.

three-dimensional path that the CPVC pipe must take and uses that path to attach the switch interface to the structural frame. As a general rule, the more direct the path (i.e., the fewer the number of turns required and the shorter the distance a pipe must cross "free space"), the more stable the mount. Using the precut lengths of pipe and the fittings in the CPVC mounting kit, the facilitator assembles the visualized mount much like using an erector set, using the length codes to assist in quickly selecting larger or smaller pipe lengths during the assembly process. As will soon become apparent to the facilitator, a small needle-nose pliers is a must for removing small lengths of pipe from CPVC fittings.

**ADAPTING THE SWITCH INTERFACE TO ACCOMMODATE A CPVC SWITCH MOUNT.** A given interface can be adapted to accommodate a CPVC switch mount in a variety of ways. In general, methods vary in:

- ❑ The relative *strength* of the adaptation (Some adaptations are better able to withstand higher forces.)
- ❑ The *weight* of the adaptation (This is especially crucial when the mount design necessitates suspending the switch a long distance out in free space.)
- ❑ The *cost* of the adaptation (Some component parts such as geno angle adapter or a saddle tee are more costly.)
- ❑ The *permanence* of the adaptation (Some methods permanently adapt the switch, thereby precluding its use in other formats.)
- ❑ The *flexibility* of the adaptation to accommodate use in a variety of therapeutic positions (One method may be preferred over another because it can accommodate the mount designs needed for both the child's wheelchair and prone stander.)

The facilitator will also find there is considerable local variability as to the availability of parts. Often the availability of component parts is a primary determinant in choosing the method of switch interface adaptation.

Visually depicted in Figure 4.17 are several methods for adapting a variety of commonly prescribed switch interfaces. Although far from exhaustive in terms of the number of switch interfaces that are now commercially available, the major types have been represented, serving as a guideline for adapting different but similar switch interfaces.

As previously discussed, numerous options may exist for adapting a particular switch to accommodate a CPVC mount. One method of switch adaptation may be preferred, depending on a variety of factors:

- ❑ The design of the wheelchair frame
- ❑ The need to utilize a specific switch with more than one control site (For example, while a child is achieving communication using a head-activated format, she may also be undergoing parallel programming with a hand-activated format designed to improve upper extremity functioning; it would be more efficient and cost-effective for both goals to be realized with the same switch.)
- ❑ The need to utilize a specific switch in a variety of therapeutic positions (For example, a child may need to achieve communication in both his wheelchair and his prone stander; it would be more efficient and cost effective if a portion of the mount could address needs of mounts required for both pieces of therapeutic equipment.)
- ❑ The availability of component parts (There are considerable regional variations in the availability of parts.)

One method of switch adaptation may be selected over another. Presented in Figure 4.18 are four options for adapting and mounting a head-activated switch on a particular wheelchair frame. Of the four options presented, Options c and d might be preferred because they permit a more stable mount to be achieved with fewer turns. If this child's therapeutic plan, however, necessitated motor training with this same switch in a lap-tray–presented, hand-activated format, Option c would not be feasible, because the switch has been permanently attached to the mounting fittings. Because Options d and e (incorporating a mounting plate) allow the same switch to be used in both a head-activated and hand-activated format, they would be the methods of choice for this particular child. In general, it is safe to say that options that allow the transition to CPVC pipe to be achieved within a short distance and with fewer fittings are more flexible and thus are more desirable.

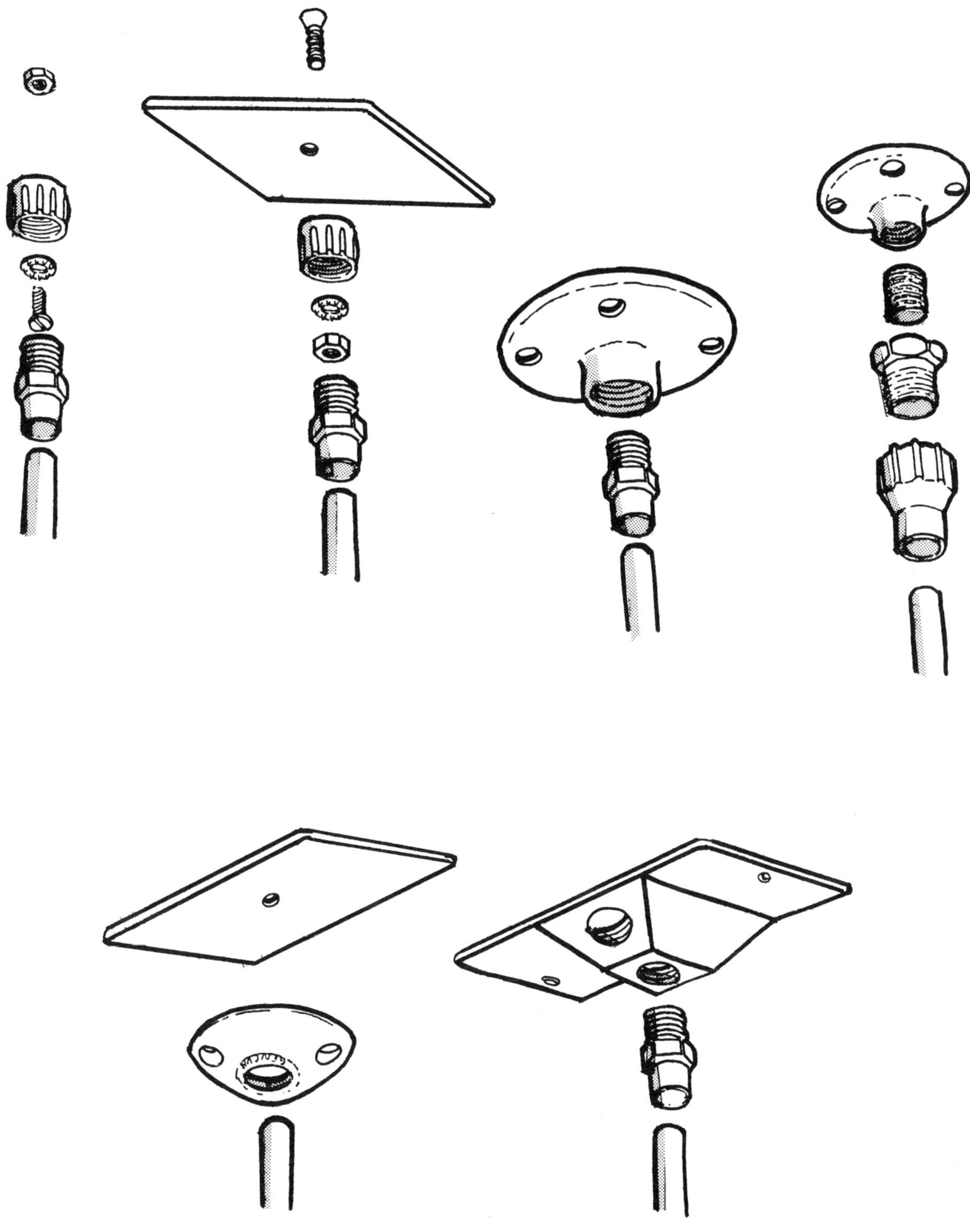

**FIGURE 4.17.** Methods of adaptation for a variety of commonly prescribed switch interfaces.

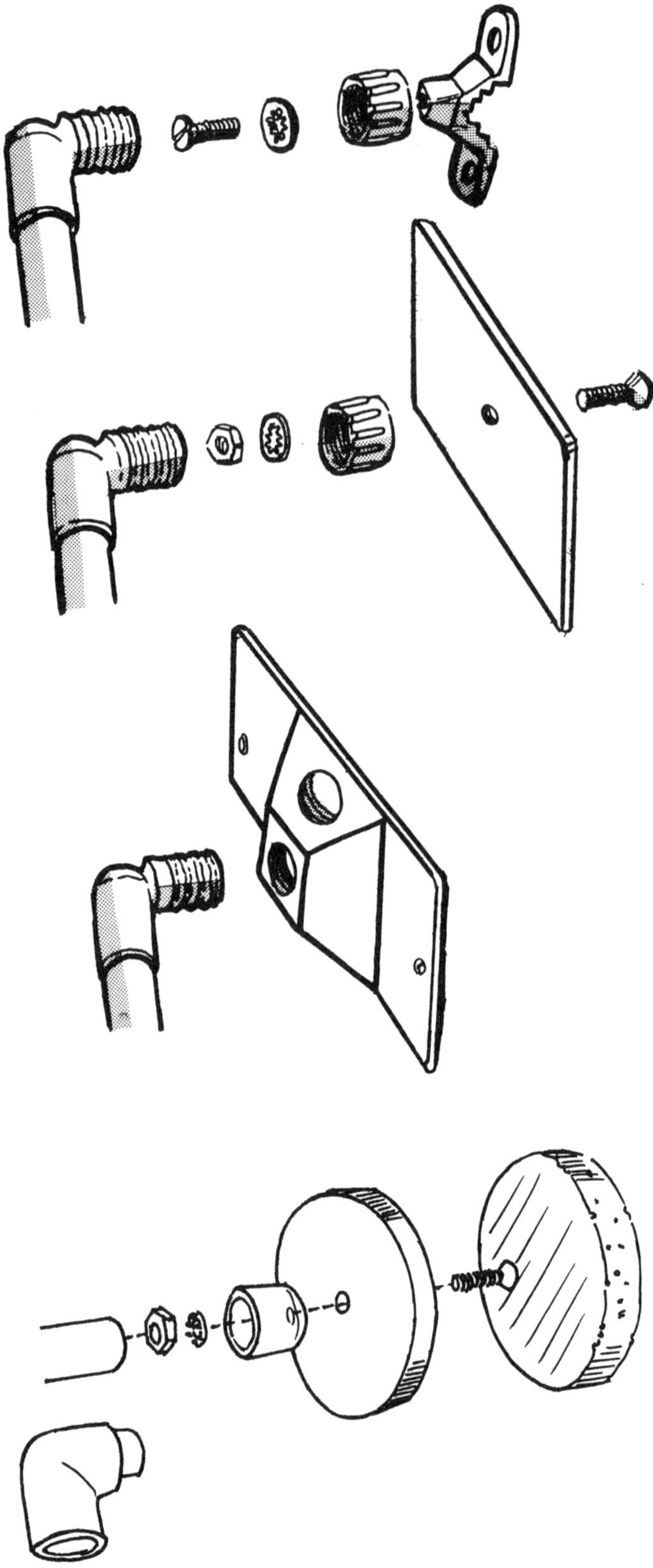

**FIGURE 4.17. (Continued)**

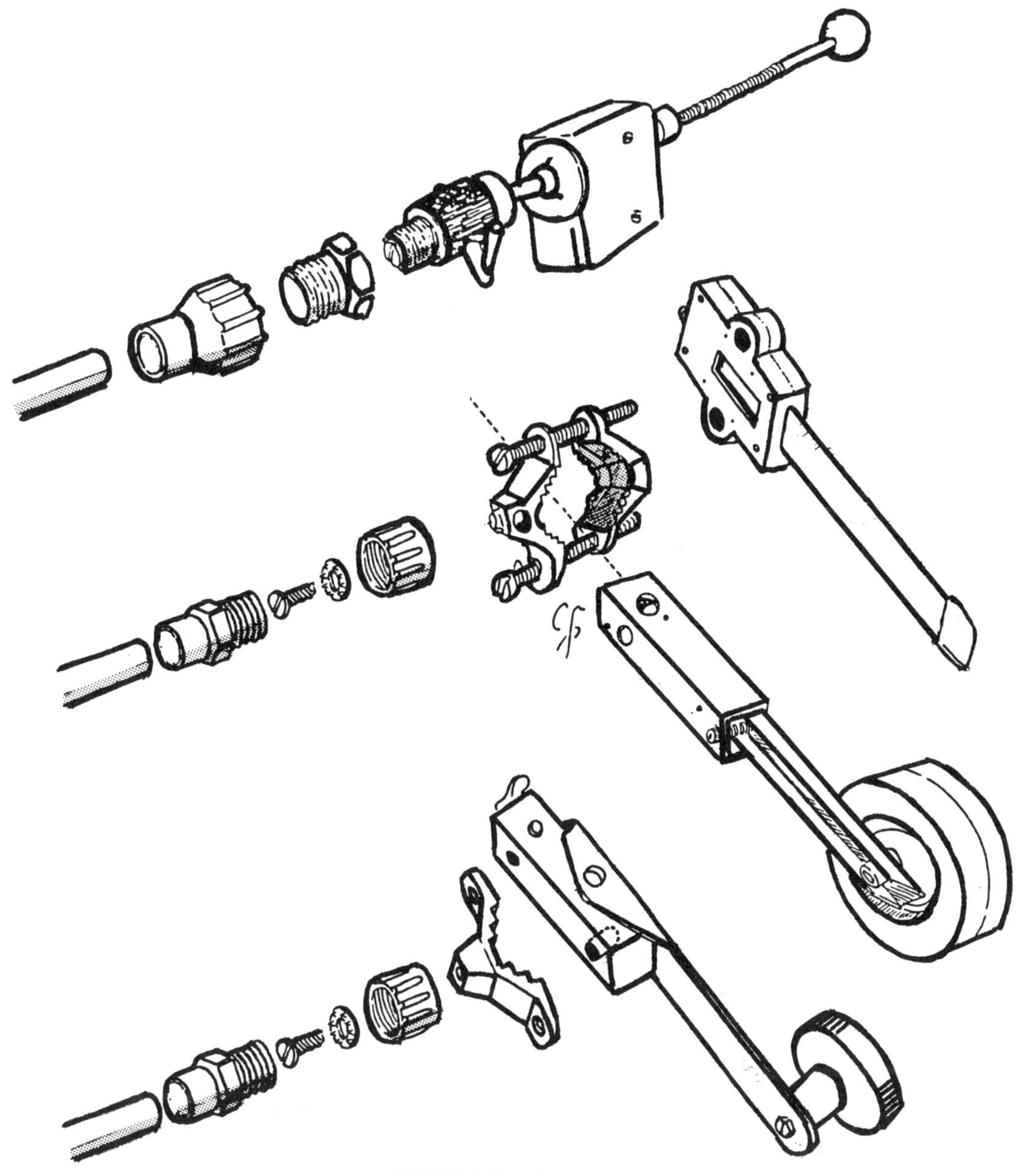

FIGURE 4.17. (Continued)

**ATTACHING THE CPVC MAINFRAME TO SUPPORTING THERAPEUTIC POSITIONING EQUIPMENT.** The typical wheelchair attachment points for the CPVC mainframe are depicted in Figure 4.19. When constructing a wheelchair mount for a head-activated switch, the vertical uprights of the wheelchair frame (supporting the back) frequently serve as the mount attachment site. Although the wheelchair handgrips can also serve as a point of attachment, this location may not be optimal if presence of the mount compromises its use as a handgrip.

When constructing a wheelchair mount for a knee-activated switch interface, the point of mount attachment is frequently the wheelchair frame supporting the armrests. This structure can also serve as a point of mount attachment to position a hand-activated switch at the end or side of the wheelchair armrest.

As illustrated in Figure 4.20, four methods can be used to attach the CPVC mainframe to the supporting structure of therapeutic positioning equipment: (a) metal ground clamps (typically used in

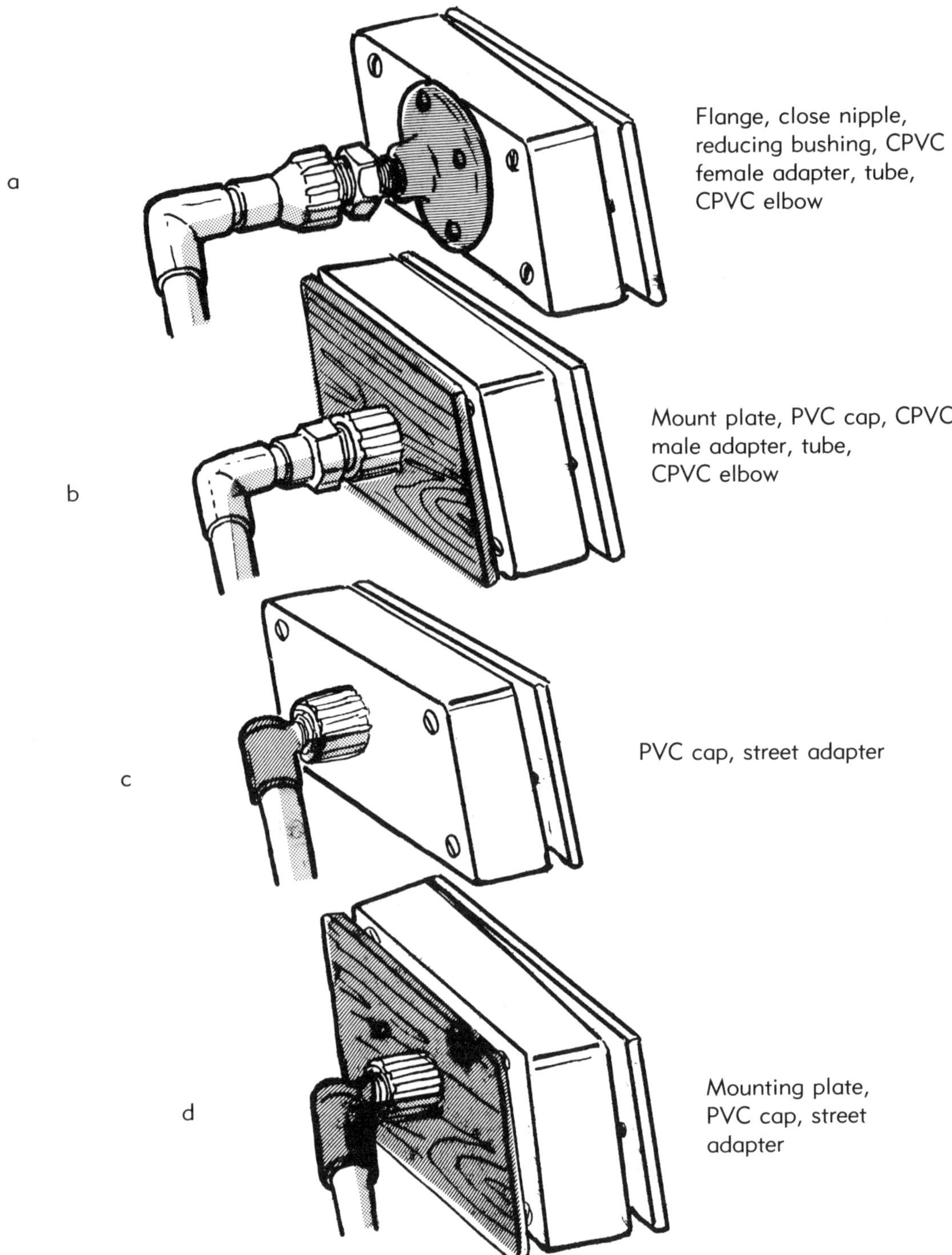


**FIGURE 4.18.** Selecting the most flexible option for accommodating a variety of therapeutic needs.

electrical work for fastening a ground wire to a grounding rod), (b) metal worm-drive or hose clamps (used in plumbing and automotive work to secure a hose), (c) commercially available wheelchair clamps (designed to attach commercially available adaptive fixtures to the wheelchair frame), and (d) plastic cable ties. When the wheelchair upholstery attaches directly to the wheelchair frame, the more expensive commercially available wheelchair clamp is, by default, the option for CPVC mount attachment.

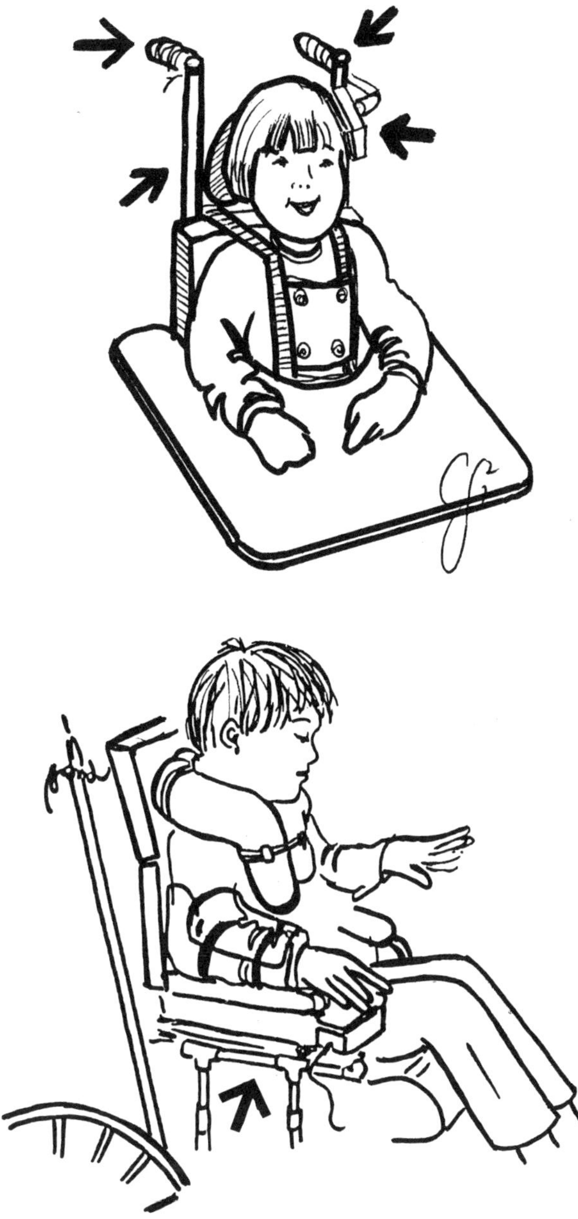

**FIGURE 4.19.** CPVC mount attachment points on the wheelchair mainframe.

The process of attaching clamps is greatly expedited when using an electric screwdriver. When attaching clamps, care should always be taken to position them at angles easily accessible for loosening and adjusting the mount during the fine-tuning that occurs later in the assessment process.

**INCREASING CPVC MOUNT STABILITY.** It is not unusual for children who are severely motorically involved to require extensive trials to acquire proficiency with a target motor response for switch access. As a general rule, the more consistency that can be built into the response required for switch activation, the faster the speed of skill acquisition. Because the CPVC mount serves as the supporting structure for the switch setup, its stability is germane to the consistency of the motor response required for switch access. As previously discussed, the more direct the path that the mount assumes, the greater its inherent stability. As depicted in Figures 4.21 and 4.22, stability is greatly enhanced when the mount design utilizes (a) more than one clamp, (b) perpendicular clamping (made possible by incorporating tee fittings), (c) pipe lengths that allow the mount to rest on or butt against existing frame structures, and (d) straight adapters or caps to ensure that the worm-drive or ground clamps do not slide (as a result of the pipe not being equidistant from the supporting structure). When constructing a head-activated switch setup, stability can be further enhanced by designing the mount to allow the switch to be partially supported by the headrest. When pursuing this option, however, care should be taken to ensure that the headrest does not interfere with optimal operation of the switch.

As illustrated in Figure 4.23, many of the currently available lightweight wheelchairs (e.g., Brio, Zippy) necessitate that the switch mount travel a substantial distance through free space (as vertical uprights are no longer available to serve as a closer attachment point). Typically, the metal back of the seat insert serves as a point of mount attachment. To enhance stability, the facilitator should (a) use perpendicular clamping at the point of attachment (to minimize shifting), (b) clamp as closely as possible to the point of exiting into free space, (c) consider constructing a parallel mount structure, and (d) consider incorporating brace bars into the design. As a precautionary note, the warranty for some chairs is voided when holes are drilled into the metal structure of the chair.

**FINE-TUNING THE CPVC MOUNT.** Having completed the preliminary mount, assessments are conducted (see Chapter 6) to determine if the mount continues to position the switch interface in a functionally viable position for the client. It is during this phase of the process that different types of switches with accompanying CPVC mounts might be subjected to systematic evaluation. When a viable setup has been approximated, fine-tuning of the mount typically

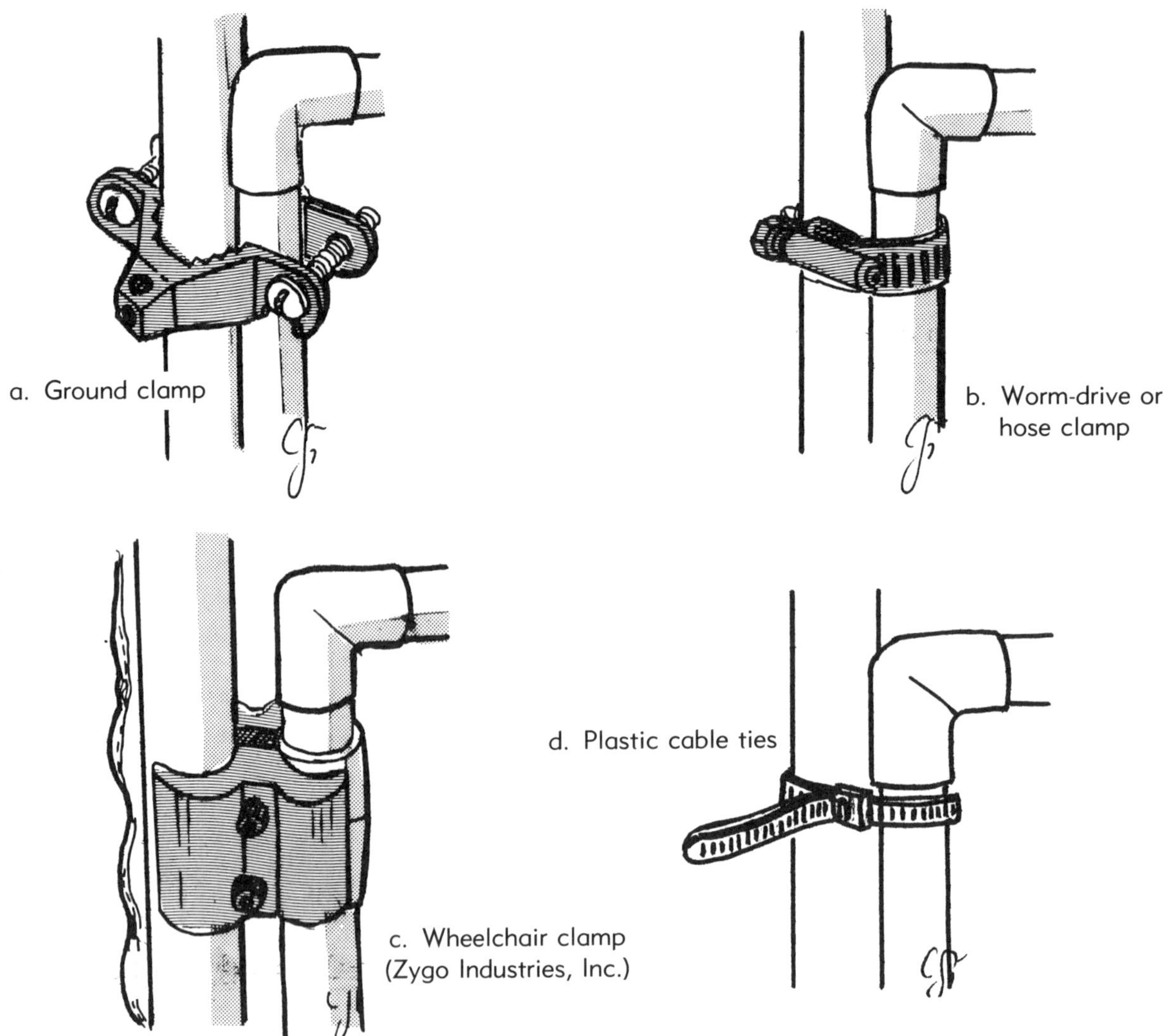


**FIGURE 4.20.** Methods for attaching the CPVC mount to the supporting structure of therapeutic positioning equipment.

occurs. For example, if accidental activations persist during assessment, the facilitator may wish to increase the distance between the control site and the switch interface. As depicted in Figure 4.24, this can be achieved by (a) substituting a shorter length of CPVC pipe to increase the distance between the control site and the switch, (b) pivoting the CPVC pipe mount away from the control site at the level of wheelchair attachment, or (c) adjusting the orientation of the switch on its Velcro or Dual Lock attachment on the mounting plate. When conducting these adjustments, care should be taken to ensure that the switch activation surface is aligned with the control site. Angled Ethafoam wedges (inserted between the mounting plate and the switch) may be required to optimize contact.

**MAKING THE CPVC MOUNT PERMANENT.** When the facilitator is sufficiently satisfied with the switch setup and mount, steps can be taken to make the mount permanent. This process is depicted in Figure 4.25. Using CPVC solvent cement, all joints are solvent-welded except one joint which serves as a "removal joint" (to be discussed in detail later). Note that the assembled precut pipes (derived from the CPVC kit) are the same pipes that will eventually be solvent-welded to form the child's permanent mount. Duplicate lengths are later cut to replenish those used from the kit. To ensure that the exact three-dimensional configuration is maintained during the solvent-welding process, a pencil can be used to mark off (a) the depth of pipe insertion and (b) the alignment of the component parts of the joint.

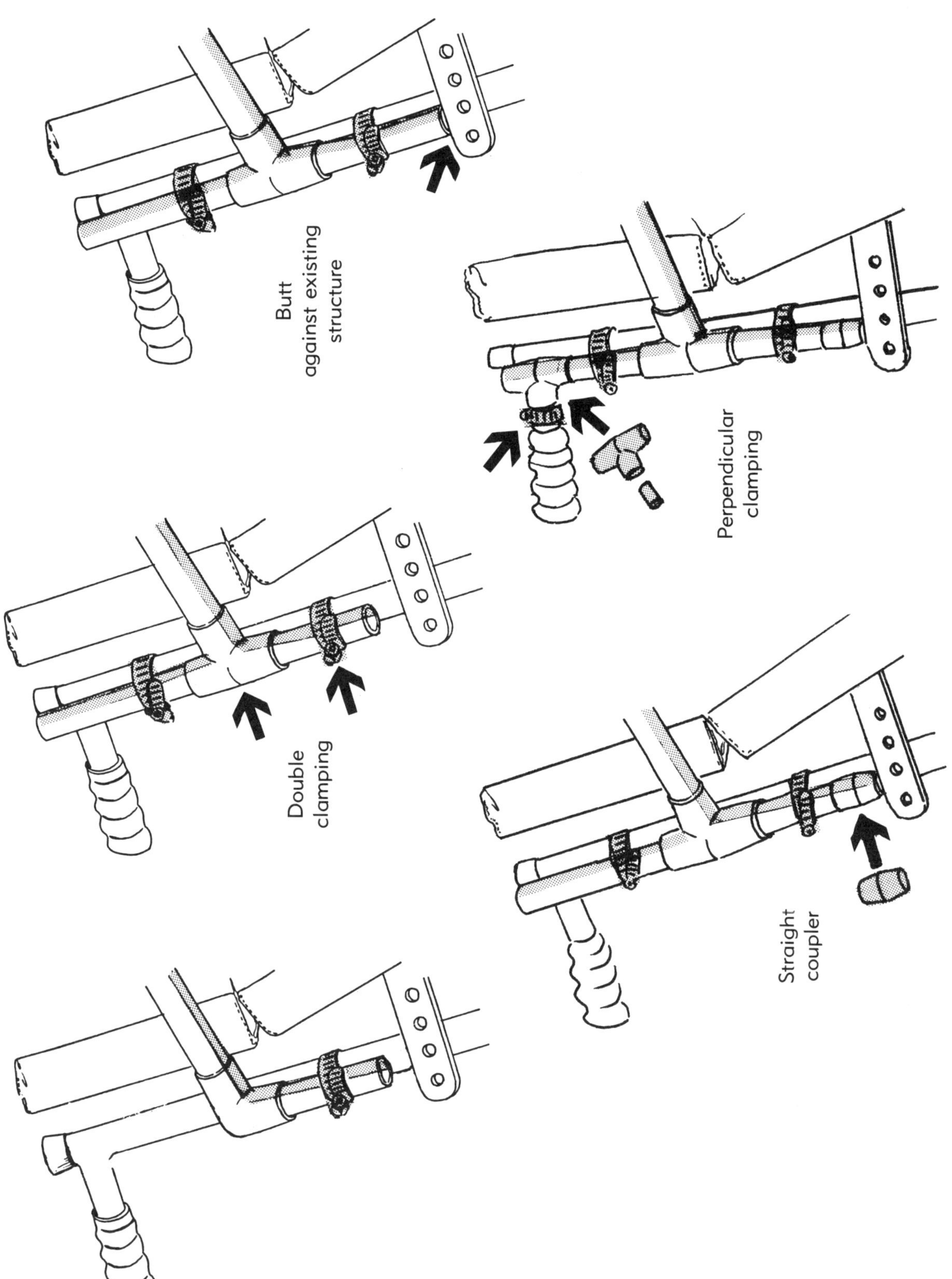


**FIGURE 4.21.** Increasing mount stability—Example 1.

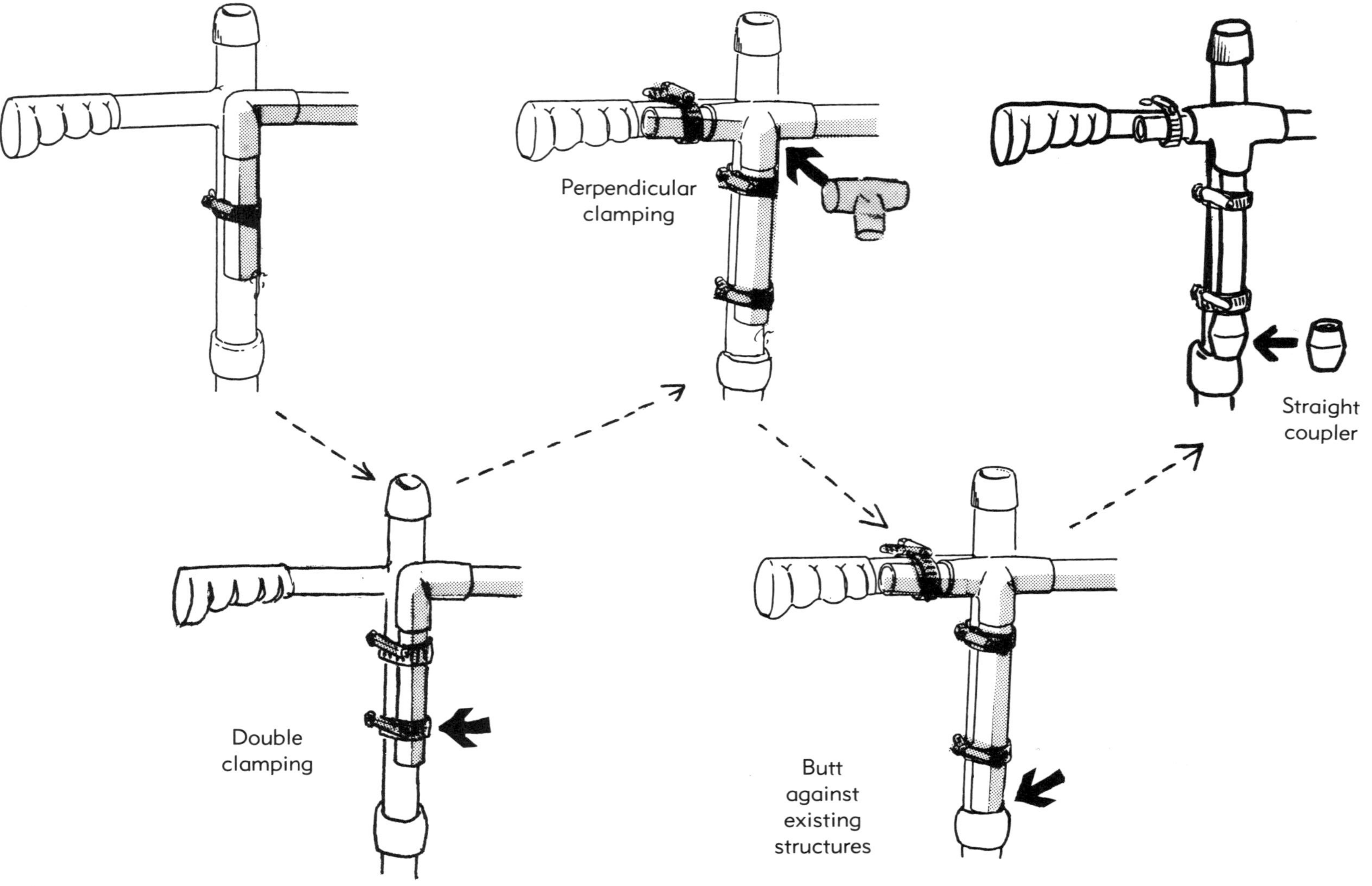


**FIGURE 4.22.** Increasing mount stability—Example 2.

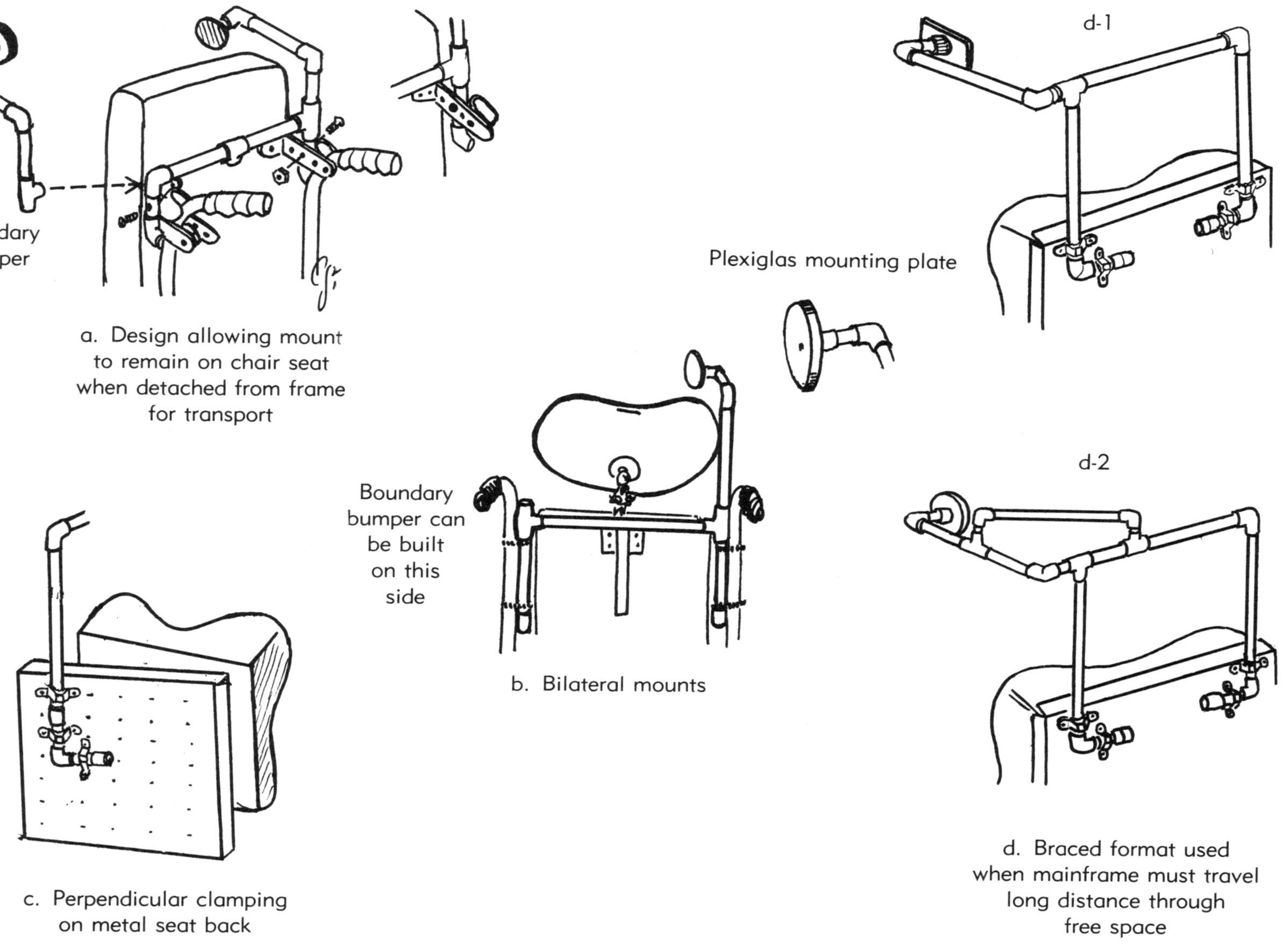


**FIGURE 4.23.** Mounting designs.

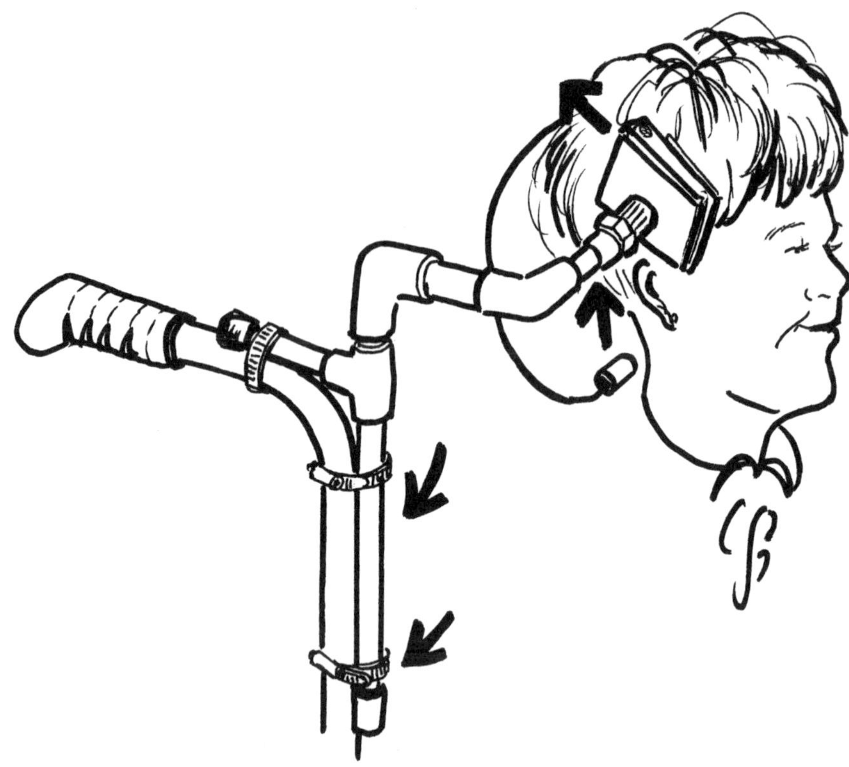

**FIGURE 4.24.** Fine-tuning the CPVC mount.

To avoid confusion, joints should be dismantled and solvent-welded one at a time. To weld a joint, the facilitator dips the end of the CPVC pipe into the solvent cement, coating it to a depth of approximately ½ inch. Because the solvent cement dries rapidly and permanently, the facilitator must quickly join the pipe and its fitting to full depth with a slight twist to bring it to its correct alignment (designated by the pencil markings). The twist breaks up insertion lines in the solvent cement. The facilitator then holds the fitting until the solvent cement seals tightly. Excess solvent cement can be removed from the mount using paper towels.

Solvent-welding is a one-way process—that is, you can "glue" a fitting but you cannot unglue it. If the facilitator accidentally incorporates the wrong fitting into the mount, the mount may still be salvaged using the correction procedure detailed in Figure 4.26. As illustrated, the facilitator must first cut the fitting out, leaving at least ½ inch of pipe to allow a straight coupler to be used to interface the cut ends. The correct fitting can then be incorporated into the design.

It is important to note that CPVC solvent cement emits toxic fumes. It is therefore highly recommended that the joining process be performed with latex gloves, either outdoors or in a well-ventilated room (with the child preferably out of the chair).

**INCORPORATING A REMOVAL JOINT IN A CPVC MOUNT.** The mount design must incorporate a method for easily and quickly removing the switch interface (a) when transferring the child in and out of the wheelchair, (b) when moving the switch from one therapeutic position (e.g., seated in wheelchair) to another (e.g., on prone stander, in side-lying), and (c) to minimize damage that might occur when transporting the wheelchair in the trunk of a car. It is, however, imperative that stability and consistency of switch presentation be maintained in the process. If a removal joint is not incorporated into the design, the facilitator must either loosen, then tighten the mount at its attachment clamps (a time-consuming process that jeopardizes attempts to maintain the required motor response highly consistent across time), or maintain looser attachment clamps that allow the entire mount to be pivoted away from the control site (compromising mount stability and consistency). As illustrated in Figure 4.27, a more acceptable alternative is to incorporate a cotter pin removal

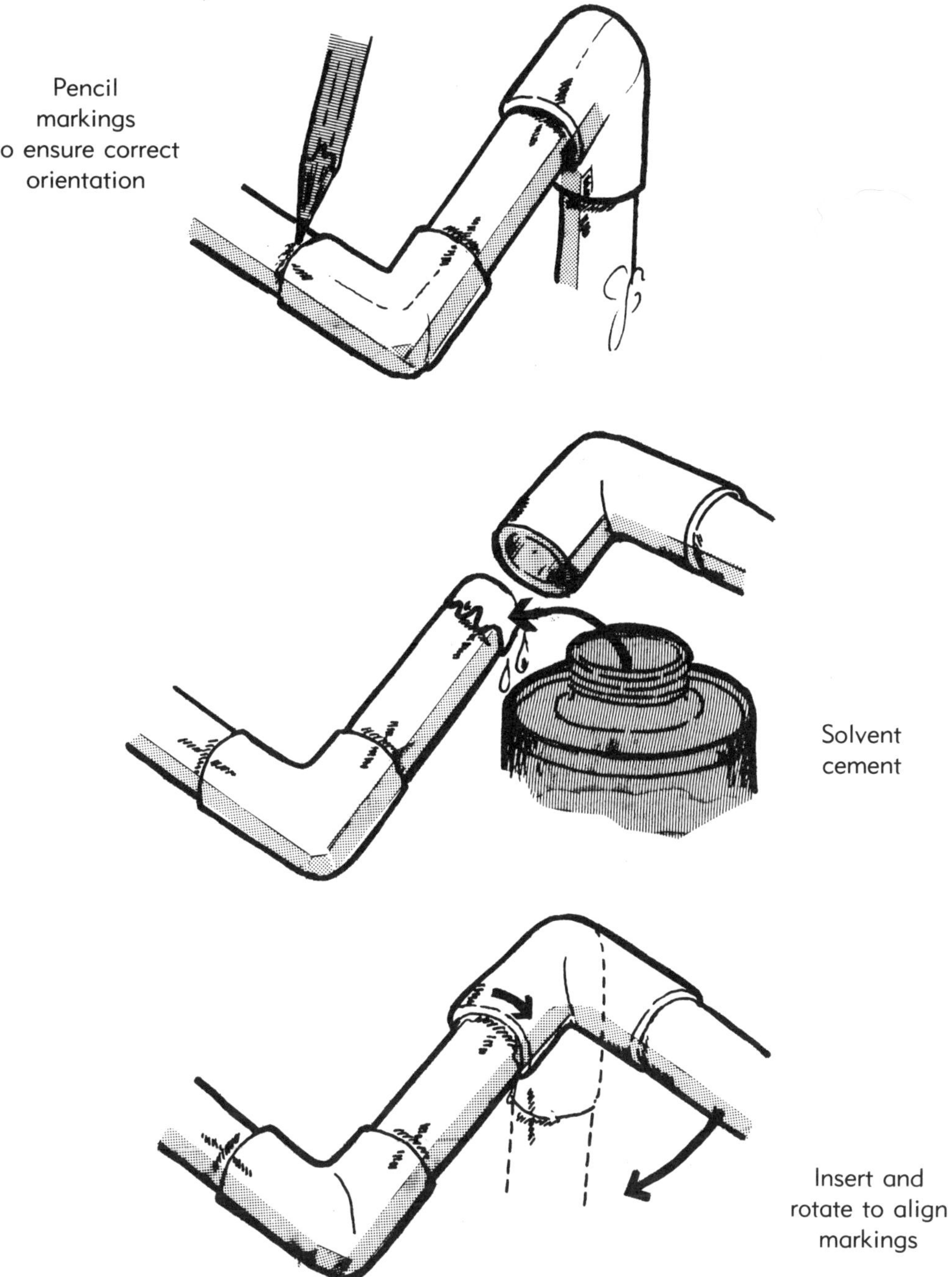


**FIGURE 4.25.** Making the CPVC mount permanent.

joint into the mount design. A cotter pin removal joint consists of a cotter pin that is inserted into a hole that has been drilled through the joint designated to serve as a removal joint. Using an electric drill, a hole is created that passes through both the fitting and the inserted pipe of the removal joint. When the cotter pin is inserted into this hole, the joint is stabilized; when the pin is removed, the switch can be easily dismantled. When drilling a hole for the cotter pin, care should be taken to ensure that the pipe is fully inserted into the fitting prior to drilling. To permit easy insertion, the cotter pin hole should be slightly larger than the outer diameter of the cotter pin. This can be achieved by using a drill bit equal in size to the cotter pin and reaming the hole slightly during the drilling process.

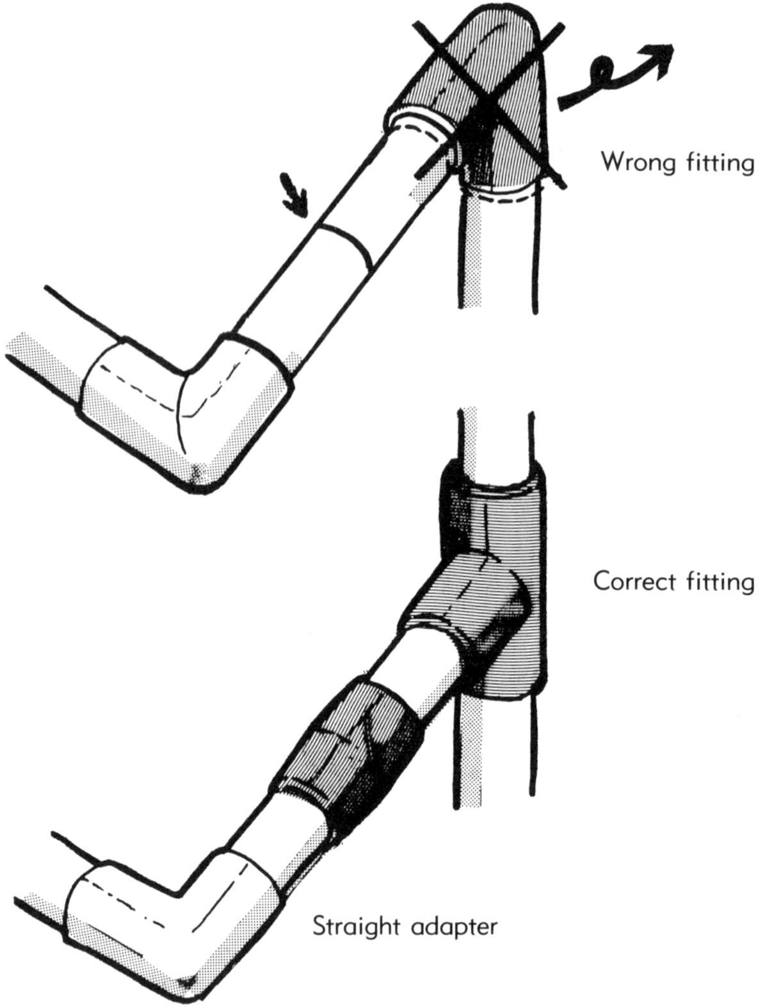


**FIGURE 4.26.** Procedure for correcting errors occurring during the solvent-welding process.

When selecting the joint to serve as a removal joint, the facilitator should select a joint that allows the switch interface to be easily removed from the CPVC mount without moving the switch into the control site. Both incorrect and correct options for head- and knee-activated formats are presented in Figure 4.28.

Vertical placement of the cotter pin hole is preferred over horizontal placement. Horizontally inserted cotter pins tend to fall out, given the vibration of wheelchair transport. When a pin is vertically inserted, gravity assists in maintaining insertion. Although vertical insertion is preferred, there are instances in which true vertical insertion is not feasible. As illustrated in Figure 4.29, limitations in the space needed to manipulate and insert the pin may preclude true vertical insertion. In such compromised situations, the cotter pin hole should be vertically angled to promote ease of insertion, while simultaneously allowing gravity to assist in keeping the pin inserted.

As illustrated in Figure 4.30, the mount requirements for alternative therapeutic positions may also dictate placement of the cotter pin hole. If the mount for an alternative therapeutic position to seated necessitates extending the pipe length, CPVC straight couplers can be used to achieve this extension.

The constraints of transport must also be taken into consideration when designing the location of the removal joint. Many wheelchairs are collapsed and transported in the trunks of cars. The size of the trunk may impose limitations on the distance that the CPVC mount can extend beyond the chair. The overhead clearance for entering the door of a van

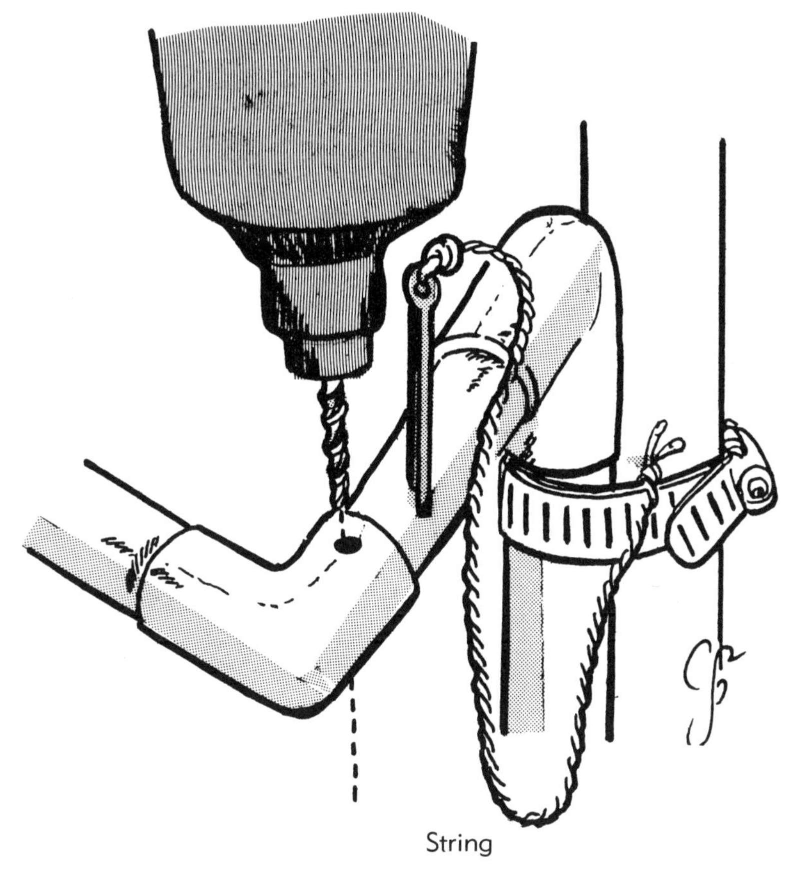


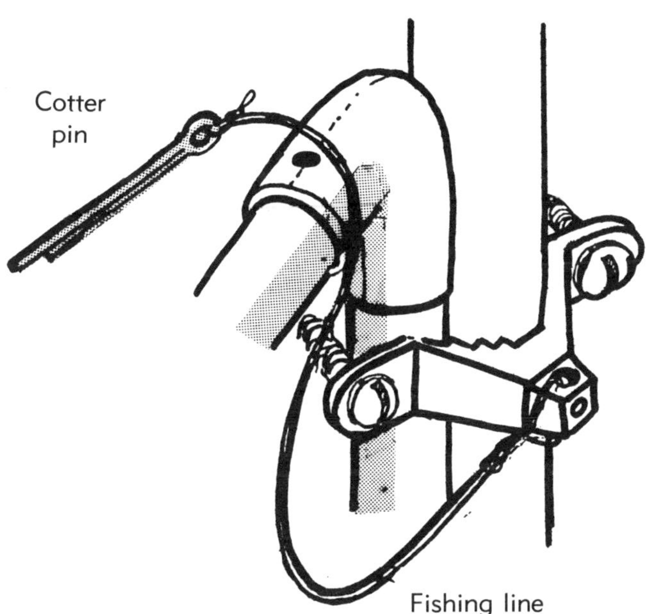


**FIGURE 4.27.** Incorporating a cotter pin removal joint into the mount design.

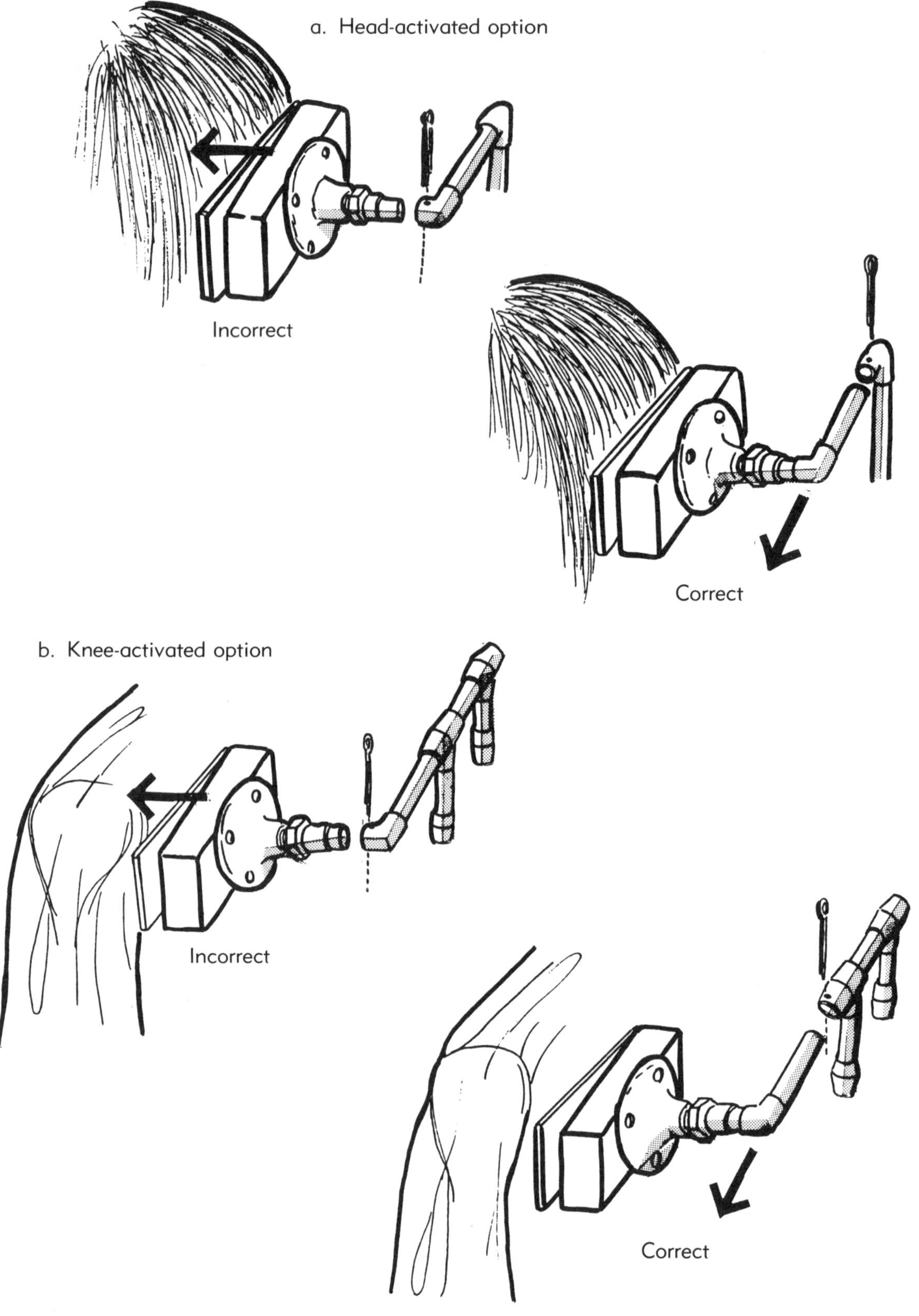


**FIGURE 4.28.** Cotter pin removal joints—Incorrect and correct options for head- and knee-activated options.

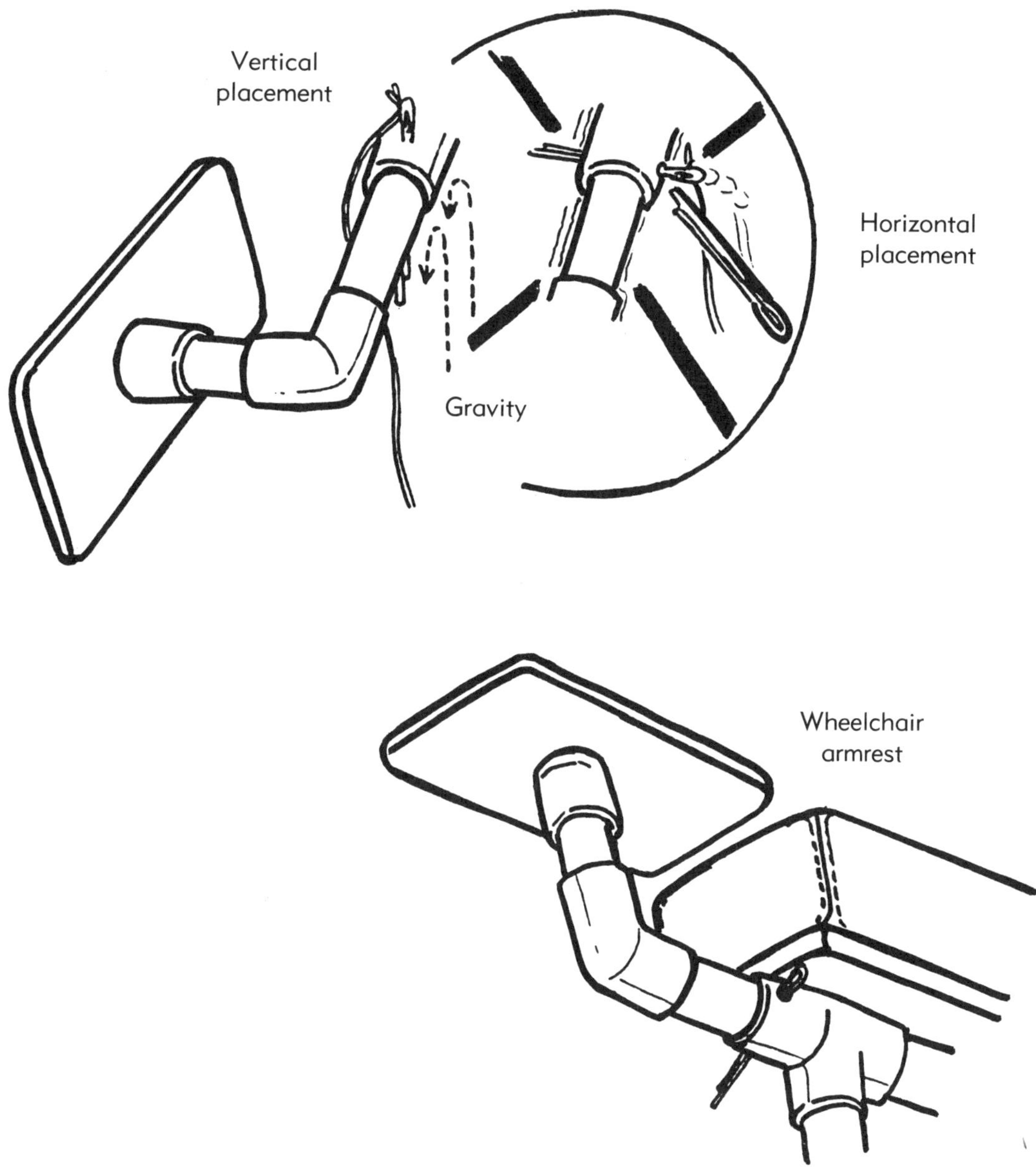


**FIGURE 4.29.** Modified vertical placement of the cotter pin in the cotter pin removal joint.

may impose similar restrictions. Given the permissible clearance, the mount may need to be designed to accommodate a removal joint lower on the CPVC mount.

As illustrated in Figure 4.31, commercially available mounting hardware can be used in conjunction with CPVC materials. In particular, a pushbutton disconnect can be incorporated into a CPVC mount design, thus providing an alternative to the cotter pin removal joint. In similar fashion, the facilitator may also wish to incorporate a commercially available swivel clamp into the mount design. With the addition of this swivel component, more-refined adjustment of the switch can be achieved relative to the control site.

**MAKING THE CPVC MOUNT AESTHETIC.** Aesthetics should not be overlooked when building CPVC switch mounts. It is important to make the mount as cosmetically appealing as possible. Illustrated in Figure 4.32 are several options for making the mount more aesthetic. CPVC pipes typically have lettering

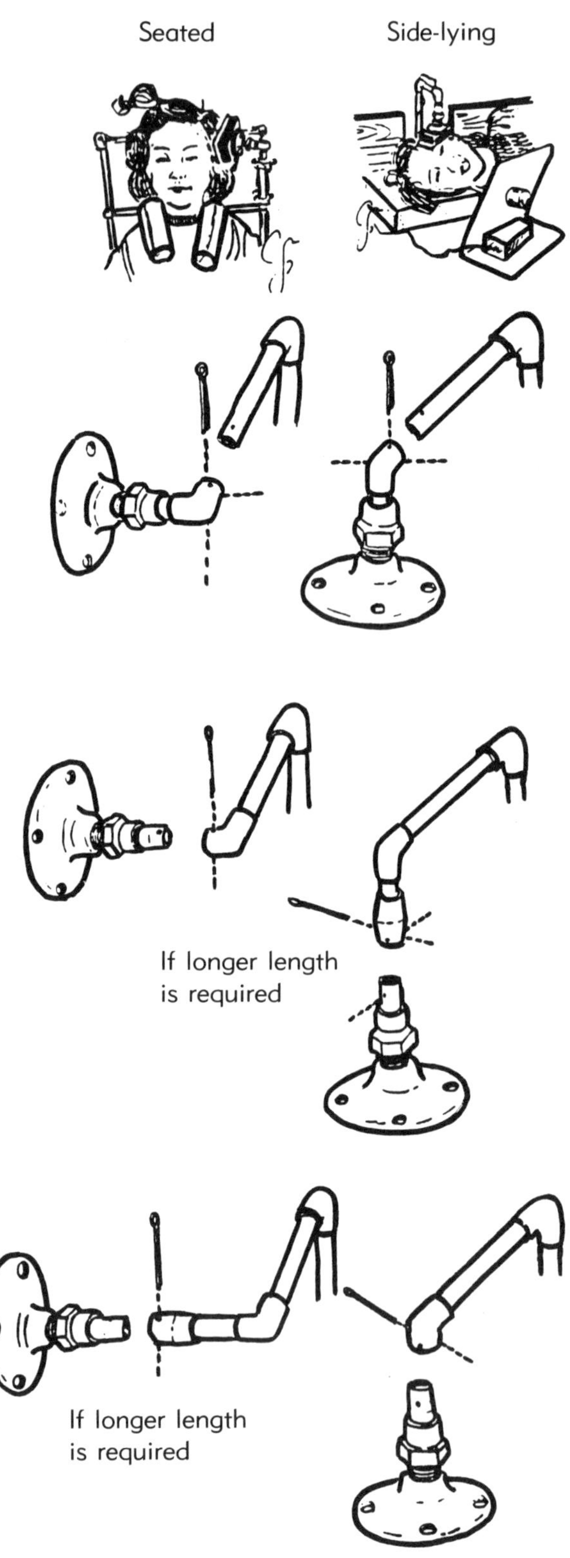


**FIGURE 4.30.** Accommodating alternate therapeutic positions in CPVC mount design.

and numbers along their length. This printing and any soiled areas can be removed using CPVC pipe cleaner or primer (Figure 4.32a). As previously discussed, steps should be taken to safeguard the facilitator and the child against potentially harmful fumes and contact with the skin.

In some instances, the facilitator may wish to spray paint the mount (Figure 4.32b). Although some families select colors to make the mount less conspicuous (e.g., selecting matte black to blend in with the wheelchair frame), others select bright colors to accentuate its ornamental presence. Paint does, however, become scratched with time. Periodic repainting may be necessary. Initial painting is always done before the mount is attached to the wheelchair.

It is also possible to coat the assembled mount with heat-shrink plastic. As depicted in Figure 4.32c, the heat-shrink plastic (available from distributors of electrical supplies) is slid onto the pipe and is then shrunk to a tight fit using a hair dryer. This option, however, is usually pursued only when the facilitator is confident that the switch setup has no further refinements.

### Headrest Switch Mounts

For some children it is feasible to unobtrusively embed a switch or multiple switches within the wheelchair headrest. Contoured head supports such as the Otto Bock one- or two-step headrests are especially amenable to this application. TASH, Inc., offers a commercially available headrest with two small, slightly protruding switches covered in foam. In other situations, facilitators have selected small switches that they have recessed in the headrest to a depth not affected by the typical movement of the head within the headrest. To activate the switch, the child must exert pressure on the headrest, causing the surface of the headrest to indent slightly to allow the head to make contact with the switch activation surface. When the switch is embedded at the back of the head support, care should be taken to ensure that placement does not trigger the involuntary reflex of total body extension that sometimes results when the occipital area of the head is stimulated.

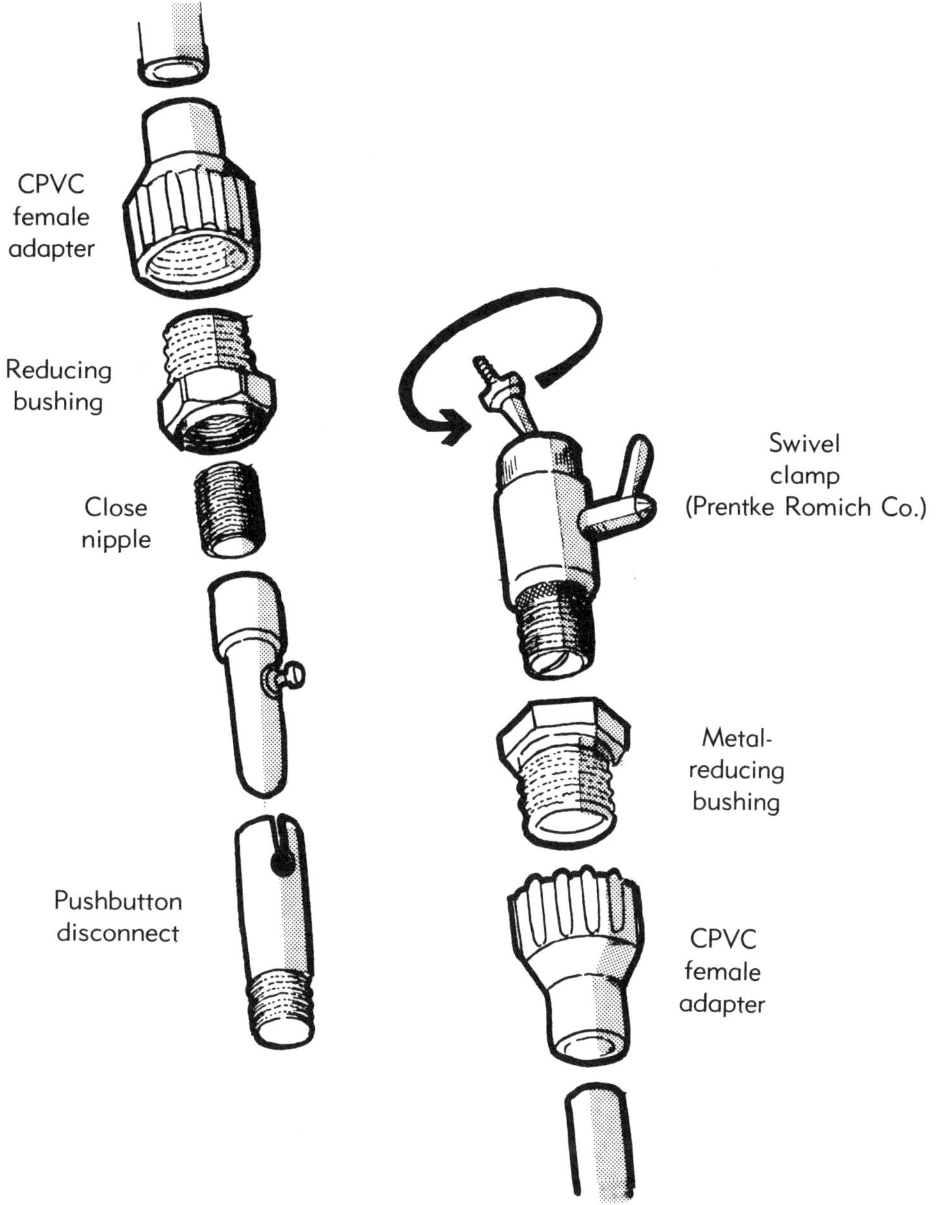


**FIGURE 4.31.** Incorporating commercially available fixtures into the CPVC mount design.

## Hand-Activated Switch Mounts Constructed with Ethafoam

As previously discussed, hand-activated switch setups that present the switch in a recessed/low-profile format and/or in a vertically angled format can greatly enhance the child's ability to access a switch interface effortlessly and reliably. When the switch is presented in a *recessed or low-profile format,* (a) the need to use shoulder elevation to get on the switch is virtually eliminated, thereby simplifying the target motor response; (b) the surrounding surface may be used to stabilize the proximal portions of the hand, thereby facilitating distal mobility required for switch access; and (c) the surrounding surface may serve as a guide, assisting the child in sliding the hand on and off of the switch interface.

When the switch is presented in a *vertically angled format,* (a) visual conflict of interest is reduced (because the switch and target system appear in the

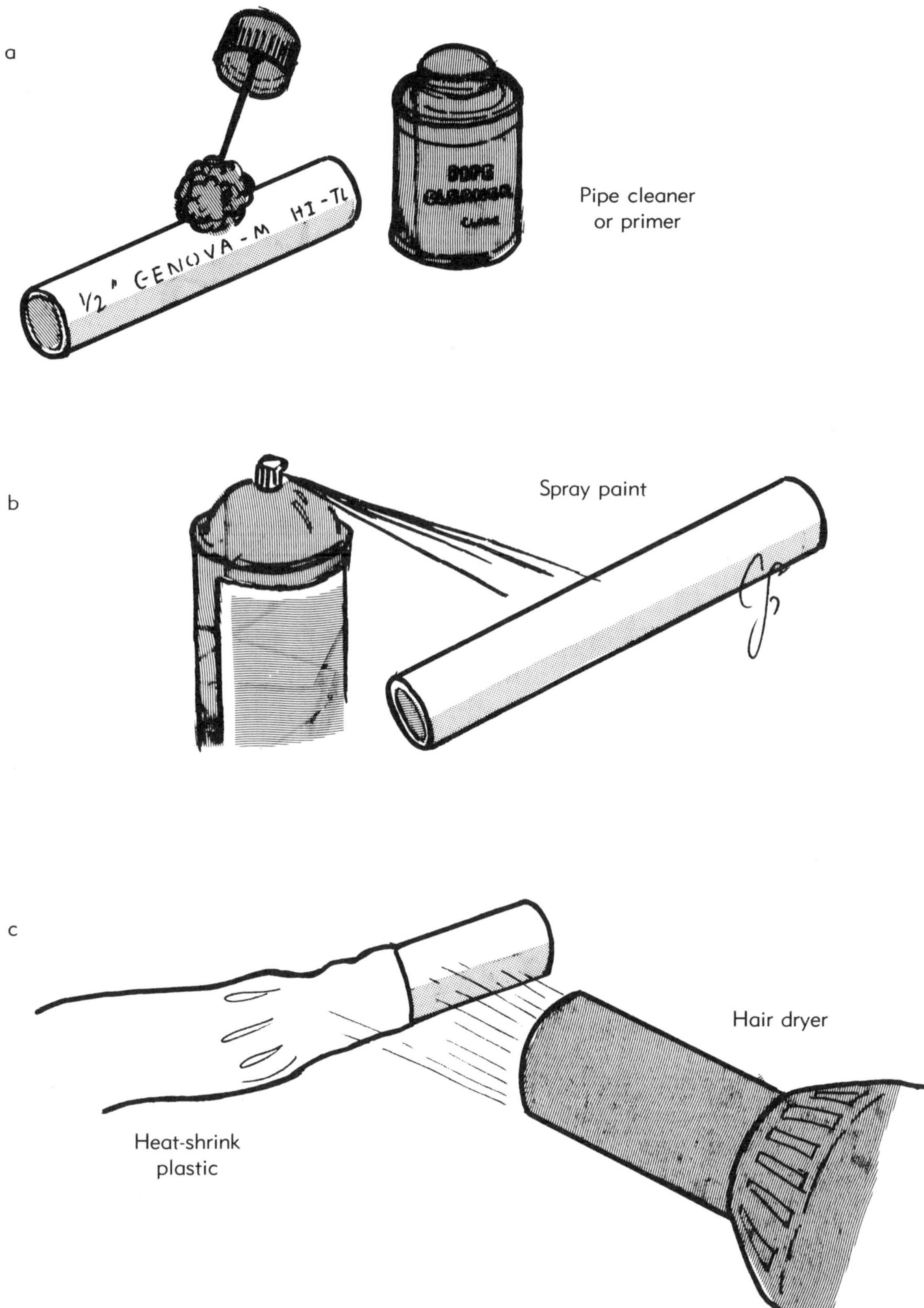


**FIGURE 4.32.** Making the CPVC mount aesthetic.

same visual plane), (b) a "head-up" posture is promoted, (c) the tendency for increased extensor tone in the arms may be reduced (because placement of the Ethafoam mount may encourage elbow flexion that tends to break up the extensor synergy pattern), and (d) ulnar deviation of the hand may no longer be operative during the switch access process (because the Ethafoam mount by design promotes elbow flexion, which in turn helps to break up the extensor synergy pattern of which ulnar deviation of the hand is a component).

Custom-made Ethafoam structures can be used to present hand-activated switch setups in a low-profile/recessed and/or an angled format. Ethafoam is a lightweight, closed-cell foam product that is available from distributors specializing in foam and plastic products. It is typically purchased in large sheets of variable thickness and density. A thickness of 1½ inches and a density of 220 have been found to be sufficient to allow construction of a mount capable of presenting most switch interfaces in a recessed format. This density also permits easy cutting with an electric kitchen knife.

When constructing an angled Ethafoam mount, the width of the child's lap tray usually dictates the width of the Ethafoam structure. There are instances, however, in which only a portion of this width may be used, to provide the child with a vertical edge to assist in stabilizing the nonindicating hand/arm. As illustrated in Figure 4.33, boundary bumpers may be added to the design to better delineate the boundaries of the target motor response.

Prior to constructing the mount, evaluation with a three-part Ethafoam assessment mount (as discussed in Chapter 3) will have determined (a) the type of switch interface to be employed; (b) its location in the Ethafoam mount; (c) the distance between the mount and the child's body; (d) the angle of the Ethafoam mount surface; and (e) the manner of presentation of the switch activation surface relative to the Ethafoam mount surface (e.g., flush, recessed, low-profile).

The basic steps employed when constructing a simple, angled Ethafoam mount are depicted in Figure 4.34. The more complex versions, previously presented in Figure 3.26, are variations of the basic design. The basic steps are as follows:

1. Using an electric knife, cut a rectangle of Ethafoam that is 8 to 10 inches wide and long enough to span the entire width of the child's lap tray.
2. Trace the dimensions of the switch interface of choice at the location previously determined to promote a viable switch performance (Figure 4.34a).
3. Using the electric knife, gradually wedge the Ethafoam along its length. This tapered edge will allow the angled mount to smoothly transition to the lap tray surface (Figure 4.33b).
4. Cut a hole ⅛ inch larger than the dimensions drawn for the switch interface. Usually, a 2-inch space is left between the tapered edge

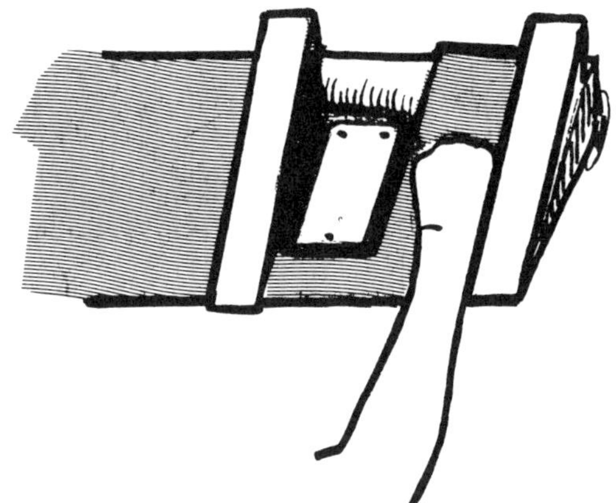

Built-up bumpers

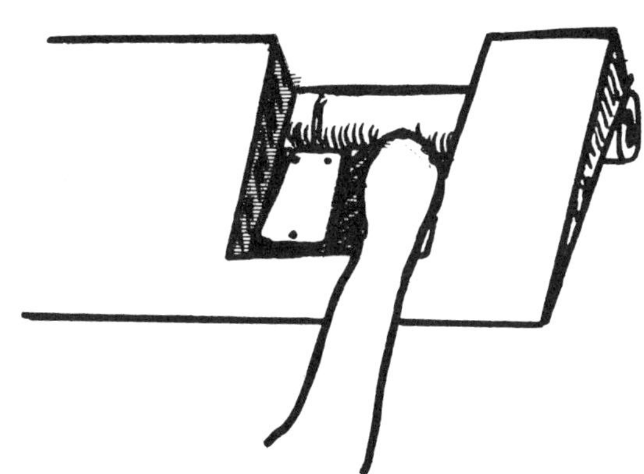

Built-in bumpers

**FIGURE 4.33.** Ethafoam hand-activated switch mounts.

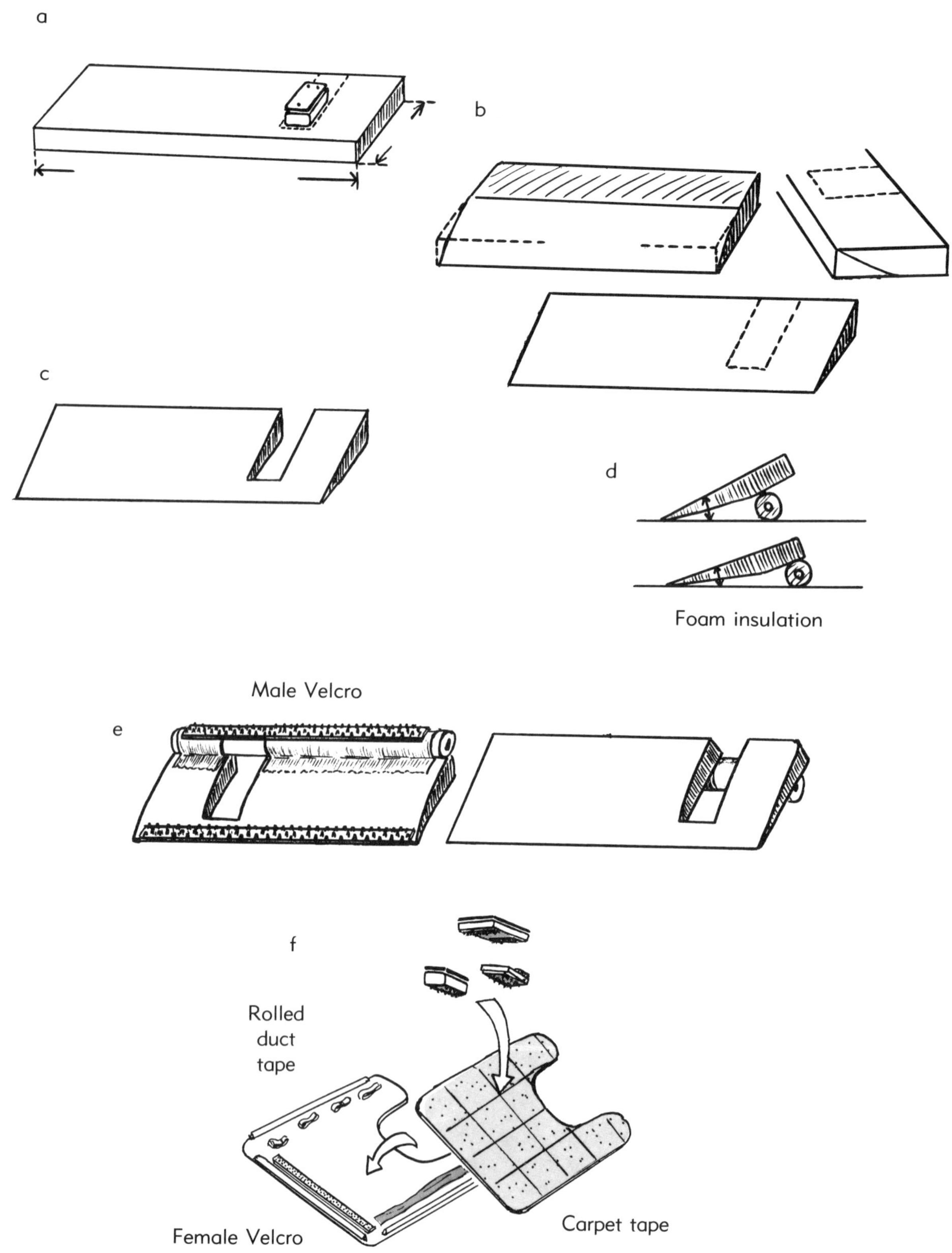


**FIGURE 4.34.** Constructing an Ethafoam switch mount.

of the Ethafoam and the switch cutout (Figure 4.34c).

5. Cut a length of foam insulation tubing equal in length to that of the Ethafoam mount.
6. Simulate the desired angle of the mount by shifting the foam insulation tubing either closer or farther away from the tapered edge of the Ethafoam mount. The closer the tubing moves toward the tapered edge, the steeper the Ethafoam mount (Figure 4.34d).
7. When the desired angle has been achieved, attach the foam insulation tubing to the Ethafoam, first with glue from a hot-glue gun, then with duct tape. Be sure to knead the duct tape into the foam surface to maximize contact and ensure full adherence of the parts to be joined.
8. Attach adhesive male Velcro to (a) the tapered edge of the Ethafoam mount and (b) the bottom of the foam tubing that will make contact with the lap tray or table surface (Figure 4.34e).
9. Line the lap tray surface (either partially or completely) with indoor/outdoor carpet. The indoor/outdoor carpet can be attached to the lap tray surface using (a) carpet tape, (b) duct tape rolled in loops, or (c) adhesive male and female Velcro (Figure 4.34f). As indoor/outdoor carpet has an affinity for male Velcro, the Ethafoam structure can be temporarily but securely affixed to the lap tray surface.
10. If boundary bumpers are desired, they can also be adhered to the Ethafoam mount using Dual Lock, glue, or adhesive Velcro.
11. The Ethafoam rectangle removed when making the switch cutout is used to construct the wedge needed for achieving the flush, recessed, or low-profile formats previously presented in Figure 3.28. The wedge is inserted into the cutout and is adhered to the indoor/outdoor carpet of the supporting surface (via adhesive male Velcro attached to its bottom).

Although Ethafoam mounts hold up well for the majority of children, some children may require a sturdier, padded, wooden version. It is also possible to cover the entire Ethafoam structure with Formafoam. The resulting structure can then be coated with Fabricoat paint (Phelps, personal communication, 1991). Both the Formafoam and the Fabricoat paint can be purchased from Danmar Products, Inc.

## Switch Mounts Positioned on the Body

Several options exist for mounting the switch on the child's body:

- ❑ Chest mounts
- ❑ Head mounts

**CHEST MOUNTS.** Chin mounts or chest plates (Figure 4.35) are commercially available from a variety of sources (e.g., Don Johnston Developmental Equipment, Inc.; Prentke Romich Company; Possum). Most options are adjustable, allowing the switch interface to be moved forward or backward, up and down relative to the chin. Although some mounts are attached to the body using Velcro straps, others are snapped around the neck as a detachable collar. As a general rule, straps necessitate extra time and steps to set up the child's switch. The facilitator should, therefore, consider attaching the chin mount to the chest harness, thereby eliminating the extra steps required to position and secure the straps. Adhesive Velcro (male Velcro on the mount; female Velcro on the chest harness) can be used to achieve a secure attachment. When pursuing this option, care should be taken to ensure that placement on the chest harness remains constant from one time to the next. If positioning periodically shifts, the Velcro attachment permits minor height adjustments.

When utilizing a chin mount, chest plate, or chest collar, mount stability is crucial to promoting optimal switch access. If the mount is not stable, difficulty may be experienced with the release aspects of switch access. Care should therefore be taken to make the chin mount's attachment to the body as stable as possible.

There are instances in which structural deviations preclude the use of traditional mounting options. This is especially evident with children who, for medical reasons, must assume a supine position or children who, due to severe kyphosis (anterior curvature of the spine) and severe arm contractures, are not functional in a seated position. Such children may be able to access a switch when the switch is presented on their chest or stomach. Movement of

a. Chin mount
(Don Johnston
Developmental Equipment)

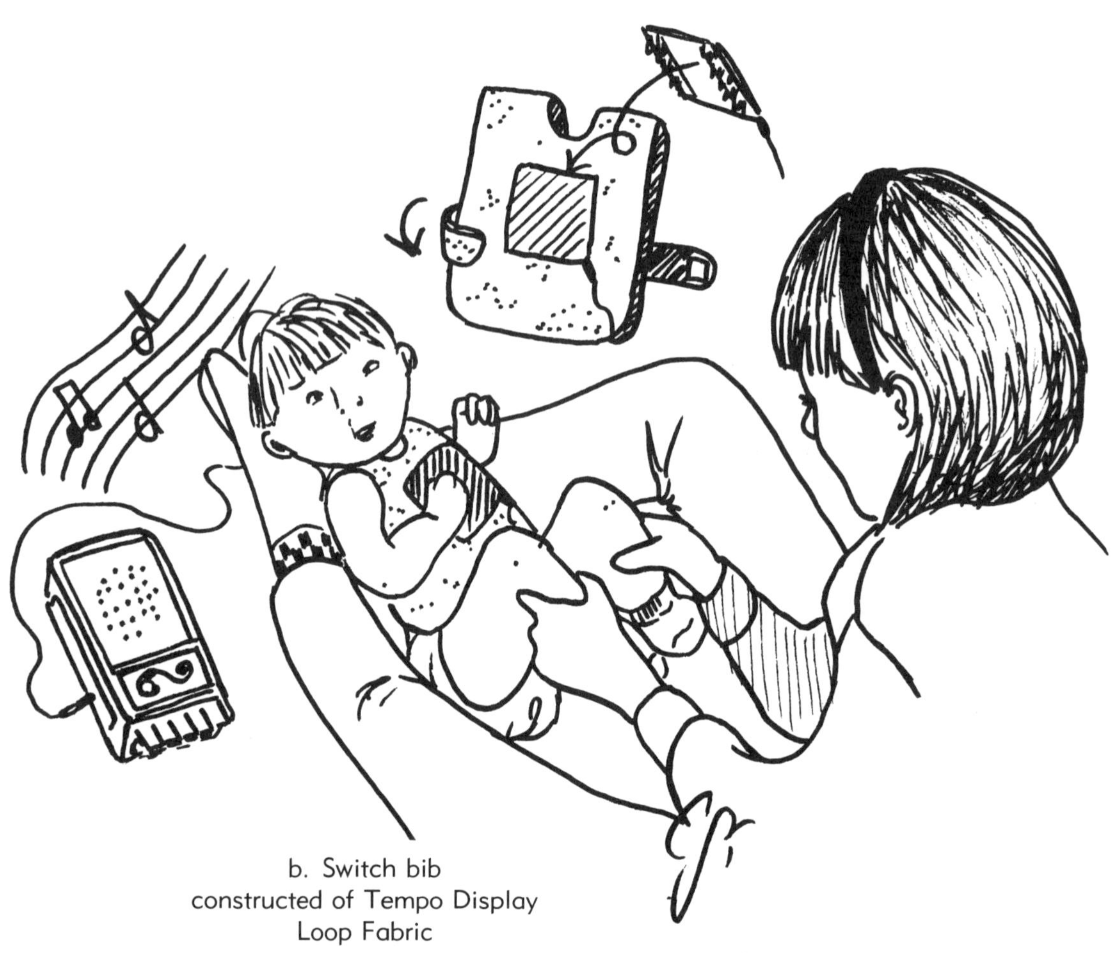

b. Switch bib
constructed of Tempo Display
Loop Fabric

**FIGURE 4.35.** Chest mounts.

the hand or arm against the body serves as the movement pattern for switch access. A switch bib (worn by the child) can serve as a convenient means for securing the switch in the desired target location. As illustrated in Figure 4.35b, switch bibs can be constructed of (a) terry cloth or Tempo Display Loop Fabric (Lockfast, Inc.), which readily couples with the male Velcro attached to the bottom of the switch, (b) cotton material with a large patch of adhesive Velcro to allow attachment of a switch lined with male Velcro, or (c) a pocket large enough to accommodate the switch without interfering with its mode of operation. To ensure consistency of switch placement, all variations include a means for anchoring the lower edge of the switch bib.

**HEAD MOUNTS.** Mercury switches are frequently used to train children to hold their head erect. Although such switches are sometimes attached to the child's hair with barrettes (Figure 4.36a) (Burkhart, 1980), they are more frequently attached to a headband worn by the child (Figure 4.36b). As one might expect, the usefulness of such an option is greatly compromised when the headgear does not maintain a constant position on the child's head. Although many of the commercially available options work well with adults, they are often less than optimal when used with children demonstrating considerable extraneous head movement.

In general, the stability of a head mount is greatly enhanced when the mount design includes a headband, two perpendicular crown bands, and a chin band (Figure 4.36c). This headband is also suitable for children using a light-beam indicator or an infrared sensor. Adhesive Velcro or loops of dressmaker elastic can be used to attach the mercury switch, light-beam indicator, or infrared sensor to the headgear (male Velcro on the mercury switch, light-beam indicator, infrared sensor; female Velcro on the headgear).

As depicted in Figure 4.36d, a chin pointer helmet can also be adapted to accommodate presentation of a tongue- or mouth-activated switch interface (Zygo Industries, Inc.). Although this option has the advantage of ensuring correct placement of the switch regardless of the movement of the head, it is more physically intrusive than the previously discussed options. As illustrated in Figure 4.36e, a visor can also be used to allow an attached roller lever switch to capitalize on movement of the eyebrow or forehead. All other factors being equal, however, switches mounted adjacent to the child's body are considered preferable to those mounted on the child's body (Wright & Nomura, 1985).

## Summary

The switch mount is the structure that positions the switch interface in a desired location relative to the control site. It must therefore be noninterfering, safe, flexible, cosmetically pleasing, and above all, stable. Switch mounts can assume a variety of forms. Several companies offer kits allowing mounts to be constructed from commercially available adaptive fixtures. A less-expensive, yet highly flexible alternative is available using CPVC pipes and fittings, which can be purchased in your local hardware store. Switches can also be embedded in the child's wheelchair headrest. For children using their hand as the control site, angled Ethafoam switch mounts can be used to simplify the required motor response. Such mounts allow the switch activation surface to be presented recessed, flush, or low profile relative to the surface of the mount. Several options also exist for positioning switches on the body. Included in this category are chin or chest mounts, glasses, various headgear, and switch bibs. It has been speculated that the more consistent the required motor response can be made, the faster the rate of acquisition. Because the switch mount is the structure that positions the switch in the path of the target movement pattern, considerable attention must be directed toward its construction.

Now that a viable switch setup has been delineated, attention can be directed toward delineating a scanning selection technique in keeping with the child's motor, visual, and cognitive strengths and weaknesses. Before this can occur, however, readers may wish to familiarize themselves with the variety of scanning selection techniques that are available. Chapter 5 provides such an overview.

a. Barrettes
(Burkhart 1987)

b. Headband
construction

c. Headgear
of dressmaker
elastic

d. Zygo Chin Pointer
modified to
accommodate a
tongue or bite switch

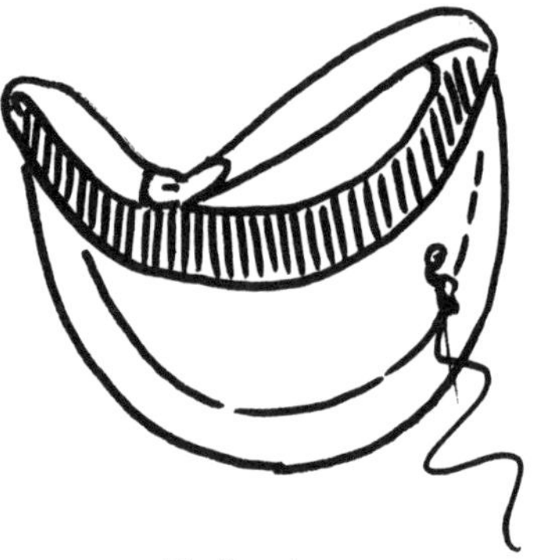

e. Roller lever
switch mounted
on underside of
sun visor

**FIGURE 4.36.** Head mounts.

chapter 5

# Scanning Selection Techniques

Technology currently offers users of electronic scanning communication devices a wide variety of scanning selection techniques—techniques that possess very different component scanning features. For example, consider the following scanning selection techniques.

Amanda, 3 years of age, utilizes a circular scanner accessed by a single switch (Figure 5.1). Initiating and releasing contact with the switch causes the scanning indicator (rotating needle) to move in a clockwise direction, scanning selection set items displayed in its circular path. Reinitiating contact with the switch stops the scanning indicator, thereby targeting a desired message element.

Keisha, 6 years of age, utilizes a personal computer with scanning software that employs a row-column scan pattern (Figure 5.2). Selection set items are arranged in a matrix of rows and columns. Keisha accesses the device using a single switch. Selection set items are initially scanned in groups, row by row in a downward direction from top to bottom of the computer screen. When Keisha activates her switch, the indicator begins to move across the selected row, proceeding element by element in a left to right direction. A second activation of the switch then stops the indicator on a desired item. After a preset length of time, the selected item is entered for voice-output communication.

**FIGURE 5.1.** Scanning selection techniques—Amanda.

**FIGURE 5.2.** Scanning selection techniques—Keisha.

Will, 12 years of age, utilizes a voice-output communication device that allows for directed scanning (Figure 5.3). Will accesses the device with a joystick control interface. Using the joystick, Will is able to control the direction of the scanning indicator, moving it up, down, left, right, or diagonally. Will is thus able to move the indicator directly to a target item in the selection set by maintaining switch activation with the joystick in the desired direction. Release of the joystick stops the indicator on the target item. Activation of an additional knee-activated single switch enters the selected item for voice output.

The fact that the techniques described differ significantly is readily apparent. The features by which the techniques differ, however, may not be as readily apparent to the novice therapist. These features must therefore be defined prior to selecting the scanning technique that best meets children's needs and is most in keeping with their visual, motor, and cognitive capabilities. As outlined in Table 5.1, scanning selection techniques can be defined relative to three major component scanning features: scan process, scan pattern, and scan mode. With respect to scan process, scanning selection techniques are categorized as either a preset scanning technique or a directed scanning technique. Provided in this chapter is a discussion of preset scanning techniques and directed scanning techniques along with their component features of scan pattern and scan mode. The discussion is limited to those techniques most frequently employed with children. For information pertaining to more elaborate scanning selection techniques, the reader is referred to Vanderheiden (1988).

**FIGURE 5.3.** Scanning selection techniques—Will.

## Preset Scanning

Preset scanning is a process in which the scanning indicator (i.e., rotating needle, cursor, light-emitting diode) moves in a predefined, predictable pattern controlled by the electronic scanning device. As indicated in Table 5.1, a number of scan patterns including linear, circular, row-column, and block are all considered preset scan patterns. When using a preset scan process, the child selects desired items in the selection set as they are systematically highlighted by the scanning indicator during the scanning process. Depending on the needs and abilities of the child, the selection set may consist of single letters, words, or phrases/sentences. When using code-based formats (abbreviated letter codes, semantic compaction), the selection set includes the code elements necessary for calling forth preprogrammed messages. Although a selection set is usually represented visually on the scanner display, the selection set can also be presented auditorially and accessed via a technique known as auditory scanning. When using auditory scanning, each item in the selection set is presented to the child via voice output throughout the scanning process. Within this chapter, attention is directed solely toward visual scanning techniques. Should readers desire further information relative to auditory scanning techniques, they are referred to the work of Beukelman et al. (1985), Blackstone (1988), and Fried-Oken (1988).

### Preset Scanning: Scan Patterns

Scan pattern is defined as the direction or path in which the scanning indicator moves during the scanning process. As reflected in Table 5.1,

**TABLE 5.1.** Scanning Selection Techniques

| Scan Process | Scan Pattern | | Scan Mode |
|---|---|---|---|
| Preset Scanning | Element | Linear | Automatic Inverse Step |
| | | Circular | Automatic Inverse Step |
| | Group-Element | Row-Column | Automatic Inverse Step |
| | | Block | Automatic Inverse Step |
| | | Page | Automatic Inverse Step |
| | Group-Group-Element | Page-Row-Column | Automatic Inverse Step |
| Directed Scanning | Element | Variable | Inverse Step |

three major types of preset scan patterns can be delineated:

- ❑ Element
- ❑ Group-element
- ❑ Group-group-element

In general, scan patterns vary with respect to the increments in which selection set items are scanned. When an element scan pattern is employed, items are sequentially scanned one by one (Lee & Thomas, 1990). When group-element and group-group-element patterns are used, items in the selection set are initially scanned as groups (e.g., row by row, block by block, page by page, page-row-column), and only later are scanned element by element within the previously selected group.[1] As presented in Table 5.1, specific patterns exist within all three major types of preset scan patterns.

**ELEMENT PATTERNS.** As illustrated in Figure 5.4, preset element scanning can be achieved using either a linear or a circular pattern. When using a linear pattern, the scanning indicator moves element by element in a linear direction across each row on the scanner display (Figure 5.4a) (Fishman, 1987; Vanderheiden, 1988). With most scanning devices, the scanning indicator advances in a left to right direction. When the scanning indicator reaches the end of the row, it reappears at the far left of either (a) the same row when scanning is conducted using a single row (unidimensional display) or (b) the following row when a matrix configuration (two-dimensional display) is employed. An exception to this left to right progression, however, is a linear pattern in which the indicator begins at the far left of the first row in a two-row, eight-location matrix, but reverses its direction, moving right to left once it drops to the following row. This linear pattern is referred to as pseudocircular (Figure 5.4b).

When a circular pattern is employed, the scanning indicator moves in a circular direction either clockwise or counterclockwise, scanning items element by element within its circular path (Figure 5.4c). Circular patterns are employed by devices known as circular, dial, rotary, or clock scanners. As depicted in Figure 5.4c, the scanning indicator on a circular scanner may be in the form of a rotating needle that scans items displayed in its circular path or a light that sequentially highlights items displayed in a circular format on the scanner display. Some rotary devices are designed to accommodate two-switch interfaces (Don Johnston Developmen-

[1]Group-element and group-group-element scanning are also referred to as two-dimensional and three-dimensional scanning, respectively (Lee & Thomas, 1990; Vanderheiden & Lloyd, 1986).

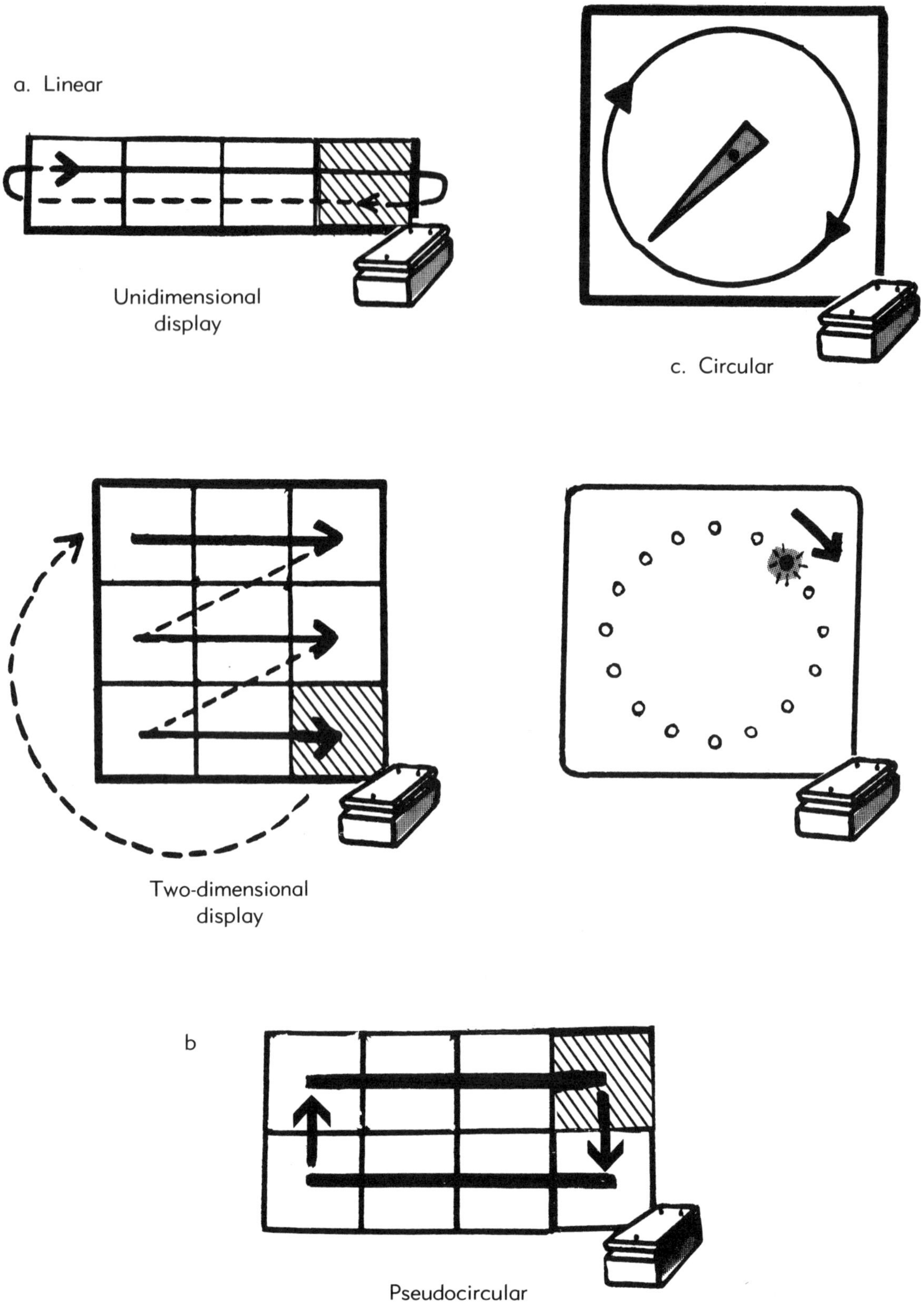

a. Linear
Unidimensional display
Two-dimensional display
c. Circular
b
Pseudocircular

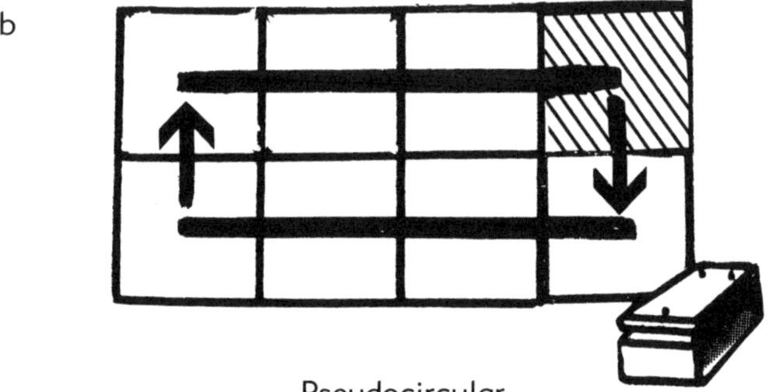

**FIGURE 5.4.** Preset element scanning.

tal Equipment, Steven Kanor, PhD, Inc.). One switch interface moves the scanning indicator in a clockwise direction; the second switch interface moves the indicator in a counterclockwise direction. As the use of two-switch interfaces allows the child to move the scanning indicator in the direction closest to the target item, selection rate is hypothetically increased.

Preset element scanning (whether it be a linear or a circular pattern) is typically considered the simplest type of scanning (Vanderheiden, 1988). "Message elements are presented one at a time and the child simply responds when the aide gets to the one he wants" (p. 33). Preset element scanning, however, is a relatively slow means of access. As a result, preset element scan patterns are usually restricted to small selection sets—that is, selection sets of fewer than 10 items (Lee & Thomas, 1990; Vanderheiden & Lloyd, 1986). Preset group-element scan patterns or directed scanning are generally preferred for selection sets beyond 10 items (Fishman, 1987; Lee & Thomas, 1990; Vanderheiden & Lloyd, 1986). Although larger selection sets should ideally employ a preset group-element pattern or a directed scanning process, many young or cognitively impaired children may not possess the motoric and cognitive abilities required by these techniques. Preset element scan patterns are thus often employed during the early stages of intervention with larger selection sets, realizing that selection rate will be slow. Maria, for example, is 3 years of age and needs more than 10 message elements for expressive communication. Because the cognitive and motoric requirements of a group-element pattern are too demanding, training was initiated using an element (linear) pattern with 20 items in the selection set.

**GROUP-ELEMENT AND GROUP-GROUP-ELEMENT PATTERNS.** As previously defined, group-element and group-group-element scan patterns highlight items in the selection set initially as groups and subsequently element by element within the selected group. Because these scan patterns, by design, decrease the number of items that must be individually scanned prior to selecting a target item, rate of selection is typically increased (Fishman, 1987; Vanderheiden & Lloyd, 1986). As indicated in Table 5.1, group-element scan patterns include row-column scanning, block scanning, and page scanning.

*Row-column scanning* is the most frequently employed group-element scan pattern (Fishman, 1987; Vanderheiden, 1988). When row-column scanning is employed, selection set items are typically arranged in a matrix of rows and columns. As visualized in Figure 5.5, items are initially scanned row by row in a downward direction on the scanner display. The switch interface is then activated to select the row containing the target item. Having selected the desired row, items are then scanned one by one in a left to right direction across the selected row. When the desired item within the row is highlighted by the scanning indicator, activation of the switch interface stops the scan process, allowing the targeted item to be entered for visual, spoken, and/or printed output. In the event the item selected is not the item of choice, some scanning devices possess a delay feature that can be employed to negate unwanted selections (Light Talker, Prentke Romich Company). A delay feature provides the child with a time period in which the scanning process can be reinitiated prior to the entry of a selected item. Corrections can thus be made prior to having unwanted items processed by the scanning device. In the absence of a delay feature, a selected item is automatically entered for visual, spoken, and/or printed output.

As illustrated in Figure 5.6, *block scanning* is a group- element pattern in which selection set items are scanned in blocks or clusters on the scanner display (Scan Pac, Adaptive Communication Systems). When using block scanning, items are scanned block by block until the child selects the block containing the desired item. Items within the selected block are then scanned one at a time until the target item is selected by a second activation of the switch.

The final group-element scan pattern to be discussed is that of *page scanning* (Vanderheiden, 1988). With page scanning, large groups of vocabulary items that exceed the space of small selection screens or displays are presented in page form on a larger display such as a computer screen. When using page scanning, the child initially selects the page containing the target item by activating a switch interface. Items within the selected page are then scanned element by element. For even larger selection sets, page scanning may take the form of a group-group-element pattern. According to Vanderheiden (1988), "this could take the form of

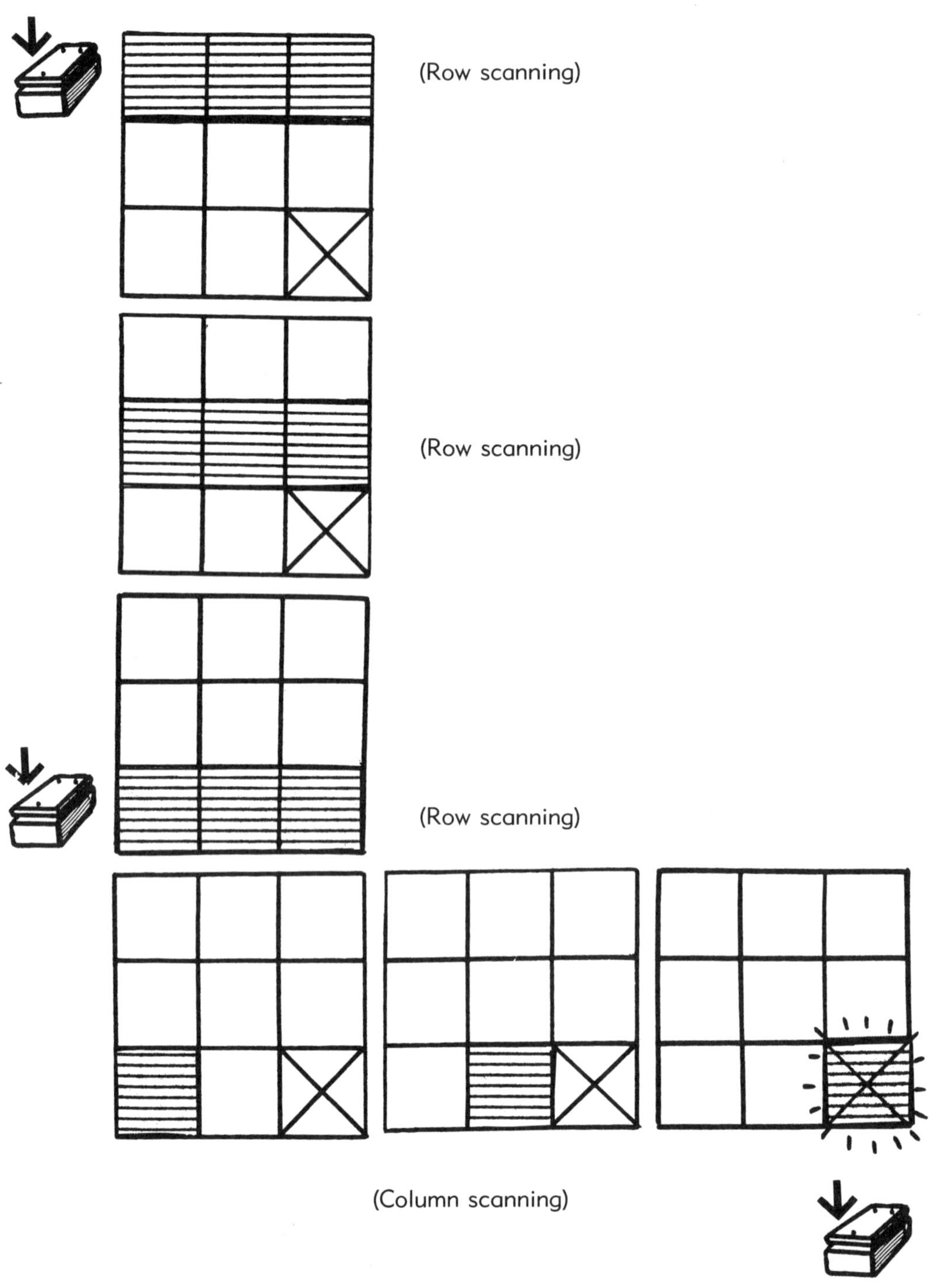


**FIGURE 5.5.** Preset row-column scanning.

page-row-column scanning, or, on very large displays, large square sections of the panel may be indicated first, followed by row and then by items'' (p. 23).

## Preset Scanning: Scan Modes

Preset scanning selection techniques also differ in the scan mode they employ. Scan mode is defined

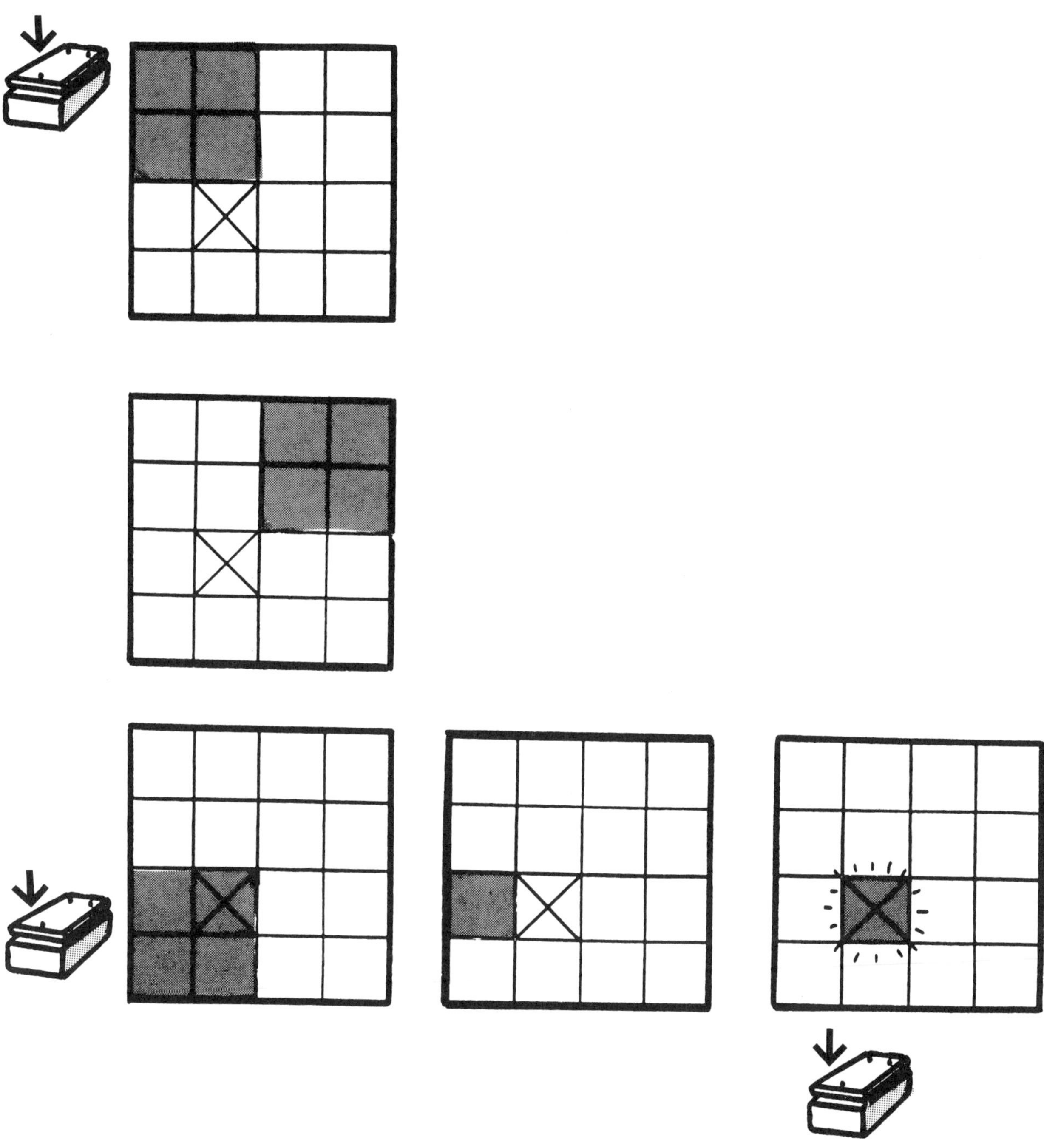

**FIGURE 5.6.** Preset block scanning.

as the manner in which the switch interface(s) operates in conjunction with the scanning device to achieve the scanning process. As reflected in Table 5.1, preset scanning can be realized using three basic techniques or modes that vary with respect to the switch accessing skills required for access (i.e., initiating, maintaining, and releasing contact with the switch interface). Scan modes also vary with respect to whether switch closure is achieved within a timed format or an untimed format (Lee & Thomas, 1990). Discussed in this section of the chapter are the three basic modes of scanning and the switch accessing skills that will be required to use each of them:

- ❑ Automatic mode
- ❑ Inverse mode
- ❑ Step mode

**AUTOMATIC MODE.** With an automatic mode, the scanning indicator advances automatically through the selection set in a predefined path, at a user-defined scanning speed. When a target item is highlighted by the scanning indicator, the child stops the scanning process by quickly initiating contact with the switch interface (Lee & Thomas, 1990).

Anticipation of the advancing cursor arriving at a target item and the subsequent timed switch activation to select that target item are thus the primary skill requirements for successful implementation of an automatic mode (Lee & Thomas, 1990). Because the scanning indicator moves automatically when the scanning process is initiated, maintained contact is not required. Table 5.2 summarizes the switch accessing skills required when using an automatic scan mode.

Many children demonstrate difficulty with the anticipatory timing component of initiating switch contact required by an automatic scan mode. For example, Tony is a child who exhibits increased tone when he is required to perform a timed initiation of switch contact. He frequently demonstrates either premature or delayed switch activations. For children such as Tony, the use of an inverse or step mode may be preferred.

**INVERSE MODE.** When an inverse scan mode is being used, the scanning indicator does not automatically advance through the selection set. Rather, the child advances the scanning indicator in its preset pattern by maintaining contact with the switch interface. When the target item is highlighted by the scanning indicator, the child stops the scanning process by quickly releasing contact with the switch interface (Lee & Thomas, 1990).

As is the case with an automatic scan mode, anticipation of the scanning indicator advancing toward and arriving at a target item is an integral feature of an inverse scan mode. In contrast to an automatic scan mode, however, the child is required to (a) maintain activation of the switch interface to sustain the scanning process and (b) perform an anticipated timed release rather than an anticipated timed activation of the switch interface to stop the scanning process on the target item. For some children, gravity can be used to assist in releasing switch contact by using an inverted or angled switch mount. With such a setup, the child exerts a small amount of extension to maintain switch activation and merely relaxes to move down off of the switch. Table 5.3 summarizes the switch accessing skills required for an inverse scan mode.

**STEP MODE.** When using a step scan mode, the child advances the scanning indicator one item at a time. Each time the child initiates contact with the switch interface, the scanning indicator advances one step in the scan pattern. When the scanning indicator highlights the target item, the child merely waits a preset length of time for the desired item to be automatically entered for visual, voice, and/or printed output (Lee & Thomas, 1990).

A step scan mode is considered to be easier than an automatic or an inverse mode for the following reasons:

1. Generally, step scanning does *not* require a true timing component to either initiate or release contact with the switch interface. The child is merely required to perform an untimed activation of the switch interface to advance the scanning indicator to the next item. Thus, the child has complete control over the scan rate and movement of the scanning indicator (Lee & Thomas, 1990). It should, however, be noted that with some scanning systems, release of the switch interface must be performed relatively quickly to prevent the scanning indicator from advancing as if it were operating within an inverse mode.
2. Step scanning does *not* involve the anticipation of the scanning indicator automatically advancing toward a target item (Lee & Thomas, 1990). As previously discussed, the child has complete control over the movement of the scanning indicator, advancing at a user-defined pace, one item at a time with each switch activation. In contrast to an automatic or an inverse scan mode in which the device presents choices and waits for the child to select a choice, a step scan mode places movement of the scanning indicator more directly under the control of the child. Because step scanning retains more of a

**TABLE 5.2.** Switch Accessing Skills Required for an Automatic Scan Mode

| To Start the Scan | To Maintain the Scan | To Stop the Scan | To Select the Target Item |
|---|---|---|---|
| Untimed activation of the switch interface | Indicator scans automatically; maintained activation of the switch interface not required | Timed activation of the switch interface | Automatic entry<br>Manual entry |

direct selection component than an automatic or an inverse scan mode, it has been described as a pseudoscanning technique (Vanderheiden, 1975).

3. Step scanning does *not* require the child to coordinate visual scanning with the motor act of accessing the switch. Instead, the child is merely required to visually attend to one item at a time as he or she advances the scanning indicator.

Although generally considered to be easier, step scanning does require repetitive switch activations. Fatigue secondary to multiple activations may therefore be a problem for some children. Summarized in Table 5.4 are the switch accessing skills required for a step scan mode.

As previously indicated in Table 5.1, all three scan modes can be utilized with a full range of scan patterns when employed in preset scanning. They can also be achieved with either one- or two-switch interfaces. As outlined in Table 5.5, the use of a second switch interface affords the child greater control over both the scanning process and the actual selection of target vocabulary items. Although the use of two-switch interfaces can provide the child with greater control and speed, the reader should be cognizant that two-switch scanning is often motorically and cognitively more difficult for the child than single-switch scanning. Single-switch scanning is therefore usually introduced prior to two-switch scanning in the intervention process.

## Directed Scanning

In contrast to preset scanning (i.e., a process that employs a predefined, device-controlled pattern), directed scanning places the scan pattern under the child's control. Using multiple switch interfaces, the child has the flexibility of moving the scanning indicator up, down, left, right, or diagonally directly toward target items in the selection array. The pattern of scan thus varies according to the location of target items on the scanner display. Because the child is not required to wait as the scanning indicator highlights unwanted items while moving in a preset pattern, the selection process may be achieved more rapidly with directed scanning than with preset scanning. Because the child is required to define the scan pattern and use multiple switch interfaces to control that pattern, however, the motor, visual, and cognitive skills required by directed scanning are typically considered to be greater than those required by preset scanning.

As previously noted directed scanning is achieved using more than one switch. A joystick control, for example, houses at least four switches, each switch

**TABLE 5.3.** Switch Accessing Skills Required for an Inverse Scan Mode

| To Start the Scan | To Maintain the Scan | To Stop the Scan | To Select the Target Item |
|---|---|---|---|
| Untimed activation of the switch interface | Maintained activation of the switch interface | Timed release of the switch interface<br>Manual entry | Automatic entry |

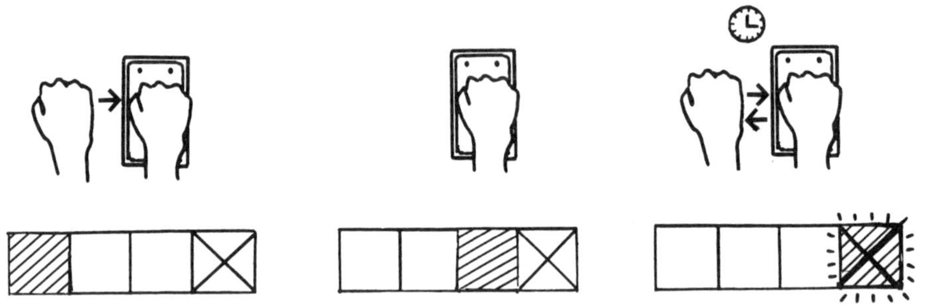

**TABLE 5.4.** Switch Accessing Skills Required for a Step Scan Mode

| To Start the Scan | To Maintain the Scan | To Stop the Scan | To Select the Target Item |
|---|---|---|---|
| Untimed activation of the switch interface | Untimed activations of the switch interface | Varies with the scanning device. For some, an untimed release is all that is required. For others, a quick release is required to prevent the scanning indicator from advancing to the next item as if operating in an inverse scan mode. | Automatic entry<br>Manual entry |

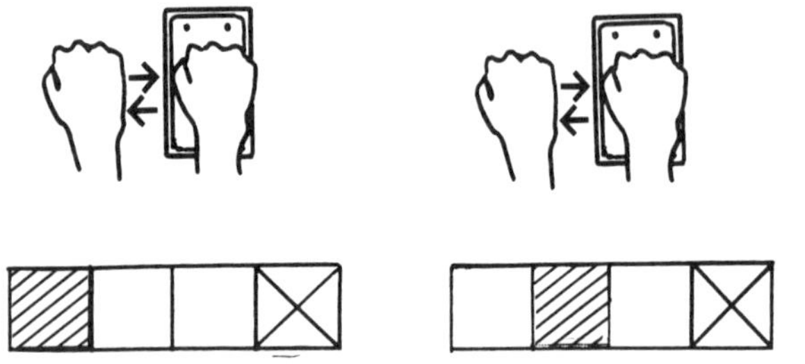

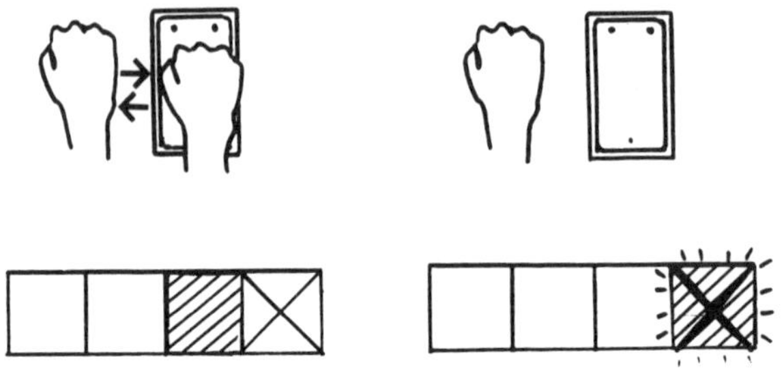

**TABLE 5.5.** Two-Switch Preset Scanning

| Scan Mode | Description |
|---|---|
| Two-switch automatic scanning | Same as automatic scanning with a single-switch interface. The addition of a second switch allows the user to exit from an incorrect row during the scanning process. |
| Two-switch inverse scanning | Maintained activation of one switch advances the scanning indicator to the target item. Timed activation of a second switch interface enters the target item for visual, voice, and/or printed output. |
| Two-switch step scanning | Repeated activation of one switch advances the scanning indicator to the target item. Timed activation of a second switch enters the target item for visual, voice, and/or printed output. |

*Note.* Adapted from *Control of Computer-Based Technology for People with Physical Disabilities* by K S. Lee and D. J. Thomas, 1990, Toronto, Canada: University of Toronto Press.

controlling a different direction. As illustrated in Figure 5.7, pushing the joystick in one of the four directions moves the scanning indicator in the corresponding direction on the scanner display. With some joysticks, pushing the joystick diagonally permits diagonal movement of the scanning indicator.

Directed scanning can also be achieved with a multiswitch array. When performing directed scanning with a multiswitch array, two to four switches are employed. As illustrated in Figure 5.8, a *two-switch array* allows the child to move the scanning indicator in at least two directions. Typically, one switch interface moves the indicator in a downward direction. The second switch interface moves the indicator to the right across the scanner display (Fishman, 1987). As illustrated in Figure 5.9, movement in all four directions (up, down, left, right) can also be achieved with two-switch interfaces, provided the scanning device possesses a reverse function feature. A reverse function allows the scanning indicator to reverse its direction when the switch interface is activated a second time (Lee & Thomas, 1990).

For the child who is capable of accessing four separate switches, a *four-switch array* can be employed. As depicted in Figure 5.10, each switch in the array moves the scanning indicator in a different direction, similar to a joystick control. In some instances, an additional switch may be added to the array to allow the child to enter a target item for processing by the scanning device. This additional

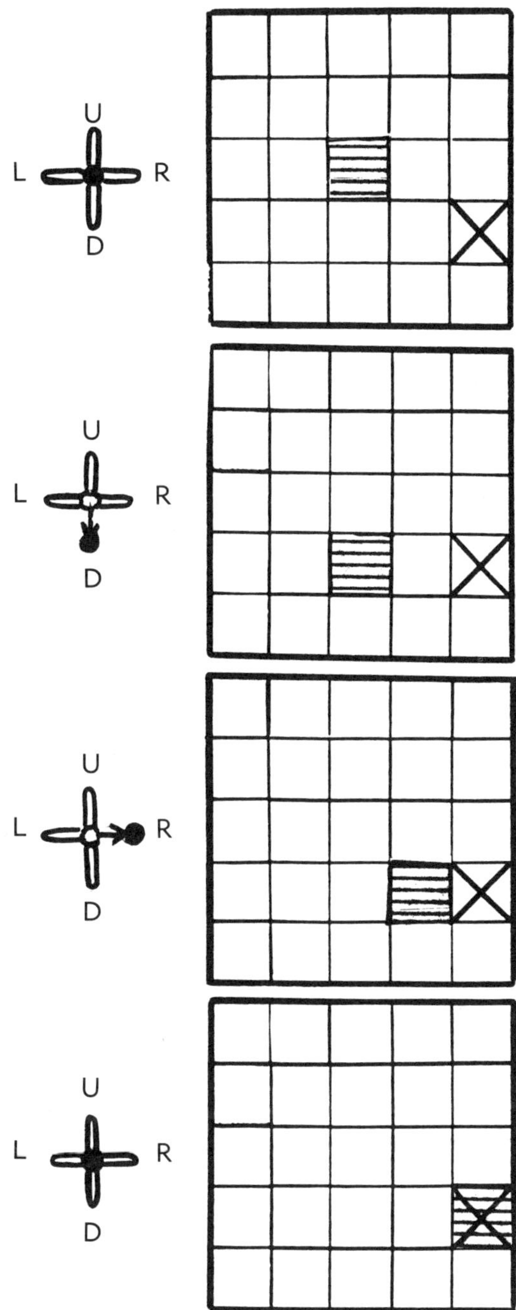


**FIGURE 5.7.** Directed scanning using a joystick control.

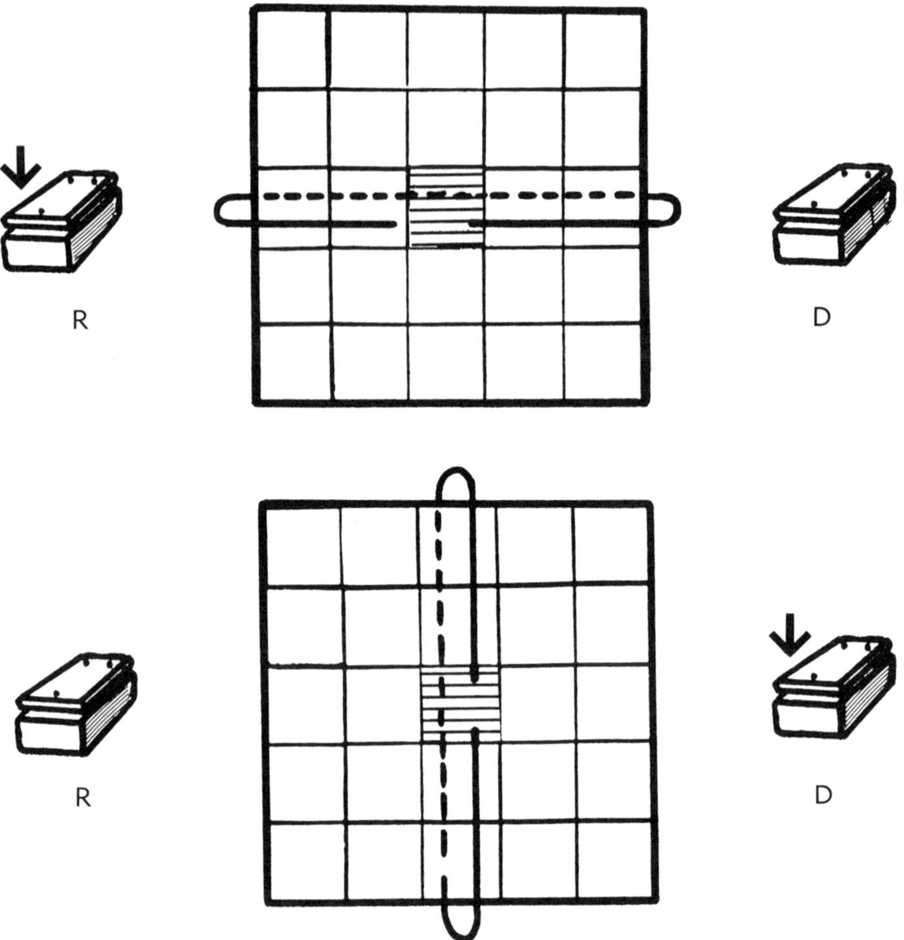


**FIGURE 5.8.** Directed scanning using a two-switch array or dual switch.

switch interface is usually referred to as the *select* or *manual entry switch.* (In some instances, the additional switch in the array may also be used as a call signal or as a means for turning the scanning device on and off.) When the target item is highlighted by the scanning indicator, the child activates the manual entry switch, thus entering that item for visual, voice, and/or printed output. When a joystick control is used for the scanning process, entry may be achieved using (a) an additional single switch, (b) a manual entry feature, or (c) an automatic entry feature. When using a *manual entry feature,* the child is required to perform an additional switch activation to enter the item for processing by the device. Although manual entry requires an additional switch activation, use of this option provides the child greater control over the selection of target items, thereby minimizing the frequency of incorrect selections (Light Talker, Prentke Romich Company). When an *automatic entry feature* is employed, the child merely waits a preset length of time after selection, after which the item is automatically entered. This time period is referred to as the *acceptance time.*

When performing directed scanning, the scanning indicator advances element by element. Although directed scanning can be achieved with either an inverse or step scan mode,[2] an inverse mode is the more frequently employed of the two modes.

Many devices employing directed scanning utilize a feature known as *centering* (Prentke Romich Company, Zygo Industries). When centering is operative, the scanning indicator automatically

[2]Also referred to as multiple step scan and single step scan modes, respectively (Fishman, 1987; Zygo Industries, Inc., 1983).

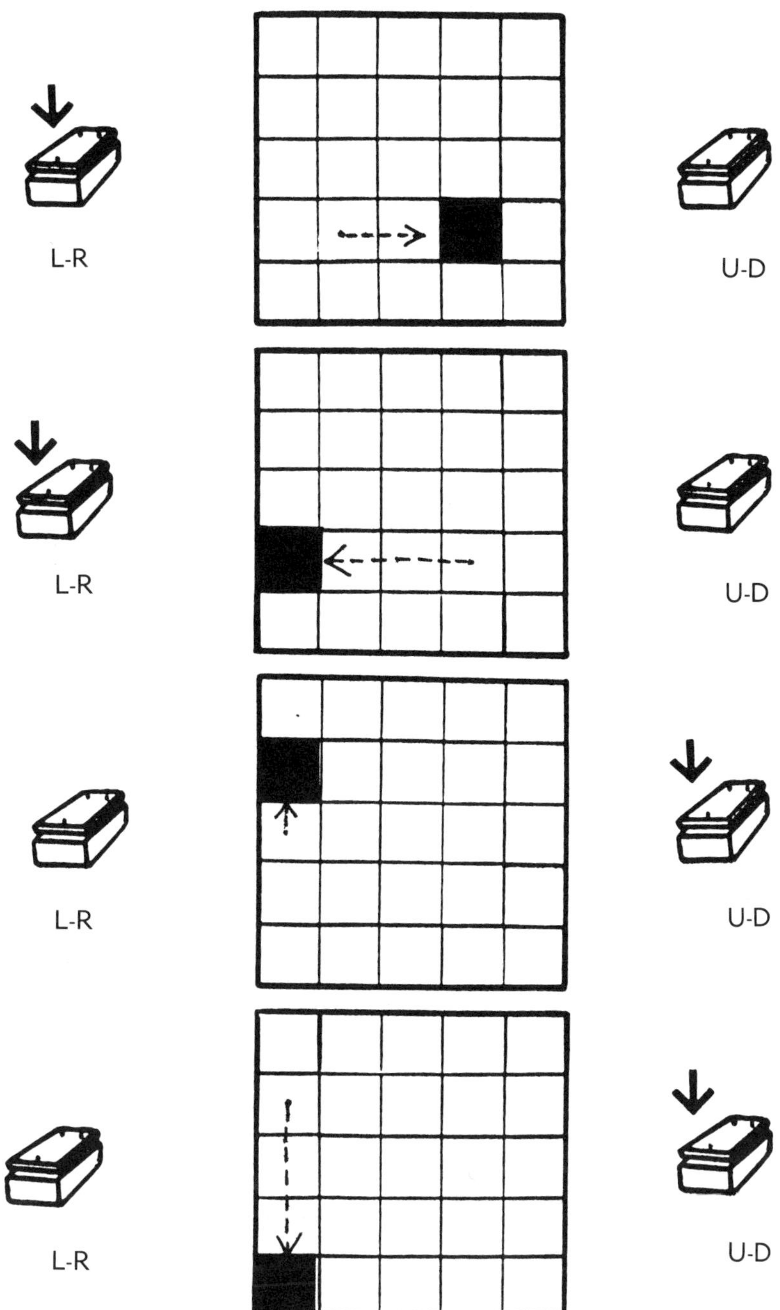


**FIGURE 5.9.** Two-switch scanning using a reverse function.

returns to the center of the scanner display after each selection. Because the "home base" for the scanning indicator is centrally located with respect to all items in the selection set, rate of selection is generally enhanced. To further accelerate the selection process, the most frequently used items can be located in the area closest to this central location. In addition to enhancing rate of selection, centering appears to play an important role in routinizing the child's cognitive and motor planning. Because the scanning process is always initiated from the same point or "home base" on the scanner display, the unique path required for selecting a particular item can remain constant across repeated selections of that particular item. Thus, the act of selecting a target item can become increasingly subconscious over repeated trials, thereby minimizing cognitive and motor planning.

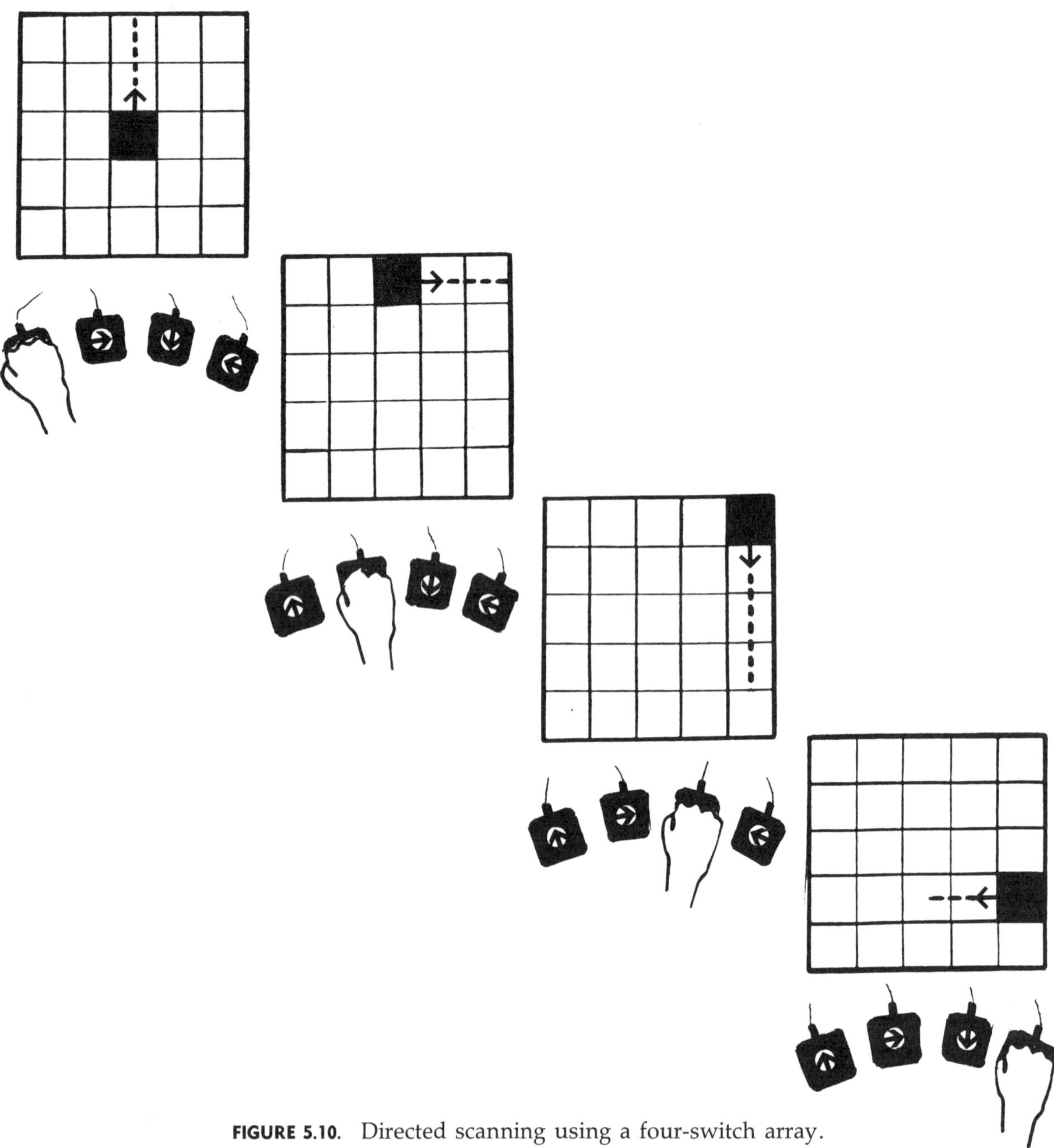

**FIGURE 5.10.** Directed scanning using a four-switch array.

## Summary

A broad range of scanning selection techniques are available to the potential user of a scanning communication device. In general, these techniques vary according to three major components: scan process (preset vs. directed), scan pattern (element vs. group-element vs. group-group-element), and scan mode (automatic, inverse, step). When using a preset scanning process, the scanning indicator moves in a predefined, predictable pattern controlled by the electronic scanning device. When using directed scanning, the scan pattern is under the user's control, allowing the child to directly move the scanning indicator up, down, left, right, or diagonally to desired items in the selection array.

Within preset scanning a variety of scan patterns are feasible: element scanning (linear, circular, pseudocircular), group-element scanning (e.g., row-column, block, page), and group-group-element scanning (page-row-column). In general, the use of element scan patterns is restricted to selection sets of fewer than 10 items; group-element and group-group-element patterns are generally preferred for selection sets larger than 10 items because rate of access is greatly enhanced. Because element scan patterns are visually and cognitively easier, however, they are frequently employed with cognitively young children.

Scanning selection techniques also differ in scan modes—that is, the manner in which the switch interface(s) operates in conjunction with the scanning device to achieve the scanning process. Whereas an automatic scan mode requires an anticipatory timed initiation to stop the scan process, an inverse scan mode requires an anticipatory timed release to stop the scanning action. Because a step scan mode merely requires the child to initiate and release contact with the switch in an untimed format, it is often the mode of choice for early intervention.

Within directed scanning, scanning is achieved using either a joystick or a multiswitch array. When a centering feature is employed, rate of selection is often enhanced because the child's cognitive and motor planning can become highly routinized. Directed scanning is often preferred over preset scanning, because it allows the child to access large arrays more quickly. Directed scanning is, however, believed to be motorically and cognitively more difficult than preset scanning.

A clear understanding of the component features and the skills required for each scanning selection technique is crucial to delineating the technique most in keeping with a child's current cognitive, visual, and motor skills. With this knowledge the facilitator is better able to assess and train an appropriate scanning selection technique. In Chapter 6, attention is directed toward providing the reader with specific strategies for systematically training various scanning selection techniques.

chapter 6

# DETERMINING AND TRAINING SCANNING SELECTION TECHNIQUES

LIGHT ET AL. (1988) described augmentative communication training as the process of acquiring operational, linguistic, and social knowledge. Very generally, the child must be able to reliably and effortlessly access an augmentative communication system (operational knowledge) to effectively utilize that system for communicative exchange (social and linguistic knowledge). Without operational knowledge, the child is unable to either acquire or successfully demonstrate social and linguistic knowledge.

To establish effective use of an augmentative communication system, considerable attention must therefore be directed toward training the accessing skills (operational knowledge) required for using a scanning communication device. This chapter provides a discussion of intervention strategies for training the accessing skills dictated by various scanning selection techniques. Because assessment strategies are often synonymous with many of our intervention strategies, the majority of tasks and issues presented are applicable to the assessment as well as the intervention process.

## General Training Issues

General training issues as discussed in this section include the following:

- ❑ Intuitive generalities
- ❑ The need for parallel programming
- ❑ The need for a layered approach

### Intuitive Generalities

Scanning selection techniques vary with respect to their visual, motor, and cognitive skill requirements. Presently, little empirical data exist regarding the relative difficulty of the various scanning selection techniques. In the absence of empirical information, however, many facilitators intuitively adhere to the following generalities regarding the skills associated with various scanning selection techniques: scan process, scan pattern, and scan mode.

**SCAN PROCESS.** Directed scanning is generally preferred over preset scanning, because it allows for faster rates of message selection. In general, however, preset scanning techniques are considered to be easier, because they do not require the child to:

- ❑ Mentally plan the scan pattern in keeping with the relative location of subsequent target items
- ❑ Utilize multiple switch interfaces to control the scan pattern

**SCAN PATTERN.** Preset group-element patterns (e.g., row-column) are often preferred over preset element patterns (e.g., linear), because they allow the child to more quickly access a larger array. Although array size is usually limited with regard to an element pattern (given the time required to scan a large array element by element), an element pattern is considered to be a cognitively easier and more straightforward pattern (Vanderheiden, 1988).

**SCAN MODE.** Automatic and inverse modes are generally preferred over a step mode, because they are more frequently employed in group-element preset scanning and directed scanning—scan patterns that allow for faster scanning of large message arrays. Because a step mode does not require the child to perform an anticipated timed initiation or release, however, it is generally easier for many children (provided the children are capable of performing repeated switch activations without fatiguing). The relative ease of performing an automatic versus an inverse scan mode is in large part dependent on children's relative ability to perform an anticipated timed initiation (automatic) versus an anticipated timed release (inverse) of switch contact.

## The Need for Parallel Programming

Ideally, a scanning selection technique should allow the child to access the largest selection set possible in the least amount of time, with the least amount of effort. As a general rule, however, techniques that allow for rapid scanning of large selection sets are cognitively and motorically more difficult than techniques that do not afford the user these benefits. Initially, a less demanding technique such as element scanning may be utilized to ensure ease of communication. Because array size and selection rate are limited when using element scanning, this technique should be viewed as an initial rather than a long-range option for many children. In preparation for advancing the child to a more efficient but more difficult technique, the facilitator should consider adopting the concept of parallel programming. When conducting parallel programming, the skills required by the next-more-advanced selection technique are trained concurrent to the child's communicative use of a less taxing technique. More specifically, parallel training efforts may be directed toward:

- ❑ Training the skills required by a more advanced or sophisticated scanning technique that will ultimately allow the child to more quickly access a larger message array
- ❑ Training the skills required by an ultimately faster selection technique such as direct selection using an optical head-pointer

Parallel programming thus ensures that the child's therapeutic plan is not shortsighted in its long-range focus. It allows the child to take the path of least resistance to mediate communicative exchange, but continues to "ready" the child to advance to the communicative use of a more sophisticated and faster technique. By conducting parallel programming, the child may more smoothly transition from one technique to another. Consider the following three children:

**CASE B.C.** B.C., a 4-year-old child with cerebral palsy, initially received training in the use of a linear scanning technique. Because B.C. exhibited difficulty with the anticipatory timing requirements of an automatic and an inverse scan mode, linear scanning was initiated using the relatively untimed switch accessing skills of a step scan mode. When B.C. was communicating with a scanning device accessed using an element scan pattern and a step scan mode, parallel motor training was initiated in establishing the skills required for performing element scanning using an automatic scan mode. It is important to note that this parallel motor training was conducted in tasks primarily possessing a motor load, with the cognitive and communication load purposely minimized to reduce the task requirements.

**CASE D.J.** It was anticipated that D.J., a 5-year-old child with cerebral palsy, would ultimately access her scanning communication device using row-column scanning. During the initial stages of intervention, however, a row-column pattern proved too difficult for D.J. Communication training was therefore initiated using an automatic scan mode within the context of a simpler element (linear) scan pattern. Parallel motor training was then initiated to give D.J. practice using an automatic mode within the context of a more sophisticated row-column pattern. Parallel training was initially conducted in tasks possessing minimal cognitive and communication requirements. When D.J. was demonstrating a high degree of success with her parallel programming, steps were taken to allow her to access her communication device using row-column scanning.

**CASE J.M.** J.M., a 6-year-old child with cerebral palsy, initiated her communication training utilizing an automatic scan mode within a row-column scan pattern. Concurrent with her use of row-column scanning, J.M. underwent parallel motor training using an optical head-pointer (a faster but more physically taxing direct selection technique). Such training was initially conducted in the context of interactive games and motivating targeting tasks with minimal communication load. When J.M. was able to reliably access her communication device using an optical head-pointer in tasks with primarily a motor load, training was initiated within the context of tasks possessing greater communicative and cognitive load. Ultimately, J.M. was able to achieve communicative exchange more quickly using an optical head-pointer.

### The Need for a Layering Approach

As summarized in Table 6.1, proficient use of a scanning selection technique requires the child to simultaneously perform a variety of skills (i.e., visual, motor, cognitive, communication) within the context of an electronic scanning device. This multiplicity of skill requirements often proves problematic for many children undergoing training in the use of a scanning selection technique. To reduce the skill requirements and thus simplify a scanning selection technique during the initial stages of intervention, training should be conducted utilizing a layering approach. With a layering approach, intervention is initially directed toward training the motor skills dictated by scan mode. As the child gains proficiency with scan mode, the additional skill requirements of scan pattern are gradually and systematically added to the training task. Ultimately, an increased cognitive and communication load (purposely minimized in previous layers) is overlaid on the motor and visual requirements of the scanning task. The layering approach to training thus allows:

- ❑ The child to focus her or his attention on gaining proficiency with one new skill at a time
- ❑ The facilitator to more quickly identify specific components of the task that are proving problematic for the child. When component skills are introduced simultaneously from the outset of intervention, the facilitator experiences difficulty isolating the source of the child's difficulty.

## Specific Training Techniques Relative to the Layering Approach

As discussed, a layering approach is employed as a means of simplifying the scanning task for initial training. Specific information is presented in this section relative to:

- ❑ Training scan mode in tasks possessing minimal visual, cognitive, and communication load
- ❑ Training scan pattern in tasks with increased visual and cognitive load, but minimal communication load

### Training Scan Mode

The initial skills to be trained in the layering approach are the switch accessing skills required by scan mode. As discussed in Chapter 5, the ability to volitionally initiate and release contact with a switch is vital to the successful performance of all three scan modes (automatic, inverse, step). When performing an automatic scan mode, an anticipatory timed initiation is required to make a selection within the scan array. An inverse mode requires the child to perform an anticipatory timed release to target an item within the scan array. In direct contrast, a step scan mode requires only the ability to repetitively initiate and release contact with the switch within a relatively untimed format.

Many of the basic skills required for mastery of scan mode (whether automatic, inverse, or step) can be taught independent of scan pattern (element, group-element) using switch-accessed battery (DC)- or AC-powered rewards and computer software. Typically, the interfaced switch operates the end reward in either a direct (momentary) or a latching mode. When operating the switch in a direct mode, the child must initiate and maintain contact with the switch to start and maintain the activity of the interfaced reward. To stop the activity, the child must release contact with the switch. This mode of switch operation is most in keeping with an inverse scan mode. When the switch is operated in a latching mode, it performs similarly to a household light switch. That is, the child must initiate contact with the switch to turn the reward on, but does not have to maintain contact with the switch to sustain the

**TABLE 6.1.** General Skills Required by Scanning Selection Techniques

| Motor | Visual | Cognitive | Communication |
|---|---|---|---|
| Access single-, dual-, or multiple-switch interfaces to input the scanning device.<br>Perform the switch accessing skills of initiating, releasing, and/or maintaining switch contact as dictated by the scan mode employed. | Visually attend to the scan array and scan pattern.<br>Focus visual attention on a target item within the scan array while using peripheral vision to visually monitor the scanning indicator, advancing toward and eventually arriving at that target item. | Mentally make a selection from available choices within the selection set.<br>Mentally anticipate the pattern of scan.<br>Exhibit the attention span required for the scanning indicator to advance along its path to a given target item within the selection set.<br>Mentally plan the scan pattern in directed scanning based on the location of a target item within the selection set. | Learn the symbol set and message content contained in the scan array.<br>Learn to use the selection set interactively.<br>Learn the conversational skills required for multiple-turn conversational exchange. |

activity of the reward. To stop the activity, the child must reinitiate contact with the switch. This mode of switch operation is most in keeping with an automatic scan mode.

Most commercially available switches operate in a direct or momentary mode. Although switches operating in a latching mode (usually referred to as on/off switches) are considerably fewer in number, numerous devices exist that are capable of imparting an on/off function to direct mode switches. When such devices are interfaced between the direct mode switch and the reward (as depicted in Figure 6.1), the switch is able to control the reward in a manner comparable to an on/off switch. Table 6.2 presents a listing of commercially available latching devices.

Numerous resources are available for adapting battery (DC)-powered rewards to permit switch access (Burkhart, 1980, 1982; Goossens' & Crain, 1986a, 1986b; Lynn, 1985; Musselwhite & St. Louis, 1988; Wright & Nomura, 1985). Two such options (nonpermanent wafer method and permanent method) are illustrated in Figure 6.2. (For information on adapting radio-controlled toys, the reader is referred to Burkhart [1980].)

When using switches to access AC-powered rewards, it is imperative that the facilitator safeguard the child from the possibility of electrical shock (Figure 6.3). Listed in Table 6.3 are several commercially available devices that allow AC-powered devices to be safely used as switch-accessed rewards.

If the computer is to serve as the interfaced reward, steps must be taken to adapt the computer to accept the switch as an alternate input device (Figure 6.4). When using an Apple computer, this can be achieved via (a) the internal 16-pin game port (Figure 6.4a), (b) the external 9-pin joystick port (Figure 6.4b), or (c) an internal circuit card (Adaptive Firmware Card by Adaptive Peripherals, Inc.) (Figure 6.4c). When using either the internal game port option or the external joystick port option, the child is able to operate only software that has been specifically designed for single switch operation. When using the Adaptive Firmware Card, the child is able to use a single switch to access all standard software. The latter is made possible through a scanning array reflecting the keyboard that will automatically appear at either the top or bottom of the computer screen. The child then uses a scanning

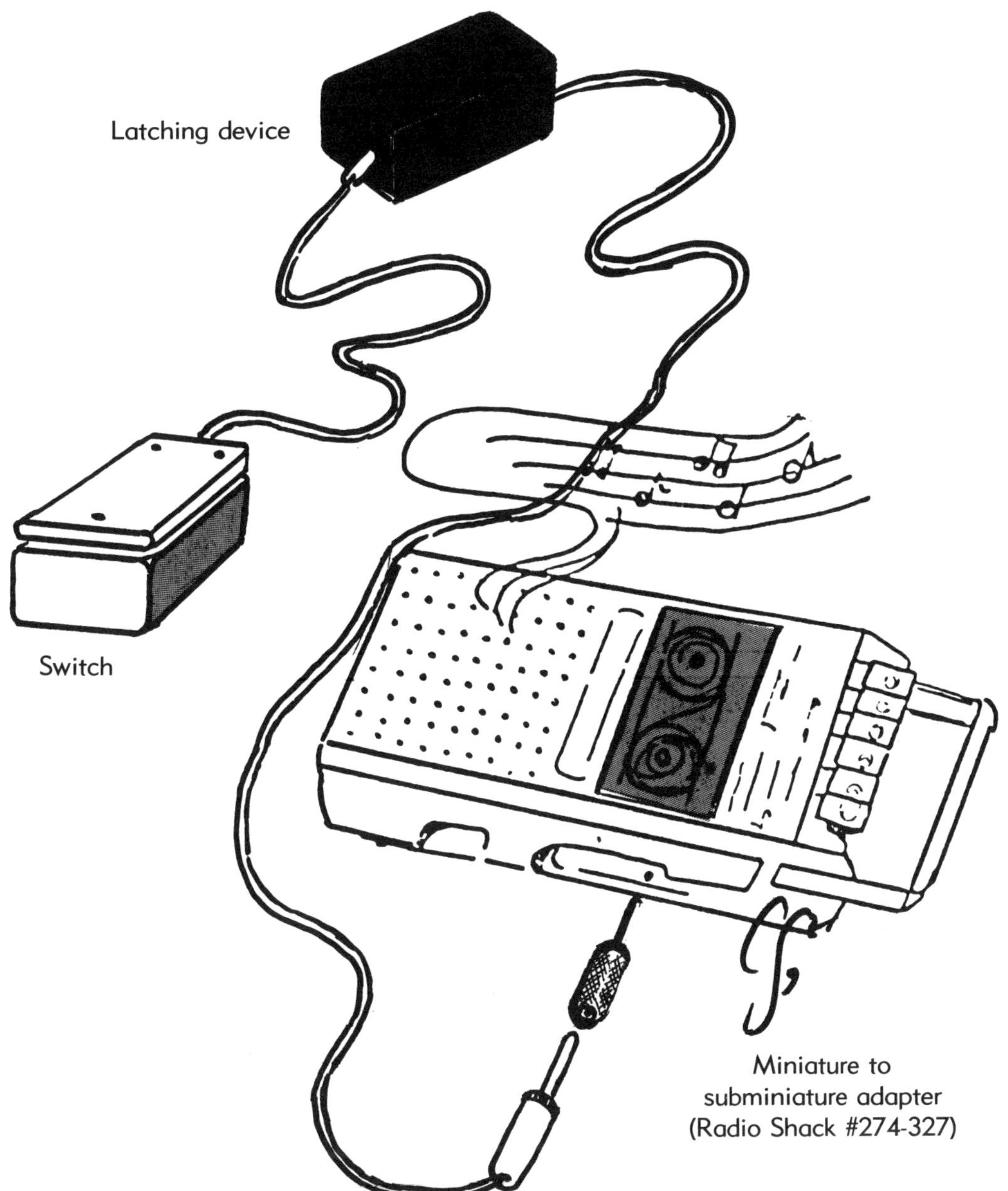


**FIGURE 6.1.** Commercially available latching devices.

selection technique (usually block scanning) to access the symbolic counterparts of the keys in the scanning array.

As illustrated in Figure 6.5, the IBM computer is typically adapted via (a) the parallel port using the PC Adaptive Interface Device (PC A.I.D.) (Figure 6.5a) or (b) the serial port using the Serial Adaptive Interface Device (Serial A.I.D.) (Figure 6.5b). When using the PC A.I.D., standard software can be accessed using either the keyboard, scanning (automatic, inverse, or step scan mode), or Morse code (1 or 2 switches). When using the PC Serial A.I.D., standard software can be accessed by all the methods possible with PC A.I.D. plus several alternate keyboards. Table 6.4 summarizes several commercially available options for adapting Apple and IBM computers to accept switch input. (For further information on accessing computers such as the Commodore 64, VIC 20, and the TRS-80 Color Computer, the reader is referred to Burkhart [1987] and Goossens' & Crain [1986a].)

In general, scan mode training activities involving switch-accessed AC- or DC-powered rewards and computer games vary in the extent to which

**TABLE 6.2.** Commercially Available Latching Devices

| Product | Distributor | Peripherals | Power Source |
|---|---|---|---|
| Switch Latch/Timer | Don Johnston Developmental Equipment | 1–2 switches | 9V battery |
| Switch Latch | TASH, Inc. | 1 switch | 9V battery |
| Training Aid 2 | Prentke Romich Company | 1–2 switches controlling 1–2 battery- or AC-powered rewards | 120V AC |
| Dual Switch Latch and Timer | TASH, Inc. | 1–2 switches controlling 1–2 battery-powered rewards | 9V battery |
| Able Net Control Unit | Able Net | Single switch operating 2 AC-powered devices; appliances can be operated momentarily or 2 to 90 seconds as if latching | 120V AC (reduces voltage to 24V at user end) |
| Dual Channel Latching Switch Interface | Hugh MacMillan Medical Center | 1–2 switches used to control 1–2 battery-powered rewards | 9V battery |
| Push-On–Push-Off Module | Steven E. Kanor, Inc. | 1 switch used to control a switch-operated reward | 2 ''D'' batteries |

*Note.* Information derived from *Communication, Control, and Computer Access for Disabled and Elderly Individuals: Resource Book 3: Software and Hardware* by S. A. Brandenburg and G. Vanderheiden, 1987, San Diego: College-Hill/Little, Brown and Company.

they (a) focus on initiating (I), maintaining (M), and releasing (R) switch contact and (b) require I or R to be performed within a predetermined time frame. By way of example, a range of activities will be discussed with reference to four basic skill clusters:

- ❑ Ability to volitionally I and M contact with the switch within an untimed format (I & M, Untimed)
- ❑ Ability to volitionally R contact with the switch within an untimed format (I & R, Untimed)
- ❑ Ability to volitionally I and R contact with the switch in rapid succession (I & R, Rapid Succession)
- ❑ Ability to volitionally I and R contact with the switch within a timed format (I & R, Timed)

Following discussion of these four skill clusters the reader will find a section on determining the scan mode to be trained.

**ABILITY TO VOLITIONALLY I AND M CONTACT WITH THE SWITCH WITHIN AN UNTIMED FORMAT (I & M, UNTIMED).** In this section we consider this skill cluster as it relates to (a) adapted battery-powered and AC-powered rewards and (b) computer software.

**Adapted DC- and AC-Powered Rewards.** Early intervention with developmentally young children frequently focuses on training cause and effect using adapted DC- and AC-powered rewards. (For more in-depth information regarding the early training of cause and effect, the reader is referred to Campbell [c. 1985] and Zuromski [1978].)

As depicted in Figure 6.6, the facilitator may wish to initiate intervention using stationary rewards, thereby eliminating the child's need to visually track the interfaced reward. Examples include initiating and maintaining contact with the switch to maintain the activity of a tape recorder playing music or a stationary mechanical bear playing a drum (Figure 6.6a). With older individuals

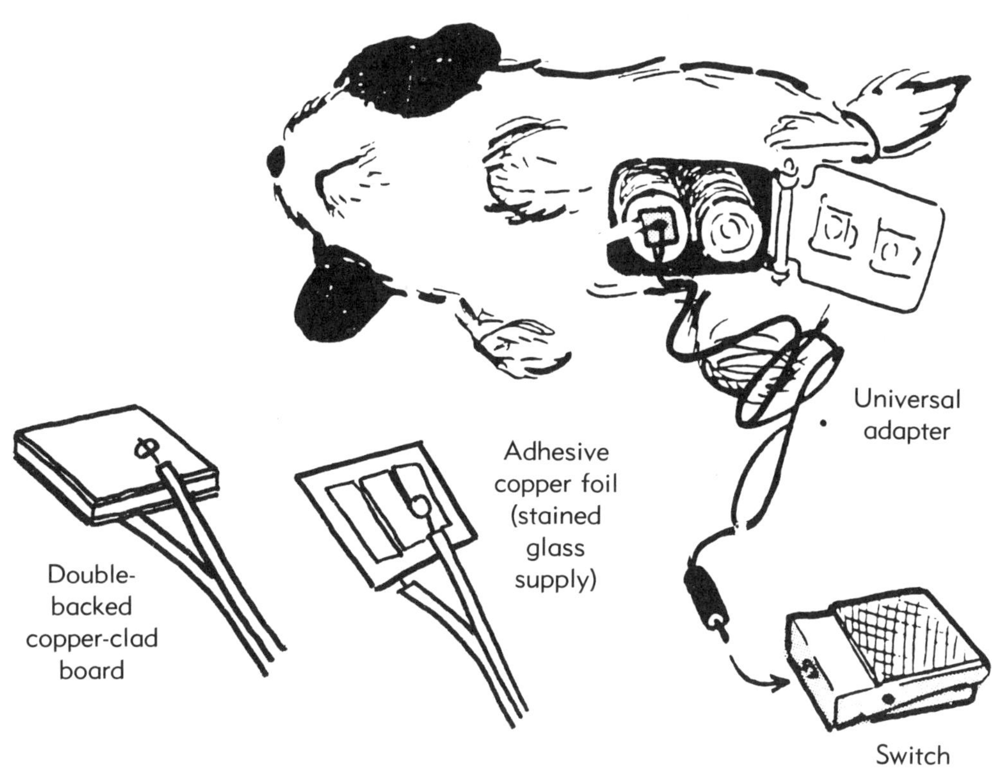


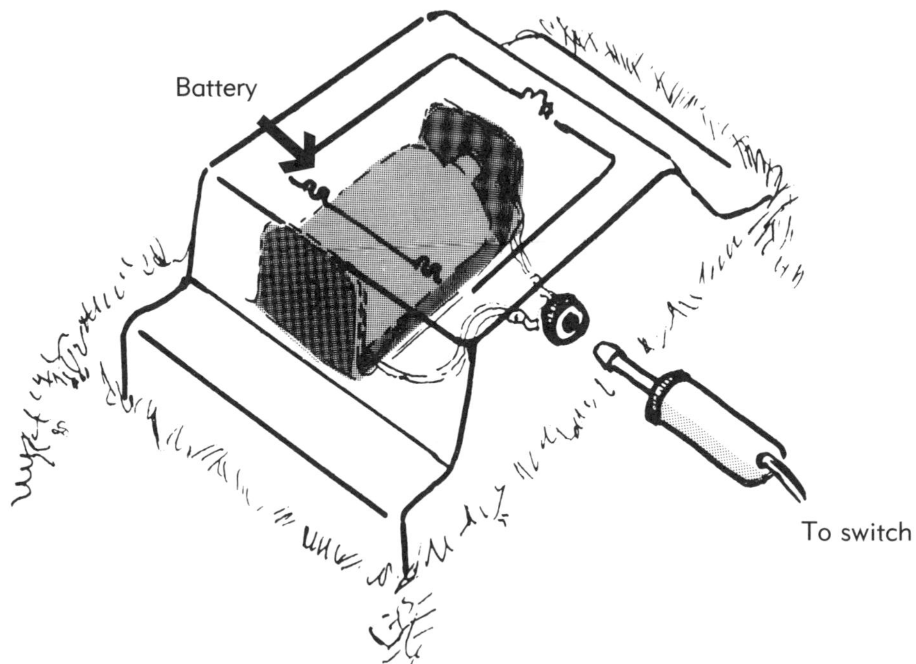


**FIGURE 6.2.** Adapting battery (DC)-powered rewards to accept switch input.

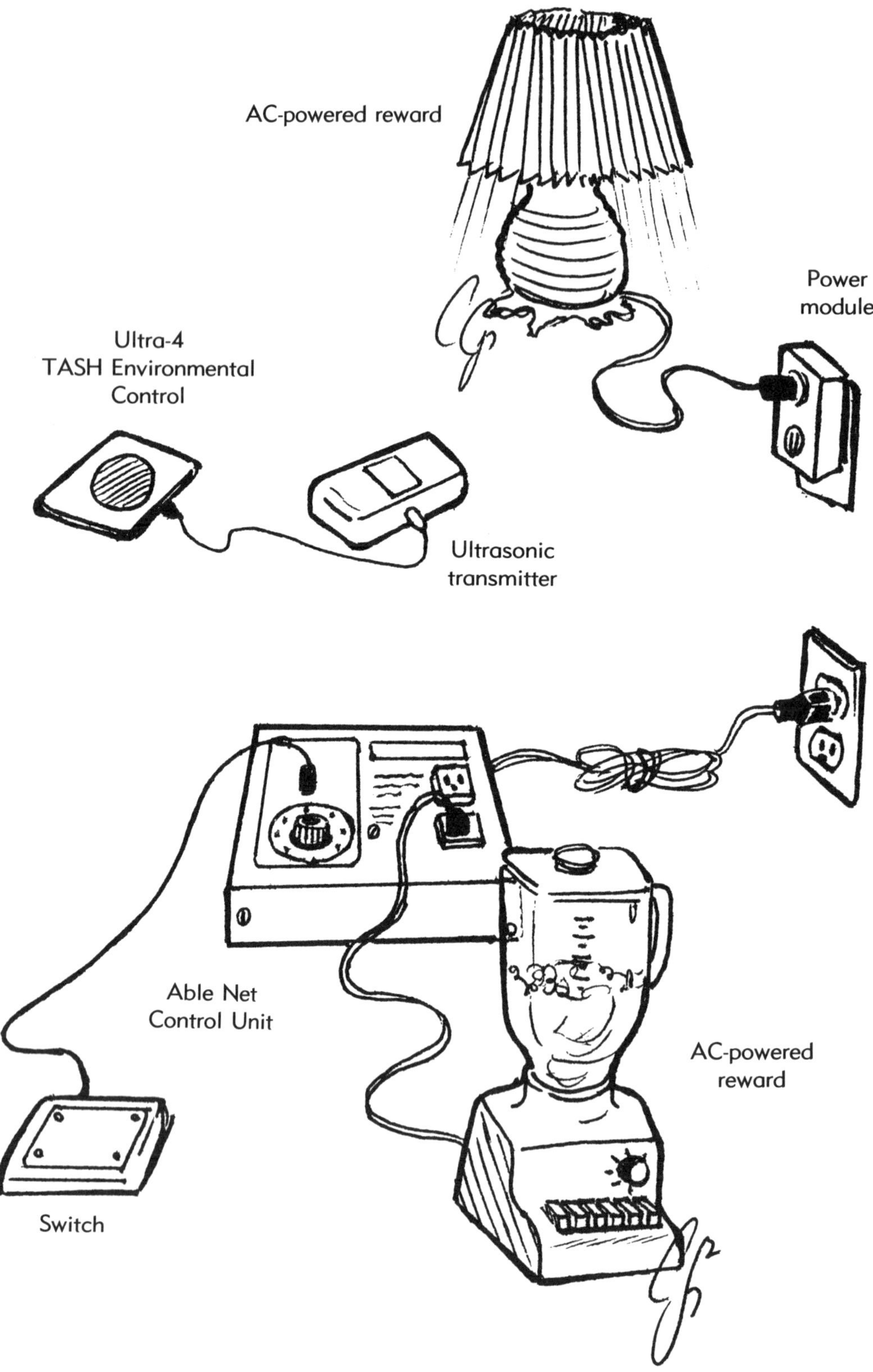


**FIGURE 6.3.** Adapting AC-powered rewards to accept switch input.

**TABLE 6.3.** Commercially Available Options for Safely Adapting AC-Powered Rewards to Accept Switch Input

| Product | Distributor | Peripheral | Power Source |
|---|---|---|---|
| Active Stimulation Programmer | Handicapped Children's Technological Services, Inc. | 1 switch controlling 1 AC- or battery-powered reward | 120V AC |
| Able Net Control Unit | Able Net | 1 switch controlling 2 AC-powered rewards (voltage at user's end is 24V) | 120V AC |
| REACH Power Control Adapter | REACH Inc. | 1–3 AC-powered rewards | 120V AC |
| Training Aid 2 | Prentke Romich Company | 1–2 switches controlling 1–2 AC- or battery-powered rewards | 120V AC |

*Note.* Information derived from *Communication, Control, and Computer Access for Disabled and Elderly Individuals: Resource Book 3: Software and Hardware,* by S. A. Brandenburg and G. Vanderheiden, 1987, San Diego: College-Hill/Little, Brown and Company.

who are functioning developmentally at a much younger level, activities might include maintaining contact with the switch to sustain the activity of a blender or mixer being used in a food preparation activity. Because stationary toys tend to be less interesting, however, the facilitator might consider incorporating the use of a device that will (a) automatically activate toys in random order (e.g., Training Aid, Prentke Romich Company) (Figure 6.6b), (b) advance to the next toy in a series of three toys each time the switch is activated (Three-Device Switch, Shafer Foundation) (Figure 6.6c), or (c) allow the facilitator to switch toys on and off by manipulating toggle switches on a relay box (Figure 6.6d).

Later in intervention (Figure 6.7), nonstationary rewards are incorporated into the therapeutic plan, thus overlaying the need for the child to visually track the interfaced reward. Examples of such activities include initiating and maintaining contact with the switch to make a fireman climb up the ladder, make a toy puppy come to the child for a hug, make the toy robot bring the child a cookie (held in the Robot's pincerlike hand), or make the toy train transport a drink to the child. Tasks that require the child to use the switch as a tool to obtain desirable rewards (e.g., cookie, drink) are very much in keeping with the means-ends tasks (using support [Piagetian Stage IV], string, or stick [Piagetian Stage V] as tools for accessing desirable out-of-reach objects). From a cognitive perspective, tasks that position the reward to move toward the child are highly desirable and motivating. It should, however, be noted that such tasks require the child to perform both eye convergence and visual pursuit. For children who experience difficulty with visual coordination, such a setup may prove problematic. In such instances, tasks that require the child to perform either vertical or horizontal visual tracking may prove to be easier. When using linear horizontal or vertical movement patterns, the facilitator should ideally structure tasks to include a clear end goal (Figure 6.8). For example, rather than merely making the dog move, the task is structured so that the dog is moving to get its bone which has been placed at a distance. In many instances, it is possible to incorporate a series of end goals. For example, the child might be required to initiate and maintain switch contact to make the puppy come out of its doghouse, move to get a bone, move to get a drink from its dish, and then return to its doghouse for a nap.

Later in intervention, the facilitator may wish to systematically overlay visual tracking within a two-dimensional plane (e.g., rotary scanner, train on a circular track) (Figure 6.9a), and only later within a three-dimensional plane (e.g., spiral movements of various toys that involve characters such as penguins or koala bears that climb stairs then move down a spiral slide) (Figure 6.9b). For children demonstrating difficulty with visual coordination, toys that use random movement patterns such as "bump-and-go" mechanical toys would be introduced last because they require more skill in visual tracking (Figure 6.10).

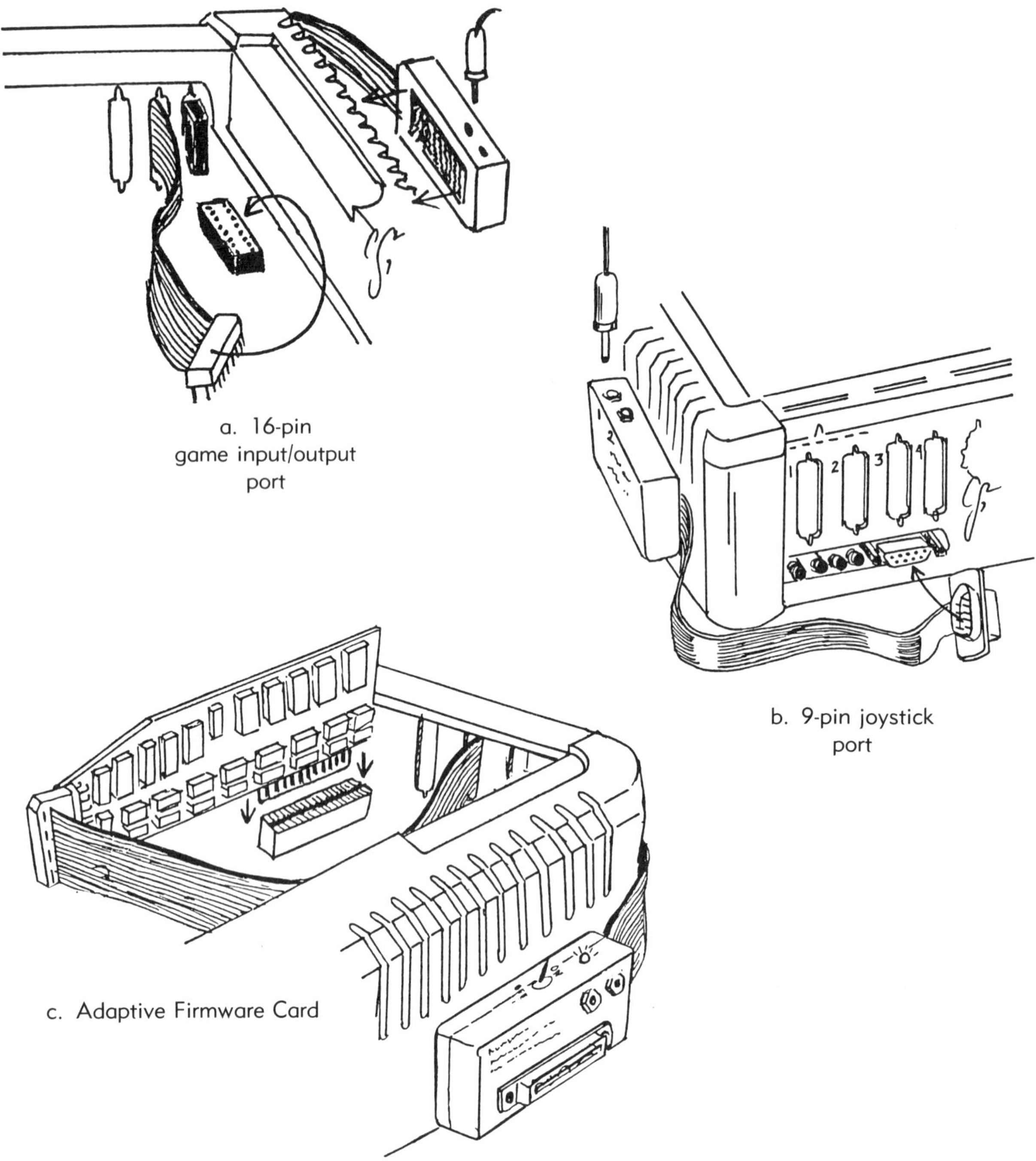


**FIGURE 6.4.** Adapting the Apple computer to accept switch input.

**Computer Software.** Many software programs are available that have been designed to give the child practice with I and M contact with the switch to achieve interesting visual and/or auditory rewards. At the earliest level software is being used to train cause and effect. Musselwhite (1988) set forth guidelines for classifying this software into beginning, intermediate, and advanced levels of cause and effect. At the *beginning level* she recommended that facilitators use software with large, simple graphics, bold movement, and ideally "blanking" of the monitor screen between switch activations. At the

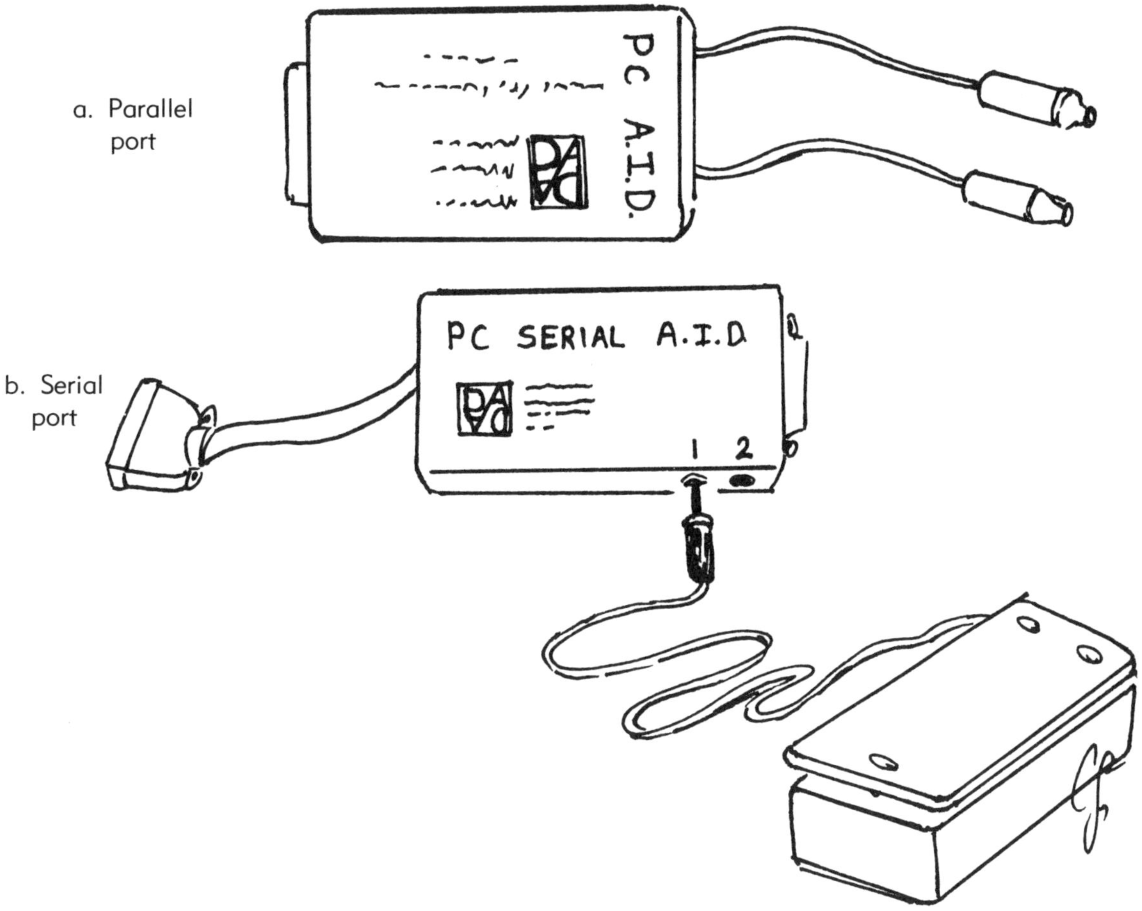


**FIGURE 6.5.** Adapting the IBM computer to accept switch input.

*intermediate level* of difficulty, software is selected that reflects the use of medium-size graphics, less bold movement, and no blanking of the monitor between activations. At the *advanced level* the software employed includes small graphics, small movement, and no blanking of the monitor between activations. Table 6.5 presents sample software that addresses skill cluster one (I & M, Untimed). A more extensive listing of software addressing this skill cluster is available in a resource by Goossens' and Crain (in press) entitled "Annotated Listing of Computer Software for Training Various Scanning Selection Techniques."

**ABILITY TO VOLITIONALLY R CONTACT WITH THE SWITCH WITHIN AN UNTIMED FORMAT (I & R, UNTIMED).** In this section we consider the R, Untimed, skill cluster as it relates to (a) DC- and AC-powered rewards and (b) computer software.

**Adapted Battery- and AC-Powered Rewards.** When the child is able to reliably initiate and maintain contact with the switch interface, therapeutic attention is shifted toward establishing volitional release in the absence of timing. As illustrated in Figure 6.11, this skill cluster can be addressed using a switch-accessed tape recorder in tasks that possess a clear incentive to start and stop the music. When engaged in "freeze-frame dancing," for example, the child is motivated to start the music because all participants in the game are required to dance wildly. Whenever the child stops the music, participants are required to hold a frozen posture until the music is reinstated, at which time the dancing is resumed. When engaged in musical chairs, the child is motivated to start the music because all participants in the game are required to march around an array of chairs. Whenever the child stops the music, participants must scurry to claim the remaining chairs. Motivation to stop the music is thus inherent to the task.

In addition to the aforementioned tasks involving a switch-accessed tape recorder, the facilitator may consider interfacing a timing device between

**TABLE 6.4.** Commercially Available Options for Adapting Apple and IBM Computers to Accept Switch Input

| Product | Distributor | Computer | Connects to | Peripherals |
|---|---|---|---|---|
| Switch Interface | Don Johnston Developmental Equipment | Apple II family | C10 game I/O port (inside) C11 Joystick game port (back) | 1–2 switches |
| Apple Computer Adapter | Steven E. Kanor, Inc. | Apple II family | Game I/O port (inside) | 1–2 switches |
| Apple IIe Input Adapter | Life Science Associates | Apple IIe | Game I/O port (inside) | 1–3 switches |
| Apple Switch Interface | Prentke Romich Company | Apple II family | Game I/O port (inside) | 1–2 switches |
| Interface Box for Apple IIe | ComputAbility Corporation | Apple II family | Game I/O port (inside) | 1–2 switches |
| Switch Adapter | TASH, Inc. | Apple II+, IIe | Game I/O port (inside) | • single switch<br>• dual switch<br>• multiple switches |
| Computer Switch Interface Box | REACH Inc. | Apple IIe<br>Apple IIc<br>Apple IIGS<br>Laser 128 | Joystick game port | |
| Multiple-Switch Box | Don Johnston Developmental Equipment | Apple family (requires Adaptive Firmware Card) | 16-pin port of Adaptive Firmware Card | 1–8 switches |
| Multiswitch Adapter Box | ComputAbility Corporation | Apple family (requires Adaptive Firmware Card) | 16-pin port of Adaptive Firmware Card | 1–8 switches |
| Porter | Don Johnston Developmental Equipment | Apple family | Game I/O port (inside) | 2 16-pin I/O ports; 2 9-pin joystick ports<br>• allows easier access to game I/O port and joystick port<br>• input devices can remain plugged in when not in use |
| Adaptive Firmware Card | Don Johnston Developmental Equipment | Apple IIGS<br>Apple IIe<br>Apple II, II+ | IIGS: + mouse emulation, large-size scan arrays, extended menu | • single switch<br>• 2-switch Morse code<br>• (Unicorn expanded keyboard, assisted keyboard) |
| PC AID (Alternate Input Device) | Don Johnston Developmental Equipment | IBM PC AT<br>IBM PC family | Parallel port | • single switch scanning using automatic, inverse, or step scan mode<br>• Morse code using single or dual switches |
| PC Serial AID | Don Johnston Developmental Equipment | IBM PC AT<br>IBM PC family | Serial port | Above plus: Alternate keyboards (Unicorn expanded TASH mini keyboard) |
| Scooter | Don Johnston Developmental Equipment | Apple family | Game I/O port | 2 16-pin I/O ports |

*Note.* Information derived from *Communication, Control, and Computer Access for Disabled and Elderly Individuals: Resource Book 3: Software and Hardware* by S. A. Brandenburg and G. Vanderheiden, 1987, San Diego: College-Hill/Little, Brown and Company.

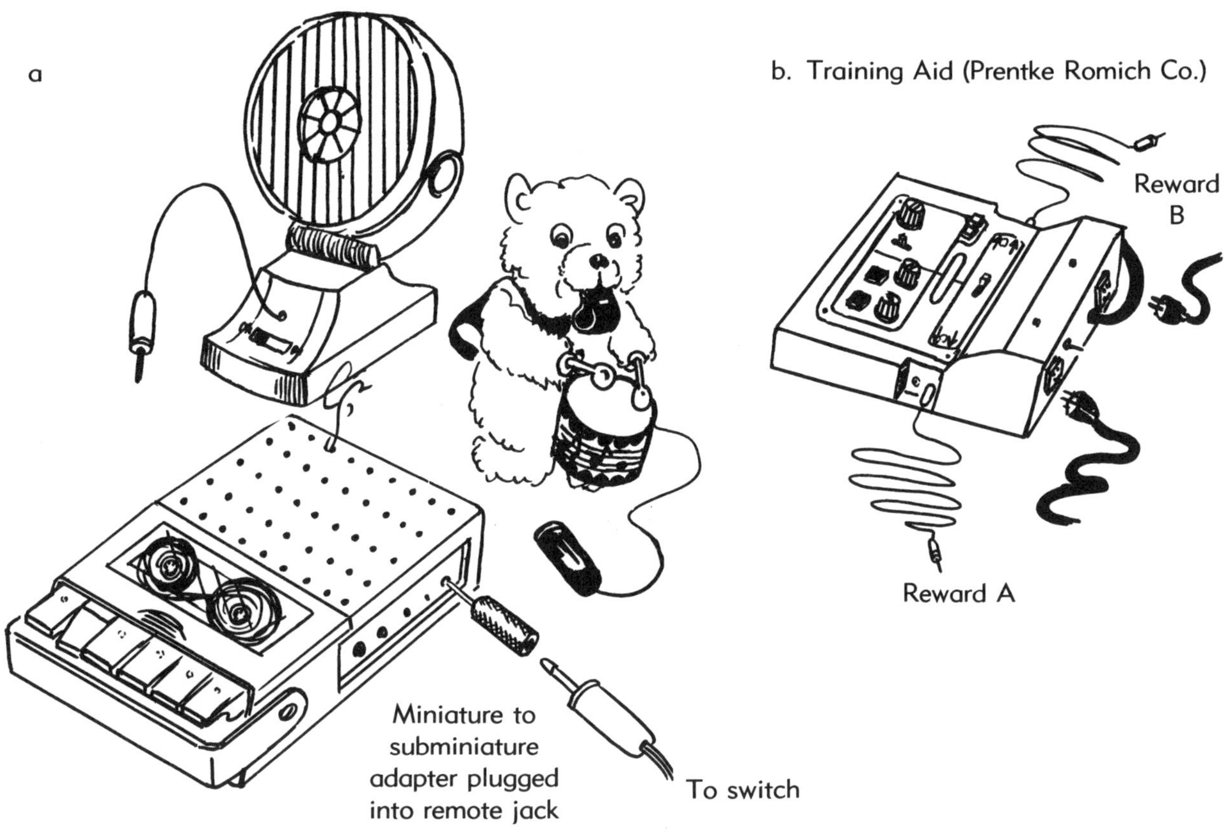


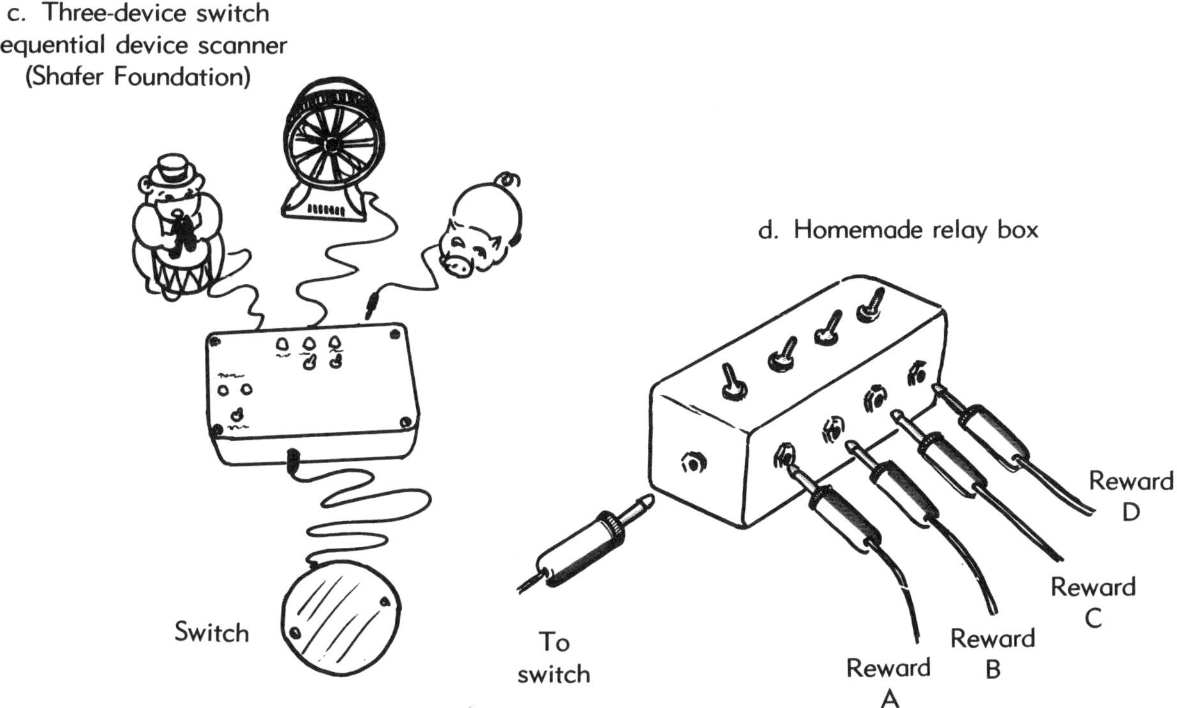


**FIGURE 6.6.** I & M Untimed: Stationary rewards.

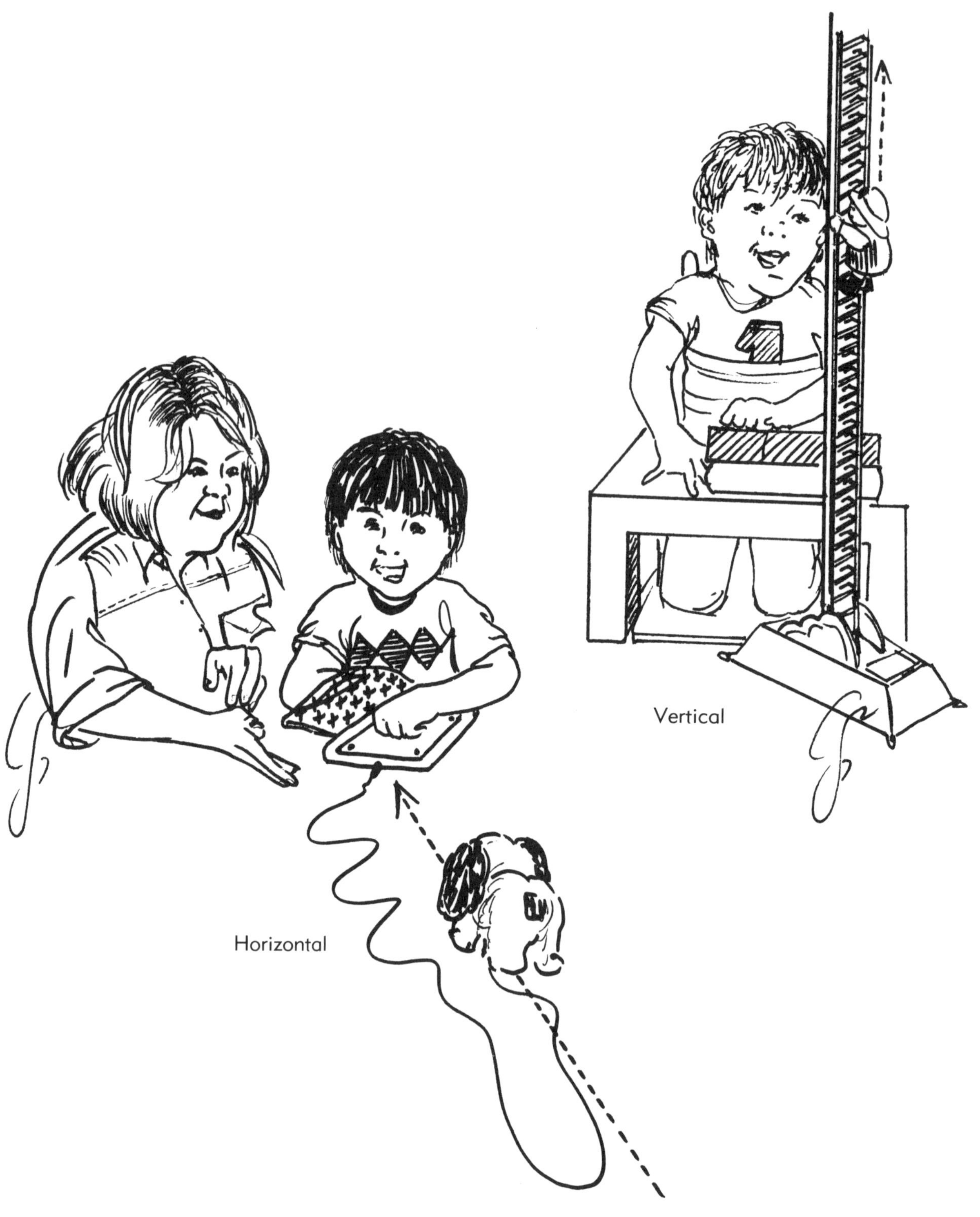


**FIGURE 6.7.** I & M, Untimed: Nonstationary rewards—Tracking within a consistent one-dimensional plane.

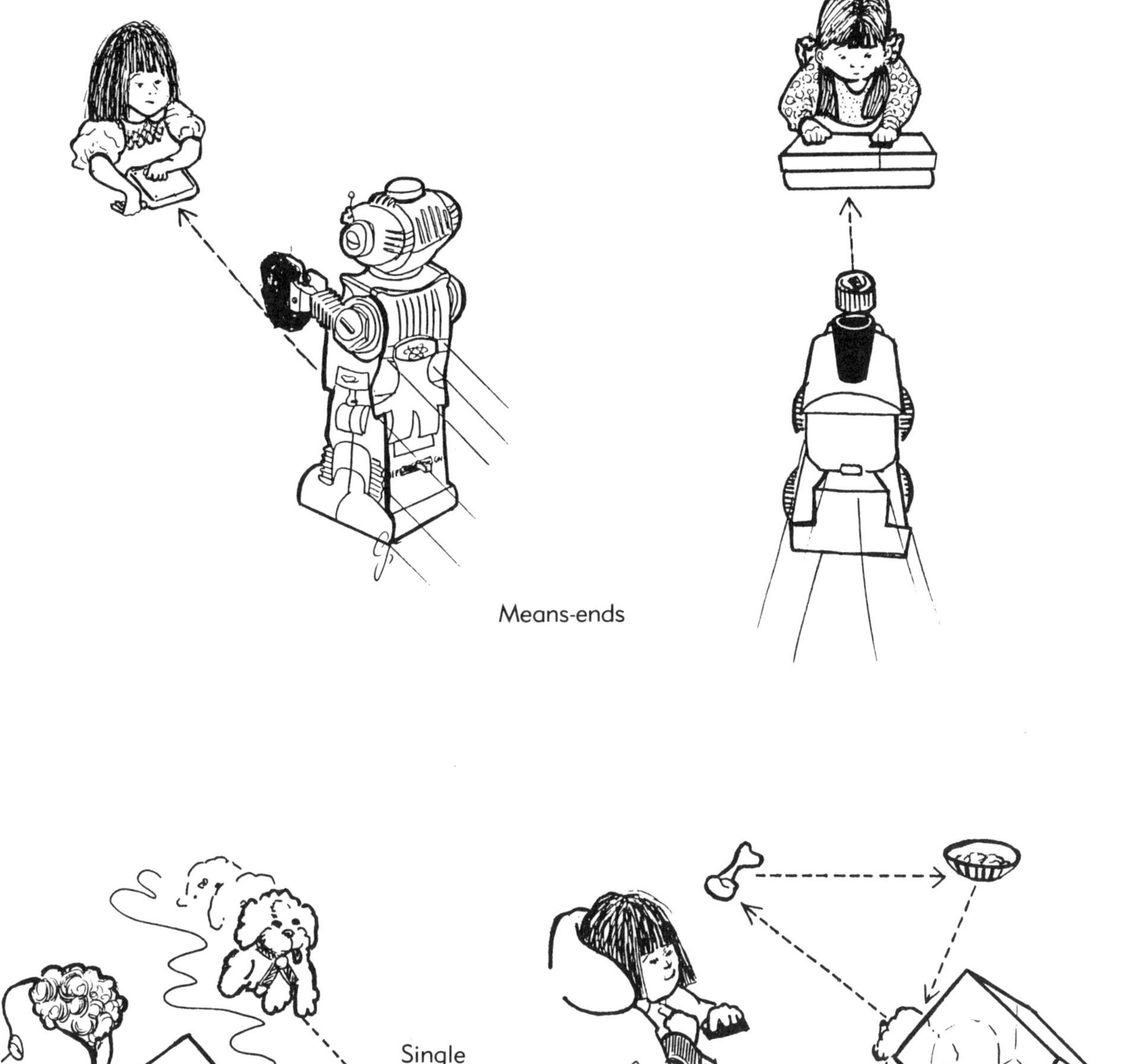


FIGURE 6.8. I & M, Untimed: Incorporating clear end goals.

the switch and the switch-accessed reward. As illustrated in Figure 6.12, such devices allow the reward to operate for a predetermined length of time, after which the reward stops and the child must release and reinitiate contact with the switch to resume the reward. Provided in Table 6.6 are several resources for commercially available timing devices that require switch release after a predetermined time.

**Computer Software.** Several computer games are reflective of this skill cluster. By way of example, Table 6.7 presents several sample software programs that address this second skill cluster (I & R, Untimed) in motivating task formats. With some programs, the ensuing visual/auditory reward is contingent upon switch release. That is, the activity will not unfold until the switch is released. With

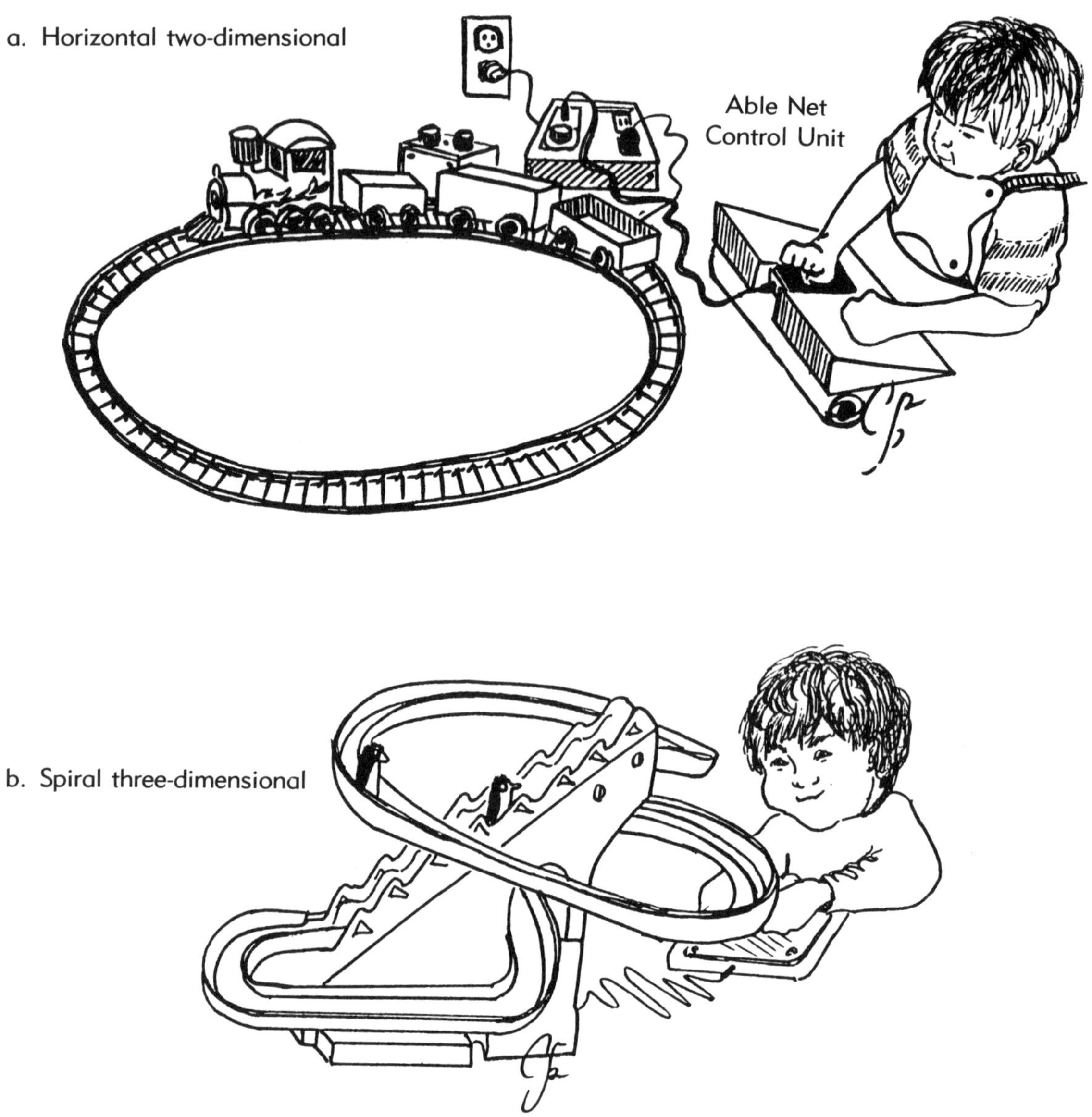


**FIGURE 6.9.** I & M, Untimed: Nonstationary rewards—Tracking within a consistent two- and three-dimensional plane.

other programs, the reward unfolds upon initiation, but release and reinitiation are required for continued or repeat play. Despite their differences, both types of programs necessitate an untimed release. An annotated listing of software programs designed to address this skill cluster is available in Goossens' and Crain (in press).

**ABILITY TO VOLITIONALLY I AND R CONTACT WITH THE SWITCH IN RAPID SUCCESSION (I & R, RAPID SUCCESSION).** Several software programs exist that require the child to repetitively I and R contact with the switch within a predetermined time frame. Presented in Table 6.8 are several software programs reflective of skill cluster three (I & R, Rapid Succession). (For a more extensive annotated listing of software addressing this skill cluster, the reader is referred to Goossens' & Crain, in press.)

**ABILITY TO VOLITIONALLY I AND R CONTACT WITH THE SWITCH WITHIN A TIMED FORMAT (I & R, TIMED).** This section contains discussion of the I & R, Timed, skill

**FIGURE 6.10.** I & M, Untimed: Nonstationary rewards—Tracking an inconsistent pattern.

cluster as it relates to (a) DC- and AC-powered rewards and (b) computer software.

**Adapted Battery- and AC-Powered Rewards.** When the child is able to volitionally release contact with the switch within untimed formats, attention can be directed toward incorporating a timing component. In general, a timed response may be required for either the R or the I aspect of switch access. A task involving a slide projector adapted to accept switch input can provide the child with considerable practice in performing a quick R. A slide projector control is commercially available from AbleNet, Inc. Illustrated in Figure 6.13 are two additional methods of adapting the slide projector to accept switch input. Instructions for the adapted remote method are provided in Appendix C. Specifics regarding training use of a slide projector adapted to accept switch input are presented in Appendix D.

Tasks involving adapted battery-powered rewards can also be modified to provide the child with practice stopping a moving toy within a predetermined time frame. As illustrated in Figure 6.14, this is typically achieved within the context of a visible response envelope depicted as a square of colored construction paper. Such tasks might include using a switch to make a mechanical puppy stop on a target (square of construction paper) on which a bone has been placed. To successfully retrieve the bone, the child must stop the toy when it is physically making contact with the square. The construction paper thus serves as a visible response envelope. That is, the child has from the time the toy first touches the square until the toy leaves the square to activate the switch. As previously discussed, when the switch interface is being operated in a direct mode, the child must perform a timed R to stop the toy. When the switch interface is being operated in a latching mode, a timed I is required. With time, the task can be made more challenging by incorporating more targets and manipulating the time required to stop on each target. The latter can be achieved by (a) keeping the size of the target square constant but using toys that move increasingly faster (e.g., toy dog [slow] vs. race car [fast]) or (b) keeping the speed of the toy constant but systematically decreasing the size of the target square. Later, the facilitator can increase the cognitive demands of the task by having a single target (e.g., bone) available within an empty array (designated by squares of construction paper).

Burkhart (1987) provided instructions for modifying a "fishing" game to create a switch-accessed horizontally rotating turntable (Figure 6.15). When a box with a cutout viewing window is placed over the turntable, the appearance of a reward in the viewing window serves as the visible cue to stop the turntable. Although the speed of rotation cannot be systematically altered (given the constraints of equipment design), the visible response envelope can be manipulated by altering the size of the box's viewing window. Initially, the facilitator may wish to provide the child with a lenient response envelope made possible by using a large viewing window. With time, the viewing window can be made increasingly smaller, thus requiring the child to respond more quickly to stop the turntable while the reward is in view. Failure to stop the turntable while the reward is in view results in a missed opportunity to gain the reward. Because this task requires considerable visual attention, it is highly recommended that a quiet musical reward be interfaced between the turntable and the switch to provide the child with a tangible measure that the activity is in progress. It is also helpful to incorporate a small light (e.g., flashlight, penlight) manually operated by the facilitator into the task. When the

**TABLE 6.5.** Sample Software Addressing Skill Cluster 1 (I & M, Untimed)

| Software | Description | Source |
|---|---|---|
| Happy Face | When the child I and M contact with the switch, he or she sees a happy face on the computer screen and hears the "When you're happy and you know it . . ." tune. When the child releases contact with the switch, the auditory and visual display is discontinued (blanking). | The New Cause and Effect Disk (Schmitt, c. 1988) (public domain) |
| Music and Boxes | When the child I contact with the switch, he or she hears a tune (e.g. "Hickory Dickory Dock," "Old MacDonald Had a Farm," "I'm a Little Teapot") and observes an everchanging series of concentric colored boxes. | Switch Access Music (public domain)<br>The New Cause and Effect Disk (public domain) |
| Frog and Fly | When the child I contact with the switch, the frog opens its mouth and its tongue shoots out to touch a fly that is animated but remains stationary. When switch closure is M'd, the frog repeatedly makes a croaking sound while repeatedly opening and closing its mouth. No blanking. | The New Cause and Effect Disk (public domain) |
| The Dancer | The child must I (but not necessarily maintain) contact with the switch to start the music and make the man dance. M results in repeat play. | The New Cause and Effect Disk (Schmitt, c. 1988) (public domain) |

reward appears in the viewing window, the light is activated via an on/off switch controlled by the facilitator. This light remains on until the reward disappears from the viewing window, at which point it is turned off by the facilitator. Thus, an opportunity to respond can be made more visually salient to the child. Such assistance can later be faded from use. The concept of a viewing window can also be applied to the use of an upright rotary scanner. This can be achieved by attaching a lightweight reward (e.g., cookie) to the rotating needle and overlaying a box with a viewing window.

**Computer Software.** Numerous software programs are available that require the child to perform an anticipatory, timed I (automatic scan mode) or timed R (inverse scan mode) when two items are aligned in some way. Table 6.9 presents a sample of software programs addressing skill cluster four (I & R, Timed). With most software, the allowable response time is not visibly apparent to the child. A visual cue (e.g., a flashing indicator) appears on the monitor suggesting "It's time to respond," but the child has no tangible indication of how much time is left for responding in the continuum of allowable time. There are, however, several software programs that provide the child with a visible response envelope. In the computer tasks Fly and Frog and Anti-Aircraft (Motor Training Games; Don Johnston Developmental Equipment), illustrated in Figure 6.16, a target (e.g., fly, airplane) appears on the far left of the computer screen and proceeds across the screen. The child must initiate contact with the switch before the target reaches the far right of the screen. When the child successfully activates the switch while the target is still on the screen, he or she is rewarded with an interesting spectacle. In the case of Fly and Frog, the frog shoots out its tongue to "catch" the fly. In the case of Anti-Aircraft, the plane "explodes" and a parachuter drifts slowly to

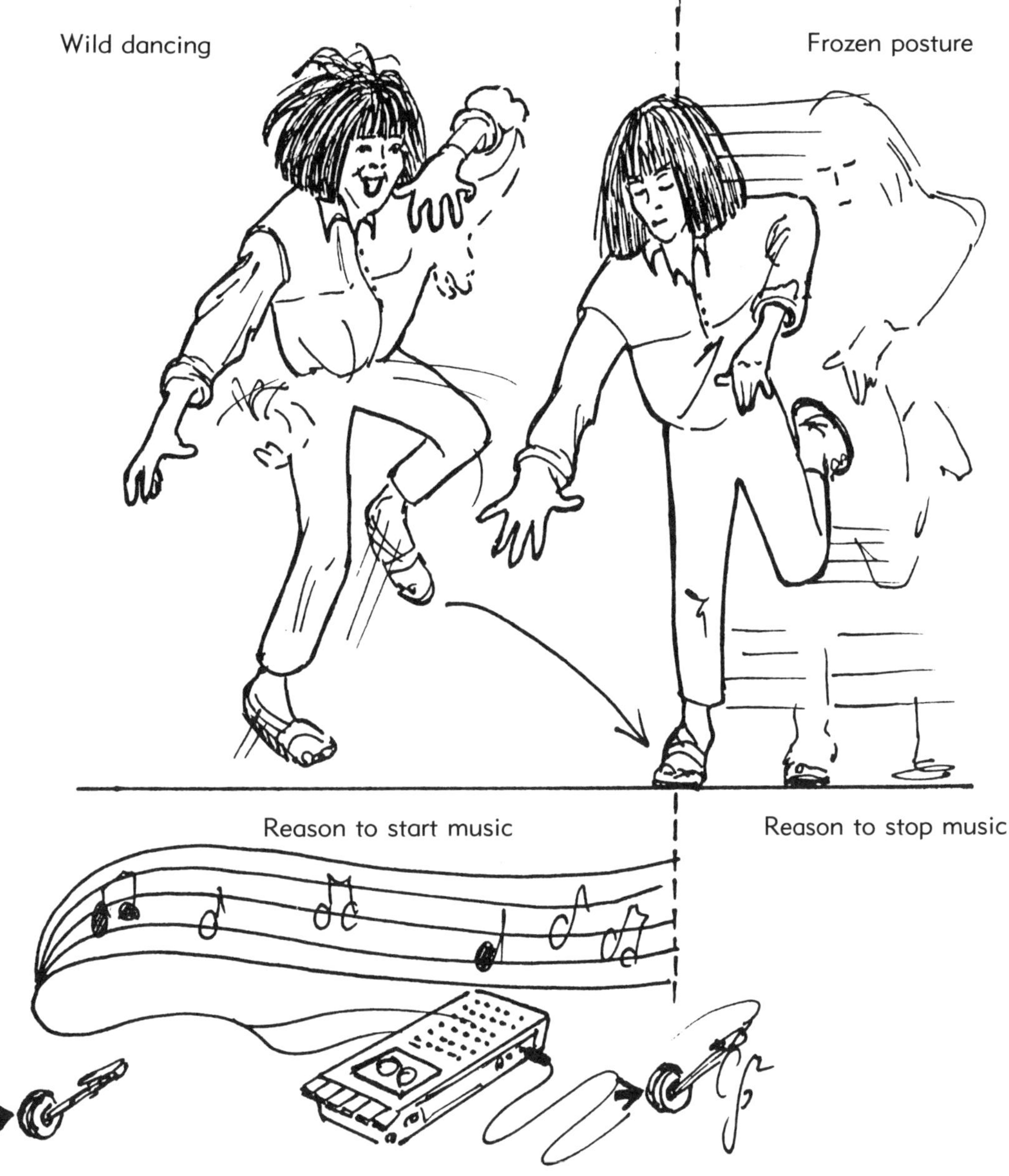


**FIGURE 6.11.** I & R, Untimed: Freeze-frame dancing.

earth. With both tasks, the allowable response time is automatically decreased with each successful trial as the speed with which the target crosses the screen increases. Whether the presence or absence of a visible response envelope aids the acquisition process is yet to be determined experimentally. An annotated listing of software addressing skill cluster four (I & R, Timed) is available in Goossens' and Crain (in press).

**DETERMINING SCAN MODE TO BE TRAINED.** Delineating the scan mode to be trained for communication access for a particular child is often a difficult decision for facilitators. There are, however, a number of variables relative to the child, the scanning device, the control site for switch access, and the scan mode itself that can assist in this decision-making process.

**Child-Related Variables.** Following a period of assessment or diagnostic training, the child's performance can serve as a guide in delineating an appropriate scan mode. For example,

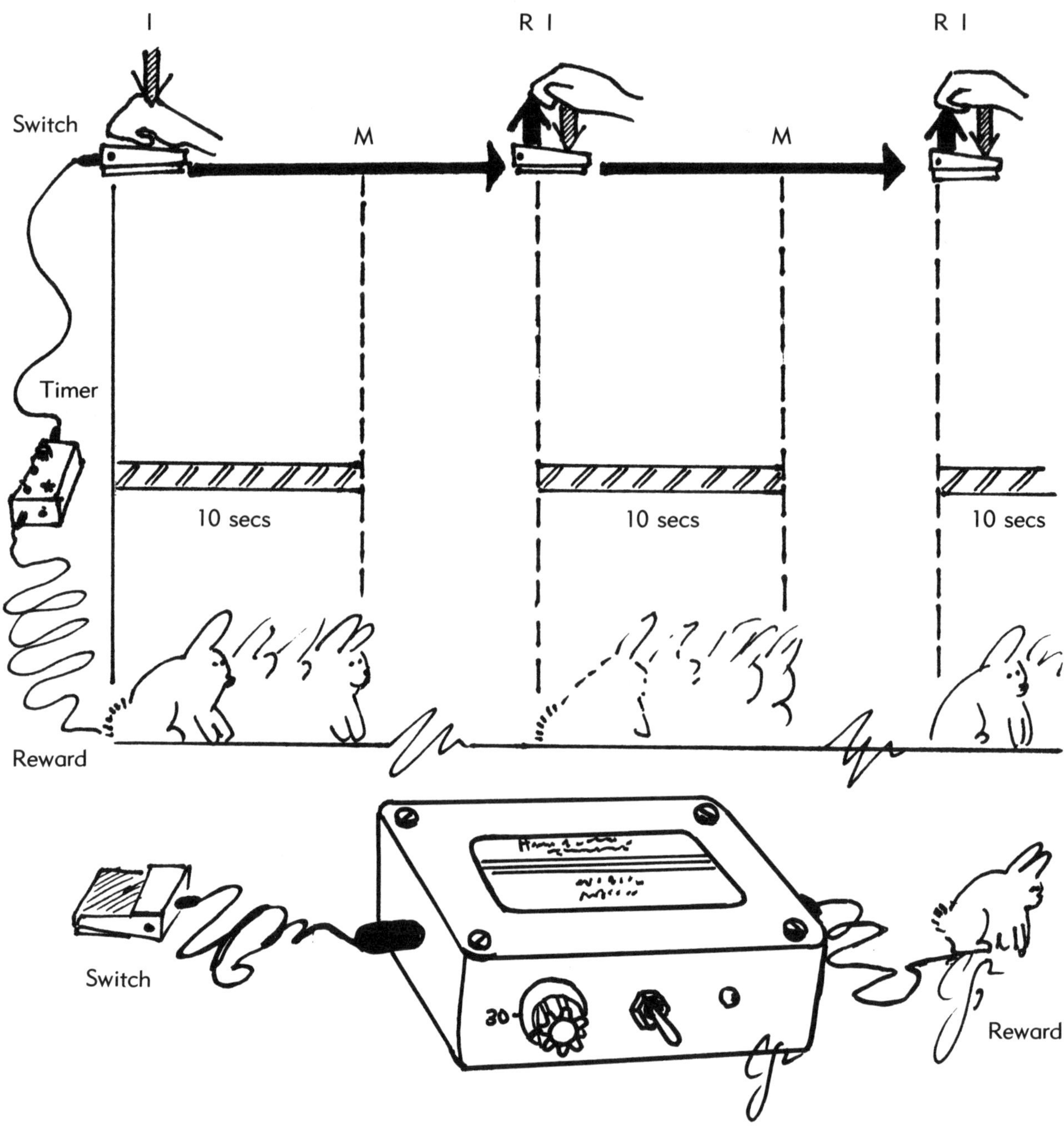


**FIGURE 6.12.** I & R, Untimed: Using a timing device.

- An *automatic mode* may be preferred for the child who exhibits better ability to *initiate* than release switch contact.
- An *inverse mode* may be preferred for the child who exhibits better ability to *release* than initiate switch contact and is able to maintain contact with the switch interface.
- A *step mode* may initially be preferred for the child who is capable of *initiating and releasing* switch contact but exhibits difficulty performing these skills within a timed format. To utilize a step mode, however, the child must be capable of performing repeated switch activations without fatiguing. When a step mode is employed to achieve communicative exchange, parallel motor training is usually conducted to establish the skills required for eventually performing an automatic or an inverse mode.

**TABLE 6.6.** Commercially Available Timing Devices

| Product | Distributor | Time | Power Source |
|---|---|---|---|
| Delay Timer | Arroyo & Associates | 1 to 60 seconds | 9V battery |
| Training Aid 2 | Prentke Romich Company | | 120V AC |
| Dual Switch Latch and Timer | TASH, Inc. | | 9V battery |
| Timer and Counter | Handicapped Children's Technological Services, Inc. | 0 to 90 seconds | 9V battery |
| Timer Module | Steven E. Kanor, Inc. | | 9V battery |

*Note.* Information derived from *Communication, Control, and Computer Access for Disabled and Elderly Individuals: Resource Book 3: Software and Hardware* by S. A. Brandenburg and G. Vanderheiden, 1987, San Diego: College-Hill/Little, Brown and Company.

**Device-Related Variables.** Some scan modes are employed more frequently than others to control a communication device. Although several devices offer a choice of scan modes, devices designed for preset group-element scanning (e.g., row-column) typically employ an automatic mode. By contrast, devices utilizing directed scanning usually employ an inverse mode. If the child will require a large selection set in the future, automatic and inverse modes are preferred because these are the modes used in conjunction with preset group-element or directed scanning (selection techniques used to access large arrays). Devices employing a step mode are generally associated with small message arrays and preset element patterns. A step mode is thus frequently viewed as an initial rather than a long-range option for accessing a communication device.

**Control Site–Related Variables.** Scan mode may also be dictated to some degree by the control site the child is using for switch access. If a lateral head turn or head tilt is being used to activate a switch interface, for example, the switch is typically mounted close to the control site, thereby minimizing the amount of head movement required. For this child an automatic, inverse, or step mode may all be considered viable options. If, however, the child exhibits extraneous head movement, the switch interface must be mounted at a distance from the control site to minimize accidental activation. As illustrated in Figure 6.17, an inverse mode requiring maintained contact with the switch interface would require this child to maintain an awkward head posture significantly away from midline. The child who experiences difficulty dissociating head and eye movement would experience difficulty visually monitoring the scanner display. With such a child, an inverse mode may be contraindicated or less than optimal.

An inverse mode would also be contraindicated for control sites that must move against gravity (e.g., hand, foot) to activate a switch interface that is mounted in an inverted position. Because maintaining switch contact against gravity would prove fatiguing, an automatic mode would be preferred. When using an automatic scan mode with an inverted switch setup, gravity can assist the child in releasing switch contact.

**Scan Mode–Related Variables.** As previously discussed, a step mode is considered the easiest of the three modes. It is therefore frequently introduced as an initial scanning technique that will allow the child to move into communication tasks as quickly as possible. Due to the slowness of this mode and the fact that it is typically associated with small selection sets, a step mode is generally reserved for early choice-making tasks involving a limited array set. For the child requiring communication beyond choice-making routines, an automatic or an inverse mode is preferred.

**TABLE 6.7.** Sample Software Addressing Skill Cluster 2 (I & R, Untimed)

| Software | Description | Source |
|---|---|---|
| Join the Circus | When the child I and R contact with the switch, a circus act (e.g., a juggling team, a magician, a lion tamer) unfolds. A green light and an auditory cue, "_____, hit your switch" serve to cue the child to initiate contact. The number of activations required to stage the entire scene can be varied from one to four. | Join the Circus (Don Johnston Developmental Equipment, 1988) |
| House Painter | The child is required to I and *R* contact with the switch interface to effect a change in the house displayed on the computer monitor. Changes to the house include turning the lights on/off and painting the house different colors. The change is then spoken (e.g., "a white house," "lights on"). The child ideally performs each switch activation spontaneously to effect a change. In the event the child does not do so in a predetermined time period, a verbal cue (e.g., "*Timmy,* press your switch") is provided. | Make It Happen (Don Johnston Developmental Equipment, 1988) |
| The Robot | The room of a house appears on the computer screen. A robot then enters the room. Whenever the child I and R contact with the switch interface, the robot performs some task in the room (e.g., dusts table, vacuums floor, turns TV on/off, answers the phone). | Make It Happen (Don Johnston Developmental Equipment, 1988) |
| Conduct a Creature Chorus | Eight creatures appear on the computer monitor, each producing a different sound. Initiating contact with the switch interface results in the creatures producing sounds as if in a chorus. To switch from one creature to another the child must R and re-I contact with the switch. | Creature Chorus (Fox & Sweig Wilson, 1976) |
| Creature Antics | In response to various verbal commands (e.g., Make Breaker dance . . . some more . . . What's next? . . . Make it throw . . . some more), the child is required to I contact with the switch to make various creatures (e.g., Blob, Boz, Breaker, Punk Poodles, and Roggi) perform a wide array of animated antics. To continue the antics the child must R and re-I contact with the switch. | Creature Antics (Fox & Sweig Wilson, 1987) |

**TABLE 6.8.** Sample Software Addressing Skill Cluster 3 (I & R, Rapid Succession)

| Software | Description | Source |
|---|---|---|
| Zig Zag 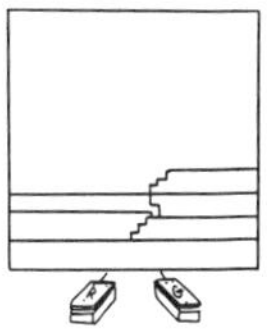 | In response to the verbal cue "(Child's name), press your switch," the child must I and R contact with the switch. Successful I is rewarded with the verbal praise, "Good work." Each child is called upon to activate his or her switch a variable number of times ("again . . . again") before the second child is given a turn. When asked to repetitively activate the switch, the child must R and re-I within a narrow time frame to lay down a bar of color on his or her side. | Interaction Games (Cooper & Koch, 1987) |
| Race 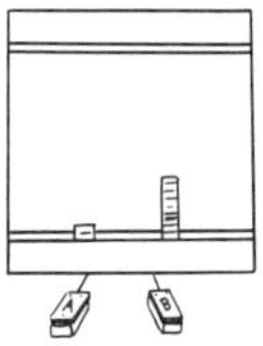 | Two children compete to have their color bar reach the top first. Each time a child I contact with his or her switch, an increment of color is added to his or her bar of color. To achieve the multiple Is required to reach the top, the child must R to re-I. Each I is accompanied by a beep. When a bar reaches the top, the winner receives verbal praise: "_____ is the winner this time." The winner bar is then widened. | Interaction Games (Cooper & Koch, 1987) |
| Bully 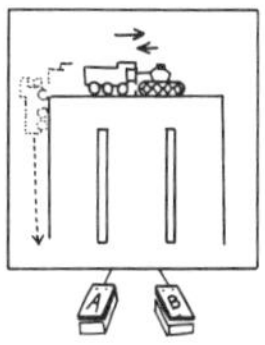 | Two children play. Each child is required to pick a vehicle (e.g., bulldozer, dump truck, tank, tractor) from a two-item array. Each child must then repetitively I and R contact with his or her switch in an attempt to achieve the greater number of activations required to push the opponent's vehicle off the platform. Each I moves the child's vehicle forward a short distance. Eventually, one vehicle pushes the other off the platform. The winner is rewarded with verbal praise: "*Child A* pushed *Child B* off the box. Good work!" | Interaction Games (Cooper & Koch, 1987) |
| Davy's Digits Simple Counting 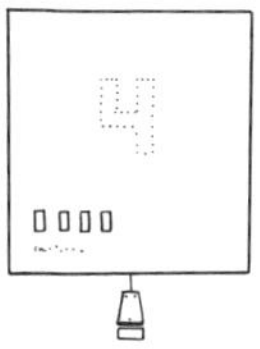 | The child must I and R contact with the switch in rapid succession. The computer then prints the corresponding number on the monitor. | Motor Training Games (Schwejda & McDonald, 1986) |
| Davy's Digits Matching 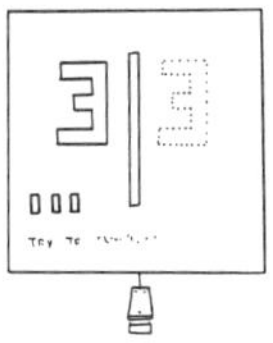 | A number is displayed on the screen. The child is required to I and R contact with the switch to "count out" the corresponding number, visually depicted as color bars at the bottom of the screen. When successful, a matched number appears on the screen followed by a fanfare and a spectacle of flashing lights. When unsuccessful, a buzzer is heard. | Motor Training Games (Schwejda & McDonald, 1986) |

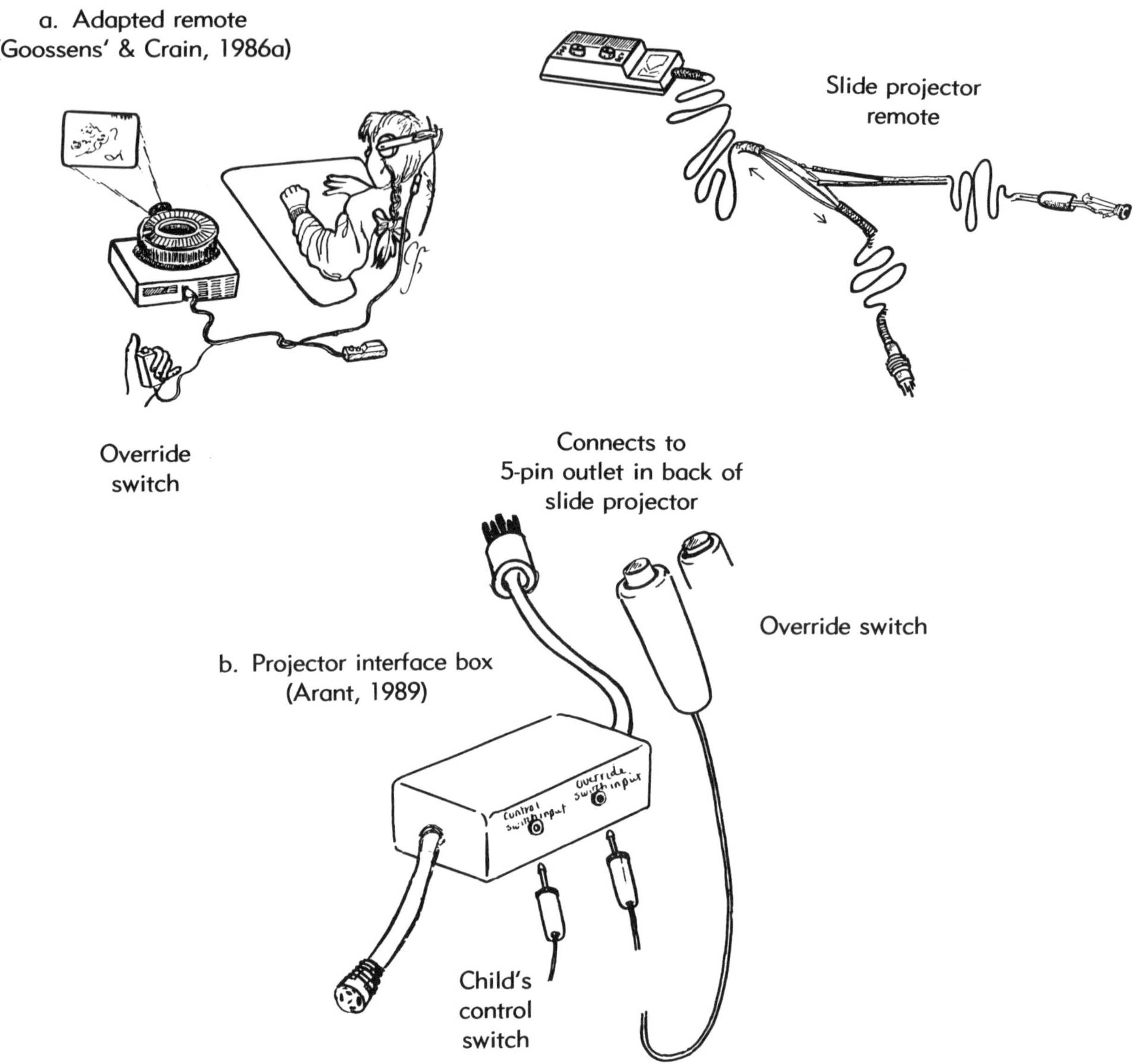


**FIGURE 6.13.** I & R, Timed: Adapted slide projector task.

### Training Scan Pattern

Having mastered the switch accessing skills dictated by a particular scan mode in timed tasks possessing primarily a motor load, the second phase of the layering approach can be initiated. Within the second phase, a scan pattern is introduced with a scanning indicator advancing through a visual array. A substantial cognitive and visual load is thus overlaid on the existing motor load dictated by scan mode. The introduction of a scan pattern increases the skill requirements of the training task, because the child must:

- ❑ Focus on a target cell while visually monitoring the scanning indicator advancing along a designated path
- ❑ Predict the path in which the scanning indicator moves in order to anticipate it advancing toward a target item
- ❑ Perceive the scanning indicator as a selection tool and recognize when that indicator is highlighting a target item
- ❑ Understand that there is a direct relationship between the scanning indicator and switch access

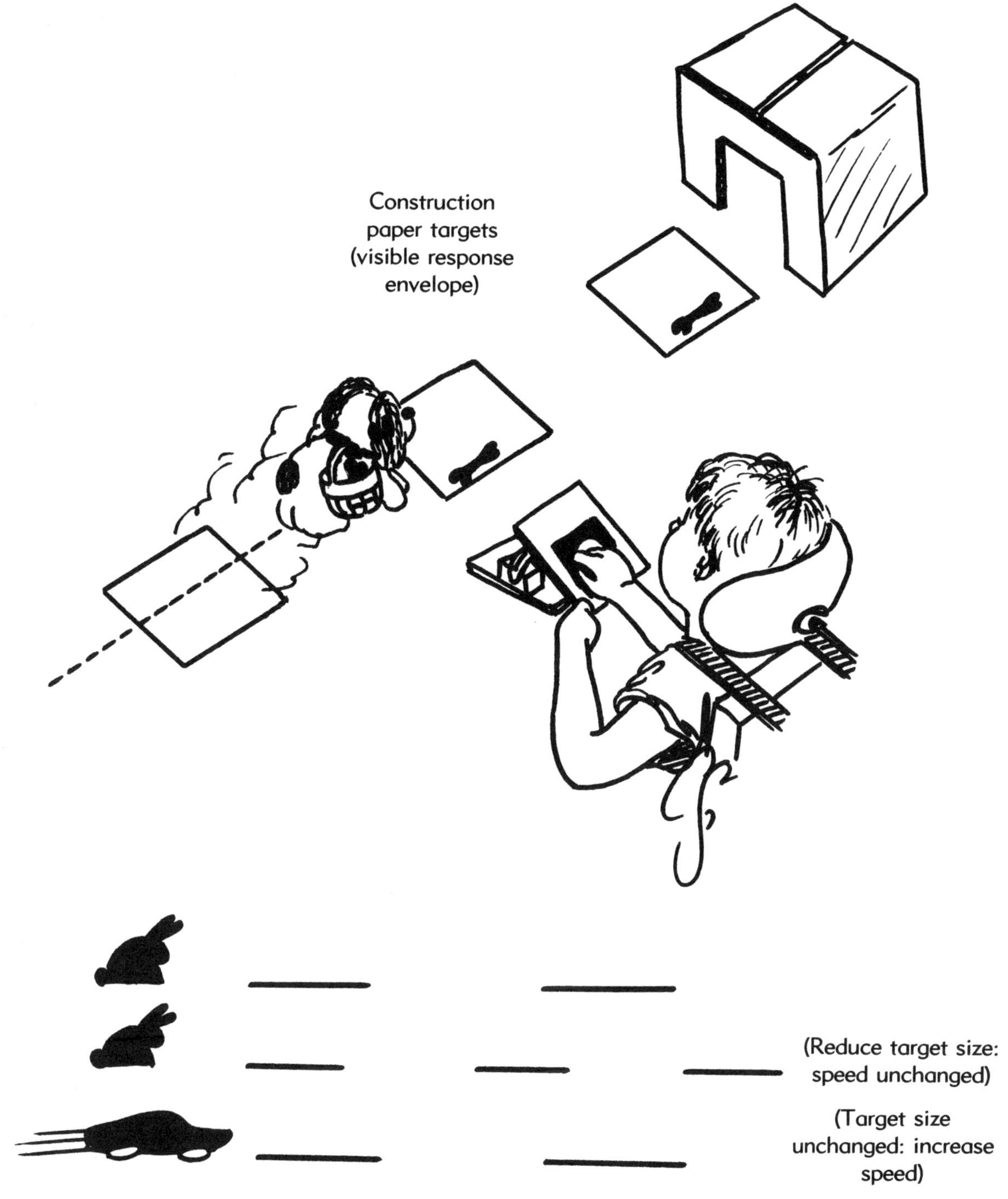


**FIGURE 6.14.** I & R, Timed: Using battery-powered rewards (visible response envelope).

- ❑ Perform the necessary motor skills (dictated by scan mode) to select a target item within a predetermined time frame

When these skills are required in combination during the early stages of intervention, the task of switch access is extremely difficult for many children who are severely physically challenged. To simplify the task of switch access, the training of scan pattern should be approached through a multiphase process.

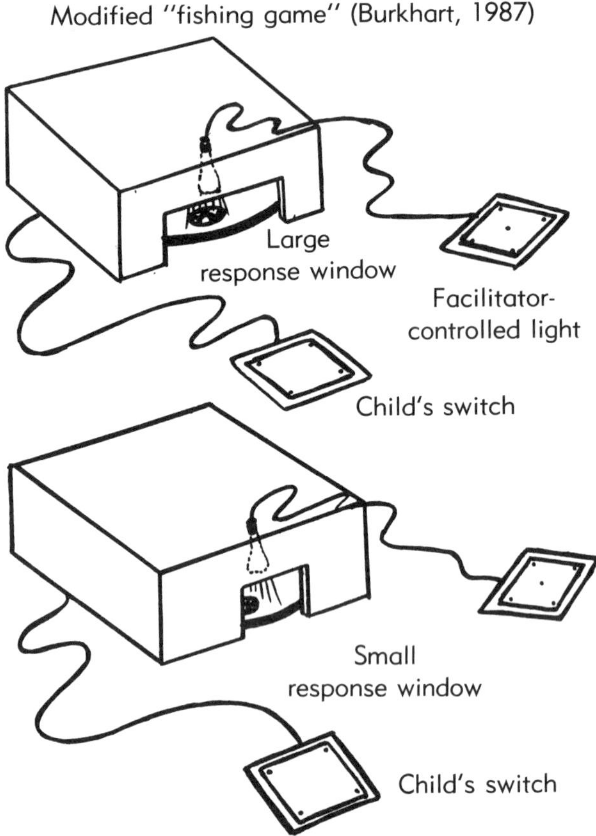


**FIGURE 6.15.** I & R, Timed: Using rotary devices (visible response envelope).

**SINGLE CELL TARGETING IN THE ABSENCE OF A VISIBLE SCAN PATTERN.** Training can be conducted in the context of a dedicated aid (Light Talker, Epson Scan Pac) or using symbol- or language-empty computer software (e.g., TARGET, Children's Hospital Medical Center of Boston; Step-By-Step, Children's Hospital at Stanford; Scan and Speak, The Psychological Corporation Harcourt Brace Jovanovich, Inc.; Talking Scanner used with the Adaptive Firmware Card; Adaptive Peripheral, Inc.).

Such programs are highly user programmable, allowing the facilitator (depending on the program) to manipulate such features as scan mode (automatic, inverse, step), scan pattern (linear, row-column, block), scan rate, scan array size, cursor type, and presence/absence of auditory feedback as the cursor moves from cell to cell. With the exception of the TARGET program, all programs cited allow voice output to be overlaid on the activity.

When training a preset scan pattern using a dedicated aid or symbol-empty computer software, the concept of a scanning indicator can initially be introduced to the child in the absence of a visible scan pattern, thus decreasing the visual requirements of the training task.[1] Only a single cell is exposed to the child at a given time on the display of either a dedicated scanning device or computer screen. As illustrated in Figure 6.18, a transparent overlay (0.020 or 0.030 mil) is constructed of polycarbonate vinyl for the scanner display. Opaque laminated cards can then be attached with Velcro to the vinyl overlay to temporarily conceal all cells except one on the scanner display. The scan pattern is thus present, but not visible to the child; only the single cell available for targeting is visible to the child. When the exposed target cell is highlighted by the scanning indicator, the child must either initiate (automatic mode) or release (inverse or step mode) switch contact to target the cell.

Only one switch activation is required when a *linear pattern* is employed. When a *group-element pattern* such as row-column scanning is being introduced (Figure 6.19), the child must make at least two switch activations. The first switch activation stops the scanning process on the target row. The second activation stops the cursor on the target cell within that row. Despite the use of a more sophisticated pattern, the child is still accessing the switch interface only when she or he sees the scanning indicator highlighting the exposed target cell. In the case of row-column scanning, access must occur twice before the target item is entered for visual and/or voice output.

As illustrated in Figure 6.20, the time that elapses between the first and second switch activation varies depending on the location of a target item in the scan array. For example, the most time elapses for those items located in the column at the far right of the scanner display. The amount of time decreases column by column as you move in a right to left direction across the display. When scanning is ongoing, the time allowed to mentally prepare for the initial switch activation also varies. As depicted in Figure 6.20, the bottom row in the matrix allows the child the maximum amount of time to mentally and motorically prepare for the initial switch activation required in the scanning process. Less time is allowed with each row as you move in an upward direction across the scanner display. These timing variables can be systematically manipulated for single cell targeting tasks. Initially, the child is required

[1]This section could have been discussed relative to training scan mode, because training is conducted in the absence of a visible scan pattern. For the sake of clarity, however, it is presented as the initial training phase of scan pattern.

**TABLE 6.9.** Sample Software Addressing Skill Cluster 4 (I & R, Timed)

| Software | Description | Source |
|---|---|---|
| Money in the Bank | The child must activate the switch when the coin is aligned (signaled by a flashing coin and beeping) with the piggy bank slot. If successful, the coin drops into the piggy bank and the amount is announced (e.g., "five cents"). If unsuccessful, the coin bounces on the table and "disappears" into a "hole" at the lower left of the screen. | Make It in Time (Don Johnston Developmental Equipment, 1988) |
| Assembly Line | The child is required to activate the switch when a package proceeding down a conveyor belt is aligned (signaled by flashing of the package and beeping) with a stamp held by a man. If successful, the package is stamped and the man's facial expression changes to a smile. A color bar is then added to the store card at the lower left of the screen. | Make It in Time (Don Johnston Developmental Equipment, 1988) |
| Duck Pond | The child is required to activate the switch when a duck is aligned (signaled by flashing of the duck and beeping) with the exit to the pond. If successful, the duck says, "Quack quack" then exits the pond. | Make It in Time (Don Johnston Developmental Equipment, 1988) |
| Make That Kick | The child must activate the switch when the kicker is adjacent (signaled by a flashing football and beeping) to the ball. If successful, the ball is kicked through the goal posts, the referee signals and announces "The kick is good!" and the scoreboard changes. If unsuccessful, the kicker bypasses the ball then walks back to his starting point. | Make It in Time (Don Johnston Developmental Equipment, 1988) |

to target only those items that allow the maximum amount of time possible to prepare for both the first and second switch activations. Items permitting less time are introduced later in the training process.

Training should always be conducted using motivating targeting tasks. Tasks might include targeting small toys or objects needed for a particular play activity such as the component parts needed to assemble a Mr. Potato Head or the color forms needed to create a composite color form picture. Small objects can be mounted to the vinyl overlay with small pieces of adhesive Velcro. Plastic color forms adhere directly to the vinyl. The overlay can be easily attached and removed from the computer monitor or scanning device using Velcro adhered to its corners.

When training is conducted in the context of a voice-output dedicated scanning communication aid, messages are programmed to provide the child with auditory feedback and reinforcement. To ensure that the voice output is provided for reinforcement only when the exposed cell has been successfully targeted, the volume of the device is manually controlled by the facilitator. As the indi-

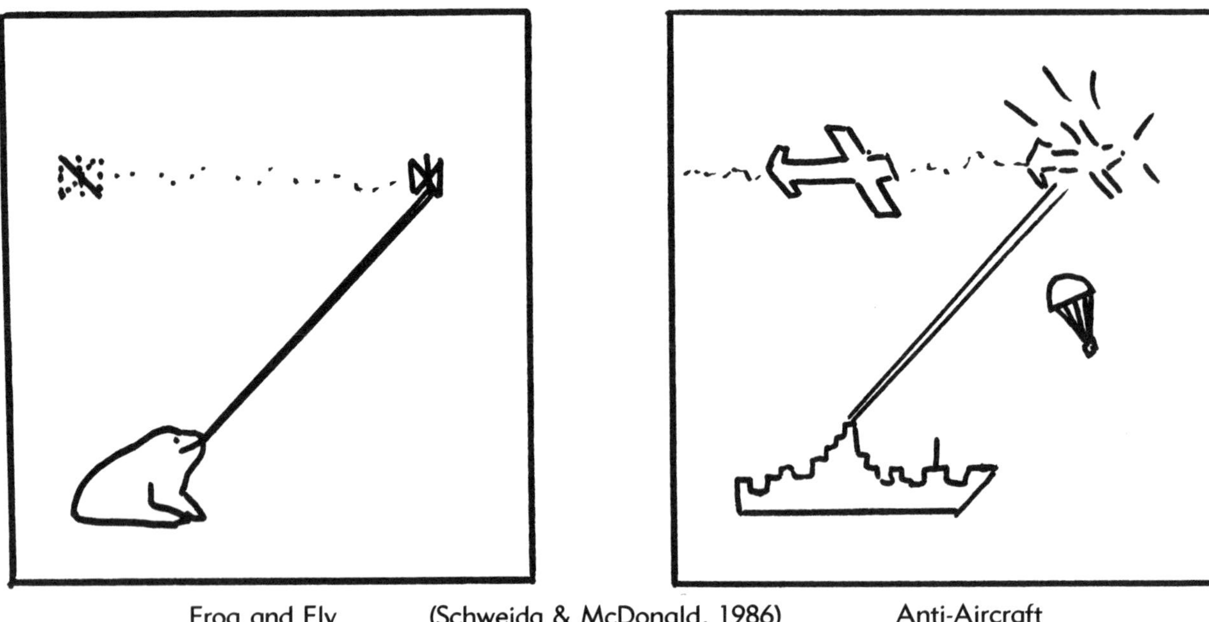

Frog and Fly (Schwejda & McDonald, 1986) Anti-Aircraft

**FIGURE 6.16.** I & R, Timed: Using computer software (visible response envelope).

cator scans to the target cell, the volume is purposely turned down. When the cell is successfully targeted by the child, the facilitator immediately adjusts the volume up, thus making the preprogrammed message audible. In the event the child fails to access the target item within the time allotted by the rate of scan, the volume is again turned down as the indicator advances to the next cell in the scan array. When voice output is not an option based on the device or the computer software being used, the facilitator provides the appropriate praise and reinforcing comments. Throughout training, data are collected regarding the child's ability to accurately access the switch interface when the exposed cell is highlighted within the time allotted by scan rate. The child's performance can be recorded directly on the vinyl overlay using erasable china markers or overhead projector pens. When an element scan pattern is employed, data are collected regarding the number of trials required to successfully select the target cell. When a group-element pattern is being trained, the data collected reflect the child's ability to make both the first and the second switch activations necessary to select the target item. Data that are documented directly on the vinyl overlay during training are later transferred to a separate data sheet, which serves as a guide for future programmatic decisions.

**SINGLE CELL TARGETING IN THE CONTEXT OF A VISIBLE SCAN PATTERN.** When the child has mastered the task of targeting a single exposed cell in the absence of a visible scan pattern, the pattern can be introduced gradually to the child using a scan pattern breakdown approach. With the *scan pattern breakdown approach,* the pattern is task-analyzed into its component parts, which are trained separately before being integrated into the full scan pattern. This approach is designed to initially minimize the cognitive and visual requirements of the scanning task and to gradually increase the task requirements as the child's skills allow. The scan pattern breakdown approach can be applied to the training of:

- ❑ Linear scanning
- ❑ Row-column scanning
- ❑ Directed scanning

**Linear Scanning.** A linear pattern can be trained using a series of tasks. In Task 1, the child undergoes training in targeting designated cells along a single horizontal row. When the child has mastered scanning along a horizontal plane, a second row is introduced creating a matrix (two-dimensional) configuration. When the child has successfully mastered scanning within a matrix of two rows, additional rows are added. Gradual exposure of

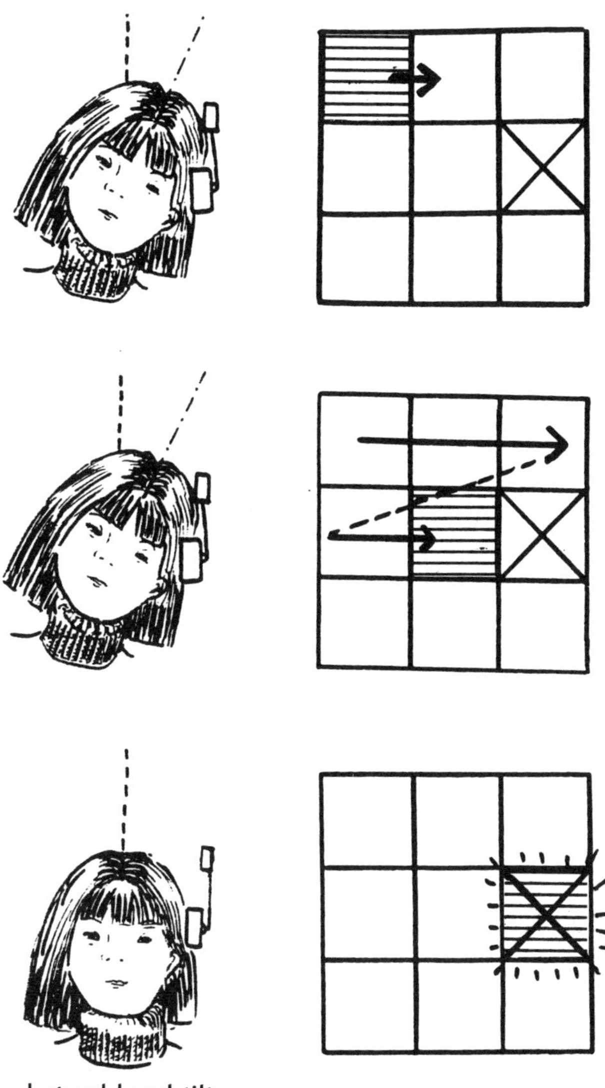


**FIGURE 6.17.** Determining scan mode: Control site variables.

each row is achieved by removing the row of opaque cards that are attached (with Velcro) to a clear 0.020-mil Lexan overlay.

**Row-Column Scanning.** As outlined in Figure 6.21, row-column scanning can also be trained in a series of tasks. In Task 1, the child is required to target cells along a single vertical row. In Task 2, targeting is introduced along a single horizontal row. In Task 3, a second horizontal row is exposed integrating the horizontal and vertical planes, thus creating a matrix configuration for two-dimensional scanning. With each task, steps are presented for systematically manipulating the timing requirements for both the first and second switch activations required in row-column scanning. Those cells providing the child with the maximum amount of time possible to access are typically considered easiest and are thus presented earliest in training. Those cells requiring the least time to prepare for targeting are reserved for later in the training sequence.

**Directed Scanning.** Although directed scanning employs a variable, user-defined pattern, it can also be trained using a breakdown approach. Depicted in Figure 6.22 are the relative times for accessing each cell in an array when using (a) a four-position joystick or four-switch array and (b) an eight-position joystick.

As illustrated in Figure 6.23, directed scanning can be task-analyzed into several component tasks. When using a four-position joystick or a four-switch array, Task 1 would focus attention on targeting cells within a single plane (e.g., left to right, up to down). This can be achieved using an Aquaplast guard (D. Southwick, personal communication, 1989) that contains a slot permitting movement of the joystick in only a single plane (e.g., left to right or up to down). When using a wafer board multiswitch array, only the switches required for targeting in the designated single plane would be simultaneously exposed (e.g., left and right or up and down). When the child has demonstrated the ability to target cells in a single plane, Task 2 is introduced. In Task 2, the horizontal and vertical planes are integrated (cross-formation), requiring the child to make a decision as to which position (left, right, up, down) must be selected to access a target cell designated by the facilitator. It is important to note that when a centering feature is employed, only one motor movement is required (i.e., either up, down, left, or right) to access cells located in the cross-formation. When the child has demonstrated the ability to target cells in a cross-formation (requiring only one motor movement), Task 3 is introduced. In Task 3, the child must target cells outside of the cross-formation. Due to their position in the array, all cells outside the cross require the child to sequence two motor movements.

When using an eight-position joystick (Figure 6.24), additional attention must be directed toward training scanning along a diagonal plane. In Task 1, attention is again focused on targeting cells within

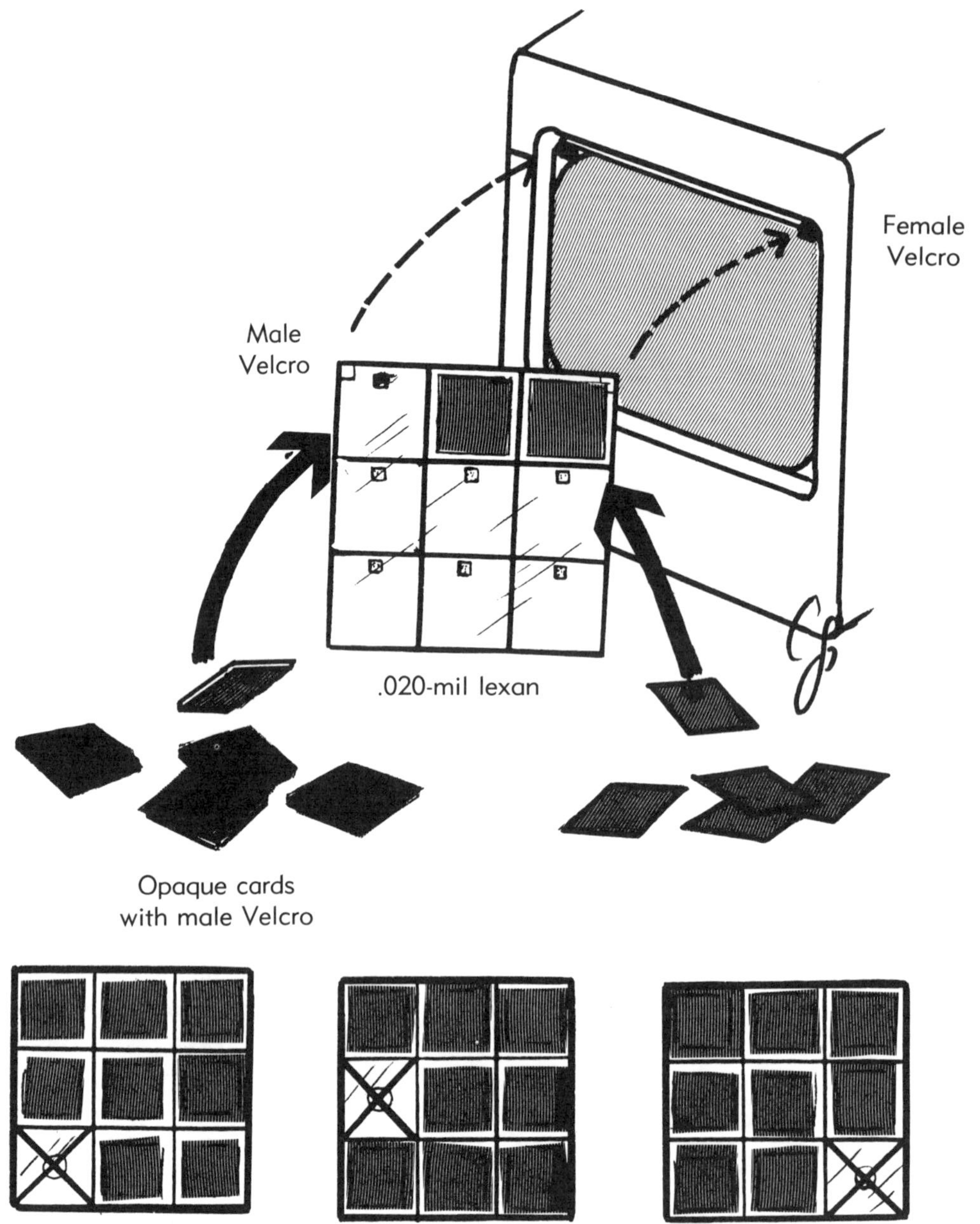


**FIGURE 6.18.** Physical setup for conducting single cell targeting in the absence of a scan pattern.

a single plane (e.g., left to right, up to down, diagonally). In Task 2, the horizontal and vertical planes are integrated (cross-formation) and the diagonal planes are integrated (X-formation), requiring the child to make a decision as to which direction must be selected to access the target cell. In Task 3, the child must target the cells outside of the cross- and X-formation. As with a four-position joystick or four-switch array, the child is now required to sequence two motor movements. Throughout each task, timing is systematically manipulated; initially targeting the items farthest from the center cell (given that a centering feature is employed), allowing the child more time to mentally and motorically prepare for accessing the target cell.

In general, training is conducted using transparent overlays that allow the child to move the scanning indicator along a defined path drawn by the facilitator using a china marker or overhead projector pen. Over time, the child assumes greater

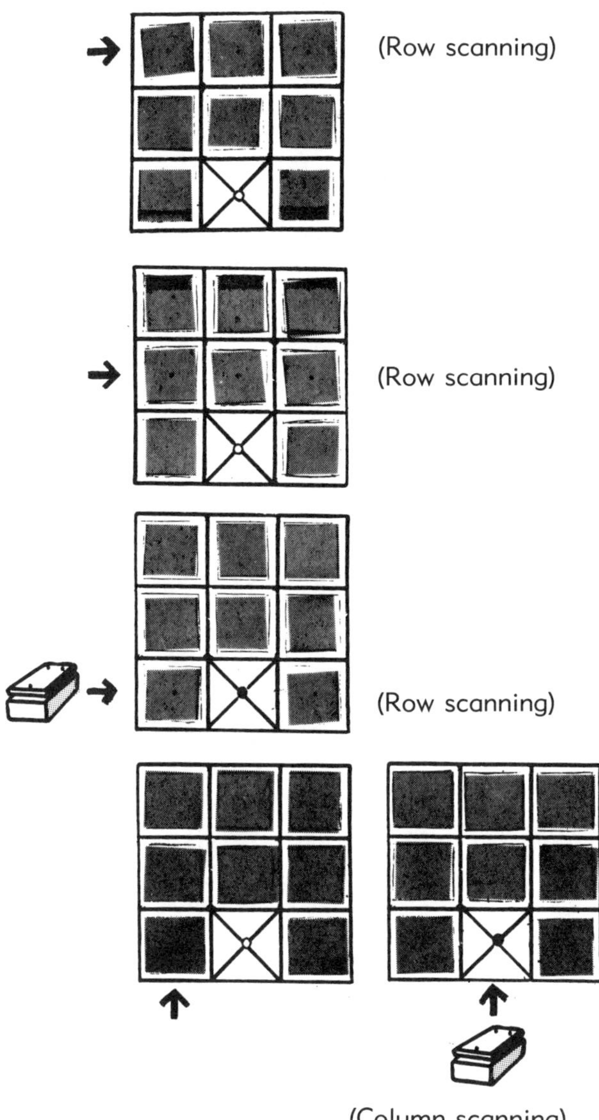


**FIGURE 6.19.** Single cell targeting: Row-column scan pattern.

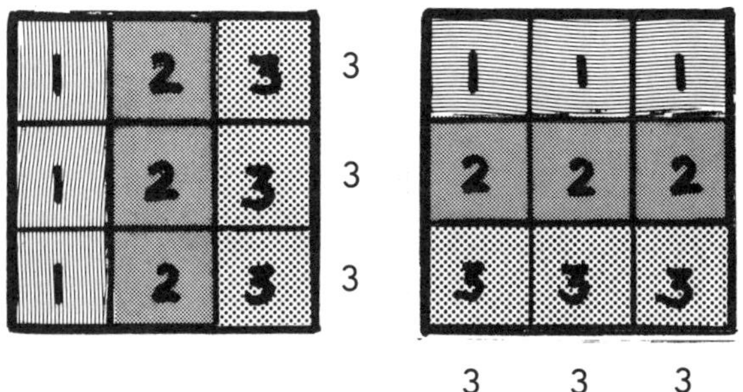


**FIGURE 6.20.** Scan array with timing variables depicted.

responsibility for mentally formulating the most direct path between the center cell and the target cell. Motivating targeting tasks are again utilized for training.

**COMPUTER SOFTWARE.** Presented in Table 6.10 is a sample listing of computer software designed to train linear scanning in motivating task formats. Many of the more exceptional programs have numerous variable features, allowing the task to be tailored to the strengths and weaknesses of the individual child. The Make It in Time software (Don Johnston Developmental Equipment), for example, can be configured to require either a timed I or a timed R, has an adjustable reaction time (delays the action subsequent to activation of the switch, thereby allowing the child to return his or her gaze to the computer monitor), has variable rate of scan, and can provide the facilitator with a printout of the child's performance. Table 6.11 presents sample software addressing row-column scanning in motivating task formats.

**PLAY.** Skills required for directed scanning can also be facilitated through adaptive play using the Blackburn Table (Blackburn, Inventor) and Customized Routes for Remote Controlled Vehicles (Hunsinger, Service De Technologie, Hospital Marie Enfant). The Blackburn Table allows a small object such as a miniature bear or game piece to be moved on the Blackburn Table using either a joystick or a multiswitch array. These options are illustrated in Figure 6.25.

## Summary

Scanning selection techniques require a child to simultaneously perform a number of motor, visual, cognitive, and communication skills. To simplify a scanning selection technique for training, a *layering approach* to intervention is recommended. With a layering approach, the multiple skill requirements of the scanning task are initially minimized. Throughout the training process, skill requirements are gradually and systematically increased. Specifically, intervention proceeds from (a) establishing the motor switch access skills required by scan mode in tasks possessing decreased visual, cognitive, and communication requirements to (b) training scan

Task 1. Targeting cells along a single vertical column

Step a

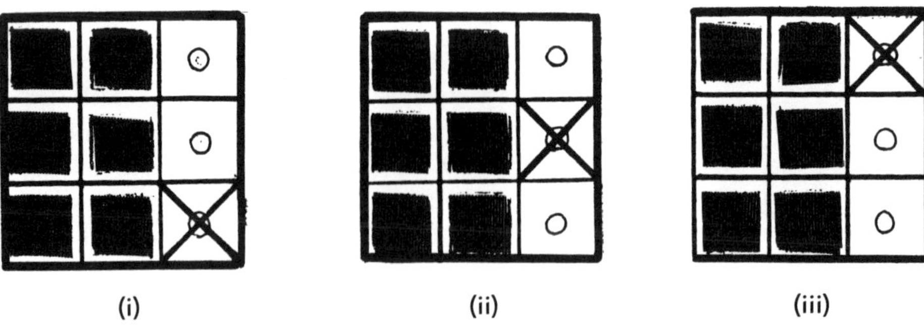


Step b

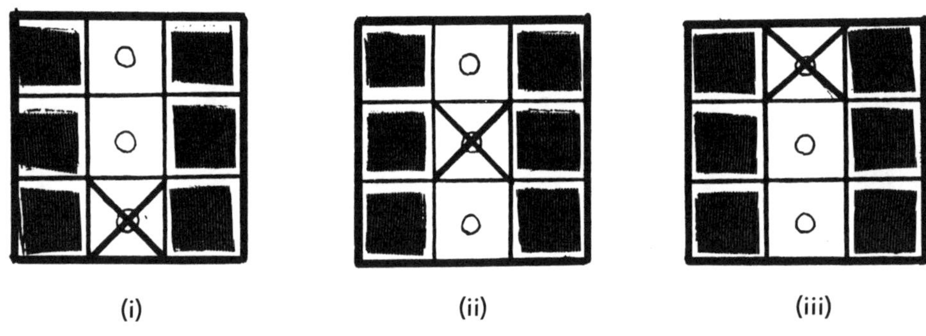


Step c

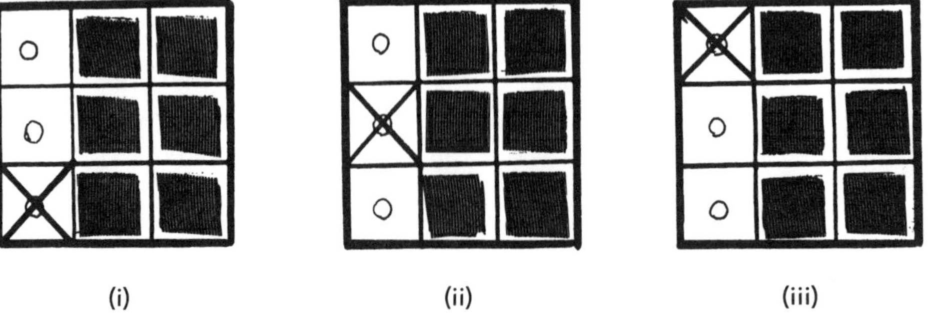


**FIGURE 6.21.** Training row-column scan pattern: Breakdown approach.

Task 2. Targeting cells along a single horizontal row

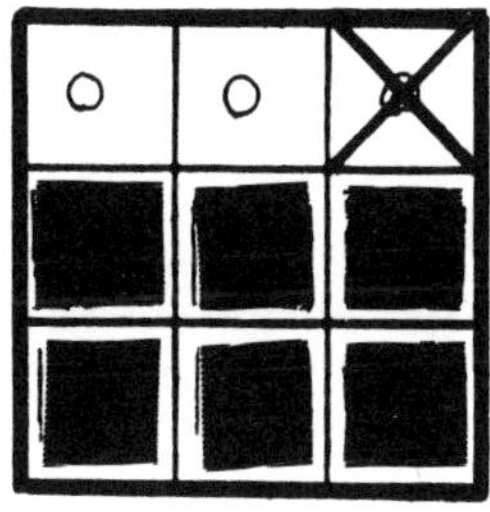
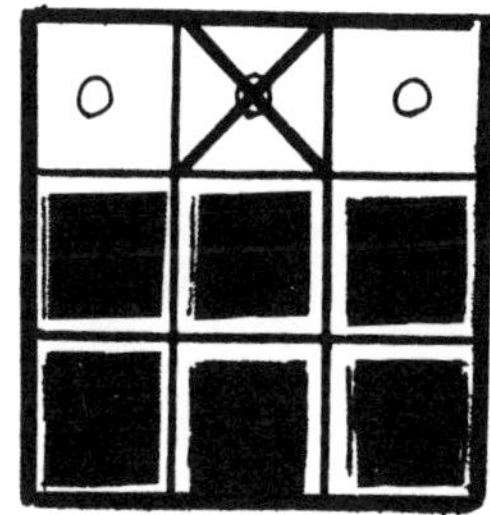
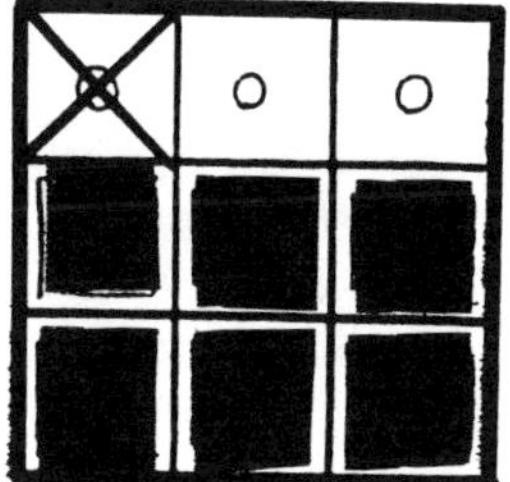

Task 3. Targeting cells within a matrix configuration

Step a

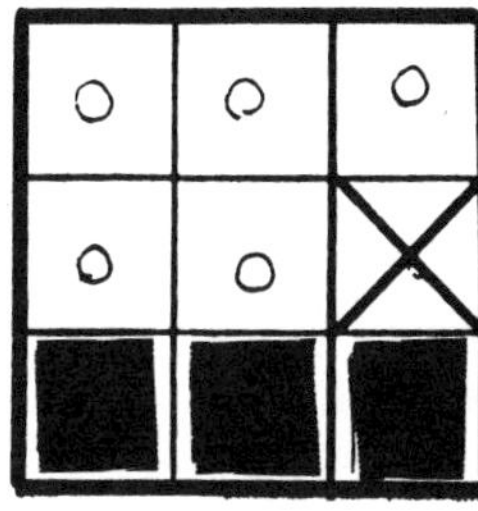
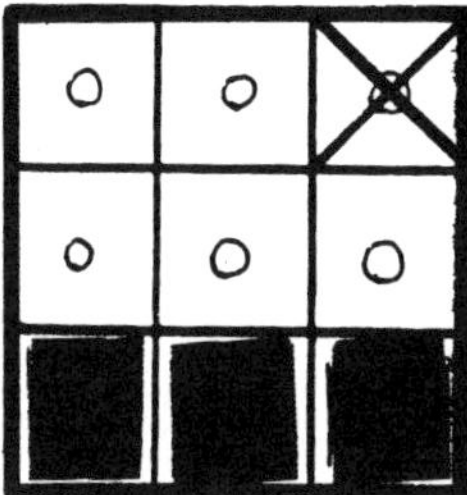

Step b

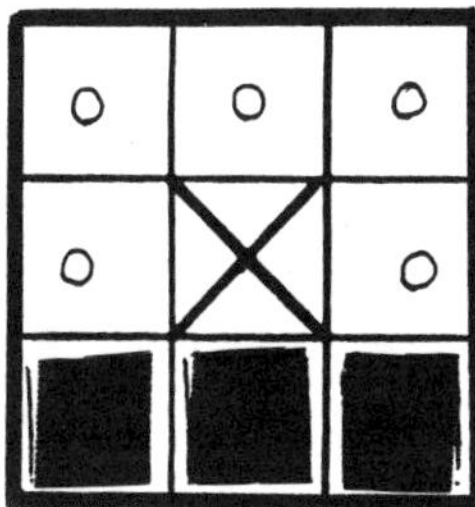
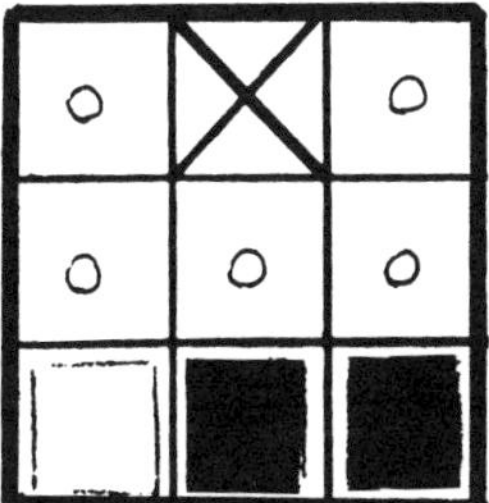

Step c

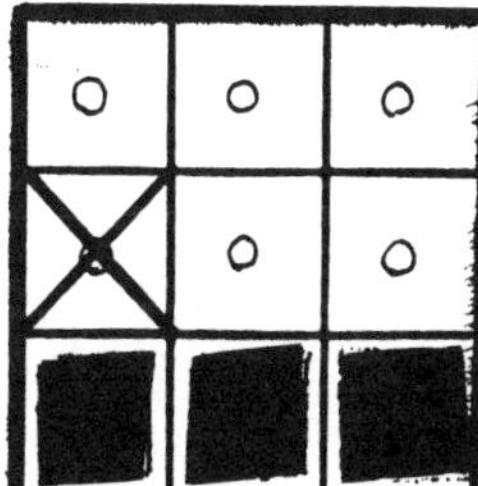
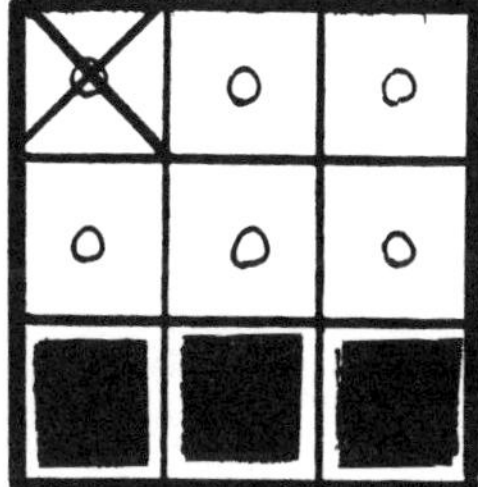

**FIGURE 6.21. (Continued)**

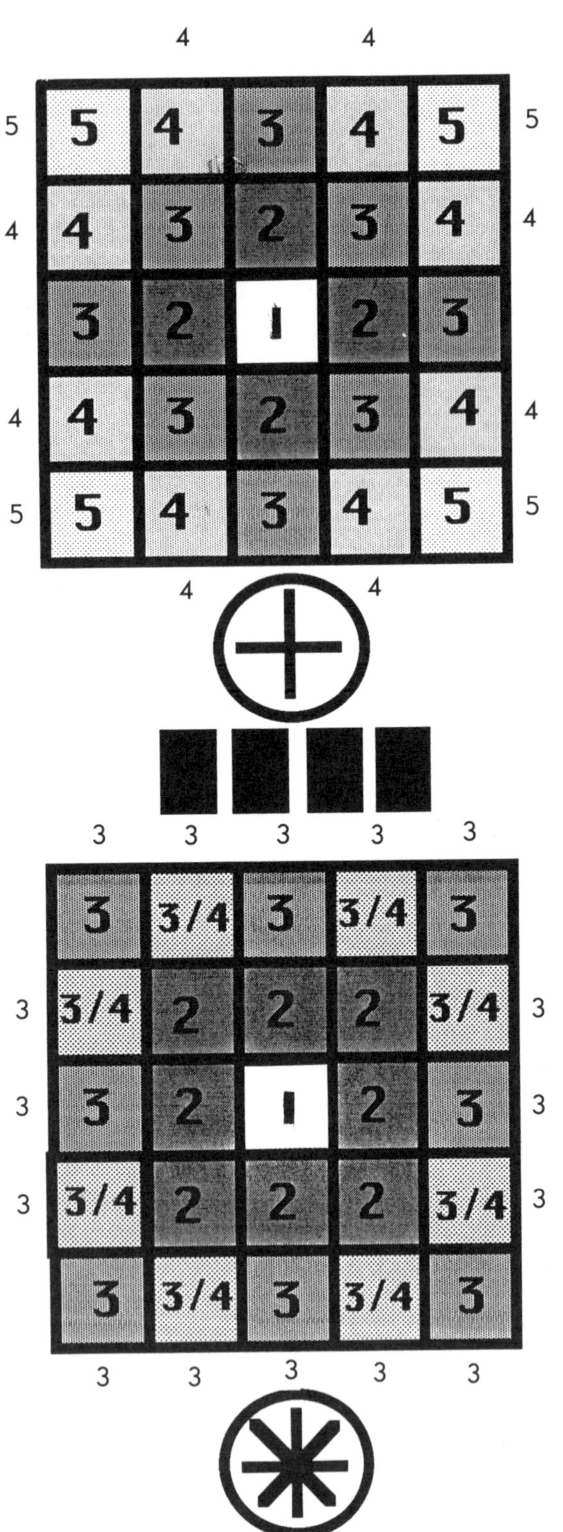


**FIGURE 6.22.** Directed scan array with timing variables depicted for a four- and eight-position joystick.

pattern in tasks with increased visual and cognitive requirements but still minimal communication demands.

Switch accessing skills dictated by scan mode are best taught within motivating formats using switch-accessed battery (DC)- or AC-powered rewards and computer software. Depending on the scan mode being trained (automatic, inverse, step), a variety of training activities are employed to address the following switch accessing skills:

- ❑ Ability to volitionally *initiate* and *maintain* contact with the switch within an *untimed* format
- ❑ Ability to volitionally *release* contact with the switch within an *untimed* format
- ❑ Ability to volitionally *initiate* and *release* contact with the switch in *rapid succession*
- ❑ Ability to volitionally *initiate* and *release* contact with the switch within a *timed* format

Once the child has mastered the switch accessing skills dictated by a particular scan mode, a scan pattern is introduced in the context of a dedicated scanning communication device or microcomputer with scanning software. It is at this point that additional visual and cognitive skills are required of the child. To simplify the skill requirements of the task, training is again initiated with single cell targeting tasks in the absence of a visible scan pattern. The scan pattern is then gradually introduced using a *scan pattern breakdown approach*. With the breakdown approach, the scan pattern is task-analyzed into its component parts, which are trained separately before being integrated into the full scan pattern. Motivating targeting tasks and computer software are again utilized for training.

Adhering to a layering approach for training, communication demands are minimized throughout the training of both scan mode and scan pattern. Having mastered (a) the motor skills dictated by scan mode and (b) the combined motor, visual, and cognitive skills dictated by scan pattern, therapeutic attention can be directed toward establishing communicative use of the child's scanning selection techniques.

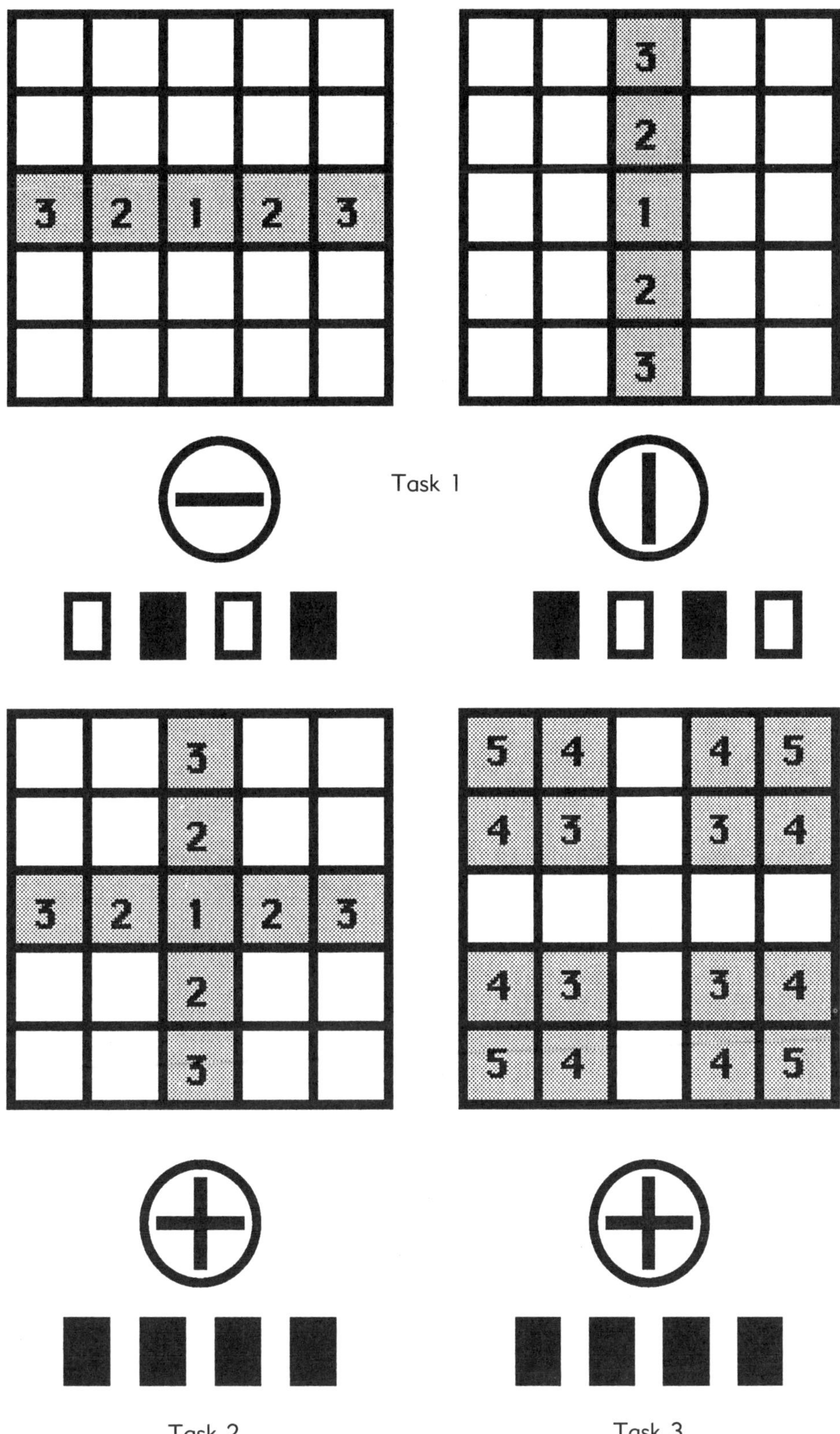


**FIGURE 6.23.** Training directed scanning within a four-position format: Breakdown approach.

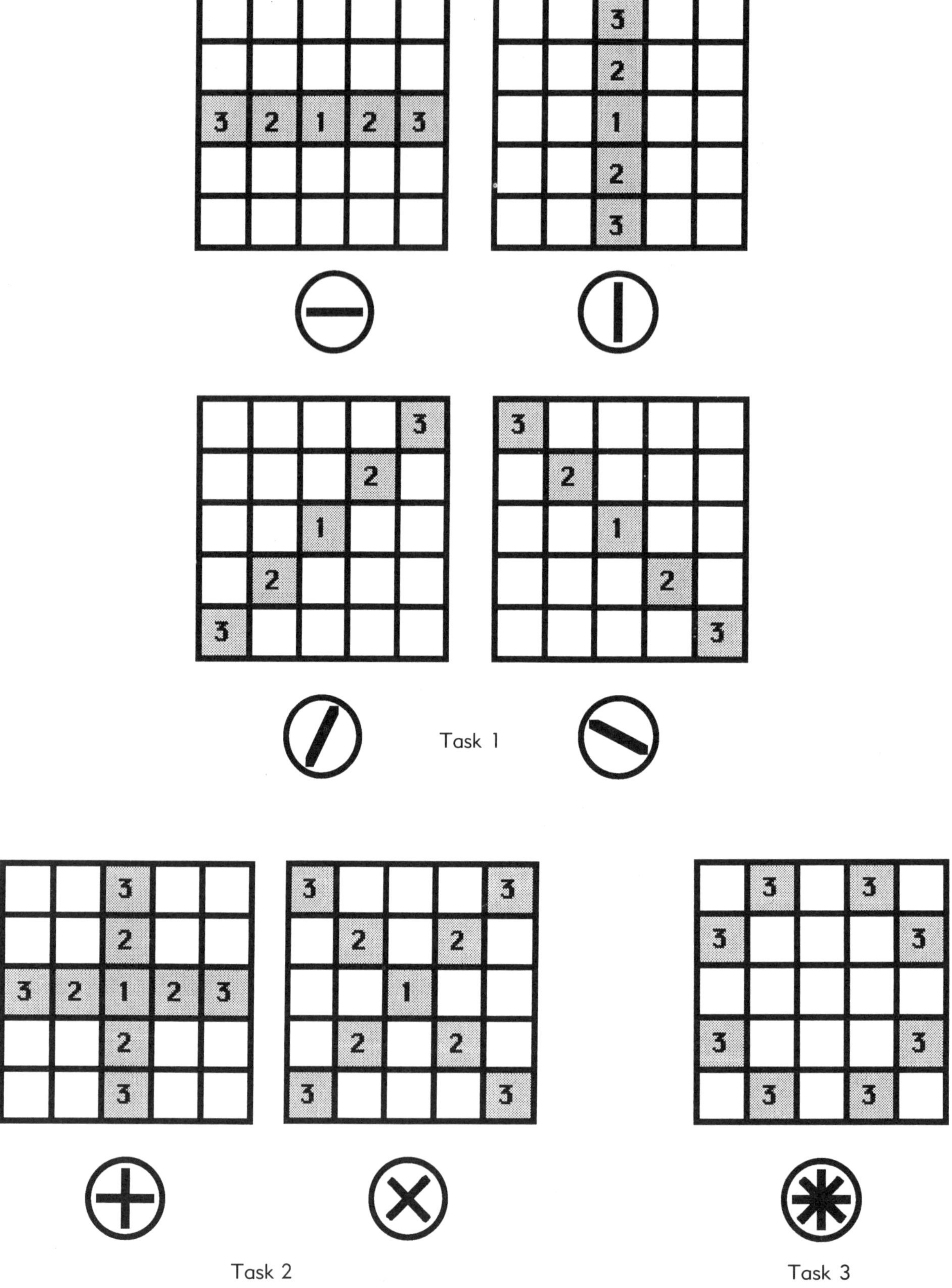


**FIGURE 6.24.** Training directed scanning within an eight-position format: Breakdown approach.

**TABLE 6.10.** Sample Software Addressing Scan Pattern: Linear Scanning

| Software | Description | Source |
|---|---|---|
| Going Fishing | The child is required to I contact with the switch when a colored version of a picture part is superimposed over its noncolored outline in a scan array. When the child successfully performs a timed activation, he or she is rewarded with the visual spectacle of the colored part being transferred to the composite picture. | Learn to Scan (Koch, 1988) Don Johnston Developmental Equipment |
| Moving On | A car, balloon, or truck appears in one of three columns either horizontally or vertically presented. A boy then automatically scans through the three columns. The child is required to initiate contact with the switch when the boy is adjacent to the target object. If successful the reward is an interesting spectacle (e.g., boy grabs bottom of helicopter and is lifted up out of the screen, boy waves goodbye and plane flies forward, rocket blasts off, boy gets in truck and drives off, boy gets on bike and rides off, boy waterskis with boat). | Learn to Scan (Koch, 1988) Don Johnston Developmental Equipment |
| Egg Layer | A bird flies over a nest and descends to the nest to deposit an egg. A linear array of colored eggs appears on the bottom of the screen. If the child successfully stops the cursor on the corresponding color, he or she is rewarded with the spectacle of watching the egg hatch. | Learn to Scan (Koch, 1988) Don Johnston Developmental Equipment |
| Hide and Scan | The child observes a door open and watches a child emerge in a wheelchair. The child in the wheelchair then passes an array of buildings each with a different-colored door. In response to the command, "Press your switch to find me," the child is required to select from an array the color of the door behind which the boy is hiding. When successful he or she receives the verbal praise, "Good watching. I am behind the blue door." The graphic of the boy then exits the successfully targeted door. | Learn to Scan (Koch, 1988) Don Johnston Developmental Equipment |
| Rabbit Scanner | The child must I contact with the switch when the moving cursor (in the shape of a rabbit) is adjacent to a target cell (designated by a carrot) in a linear array. When successful the child is rewarded by the rabbit performing a somersault. | Rabbit Scanner (Rettig, 1987) Don Johnston Developmental Equipment |

**TABLE 6.11.** Sample Software for Training Scan Pattern: Row-Column Scanning in Motivating Task Formats

| Software | Description | Source |
|---|---|---|
| Scancentration | A 4 × 4 matrix of paired symbols appears on the screen. After studying the array for a user-decided length of time, each symbol is covered to be accessed through row-column scanning. The object of the game is to uncover a matched set. When successful the child is verbally praised: "They are the same" accompanied by a trilled sound. When unsuccessful the child hears a buzzer and the comment, "They are different." | Interaction Games (Cooper & Koch, 1987) Don Johnston Developmental Equipment |
| Tic-Tac-Toe | Two players. Each child is required to I contact with the switch twice to select a square. The first activation selects the row; the second activation selects the column. Having selected the desired row and column, the child is assigned a token (either X or O), which is inserted on the display. | Interaction Games (Cooper & Koch, 1987) Don Johnston Developmental Equipment |
| Catch the Cow | The child must I and R contact with Switch A to advance the arrow cursor to select the box containing the cow. The child must then I contact with Switch B to enter this selection. If successful the child is rewarded with a trilling sound and the cow changes from orange to green and moves off the screen to reappear below as a success count. If unsuccessful, the child hears a buzzer sound and loses previously accumulated cows. When three cows are accumulated, a more sophisticated scan array is introduced. | Single Switch Games: Matching and Manipulating (public domain) |

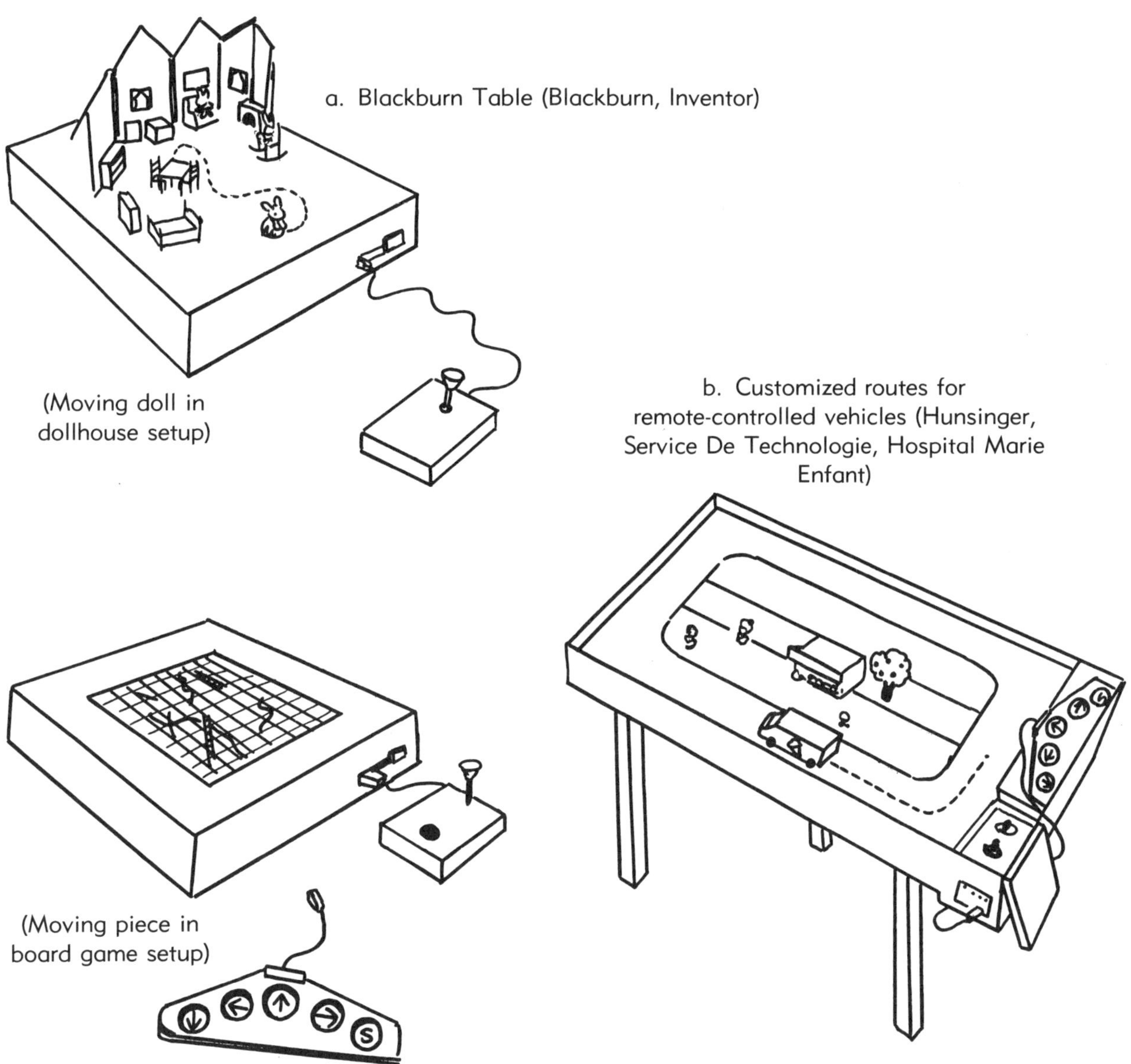


**FIGURE 6.25.** Training directed scanning through adaptive play.

chapter 7

# Communication Training: Early Choice Making

CHILDREN WHO ARE severely physically challenged are frequently observed to be somewhat passive, with an overriding tendency to sit back and let the world come to them. The seeds for this passivity or "learned helplessness" are believed to be sown within the first year of the severely handicapped child's life. During this first year, there is much that children with severe physical limitations are unable to do for themselves. It is therefore not surprising that caregivers come to anticipate and address the child's every need, in the absence of the child's active participation.

In the past decade, the therapeutic emphasis in early intervention programs has focused on establishing avenues of active control from the earliest months of life. Attempting to compensate for poor motor control, children with severe physical involvement are being exposed to switch-operated toys (Burkhart, 1980, 1982) and are being provided with play materials adapted to circumvent an inadequate grasp, poor coordination, or lack of muscle strength (Musselwhite, 1986). Further augmenting the impact of these adapted materials are strategies for breaking up patterns of abnormal tone, allowing the child, with facilitation, to manipulate objects more effortlessly and in a more normalized fashion.

Children are also being therapeutically positioned at an earlier age. Given the benefit of therapeutic positioning, they are better able to move their head and upper extremities against the forces of gravity, and are thus experiencing greater success acquiring the motor skills necessary for nurturing their overall development.

From a communication perspective, steps are being taken to teach children with severe physical handicaps to signal a desire for more of a pleasurable object or activity. These children are also from an early age being taught to assume some measure of control over their environment by engaging in choice-making activities. Prior to the developmental age of 12 months, choice making is primarily realized using real objects, for example, "Let's play . . . BALL? (holding up the ball) . . . SLINKY? (holding up the slinky). You pick." Selection can be achieved through a variety of avenues, depending on the degree of motor involvement: eye point, reach, fist point, finger point, light pointer, head stick. Later, emphasis may be placed on achieving choice making using increasingly more sophisticated levels of symbolic representation (e.g., colored photographs, black and white photographs, realistically colored line drawings, black and white line drawings).

Ideally, cognitively young children with a severe physical handicap should be readily engaging in choice-making activities interspersed throughout the course of their routine day. This goal, however, will be realized only when considerable time is devoted to designing the overall communication system and teaching its use within interactive paradigms.

## Designing the System

When designing a choice-making system (for use in the home and/or the school environment), a systematic approach is required. We have found it helpful to address the task of system setup for choice making using a five-phase, environmentally based approach.

- ❑ Phase I. Delineating the overall communication environment to be impacted
- ❑ Phase II. Delineating and prioritizing potential choices within the overall communication environment
- ❑ Phase III. Establishing the symbolic representations for the previously delineated choices
- ❑ Phase IV. Establishing readily accessible storage displays within the communication environment
- ❑ Phase V. Establishing flexible display formats for choice making

## Phase I. Delineating the Overall Communication Environment to Be Impacted

During Step 1 of Phase I, attention is directed toward documenting the child's daily routine. Presented in Table 7.1 is a form that can be used to glean information from the facilitator(s) regarding (a) routine daily activities (e.g., snack time, toileting, music time), (b) activities frequently engaged in outside the home or school environment (e.g., visiting Grandma, going to McDonald's, going to the park), and (c) activities occasionally engaged in outside the home or school environment (e.g., visiting the zoo).

During Step 2 of Phase I, the facilitator is asked to prioritize activities for system setup. In general, it is suggested that priority be given to activities that (a) occur frequently in the child's routine, (b) are highly motivating activities for the child, and (c) reflect a high priority need based on past frustrations stemming from the inability to communicate effectively.

## Phase II. Delineating and Prioritizing Potential Choices Within the Overall Communication Environment

During Phase II, attention is directed toward delineating juncture points in the target activities where choices might be provided. During music time, for example, children might be given a choice of who to sit beside (Jimmy vs. Judy), what musical instrument they wish to play (drum vs. shaker), what song to sing (''Wheels on the Bus'' vs. ''The Rainbow Song''), what color scarf they wish to wave during ''The Rainbow Song'' (red vs. blue), what animal will be next in the Old MacDonald song (cow vs. cat), and who gets to pick the next animal in the Old MacDonald song (Judy vs. Benjamin). During snack time, children might be given a choice of what they want on their cracker (Cheeze Whiz vs. peanut butter), or what they wish to drink (water vs. milk). On the playground, children might be given a choice of what playground equipment they wish to play on (swing vs. rocker) and who will push them on the swing (Miss Nancy or Miss Ellen). During an individual physical therapy session, they might be given a choice of what exercise they wish to do next (balancing on the ball vs. weight bearing on their knees). Having selected weight bearing on their knees, they might be given a further choice of what toy they wish to play with while they are engaged in this exercise (discovery cottage toy vs. ring-stacking toy).

When delineating objects or activities that can be included in a choice-making paradigm, it is important to delineate not only those objects or activities that are high preference for the individual children, but also objects or activities that are low preference or that they perhaps dislike. As will be discussed later in this chapter, a low-preference object or activity may be paired with a high-preference object or activity to heighten the child's awareness of the need to pay closer attention to the symbolic representation. When choosing between two high-preference objects or activities, the consequence of a haphazard choice is not as marked as when choosing between a high- and a low-preference choice.

When choice-making paradigms are being established within a classroom setting where several children are candidates for training, all toys and activities can potentially serve a role as either high-preference or low-preference activities for a given child. Because preferences vary greatly across children and individual preferences shift over time, it is highly advisable to establish a broad array of objects and activities within the classroom as potential items for choice making through the course of the day.

**TABLE 7.1.** Daily Communication Schedule

| Activity | No. of Times/ Day | Brief Description | | | Present Communication | | | | | Communication Success | | | | | | | | |
|---|---|---|---|---|---|---|---|---|---|---|---|---|---|---|---|---|---|---|
| | | Who/ | What/ | Where | Minimal | Objects | Pics Only | Device | Other | Poor | 1 | 2 | 3 | 4 | 5 | 6 | 7 | Superior |
| | | | | | | | | | | | | | | | | | | |

*Note.* From C. R. Musselwhite, 1990, (personal communication). Ashville, NC: Irene Wortham Center.

### Phase III. Establishing the Symbolic Representations for the Previously Delineated Choices

During Phase III attention is directed toward securing symbolic representations for the previously delineated objects or activities that will serve as potential choices throughout the day. When working with a cognitively young child, choice making is typically initiated first with real objects and only later with pictorial representations such as colored photographs, black and white photographs, or black and white line drawings. As indicated by Mirenda and Locke (1989), the aforementioned symbolic representations of objects are not equivalent in terms of their relative difficulty. According to their study involving 40 nonspeaking clients ranging in age from 3-11 to 20-10 years, the relative hierarchy of receptive recognition for noun labels (easiest to hardest) is as follows: nonidentical objects, colored photographs, black and white photographs, miniature objects, black and white line drawings (Picsyms, Self-Talk, Picture Communication Symbols, and Rebus, in that order), Blissymbols, and written words. This ordering occurred regardless of the disability type (mild, moderate, and severe mental retardation; autism) of the nonspeaking individuals involved in the study.

The symbolic representation employed with a given child will vary depending on the child's cognitive level. When engaged in early intervention, we have tended to use photographs with children functioning cognitively between a 12- and 18-month level with the intent of transitioning to line drawings before 24 months of age. Once the child is able to relate to line drawings, the ready availability of numerous commercially available symbol sets greatly facilitates the task of system setup.

Realistic pictorial representations can be derived by (a) taking colored photographs of the various objects or activities, (b) cutting realistic pictures from the box in which the toy or food item was purchased (Van Tatenhove, 1985), or (c) cutting realistic colored pictures out of magazine advertisements. When taking photographs of referents, it is advisable to use a 35-mm camera and to place the object on a plain (yellow) poster board to enhance the picture's figure-ground differential. Ideally, these photographs should be taken using unidirectional artificial light or window light. Because unidirectional light tends to cast a slight shadow under the object, objects photographed according to this procedure tend to appear more three-dimensional than photographs shot with multidirectional light. Once the photographs for the various choices previously delineated in Phase II are successfully secured, the corresponding line drawing versions can be derived by placing a photocopy version of the photograph face up on a light box or against a window to facilitate the process of tracing its major features to create a simple line drawing version. The line drawing version of the identical referent is then placed on file serving as a master. This master can be subsequently photocopied for use during choice-making activities.

Moving further up the scale of abstractness, the corresponding pictographic symbols can be derived from commercially available symbol sets. To enhance the figure-ground differential of (a) the black and white line drawings created from photographs and (b) the black and white pictographic symbols derived from commercially available symbol sets, it is recommended that the facilitator color the background, leaving the figure white.

Within the classroom setting, three types of symbol representations have proven to be beneficial to the intervention process: colored photographs (or realistic box pictures) of the identical referent, black and white line drawings of the identical referent (with color-enhanced background), and black and white pictographic symbols derived from a commercially available pictographic symbol set (with color-enhanced background). This range of symbolic representations is summarized in Figure 7.1.

Many interventionists tend to embrace a particular commercially available symbol set and to select symbols from other sets only when they are dissatisfied with a particular exemplar within the core set. Whereas we initially agonized over what symbol set to use with what child within the classroom setting, we have since adopted a strategy of selecting one highly pictographic set that is used with all children within the classroom setting. The children in the class are thus better able to benefit from seeing their symbols being used by other children within the classroom setting. Generally, the extent to which children see their symbols being used interactively day in and day out is the greatest determinant of the acquisition of spontaneous, self-initiated use.

To enhance the longevity of these symbolic representations, it is recommended that they be

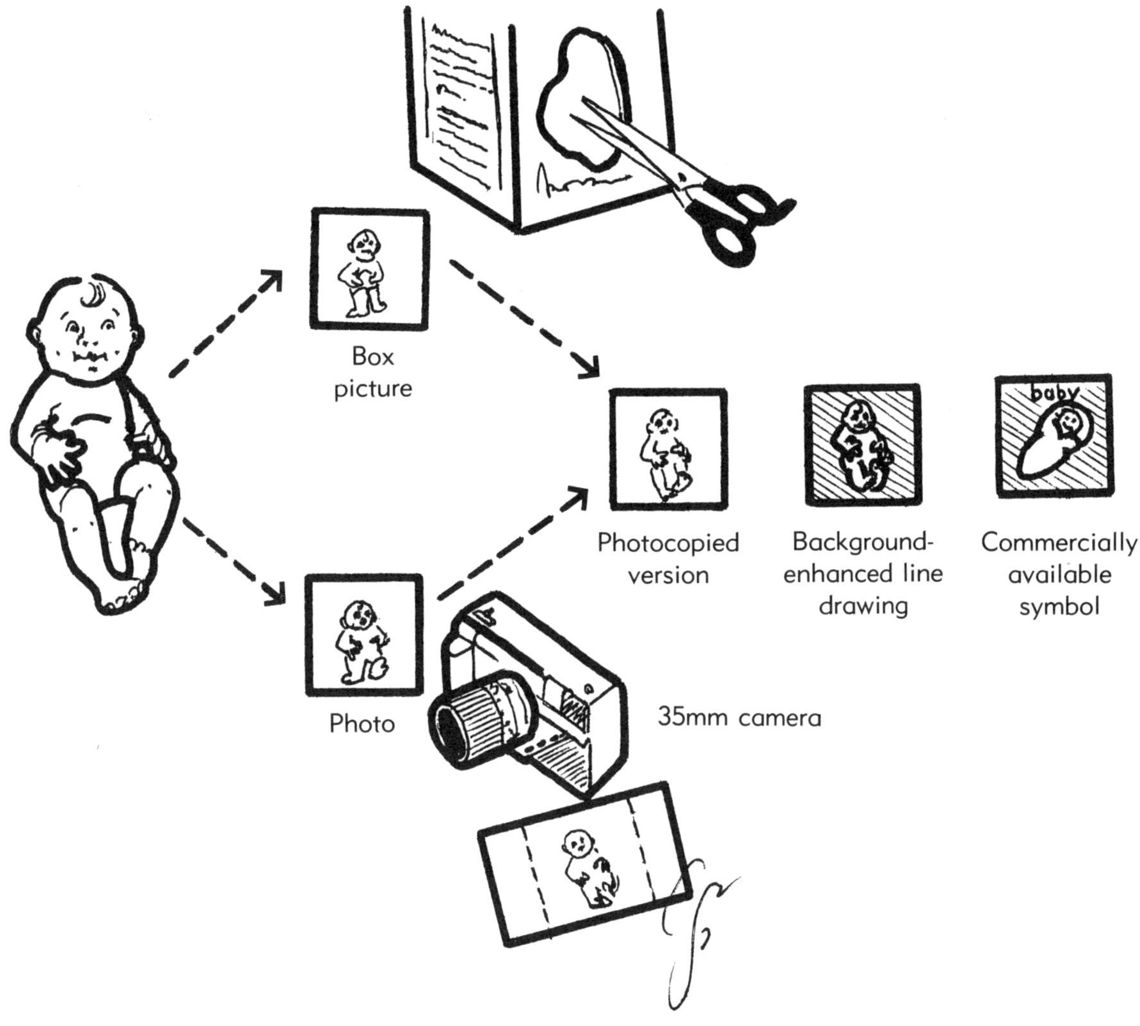


**FIGURE 7.1.** Range of symbolic representations.

laminated or covered on both sides with clear contact paper. A 1-inch square of adhesive male Velcro is then attached to the back of each symbolic representation, allowing it to be attached to both the storage displays and the communication displays to be discussed in Phases IV and V, respectively.

### Phase IV. Establishing Readily Accessible Storage Displays Within the Environment

If a choice-making paradigm is to be successfully implemented within the environment, the symbolic representations for the choice options must be readily accessible. In the past, attempts to use a three-ring binder that stored all potential choices and their range of symbolic representations proved unsuccessful, because it required too much time to find the book, leaf through its alphabetical listing, and locate and pull out the desired pictures. If choices are to be presented as they arise at key juncture points in the daily routine, formats are required that store the visual representations (a) in the area where they are most likely to be needed and (b) in a format that minimizes the time required to locate the desired visual representation. Toward addressing the first concern, the visual representations reflecting choices that can occur within the bathroom routine should be stored in the bathroom; choices relative to mealtime or snack time would be stored in the area where eating typically occurs or where the snacks are typically stored; choices unique to watching TV would be stored in the room where the family watches TV; choices relative to classroom circle-time activities would be stored in the general area where circle time is conducted; choices relative to the playground would be stored in the general vicinity of the exit to the playground.

Illustrated in Figures 7.2 and 7.3 are several storage options that address the need to minimize the time required to locate and select the desired visual representations within the home and classroom settings. In general, storage displays are constructed of (a) plastic pockets (cut-apart photo protector sheets) that are adhered to a surface with adhesive, double-backed foam tape; (b) strips of adhesive female Velcro applied directly to a surface or applied to a clear vinyl sheet that is then attached to a surface with hooks (adhesive, screw, or suction cup); (c) indoor/outdoor carpet adhered to a surface with heavy-duty staples, glue, or hooks; or (d) Tempo display-loop fabric, a fabric (available in many colors) that couples with male Velcro.

When designing a choice-making paradigm for the home setting, aesthetic issues must be addressed in addition to functional issues. Although some families have no reservations about their home turning into a large environmental communication display, others prefer that the visual representations be readily accessible, but concealed. Several accessible, but concealed storage options are visually depicted in Figure 7.4.

When a concealed storage option is not immediately accessible, steps can be taken to move the storage display to a more accessible location for the duration of the activity. In the kitchen, for example, adhesive hooks mounted on the refrigerator allow the concealed, but not readily accessible storage display to be placed within easier reach for the duration of the activity. Upon completing the meal or snack, this mobile storage display is then returned to its habitual storage location. In the bathroom, suction cup hooks mounted on the mirror allow the storage display to be made more accessible during the activity. When the bathroom routine has been completed, the storage display is returned to its habitual location.

In many instances, duplicate pictures may be needed in several storage locations. Multiple arrays of people are typically required in several locations throughout the home or school setting. During mealtime for example, the child might be given the choice, ''Who do you want to feed you (Mom or Dad)?''; while watching TV the child might be given the choice, ''Who do you want to hold you while watching TV (Mom, Dad, or sister)?''; when getting ready for bed, the child may be given the choice, ''Who do you want to give you your bath?''; while involved in the bedtime routine, the child might be given the choice, ''Who do you want to read the bedtime story?'' The need for making choices between people across a wide variety of activities thus necessitates that the visual representations for people be replicated on several storage displays throughout the home or school.

### Phase V. Establishing Flexible Display Formats for Choice Making

Choice making can be achieved using a variety of selection techniques. As illustrated in Figures 7.5 and 7.6, several options exist for choice making using a nonelectronic display format. Although most nonelectronic formats reflect the use of a direct selection technique, partner-assisted scanning is also possible.

As visually represented in Figures 7.7, 7.8, and 7.9, several options also exist for conducting choice making within an electronic format. Although some options involve direct selection, others use a scanning selection technique. Many options provide the motivation of voice output (e.g., Parrot JK, Remote Switch IntroTalker, Powerpad, AIPS Wolf); others, such as rotary scanners and electronic choice boxes, do not. Although some options are highly portable, those involving software on a personal computer tend to limit communication to activities that can be conducted in the general vicinity of the personal computer.

When deciding what display format to use when, several factors must be taken into consideration. These factors can be discussed as three broad categories: child factors, time factors, and situation factors.

**CHILD FACTORS.** Choices achieved via direct selection are typically considered to be cognitively easier than choices achieved through scanning. Being cognizant of this fact, many facilitators strive to give cognitively young children experience making choices via direct selection techniques before the additional operational knowledge that is required to make choices using a scanning selection technique is superimposed on

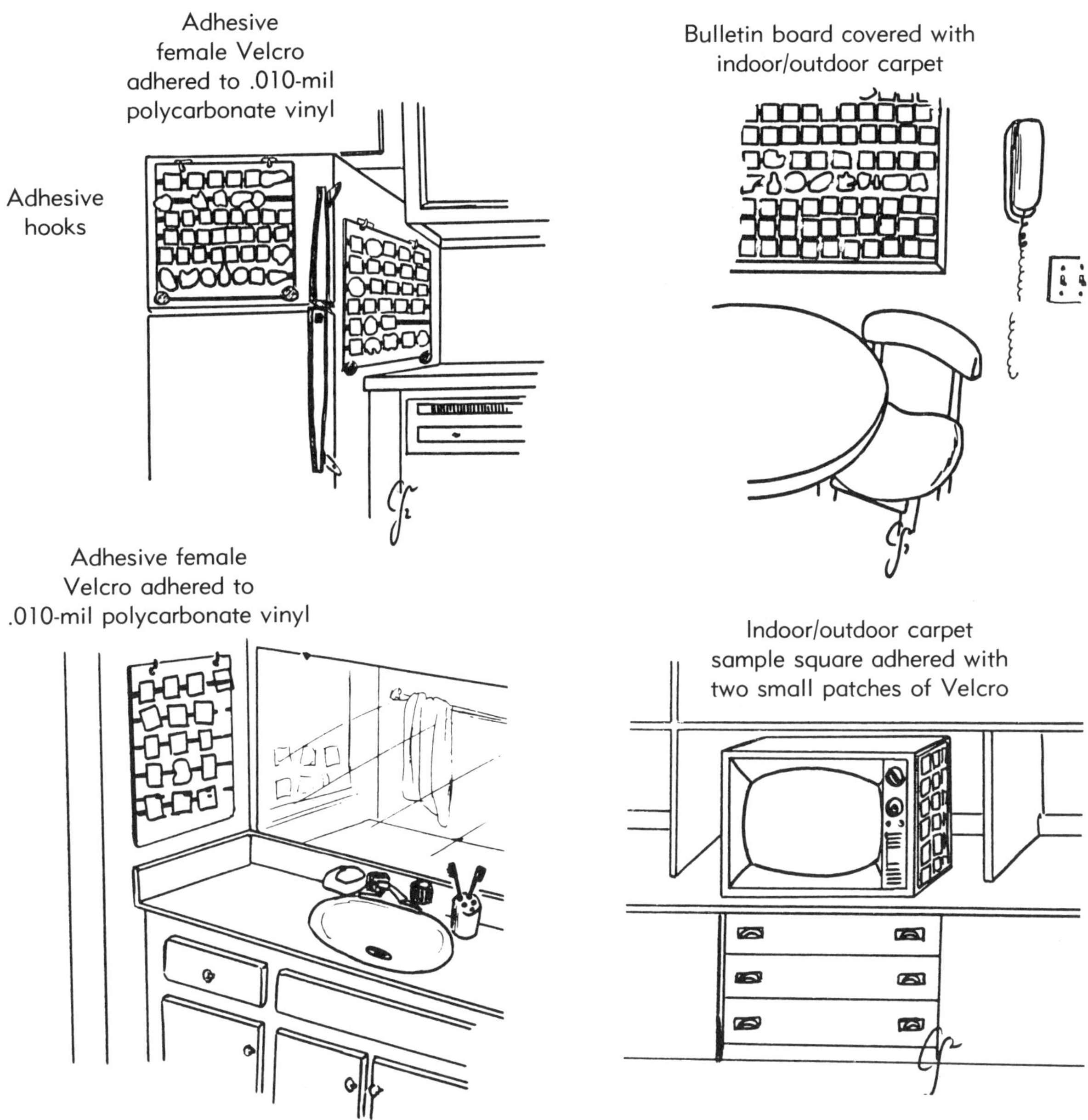


**FIGURE 7.2.** Readily accessible storage options for the home.

the choice-making task. As choice array size is increased, however, direct selection options may no longer be feasible. A child with strabismus, for example, may be able to give readily interpretable eye-pointing responses when the facilitator is holding two choices that are widely spaced. When the child's therapeutic plan necessitates an increase in choice array size, however, the child's eye-pointing responses may no longer be intelligible. A scanning selection technique is therefore warranted. Similarly a severely motor-involved child may be able to use a fist point to reliably select one of three choices. When array size is increased beyond this number, however, motor difficulty necessitates the use of either nonelectronic, partner-assisted scanning, or electronic scanning.

**TIME FACTORS.** Time is perhaps the most important single determinant of whether a given choice will be conducted within a nonelectronic or an electronic format. Within the busy home or classroom schedule, nonelectronic formats tend to be used more fre-

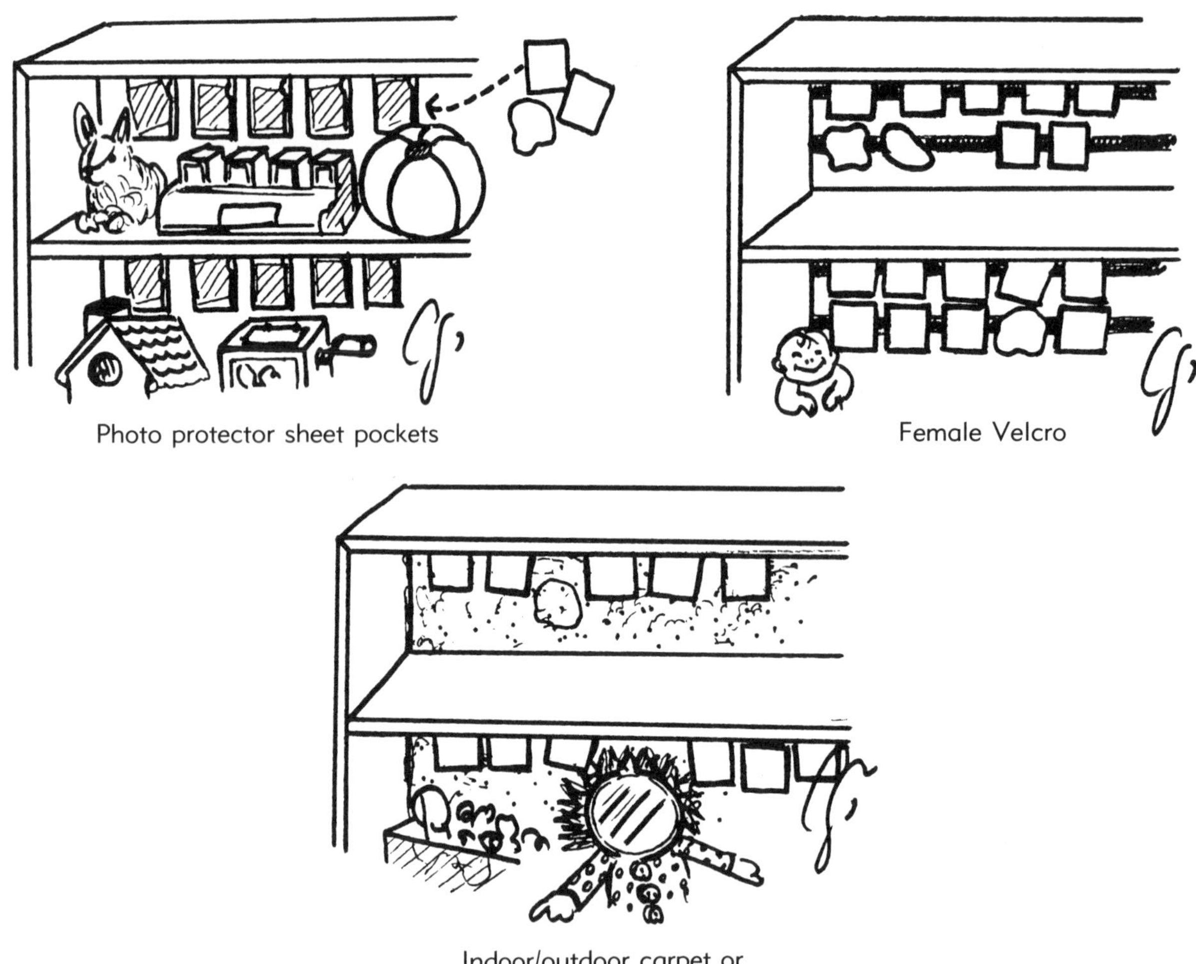


**FIGURE 7.3.** Readily accessible storage options for the classroom.

quently, because they require considerably less time to implement. Although choice making may be more easily achieved within a nonelectronic format, the highly motivating nature of voice output should not be overlooked in the decision process. Furthermore, if the child is to ultimately benefit from being able to call forth preprogrammed sentences to achieve conversational exchange, early choice making achieved through a scanning communication device is a necessary first step. Choice making achieved through electronics, specifically scanning, is thus a necessary means to an end.

**SITUATION FACTORS.** Situation factors also play an important role in the decision to use a nonelectronic instead of an electronic format for a given choice opportunity occurring within the flow of the day's routine. Some choices simply are not feasible within an electronic format. Bath time, for example, is a time replete with opportunities for meaningful choice making. Unfortunately, the use of an electronic device is not feasible within this context.

For many families, mealtime is a slow, labor-intensive process. Although many families are amenable to incorporating a rapidly achieved nonelectronic direct selection format such as eye pointing into this already time-consuming routine, many prefer not to slow the process further by overlaying a scanning selection technique.

In the final analysis, it is a combination of child variables, time variables, and situation variables that will dictate what display format will be used to mediate a particular choice at a key juncture point in the flow of the daily routine. Because electronic formats (especially voice-output options) often require more steps to set the choice contingency in place, varied choices simply would not be frequently offered throughout the course of the day if choice

**FIGURE 7.4.** Accessible, but concealed storage options.

making had to be realized solely through electronic means. However, steps can be taken to facilitate use of a voice-output format within an environmental approach. In current practice, dedicated aids or personal computers are typically programmed as *specific choice sets.* When programmed as a specific choice set, the exact verbal labels for the choice items or activities are programmed into the device. During snack time, for example, the child might be given a choice of CRACKER, MILK, JUICE, PEANUT

**FIGURE 7.5.** Choice making with nonelectronic displays—Manual pointing, chin pointer, light pointer, partner-assisted scanning.

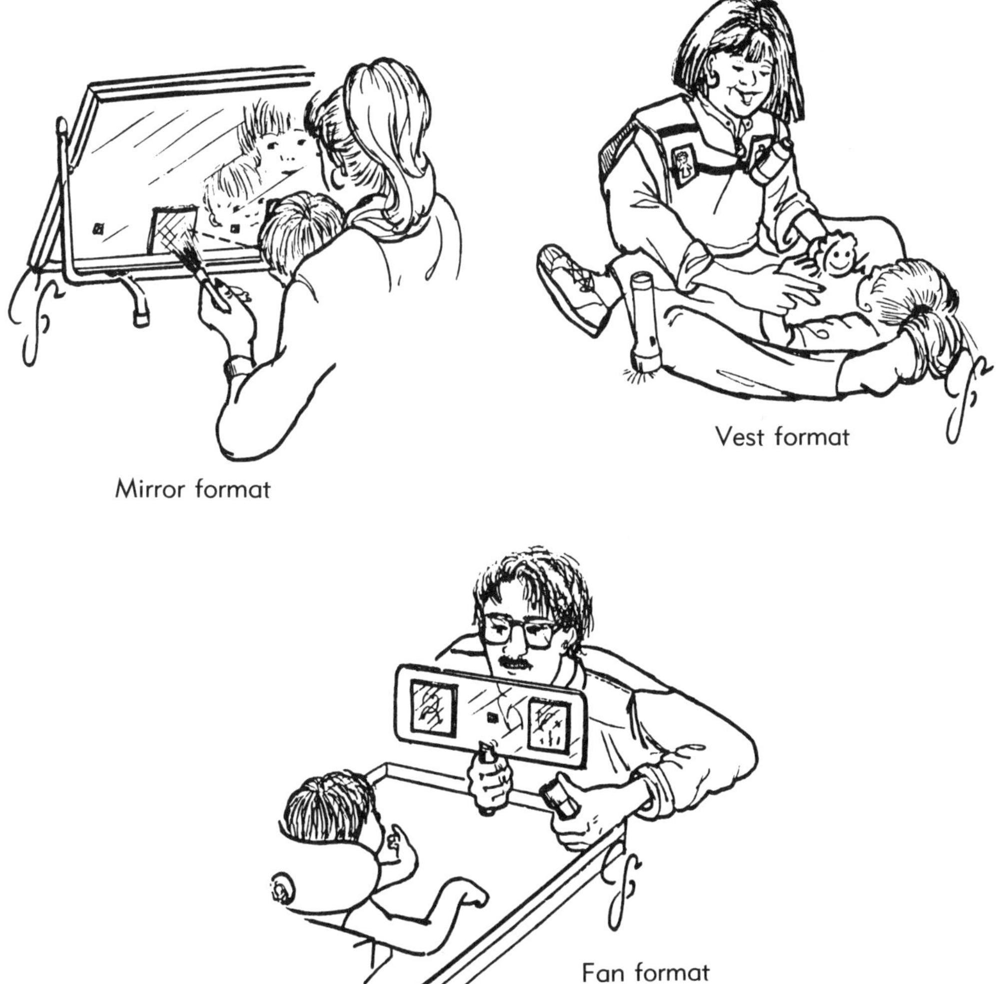


**FIGURE 7.6.** Choice making with nonelectronic displays—Eye pointing.

**FIGURE 7.7.** Choice making achieved electronically—No voice output.

**FIGURE 7.8.** Choice making achieved electronically with voice output—Direct selection.

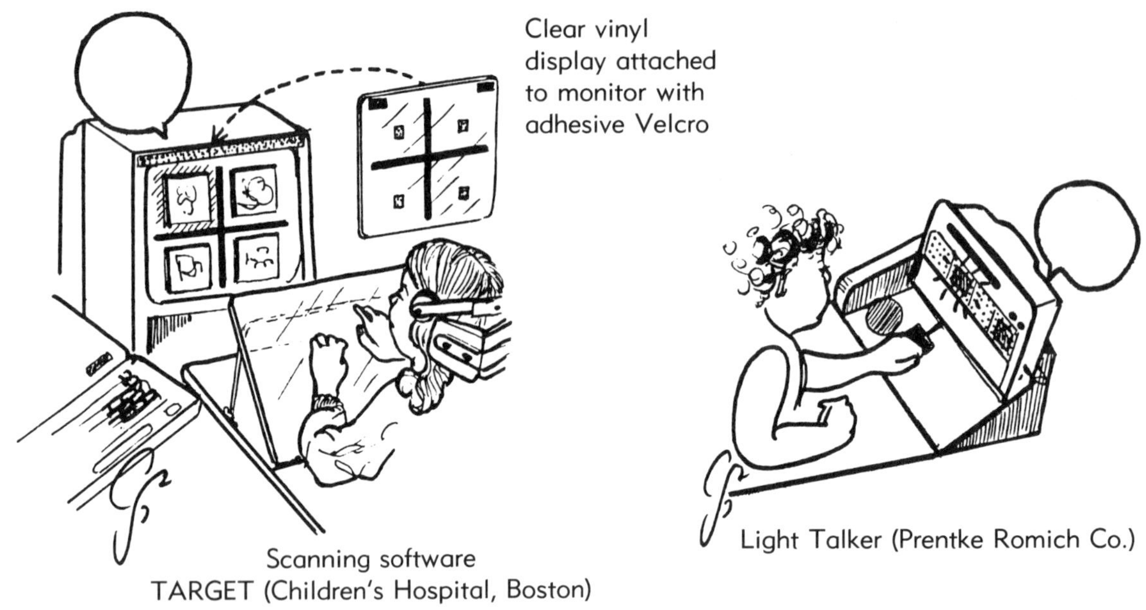


**FIGURE 7.9.** Choice making achieved electronically with voice output—Scanning.

BUTTER. During play time he or she might be given a choice of BALL, BOOK, MUSIC, ROBOT. When specific choice sets are being used, the provision of specificity results in a concomitant loss of flexibility. Although the facilitator could create numerous permutations of various choice sets of specific activities or objects, extra setup time would be required to delineate which preprogrammed permutation best suits the needs of that particular choice juncture. As a supplement to or an alternative to specific choice sets, the facilitator may wish to use more *generic choice sets.* A generic choice set for food-based items, for example, might include the messages, "Gimme this," "Want this," "More please," "Want some." When using a generic choice set, the full array of foods can be easily accommodated within one shared format. A generic choice set for people-based choices might include repetitions of, "I pick her," "I pick him." Using this format all persons in the class could serve as potential choices, in any combination. The generic choice set for toy-based items might include, "Get me this," "Want this one," "I pick this," "Wanna play with this." All toys, in any combination, can now be used for choice making. Choices relative to therapeutic positioning might include, "Wanna do this," "I pick this," "Put me here," "Move me here."

In contrast to specific choice sets, generic choice sets allow the facilitator (a) access to a broader array of choice alternatives (i.e., choice alternatives are not limited to those preprogrammed in the device) and (b) greater flexibility in manipulating choice alternatives within a high- versus low-preference continuum. Generic choice sets work well with older children for whom choice making is being used to assist in training alternate selection techniques. For cognitively younger children who are just acquiring language, specific choice sets are definitely the preferred option.

When several specific choice sets (e.g., toy choice set A, B, C, D; music choice set A, B, C; lunch choice set; snack choice set) are programmed into a device, it is also feasible to designate a generic message such as, "Wanna play with this" (for the toy choice set) or "Let's sing this" (for the music choice set) to a specific location on the device. When displays are constructed with symbols as detachable units fastened with Velcro, a symbol representing either a new toy or a toy from toy choice set B can be paired with any choice on toy choice set A. This symbol is merely placed on the generic message location of the device or on the remote switch corresponding to this location. In this fashion the facilitator is able to quickly offer a new choice that is not currently programmed into the device or is able to functionally straddle two pages on the device by quickly moving a choice from one choice set to another (e.g., moving "Old MacDonald" from music choice set

A to the generic message location on music choice set B for a particular choice-making opportunity). A generic message cell thus adds greater flexibility into specific choice sets.

As illustrated in Figure 7.10, the communication display formats for generic choice sets can be constructed of clear vinyl (0.10 or 0.20 mil) that is attached to the computer monitor or Plexiglas faceplate of the portable dedicated communication device (adhesive female Velcro on the device; adhesive male Velcro on the vinyl display). Narrow strips of colored plastic tape can be used to delineate the target cells. A 1-inch square of adhesive female Velcro can be affixed to each choice cell to serve as the point of attachment for the symbolic representations previously constructed in Phase III. If the device is configured in an eight-location format, the possibility exists to program in two related generic choice sets, thereby further eliminating the need to call forth a new level when a new choice set is required. A lightweight cardboard bar can be used to block out the top or the bottom row, depending on the generic choice set required.

## Training Use of the System

Ideally, we would like to see cognitively young children who are severely physically challenged given numerous opportunities to make meaningful choices throughout the course of the day. For this to occur, attention must be directed toward the following issues:

- ❑ Conducting training within versus outside the target environment
- ❑ Utilizing intermittent versus massed trials
- ❑ Using electronic versus nonelectronic options
- ❑ Manipulating choice array size
- ❑ Presence versus absence of the choice referents
- ❑ Utilizing high- versus low-preference choices
- ❑ Utilizing free- versus restricted-choice format
- ❑ Providing models of spontaneous self-initiated use
- ❑ Utilizing a prompt hierarchy to establish the choice-making behavior
- ❑ Transitioning from real objects to photographs to line drawings

### Conducting Training Within Versus Outside the Target Environment

Typically, students undergo augmentative communication training outside the setting in which they must ultimately use their system to achieve social interaction. Ideally, the majority of communication programming should be conducted in the natural environment with environmentally relevant communication partners (Calculator, 1988). This practice eliminates many of the problems noted in generalizing learning from the "training environment" to the "target environment" (Warren, Horn, & Hill, 1987). As advocated by many authors (e.g., Brown, Nietupski, & Hamre-Nietupski, 1976; Falvey, Bishop, Grenot-Scheyer, & Coots, 1988; Guess & Helmstetter, 1986), communication programming should concentrate on establishing the communication skills (that are required for viable communication within the natural settings) in the same settings in which they will ultimately be used. When addressed within these natural settings, communication skills can be developed in response to the natural cues and the natural consequences within the natural environment (Halle, 1987).

### Utilizing Intermittent Versus Massed Trials

When an environmentally based approach is being used, the potential exists for choice making to occur interspersed across the day, thus permeating all aspects of ongoing home or classroom activities. Children who are severely physically challenged and/or who have multiple handicaps are frequently highly distractible and tend to fatigue more quickly than children without motor impairments. Both factors tend to contraindicate the use of a massed trials approach with the cognitively young child. Within an environmentally based approach, the child's therapeutic plan may designate that a specific child be given a minimum of 10 opportunities to make meaningful choices throughout the course of the day. Similarly, within the home setting the family may strive to provide the child with five opportunities to make environmentally relevant choices during the course of the after-school hours. The number of choice opportunities provided will vary depending on the needs of the individual child and the time constraints of busy schedules. With time,

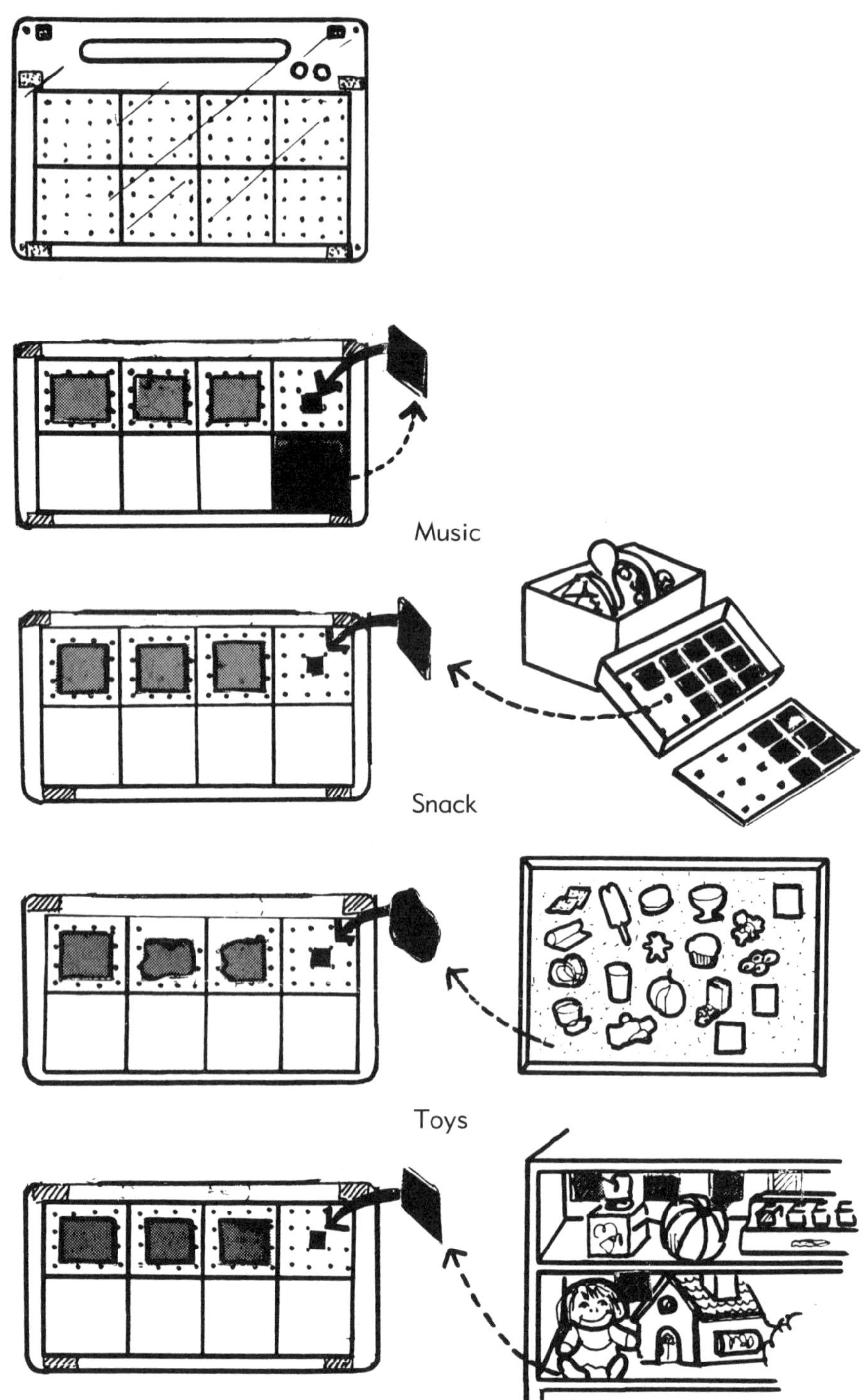


**FIGURE 7.10.** Templates for generic choice sets.

however, most facilitators tend to subconsciously increase the number of choice opportunities provided over the course of the day. This is especially true when the environment has been designed to make the visual representations readily accessible to the facilitator.

## Using Electronic Versus Nonelectronic Options

As previously discussed, a combination of child variables, time variables, and situation variables dictate what display format will be used when, during the course of the day. Although the choice of what toy to play with might be achieved within a voice-output electronic format, the decision of what therapeutic position will be assumed next might need (due to time constraints) to be achieved more quickly using an eye-pointing response. During snack time sufficient time might be available to set up the voice-output device to mediate choice making during snack. The decision of who the child will sit beside during snack, however, might need to be quickly achieved using an eye-pointing response. It is ultimately the facilitator's skillful manipulation of display formats in keeping with the situation and the time constraints of the moment that determine whether the overall choice-making system allows children to truly impact their environment in a meaningful way.

### Manipulating Choice Array Size

During the initial stages of intervention, it is best to limit array size. Early choice making is thus frequently initiated using two items. With an increase in array size, there is concomitant increase in the cognitive, visual, and motor demands of the choice-making task. To facilitate visual scanning of all the choice alternatives prior to selection, it is recommended that a flashlight be used to visually highlight each choice as it is presented, for example, "Mama's got GRAPES (shines light on symbolic representation for grapes) and BANANA (shines light on symbolic representation for banana). You pick." To facilitate left to right visual scanning of the choice array, it is recommended that the facilitator always highlight the choice alternatives in a left to right direction. With repeated exposure to the choice-making paradigm and with increased familiarity with the visual representation, visual cuing can be faded from use.

### Presence Versus Absence of the Choice Referents

According to Chapman and Miller (1980), normally developing children are able, by approximately 15 months of age, to respond to verbal labels of familiar objects and people when the referents are immediately present. It is only when children are beyond 18 months of age that they are believed to understand spoken words out of routine context. During the initial stages of choice-making intervention, presence of the referent can greatly facilitate the learning process. We have found it helpful to have the referent items visible, but just out of reach. When the child reaches, points to, or eye-points to the desired object, the facilitator can then capitalize on this nonverbal communicative intent by either (a) hand over hand assisting the child in selecting the corresponding symbolic representation for the desired choice item or (b) light-cuing the visual representation corresponding to the child's nonverbal communicative intent. Later, as intervention progresses, presence of the choice referents may no longer be necessary, because the child has come to comprehend the meaning of the pictures in the absence of their corresponding referents.

### Utilizing High- and Low-Preference Choices

Early in intervention, many facilitators strive to increase the likelihood of the child being positively reinforced by using only high-preference items as choice alternatives. When presented with two equally high-preference choices (e.g., GRAPES, BANANA), however, the child is faced with a "no-lose" situation. There is no real need to attend to the pictures at all; the child merely selects a picture, any picture, and is reinforced with its corresponding referent.

Later in intervention, the facilitator may wish to manipulate choices along a high- to low-preference continuum. When the child is presented a high-preference choice (BANANA) paired with a low-preference choice (GRAPEFRUIT), there is a definite consequence to inadvertently selecting the low-preference item. The manipulation of choices along a high- to low-preference continuum thus forces the child to direct greater attention to the symbolic representations.

### Utilizing Free- Versus Restricted-Choice Formats

When choice alternatives are presented within a free-choice format, the child is at liberty to select either choice. When choice alternatives are presented within a restricted-choice format, one of the choice alternatives is the preferred choice by virtue of context. Consider, for example, a situation in which the symbolic representations for two toys are presented as choice alternatives. The facilitator then proceeds to play with one of the two toys, thereby heightening the child's desire to play with that choice alternative. Because the child is nonverbally indicating a desire for a turn with a specific toy, the choice format (previously a free-choice format) has now been converted into a restricted-choice format.

### Providing Models of Spontaneous Self-Initiated Use

During the earliest stages of choice-making intervention, there is value in the child being exposed to models of spontaneous self-initiated use. This is most easily achieved by having the facilitator or a second individual use the choice array to request a turn with the object or activity. For example: "Let's have a snack. Mama's got GRAPES . . . and a BANANA. Let's see . . . Mama wants GRAPES . . . (selects the symbolic representation for GRAPES then rewards herself with grapes) . . . mmmm, good. Tastes good . . . (child's sibling points to the visual representation for *banana*) . . . Oh look, BANANA . . . Bobby (child's brother) wants BANANA . . . . Here, Bobby . . . BANANA."

Peer competition can be extremely motivating for the child. With the assistance of a multiswitch box (Kanor), several children can take turns requesting objects or activities from a shared display. In other instances we have found it beneficial to use a "nonspeaking, helping doll." When both the child's switch and the doll's switch are interfaced with a multiswitch box, the doll can be used to model self-initiated choice-making behavior. When, for example, the choice alternatives have been presented and the child has failed to initiate the choice-making process, the doll proceeds to make a choice, thus modeling the desired behavior: "Oh! Billy (helping doll) you got something to say? OK, Billy we're watching . . . (Billy selects the visual representation for banana) Oh, BANANA! . . . Billy wants BANANA . . . Here, Billy. Here's some banana."

### Utilizing a Prompt Hierarchy to Establish the Choice-Making Behavior

During the early stages of intervention, cuing may prove beneficial in establishing the desired response. When working with children who are severely physically challenged, however, excessive verbal cuing may prove to be counterproductive. When bombarded with a barrage of verbal directives, many children experience an increase in overall body tone that negatively affects their ability to perform. Furthermore, verbal directives (e.g., "Pick this one," "Stop it here," "Tell her you want the slinky") tend to be intrusive and/or pragmatically inappropriate. As an alternative to verbal cuing, the facilitator should consider the use of a less intrusive light cue. In instances in which choice making is occurring within a restricted-choice format, the facilitator may cue the target choice by shining a constant light on its visual representation within the choice array. Eventually, the child assumes a behavior set of selecting the visual representation that is visually highlighted by the facilitator's flashlight. Later, steps are taken to systematically wean the child of her or his dependence on this light cue. When a choice opportunity is presented, the child is first given an opportunity to demonstrate a spontaneous, self-initiated selection. If the child fails to capitalize on this opportunity, the facilitator provides a *search light cue.* When providing a search light cue, the facilitator uses a circular motion to scan the choice array. A search cue implies the unspoken message, "Let's use the pictures." If after a predetermined number of seconds (depending on the child's latency of response), the child has still failed to capitalize on this choice-making opportunity, a momentary light cue is provided. When providing a *momentary light cue,* the facilitator shines the light on the target choice for a brief period and then removes the light cue. A momentary light cue implies the unspoken message, "Let's cheat . . . Is this the one you're looking for?" If after a predetermined number of seconds the child has still not successfully targeted the choice, a *constant light cue* is provided. When a constant light cue is provided, the facilitator continues to shine the light on the target choice until it has been successfully targeted by the child. A constant light cue implies the unspoken message, "Let me help you. This is the one you want. I'll keep the light on it to help you target it."

### Transitioning from Real Objects to Photographs to Line Drawings

Ideally, the transition from one representational level to the next should be a smooth process. To ensure a smooth transition, the facilitator might consider using the pairing process suggested by Van Tatenhove (1978). When using a pairing process, the child is always exposed to a transitionary period before progressing on to a higher representational level. Initially, the child might be required to make choices involving the real objects. Once the child is reliably making choices using real objects, the colored photographs of these real objects are paired with the real-life referents within the previously established choice-making paradigms. Thus, although the child continues to make choices relative to the real objects, he or she is simultaneously being exposed to their higher level symbolic representations. Later in intervention, the real objects are no longer present in the choice-making paradigm and the child is required to relate to the colored photographs within the context of the choice-making paradigm. Once the child is reliably using colored photographs to make choices within a given context, a higher level symbolic representation such as background-enhanced black and white line drawings might undergo a transitionary pairing process. In this fashion each level of representation serves as scaffolding for the next-higher level of representation.

## Summary

Children who are severely physically challenged are now being provided with avenues for controlling their environment. In the communication realm, this frequently assumes the form of early choice making interspersed throughout the course of the child's routine day. For this to occur, attention must be directed toward designing a communication system conducive to environmental impact. A five-phase environmentally based approach is advocated. During Phase I, the facilitator delineates the overall communication environment to be impacted. In Phase II, attention is directed toward delineating and prioritizing potential choices within the overall communication environment. During Phase III, symbolic representations (photographs, line drawings) are established for the previously delineated choices. Phase IV is devoted to establishing readily accessible storage displays within the communication environment. During Phase V, flexible display formats are established to accommodate environmentally based choice making. By design, this system can flexibly accommodate the following:

- ❑ A wide array of environmentally relevant choices in keeping with the needs and interests of the individual child
- ❑ A continuum of symbolic representations in keeping with the present and future cognitive needs of the individual child
- ❑ A wide array of selection techniques in keeping with the present and future motor abilities of the individual child
- ❑ Both nonelectronic and electronic formats

A good system setup in and of itself, however, is not sufficient to guarantee successful environmental use. Ideally, choice making should be established first within a direct selection format, and only later using scanning (given the additional motor and visual demands necessitated by scanning). Ideally, training should occur primarily within the target environment using intermittent as opposed to massed trials. Array size is usually gradually increased over time. Often, it is the skillful manipulation of high- and low-preference choices and the use of both free- and restricted-choice formats that contribute to successful acquisition. Initially, there appears to be value in having the choice referents visible but just out of reach, thus forcing the nonverbal behavior that can then be shaped into the symbolic use of pictures. The strategy of having significant others model the desired behavior and using a prompt hierarchy involving a small penlight has also been found to be extremely useful in nurturing more spontaneous use. The task of shifting from one level of representation to another is difficult for many cognitively young children. To facilitate this transition, we advocate using a pairing process.

Prior to the developmental age of 2 years, choice making assumes a central role in the child's therapeutic plan. Viable communication, however, includes considerably more than this request for object or activity function. Attention must therefore also be directed toward training the child to use a scanning communication device to achieve communication above and beyond choice making. Chapter 8 is devoted to establishing scanning communication systems to address conversational needs, above and beyond choice making.

chapter 8

# Communication Training: Beyond Choice Making

During the earliest stages of communication training, choice making (reflecting the request for object or activity function) assumes center stage in the intervention process. Normal communicative exchange, however, involves much more than the communication of basic needs and desires. If children who are severely physically challenged are to begin to approximate normal communicative exchange, communication systems must be designed that allow children to impact their environment using a more complete range of pragmatic functions—functions that extend above and beyond the request function in activities above and beyond choice making.

In the previous chapter, information was imparted to assist the reader in implementing contextually relevant choice-making activities within an environmentally based framework. In the present chapter, attention is shifted toward designing and implementing communication systems that extend the child's communicative impact beyond choice making.

Ideally, we would like to see children demonstrating frequent, spontaneous, self-initiated use of their augmentative communication system throughout the course of their daily routines. This goal, however, will be realized only when considerable attention is devoted to (a) designing communication systems that allow children to impact their environment frequently and interactively and (b) teaching children to use these well-designed systems in a manner that does indeed nurture spontaneous, self-initiated use.

## Designing the System

Regarding design of a communication system, this section contains information related to:

- ❑ General considerations
- ❑ Electronic versus nonelectronic formats
- ❑ Level- versus code-based voice-output electronic formats
- ❑ Specific guidelines
- ❑ Transition from nonelectronic to electronic format
- ❑ Transition from level- to code-based format
- ❑ Transition from 8- to 32- to 128-location formats within a code-based format

### General Considerations for System Design

This section includes discussion of the following areas as they relate to design of the communication system:

- ❑ Conversational versus language/academic tool
- ❑ Flexibility versus speed
- ❑ Diluted versus concentrated message sets
- ❑ Script- versus dialogue-generated message sets

**CONVERSATIONAL VERSUS LANGUAGE/ACADEMIC TOOL.** When designing a system for a nonspeaking child who is severely physically challenged, primary attention should be directed toward designing the system to serve the child first and foremost as a conversational tool. For most facilitators, however, the task of trying to emulate the flexible and spontaneous nature of naturally spoken conversation, within the many limitations of an augmentative communication format, seems insurmountable. It is little wonder that facilitators, overwhelmed by the enormity of the task, tend to design systems that are best described as language learning or academic tools, rather than true conversational aids.

Lest we judge ourselves too severely, it is important to note that within the constraints of existing technology, even the most well-designed scanning system falls far short of emulating the flexibility and speed of conversation achieved through natural speech. The fact that we cannot replicate the natural conversational model, however, should in no way preclude our efforts to maximize conversational impact through system design.

**FLEXIBILITY VERSUS SPEED OF COMMUNICATION.** Ideally, communication should allow children to convey what they wish to say, how they wish to say it, with whom they wish to say it, and when they wish to say it. When a system is being designed for a nonspeaking child who is severely physically challenged, however, flexibility of communication can be achieved only at the expense of speed of communication and vice versa. As illustrated in Figure 8.1, a letter-based format affords the literate child ultimate flexibility of communication. Using the letters of the alphabet, generative power is maximized. That is, children are able to communicate what they wish to say, exactly how they wish to say it. This flexibility of communication, however, is achieved at considerable cost to speed of communication. Because several selections are required to communicate each message and time is required to make each selection, viable conversational exchange is not feasible using solely a letter-based format. It should, however, be noted that some scanning devices possess a feature called *predictive linguistics.* When this feature is in effect, the device predicts the next letter or word based on the frequency with which certain letters coexist with other letters, or with words.

When using a predominantly word-based format, speed of communication is substantially increased over a letter-based format. As illustrated in Figure 8.1, however, a word-based format lacks the generative power of the letter-based format. A gain in speed of communication is achieved with some loss of generative power, unless the child also has access to a letter-based format when the word is not within the system.

When using a predominantly phrase- or sentence-based format, speed of communication is maximized. The increase in speed of communication, however, is achieved with a substantial loss in generative power.

Children who are severely physically challenged are often relegated to using scanning communication systems. Scanning selection techniques, by nature, are inordinately slow compared to their direct selection counterparts. When the child is using a scanning selection technique, the time required to make each selection precludes sole reliance on a letter- or word-based approach for conversational exchange. The reader should not misconstrue this statement to negate the use of a letter- or word-based approach for non–time-dependent activities. In an attempt to maximize speed of "real-time" communication, a scanning-based system for a preliterate child should be designed according to a predominantly phrase- or sentence-based format and should generally limit the number of selections needed to call forth a message to one, and only occasionally two, selections per message.

**DILUTED VERSUS CONCENTRATED MESSAGE SETS.** Children who are developing normally demonstrate conversational exchange characterized by multiple turns within a relatively narrow time frame. In marked contrast, nonspeaking children using augmentative communication systems are noted to use their systems infrequently, seldom for multiple turns, and only when obligated to do so ("Tell me what you want. Tell me with your machine"). Typically, the more physically challenged the child, the greater the tendency for this scenario to unfold.

Although much of the blame for this phenomenon may be attributed to the slowness of scanning as a selection technique, the manner in which facilitators select message content is also worthy of scrutiny. As illustrated in Figure 8.2, there is a pervasive tendency in current clinical practice to design augmentative communication systems that reflect diluted message sets. That is, the provided messages allow the child to say a little about a lot of different topics, but they do not allow the child to say a lot about any one activity or topic. Because the system is not designed to promote multiple

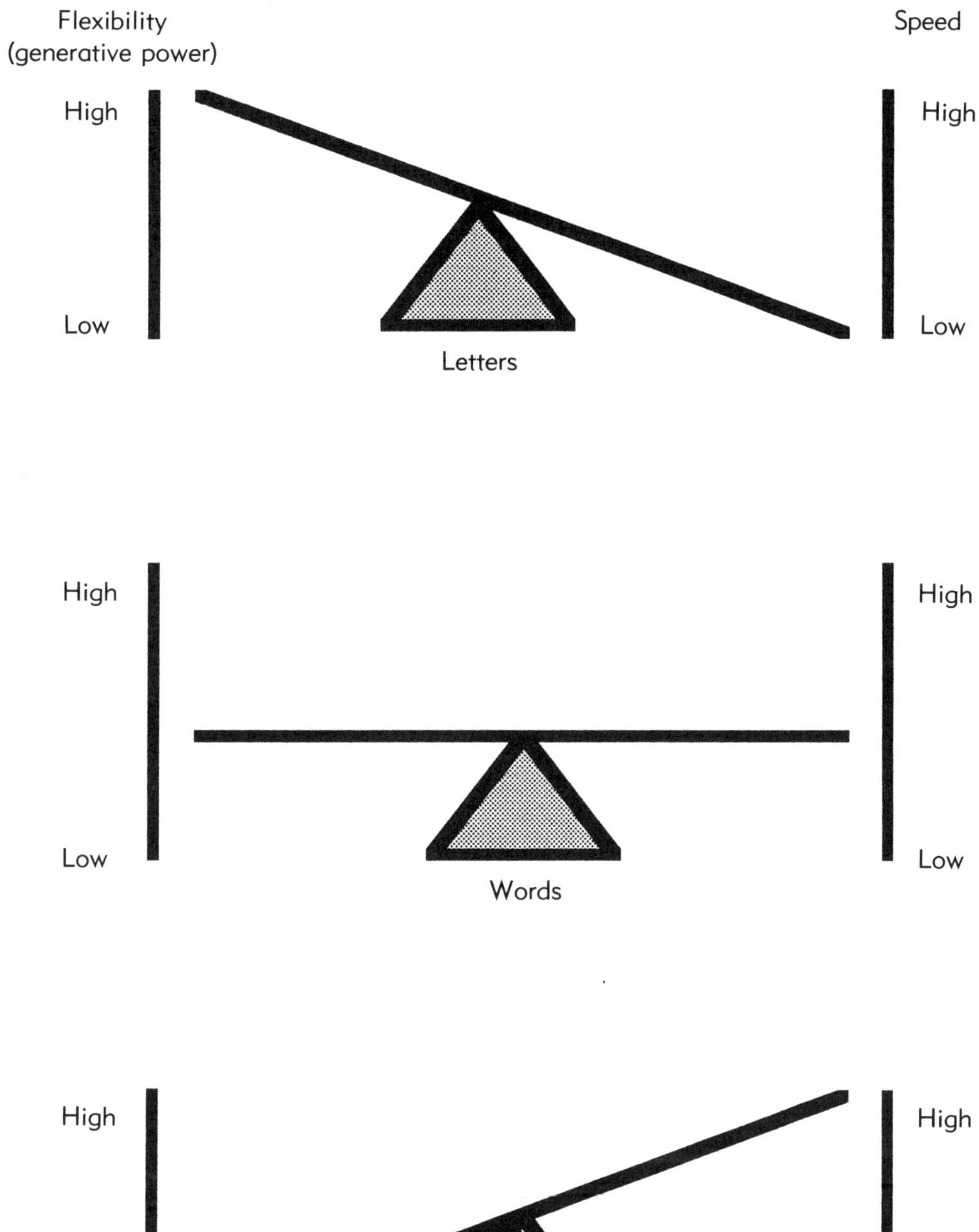


**FIGURE 8.1.** Flexibility versus speed of communication for letter- versus word- versus phrase/sentence-based formats.

turns within a narrow time frame, the lack of this skill should not be surprising. If the goal of system design is to maximize the system's utility as a conversational tool, attention must be directed toward providing children with *concentrated message sets.* A concentrated message set is activity- or topic-based and is basically a collection of messages that allow the child to fulfill multiple communication turns while engaged in the target activity or topic. In contrast to diluted message sets, concentrated message sets allow the child to say a lot about a given topic. They are also more amenable to inter-

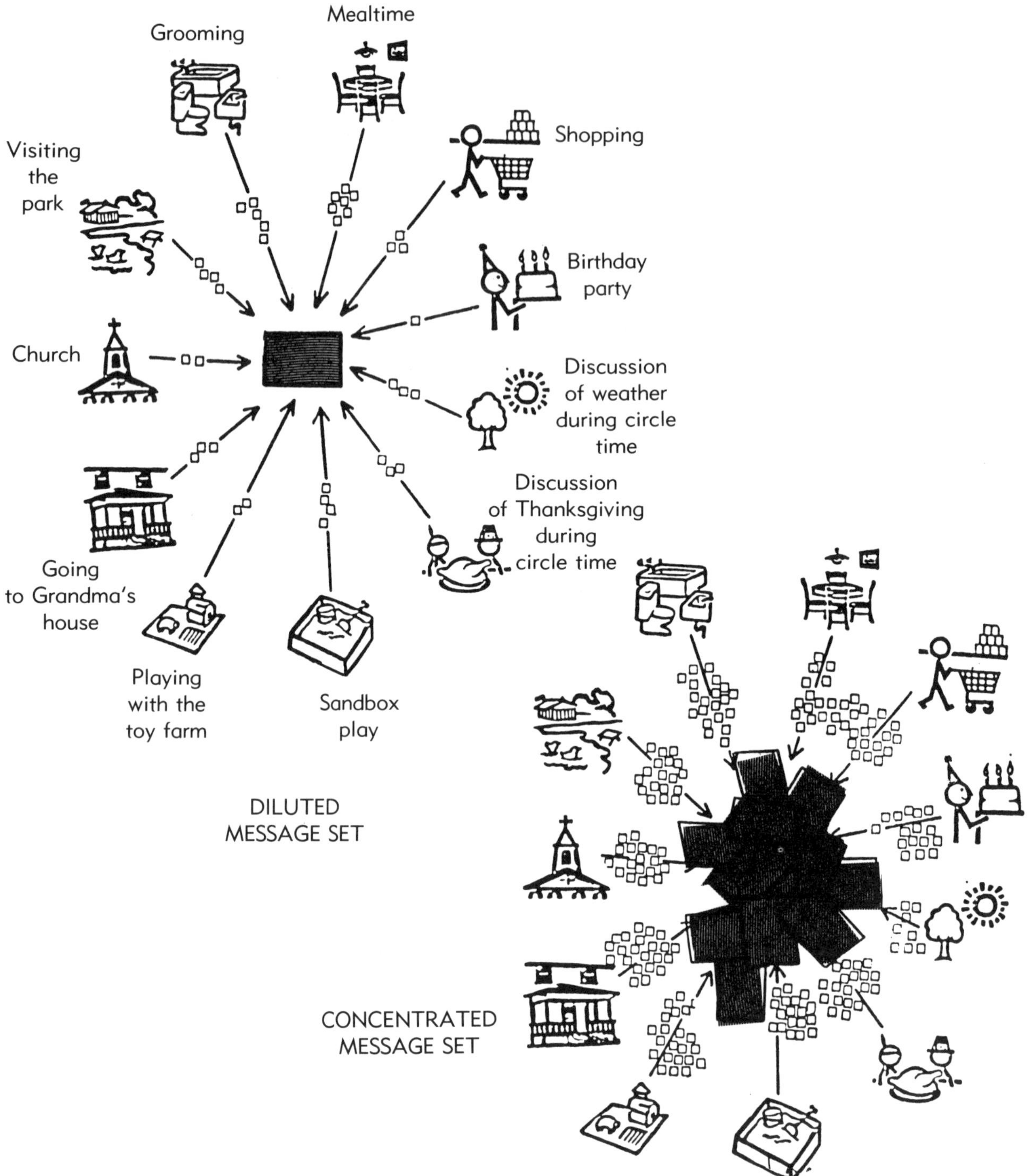


**FIGURE 8.2.** Diluted versus concentrated message sets.

vention. With a diluted message set, intervention is greatly confounded by the fact that the facilitator literally cannot "get a handle on" the messages for training in a contextually relevant format. As illustrated in Figure 8.3, a diluted message set is analogous to a scattered collection of beads with no string to make them a cohesive functional unit. A concentrated message set, in contrast, is analogous to a collection of beads with a unifying string that allows them to be linked to form a functional unit. Just as the beads cannot become a functional entity in the absence of a string, likewise, the facilitator

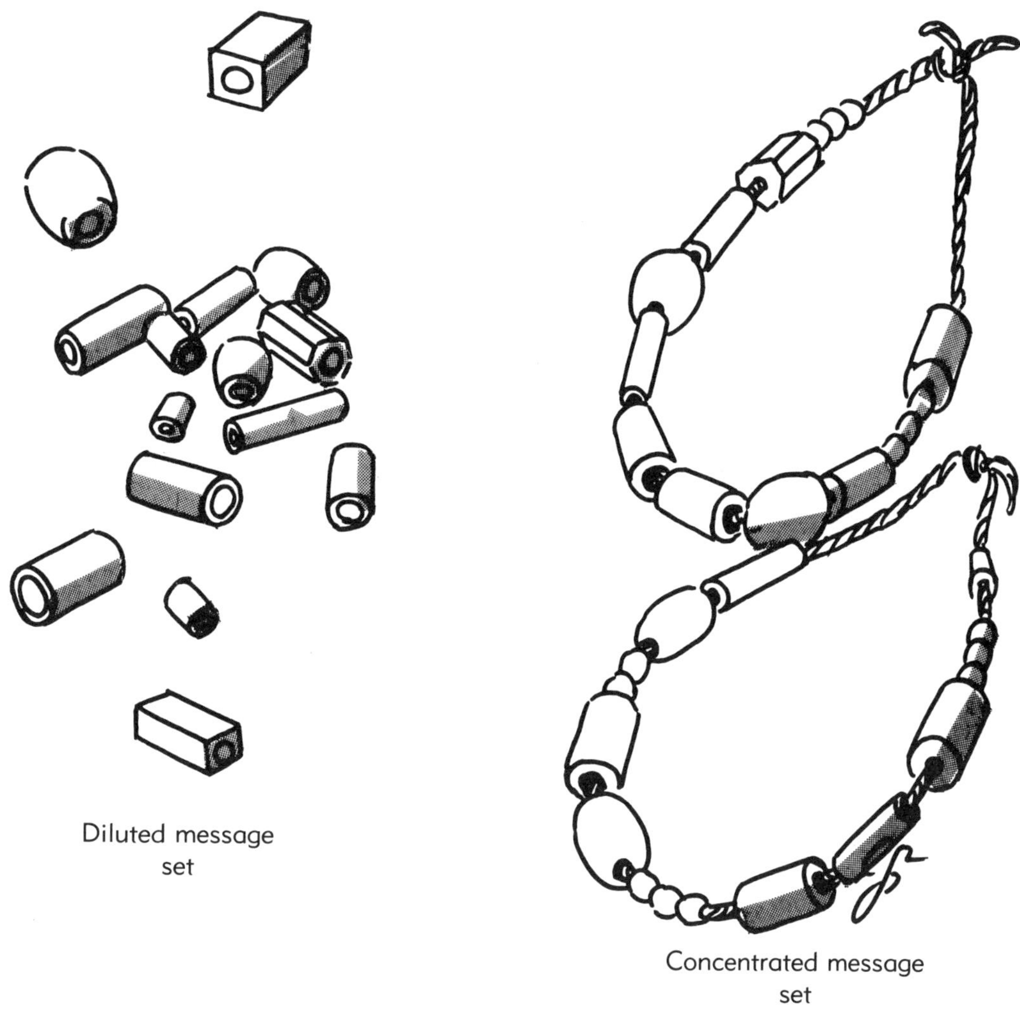


**FIGURE 8.3.** Analogy of diluted versus concentrated message sets.

cannot nurture multiple turns in the absence of a unifying theme that temporally links messages into a functional unit with communicative impact. To nurture the multiple turns characteristic of normal conversational exchange, scanning-based systems should reflect the use of multiple, concentrated message sets.

**SCRIPT- VERSUS DIALOGUE-GENERATED MESSAGE SETS.** Concentrated message sets can be derived using either a script-generated or a dialogue-generated approach. When using a script-generated approach, the facilitator selects a pool of messages that will allow the child to engage in multiple communication turns and be highly interactive within a relatively narrow time frame. In an attempt to approximate normal conversational exchange, various facilitators advocate tape-recording normally speaking children engaged in similar activities or topics. The resulting messages then serve as a base for the target message pool. In summary, script-generated messages are best described as a smorgasbord of messages relevant to a particular topic or activity.

When a dialogue-generated approach is being used, additional attention is directed toward selecting messages that reflect the conversational dyad. In contrast to a script-generated message pool, a dialogue-generated message pool is bidirectional in nature, reflecting the temporally linked messages of a hypothetical conversational Partner A relative to a hypothetical conversational Partner B and vice versa. According to B. Baker (personal communication, 1989), a typical dialogue reflects six to eight turnovers of the ''conversational floor.'' As illustrated in Figure 8.4, a script-generated message pool is analogous to a collection of beads equally accessible to both Partner A and Partner B. Partners A and B take turns selecting and adding beads to their

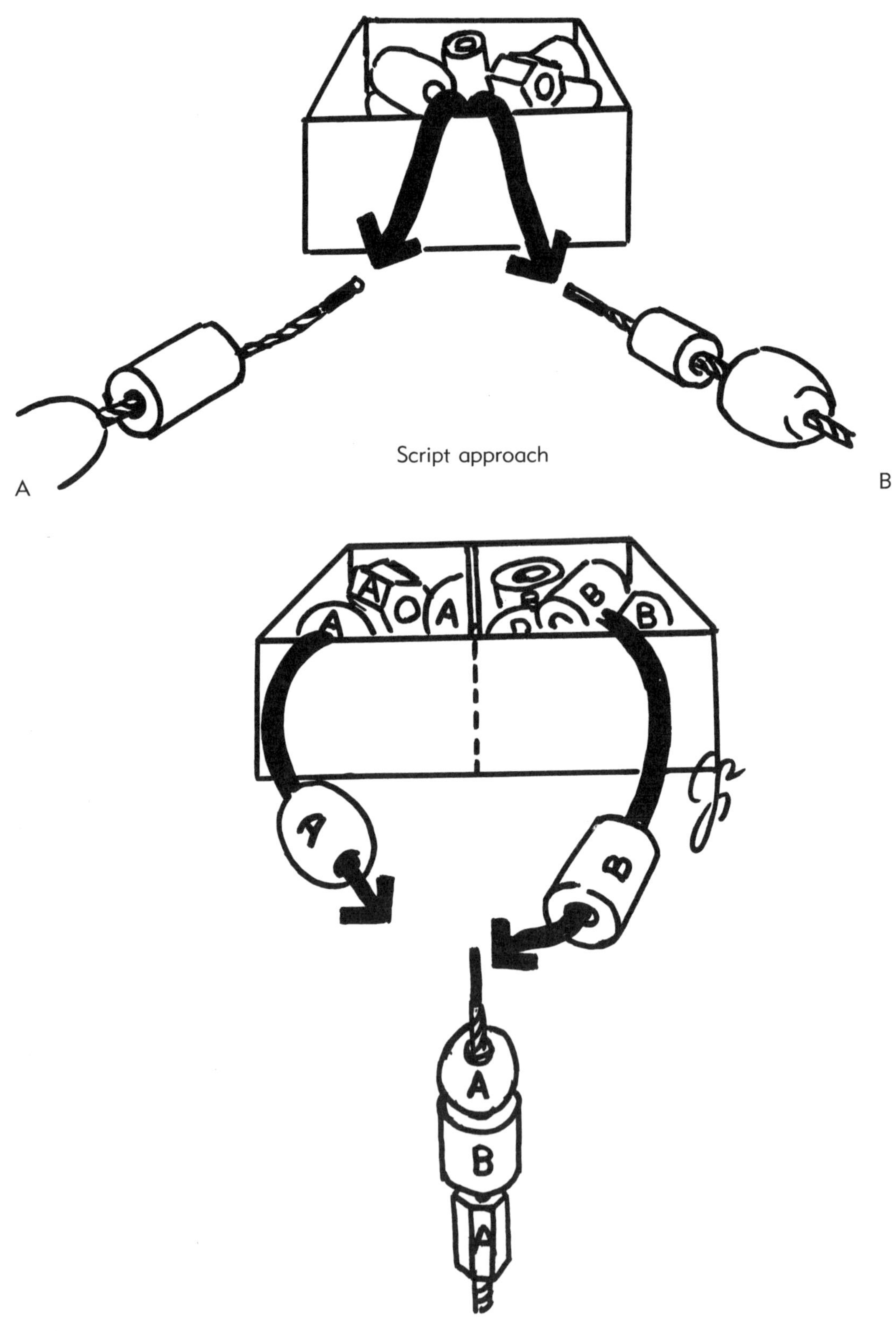


**FIGURE 8.4.** Analogy of script approach versus a dialogue approach to generating concentrated message sets.

own individual strings. A dialogue-generated message pool is analogous to a collection of beads that are already coded as being beads for Partner A or beads for Partner B. In contrast to the script-generated approach, a dialogue-generated approach allows Partner A and Partner B to take turns adding beads to a shared string.

In deciding whether to generate a concentrated message set using a script- versus a dialogue-generated approach, several factors must be taken into consideration. As a general rule, the nature of the situation itself often mandates the best approach. A food preparation activity, for example, is best mediated using a script approach, because both communication partners are primarily commenting on an ongoing activity. A scenario involving playing checkers, in contrast, would be best addressed in a predominantly dialogue-generated approach, because the communicative interaction that unfolds when individuals are engaged in that activity tends to be more conversational in nature. This is not to suggest that a predominantly dialogue-generated message set might not include several messages that are scriptlike in their focus or vice versa. As illustrated in Figure 8.5, the age of the child also is a determining factor. We have found the script-generated approach to be most successful in our intervention with preschool children. Although some dialogues are employed, they are usually reflective of one to two turnovers, and are typically embedded within a predominantly script-generated approach. As the child matures, however, emphasis tends to shift in the direction of functional clusters of dialogues, each six to eight turnovers in length.

## Electronic Versus Nonelectronic Formats

Electronic communication aids hold much promise for functionally nonspeaking children who are severely physically challenged. Because many electronic devices possess voice-output capability, children utilizing these communication options are able to communicate (a) independently, not having to rely on the communication partner to interpret symbol selections; (b) at a distance, not having to be in close proximity to the communication partner; and (c) in a more normalized and salient fashion. In addition, many of the currently available electronic communication devices possess printed output capabilities. Thus, the potential exists for addressing not only children's spoken communication needs, but their written needs as well.

Although electronic options can be used to address the communication needs of a wide array of communication situations, there are numerous instances in which a nonelectronic option may be the required and/or preferred option. Bath time, for example, is an excellent opportunity to promote communication between caregiver and child. The use of an electronic communication device, however, is not feasible within this context, because water could potentially damage the device. In such instances, a nonelectronic option is required if communication is to be realized within this potentially rich communication situation. Similarly, not all therapeutic positions that the child assumes during the course of the day may be amenable to the use of an electronic option. If, for example, a seated child uses a knee-activated switch setup to access an electronic device, he or she will not have access to this movement pattern when therapeutically positioned in a prone stander. If a viable alternate control site cannot be delineated for controlling the device when in prone standing, a nonelectronic option is required to mediate communication in this therapeutic position. Additionally, when using a nonelectronic alternative such as eye pointing, a cognitively young child may have access to a larger message array that can be accessed more quickly, reliably, and effortlessly than is possible using an electronic alternative. The latter is especially true in instances in which (a) the child has not yet mastered the operational knowledge required to reliably use a scanning selection technique or (b) the child's current scanning selection technique (e.g., linear scanning) severely limits message array size.

When learning to use an augmentative communication aid (whether electronic or nonelectronic), the child must acquire knowledge in three domains: operational, linguistic, and social (Light, 1989). In most instances, the operational skills required for accessing an electronic scanning communication device are considerably greater than those required for accessing nonelectronic counterparts. Rather than implementing a scanning electronic option that requires the child to simultaneously acquire knowledge in three challenging domains, the facilitator may opt to select a nonelectronic display format with a simpler operational mode such as direct

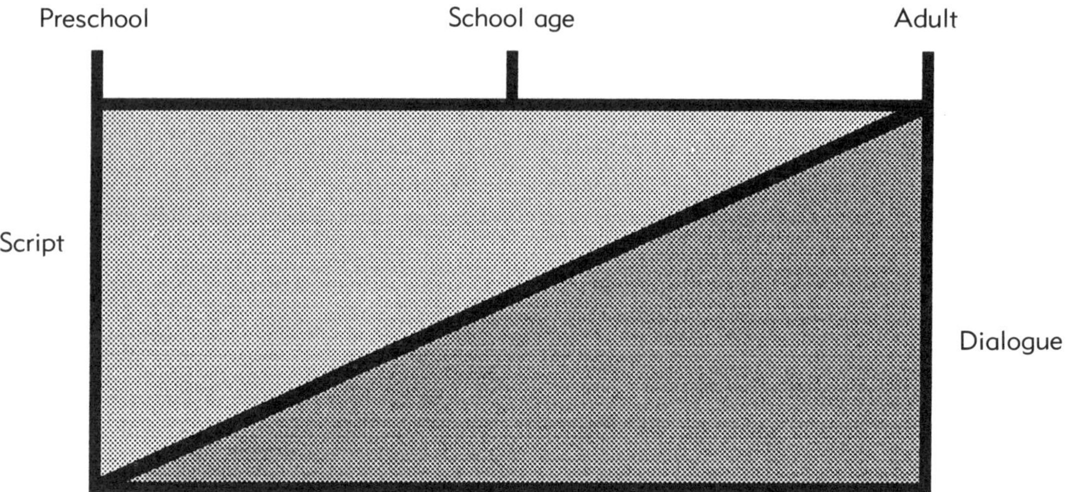


**FIGURE 8.5.** Script- versus dialogue-generated approach relative to age.

selection eye pointing. Thus, the facilitator is better able to focus the child's full attention on the linguistic and social aspects of system use without further confounding the acquisition process by overlaying a more difficult operational mode. Eye pointing often serves as an alternate selection technique when an electronic option such as scanning is not feasible or is a less desirable alternative. An in-depth discussion of eye-pointing display formats is beyond the scope of this book. Should readers desire further information, they are referred to Goossens' and Crain (1986b), Goossens' and Elder (1988), and Goossens' (1989).

In summary, there are numerous instances in which a nonelectronic option may be the required and/or preferred option. Although electronic options may appear to be the ultimate, nonelectronic options will continue to be an important part of the constellation of augmentative communication techniques that make up the severely physically challenged child's overall augmentative communication system. It is for this reason that the procedures for system development discussed later in this chapter recommend that communication need be determined first, before the nonelectronic, electronic, or combined format necessary to address that situational need is decided.

## Level- Versus Code-Based Voice-Output Electronic Formats

Numerous voice-output scanning communication devices are available for use with individuals who are severely physically challenged (Brandenburg & Vanderheiden, 1987a). Voice-output scanning communication devices differ not only in the scanning selection techniques that they offer, but also in the manner in which preprogrammed messages are represented and called forth on the device. Two broad types of formats can be delineated:

- ❑ Level-based formats
- ❑ Code-based formats

**LEVEL-BASED FORMATS.** Most voice-output scanning communication devices used with cognitively young children operate in a level-based format. As illustrated in Figure 8.6, level-based formats can be visualized as a series of levels or pages to which messages are assigned in functional groupings. When designing a level-based format for a 4-year-old child, for example, all message units required to mediate communication during mealtime might be assigned to one level on the device; all messages related to changing the baby doll's diaper might be assigned to another level; and all message units required for communicating while helping mom bake cookies might be assigned to yet another level. Because the content of each level is unique, several communication displays must be designed to uniquely reflect the message content of each level. Whenever the child progresses to a new activity, two steps must occur: (a) The level assigned to that activity must be called forth on the device, and (b) the communication display unique to that activity must be placed on the device to serve as a guide for message retrieval while the child is engaged in

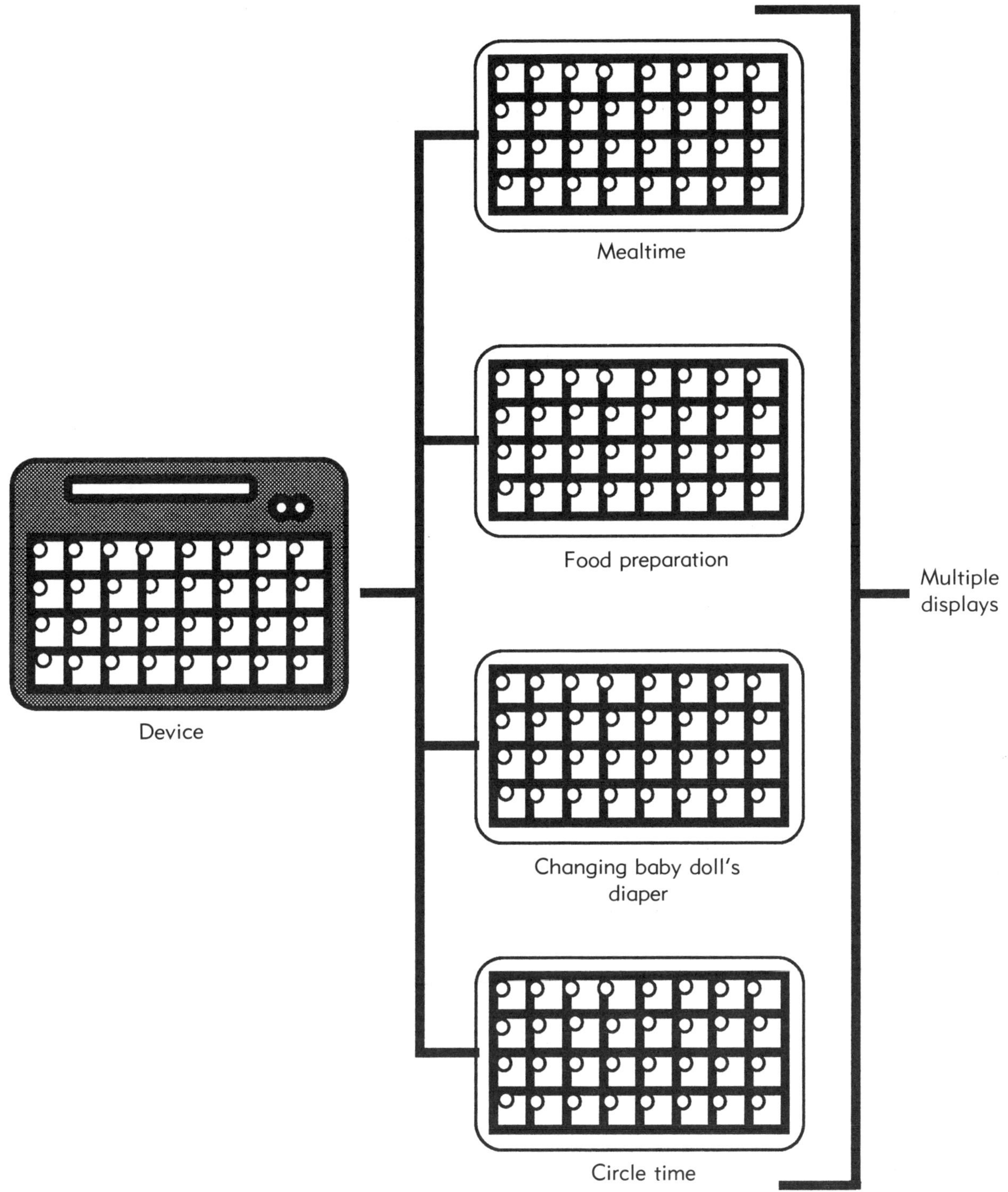


**FIGURE 8.6.** Level-based formats.

the target activity. Given the motor involvement of children using scanning systems, however, it is usually the facilitator who assumes primary responsibility for changing levels and communication displays throughout the course of the day. Although many children will require the assistance of a second individual to physically change communication displays, steps can be taken to allow the child to signal a desire to change activities. This can be achieved by assigning a message such as "Let's switch" to all levels on the device. A symbolic representation for each level mounted on the child's lap tray or on a clear vinyl overlay (held vertically by the facilitator) can be used to specify the desired level on the device. When using the clear vinyl display, an eye-link procedure (Drinker & Kropoff, 1981) can be employed to give the child access to a larger symbol array than is typically possible using an eye-point. When using this technique, the child eye-points to the desired visual representation, then maintains his or her gaze on the target symbol while the facilitator moves the display slightly right, left, up, or down. The manner in which the child's eyes track each adjustment provides the facilitator with the necessary information for determining the target symbol to which the child is eye pointing. This procedure is summarized in Figure 8.7.

Level-based formats have the advantage of allowing the full message array for an activity to be simultaneously presented. This allows the child to employ recognition, as opposed to recall memory, in deciding what message will be used at a key juncture point in the interaction. Level-based devices do, however, have the disadvantage of leaving the child highly dependent on a second individual (usually a facilitating adult) to change level-based communication displays. Although it is possible to composite the information of four levels into one display (assigning each level to a specific quadrant of each cell on the communication display), the result is visually confusing for many young children.

**FIGURE 8.7.** Eye-link procedure being used to denote a change in activity for a level-based device.

**CODE-BASED FORMATS.** Several scanning devices use either number codes (VOIS 150 of Phonic Ear, Inc.), letter codes (Epson Scanpac of Adaptive Communication Systems), or multimeaning icon codes (LightTalker or Liberator Minspeak software of Prentke Romich Company) to store and call forth preprogrammed messages. In contrast to level-based formats, code-based formats require either no display (as is the case with Morse code) or only one communication display depicting a limited set of code elements (Figure 8.8). These code elements are joined in different permutations to represent a broad array of messages. When using abbreviated letter codes or icon codes, the code element(s) selected to represent a given message usually reflects some meaningful relationship with the target message. When using number codes, the relationship between the number codes selected and the message is primarily arbitrary. When using Morse code, messages are composed letter by letter using different permutations of dots and dashes for each letter. When the system is switch-accessed, two switches are employed: one controlling the dots in the code, the other controlling the dashes. When using abbreviated letter codes, the letters selected to form the code sequence usually include the first letter of several key words in the message. When using icon codes (Minspeak/semantic compaction; Semantic Compaction Systems), the icons selected to form the code usually bear some association with key concepts within the message (Baker, 1982). This process of selecting meaningful code sequences is visually represented in Table 8.1.

Currently, there is very little research to guide the facilitator in deciding when to introduce a code-based format. To utilize abbreviated letter codes, it is generally believed that literacy skills are required. To utilize a Morse-code–based system, at least a Grade-4 level of spelling proficiency is believed necessary for viable communicative use (Beukelman et al., 1985). Although literacy skills are not required to utilize icon codes (semantic compaction), children must be capable of comprehending multimeaning icons. That is, they must appreciate that an icon

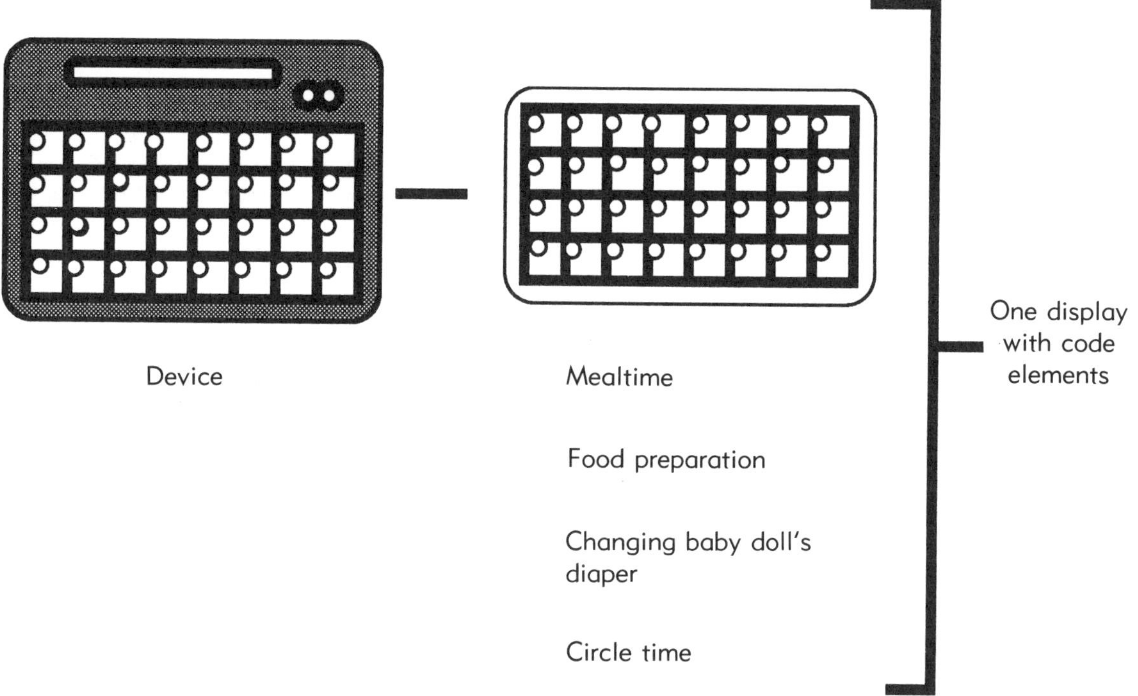


**FIGURE 8.8.** Code-based formats.

**TABLE 8.1.** Selecting Meaningful Code Sequences

| Method of Coding | Message | Code |
|---|---|---|
| Abbreviated letter codes | 1. Put it in | PI |
| | 2. Gotta be careful | BC |
| | 3. Open it | OI |
| | 4. Let me | LM |
| | 5. No don't | ND |
| | 6. Uh oh | UO |
| | 7. It's yuckie | IY |
| | 8. Let me taste | MT |
| Semantic compaction | 1. Put it in | |
| | 2. Gotta be careful | |
| | 3. Open it | |
| | 4. Let me | |
| | 5. No don't | |
| | 6. Uh oh | |
| | 7. It's yuckie | |
| | 8. Let me taste | |

*Note.* Pictures derived from Minsymbols (Minspeak Corporation/Prentke Romich Company). Reprinted by permission.

such as BED can be used to symbolize not only the obvious concept of *bed,* but also associated concepts such as *warmth, tired, sleep, blanket, pillow, sick, lazy,* and *blue* (if the bed depicted in the icon happens to be blue in color). At the present time, there are no definitive data to assist facilitators in deciding (a) how early a code-based format such as semantic compaction can be introduced; (b) whether it is advantageous to begin communication training within a level-based format, advancing later to a code-based format; or (c) whether initial exposure to a code-based format would, in the long run, be less confusing for the child than starting with a level-based format and later shifting to a code-based format. An assessment instrument called the Semantic Compaction Competency Profile (Elder, Goossens', & Bray, 1989, 1990) has been developed and is currently being used to assess cognitively based skills in five areas: icon flexibility, icon association strategies, two-icon sequencing, three-icon sequencing, and icon theming. Results of a preliminary study (Elder et al., 1989) involving 80 normally developing 3-, 4-, 5-, and 6-year-olds revealed ordinal patterns of performance across the five skill areas. A training study involving 24 normally developing 4-year-olds (Goossens', Elder, & Bray, 1990) provided further support for these ordinal patterns of performance and further substantiated the validity of the instrument. Research is currently under way extending this research to children who are functionally nonspeaking.

Because code-based formats use only one communication display, the need to repeatedly change activity-based communication displays is eliminated. Thus, the child is no longer dependent on a second individual to physically change levels and displays on the device, and is able to access all messages regardless of their activity or topic of origin. Code-based formats thus have the advantage of being highly flexible, with respect to the ease of accessing messages across activity boundaries, and they eliminate the need to continually change displays as the child progresses from one activity or topic to the next. Code-based formats, however, are generally considered to be cognitively more demanding. When using a level-based format, the full array of messages for a particular topic or activity are represented by the symbols with which they bear a one-to-one correspondence. Because these messages are directly represented in a one-to-one relationship with their corresponding symbols, the full array of potential messages for an activity is reflected on the level-based communication display. Thus, when a communication situation arises at a key juncture point in an ongoing interaction, children are able to visually scan the symbol array to help them decide what message is appropriate to the interaction (recognition memory). When using a code-based format, messages are indirectly represented on the communication display. That is, when a communication situation arises, children must use recall memory to formulate the message they wish to communicate. Having mentally delineated what message they wish to communicate, they must then use recognition memory to select the icon or icon sequence necessary to retrieve the desired target message.

Although the level-based format is less flexible with respect to message access across activity boundaries, the relationship between the symbol and its corresponding message is less abstract. For this reason, in current clinical practice facilitators typically strive to give preschool children experience with a level-based format prior to introducing a code-based format. However, there are as yet no empirical data to support this contention.

## Specific Guidelines for System Design

The guidelines for designing a communication system are described here as follows:

- ❑ Phase I. Delineating the environment
- ❑ Phase II. Delineating and prioritizing activities to be targeted
- ❑ Phase III. Delineating and prioritizing messages for each target activity
- ❑ Phase IV. Delineating a key concept for each message
- ❑ Phase V. Delineating the augmentative communication technique for each target activity
- ❑ Phase VI. Preparing the communication display
- ❑ Phase VII. Gradual introduction of messages within the message set

**PHASE I. DELINEATING THE OVERALL COMMUNICATION ENVIRONMENT TO BE IMPACTED.** For the very young, severely motor-involved child, a viable *augmentative communication system* often includes a constellation of augmentative communication techniques (e.g., facial expression, bodily gestures, eye pointing, scanning) and display formats (e.g., eye-gaze frame, eye-gaze vest, eye-gaze easel, partner-assisted scanning, device-assisted scanning). A viable augmentative communication system can, however, be achieved only when the child's communication needs dictate the nature of the system, not the reverse. The child's communication needs are, in large part, determined by the environment(s) in which the child must function communicatively. To best delineate the communication needs crucial to designing a viable augmentative communication system, all facilitators charged with system setup must be cognizant of the child's routine schedule. Previously presented in Table 7.1 is a form (C. Musselwhite, personal communication, 1990) that can be used to interview parents (teachers) to glean general information regarding (a) routine daily activities and (b) activities frequently engaged in outside the home (school) environment.

During Step 2 of Phase I, the facilitator is asked to select and prioritize the activities or topic clusters that will be the primary focus of initial system setup. When selecting the target activities/topics, facilitators are instructed to give priority to activities or clusters of topics that (a) occur frequently in the child's routine, (b) are highly motivating activities/ topics for the child, or (c) reflect a high-priority need based on past frustrations resulting from an inability to communicate effectively.

**PHASE II. DELINEATING AND PRIORITIZING ACTIVITIES/ TOPICS TO BE TARGETED WITHIN THE OVERALL COMMUNICATION ENVIRONMENT.** During Step 1 of Phase II of system design, the previously designated schedule is used to delineate activities or topics that hold potential for being mediated with concentrated sets of messages. As previously discussed, a concentrated message set is a collection of messages that (a) is conducive to multiple communication turns within a manageable time frame and (b) has a temporal or sequential "communication string" that links the messages together into a cohesive unit for training.

Considerable time and energy are required to establish a viable augmentative communication system. To reap the most from our efforts, it is imperative that first priority be given to targeting those communicative needs that will maximally impact and substantially alter the quality of the child's life.

**PHASE III. DELINEATING AND PRIORITIZING MESSAGES FOR EACH TARGET ACTIVITY/TOPIC.** Phase III consists of two steps. In Step 1, a script or dialogue approach is used to generate a concentrated set of at least 20 and usually no more than 36 messages (phrases/ sentences) for each target activity/topic to provide good (yet not overwhelming) coverage of many activities. Thirty-six was selected as the maximum number of messages generated because many of the frequently prescribed scanning devices are able to configure the device into a 32- or 36-cell format.

When generating a concentrated message set using a *script approach*, care should be taken to select up to 36 messages that (a) provide adequate coverage of the communication needs for that activity (e.g., cooking activity—PUT IT IN, TURN IT ON); (b) are high in conversational impact (e.g., cooking activity—LET ME SEE, I WANNA TASTE, BE CAREFUL, SILLY YOU FORGOT); and (c) are generic enough to promote their repeated use within the targeted activity (e.g., cooking activity—PUT IT IN + an eye-point toward the intended referent would be more "economical" to the message set than three highly specific, although functionally similar, messages such as, PUT IT IN THE BOWL, PUT IT IN THE MEASURING CUP, PUT IT IN THE OVEN). Table 8.2 presents the script-generated message sets for three activities.

When generating a concentrated message set using a *dialogue approach*, up to 36 messages are selected to reflect a functional unit of five or six subdialogues, each consisting of six to eight conversational turns (i.e., ABABAB or ABABABAB). Although dialogues can be trained as isolated entities, we have found it to be advantageous to address dialogues in clusters of related subdialogues to (a) facilitate their categorization on both level- and code-based formats and (b) promote training that is long range in its focus. Table 8.3 presents the dialogue-generated message sets for three activities.

During Step 2 of Phase III, the messages generated for each target activity or topic are rank-ordered based on their perceived relative importance to the target activity or dialogue cluster (a rank of 1 reflecting the highest end of the priority continuum). As will be discussed in greater detail later, this priority ranking will be used to assist the facilitator in deciding (a) which messages will be included on the communication display (based on maximum symbol capacity), (b) where messages will be assigned on

**TABLE 8.2.** Script-Generated Message Sets for Three Activities

| | Frequency | Saliency | Cumulative |
|---|---|---|---|
| **Activity: Mealtime** | | | |
| 1. Want some more please. | 3 | 3 | 6 |
| 2. It's yuckie. | 3 | 3 | 6 |
| 3. I'm done. | 3 | 3 | 6 |
| 4. How much do I hafta eat? | 3 | 3 | 6 |
| 5. Give me a lot. | 3 | 3 | 6 |
| 6. "The Blessing" | 3 | 2 | 5 |
| 7. Tickler #1 | 2 | 3 | 5 |
| 8. Response #1 | 2 | 3 | 5 |
| 9. How come? | 3 | 2 | 5 |
| 10. Tickler #2 | 2 | 2 | 4 |
| 11. Response #2 | 2 | 2 | 4 |
| 12. What'd you do today? | 2 | 2 | 4 |
| 13. Let me. | 2 | 2 | 4 |
| 14. Quit bugging me. | 1 | 3 | 4 |
| 15. No, don't. | 3 | 1 | 4 |
| 16. Don't want to. | 1 | 2 | 3 |
| 17. Thank you. | 2 | 1 | 3 |
| 18. I'm ready for dessert. | 1 | 2 | 3 |
| 19. Tastes good. | 1 | 1 | 2 |
| 20. What's for dessert? | 1 | 1 | 2 |
| 21. Not again. | 1 | 1 | 2 |
| 22. Can I watch TV? | 1 | 1 | 2 |
| 23. Excuse me. | 1 | 1 | 2 |
| 24. I'm in the clean plate club. | 1 | 1 | 2 |
| **Activity: Food Preparation** | | | |
| 1. Put it in. | 3 | 3 | 6 |
| 2. Gotta be careful. | 3 | 3 | 6 |
| 3. Open it. | 3 | 3 | 6 |
| 4. Let me. | 3 | 3 | 6 |
| 5. No, don't. | 3 | 3 | 6 |
| 6. Uh-oh. | 3 | 3 | 6 |
| 7. It's yuckie. | 3 | 3 | 6 |
| 8. Let me taste. | 2 | 3 | 5 |
| 9. Let me see. | 3 | 2 | 5 |
| 10. I wanna stir. | 3 | 2 | 5 |
| 11. Turn it on. | 3 | 2 | 5 |
| 12. No, it's not. | 2 | 3 | 5 |
| 13. Give me a lot. | 2 | 3 | 5 |
| 14. Take it out. | 2 | 2 | 4 |
| 15. Don't forget. | 2 | 2 | 4 |
| 16. Is it done yet? | 2 | 2 | 4 |
| 17. Need some more. | 2 | 2 | 4 |

*(Table continues)*

**TABLE 8.2.** *(continued)*

| | Frequency | Saliency | Cumulative |
|---|---|---|---|
| **Activity: Food Preparation** *(continued)* | | | |
| 18. Help me please. | 2 | 2 | 4 |
| 19. It's hot. | 2 | 1 | 3 |
| 20. I know how. | 1 | 2 | 3 |
| 21. Good. | 2 | 1 | 3 |
| 22. I think it's burning. | 1 | 2 | 3 |
| 23. Set the timer. | 1 | 1 | 2 |
| 24. Turn it off. | 1 | 1 | 2 |
| 25. It's done. | 1 | 1 | 2 |
| 26. It's not done. | 1 | 1 | 2 |
| 27. This is fun. | 1 | 1 | 2 |
| 28. That's enough. | 1 | 1 | 2 |
| 29. That's too much. | 1 | 1 | 2 |
| **Activity: Arts and Crafts** | | | |
| 1. Look at mine. | 3 | 3 | 6 |
| 2. Let me. | 3 | 3 | 6 |
| 3. Give me a lot. | 3 | 3 | 6 |
| 4. Need some more. | 3 | 3 | 6 |
| 5. It's yuckie. | 3 | 3 | 6 |
| 6. Want a different one. | 3 | 3 | 6 |
| 7. That's mine. | 3 | 3 | 6 |
| 8. That's not right. | 3 | 3 | 6 |
| 9. Where's mine? | 3 | 2 | 5 |
| 10. No, don't. | 2 | 3 | 5 |
| 11. Mine's the best. | 2 | 3 | 5 |
| 12. Gotta be careful. | 3 | 1 | 4 |
| 13. It's neato. | 2 | 2 | 4 |
| 14. Help me please. | 2 | 2 | 4 |
| 15. That's my favorite. | 2 | 2 | 4 |
| 16. Don't like it. | 2 | 2 | 4 |
| 17. No, it's not. | 2 | 2 | 4 |
| 18. How come? | 2 | 2 | 4 |
| 19. You like mine? | 2 | 2 | 4 |
| 20. Let me see yours. | 1 | 2 | 3 |
| 21. I'm done. | 1 | 2 | 3 |
| 22. I'm making this for someone. | 1 | 2 | 3 |
| 23. I know how. | 1 | 1 | 2 |
| 24. This is fun. | 1 | 1 | 2 |
| 25. That's enough. | 1 | 1 | 2 |
| 26. That's too much. | 1 | 1 | 2 |
| 27. Do it again. | 1 | 1 | 2 |
| 28. Can I take it home? | 1 | 1 | 2 |
| 29. It's not done yet. | 1 | 1 | 2 |
| 30. Thank you. | 1 | 1 | 2 |

**TABLE 8.3.** Dialogue-Generated Message Sets for Three Activities

**Topic: Running Errands at School**

A. Hi there, how're you doing?
B. Doing good.
A. Where are you heading?
B. I'm running errands
—Gotta get the mail.
—Gotta turn in the lunch list.
—Gotta make some copies.
A. Well, I won't keep ya.
B. See ya later, alligator.
A. See ya soon, big baboon.

A. You're lookin' good.
B. Thanks.
A. Is that new?
B. How do you like it?
A. Look neat!
B. I like it too.
A. Notice anything different about me?
B. Let me guess. (with my eyes)
—You've lost weight.
—Your hair is different.
—You're wearing something new.
A. Keep guessing.
B. (eye pointing or guessing with voice output)
A. Do you give up?
B. No way!
A. Bingo . . . you got it!

A. Is there any mail for Mrs./Mr. _______?
B. Sure is.
A. Just stuff it in my book bag.
B. Is that all?
A. Gotta make some copies.
B. Here you go.
A. Thanks.
B. Have a good day.
A. See you later.

**Topic: Jokes/Teasing**

A. Heh, come here.
B. What do you want?
A. Got something to show ya.
B. Let me see.
A. It's under my lap tray (e.g., a fake spider).
B. Ooh, that's gross!
A. Gotcha!
B. That's not funny.
A. It's just fake.

**Topic: Jokes/Teasing** *(continued)*

A. Know any good jokes?
B. I got one.
A. Let me hear it.
B. Joke #1
A. I've heard that one
B. Joke #2
A. (Answer)
B. Aak! wrong answer
B. Do you give up?

A. I give
B. Joke answer #1

A. I give up tell me
B. Joke answer #1

A. No way
B. Oh, you got it.

A. Knock, knock.
B. Who's there?
A. (Part 1 of knock, knock joke)
B. _______ who?
A. (Part 2 of knock, knock joke)
B. Boy, that was stupid.

**Topic: I've Got a Secret/Girlfriend**

A. Heh, come here.
B. What do you want?
A. I know a secret.
B. Let me hear it.
A. Promise not to tell?
B. I won't tell.
A. Cross your heart?
B. Cross my heart and hope to die.
A. I'll get you if you tell.
B. I won't tell.
A. Look in the pocket on the back of my wheelchair (note with secret printed on it).
B. —Really?
—No way!
—That's neat!
A. Remember, you promised not to tell.
B. I'm gonna blab it (teasing).
A. I'll get you if you tell.

A. Heh, guess what.
B. What?
A. I've got a girlfriend.

*(Table continues)*

**TABLE 8.3.** *(continued)*

**Topic: I've Got a Secret/Girlfriend** *(continued)*

B. Who is it?
A. —Can you guess? . . . Ask me questions about her.
B. (asks close-ended questions re: girlfriend)
A. —Nope . . . keep guessing.
 —That's right . . . you're getting warmer.
 —Do you give up?
B. (names girlfriend or gives up)
A. Look in the pocket of my wheelchair (note with girlfriend's name written on it)
B. —Really? . . . Does she like you?
 —No way!
 —That's neat!
A. Remember, you promised not to tell.
B. I'm gonna blab it.
A. I'll get you if you tell.

A. Who's your best friend?
B. You're my best friend.
A. You're my best friend.
B. We're BFFs . . . Best Friends Forever.
A. Can you come over to play?
B. Gotta ask my mom.
A. What'd she say?
B. —No, I can't . . . maybe tomorrow.
 —It's okay.
A. Yeah, yeah, yeah!

the communication display (based on relative ease of access), and (c) the relative order in which messages will be introduced for training in the therapeutic process.

When ranking a *script-generated message set,* messages that are (a) frequently occurring, (b) highly interactive, and/or (c) highly time-dependent are weighted in the direction of the highest rank of 1. In direct contrast, messages that occur infrequently, are not as salient in conversational impact, and are not time-dependent are weighted toward the lowest rank.

When ranking a *dialogue-generated message set,* thought must be given to the manner in which the dialogue will be trained. With some dialogue clusters, the facilitator may merely rank dialogues according to their perceived relative importance or the temporal order in which the dialogues unfold within the dialogue cluster. With other clusters, it may be possible to break the full message set into a basic version (approximately 12 messages) and an intermediate version (approximately 24 messages) of the full 36-message scenario. When delineating the basic version, attention is directed toward selecting those messages that are basic or core to the interaction. Given their pivotal importance to the scenario as a whole, they are assigned the highest rankings. When delineating the intermediate version, attention is directed toward selecting those messages that further enhance the basic version. Because these messages are less vital to the scenario (but more important to the scenario than those added to form the full version), they are given intermediate rankings on the continuum.

Although the process of ranking messages according to their perceived relative importance to the target activity/dialogue cluster may appear to be subjective, the process is not unlike what typically occurs repetitively during system setup. Early in the process of system setup, we must make decisions as to what messages to include on the display. We are therefore forced to make decisions as to what messages are more important than others. Later, we must decide what messages will be placed in the easiest versus hardest points of access on the display. Again, we are forced to make decisions as to what messages are more important than others to warrant the points of easiest access. Once intervention is begun, decisions must be made regarding what messages will be introduced first in the therapeutic process. Again, the facilitator must make decisions regarding the relative importance of the messages in the message set. Typically, those messages with the highest likelihood of success (those considered to be most vital to the interaction) are introduced earliest in the intervention process.

Although the process of rank-ordering messages according to their perceived relative importance to the target activity/dialogue cluster is time-consuming, it is a procedure that allows repetitive decision points to be addressed systematically and effortlessly.

**PHASE IV. DELINEATING A KEY CONCEPT FOR EACH MESSAGE IN A TARGET-MESSAGE SET.** Eventually, a graphic representation (in the case of a level-based format) or a sequence of graphic representations (in the case of a code-based format) will be required to symbolically and differentially represent each message in the message set. In preparation for this process, the facilitator is asked to underline a key concept in each message. Ideally, the key concept should embody the essence of that message, making it unique from all other messages in the set. In instances in which two messages share the same logical key concept (e.g., PUT IT IN, IT'S INSIDE), steps are taken to delineate a second priority concept for one of the semantically similar messages.

It is important to note that the process of delineating the key concept in the message is performed irrespective of (a) the child for whom the communication display is being developed; (b) the type of selection technique (or display format) that will ultimately be pursued (e.g., electronic vs. nonelectronic, 8-location vs. 36-location); and (c) the type of format that an electronic alternative might assume (e.g., level- vs. code-based).

**PHASE V. DELINEATING THE AUGMENTATIVE COMMUNICATION TECHNIQUE/DISPLAY FORMAT FOR EACH TARGET ACTIVITY OR TOPIC.** During Phase V, more in-depth information is gleaned from the parent (teacher) regarding the physical logistics of engaging the child in the target activity. As previously discussed, the communicative needs of some activities (e.g., bath time, dressing/undressing) (a) may not lend themselves to being mediated by an electronic communication device or (b) may be more efficiently or effectively mediated using a nonelectronic format. Rather than ignoring these high-priority needs because they are not amenable to using an electronic device, the proposed format for system design dictates that an appropriate selection technique/display format be delineated to mediate these priority needs.

Based on information derived from the family/school, a decision is made regarding what selection technique (e.g., direct selection—eye gaze) and what display format (e.g., eye-gaze vest, eye-gaze frame, eye-gaze easel) will allow the child to most efficiently access messages when engaged in the target activity or topic. Presented in Table 8.4 are several priority target activities/topics for a given child and the selected techniques/display formats that were required to mediate communication during these activities.

**PHASE VI. PREPARING THE COMMUNICATION DISPLAY.** The communication display may be either level-based or code-based.

**If Level-Based.** A level-based communication display requires the following considerations: (a) planning a maximum capacity display, (b) selecting message content, (c) selecting visual representation, (d) assigning messages/symbols to the display, (e) color-coding symbols, (f) laminating the display, (g) designing the layout of exposed LEDs, and (h) facilitating the interchange of displays.

*Planning maximum capacity displays.* When preparing communication displays for a target activity or topic, it is advisable to prepare displays that are more long range than the child's current level of performance. Generally, the child's current selection technique/display format determines the maximum number of symbols (messages) that the communication display can functionally support. If a 14-pocket eye-gaze vest were selected to mediate communication during Target Activity A, a maximum capacity display of 14 symbols (messages) would be prepared for this target activity. If a mirror format were delineated to mediate communication during Target Activity B, a maximum capacity polycarbonate vinyl display of 13 symbols (messages) would be prepared. If element scanning within an eight-location electronic format were prescribed for use in conjunction with a three-sided transparent eye-gaze frame, two displays would be prepared: an eight-symbol (message) maximum capacity display for the electronic device plus a 13-symbol (message) maximum capacity display for the eye-gaze frame. The process of preparing maximum capacity displays is analogous to a parent striving to buy clothes that a child can grow into, as opposed to clothes that the child will soon outgrow. If a parent buys clothes only for the present, considerable time and money must be spent shopping for clothes.

*Selecting message content for maximum capacity displays.* Messages to be included on the communication display for a target activity/cluster of dialogues are selected according to their relative rankings. If the communication display format selected for a target topic is able to accommodate a maximum of eight symbols/messages, the top-ranked eight messages would be selected for inclusion on the display. If the display format for a target activity is able to accommodate 14 symbols, the top-ranked 14 messages in the ranked message set would be selected. If the communication display format for a target activity is able to accommodate 32 symbols (messages) at maximum capacity, the top-ranked 32 messages would be selected from the

**TABLE 8.4.** Priority Target Activities/Topics for a Hypothetical Child and the Selected Techniques/Display Formats

| Activity/Topic | Selection Technique | Display Format |
|---|---|---|
| bath time | eye pointing | vest |
| playtime (washing a baby doll) | eye pointing | vest + frame |
| mealtime | eye pointing | vest + frame |
| arts/crafts | eye pointing + scanning | frame + eight-location linear scanning on level-based display |
| circle time (current events: "Guess what I did this weekend") | scanning | eight-location linear scanning on level-based display |

36-item message set previously delineated for that activity.

*Selecting visual representation for communication displays.* In preparing the communication display, a visual representation (usually a pictographic symbol) is selected to reflect the key concept previously underlined in each message. Numerous symbol sets from which symbols can be derived are commercially available. Many are now available in a stamp format (e.g., Rebus, Picture Communication Symbols). Still others (e.g., Picture Communication Symbols) can be generated in various sizes using software programs (e.g., Boardmaker by Mayer-Johnson Company) compatible with the Macintosh computer system. It should, however, be noted that symbol sets are predominantly word-based. Symbols denoting full sentences (e.g., "I don't know," "I don't understand") are few in number in the majority of symbol sets. Although a word-based symbol corresponding to the key concept in a message is often sufficient to capture the essence of a target message, there are instances in which the facilitator may wish to combine two symbols into one (e.g., I WANNA DO IT vs. YOU DO IT) or to embellish an existing word-based symbol to better represent the essence of the message.

*Assigning messages/symbols to communication displays.* Assignment of messages is based on whether the message set is script- or dialogue-generated.

*If script-generated.* When a communication display for a script-generated message set is being designed, messages are assigned to cells on the blank overlay according to their previously ranked order in the temporal sequence of the path of scan. As illustrated in Figure 8.9, the path of scan (i.e., scan pattern) will vary with the type of scanning technique employed. When a linear scan pattern is employed, the cursor moves through each successive cell in a left to right direction. When a selection is made, the scanning indicator typically returns to its initial starting point in the upper left-hand corner of the display. When a row-column scan pattern is employed, the number of steps required to reach each cell varies. In general, cells positioned in the upper left-hand corner can be accessed quicker than cells progressively lower and to the right in the scanning array. When a selection has been made, the cursor automatically reverts to its starting point.

*If dialogue-generated.* When the message set is primarily dialogue-generated, messages are assigned to cells on the blank overlay clustered according to the corresponding subdialogues. Most dialogues are temporal in nature, that is, the scenario they reflect tends to unfold in a sequentially ordered time frame. Dialogues are assigned to the path of scan, clustered according to the temporal order in which the dialogue unfolds. Figure 8.10 depicts the assignment of ranked script-generated messages to a device using a linear scan pattern versus a device using a row-column scan pattern. When symbols have been assigned to cells on the level-based display according to the rank of their corresponding messages, they should be taped in place using Scotch Magic Tape. Care should be taken to ensure that all edges are taped down to avoid trace lines when photocopied. The photocopied version of the target display and the original pasteup version of the display are then stapled

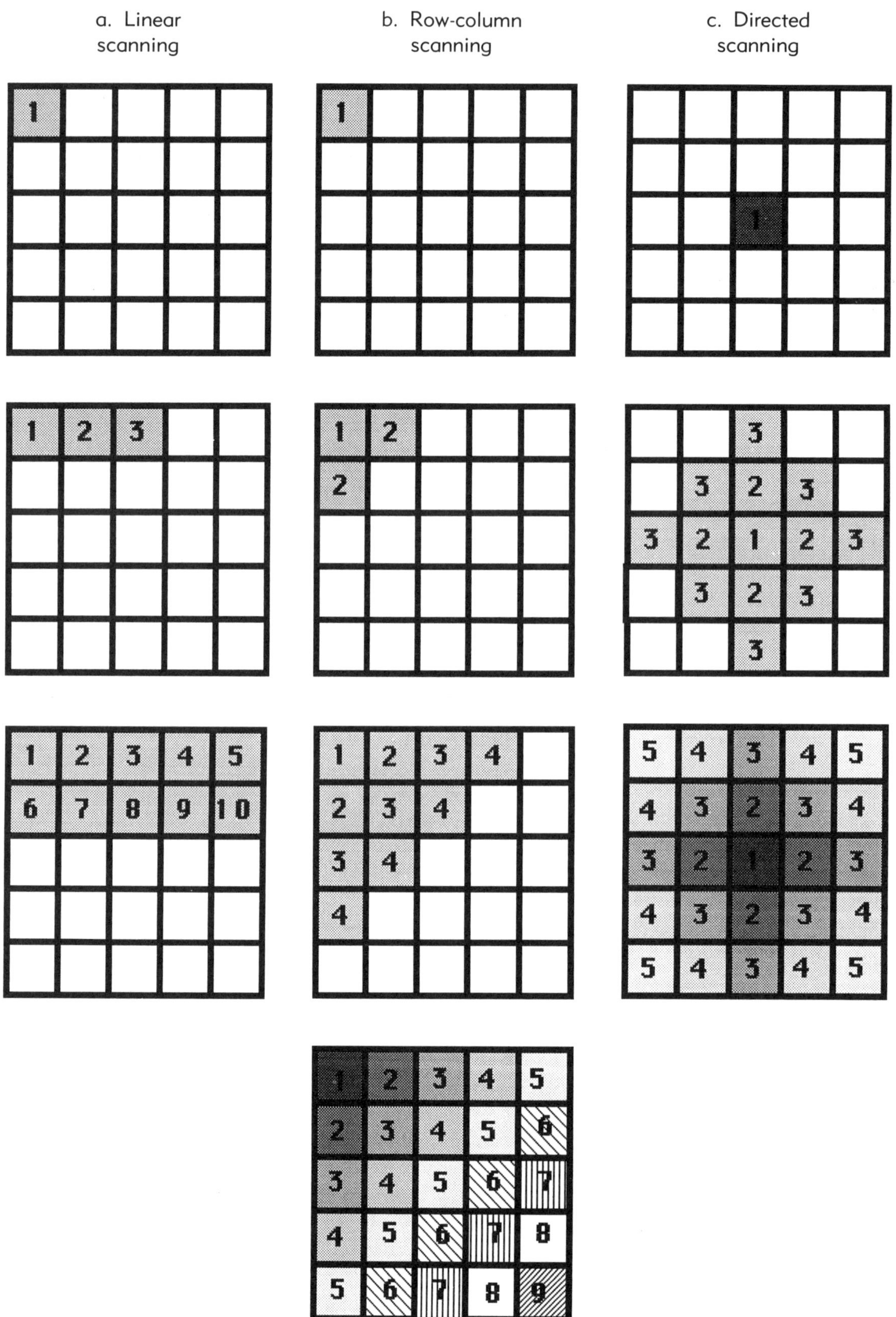


**FIGURE 8.9.** Path of scan.

Linear scan pattern

| | | | | |
|---|---|---|---|---|
| 1 | 2 | 3 | 4 | 5 |
| 6 | 7 | 8 | 9 | 10 |
| 11 | 12 | 13 | 14 | 15 |
| 16 | 17 | 18 | 19 | 20 |
| 21 | 22 | 23 | 24 | 25 |

Row-column scan pattern

Topic: ______________________

| | | |
|---|---|---|
| 1. ______ | 13. ______ | 25. ______ |
| 2. ______ | 14. ______ | 26. ______ |
| 3. ______ | 15. ______ | 27. ______ |
| 4. ______ | 16. ______ | 28. ______ |
| 5. ______ | 17. ______ | 29. ______ |
| 6. ______ | 18. ______ | 30. ______ |
| 7. ______ | 19. ______ | 31. ______ |
| 8. ______ | 20. ______ | 32. ______ |
| 9. ______ | 21. ______ | 33. ______ |
| 10. ______ | 22. ______ | 34. ______ |
| 11. ______ | 23. ______ | 35. ______ |
| 12. ______ | 24. ______ | 36. ______ |

**FIGURE 8.10.** Assigning ranked messages to the path of scan—Linear scan pattern versus row-column scan pattern.

onto a clear plastic page-protector sheet and placed on file for making duplicate copies, or modified versions as dictated by future needs. When using a software program such as Boardmaker, this cut and paste procedure is eliminated because symbols are assigned to locations on a grid.

*Color-coding symbols on displays.* Color-coding is used primarily to assist the child in visually locating symbols on the communication display. The manner in which symbols are color-coded, however, will vary depending on whether the underlying message set is script-generated or dialogue-generated.

*If script-generated.* When the message set is predominantly script-generated, symbols can be color-coded according to the grammatical category of the key concept used to symbolically encode the target message (e.g., nouns might be color-coded yellow; verbs, pink; descriptors and adverbs, blue; prepositions, green). Because messages are assigned to the path of scan according to their rank in the message set, the corresponding color-coded symbols will not fall out neatly into grouped grammatical categories as is the case with direct selection displays that utilize a Fitzgerald Key arrangement. Although grammatical groupings are not utilized, the color-coding does help to break up the display, allowing color to serve as a mnemonic for quickly locating messages on the communication display.

When color-coding symbols according to grammatical category, we have found it helpful to color only the background of the symbol, leaving the figure white. This procedure tends to enhance the symbol's figure-ground differential, thus assisting the child in more quickly locating a target symbol amid a large symbol array.

*If dialogue-generated.* Message sets that are predominantly dialogue-generated should be color-coded to enhance differentiation between (a) each subdialogue in the dialogue and (b) the messages of conversational Partner A versus the messages of conversational Partner B. To differentiate the various subdialogues within the overall dialogue, it is recommended that each be assigned a different color. To further differentiate conversational Partner A's messages from conversational Partner B's messages within a particular subdialogue, color intensity can be varied (e.g., light blue for Partner A's messages and darker blue for Partner B's messages within subdialogue 1; light red for Partner A's messages and darker red for Partner B's messages within subdialogue 2).

*Laminating displays.* The color-coded communication display should be laminated (a) to promote longevity of the display and (b) to provide a surface for directly documenting data on the display using nonpermanent pens or pencils (e.g., overhead projector pens, erasable crayons, china markers). The data documented directly on the display can be later transferred to a data sheet, providing a more permanent record of the child's performance.

*Designing the layout of exposed LEDs on displays.* Many scanning devices (e.g., Epson Scan Pac, Light Talker) allow the facilitator to manipulate symbol array size. For example, within a 128-cell format, array sizes of eight (combining 18 LED lights into one cell) and 32 (combining four LED lights) are frequently employed as smaller alternatives to the larger array. When this occurs, the aforementioned devices are also able to increase the size of the scanning indicator and the corresponding size of the visual representation. A decision must then be made as to how many and which lights will be exposed on the communication display. Illustrated in Figure 8.11 are several options for arranging lights on the communication display for scanning devices able to reconfigure cursor size.

It should, however, be noted that there are several devices that do not possess the capability to reconfigure cursor size (e.g., ScanWolf). When array size is decreased (by collapsing several component lights [LEDs] to form one larger unit), the LEDs within the newly formed large block are not activated simultaneously as a unit. Instead, the cursor maintains the status quo, scanning light by light in its usual element scan pattern. As depicted in Figure 8.12, this creates four chances to activate each composite cell, if all four lights are exposed. Although this works well for some children, it is confusing for others. If only one light is exposed in each composite cell (e.g., upper left-hand corner), there is only one chance per cell and a long delay between exposed light activations. This often necessitates increasing scan speed. With most devices, the speed with which the scanning indicator moves from light to light is inextricably bound to the amount of time each light remains activated. Thus, the faster the scan speed, the shorter the time available for the user to respond when a light is activated. For many children, it is beneficial if the unexposed lights shine

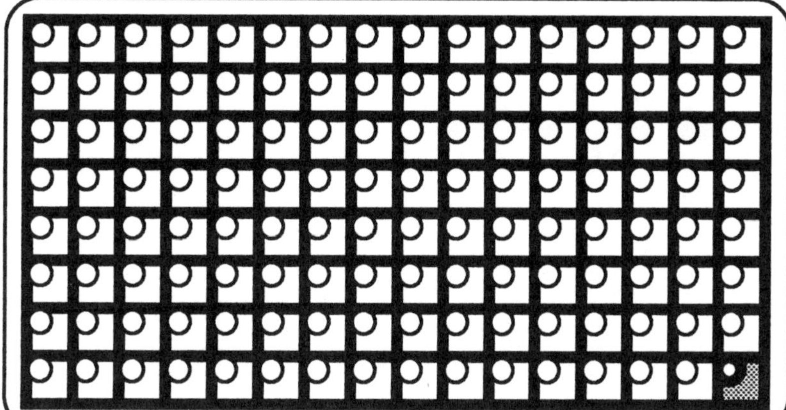


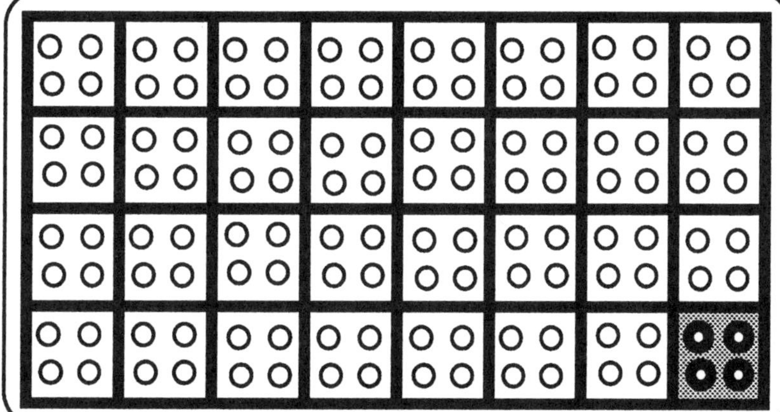


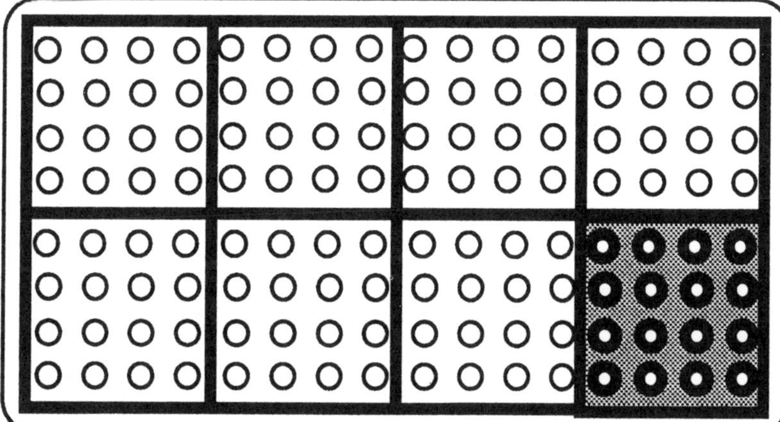


**FIGURE 8.11.** Variable cursor size.

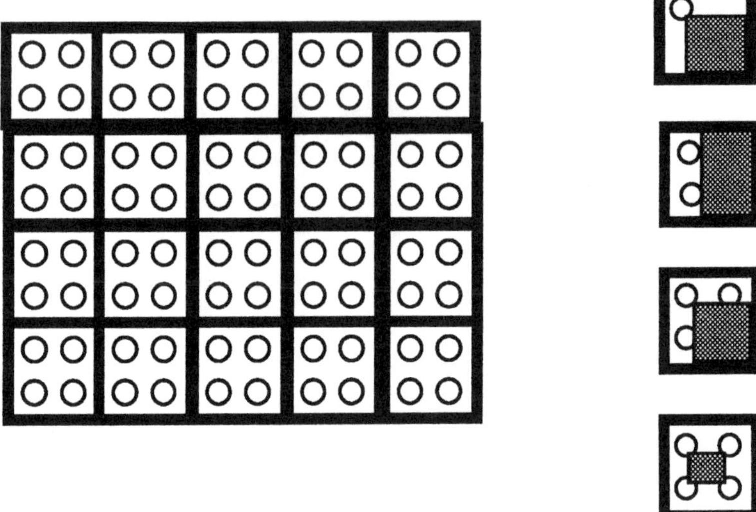

**FIGURE 8.12.** Options for arranging lights on scanning devices able to reconfigure cursor size.

faintly through the communication display constructed of thin paper, because it provides the child with additional feedback regarding the status or location of the scanning indicator within the scan pattern.

Once a decision has been made regarding which lights will be exposed, holes can be punched in the display by (a) using a hole punch with a longer carriage (Burkhart, 1987; Nomura & Wright, 1985) or (b) folding the paper display along the light lines and using a regular hole punch. This option for exposing lights is depicted in Figure 8.13.

*Facilitating the interchange of displays.* When implementing a level-based format, steps should be taken to allow the facilitator to quickly change out displays when transitioning from activity to activity. Ease of setup can be assured if steps are taken to document on the display the successive steps required to call forth the target level. This can be achieved by using fluorescent signal dots that are placed on cells and numbered according to the sequence in which they must be activated to retrieve the target level.

**If Code-Based.** A code-based communication display involves the following considerations: (a) symbol selection, (b) coloring of symbols, (c) selection of theme and subtheme icons, (d) selection of concept icons, and (e) selection of icon sequences for messages.

*Selecting symbols for the display.* When using abbreviated letter codes as the memory retrieval technique, the alphabet serves as the code elements. When using semantic compaction, a Minsymbol set is typically delineated in its entirety in advance of programming messages into the device. Although an array of symbols typically referred to as icons is provided by the manufacturer, Minsymbols can be hand-drawn or derived from the numerous commercially available symbol sets.

When using a 128-location format, symbol set size is typically limited to fewer than 70 icons. The number of different icon sequences that can be generated from a limited set is substantial. When using a set of 50 icons, for example, there are 50 possible one-icon sequences, 2,500 possible two-icon sequences, and 125,000 possible three-icon sequences (E. Nyberg, personal communication, 1989). Although the number of unique sequences possible is substantially increased when the length of the icon sequence is increased, speed of access is compromised. The need to limit access to primarily one and occasionally two selections per message cannot be overstated when using a scanning selection technique.

When selecting the Minsymbol set, care should be taken to select symbols that are rich in associational value. An icon depicting a sun with a smiling face, for example, can conjure up numerous associations such as *happy, yellow, smile, eyes, hot, outside,*

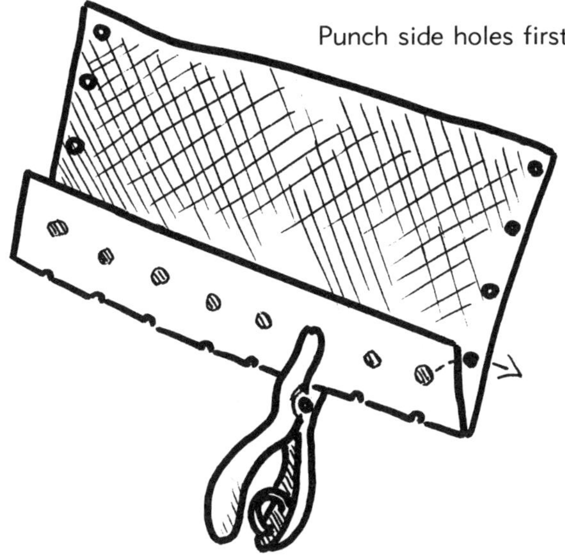


**FIGURE 8.13.** Folding procedure for exposing LEDs.

*face.* Figure 8.14 presents Minsymbol sets currently being used by several authors within both 32- and 128-location formats. For more in-depth information regarding the design of displays for semantic compaction, the reader is referred to Goossens', Elder, Caldwell, and Page (1988).

*Coloring symbols (icons).* Minsymbols are typically realistically colored to enhance their semantic richness. Because a Minsymbol must conjure forth several associated meanings, realistic coloring of the figure assists in making the surface features of the icon more salient.

*Selecting theme and subtheme icons.* Code-based formats utilizing semantic compaction typically use a theme format to organize the large numbers of preprogrammed messages that will ultimately make up the extended message pool. Messages are organized according to (a) the situations or activities in which they are used (e.g., watching TV, mealtime, playing Go Fish, school circle time, meeting someone new) and (b) categories or listings in which they have shared membership (e.g., days of the week, months of the year, names of friends, names of family members, colors). All messages pertaining to a mealtime activity, for example, might be represented by icon sequences that begin with the icon. Within this broad category of mealtime (denoted by the theme icon ), large numbers of messages might be further categorized under subthemes. Messages pertaining to eating at home might be represented by icon sequences that include the theme icon plus the subtheme icon . All messages pertaining to eating at a restaurant might be denoted by icon sequences that begin with the theme icon followed by the subtheme icon (associated with the act of going out to eat). Messages selected to mediate communication during eating at a fast-food restaurant might be represented by icon sequences that include the theme icon plus the subtheme icon (associated with crinkle-cut french fries). The individual food items might then be assigned to category subthemes. An extensive listing of vegetables might be represented by icon sequences that begin with the theme icon and are followed by a category subtheme icon of (associated with something plantlike). Similarly, a category listing of fruits would be called forth using the theme icon followed by the category subtheme icon, also the followed by the unique icon selected to represent each fruit in the listing.

Scanning devices that use semantic compaction as a memory retrieval technique (e.g., Light Talker) possess a theme function capability that is extremely helpful when setting up the system. This feature allows the user or facilitator to "lock" the device into a theme or subtheme by selecting either the ONE- or TWO-SYMBOL THEME function, followed by the appropriate theme and subtheme icons. When locked into the mealtime theme (achieved by selecting the ONE-SYMBOL THEME function, then selecting the APPLE icon), mealtime messages programmed into the device as two- or three-icon sequences can now be called forth with one less selection per icon sequence. That is, when locked into a ONE-SYMBOL THEME, there is no need to begin icon sequences with the APPLE theme icon; it is automatically entered by the device. When locked into a TWO-SYMBOL THEME (e.g., eating out at a restaurant—APPLE + TRUCK), the mealtime messages required to mediate communication at a sit-down restaurant (programmed into the device as three- and possibly four-icon sequences) can now be called forth more quickly using one- or two-icon sequences. If the child wishes to communicate a message outside of the currently operative theme, she or he merely selects the CLEAR function, then enters the theme + message icon

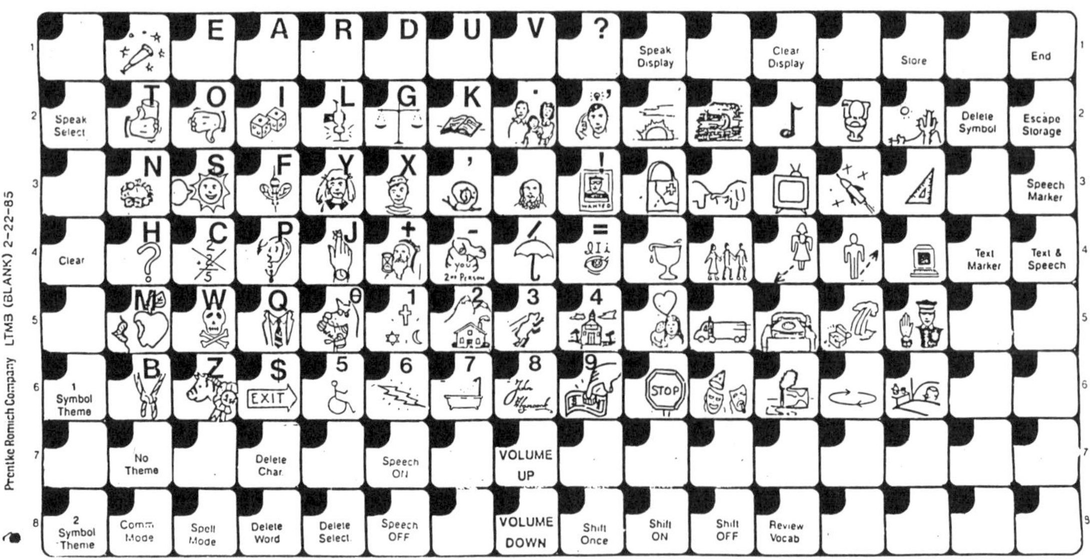


a. Minsymbols (Minspeak Corporation/Prentke Romich Co.)

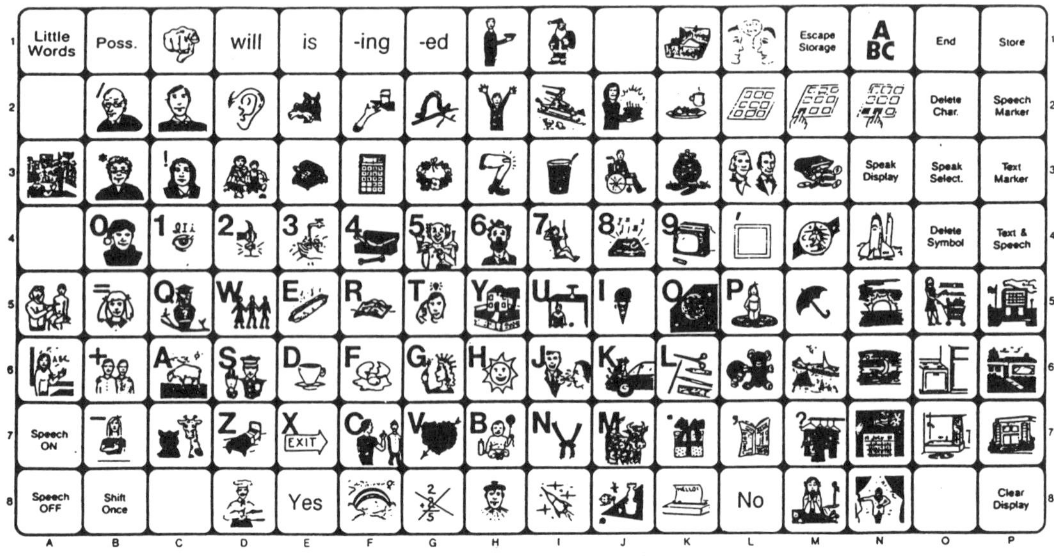


b. Interaction Education and Play (Bruno, c. 1989, Prentke Romich Co.)

**FIGURE 8.14.** Minsymbol sets from several sources.

sequence for the desired message. Having received this selection, the device automatically reinstates the previously operative ONE- or TWO-SYMBOL THEME. When the child wishes to change themes, she or he merely reestablishes a new theme by selecting the ONE- or TWO-SYMBOL THEME function or the NO THEME function. The theme function capability allows devices such as the Light Talker to be designed as either a level-based or code-based format depending on the needs of the child.

When establishing a code-based format utilizing semantic compaction, attention must be directed toward the overall hierarchical structure of themes and subthemes. Information derived during Phases I and II of the seven-phase process is now taken into consideration in delineating what major activity or category groupings are required and what subthemes will be embedded within each major grouping. Major groupings such as mealtime, homework, games, or watching TV are then designated by mutually exclusive theme icons. Subgroupings within these major groupings are then assigned subtheme icons. This process is visually depicted in Table 8.5.

With many children we have found it helpful to establish a core theme that includes basic needs and, perhaps more important, messages fulfilling the function of social closeness (Beukelman, 1987). This grouping typically includes highly interactive generic messages that cut across situations. When not engaged in a particular activity, the child is typically "locked" into the basic needs/social closeness theme. Table 8.6 presents examples of messages that might be included in this core basic needs/social closeness theme.

*Selecting concept icons.* Selecting icon sequences to denote the messages previously delineated in Phase III is best done on the basis of their perceived semantic links to the key concepts within the message, previously designated in Phase IV. To ensure internal consistency and to minimize the memory load involved in calling forth preprogrammed messages, we have found it helpful to select the icons for key concepts in advance of actually selecting the icon sequences for specific messages (Goossens' & Crain, 1987). When a concept-listing approach is not employed, the system is frequently plagued with numerous inconsistencies. These inconsistencies greatly confound the required memory load. When key concepts are consistently represented by the same icons throughout the system, the memory load is reduced to learning a relatively limited set of "building blocks." The efficiency of a concept-listing approach is depicted in Table 8.7. In general, familiarity with the icons used to denote key concepts in the concept listing can greatly facilitate children's ability to recall icon sequences. When children wish to recall the icons for a particular preprogrammed message, they mentally delineate the key concept or concepts in the message then scan the icons on their Minsymbol array for the icon typically associated with that key concept. Similarly, a concept-listing approach can greatly facilitate the ease with which a facilitator can capitalize on environmental opportunities for message use. Imagine an instance in which Johnny has begun to whimper and cry because his father and sister are about to leave for the store without him. In this scenario, an ideal opportunity exists for Johnny's mother to cue him to generate the preprogrammed message, "Heh, don't forget me." Knowing that the key concept FORGET is routinely represented by the icon FORGET (  ), Johnny's mother is able to quickly recall and cue Johnny to access the icon necessary to retrieve the preprogrammed message, "Heh, don't forget me!"

When using a concept-listing approach to system setup, the facilitators, in conjunction with the child (when feasible), select the icon that will be consistently used to denote each concept in an extensive concept listing. The concept listing we employ is derived from the word-listing employed in Words Strategy (Semantic Compaction Systems; Prentke Romich Company). Words Strategy is a word-based approach to message compilation. When using Words Strategy, the user composes messages word by word using one or two icons in conjunction with grammar label icons. Until recently the slowness of single-switch scanning precluded the use of Words Strategy for "real-time" communicative exchange with children employing row-column scanning. A device called Liberator (Semantic Compaction Systems; Prentke Romich Company) capable of predictive scanning has appeared on the market. Using predictive scanning, Words Strategy is now viable for individuals using single-switch scanning. Row-column or block scanning is used to select the first icon in the sequence. Depending on the icon selected, the device then presents (via highlighted lights) the probable alternatives for the second icon in the sequence. Linear scanning is used to scan

**TABLE 8.5.** Selecting Theme and Subtheme Icons

| Theme | Minsymbol | Subtheme | Minsymbol |
|---|---|---|---|
| School |  | Homework |  |
| | | Math |  |
| | | Spelling |  |
| Mealtime |  | Fast food |  |
| | | Restaurant |  |
| | | Meats |  |
| | | Fruit |  |

**TABLE 8.6.** Sample Messages Included in a Core Basic Needs/Social Closeness Theme

Is it time yet?
It's time.
It's not time.
Heh, come here.
Quit bugging me.
Get out of my face.
Got something to tell you.
I'm not gonna tell.
Hi, how are you?.
I'm fine.
What about me?
I know.
I don't remember.
I don't know.
I'm all done.
Not done yet.
Want something different.
Let's do it again.
I like it.
I love it.
I hate it.
Let me.
No, don't.
Don't wanna.
Need help.
I can do it by myself.
That's right.
That's not right.
More please.
No, thank you.
That's mine.
It's for you.
Leave it alone.
You can have it.
Ready to go.
I'm not ready.
What's to eat?
I'm thirsty.
You're my friend.
I wanna.
Do I have to?
No, it's not.
Yes, it is.
What?
When?
Where?
Why (How come)?
I don't feel good.
Awesome!
That's neat.
Gross!
You're not my best friend anymore.
Can I please, please, please?
Give me a break.
I'm gonna tell.
You're a tattle tale.
You're gonna get it.
That makes me mad.
You're just jealous.
I'm sorry.
I won't do it again.
I promise.
Pick me.
You never pick me.
Show me.
Maybe.
I forgot.
That's okay.
I wanna sit by . . .
Thank you.
Gotta go to the bathroom.
I don't feel good.

through this restricted array. After the second selection in the sequence is made, a more restricted array of probable icons is presented as highlighted lights on the device. Linear scanning of this restricted array then results in selection of the third icon. When using icon prediction in conjunction with a variable scan pattern, speed of icon retrieval is greatly enhanced. With the advent of the Liberator, Words Strategy software is now viable for individuals using single-switch scanning as a selection technique.

There are also instances in which a child presently using a scanning selection technique may (as a result of parallel motor training discussed in

**TABLE 8.7.** Efficiency of a Concept-Listing Approach

| Theme | Theme Message | Theme Minsymbol | Message Minsymbol |
|---|---|---|---|
| *Before concept coding* | | | |
| Dressing | Please change me. |  |  |
| TV | Please change the channel. |  | 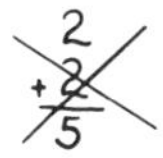 |
| Weather | Boy, the weather has sure changed! |  |  |
| *After concept coding* | | | |
| Dressing | Please change me. |  |  |
| TV | Please change the channel. |  |  |
| Weather | Boy, the weather has sure changed! |  |  |

Chapter 6) acquire the skill necessary for using a head-mounted infrared sensor (OH2). Having progressed from scanning to direct selection, the child is now a candidate for the increased flexibility of communication that is possible when using Words Strategy. In instances in which such a transition is likely, the facilitator may wish to anticipate this transfer by using icons for the concept listing derived from icon sequences employed to call forth the corresponding words in Words Strategy. In so doing, children are not required to learn a new set of associations when they transition to Words Strategy. This process is visually summarized in Table 8.8.

It is important to note that the mnemonics employed in Words Strategy reflect an adult perspective. Should the facilitator decide to derive icons for the concept listing from those employed in the word listing for Words Strategy, it will be necessary to reframe these mnemonics in terms more easily understood by children.

*Selecting icon sequences for messages.* In Phase IV, a key concept or concepts are delineated for each message in the concentrated message set for a specific topic or activity. During Phase IV, the facilitator delineates the icon sequence that will be used to denote each message in the set. The first icon in the sequence is typically the theme icon for the activity or topic under which the message set is subsumed. In instances in which subcategorization is occurring, the second icon in the sequence reflects the subtheme icon. The third icon in the sequence is typically the icon for the key concept (derived from the concept listing). In instances in which the designated key concept for a message is not represented in the concept listing, an icon is selected for this key concept and both the concept and its selected icon are added to the concept listing.

**PHASE VII. GRADUAL INTRODUCTION OF MESSAGES WITHIN THE MESSAGE SET.** When, as advocated, a communication display is planned long range to reflect the maximum number of symbols that it is able to support, the long-range direction of therapy is clearly defined. Regardless of whether the child is using a level-based or a code-based format, however, full exposure to all messages in the concentrated message set may prove to be overwhelming. With most

**TABLE 8.8.** Selecting Icon Codes from Words Strategy

| Word | Words Strategy Minsymbol Code Key 1 | Key 2 | Key 3 | Phrase/Sentence Strategy Minsymbol for Concept |
|---|---|---|---|---|
| Come |  | verb | |  |
| Hungry |  | adj | |  |
| Need |  |  | verb |  |
| Good |  | adj | |  |

children, there is value in gradually exposing messages over time. Ideally, when introducing a message set, the facilitator begins intervention with those messages that can be used frequently with considerable impact. During Phase III, messages within the message set were rank-ordered according to their relative importance to the targeted interaction. This rank order now serves as a guide in determining the order in which messages are introduced in the training process. Initially, the facilitator might introduce only the highest ranked 10 messages in the target message set. When the child is demonstrating spontaneous, self-initiated use of these 10 messages in context, the messages ranked 11 through 20 are introduced for training. The process continues until all messages in the target message set have been introduced. How many new messages are simultaneously introduced and when they are introduced in the therapeutic process should be individualized according to the specific needs of the child. Patches of duct tape or paper "window templates" (Smith, 1983) can be used to gradually expose symbols. Presented in Table 8.9 is a generic data sheet that can be used to document system setup and progress in gradually exposing messages.

**If Level-Based.** As previously discussed, script-generated messages are assigned to the path of scan using their relative rankings to guide assignment. Because messages are introduced according to their relative rankings, symbols are gradually introduced by cutting away the paper template in the direction of the path of scan. Figure 8.15 illustrates the gradual introduction of messages for an activity/topic when using an element versus a row-column scanning pattern. When a device is being used by only one child, the facilitator may (a) program in the entire message set or (b) decide to program in messages gradually as they are introduced in the therapeutic process. The latter approach is especially useful with young children new to the therapeutic process because the activation of blocked-out symbols will not result in voice output. The need to target cells depicted with a symbol is, therefore, highlighted. When a device is being used by sev-

**TABLE 8.9.** Data Sheet Documenting System Setup

Child: ______________________ Device: ______________________

Facilitator(s): ______________________ Display Format: ______________________

| Activity/Topic | Ranking of Messages | | | | | | | | | | | | | | | | | | | | | | | | | | | | | | | | | | | |
|---|---|---|---|---|---|---|---|---|---|---|---|---|---|---|---|---|---|---|---|---|---|---|---|---|---|---|---|---|---|---|---|---|---|---|---|---|
| | 1 | 2 | 3 | 4 | 5 | 6 | 7 | 8 | 9 | 10 | 11 | 12 | 13 | 14 | 15 | 16 | 17 | 18 | 19 | 20 | 21 | 22 | 23 | 24 | 25 | 26 | 27 | 28 | 29 | 30 | 31 | 32 | 33 | 34 | 35 | 36 |
| 1 | | | | | | | | | | | | | | | | | | | | | | | | | | | | | | | | | | | | |
| 2 | | | | | | | | | | | | | | | | | | | | | | | | | | | | | | | | | | | | |
| 3 | | | | | | | | | | | | | | | | | | | | | | | | | | | | | | | | | | | | |
| 4 | | | | | | | | | | | | | | | | | | | | | | | | | | | | | | | | | | | | |
| 5 | | | | | | | | | | | | | | | | | | | | | | | | | | | | | | | | | | | | |
| 6 | | | | | | | | | | | | | | | | | | | | | | | | | | | | | | | | | | | | |
| 7 | | | | | | | | | | | | | | | | | | | | | | | | | | | | | | | | | | | | |
| 8 | | | | | | | | | | | | | | | | | | | | | | | | | | | | | | | | | | | | |
| 9 | | | | | | | | | | | | | | | | | | | | | | | | | | | | | | | | | | | | |
| 10 | | | | | | | | | | | | | | | | | | | | | | | | | | | | | | | | | | | | |
| 11 | | | | | | | | | | | | | | | | | | | | | | | | | | | | | | | | | | | | |
| 12 | | | | | | | | | | | | | | | | | | | | | | | | | | | | | | | | | | | | |

**Mastery Criteria:** ______________________ will demonstrate spontaneous, self-initiated use of __________% of the symbols exposed, across two consecutive sessions.

**Introduction Date:** Coded in blue.

**Mastery Date:** Coded in red.

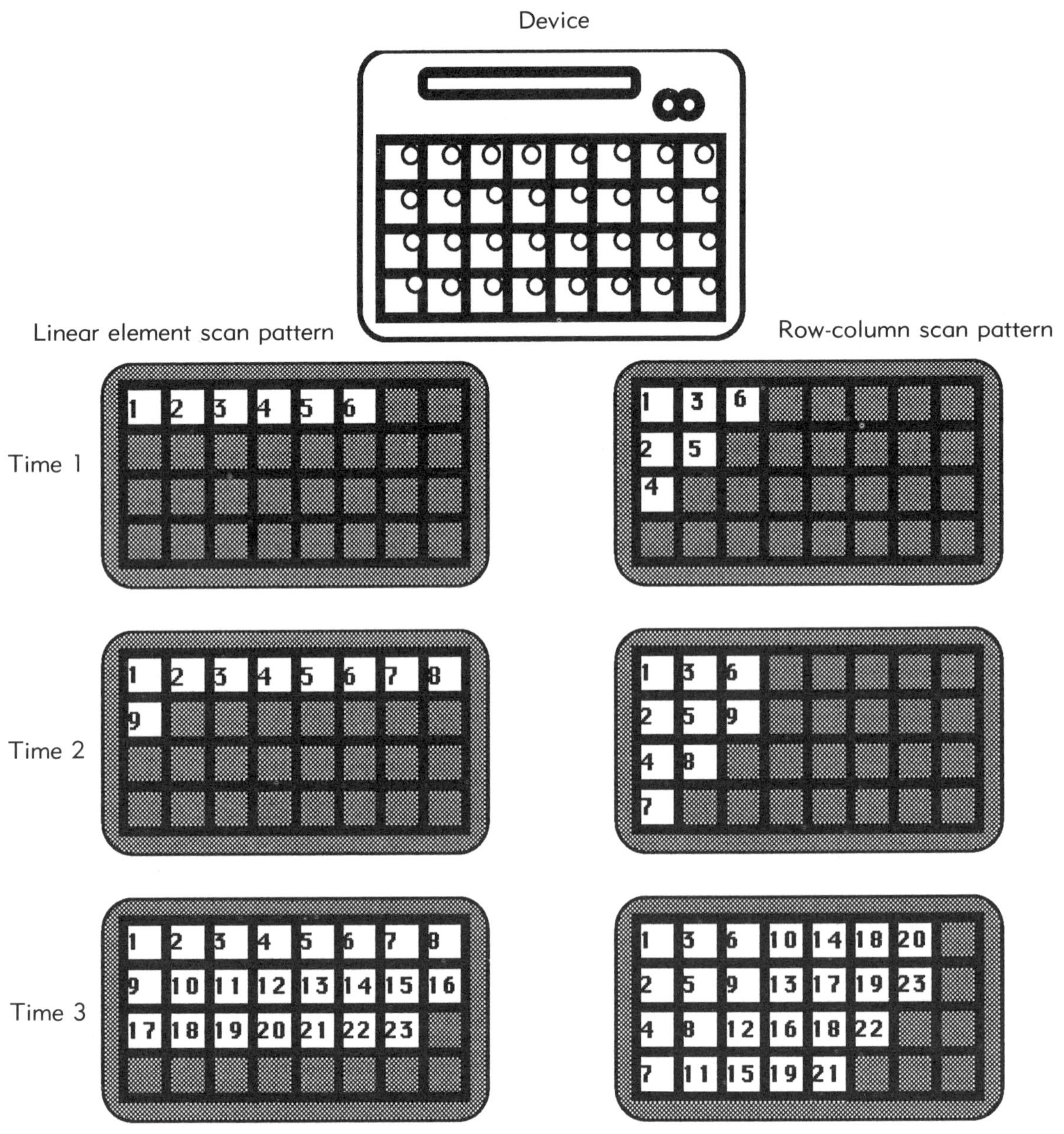


**FIGURE 8.15.** Gradual exposure of messages for an activity/topic when using an element versus a row-column scan pattern.

eral children reflecting variable rates of acquisition (as is often the case in classroom settings), the message set is programmed into the device in its entirety. Paper cut-out templates thus allow the exposure of symbols to be individualized for children progressing at variable rates. As children progress at their own rate, their individual templates are altered according to the path of scan to expose the desired number of messages. This process is visually represented in Figure 8.16.

**If Code-Based.** When using a code-based format, messages cannot be assigned to the path of scan according to their ranks as was the case with level-based formats. Instead, the Minsymbol icons occupy fixed positions on the communication display. The icon sequences differentiate one message from the next in the message set within a code-based format based on semantic compaction. As was the case with level-based formats, however, messages can be gradually exposed in the order of their previously

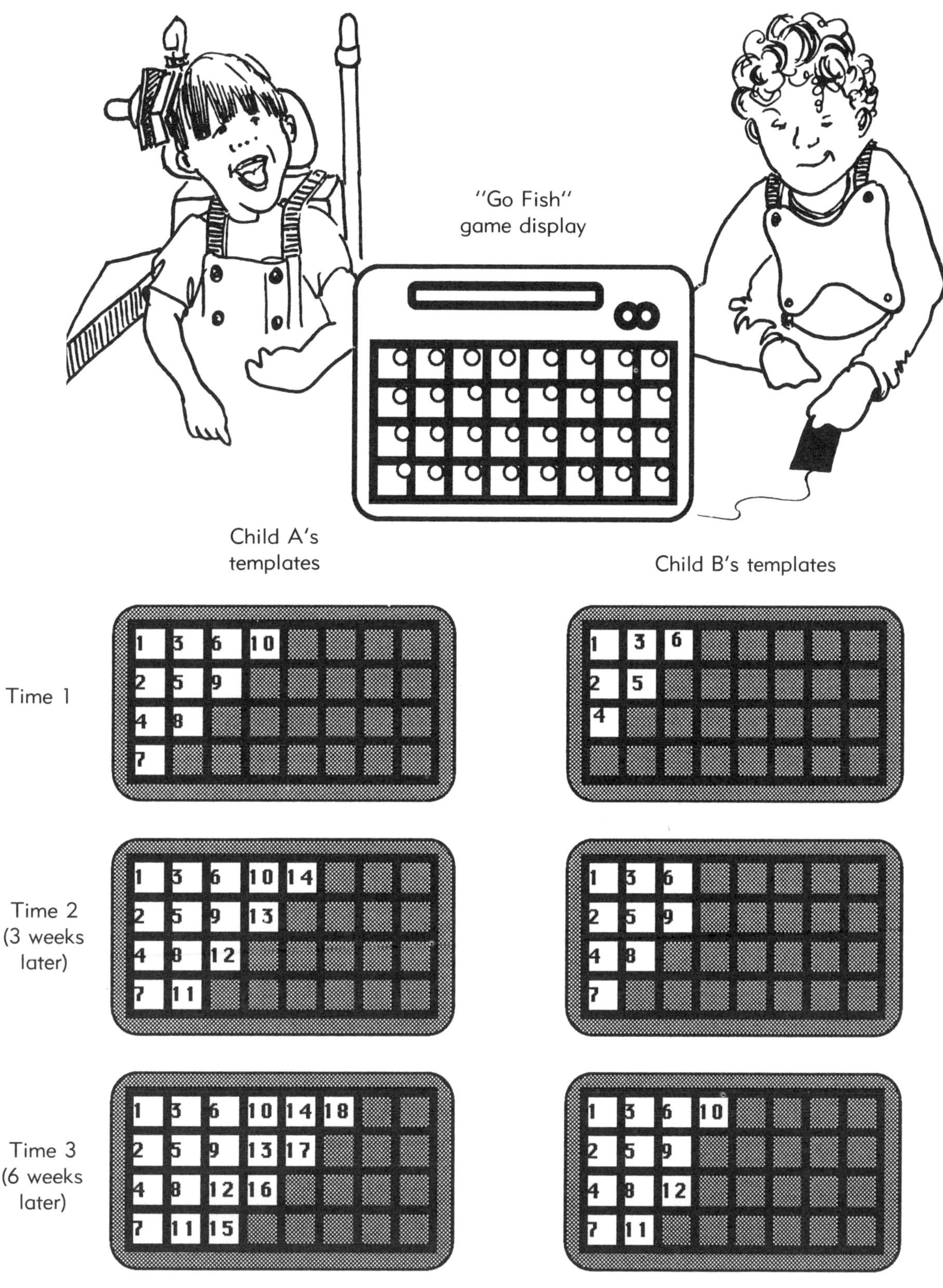


**FIGURE 8.16.** Individualizing rate of exposure of messages.

determined relative ranking. When introducing the first-ranked 10 messages in the message set, for example, the facilitator may choose to obliterate all icons except those required to retrieve the top-ranked 10 messages. Once the child is demonstrating spontaneous self-initiated use of these messages, the facilitator may choose to introduce an additional 10 messages. Steps are then taken to expose the additional required icons by cutting out their corresponding windows on the paper template designated for that particular activity. As was previously discussed, these paper cut-out window templates are developed (a) unique to each concentrated message set and (b) according to each child's unique rate of learning. Figure 8.17 summarizes the use of paper window templates with code-based formats.

As previously discussed, the process of preparing long-range, maximum capacity symbol displays is analogous to buying clothes with potential for future growth. Much like the parent who tries to functionally accommodate for the larger size by rolling up the pant legs or providing the child with a belt, so the facilitator attempts to address the child's current needs by using tape or paper cut-out window templates to expose symbols in a gradual process.

## Transitioning from Nonelectronic to Electronic Format

Frequently, the type of scanning technique the child is able to perform reliably and effortlessly may greatly limit the number of messages simultaneously available for access. If, for example, the child is currently able to perform only linear scanning (depending on the type of device), array size may be limited to eight symbols. If the child is capable of using eye pointing as a selection technique, the possibility exists to supplement this electronic format with a simultaneously presented nonelectronic format. When a three-sided eye-point frame (capable of accommodating 13 messages) is used in conjunction with an eight-location electronic format, 21 of the 36 messages previously delineated for a target activity or topic can now be employed to mediate communicative exchange during the target activity or topic. When using a partner-assisted Talking EyePoint Board (InvoTek), the eye-pointing format can be mediated using voice output. This can be achieved in two ways: (a) by using an Apple IIe, IIgs computer and the Adaptive Firmware Card or (b) by using a Super Wolf communication device and an Expanded Keyboard Interface (InvoTek). Thus, each target activity or topic would have two displays: (a) a clear polycarbonate vinyl (.020-mil) display with double-backed symbols for the nonelectronic eye-point frame or the electronic Talking EyePoint Board (InvoTek) and (b) an eight-symbol display for the electronic voice-output device. When the nonelectronic version of the eye-point frame is being used, the highest ranked messages are typically assigned to the scanning device, allowing these high-priority items to be mediated with voice output. When the Talking EyePoint Board is being used, the top-ranked items are usually assigned to the frame, because communication can be mediated much faster via the frame than the device. Typically, children using linear scanning for communicative exchange are undergoing parallel motor training to acquire proficiency in row-column scanning. When the child is capable of proficiently using row-column scanning in tasks with minimal communication load, this more advanced selection technique replaces linear scanning as the primary selection technique for communicative exchange. With the transition from linear scanning to row-column scanning, array size can be substantially increased. Messages previously presented within a combined eight-symbol electronic format and a 13-symbol electronic or nonelectronic eye-point frame format can now be made available within a larger array format (typically 32 or 36) on the electronic device.

When a *script approach* is being used within a level-based format, messages are presented rank-ordered according to the path of scan. When a *dialogue approach* is being used within a level-based format, messages are frequently assigned to the path of scan in the approximate temporal order in which they unfold in the dialogue. When a *code-based format* is being used, the communication display is typically determined in advance and remains constant across activities or topics.

In some instances, the facilitator may wish to use an eye-point display format as a springboard for gradually introducing messages on the electronic device. Newly introduced items might be introduced in the context of the eye-point frame. Because eye pointing is a direct selection technique, the child is able to "enter the communication game" more

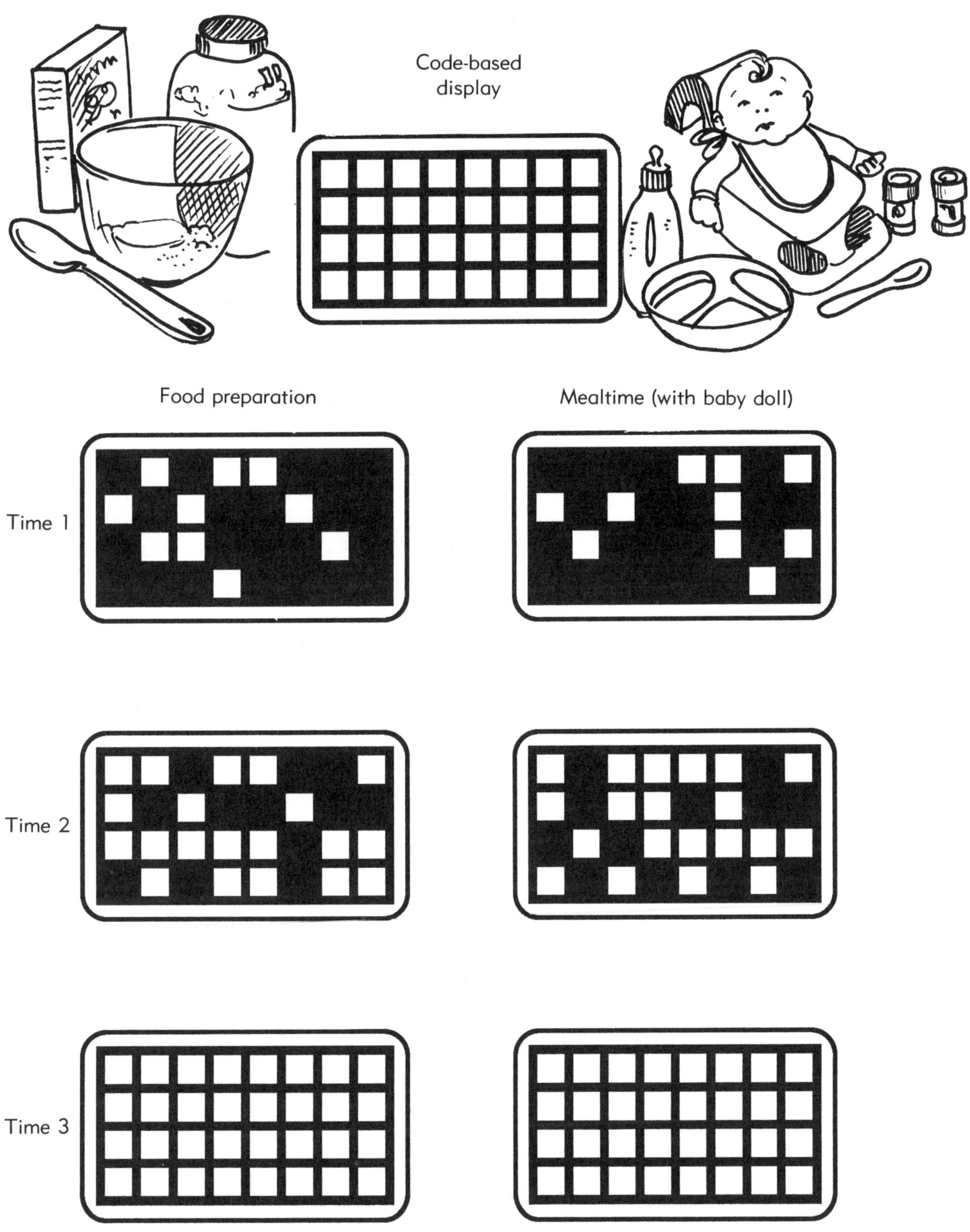


**FIGURE 8.17.** Using paper window templates within a code-based format.

quickly and effortlessly. Having experienced the power of using these messages communicatively in a less physically taxing format, children can be reintroduced to these same messages within a more physically challenging electronic format. Given the saliency of voice output, however, it is hoped that the extra effort required would be counterbalanced by the motivation of voice output. This process is visually reflected in Figure 8.18.

### Transitioning from a Level-Based to a Code-Based Format

When using a level-based format, a second individual is required to physically change displays for the child who is severely physically challenged. When a code-based format is employed, the child is theoretically able to access all coded messages from a single display, eliminating dependence on a second individual. When semantic compaction (i.e., Light Talker) is being used as the memory retrieval format, the CLEAR function capability of the device permits the user to retrieve messages outside of the currently operative theme. This ease of accessing preprogrammed messages across message sets infuses greater flexibility into the child's communication repertoire when a code-based format is being used.

The changeover from a level-based to a code-based format is typically a gradual process. In keeping with the tenets of good intervention, this transition should be as smooth as possible. Given that the child is already demonstrating spontaneous, self-initiated use of messages within a given target activity, the facilitator may wish to introduce semantic compaction as a parallel program. That is, within the context of a level-based activity with which the child is already proficient, he or she is now taught to call forth the same messages using multimeaning icons. Within the context of mealtime, for example, the device would be "locked" into a ONE-SYMBOL theme of (the theme icon for mealtime), thus minimizing the number of selections per message to primarily one and occasionally two icons. The child is then taught to use a "secret code" to call forth his or her mealtime messages using a "secret code message display" (i.e., the Minsymbol display). As was previously discussed, messages can be introduced gradually according to their relative rankings, using cut-out window paper templates to facilitate the process of exposing only those icons required to call forth the targeted messages.

### Within a Code-Based Format: Transition from 8- to 32- to 128-Location Format

Frequently, children who are severely physically challenged progress through several displays of variable array size depending on their current selection technique(s). If the child is using a Light Talker, for example, use of a linear scan pattern limits array size to eight symbols. It is only when the child has mastered row-column scanning that she or he has access to an array size of 32 or 128. When a target message set is being assigned to an 8-location format, only the top-ranked eight items in the concentrated message set would be employed. When the messages for a target activity are being assigned to a 32-location format, the top-ranked 32 items in the concentrated message set would be selected for programming. When messages for a target activity are being assigned to a 128-location format, all 36 messages are available for use. The previously discussed concept-listing approach can be used regardless of the symbol array size. Ideally, however, the Minsymbol codes established within an eight-location format should continue to be operative for the 32-location format and should continue to be viable when the child progresses to a 128-location format.

Goossens', Elder, Caldwell, and Page (1988) presented a continuum of semantic compaction overlays designed to achieve this goal. As illustrated in Figure 8.19, the individual icons available within a 128-location format are available as composite icons within a 32-location format and are available as clustered composite icons within an 8-location format. By ensuring that most of the icons that will ultimately be available to the child within a 128-location format are also present within the earlier 32- and 8-location formats, the concept-listing approach to designing code-based (semantic compaction) formats allows a gradual building of messages across a continuum of formats. Presented in Figure 8.20 are several messages from a mealtime script and their accompanying icon sequences when an 8- versus a 32- versus a 128-location format is being used. As illustrated, the key concepts (delin-

**FIGURE 8.18.** Using a combined electronic and nonelectronic format.

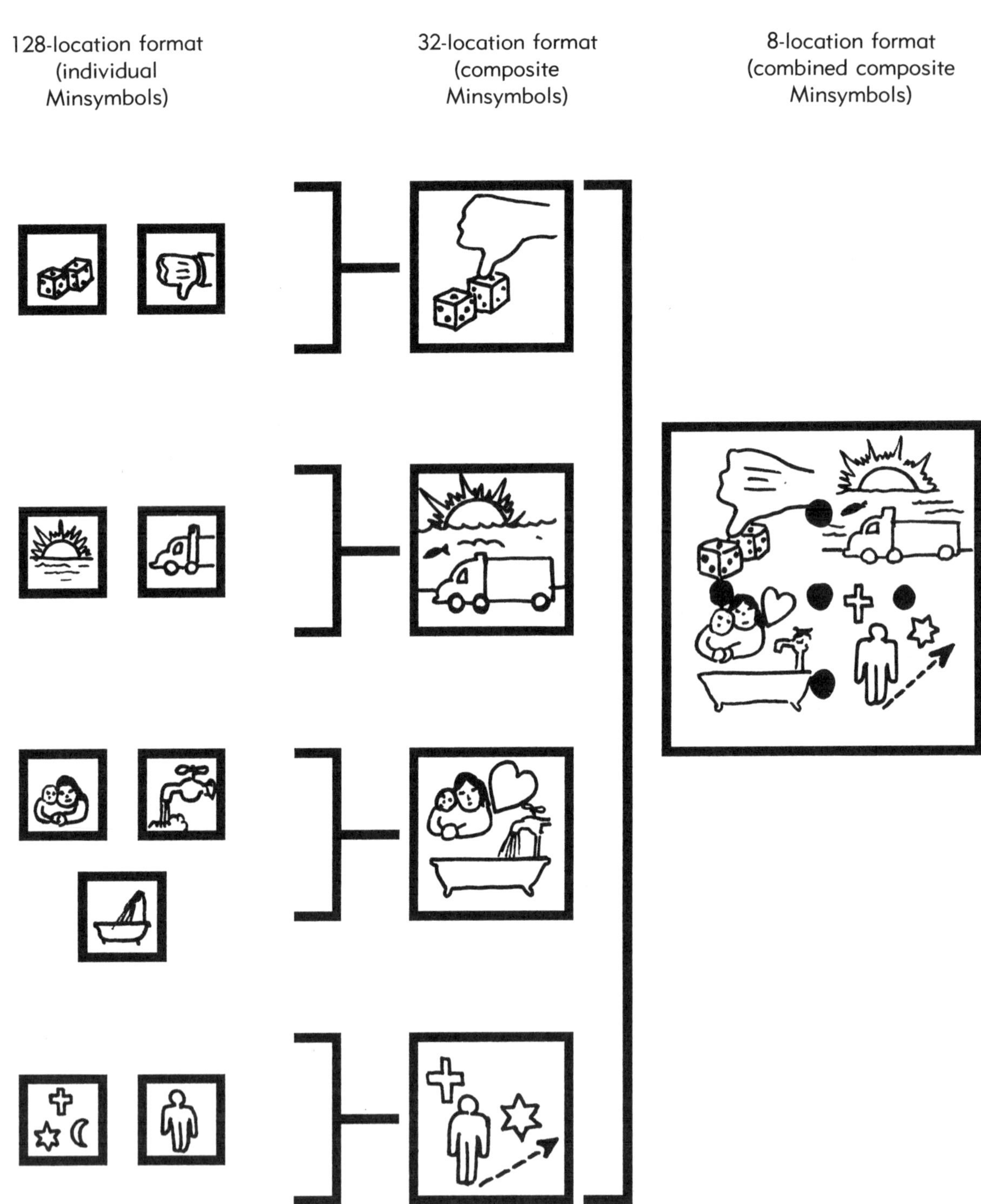


**FIGURE 8.19.** Continuum of minsymbols across 8-, 32-, and 128-location formats.

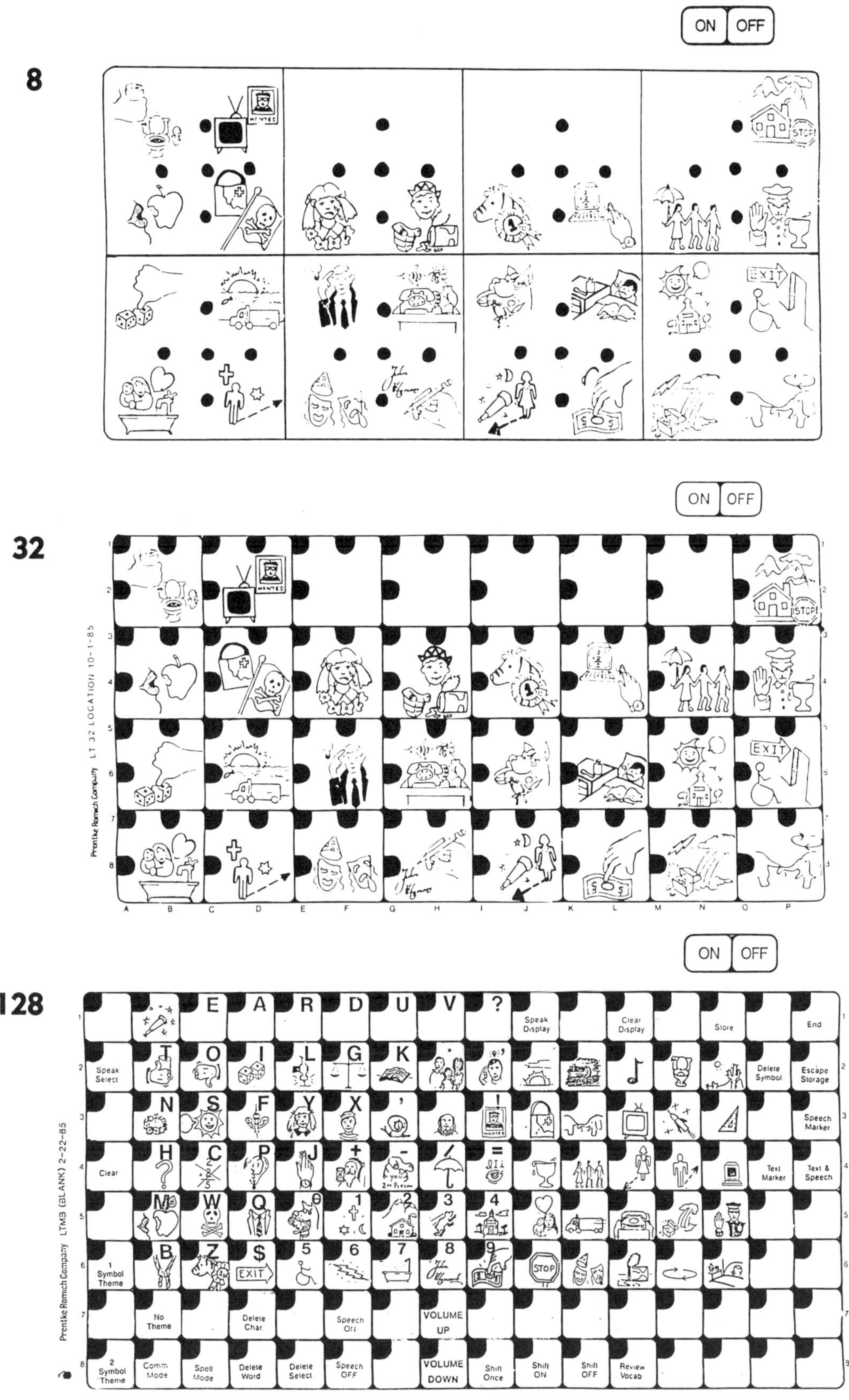


**FIGURE 8.19. (Continued)**

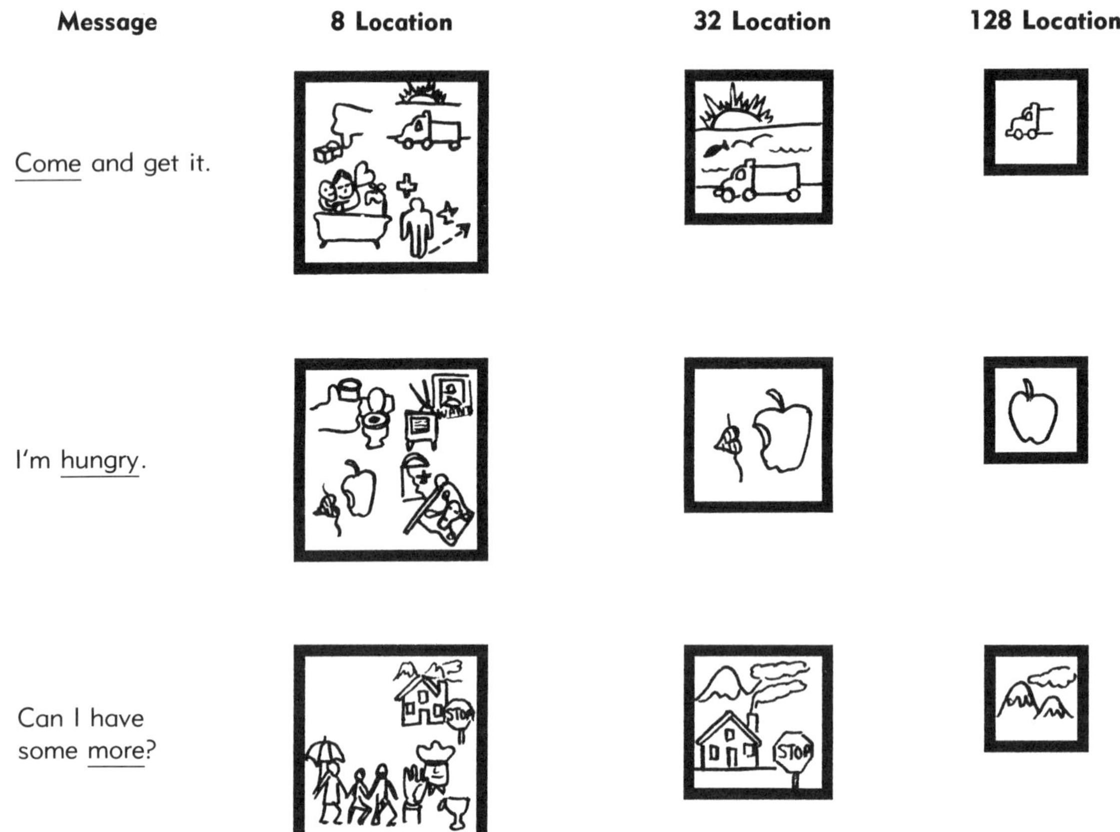


**FIGURE 8.20.** Consistency of icon codes when utilizing an 8- versus 32- versus 128-location format.

eated in Phase IV) remain consistent across the continuum, as do the mnemonic aspects of the icons used to code these key concepts.

## Training Spontaneous, Self-Initiated Use of the System

Ideally, children who are functionally nonspeaking should be using their augmentative communication systems frequently and spontaneously to impact the many environments in which they must function. Unfortunately, this is more often the exception than the rule with children who are using scanning selection techniques.

Frequent interactive use can occur only when systems are designed and trained in a manner conducive to promoting frequent interactive use. As previously discussed, when designing a scanning system care should be taken to (a) use predominantly phrase- or sentence-based messages (to expedite rate of communicative exchange), (b) minimize the number of selections required to call forth a preprogrammed message (to better approximate "real-time" communicative exchange), (c) select concentrated, activity-based message sets (to promote multiple turns within a narrow time frame), and (d) load messages in the path of scan according to their perceived relative importance to the interaction. A good design in and of itself, however, is not sufficient to guarantee success. Discussed below are both general and specific training issues relative to the act of training spontaneous, self-initiated use.

### General Issues

As a general rule, we have found intervention to be more successful when primary emphasis is placed on creating opportunities to communicate rather than obligating communication through the frequent use of directives and questions (e.g., "Tell me with your machine," "What do we do next?" "What do you want?"). Rather than pose the question, "What do we need?" in a food preparation activity, for example, the facilitator might set the stage for a self-initiated communication by looking in the bowl and commenting "Uh-oh, we forgot something!" Instead of issuing the directive, "Tell me what we need to do with this," the facilitator might comment, "We've got to do something with this." In many instances, a nonspeaking, naive helping doll can be used to model initiating behavior and set the stage for self-initiated use through sabotage routines. In a food preparation activity, for example, the helping doll might spontaneously point (on the child's display) to the LET ME TASTE symbol. Thus, the doll is modeling for the child a potentially useful message at this point in the scenario. Similarly, the helping doll might set the stage for the message OPEN IT by mistakenly placing the brownie mix box into the bowl without having first opened it (sabotage routine). The latter situation then creates an opportunity for the facilitator to set the stage by commenting, "Billy! I can't believe what he just did! He put the box in the bowl. He's really mixed up. He needs help."

Children must be provided with models of interactive use if they are to learn to use their systems frequently and interactively. Several authors have noted the need to provide users of augmentative communication systems with augmented input (Beukelman & Garrett, 1988; Romski & Sevcik, 1988).

## Specific Procedures

When an augmentative communication system configured in a word-based format is being used, frequent models of interactive use can be provided via aided language stimulation techniques (Goossens', 1989; Goossens', Crain, & Elder, 1988a, 1988b). When engaged in this form of augmented input, the facilitator points out symbols on the child's communication display in conjunction with her or his ongoing verbal language stimulation (e.g., "POUR . . . gotta POUR the CAKE MIX . . . IN . . . IN the BOWL"). Because the display is word-based, the facilitator can easily mix and match component words to create an extensive pool of novel messages.

When using an augmentative communication system reflecting a predominantly phrase- or sentence-based format, however, the task of providing augmented input is somewhat more challenging. Given the reduced generative power of sentence-based units, it is no longer feasible to combine and recombine symbols to model an exhaustive pool of novel messages during the ongoing interaction. In contrast to word-based formats, phrase- or sentence-based formats necessitate the insertion of complete messages at key points in the interactional flow. Thus, a procedure is required that will allow the facilitator to unobtrusively cue the child (a) when a message juncture point occurs and (b) as to what message can be appropriately employed at this key point during the course of in-context training. Both goals can be achieved using a *shadow light cuing* approach (Figure 8.21). When this approach is being used, the facilitator serves as a nonverbal shadow to the child, visually highlighting various symbols (depicting messages) on the scanning display. The child is, therefore, being unobtrusively cued to capitalize on opportunities for use as they unfold during key juncture points in the ongoing interaction. Highlighting of symbols can be achieved using either a finger point or a small penlight with a concentrated beam (e.g., EverReady Squeeze Light, Brinkman flashlight). Of these two options, the penlight is preferred because it is more visually salient and does not obliterate the child's view of the highlighted picture symbol. In an attempt to make this cuing as unobtrusive as possible, the facilitator refrains from using distracting verbal cues such as, "Get this one," "Say this one," or "Tell 'em you wanna do it." Such extraneous verbal directives tend to be pragmatically inappropriate and tone-increasing. They often inadvertently confound the task that they set out to facilitate.

During the initial stages of intervention, the light cue is presented as a constant cue. That is, when a communicative opportunity arises, the facilitator shines the light on the target symbol (message). This light cue is then maintained until the child has successfully accessed the target symbol's underlying preprogrammed message. Later in intervention, a hierarchy of prompts can be employed to fade the child's dependence on the light cue. When, for example, an opportunity arises to communicate "Let me do it," the child is first given an opportunity to spontaneously self-initiate a production at this key juncture point. If, after a predetermined length of time (based on the child's typical latency of response), the child has not demonstrated

**FIGURE 8.21.** Shadow light cuing format—Two facilitators.

a spontaneous, self-initiated production, the facilitator unobtrusively cues the child to use the device by scanning the penlight across the communication display using a rapid circular motion (*search light cue*). If, after a predetermined length of time, the child has still not capitalized on this opportunity to use a preprogrammed message, the facilitator provides a *momentary light cue.* When providing a momentary light cue, the facilitator shines the penlight on the target symbol for a 2- to 3-second period. Because the light cue is removed prior to successful access, a momentary light cue provides the child with assistance in deciding what message to access, but leaves the task of visually and physically targeting the correct cell to the child. If the child fails to initiate access after a predetermined length of time, the facilitator provides the child with a *constant light cue.* In contrast to the momentary light cue, the constant light cue assists the child in maintaining visual focus on the target symbol while simultaneously monitoring the scanning process. Figure 8.22 summarizes the prompt hierarchy for the shadow-cuing procedure.

Logistically, the aforementioned procedures are more easily conducted when two facilitators are involved in the training process. This is especially true during the early stages of intervention when (a) the act of serving as a ''straight man,'' setting the stage for self-initiated use, must be conducted concurrently with (b) the provision of shadow cuing according to a hierarchy of prompts and (c) the documenting of reliable data regarding productive use. In the context of a group activity such as food preparation, one adult (teacher or speech/language pathologist) typically serves as the primary facilitator. A second individual then serves the role of shadow light cuer for the children making up the group.

With experience, it is feasible to perform all three tasks simultaneously. The reader should, however, be cognizant that it is pragmatically false from the child's perspective for the facilitator to serve as both the ''straight man'' and the shadow cuer. That is, the act of setting the stage for a communication using a sabotage technique then doing an ''about face'' to cue the child as to the appropriate production may dilute the saliency of the exchange. In the event that only one facilitator is being employed during a training activity, the facilitator may wish to incorporate a helping doll who (with indirect assistance from the facilitator) performs the role of shadow cuer. When using a helping doll in the role of shadow cuer, it is advisable to (a) permanently attach the penlight to the doll's hand and (b) use a long stick (attached to the doll's wrist) to manipulate the doll's arm as if it were a stick puppet. Given these adaptations, cuing can be provided that does not appear (from the child's perspective) to be mediated by the facilitator. These adaptations of the helping doll are depicted in Figure 8.23.

In instances in which message array size is severely limited by selection technique (e.g., when using linear scanning), the facilitator may wish to supplement the high-priority messages presented within an electronic format with lesser priority messages presented in a nonelectronic format such as an eye-gaze frame. The facilitator now has access to a larger message pool with which to provide augmented input during the ongoing target activity. Once the child (as a result of parallel programming) is able to access the device using a selection technique that permits access to a larger message array

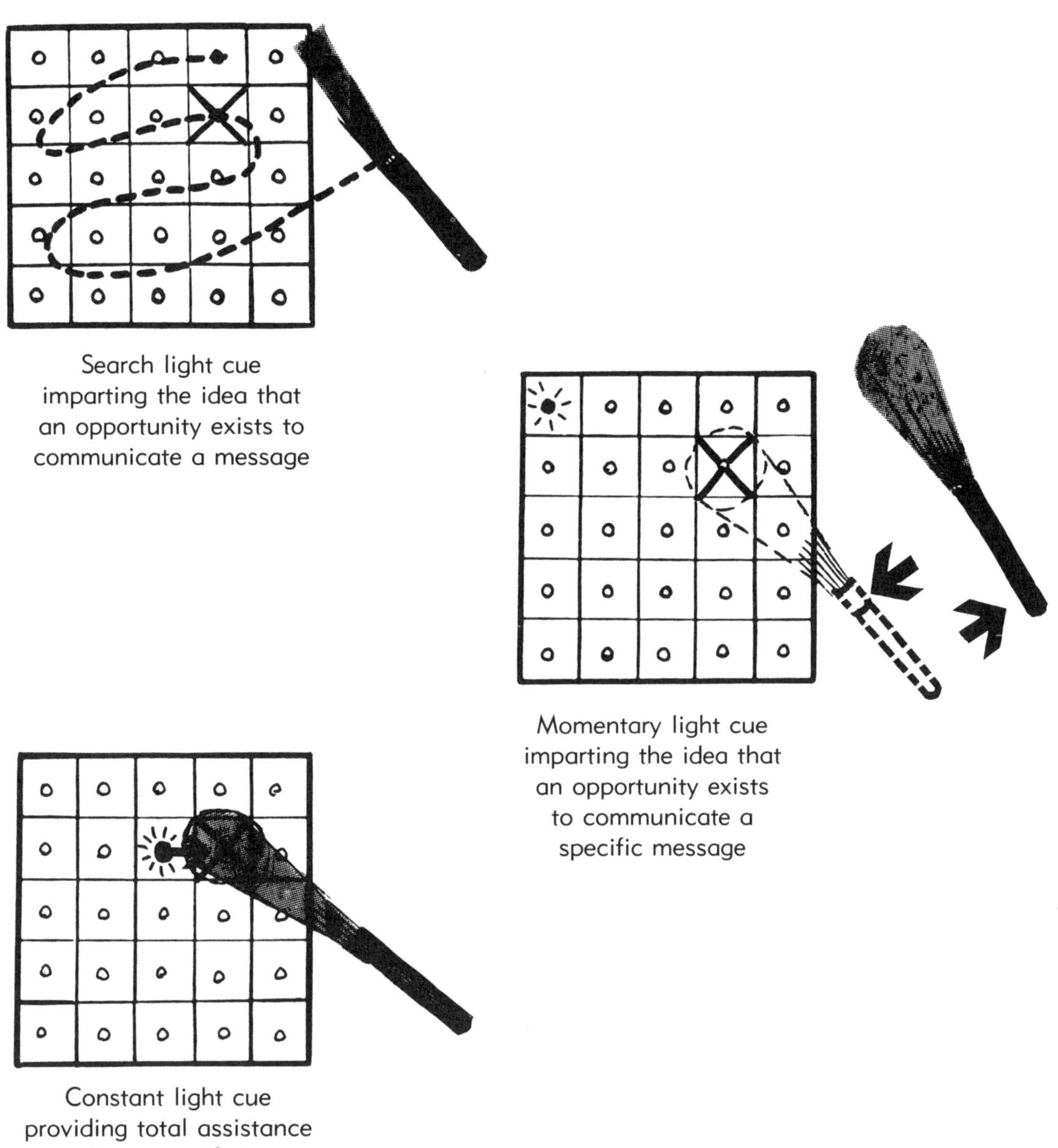


**FIGURE 8.22.** Prompt hierarchy for shadow cuing.

(e.g., row-column scanning, 32-cell format), the messages previously accessed in a nonelectronic frame format can now be accessed by the child using the voice-output capabilities of the device. This combined device plus eye-gaze frame format is visually depicted in Figure 8.24.

When using a level-based format, shadow cuing is performed by highlighting the single meaning symbol corresponding to the target message on the level-based display unique to that activity or topic. When using a code-based format such as abbreviated letter codes, shadow cuing is achieved by highlighting the corresponding letter code(s). When using a code-based format such as semantic compaction, shadow cuing is achieved by highlighting the multimeaning icon corresponding to the target message on the single semantic compaction display.

**FIGURE 8.23.** Shadow cuing format—One facilitator using a helping doll.

## Data Collection

Data collection is frequently a difficult process, especially when intervention is being conducted within a highly dynamic, interactive format. In general, data collection strategies are required that are (a) quick, (b) accurate, and (c) as unobtrusive as possible. Toward achieving this end, it is recommended that the facilitator consider using an erasable china marker or overhead projector pen to mark data directly on the protective acrylite face of the device, or on the laminated, activity-based scanning communication display adhered directly to the face of the device (Figure 8.25). Each production or failed

**FIGURE 8.24.** Shadow-cuing format—Combined electronic plus nonelectronic format.

attempt on the part of the child is immediately documented on the display in relation to its corresponding target symbol (message). Productions can be generally classified as those reflective of spontaneous, self-initiated use (both contextually appropriate, [✓], and contextually ambiguous or inappropriate, [X]) and those categorized as cued productions (following the adult's model, [A]; following the helping doll's model, [D]; following a generic spotlight cue, [S]; following a constant light cue, [C]; following a momentary light cue, [M]). In the event that more than one attempt is required to produce a successfully cued production, these failed attempts are indicated as (−). Upon completing data collection, the data documented directly on the display are then transferred to a data sheet.

When conducting classroom data collection across the course of the day, facilitators (classroom teacher, aides) may wish to use Velcro to attach both the penlight (required for shadow cuing) and the china marker (required for data collection) to the device. This ensures that these materials are readily accessible. During storytime, for example, a classroom assistant might assume responsibility for (a) placing the appropriate storytime display on the child's scanning device (by using Velcro to attach the display to the acrylite faceplate of the device), (b) "locking" the device into the storytime page or level on the device (using the code dots on the storytime display to visually cue level/page setup), (c) shadow light cuing appropriate productions at key points in the storytime activity (using the penlight mounted on the device), and (d) documenting directly on the display the nature of the child's productions during these activities (using the china marker or nonpermanent marker mounted on the device). Having completed storytime, the teacher or the assistant then repeats this process for snack time to be followed by a similar chain of events for music time. At the end of the day, data marked on the communication displays are transferred to data sheets summarizing the day's communicative per-

**FIGURE 8.25.** Collecting data directly on the communication display. Pictures derived from Picture Communication Symbols, Mayer-Johnson Company; Rebus (Clark, Davies, & Woodcock); American Guidance Service.

formance. Based on the child's performance, decisions are made regarding whether to introduce additional messages in the concentrated message set.

When the device is interfaced with a portable printer, the printer can be used to document the child's productions. Although such an approach does document the quantity of productions across the course of the day, information relative to the appropriateness of the responses and the level of cuing required is lost in the process. Use of the printer for data collection is therefore most beneficial in activities in which shadow cuing is no longer necessary.

## Summary

Augmentative communication systems must be designed to allow children to impact their environment using a broad range of pragmatic functions within a broad range of activities/topics. Ideally, children should be using such systems frequently, spontaneously, and interactively. Toward achieving these goals, considerable attention must be devoted to (a) designing the communication system to allow children to impact their environment frequently and interactively and (b) teaching children to use the well-designed system in a format that promotes spontaneous, self-initiated use.

In general, a number of issues must be carefully considered when designing an augmentative communication system. Issues in need of consideration include:

- ❑ The function of the system as a conversational versus a language learning/academic tool
- ❑ The flexibility versus speed of communication (letter-based formats vs. word-based formats vs. phrase/sentence-based formats)
- ❑ Diluted versus concentrated message sets
- ❑ Script-generated versus dialogue-generated message sets
- ❑ Electronic versus nonelectronic formats
- ❑ Level-based versus code-based voice-output electronic formats

More specifically, communication systems can be designed using the following seven-phase process:

- ❑ Phase I. Delineating the overall communication environment to be impacted
- ❑ Phase II. Delineating and prioritizing activities/topics to be targeted within the overall communication environment
- ❑ Phase III. Delineating and prioritizing messages for each target activity/topic
- ❑ Phase IV. Delineating a key concept for each message in a target message set

- ❑ Phase V. Delineating the augmentative communication technique/display format for each target activity or topic
- ❑ Phase VI. Preparing the communication display
- ❑ Phase VII. Gradual introduction of messages within the message set

Both general and specific issues relative to the task of training spontaneous, self-initiated system use are discussed in this chapter. Issues addressed include (a) the need to utilize training paradigms that foster spontaneous, self-initiated use and (b) the need for augmented input. In general, intervention is conducted with primary emphasis on creating opportunities to communicate rather than obligating the child to communicate through the frequent use of directives and questions. A number of strategies can be used to actively create opportunities for communication to occur. A ''shadow cuing'' procedure can then be employed as a means of unobtrusively cuing the child to insert appropriate messages when such opportunities arise in the conversational flow. A manageable data collection system relative to the shadow-cuing procedure is presented.

# APPENDIX A
## Guidelines for Switch Setups Involving Alternate Control Sites

| Movement Pattern | Contact Site | Distance from Contact Site | Alignment | Boundary Bumper |
|---|---|---|---|---|
| Lateral head turn | Side of forehead 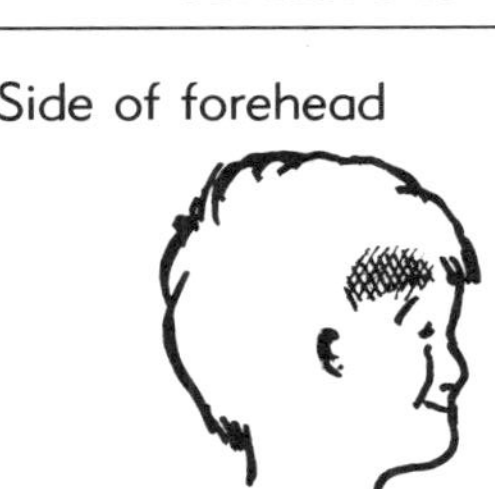 • Avoid eye and ear<br>• If child "rears up" in chair (despite efforts to stabilize pelvis), placement may need to be compromised to a height somewhere between the testing and reared position; this is also sometimes necessary when child has glasses  <br>• If "rearing up" is due to the newness or excitement of the task, may start out with a compromised position then move it down to the optimal position over time | • Position relatively close to minimize the distance the control site must deviate from midline 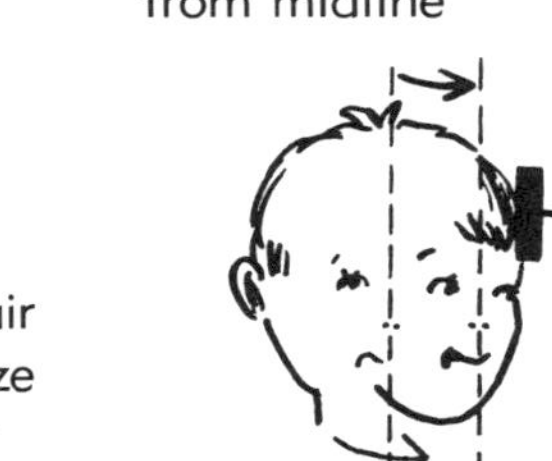<br>• Is positioned closer when using a lateral head turn as opposed to a lateral head tilt | • Align switch activation surface parallel with contour of head in forehead area<br>• Wedge may be necessary to achieve an alignment that maximizes contact between the switch and control site | • Boundary bumper in temporal area of opposite side works well; usually boundary bumper is constructed to promote midline placement of head<br>• Lateral head turn works well with contoured headrests such as Otto Bock, because headrest serves as guide for rotating on and off switch <br>• Discourage movement pattern that involves moving head out of headrest  |

*(Appendix continues)*

## APPENDIX A. Continued

| Movement Pattern | Contact Site | Distance from Contact Site | Alignment | Boundary Bumper |
|---|---|---|---|---|
| | Cheek | • Position relatively close to minimize the distance the control site must deviate from midline<br>• Distance from control site will vary depending on the amplitude of child's extraneous head movements<br>• Child may initially mouthe on switch; with many children this tendency extinguishes with time<br>• If drooling is a problem a hermatically sealed switch is desired | • Align switch activation surface with contour of cheek<br>• Wedge may be necessary to create angle that maximizes contact | • Boundary bumper in temporal area of opposite side works well<br>• Strive to create midline placement of head |

(Appendix continues)

## APPENDIX A. Continued

| Movement Pattern | Contact Site | Distance from Contact Site | Alignment | Boundary Bumper |
|---|---|---|---|---|
| Lateral head tilt | • Temporal area above ear 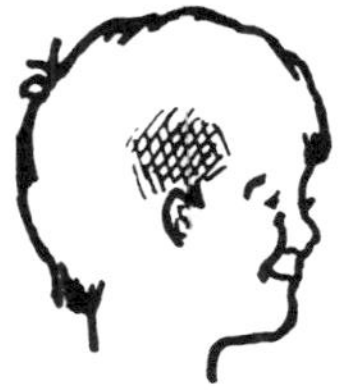<br>• Care must be taken to avoid the eye area and the ear<br>• If the child wears glasses, optimal placement may need to be compromised to avoid hitting the glasses<br>• With time, as the child grows accustomed to the switch, optimal placement can be approximated | • Can be placed farther from head than for lateral head turn 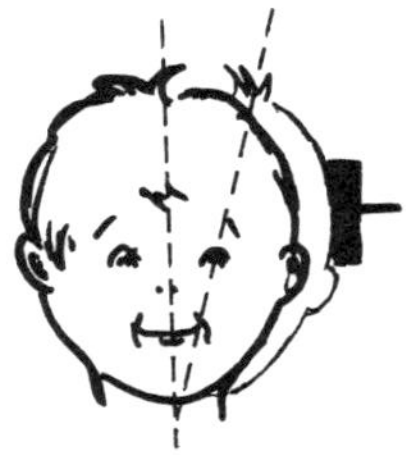<br>• Distance from head will vary depending on the amplitude of the child's extraneous head movements | • Align with contour of child's head  | • Usually, boundary bumper is constructed to promote midline placement of the head<br>Boundary bumper 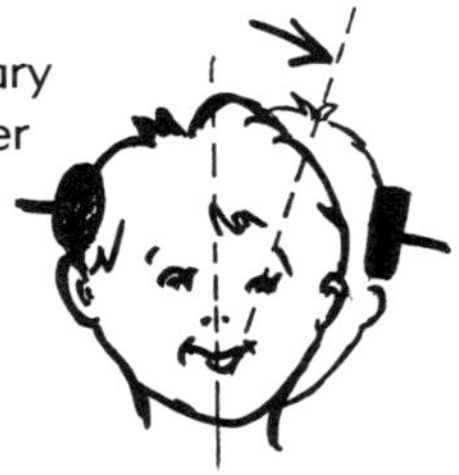<br>• Boundary bumper in temporal area works well<br>• If child wears glasses, placement of boundary bumper on the side of forehead is preferred |
| Head flexion | • Bottom of chin  | • Care must be taken to avoid placement that is too close to the neck 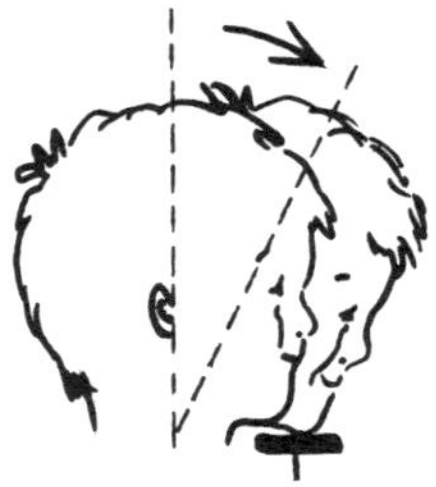 |  | • Headrest serves as a natural boundary bumper 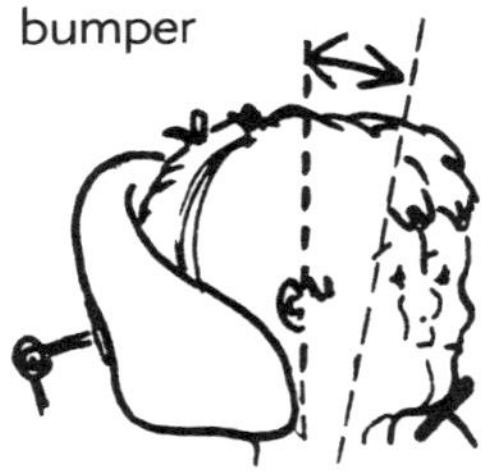 |

(Appendix continues)

## APPENDIX A. Continued

| Movement Pattern | Contact Site | Distance from Contact Site | Alignment | Boundary Bumper |
| --- | --- | --- | --- | --- |
| | • Tip of chin  | • Minimal movement is preferred to avoid total extension<br>• Chest harness may need to be loosened to facilitate free movement | • A wedge may be needed to present the switch more vertically angled to allow activation with capital flexion  | • Headrest serves as a natural boundary bumper  |
| Head extension | • Back of head<br>• Avoid the occipital area of the head  | • May be slightly recessed within a contoured headrest 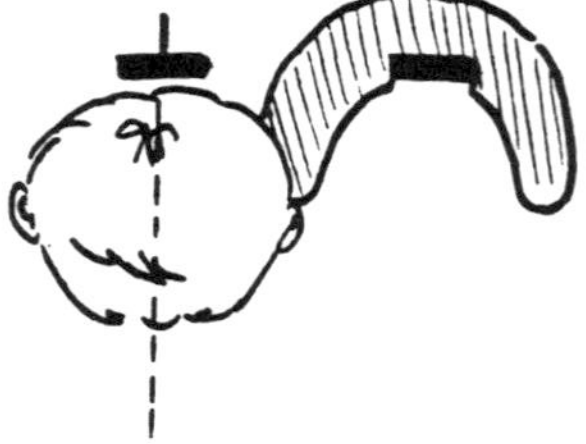<br>• If not recessed in the headrest, it may be a free-standing mount with a neck collar being used to support the head  | • Align with contour of head at point of contact 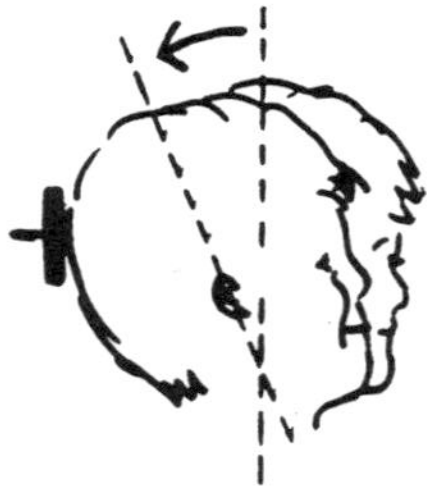 | |

*(Appendix continues)*

## APPENDIX A. Continued

| Movement Pattern | Contact Site | Distance from Contact Site | Alignment | Boundary Bumper |
|---|---|---|---|---|
| Knee adduction  | Medial side of knee 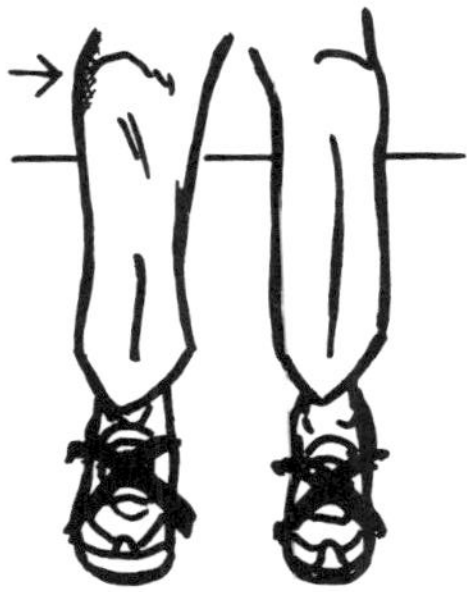 | • Can be positioned closer if using lateral tilt as opposed to lateral shift as tilt tends to be more controlled 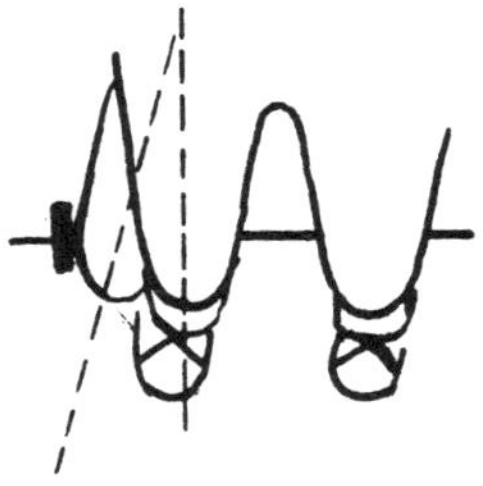<br>• Distance from control site will vary depending on amplitude of the child's extraneous knee movements (especially if athetoid) | • Align switch parallel with side of leg making sure to maximize contact between switch and side of the knee at point of contact 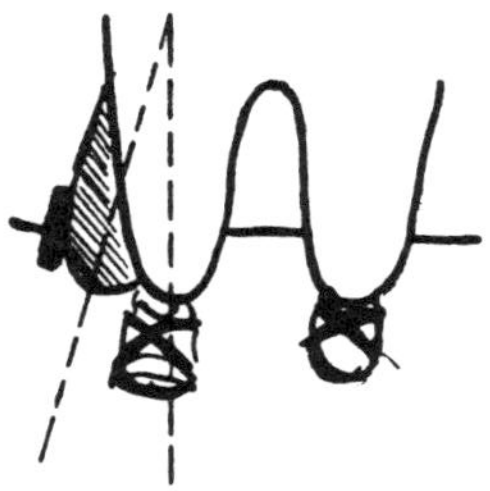 | • The boundary bumper is typically positioned in a location that promotes alignment of the leg in its typical resting position<br>• In some instances, leg adductor pads (already part of child's positioning system) may serve as natural boundary bumper<br>• Boundary bumper may be suspended down from the underside of the lap tray |
| Knee abduction  | Lateral side of knee 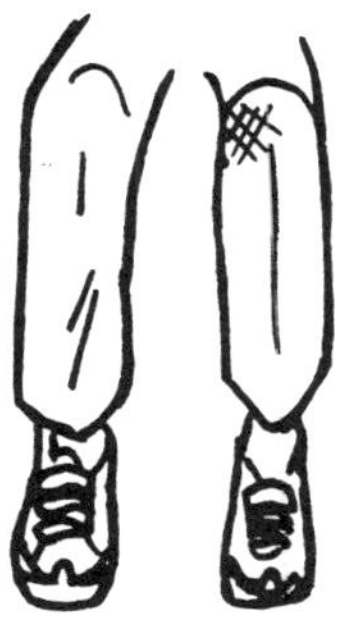 | • Can be positioned closer if using a lateral tilt as opposed to a lateral shift as tilt tends to be more controlled | • Align switch parallel with side of leg making sure to maximize contact between switch and knee at point of contact | • The boundary bumper is typically positioned to promote neutral leg alignment<br>• In some instances, an abductor pommel serves as a natural boundary bumper<br>• The boundary bumper may be suspended down from the underside of the lap tray |

*(Appendix continues)*

## APPENDIX A. Continued

| Movement Pattern | Contact Site | Distance from Contact Site | Alignment | Boundary Bumper |
|---|---|---|---|---|
| Hip flexion | Top of knee  | • Switch is usually attached to underside of lap tray<br>• A padded switch can also be strapped to child's knee, making contact with underside of lap tray<br>• Distance from control site will vary with the amplitude of child's extraneous movements<br>• Spacer block may be inserted between switch and lap tray to achieve correct distance | • Switch is usually attached to the underside of wheelchair lap tray 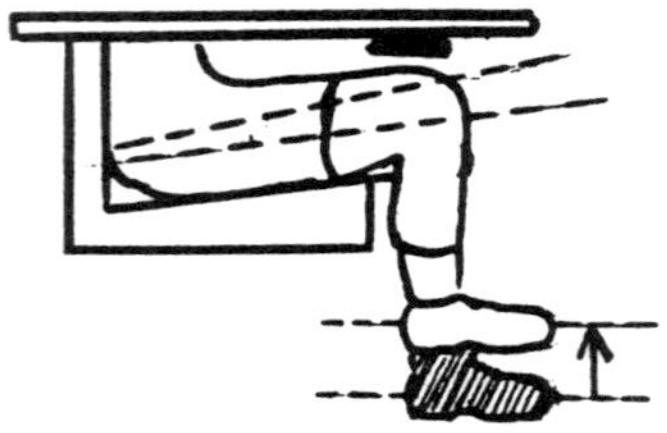<br>Lifting foot <br>Toe pivot<br>• Spacer block may need to be wedged to maximize contact between knee and switch activation surface | • Chair seat serves as natural boundary bumper<br>• Gravity assists the release aspect of switch access |

*(Appendix continues)*

## APPENDIX A. Continued

| Movement Pattern | Contact Site | Distance from Contact Site | Alignment | Boundary Bumper |
|---|---|---|---|---|
| Dorsiflexion | Top of foot | • When an up-down heel pivot arrangement is used, the switch can be positioned closer to the control site than when a nonpivot arrangement is used | • Align at an angle parallel to that of the dorsiflexed foot | • The footplate serves as a natural boundary bumper |
| Plantarflexion | Bottom of foot | • Bottom of foot is typically positioned on the switch activation surface<br><br>Heavy-duty switch or recessed format | • Switch is often placed on a slight wedge | • No boundary bumper is required, as the foot ideally does not lose contact with the switch |

*(Appendix continues)*

## APPENDIX A. Continued

| Movement Pattern | Contact Site | Distance from Contact Site | Alignment | Boundary Bumper |
|---|---|---|---|---|
| Foot adduction | Medial side of foot 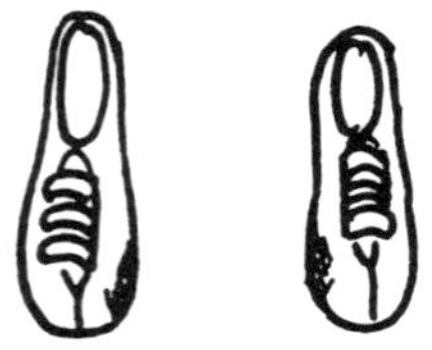 | • When a L-R heel-pivot arrangement is used, the switch can be positioned closer to the control site than when a nonpivot arrangement is used<br>• Heel cup greatly facilitates this setup <br>Tilt (heel pivot) 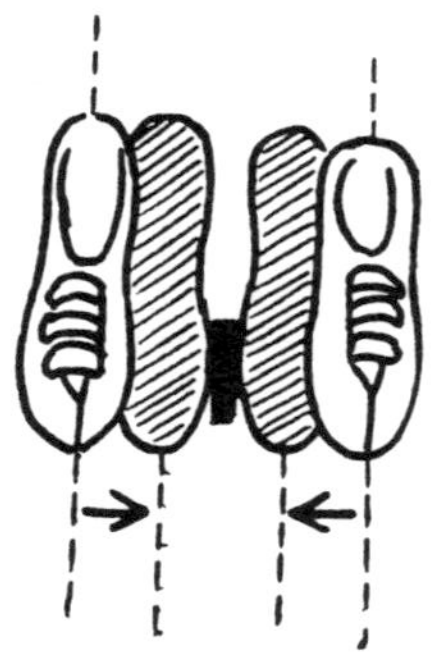<br>Shift | • When a heel-pivot arrangement is used, align switch at an angle comparable to that which the pivoted foot assumes at the point of contact<br>• When a nonpivot arrangement is used, the switch is typically aligned parallel to the foot at the point of contact | • When a nonpivot arrangement is used, a block can be mounted on the footplate to control the maximum excursion of the foot away from switch, positioned on its side<br>• Ethafoam can be used to build up on the footplate to serve as a boundary bumper   |

(Appendix continues)

## APPENDIX A. Continued

| Movement Pattern | Contact Site | Distance from Contact Site | Alignment | Boundary Bumper |
|---|---|---|---|---|
| Foot abduction | Lateral side of foot | • Same as above | | • An Ethafoam structure can be made with a guiding heel cup |
| | 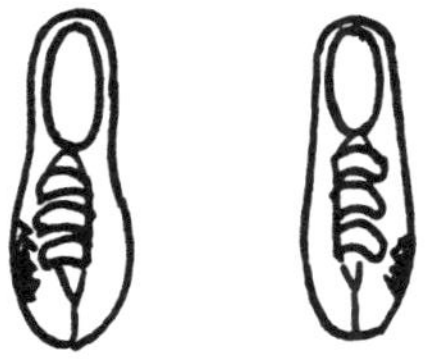 | 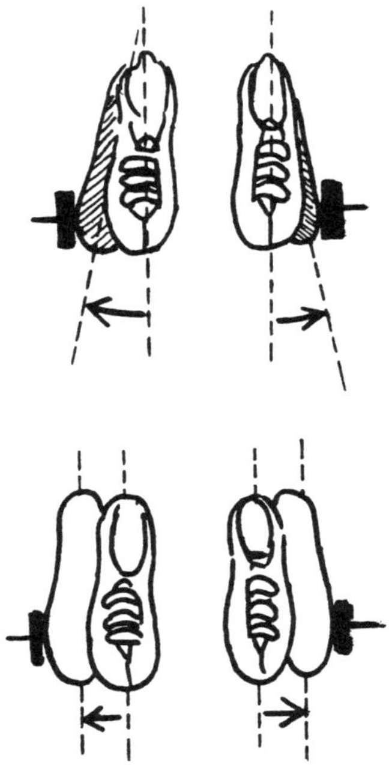 | 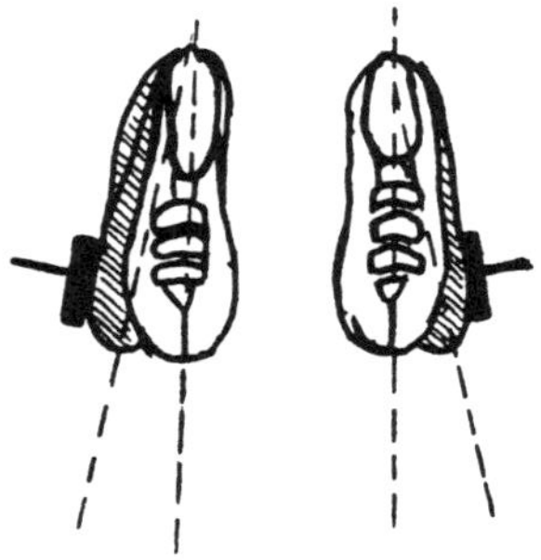 | 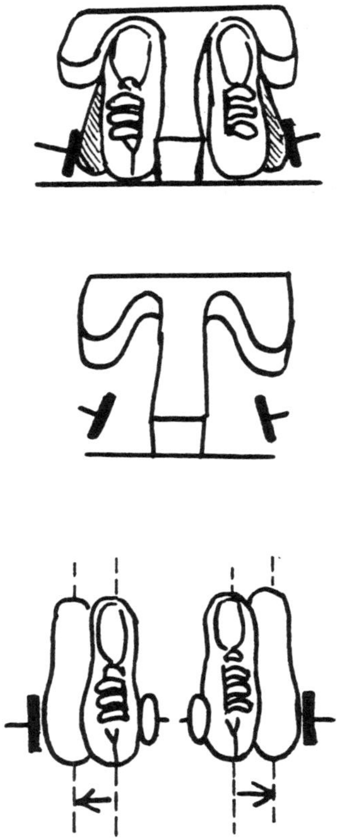 |

# APPENDIX B
## Supplies for Making CPVC Switch Mounts

| Diagram | Name | No. | Function |
|---|---|---|---|
| CPVC components  | ½″ CPVC plastic pipe (two sets ½″ to 12″ in ½″ increments) | 24′ | |
|  | ½″ CPVC 90 elbows (ells) | 12 | to achieve a 90° turn in a CPVC switch mount |
|  | ½″ CPVC 45 elbows (ells) | 6 | to achieve a 45° turn in a CPVC switch mount |
|  | ½″ CPVC tee | 6 | to permit simultaneous joining of three pipe lengths |
|  | ½″ CPVC straight coupler | 6 | • to increase pipe width to accommodate commercially available wheelchair clamp<br>• to join pipe lengths or extend a pipe length |

(Appendix continues)

## APPENDIX B. Continued

| Diagram | Name | No. | Function |
|---|---|---|---|
| CPVC components (cont.)  | ½″ CPVC female adapter | 6 | to transition to CPVC pipe from a ¾″ metal floor flange via a reducing bushing and a close nipple |
|  | ½″ CPVC male adapter | 6 | used in conjunction with weather-proof box to support mounting of a pressure switch |
|  | ½″ PVC<br>½″ CPVC cap | 6<br>6 | used in conjunction with half of a ground clamp to adapt switches to accommodate a CPVC pipe mount |
|  | street adapter | 6 | to attach CPVC mount to switch via a CPVC or PVC ½″ cap |
| 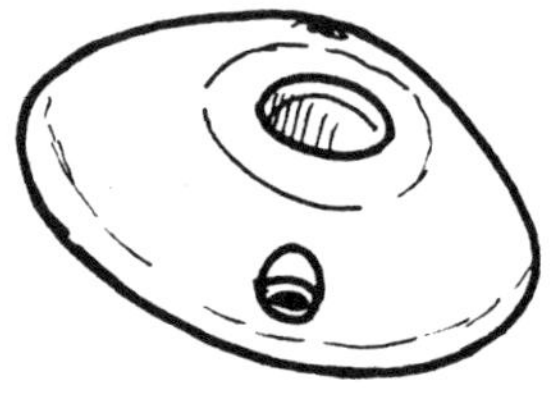 | ½″ torque flange | 2 | to attach switch interface to CPVC pipe; with a false bottom it may attach directly to the switch or may be attached to a wooden or acrylic plate that accommodates a Velcro attachment of a switch |

*(Appendix continues)*

## APPENDIX B. Continued

| Diagram | Name | No. | Function |
|---|---|---|---|
| Metal components  | ½″ to ⅜″ reducing bushing | 6 | to transition from a ⅜″ metal floor flange to a ½″ CPVC female adapter via a ⅜″ close nipple |
|  | ⅜″ close nipple | 6 | to transition from a ⅜″ metal floor flange to a CPVC female adapter via a reducing bushing |
| 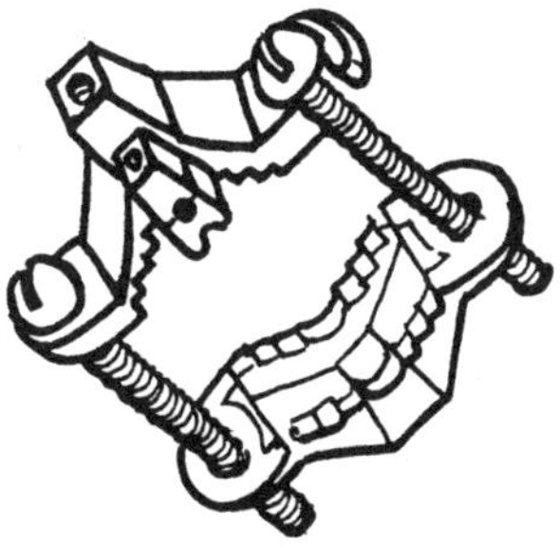 | ground clamps | 6 | to attach CPVC switch mount to frame of therapeutic positioning equipment |
|  | ¼″ × 2½″ machine screws | 6 | used in conjunction with ground clamps to accommodate a larger frame |

*(Appendix continues)*

## APPENDIX B. Continued

| Diagram | Name | No. | Function |
|---|---|---|---|
| Metal components (cont.)  | $^{10}/_{32}$ × ¾″ flat-head machine screws with nuts | 12 | to attach half of the ground clamp assembly to PVC cap (to adapt switches to accommodate CPVC pipe) |
|  | $^{10}/_{32}$ × ½″ flat-head machine screws with nuts | 12 | to attach PVC cap to wood/acrylic plate |
|  | 1½″ stainless steel worm-drive clamps | 6 | to attach pipe to frame of therapeutic positioning equipment |
|  | tooth lock washers, star lock washer, flat lock washer, split lock washer (Size 10 INT) | 1 pkg | used when modifying a PVC/CPVC cap to transition to half a ground clamp; lock washers exert a constant pressure on nuts so they won't thread off inside the cap |
| 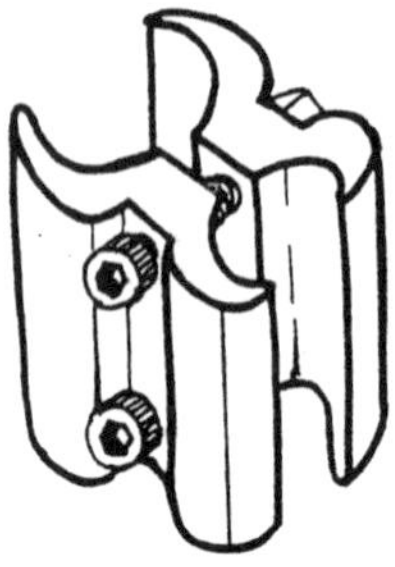 | wheelchair clamp (Zygo Industries, Don Johnston Developmental Equipment) | 2 | to attach mount to frame of therapeutic positioning equipment |

*(Appendix continues)*

## APPENDIX B. Continued

| Diagram | Name | No. | Function |
|---|---|---|---|
| Metal components (cont.) 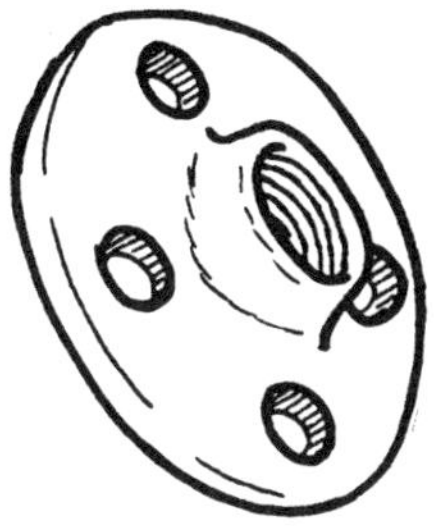 | 3/8″ or 1/2″ metal floor flange (the lighter, less bulky versions are preferred) | 2 | serves as a base for mounting a pressure switch |
| 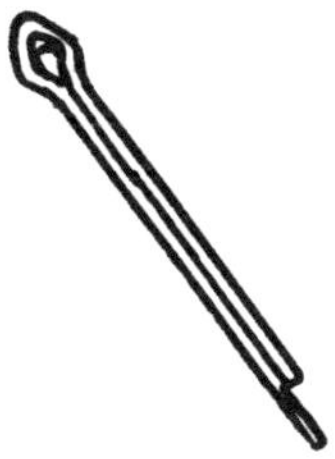 | cotter pins | 12 | used to stabilize a removal joint in the CPVC mount |
|  | pushbutton disconnect (available at audio supply or camera supply stores) | 1 | used as a removal joint in a CPVC mount; requires a close nipple, a metal reducing bushing, and a CPVC female adapter to transition |
| Equipment 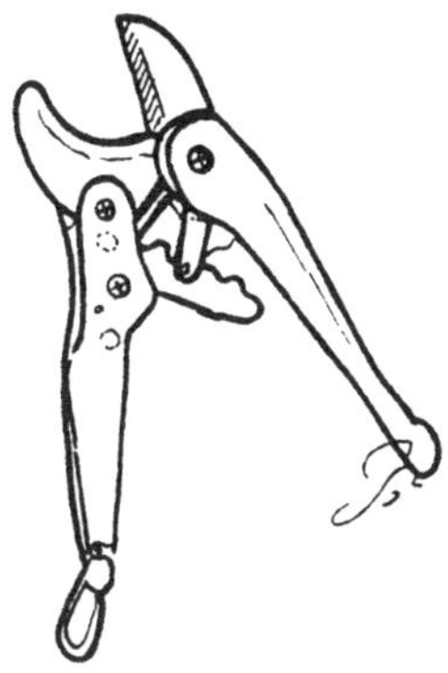 | CPVC pipe cutter (or hacksaw/ jeweler's saw)—a tubing cutter that has a special wheel for use in cutting rigid plastics | 1 | |

*(Appendix continues)*

## APPENDIX B. Continued

| Diagram | Name | No. | Function |
|---|---|---|---|
| Equipment (cont.) | electric drill | 1 | to drill cotter pin hole in removal joint |
| | screwdriver (electric is ideal but optional) | 1 | to attach ground clamps to therapeutic positioning frame |
| 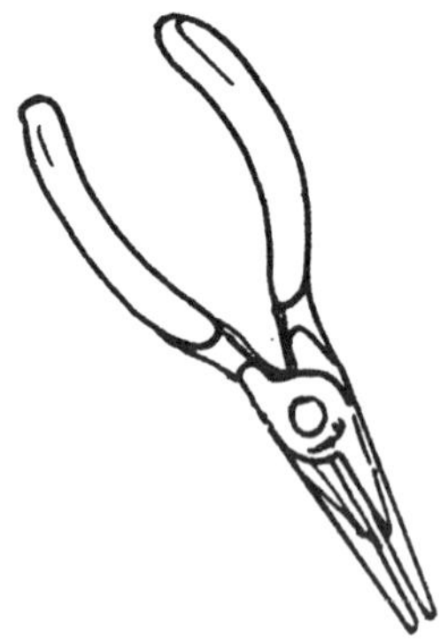 | $4\frac{3}{4}''$ needle nose pliers | 1 | to assist in removing small lengths of pipe from fittings |
|  | 8-piece hex-key wrench set ($\frac{1}{16}''$ to $\frac{1}{4}''$) | 1 | to attach wheelchair clamps to frame of therapeutic positioning equipment |
| 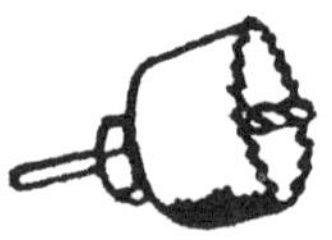 | $2\frac{1}{2}''$ diameter hole saw | | |
| Other 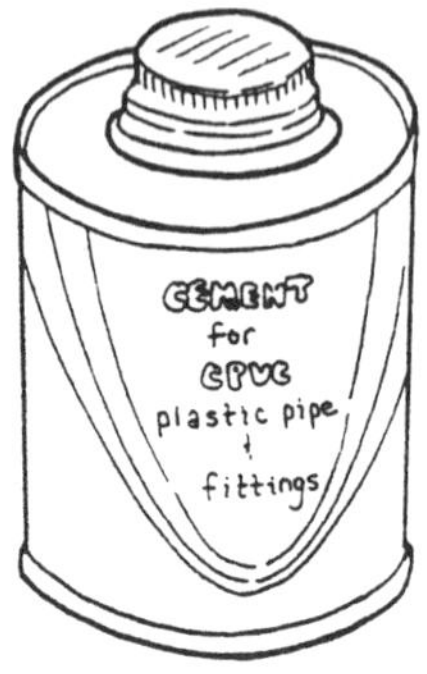 | ASTM-rated solvent cement, CPV or all purpose | 1 | to solvent-weld pipe and fittings together |

*(Appendix continues)*

## APPENDIX B. Continued

| Diagram | Name | No. | Function |
|---|---|---|---|
| Other (cont.)  | CPVC cleaner | 1 | to remove grease, oil, and dirt, and to prepare the mating surfaces for solvent cement action |
| 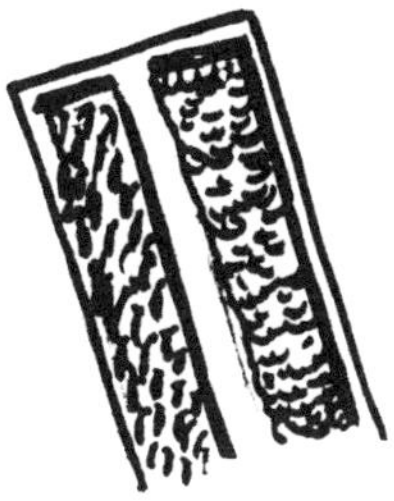 | Adhesive Velcro (male & female) | 3 yds. of each | to attach switch to mounting plate |
| 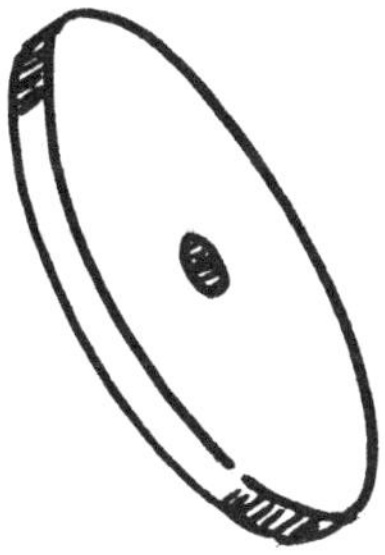 | 2½″ diameter discs cut from ⅛″ thick Plexiglas or Masonite using a hole saw; each disc has $^{10}/_{32}$″ diameter hole drilled in center | | to make mounting plates |
|  | plastic cable ties | 1 pkg. (100) | to attach CPVC mount to wheelchair frame |

*(Appendix continues)*

## APPENDIX B. Continued

| Diagram | Name | No. | Function |
|---|---|---|---|
| Other (cont.) | braided nylon cord or heavy-gauge fishing line | | to attach cotter pin to mount |
| | 12″ metal ruler | | |
| | pencil | | to mark alignment of pipe and fittings prior to solvent-welding |
| | small scissors or pocket knife | | to cut string for cotter pin |
| | small notepad | | to document replacement parts for kit |

# APPENDIX C
## Adapting a Slide Projector Remote Unit to Accept Switch Input

**Description:** Utilizing the following simple procedures, the remote unit of a slide projector can be modified to allow a child's switch interface to control a slide projector. In addition to providing the child with a particularly motivating end reward, this setup provides individuals with considerable practice in timing their release from the switch interface. (*Note.* When the client sustains contact with the switch interface, the slides advance rapidly precluding adequate viewing.)

### Materials

Remote unit of slide projector
22-gauge double-stranded speaker wire
Radio Shack miniature jack
Electrical tape
Solder
Soldering iron

### Construction

1. Cut 45″ of double-stranded speaker wire. Separate strands (both ends) at least 3″. Strip plastic coating from each end of wire (approximately ¼″).
2. Place miniature jack covering over ends of wires (inside treads facing the end to which jack terminal is to be attached). Solder loose ends of wire to terminals of the miniature jack. Bind terminals with small amounts of electrical tape to ensure exposed wires cannot make contact with each other. Screw miniature jack covering around terminals.
3. Using a utility knife, carefully remove approximately 1½″ of the outer casing of remote cord, thereby exposing the three colored leads (red, yellow, white) housed within.
4. Carefully remove approximately ⅜″ of the outer casing of the red and yellow leads thereby exposing their inner copper wires.
5. Solder one strand of the speaker wire to the exposed copper wires of the yellow lead; solder the other strand of the speaker wire to the exposed copper wires of the red lead.

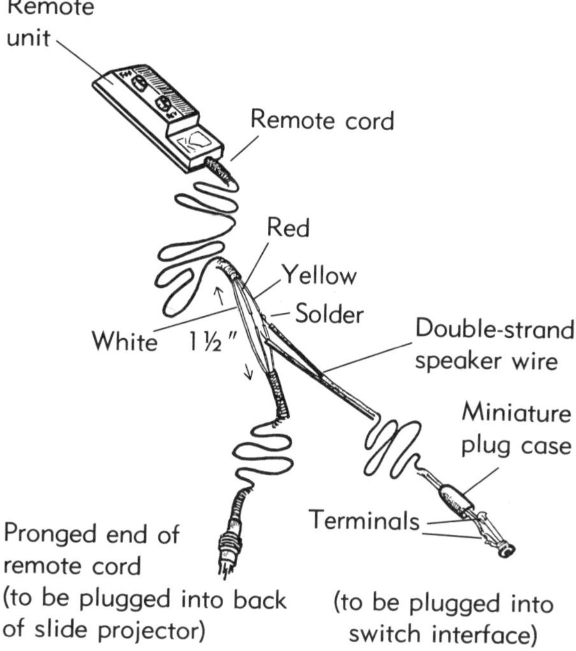

6. Wrap red and yellow leads with electrical tape to prevent contact between them.
7. Plug pronged end of remote cord into back of slide projector. Insert miniature plug of adapted remote into switch interface. Test adapted unit.
8. Wrap speaker wire and remote cord with electrical tape thereby molding them into one unit.

---

# APPENDIX D
## Training I & R: Adapted Slide Projector Task

Regardless of the type of scan mode employed, the child must be skilled in initiating and releasing contact with the switch interface. As previously illustrated in Figure 6.13, a slide projector, adapted to accept switch input, can be used to train a child to reliably, accurately, and quickly initiate and release contact with a switch interface. As an initial training task, an adapted slide projector possesses a number of advantages:

- ❑ Because there is no visual array, no scanning indicator, and no scan pattern, the task requires minimal visual scanning skills. The child merely focuses visual attention on a single slide image. Although the slides are changed with each switch activation, the visual image remains at a fixed location on the projector screen or wall. The process can thus be described as "scanning in place," as opposed to scanning along a path with a scanning indicator advancing through a visual array.
- ❑ The task is cognitively and communicatively less demanding than a true visual scanning task because the child is not required to select a target item from an array of possible choices. The child is simply required to perform the switch accessing skills necessary to advance the next available slide.
- ❑ Although a quick release of switch contact is required to prevent slides from advancing at a rate too rapid to appreciate, the adapted slide projector does not require an "anticipated" timed release in contrast with true scanning. With a true scanning task, the child is required to perform either a timed initiation or a timed release (depending on the scan mode employed) to select a target item following the anticipation of the scanning indicator advancing toward and eventually highlighting that item.

There are a number of creative ways in which an adapted slide projector can be used during both individual and small group activities within the school and home environments. For example, the child can use the adapted slide projector in a "show and tell" type of activity, presenting slides of family members and family events (e.g., vacations, holidays, birthday parties, visiting grandparents, getting a new pet) as well as school events (e.g., field trips, class parties, classroom activities). Within both environments, new slides can be added continually to an inventory of slides available for switch training and practice. Picture storybooks can also be converted into a slide format. As the child advances a slide for viewing, the facilitator reads the accompanying story lines. Slide images projected onto the wall can be interacted with by the facilitator, thereby making the story characters more realistic and the storytelling process highly interactive. Story slides can also be used to pace role-play situations performed with props. The child is thus able to assume a more active role in looking at books and reading stories either in individual or group situations.

In group activities, turn-taking is facilitated through the use of relay boxes such as the Multi-Switch Box by Steven Kanor or the Multi-Input Selector by Zygo Industries, Inc. (Musselwhite & Showalter, 1990). As illustrated in Figure D.1, the Multi-Switch Box simultaneously accommodates several switch interfaces, each controlled by an on/off toggle switch. To allow only one switch interface to be operative at a given time, the remaining three toggle switches are manually turned off by the facilitator. The Multi-Switch Box thus allows several children to take turns advancing the slides when engaged in a storytelling or "show and tell" activity.

When using an adapted slide projector for switch training, a variety of techniques can be employed for cuing the child to initiate and release switch contact. Two types of cuing techniques exist: direct and indirect. Direct cuing, as the name implies, directly cues the child to activate the switch interface and is highly reflective of the motor act required of the child. Examples of direct cuing include, "Pop your switch," "Hit your switch," or "Push your switch." In contrast, indirect cuing is more reflective of the training activity itself. Examples of indirect cuing include, "Next picture," "I

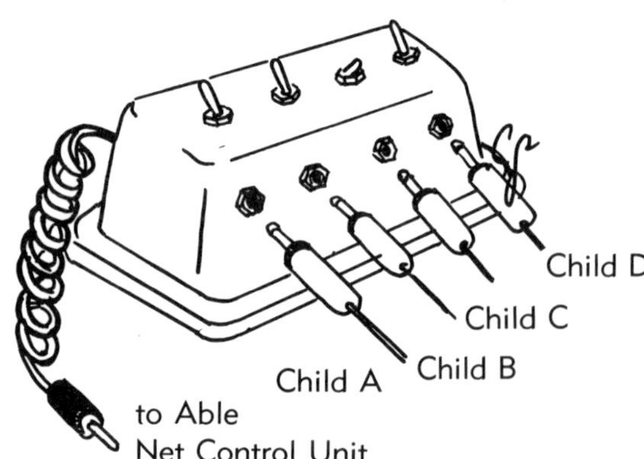


**FIGURE D.1.** Multi-Switch Box (Kanor, Inc.).

wonder what's next,'' or ''Let's see what happens.'' Although direct cuing is cognitively easier than indirect cuing, it tends to be tone-increasing for many children. As a result, indirect cuing is typically preferred given that the child's cognitive level does not dictate the use of direct cuing options. To assist the facilitator in the cuing process, a backward chaining approach is recommended. With a backward chaining approach, cues are presented along a continuum of least to most direct. Initially, an indirect cue is given following the facilitator's live narration of the visible slide (e.g., ''Let's see what's next''). In the event the child does not attempt to advance the next slide within a predetermined time period (e.g., 5 seconds), a direct cue is provided (e.g., ''Hit your switch'').

When using storybook slides, an additional indirect cuing option exists. Audiotapes of the story lines can be made with chime cues inserted for advancing the next slide. These audiotapes are not unlike the commercially available ''talking storybooks.'' Because commercially available tapes typically issue a page-turning signal every other page (i.e., when the page needs to be turned), facilitators must either modify the commercially available audiotape (inserting a signal after each picture) or produce their own narrated version to accommodate the need for a signal after each slide. In creating a homemade version, the facilitator narrates the story line for each slide and inserts some type of chime cue (e.g., bells, musical triangle).

In contrast to live narration, audiotape narration imposes a timing requirement for accessing the switch interface. If the child does not quickly and accurately initiate and release switch contact within the time required to narrate the slide's story line, the slides will not be in synchrony with the audiotape. Given the greater timing demands of audiotape narration, the latter is typically reserved for the child who is experiencing a high degree of success with switch access with live narration, a more accommodating format.

During initial training, many children experience difficulty accurately initiating and/or releasing contact with the switch interface. Specifically, some children are prone to:

- *Premature switch activations,* in which they either initiate contact too early in anticipation of advancing the next slide or they initially experience difficulty controlling their involuntary movements, resulting in accidental switch activation.
- *Multiple switch activations,* in which children make several activations in rapid succession, rapidly advancing a cluster of slides
- *Delayed release,* in which children exhibit difficulty releasing and/or are slow to release contact, thereby rapidly advancing a cluster of slides

In all three instances, the child is not successful in advancing the slides for adequate viewing. The task thus becomes frustrating for both the child and the facilitator, particularly when storybook slides are being used. To minimize the interfering effect of these unwanted activations and their accompanying frustration, a facilitator-controlled override switch can be employed (D. Southwick, personal communication, 1990). Using the override switch, the facilitator is able to supersede or block out unwanted activations before they occur. To eliminate premature activations (Figure D.2), the facilitator activates the override switch immediately following the child's advancement of the slide. The override switch then remains operative until the verbal cue to advance a slide is given. Upon delivering the verbal cue (e.g., ''Let's see what's next''), the facilitator immediately deactivates the override switch, allowing the child's switch to become operative. After the child successfully advances the next slide, the facilitator then reactivates the override switch again, partialing out the interfering effects of any premature activations that may occur. It is also important to note that children who experience difficulty with premature activations may benefit from the use of a switch setup that includes a

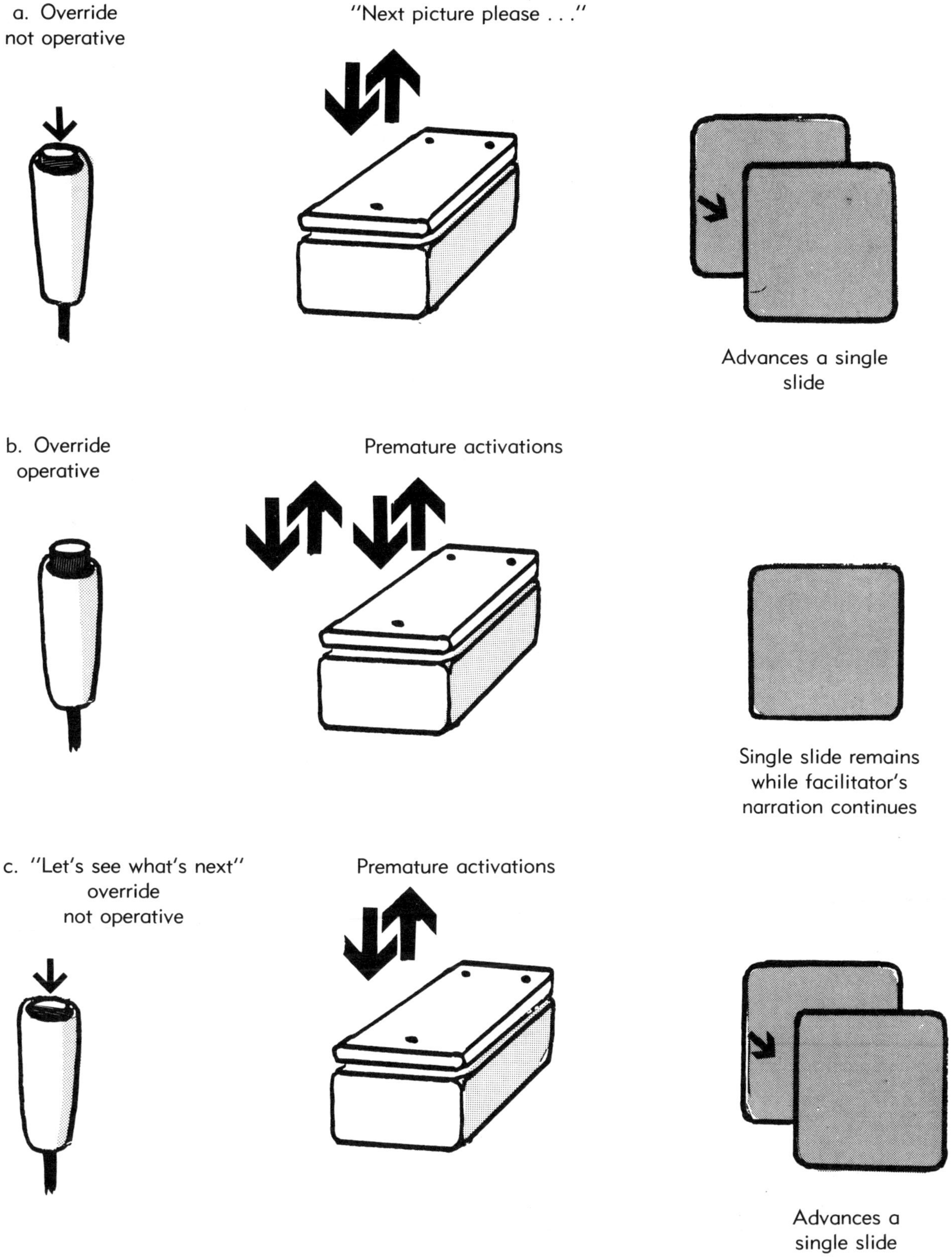

a. Override
not operative

"Next picture please . . ."

Advances a single
slide

b. Override
operative

Premature activations

Single slide remains
while facilitator's
narration continues

c. "Let's see what's next"
override
not operative

Premature activations

Advances a
single slide

**FIGURE D.2.** Using the override switch to control the consequences of premature activations.

boundary bumper. The boundary bumper serves to minimize premature activations by functioning as a tangible home base for the control site when not actively involved in the process of activating the switch interface (see discussion of boundary bumpers in Chapter 3).

To counteract multiple activations or delayed release, the facilitator activates the override switch immediately after the child initiates switch contact. Multiple activations and delayed release are thus ignored by the slide projector, and a single slide advances. The override switch remains operative until the child has released contact with the switch interface or until the verbal cue to advance the next slide is given. The use of the override switch to counteract multiple activations and delayed release is visually summarized in Figures D.3 and D.4, respectively. The use of an override switch thus allows the child to perform with a high degree of success during the initial stages of training. As the child gains proficiency with the skills of initiating and releasing, use of the override switch is reduced and eventually eliminated. The Multi-Switch Box (Kanor, Inc.) previously discussed can also serve as an interrupter switch. The facilitator merely turns the toggle switch controlling the child's switch interface to the OFF position, thereby superseding unwanted switch input.

Throughout training, objective data are collected regarding the child's ability to accurately and reliably initiate and release contact with the switch interface. These can be collected with or without the override switch operative. When the override switch is not employed, data regarding the child's premature activations, multiple activations, and/or delayed release are collected based on their subsequent effects on the action of the slide projector (e.g., by counting the number of slides advanced when the child attempts to initiate and/or release switch contact). When the override switch is employed, the subsequent action of the projector no longer assists in the data collection process relative to unwanted switch input. Instead, the facilitator must closely visually and auditorily (in the event the child is using a switch interface possessing auditory feedback) monitor the child's switch accessing performance to count the number of premature activations, multiple activations, and/or delayed release. The type of cuing provided (indirect vs. direct) is also documented during the data collection process. A sample data sheet is presented in Table D.1.

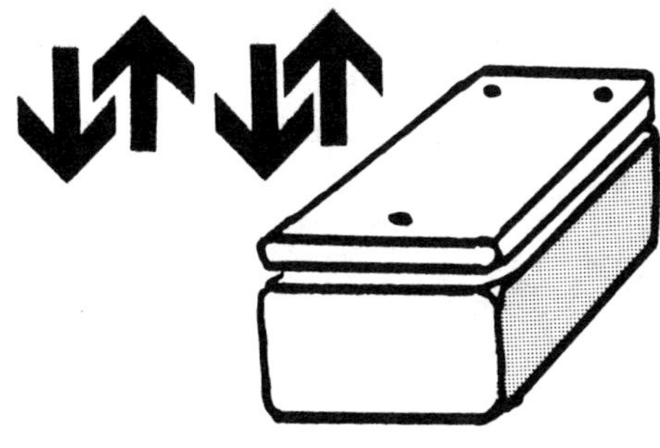

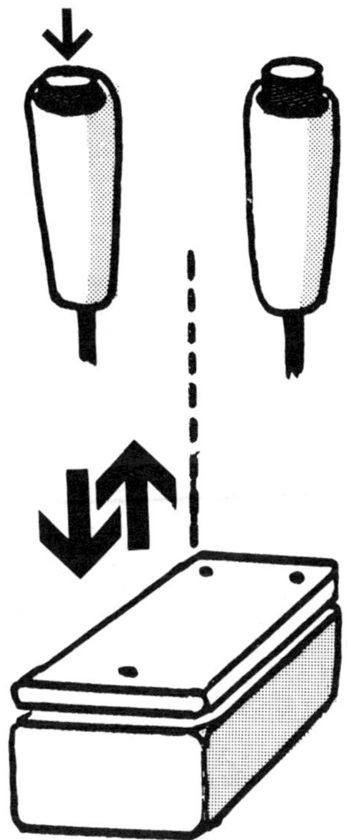

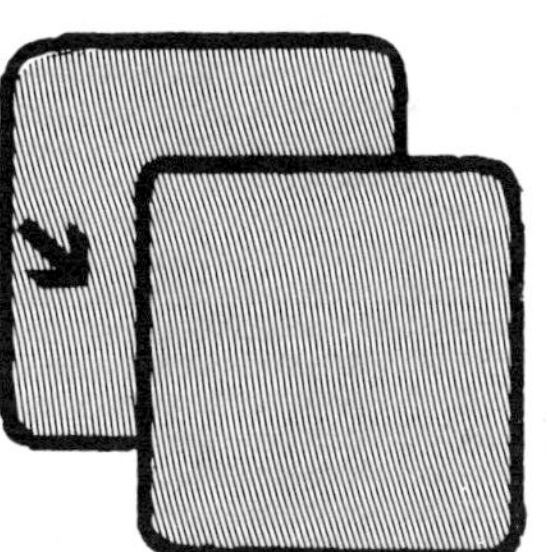


**FIGURE D.3.** Using the override switch to control the consequences of multiple activations.

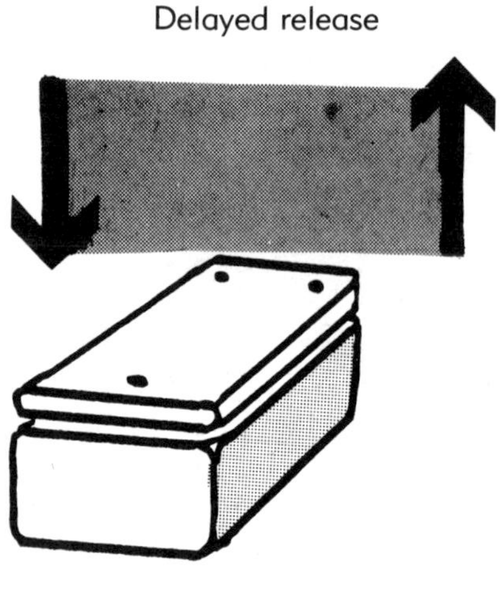

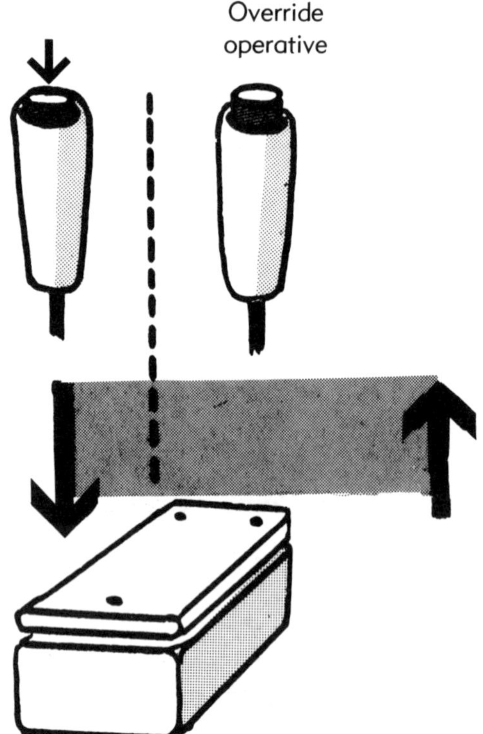


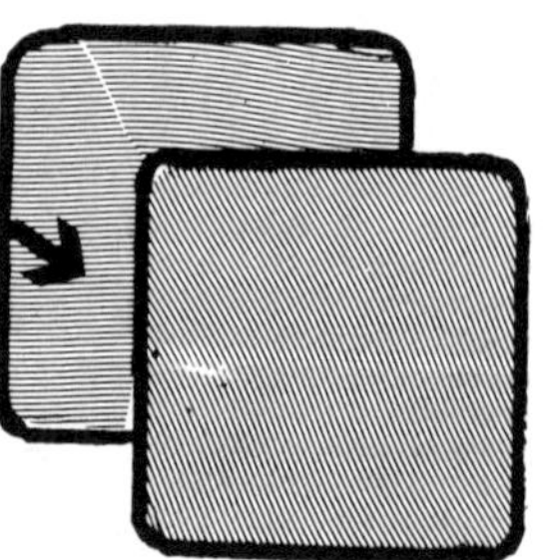


**FIGURE D.4.** Using the override switch to control the consequences of delayed release.

**TABLE D.1.** Data Sheet for Adapted Slide Projector Remote

Client: ______________________ Date: ______________________

Facilitator: ______________________ Picture stimuli: ______________________

Interrupter switch: ______________________

No ________

Yes ________ to control premature activation

________ to control multiple activations/ delayed release

Switch: __________ Control site: __________ Presentation format: __________

| Trials | Premature Activation | Time Delay Following Cue to Advance | Single Activation | Multiple Activation | Delayed Release Activation |
|---|---|---|---|---|---|
| 1 | | | | | |
| 2 | | | | | |
| 3 | | | | | |
| 4 | | | | | |
| 5 | | | | | |
| 6 | | | | | |
| 7 | | | | | |
| 8 | | | | | |
| 9 | | | | | |
| 10 | | | | | |
| 11 | | | | | |
| 12 | | | | | |
| 13 | | | | | |
| 14 | | | | | |
| 15 | | | | | |
| 16 | | | | | |
| 17 | | | | | |
| 18 | | | | | |
| 19 | | | | | |
| 20 | | | | | |

**Performance**

% trials demonstrating premature activations /20 = ________%

% trials—single activations /20 = ________%

% trials—delayed activations /20 = ________%

% trials—multiple activations /20 = ________%

Average time delay per trial _____ sec. per trial

**Scoring**

✓ Correct

X Incorrect

# APPENDIX E
## Glossary of Terms

**abduction**—movement away from the middle of the body.

**abnormal posture**—denotes a position a body part assumes that is not demonstrated in the normal population; way of holding one's body, or part of the body that is not typically demonstrated in the normal population.

**adduction**—movement toward the middle of the body.

**anterior**—belly surface, or front of the body.

**anterior pelvic tilt**—a tilt of the pelvis in which the top portion is tipped anteriorly and the sacrum moves posteriorly resulting in an increased lordosis of the lumbar spine.

**asymmetrical tonic neck reflex (ATNR)**—a lateral head turn that elicits increased extension in the extremities on the skull side and flexion in the extremities on the face side (see Figure 2.7).

**athetosis**—a condition of fluctuating tone often demonstrated as involuntary writhing movements, especially observed in the fingers.

**caudal**—relating to the tail.

**cephalo**—relating to the head.

**distal**—farthest, farther from the point of reference; used to denote a body part farther from the center of the body.

**hypertonia**—having excessive muscle tone, increased resistance to passive stretching.

**hypotonia**—having diminished muscle tone, reduced resistance to passive stretching.

**kyphosis**—a posterior curve, convex curve of the thoracic spine as viewed from the side; hunchback.

**lordosis**—anterior curve of the spine as viewed from the side; normally observed in the lumbar and cervical areas of the spine.

**occiput**—back part of the head, base of skull.

**positive supporting reaction**—pressure on the ball of the foot that elicits a pattern of mass extension.

**posterior**—back surface of the body.

**posterior pelvic tilt**—a tilt of the pelvis in which the top portion is tipped posteriorly and the sacrum moves anteriorly resulting in a flattening of the lumbar spine.

**prone**—lying face down, lying on the stomach.

**proximal**—nearest, closer to a point of reference; used to denote a body part closer to the center of the body.

**righting reactions**—automatic responses to maintain the head in midline and to maintain the normal alignment of the head and neck with the trunk.

**scoliosis**—a lateral curvature deformity of the spine usually with a rotational component.

**supine**—lying face up, lying on the back.

**symmetrical tonic neck reflex (STNR)**—flexion of the head that elicits increased flexor tone in the upper extremities and extensor tone in the lower extremities; extension of the head elicits increased extensor tone in the upper extremities and increased flexor tone in the lower extremities (see Figure 2.8).

**tonic labyrinthine reflex**—occurs when the child is placed in the supine position, extensor tone increases throughout the body; when the child is placed in the prone position, flexor tone increases throughout the body.

# APPENDIX F
## Distributors and Trademarks

Able Net
1081 10th Avenue S.E.
Minneapolis, MN 55414-1312
Phone: (800) 322-0956

ADAMLAB
Wayne County Intermediate School District
33500 Van Born Road
Wayne, MI 48184
Phone: (313) 467-1415

Adaptive Communication Systems, Inc.
Box 12440
Pittsburgh, PA 15231
Phone: (412) 264-2288

Arant, R.
Projector Interface Box
2120 Diane Circle
Alabaster, AL 35007
Phone: (205) 663-5174

Arroyo & Associates
88-45 79th Avenue
Glendale, NY 11385
Phone: (718) 849-9306

Bainum Dunbar, Inc.
Brainz Software
6427 Hillcrost, Suite 133
Houston, TX 77081
Phone: (713) 988-0887

Birch, J.
2346 Wales Drive
Cardiff, CA 90027
Phone: (619) 942-3343

Blackburn, R.
830 Rue Travers
Lac Comté Rortneus
Quebec, Canada G0A 2J0

Brown & Sharpe Manufacturing Co.
702 Rathway Avenue
Union, NJ 07083
Phone: (201) 686-8750

Burkhart, L. J.
8503 Rhode Island Avenue
College Park, MD 20740
Phone: (301) 345-9152

Communication Enhancement Clinic
Children's Hospital Medical Center
Boston, MA 02115
Phone: (617) 735-6466

ComputAbility Corporation
A Division of Preston
101 Route 46 East
Pine Brook, NJ 07058
Phone: (201) 882-0171

Creative Rehab Equipment
609 NE Schuyler Street
Portland, OR 97212
Phone: (800) 547-4611

Crestwood Company
P.O. Box 04606
Milwaukee, WI 53204-0606
Phone: (414) 461-9876

Don Johnston Developmental Equipment, Inc.
P.O. Box 639
1000 N. Rand Road 115
Wauconda, IL 60084
Phone: (708) 526-2682/(800) 999-4660

Dunamis, Inc.
2856 Buford Highway
Duluth, GA 30136
Phone: (404) 476-4934

Exceptional Children's Software
P.O. Box 4758
Overland Park, KS 66204
Phone: (816) 363-4606

Handicapped Children's Technological
Services, Inc.
P.O. Box 7
Foster, RI 02825
Phone: (401) 861-6128

Henri Hunsinger
Service de Technologie
Hospital Marie Enfant
5200 Belanger
Montreal, Quebec, Canada H1T 1C9

Hugh MacMillan Medical Centre
350 Rumsey Road
Toronto, Ontario, Canada M4G 1R8
Phone: (416) 425-6220

InvoTek
700 West 20th Street
Engineering Research Center
Fayetteville, AR 72701
Phone: (501) 575-7227

Laureate Learning Systems
110 East Spring Street
Winooski, VT 05404
Phone: (802) 655-4755

Life Science Associates
1 Fenimore Road
Bayport, NY 11705
Phone: (516) 472-2111

Lock Fast Inc.
801-K Blacklawn Road
Conyers, GA 30207
Phone: (404) 929-8080

Microcomputer Systems for the Handicapped
10418 Armstrong Street
Fairfax, VA 22030
Phone: (703) 352-3611

Otto Bock Orthopedic Industries, Inc.
3000 Xenium Lane North
Minneapolis, MN 55441
Phone: (800) 328-4058

Phelps, J.
Wayne County Regional Educational
Service Agency
Riley School
9601 Vine
Allen Park, MI 48101

Pindot Products
6001 Gross Point Road
Niles, IL 60648
Phone: (800) 451-3553

Prentke Romich Company
1022 Heyl Road
Wooster, OH 44691
Phone: (216) 262-1984/(800) 642-8255

The Psychological Corporation
Harcourt Brace Jovanovich, Publishers
555 Academic Court
San Antonio, TX 78204-9990
Phone: (512) 270-0540/(800) 228-0752

R. J. Cooper & Associates
24843 Del Prado
Dana Point, CA 92629
Phone: (714) 240-1912

REACH, Inc.
890 Hearthstone Drive
Stone Mountain, GA 30083
Phone: (404) 292-8933

Rushakoff, G. E.
Clinical Microcomputer Laboratory
Box 3W
Department of Speech
New Mexico State University
Las Cruces, NM 88003
Phone: (505) 646-2801

Schmitt, D.
Colorado Easter Seals
5755 West Alameda Avenue
Lakewood, CO 80226
Phone: (303) 233-1666

Shafer Foundation
140 Naples
Corpus Christi, TX 78404

Steven Kanor, Inc.
8 Main Street
Hastings-on-Hudson, NY 10706
Phone: (914) 478-0960

TASH, Inc.
70 Gibson Drive, Unit 1
Markham, Ontario, Canada L3R 2Z3
Phone: (416) 475-2212

UCLA/LAUSD Microcomputer Team
23-10 Rehabilitation Center
Los Angeles, CA 90024
Phone: (213) 825-4821

Washington Research Foundation
Suite 322, U-District Building
1107 N.E. 45th Street
Seattle, WA 98105
Phone: (206) 633-3569

Zygo Industries, Inc.
P.O. Box 1008
Portland, OR 97207
Phone: (503) 684-6006

**Trademarks**

Scotchmate™ Hook and Loop Fastening Systems is a trademark of 3M Company, St. Paul, MN 55144.

Velcro, Velcro USA Inc., 406 Brown Avenue, Manchester, NH 03108.

Polaroid is a registered trademark of Polaroid Corporation, Cambridge, MA, ''Polaroid''®.

Tempo® Display Loop Fabric, 3M Company, St. Paul, MN 55144.

Zippy

Quicky Designs

Ethafoam

Dual Lock™, 3M Company, St. Paul, MN 55144.

Kydex Plastic

# References


Arant, R. (1989). *Projector Interface Box.* Birmingham: Sparks Center, University of Alabama at Birmingham.

Baker, B. (September, 1982). Minspeak: A semantic compaction system that makes self-expression easier for communicatively disabled individuals. *BYTE,* pp. 186–202.

Bergen, A. F., & Colangelo, C. (1985). *Positioning the client with central nervous system deficits: The wheelchair and other adapted equipment* (2nd ed.). New York: Valhalla Rehabilitation Publications.

Bergen, A. F., Presperin, J., & Tallman, T. M. (1990). *Positioning for function: Wheelchairs and other assistive technologies.* New York: Valhalla Rehabilitation Publications.

Bergman, J. S. (1990). *How to position people with severe disabilities: Instructors' guide.* (Available from Minnesota Governor's Planning Council on Developmental Disabilities, 300 Centennial Office Building, 658 Cedar Street, St. Paul, MN 55155)

Bergman, J. S., Drews, J. E., & Jensen, A. S. (1990). *Therapeutic positioning and mobility resource manual* (3rd ed.). (Available from author, University of Alabama at Birmingham, P.O. Box 313, UAB Station, Birmingham, AL 35294)

Beukelman, D. (1987). *Augmentative and alternative communication: Serving the nonspeaking person with adult onset etiologies.* Paper presented at the Eighth Annual Southeast Augmentative Communication Conference, Birmingham, AL.

Beukelman, D., & Garrett, K. (1988). Augmentative and alternative communication for adults with acquired severe communication disorders. *Augmentative and Alternative Communication,* 4(2), 104–121.

Beukelman, D. R., Yorkston, K. M., & Dowden, P. A. (1985). *Communication augmentation: A casebook of clinical management.* Austin, TX: PRO-ED.

Blackstone, S. W. (1988). Auditory scanning techniques: Listener-assisted and automatic. *Augmentative Communication News, 1*(5), 4–5.

Bobath, B. (1978). *Adult hemiplegia: Evaluation and treatment.* London: Heinemann Medical Books.

Boehme, R. (1988). *Improving upper body control: An approach to assessment and treatment of tonal dysfunction.* Tucson: Communication Skill Builders.

Brandenburg, S. A., & Vanderheiden, G. C. (Eds.). (1987a). *Communication, control, and computer access for disabled and elderly individuals. Resource book 1: Communication aids.* Boston: College-Hill Press.

Brandenburg, S. A., & Vanderheiden, G. C. (Eds.). (1987b). *Communication, control, and computer access for disabled and elderly individuals. Resource book 2: Switches and environmental control.* Boston: College-Hill Press.

Brandenburg, S. A., & Vanderheiden, G. C. (Eds.). (1987c). *Communication, control, and computer access for disabled and elderly individuals. Resource book 3: Hardware and software.* Boston: College-Hill Press.

Branton, P. (1966). *The comfort of easy chairs.* Stevenage, Hertfordshire, England: The Furniture Industry Research Assn.

Brown, L., Nietupski, J., & Hamre-Nietupski, S. (1976). Criterion of ultimate functioning. In M. Thomas (Ed.), *Hey don't forget about me! Education's investment in the severely, profoundly, and multiply handicapped* (pp. 2–17). Reston, VA:

Division of Mental Retardation, The Council for Exceptional Children.

Bruno, J. (c. 1989). *Interaction, education and play. A Minspeak™ application program* [Computer program]. Wooster, OH: Prentke Romich.

Burkhart, L. (1980). *Homemade battery-powered toys and educational devices for severely handicapped children.* (Available from author, 8503 Rhode Island Ave., College Park, MD 20740)

Burkhart, L. (1982). *More homemade battery devices for severely handicapped children with suggested activities.* (Available from author, 8503 Rhode Island Ave., College Park, MD 20740)

Burkhart, L. (1987). *Using computers and speech synthesis to facilitate communicative interaction with young and/or severely handicapped children.* (Available from author, 8503 Rhode Island Ave., College Park, MD 20740)

Calculator, S. N. (1988). Promoting the acquisition and generalization of conversational skills by individuals with severe intellectual disabilities. *Augmentative and Alternative Communication, 4*(2), 94–104.

Campbell, P. (c. 1985). *Training manual for the Training Aid.* Wooster, OH: Prentke Romich.

Chapman, R., & Miller, J. (1980). Analyzing language and communication in the child. In R. Schiefelbusch (Ed.), *Nonspeech language and communication: Analysis and intervention* (pp. 159–176). Austin, TX: PRO-ED.

Cooper, R. J., & Koch, R. (1987). *Interaction games* [Computer program]. Wauconda, IL: Don Johnston Developmental Equipment.

Curry, J., & Exner, C. (1988). Comparison of tactile preferences in children with and without cerebral palsy. *The American Journal of Occupational Therapy, 42*(6), 371–377.

Don Johnston Developmental Equipment. (1988). *Make it in time* [Computer program]. Wauconda, IL: Don Johnston Developmental Equipment.

Don Johnston Developmental Equipment. (1988). *Make it happen* [Computer program]. Wauconda, IL: Don Johnston Developmental Equipment.

Drinker, P. A., & Kropoff, S. (1981). *Eye-link for nonvocal communication: Direct selection by eye contact.* Paper presented at the Fourth Annual Conference on Rehabilitation Engineering, Washington, DC.

Elder, P., Goossens', C., & Bray, N. (1989). The semantic compaction competency in normal preschoolers. *Proceedings of the Fourth Annual Minspeak Conference.* Wooster, OH: Prentke Romich.

Elder, P., Goossens', C., & Bray, N. (1990). *Semantic compaction competency profile: Experimental edition.* Wooster, OH: Prentke Romich.

Erhardt, R. (1982). *Developmental hand dysfunction: Theory, assessment, treatment.* Laurel, MD: Ramsco.

Erhardt, R. (1986, March). *A neurodevelopmental approach to the treatment of hand dysfunction.* Workshop conducted in New Orleans.

Falvey, M., Bishop, K., Grenot-Scheyer, M., & Coots, J. (1988). Issues and trends in mental retardation. In S. Calculator & J. Bedrosian (Eds.), *Communication assessment and intervention for adults with mental retardation* (pp. 45–66). Austin, TX: PRO-ED.

Farber, S. (1982). *Neuro rehabilitation: A multisensory approach.* Philadelphia: Saunders.

Finn, N. (1986). *Don't dream it's over* [Recording]. Crowded House. Capitol Records.

Fiorentino, M. R. (1976). *Normal and abnormal development: The influence of primitive reflexes on motor development.* Springfield, IL: Thomas.

Fishman, I. (1987). *Electronic communication aids: Selection and use.* Austin, TX: PRO-ED.

Fox, B., & Sweig Wilson, M. (1987a). *Creature antics* [Computer program]. Winooski, VT: Laureate Learning Systems.

Fox, B., & Sweig Wilson, M. (1987b). *Creature chorus* [Computer program]. Winooski, VT: Laureate Learning Systems.

Frazer, B. A., Hensinger, R. N., & Phelps, J. A. (1983). *Managing physical handicaps: A practical guide for parents, care providers and educators.* Baltimore: Brookes.

Frazer, B. A., Hensinger, R. N., & Phelps, J. A. (1987). *A professional's guide to physical management of multiple handicaps.* Baltimore: Brookes.

Fried-Oken, M. (1988). The auditory scanner for visually impaired nonspeaking persons. In L. Bernstein (Ed.), *The vocally impaired: Clinical practice and research* (pp. 249–264). Philadelphia: Grune & Stratton.

Goossens', C. (1989). Aided communication intervention before assessment: A case study of a child with cerebral palsy. *Augmentative and Alternative Communication, 5*(1), 14–26.

Goossens', C., & Crain, S. (1986a). *Augmentative communication assessment resource.* Wauconda, IL: Don Johnston Developmental Equipment.

Goossens', C., & Crain, S. (1986b). *Augmentative communication intervention resource.* Wauconda, IL: Don Johnston Developmental Equipment.

Goossens', C., & Crain, S. (1987, November). Guidelines for customizing Minspeak based communication systems in a cost and time efficient manner. *Proceedings of the Second Annual Minspeak Conference.* Wooster, OH: Prentke Romich.

Goossens', C., & Crain, S. (in press). *Annotated listing of computer software for training various scanning selection techniques.* Birmingham, AL: Southeast Augmentative Communication Conference Publication.

Goossens', C., Crain, S., & Elder, P. (1988a, October). *Engineering the preschool classroom environment for interactive symbolic communication.* Short course presented at the Fifth Biennial International Conference of the International Society for Augmentative and Alternative Communication: Animations of the mind, Anaheim, CA.

Goossens', C., Crain, S., & Elder, P. (1988b, November). *Engineering the preschool classroom environment for interactive symbolic communication.* Short course presented at the Annual Convention of the American Speech-Language-Hearing Association Convention, Boston.

Goossens', C., & Elder, P. (1988). *Fostering interactive communicative play using a combined eye-gaze vest and frame format.* Rockville, MD: American Speech-Language-Hearing Association.

Goossens', C., Elder, P., & Bray, N. (1990). *A preliminary validity study of the Semantic Compaction Competency Profile* (Fifth Annual Minspeak Conference Proceedings). Wooster, OH: Prentke Romich.

Goossens', C., Elder, P., Caldwell, M., & Page, J. (1988). Long range planning: A continuum of semantic compaction overlays. *Proceedings of the Third Annual Minspeak Conference.* Wooster, OH: Prentke Romich.

Guess, D., & Helmstetter, E. (1986). Skill cluster instruction and the individualized curriculum sequencing mode. In R. Horner, L. Meyer, & H. D. Fredericks (Eds.), *Education of learners with severe handicaps: Exemplary service strategies* (pp. 221–248). Baltimore: Brookes.

Halle, J. (1987). Teaching language in the natural environment: An analysis of spontaneity. *The Journal of the Association for Persons with Severe Handicaps, 12,* 28–37.

Hehner, J., & McNaughton, S. (1975). *Handbook of Blissymbolics.* Toronto, Ontario, Canada: Blissymbolics Communication International.

Henderson, B. (1989, March). *Seating in review: Current trends for the disabled.* Winnipeg, Manitoba, Canada: Otto Bock Orthopedic Industry of Canada, Premier Printing.

Illingworth, R. S. (1975). *The development of the infant and young child.* New York: Churchill Livingstone.

Koch, R. (1988). *Learn to scan* [Computer program]. Wauconda, IL: Don Johnston Developmental Equipment.

Koch, R. (1988). *Make it happen* [Computer program]. Wauconda, IL: Don Johnston Developmental Equipment.

Lee, K., & Thomas, D. (1990). *Control of computer-based technology for people with physical disabilities.* Toronto, Ontario, Canada: University of Toronto Press.

Light, J. (1989). Toward a definition of communicative competence for individuals using augmentative and alternative communication systems. *Augmentative and Alternative Communication, 5*(2), 137–144.

Light, J., Collier, B., Kelford Smith, A., Norris, L., Parnes, P., Rothschild, N., & Woodall, S. (1988, October). *Developing the foundations of communicative competence with users of augmentative and alternative communication systems.* Short course presented at the Fifth Biennial International Conference on Augmentative and Alternative Communication: Animations of the Mind, Anaheim, CA.

Lynn, W. M. (1985). *Switching mechanisms for special needs: A project manual.* (Available from author, National Clearinghouse of Rehabilitation Materials, 115 Old USDA Building, Oklahoma State University, Stillwater, OK 74078)

Margolis, S. A., Jones, R. M., & Brown, B. E. (1985). The subasis bar: An effective approach to pelvic stabilization in seated positioning. *Proceedings of the RESNA Eighth Annual Conference* (pp. 45–47). Washington, DC: RESNA Press.

Mirenda, P., & Locke, I (1989). A comparison of symbol transparency in nonspeaking persons with intellectual disabilities. *Journal of Speech and Hearing Disorders, 54*(2), 131–140.

Monahan, L. C., Taylor, S. J., & Shaw, C. G. (1989). Pelvic positioning: another option. *Proceedings of the Fifth International Seating Symposium* (pp. 32–38). Memphis: University of Tennessee.

Musselwhite, C. (1986). *Adaptive play for special needs children: Strategies to enhance communication and learning.* Austin, TX: PRO-ED.

Musselwhite, C. (1988). *Toward the development of a switch hierarchy.* The Irene Wortham Conference. Asheville, NC.

Musselwhite, C. (1990, personal communication) *Daily communication schedule.* Irene Wortham Center, Asheville, NC.

Musselwhite, C. (1991). *Mini-grants and volunteers: Developing support for augmentative communication programs.* Birmingham, AL: Southeast Augmentative Communication Conference Publications.

Musselwhite, C. R., & St. Louis, K. W. (1988). *Communication programming for persons with severe handicaps: Vocal and augmentation strategies* (2nd ed.). Austin, TX: PRO-ED.

Musselwhite, C., & Showalter, S. (1990, September). *Microcomputers.* The Irene Wortham Center Conference. Ashville, NC.

Nwoabi, O. M. (1987). Seating orientation and upper extremity function in children with cerebral palsy. *Journal of Physical Therapy, 67,* 1209–1212.

Rettig, M. (1987). *Rabbit scanner* [Computer program]. Overland Park, KS: Exceptional Children's Software.

Reymann, J. (1985a). Arm band control for upper extremity posturing. *Developmental Disabilities Special Interest Section Newsletter of The American Occupational Therapy Association, 8*(2), 4.

Reymann, J. (1985b). The sof-splint. *Developmental Disabilities Special Interest Section Newsletter of The American Occupational Therapy Association, 8*(2), 1–2.

Riley, M. (1970). The effect of an arm restrainer on involuntary movements. *The American Journal of Occupational Therapy, 23*(2), 116–118.

Romski, M., & Sevcik, R. (1988). Augmentative and alternative communication systems: Considerations for individuals with severe intellectual disabilities. *Augmentative and Alternative Communication, 4*(2), 66–82.

Schmitt, D. (c. 1988). *The new cause and effect disk* [Computer program]. Lakewood: Colorado Easter Seals.

Schwejda, P., & McDonald, J. (1986). *Motor training games* [Computer program]. Wauconda, IL: Don Johnston Developmental Equipment.

Smart, M. S., & Smart, R. C. (1977). *Children: Development and relationships.* New York: Macmillan.

Smith, L. (1983). *Practical hints for evaluation and programming with alternative communication systems.* Paper presented at the Fourth Annual Southeast Nonspeech Communication Conference, Birmingham, AL.

Snook, J. (1981). Spasticity reduction splint. *American Journal of Occupational Therapy, 33,* 648–651.

Stockmeyer, S. (1967). An interpretation of the approach of Rood to the treatment of neuromuscular dysfunction. In H. D. Bouman (Ed.), *Proceedings: An exploratory and analytical survey of therapeutic exercise* (Northwestern University Special Therapeutic Exercise Project). *American Journal of Physical Medicine, 46*(1), 906.

TASH. (c. 1987). *Catalogue.* (Available from TASH, Inc., 70 Gibson Drive Unit 1, Markham, Ontario, L3R 2Z3, Canada)

Trachdjian, M., & Minear, W. (1958). Sensory disturbance in the hands of children with cerebral palsy. *Journal of Bone and Joint Surgery, 40,* 85–90.

Trefler, E. (1982). Arm restraints during functional activities. *The American Journal of Occupational Therapy, 36*(9), 599–600.

Trefler, E. (Ed.). (1984). *Seating for children with cerebral palsy: A resource manual.* (Available from Rehabilitation Engineering Program, 682 Court Avenue, University of Tennessee, Center for the Health Sciences, Memphis, TN 38163)

Trefler, E., & Taylor, S. (1984). Decision making guidelines for seating and positioning children with cerebral palsy. In E. Trefler (Ed.), *Seating for children with cerebral palsy: A resource manual.* (Available from Rehabilitation Engineering Program, 682 Court Avenue, University of Tennessee, Center for the Health Sciences, Memphis, TN 38163)

Vanderheiden, G. C. (1975). Providing the child with a means to indicate. In G. C. Vanderheiden & K. Grilley (Eds.), *Non-vocal communication techniques and aids for the severely physically handicapped* (pp. 20–76). Austin, TX: PRO-ED.

Vanderheiden, G. (1988). Overview of the basic selection techniques for augmentative communication: Present and future. In L. Bernstein (Ed.), *The vocally impaired: Clinical practice and research* (pp. 5–39). Philadelphia: Grune & Stratton.

Vanderheiden, G. C., & Lloyd, L. L. (1986). Communication systems and their components. In S. Blackstone (Ed.), *Augmentative communication: An introduction* (pp. 49–162). Rockville, MD: American Speech-Language-Hearing Assn.

Van Tatenhove, G. (1978). *Augmentative communication board development: A response training protocol.* Paper presented at the Annual Convention of the American Speech-Language-Hearing Association, Atlanta.

Van Tatenhove, G. (1985, October). *Building a powerbase.* Short course presented at the Fourth Annual Southeast Augmentative Communication Conference, Birmingham, AL.

Ward, D. E. (1984). *Positioning the handicapped child for function* (2nd ed.). Chicago: Phoenix Press.

Warren, S. F., Horn, E. H., & Hill, E. W. (1987). Some innovative educational applications of advanced technologies. In L. Goetz, D. Guess, & K. Stremel-Campbell (Eds.), *Innovative program design for individuals with dual sensory impairments* (pp. 283–309). Baltimore: Brookes.

Wengert, M. E., & Margolis, S. A. (1987). A design for the back of seated positioning orthoses that controls pelvic positioning and increases head control. *Proceedings of the RESNA Tenth Annual Conference* (pp. 216–218). Washington, DC: RESNA Press.

Williams, J., Csongradi, J., & LeBlanc, M. (1982). *A guide to controls: Selection, mounting, applications.* Palo Alto, CA: Rehabilitation Engineering Center, Children's Hospital at Stanford.

Wright, C., & Nomura, M. (1985). *From toys to computers: Access for the physically disabled child.* Wauconda, IL: Don Johnston Developmental Equipment.

York, J., Nietupski, J., & Hamre-Nietupski, S. (1985). A decision making process for using micro switches. *Journal of the Association for Persons with Severe Handicaps, 10*(4), 214–223.

Zacharkow, D. (1988). *Posture sitting, standing, chair design and exercise.* Spingfield, IL: Thomas.

Zuromski, E. S. (1978). *Introduction to active stimulation.* Warwick, RI: Technical Newsletter #1, Trudeau-Zambarano Active Stimulation Program.

Zygo Industries, Inc. (1983). *Computer products brochure.* Portland, OR: Author.

# INDEX

*Page numbers in italics refer to figures. Page numbers followed by "t" refer to tables.*